# HEALING AND THE INVENTION OF METAPHOR

It has long been understood that illness is influenced not only by our bodies' physiology, but also by language, culture, and meaning. This book, written by renowned cultural psychiatrist Laurence Kirmayer, explores the influence of metaphor, narrative, and imagination in experiences of suffering and processes of healing across cultures. It emphasizes how metaphor can open a window to the hidden mechanisms of healing driven by meaning and symbolism, myth and imagination. At the same time, it offers a rigorous critical account of the metaphors embedded in the epistemology and practice of contemporary biomedicine, psychiatry, and psychotherapy. In doing so, it exposes the sociomoral and political dimensions of these dominant approaches to understanding and treating illness.

LAURENCE J. KIRMAYER is Distinguished James McGill Professor and Director of the Division of Social and Transcultural Psychiatry at McGill University. He directs the Culture & Mental Health Research Unit at the Institute of Community and Family Psychiatry of the Jewish General Hospital in Montreal. He is a fellow of the Canadian Academy of Health Sciences and the Royal Society of Canada.

# HEALING AND THE INVENTION OF METAPHOR

*Toward a Poetics of Illness Experience*

LAURENCE J. KIRMAYER

*McGill University*

CAMBRIDGE
UNIVERSITY PRESS

CAMBRIDGE
UNIVERSITY PRESS

Shaftesbury Road, Cambridge CB2 8EA, United Kingdom

One Liberty Plaza, 20th Floor, New York, NY 10006, USA

477 Williamstown Road, Port Melbourne, VIC 3207, Australia

314–321, 3rd Floor, Plot 3, Splendor Forum, Jasola District Centre, New Delhi – 110025, India

103 Penang Road, #05–06/07, Visioncrest Commercial, Singapore 238467

Cambridge University Press is part of Cambridge University Press & Assessment, a department of the University of Cambridge.

We share the University's mission to contribute to society through the pursuit of education, learning and research at the highest international levels of excellence.

www.cambridge.org
Information on this title: www.cambridge.org/9781009617789

DOI: 10.1017/9781009617802



When citing this work, please include a reference to the DOI 10.1017/9781009617802

First published 2025

*A catalogue record for this publication is available from the British Library*

*Library of Congress Cataloging-in-Publication Data*
NAMES: Kirmayer, Laurence J., 1952– author.
TITLE: Healing and the invention of metaphor : toward a poetics of illness experience / Laurence J. Kirmayer.
DESCRIPTION: New York, NY : Cambridge University Press, 2025. | Includes bibliographical references and index.
IDENTIFIERS: LCCN 2024056454 | ISBN 9781009617789 (hardback) | ISBN 9781009617796 (paperback) | ISBN 9781009617802 (ebook)
SUBJECTS: LCSH: Metaphor – Health aspects. | Metaphor – Therapeutic use. | Psychotherapy – Methodology. | Cognitive grammar.
CLASSIFICATION: LCC P301.5.M48 K57 2025 | DDC 306.4/61014–dc23/eng/20250221
LC record available at https://lccn.loc.gov/2024056454

ISBN 978-1-009-61778-9 Hardback
ISBN 978-1-009-61779-6 Paperback

*For Elizabeth*

# Contents

# *Figures and Tables*

# Preface

> Without contraries is no progression.
>
> –William Blake[1]

> Metaphor is the great human revolution at least on a par with the invention of the wheel.
>
> –Yehuda Amichai[2]

This is a book about the place of language in illness experience and healing. My aim is to examine how metaphors structure illness experience and symbolic healing. I come at this as a practitioner and participant-observer, trained in psychiatry and psychotherapy, but also engaged in medical and psychological anthropology and the philosophical critique of psychiatry. The twin tasks of this book, then, are to illustrate the ways in which metaphors can constitute and transform experience in illness and healing and to examine some of the central or root metaphors of contemporary medical, psychological, and psychiatric practice for their social and rhetorical implications. Throughout, my goal is to advance an embodied and enactive theory of language that can deepen our understanding of the poetics of illness experience and the process of healing.

To be clear, this is not a manual or handbook on the use of metaphor in psychotherapy or other clinical settings. There are several useful texts that provide such guidance for work in various contexts.[3] The focus on metaphor in this book—and on the images and narratives through which metaphoric meaning is elaborated—aims to get at the pivotal processes in illness experience and healing to both allow critique and open the door to creative rethinking of our institutions and practices.

My approach shares the concerns of medical humanities and narrative medicine with lived experience and the moral significance of illness. This work is sometimes sharply contrasted with the focus in biomedicine on molecules and mechanisms of disease. In these chapters, though, I want bridge the divide between meaning and mechanism by drawing from the methods and perspectives of cognitive science and anthropology that allow us to examine the biological, psychological, and social processes of sense- and meaning-making. Metaphor theory provides ways to link mind and mechanism, content and process, connecting personal and cultural history with the unfolding of illness experience.

The last fifty years has seen a wealth of innovative work on metaphor in philosophy, cognitive science, and the humanities. This work reveals metaphor to be central to conceptual thought, to the texture of everyday experience, and to the evocative and rhetorical powers of language. Metaphors are constructive, mutative, and sometimes also corrosive to the experience of self and other. Approaching illness experience and healing through the study of metaphor can help lay bare the cognitive machinery, discursive practices, cultural histories, and forms of life that constitute and transform experience in sickness and in health.

Illness and healing are central to the human condition. Illness is among the most obdurate and insistent predicaments that shape our lives. We are biologically constructed to give priority to pain, nausea, vertigo, and other forms of distress over and above our everyday experiences of hunger, thirst, anger, fear, sexual arousal, and other desires or motivations. All of these experiences command attention, prompt a search for meaning, evoke memories, and elicit action. When intense and persistent, though, illness experience can occupy consciousness in ways that are profoundly distressing, disorienting, and disabling. The resultant suffering and difficulties in functioning prompt a search for resolution or respite by taking curative action and, if that does not bring immediate relief, by seeking help and healing.

*Healing* differs from *cure*, which in everyday use is tied to a biological definition of affliction as disease. Cure aims to eliminate the underlying disease once and for all. As such, it implies a singular, punctual event. Healing, in contrast, has the connotations of an ongoing process that may occur partially or in stages that are often characterized as a journey. While healing may address underlying processes of affliction, it is not defined exclusively in opposition to affliction but, on analogy to the body's capacity to heal a wound, in terms of recuperative, reparative, or restorative powers. Accordingly, healing covers a broad territory from symptom relief and remoralization, to improved or restored bodily, personal, and social functioning. In bodily and mental illness, then, the metaphor of healing stands not simply for the cessation of symptoms and suffering but for the many processes that may underlie such change, including learning, behavioral change, growth, restitution, and recovery. No single mechanism or process can account for such a wide range of phenomena, yet words and symbols can have impact on all of these levels.

Most of the anthropological literature on healing examines practices and traditions to explore their symbolic meaning. Biomedical researchers are interested in such studies mainly in terms of their evidence for the potential efficacy of traditional healing. But healing practices also have ethics, aesthetics, pragmatics, and politics that deserve close attention. Ethics is central to the ways we assess healing practices in terms of their impact on individuals' well-being and social personhood. Aesthetics draws attention to the sensory and affective qualities of illness experience that allow empathy and understanding. Aesthetics is also central to how healing practices change illness experience and identity. The pragmatics of healing involve all of the material circumstances that are mobilized in the healing process, including bodily physiology, cognition, interpersonal interaction, and wider social dynamics. The politics have to do with the ways in which the various forms of social power are mobilized by the institutions, practices, and performance of healing.

This book considers all of these dimensions of healing to show how they are related through the metaphoric mediation of bodily experience and discourse. Central to this is the human capacity for imaginative invention—the ability to construct new tools, conceptual models, and forms of life. Metaphor is the most basic and flexible of our tools for invention.

The title of this book alludes to two kinds of invention: the evolutionary emergence of the capacity for metaphor as a way to fashion an infinite variety of cognitive tools, and the inventive possibilities provided by each specific metaphor. The evolutionary invention of metaphor came along with the most basic, embodied forms of perception and cognition—of seeing and thinking *as if.* Metaphor in turn provides a workshop or tinker's shed, an infinitely extendable toolkit with which to respond to the endless occasions for invention. When invention coincides with reality it becomes discovery.

Metaphor—whether it serves inquiry, invention, or discovery—is always perspectival, yielding partial truths and opening up new ways of looking at the world. One of the crucial realizations that comes from attention to metaphor is that every description of experience has hidden and unexpected connotations. Every metaphor also conjures many "contraries" in terms of sensory or affective qualities and conceptual dimensions. This richness and evocative power of metaphoric thinking is at the root of human imagination and creativity. Reflecting these dynamics of metaphor, each of the chapters begins with quotations that point to the tension of opposites inherent in metaphoric language. The winding path we will follow aims to steer between the polarities represented by these dual epigraphs without resolving their productive tension. This is akin to William Blake's stance in *The Marriage of Heaven and Hell*, where he valorizes the tension of opposites as the source of creative energy.

The dilemma in Blake's Romantic embrace of contraries is that it risks sacrificing the virtues of Enlightenment rationality, science and technical reason, as well as the forms of critical thinking, dialogue, and debate that enable an inclusive civil society.[4] The question then is how critique can be coupled with the poetic play of opposites so that we sacrifice neither the clarity of technical knowledge and moral vision nor the energy of creative ferment. The answer lies in our ability to move back and forth between different modes of engagement to bring them into dialogue. In that spirit, I hope that the reflections offered here honor the critical and poetic faculties of both sufferer and healer. The critic has the acuity to see the difference between words and things and thus to open space for new metaphors and inventions. Through the poet, who loves both words and world with equal passion, our divided selves may, for a time, be healed.

# *Acknowledgments*

This book is based on essays that have appeared over the past thirty years. Over that time, I have been gifted with colleagues and friends who have shared my interests in language, poetics, and healing. They have been generous with their time, conversations, and critical reflections, which have enriched this work at each stage in its evolution. It is a pleasure to acknowledge them here. For their many contributions to the earlier papers on which these chapters are based I thank: Gadi BenEzer, Gilles Bibeau, Ellen Corin, René Devisch, Byron Good, Mary-Jo Delvecchio Good, Jess Groesbeck, Barbara Hayton, Alex Hinton, Doug Hollan, David Howes, Sushrut Jadhav, Arthur Kleinman, John Leavitt, Roland Littlewood, Margaret Lock, Tanya Luhrmann, Gretty Mirdal, Joel Paris, Amir Raz, Jim Robbins, Zeev Rosberger, Cécile Rousseau, Radhika Santhanam-Martin, Margaret Schibuk, Vieda Skultans, and Allan Young. In reworking these papers into chapters for this book, I am deeply indebted to current colleagues and friends for critical readings and conversations: Henry Abramovitch, Suze Berkhout, Suparna Choudhury, Samuele Collu, Connie Cummings, Danny Frank, Phoebe Friesen, Raymond Gibbs, Cristiana Giordano, Ian Gold, Deborah Golub, Ana Gómez-Carrillo, Joseph Gone, Jaswant Guzder, Devon Hinton, Eric Jarvis, Carol Kidron, Boon Ooi Lee, Robert Lemelson, Bradley Lewis, Roberto Lewis-Fernández, Omri Moses, Shane Neilson, Mark Nichter, Melissa Park, Eugene Raikhel, Maxwell Ramstead, Louis Sass, William Sax, Rebecca Seligman, Constantin Tranulis, Samuel Veissière, and Carol Worthman. Special thanks to Antonella Clerici, who assisted with the bibliography and to Brad Allard for his careful copyediting.

Elizabeth Anthony has been a constant presence and support in this work, and her love the greatest sustenance. For that, and for her playful poiesis, I dedicate this book to her.

# *Sources*

Much of this book is based on previously published essays, which have been extensively revised, adapted, and updated and are included here with permission from the publishers.

*Chapter 1*: Kirmayer, L. J. (1993). La folie de la métaphore. *Anthropologie et Societé*, 17(1–2), 43–55; Kirmayer, L. J. (1989). Review of the illness narratives by A. Kleinman. *Transcultural Psychiatric Research Review*, 26(3), 202–204; Kirmayer, L. J. (2023). Cultural poetics of illness and healing. *Transcultural Psychiatry*, 40, 248–277.

*Chapter 2*: Kirmayer, L. J. (1992). The body's insistence on meaning: Metaphor as presentation and representation in illness experience. *Medical Anthropology Quarterly*, 6(4), 323–346; Kirmayer, L. J. (1993). La folie de la métaphore. *Anthropologie et Societé*, 17(1–2), 43–55; Kirmayer, L. J. (2023). Cultural poetics of illness and healing. *Transcultural Psychiatry*, 40, 248–277.

*Chapter 3*: Kirmayer, L. J. (2000). Broken narratives: Clinical encounters and the poetics of illness experience. In C. Mattingly & L. Garro (Eds.), *Narrative and the cultural construction of illness and healing* (pp. 153–180). University of California Press.

*Chapter 4*: Kirmayer, L. J. (2003). Reflections on embodiment. In J. Wilce (Ed.), *Social and cultural lives of immune systems* (pp. 282–302). Routledge; Kirmayer, L. J. (2004). The cultural diversity of healing: Meaning, metaphor and mechanism. *British Medical Bulletin*, 69(1), 33–48; Kirmayer, L. J. (2008). Culture and the metaphoric mediation of pain. *Transcultural Psychiatry*, 45(2), 318–338; Kirmayer, L. J. (2011). Unpacking the placebo response: Insights from ethnographic studies of healing. *The Journal of Mind-Body Regulation*, 1(3), 112–124; Kirmayer, L. J. (2023). Cultural poetics of illness and healing. *Transcultural Psychiatry*, 40, 248–277.

*Chapter 5*: Kirmayer, L. J. (1993). Healing and the invention of metaphor: The effectiveness of symbols revisited. *Culture, Medicine and*

*Psychiatry*, 17(2), 161–195; Kirmayer, L. J. (1996) Review: Therapeutic conversations by Stephen Gilligan and Reese Price (Eds.). *International Journal of Clinical and Experimental Hypnosis*, 44(1), 89–92; Kirmayer, L. J. (1999). Myth and ritual in psychotherapy. *Transcultural Psychiatry*, 36(4), 451–460.

*Chapter 6*: Kirmayer, L. J. (1996). Landscapes of memory. In P. Antze & M. Lambek (Eds.), *Tense past: Cultural essays in trauma and memory* (pp. 173–98). Routledge; Kirmayer, L. J. (2015). Wrestling with the angels of history: Memory, symptom intervention. In D. Hinton & A. Hinton (Eds.), *Genocide and mass violence: Memory, symptom, and recovery* (pp. 388–420). Cambridge University Press.

*Chapter 7*: Kirmayer, L. J. (2001). Failures of imagination: The refugee's narrative in psychiatry. *Anthropology & Medicine*, 10, 167–185; Kirmayer, L. J. (2002). The refugee's predicament. *L'Évolution Psychiatrique*, 67, 724–742; Kirmayer, L. J. (2008). Culture and the metaphoric mediation of pain. *Transcultural Psychiatry*, 45(2), 318–338; Kirmayer, L. J. (2015), Wrestling with the angels of history: Memory, symptom intervention. In D. Hinton & A. Hinton (Eds.), *Genocide and mass violence: Memory, symptom, and recovery* (pp. 388–420). Cambridge University Press.

*Chapter 8*: Kirmayer, L. J. (2006). Culture and psychotherapy in a creolizing world. *Transcultural Psychiatry*, 42(3), 163–168; Kirmayer, L. J. (2007). Celan's poetics of alterity: Lyric and the understanding of illness experience in medical ethics. *Monash Bioethics Review*, 26(4), 21–35; Kirmayer, L. J. (2008). Culture and the metaphoric mediation of pain. *Transcultural Psychiatry*, 45(2), 318–338. Kirmayer, L. J. (2011). Unpacking the placebo response: Insights from ethnographic studies of healing. *The Journal of Mind-Body Regulation*, 1(3), 112–124; Kirmayer, L. J. (2015). Wrestling with the angels of history: Memory, symptom intervention. In D. Hinton & A. Hinton (Eds.), *Genocide and mass violence: Memory, symptom, and recovery* (pp. 388–420). Cambridge University Press.

*Chapter 9*: Kirmayer, L. J. (2003). Asklepian dreams: The ethos of the wounded-healer in the clinical encounter. *Transcultural Psychiatry*, 40, 248–277.

*Chapter 10*: Kirmayer, L. J. (2023). Cultural poetics of illness and healing. *Transcultural Psychiatry*, 40, 248–277; Kirmayer, L. J. (2006). Toward a medicine of the imagination. *New Literary History*, 37(3), 583–605.

Some of these papers date back decades and my own subsequent work, along with the contributions of many others to the literature, has guided the transformation of these essays into chapters with a larger narrative arc. In the process, it has been encouraging to see that most of these arguments have held up well over the years—and still more gratifying to see that others have made use of these papers to advance their own work. I hope that organizing these essays in this way has added value in showing how body, speech, and mind come together in the playing field of cultural poiesis.

CHAPTER I

# *Into the Backcountry*

There arises from a bad and unapt formation of words a wonderful obstruction to the mind.

– Francis Bacon[1]

*D'un point de plus dans l'arrière-pays, dans l'inconscient du vouloir dire . . .*

– René Char[2]

Language is the most distinctive feature of the human mind, the skill with which we fashion our lifeworlds through acts of poiesis, giving voice to suffering, making sense of our predicaments, and finding ways to heal. Every language of suffering and affliction is deeply rooted in a cultural history, geography, and community. Every expression of distress and effort at transformation draws from these shared languages, even as individuals improvise new hybrid forms. Understanding the creative functions of language must be central to a medicine or psychiatry for the whole person.

A wealth of work in cultural psychiatry and anthropology shows how metaphor, image, and imagination can articulate, express, transform, and sometimes resolve experiences of suffering and affliction. This work springs from the recognition that metaphor is ubiquitous. Far from being a special, artful, or ornamental use of language, cognitive linguistics makes it clear that metaphor reflects the basic structure of human cognition, that is, our capacity to think of one thing in terms of another. Developmentally, this allows us to build up complex and abstract thought on a scaffolding of earlier and simpler knowledge and experience. Culturally, it allows us to extend shared metaphors to construct the elaborate models and stories that constitute our individual and collective identities and the institutions of the social world. Tracing the origins and consequences of the metaphors we use to articulate experience and explain our actions to each other can uncover the latent or implicit meaning in our models and point the way to new metaphors that lead to new ways of thinking.[3]

Consider the following vignettes:

> It is a Wednesday evening in Singapore, and people are gathering at a local temple to await their consultation with the *dang-ki* healer. Following preparatory rituals, the *dang-ki* is possessed by a deity who speaks through him to divine the nature of the diverse problems and afflictions people have brought and to provide help in the form of advice, magical inscriptions, and medicines. A father describes his daughters' disobedient behavior, and the *dang-ki* encourages him to accept that the world is changing and he should allow her more autonomy.[4]
>
> Allison, a fifteen-year-old student, is brought to the pediatric hospital emergency room by her parents after she deliberately cuts herself at school. She explains to the psychiatrist that she is being bullied, fighting constantly with her mother, and sleeping poorly. The psychiatrist tells Allison and her parents that she is suffering from depression and prescribes antidepressant medication to help with what he describes as a chemical imbalance caused by the stressful situation she is experiencing.[5]
>
> A psychodynamic psychotherapist tells a client that his problems stem from unconscious conflicts and that exploring the manifestations of unconscious will reveal the nature of the conflict and lead to a resolution or cure. To reveal unconscious material, the patient is advised to record his dreams in a diary and bring them to therapy to discuss. The dreams are interpreted as providing knowledge that is compensatory to the patient's conscious attitude—evidence of an inner healer that aims to help the patient recover and integrate repressed aspects of the self.[6]
>
> A cognitive behavioral therapist tells a client that her problems stem from maladaptive thoughts. He asks her to keep a diary of "automatic thoughts" that come unbidden. Together, they identify the metaphors in these self-statements and their negative effects and consider alternative metaphors that may be more accurate or conducive to problem solving, self-esteem, and adaptation.[7]
>
> At a hearing of the Truth and Reconciliation Commission of Canada (TRC), an Indigenous elder recounts his suffering in Indian Residential School and the impact it has had on his life. Grief-stricken, he describes how the abuse and loss he experienced led to his own problems of substance use and depression. The commissioners listen closely and his testimony is transcribed to be added to an archive documenting what the TRC Final Report will call Canada's history of "cultural genocide" against Indigenous Peoples.[8]

These vignettes illustrate the varied kinds of suffering and healing explored in this book, including ritual healing, contemporary psychiatric and psychotherapeutic practice, and the larger social and political arenas in which psychiatric language is deployed. In each case, the metaphors used to describe affliction are meant to point to its origins based on particular ontologies—notions of what the world is made up of—that can explain the nature of the problem and the process of healing.

For the *dang-ki*, a kind of healer following a syncretic Taoist–Buddhist tradition, affliction can arise from many different proximate causes, but the deity has the power to discern its ultimate nature and intervene in ways that can restore health and harmonious relationships.[9] The process of healing is embodied through the process of *possession*: the deity takes ownership of and inhabits the body of the *dang-ki*. For the *dang-ki* and their clients, of course, this is not a metaphor but a literal description of events. The ritual implements, setting, chants, and prescriptions all fit with a cultural and religious ontology and understanding of the world that is shared, at least in part, by healer and supplicant. At times, the *dang-ki*'s interventions may include practical advice on how to navigate a changing social world.

For the psychiatrist in the emergency room, depression is a neurobiological disorder. Calling it a "chemical imbalance" provides an inaccurate but useful metaphor that warrants the use of medication to correct the imbalance.[10] A more accurate model would characterize mood as the outcome of a neurobiological regulatory system that has become dysregulated, with problems occurring at the level of functional brain circuitry. For the adolescent and her family, the neurobiological explanation implies her problem is not something she did but something that happened to her. Taking medication is an opportunity for her to reestablish control over her own mood and behavior.

The psychodynamic psychotherapist invokes a model of the self that has passed from psychoanalytic theory to everyday folk psychology. On this view, the unconscious is a repository of repressed conflicts that result in maladaptive behavior. Plumbing the depths of the unconscious through dreams, reverie, or free association can reveal repressed conflicts and defuse their power through exposure or point to corrective actions. While classical psychoanalysis saw the unconscious mainly as a site (or consequence) of conflict, in other therapies, the unconscious may be framed as a source of strength and resources that includes an "inner healer."[11]

For the cognitive therapist, the sources of affliction lie not in the depths of unconscious but in bad habits of thought. Many of these are evident in ordinary conversation or in the private soliloquy of self-appraisal. They can be explicitly identified and replaced by more salutary statements, images and metaphors. In the case of third-wave cognitive therapies, like dialectical behavior therapy (DBT) or acceptance and commitment therapy (ACT), the recognition of the metaphoric nature of cognition and the deliberate use of metaphors to promote cognitive flexibility are key strategies.[12]

For the TRC commissioners, bearing witness to the history of state-mandated violence against Indigenous Peoples through policies of forced assimilation provides an explanation for the high prevalence of mental health problems, a way of demanding accountability and restitution, and the beginning of a long process of collective healing and reconciliation, which will benefit nations, communities, families, and individuals. Here, the metaphor of healing implies a recognition of injury and of the responsibility for care in relationships that have been governed by a politics of domination and exploitation.

In each of these situations, specific metaphors frame the nature of affliction in terms of causes rooted in a *cultural ontology*—that is, a locally shared view of what kinds of agents and entities constitute the world—and guide the process of healing by suggesting actions that address the underlying problem. Key metaphors in one context may be viewed as inapt, irrelevant, counterproductive, or even unintelligible in another context. Exploring the personal and social effects of these metaphors can clarify some of the mechanisms of suffering and healing. Critical analysis of these metaphors can reveal their underlying assumptions, limitations, and unintended consequences.[13] Critique can also serve the creative function of generating alternative metaphors that may better capture facets of experience and provide new possibilities for transformation.

## The Ubiquity of Metaphor

Metaphors are present in every form of thought and communication. Many of these are "dead" metaphors that go unrecognized as such because they have become literal expressions. As the philosopher Owen Barfield put it:

> [E]very modern language, with its thousands of abstract terms and its nuances of meaning and association, is apparently nothing from beginning to end, but an unconscionable tissue of dead or petrified metaphors . . . . A man cannot utter a dozen words without wielding the creation of a hundred named and nameless poets.[14]

In everyday speech, the bare bones of dead metaphors are animated by a living tissue of novel tropes and images that enrich and enliven thought and charge it with emotion. Studies of natural language find about one explicit metaphor for every ten to twenty-five words in everyday talk and about one metaphor for every twenty-five words on TV.[15] Situations that are emotionally charged or in which people struggle to describe unfamiliar experiences tend to have still higher rates of metaphor use. In psychotherapy, patients may produce about six metaphors a minute.[16]

Profound experiences of affliction evoke rich metaphoric language. Here is how the novelist William Styron described his own experience with severe depression in his memoir *Darkness Visible*:

> [the] despair, owing to some evil trick played upon the sick brain by the inhabiting psyche, comes to resemble the diabolical discomfort of being imprisoned in a fiercely overheated room. And because no breeze stirs this caldron, because there is no escape from this smothering confinement, it is entirely natural that the victim begins to think ceaselessly of oblivion.[17]

In this passage, metaphor is used to convey some of the bodily feeling and existential predicament of depression ("being imprisoned in a fiercely overheated room"), to sketch a theory of the underlying problem (an "evil trick upon the sick brain by the inhabiting psyche"), and to point to ongoing dynamics in which the person's response contributes to the symptoms and course of the illness ("because there is no escape . . . it is entirely natural . . . to think ceaselessly of oblivion"). In invoking a "sick brain," Styron acknowledges the dominant theories of current biological psychiatry, which explain depression as a brain disorder (A BROKEN BRAIN; A CHEMICAL IMBALANCE).[18] But by describing depression as an evil trick by the psyche that inhabits the brain, he leaves room for psychology, including processes of self-understanding, interpretation, and personal agency (Who is playing the trick?). The choice of metaphors reveals important dimensions of his ongoing struggle with the illness, as well as the ways that the conceptual resources of medicine and popular culture can be used to make sense of experience.[19]

A metaphor can point to an explicit analogy or explanation for an experience or an event. It can change our perspective on a situation or event by drawing attention to aspects we have ignored or charging it with new meaning and connotations. Viewing a person in terms of a sensory metaphor (e.g., "SHE IS A WARM PERSON"; "SHE HAS A SUNNY SMILE")[20] modifies our way of relating to them. Evocative metaphors provided by psychiatry and psychology like BROKEN BRAINS, CHEMICAL IMBALANCES, TRAUMA, and RESILIENCE can reshape our sense of agency and subjectivity. In recent years, thinking about the brain as a computer has inspired a rich body of scientific work in computational neuroscience and psychiatry[21]; in popular culture, thinking about one's own brain as a computer leads to modes of self-reflection that can change our way of being in the world, allowing distance from affliction, deliberate attempts at self-modification, or leading to self-estrangement.[22]

While some of the chapters in this book explore patients' metaphors for illness, equal attention is given to the discourse of healers and clinicians, especially to the metaphors of biomedicine, psychiatry, and psychotherapy, whether implicit in theory or explicit in clinical conversation. My interest is in two related aspects of metaphor: its place at the center of conceptual models and its use as a powerful tool in rhetoric, that is, in speech aimed to influence others and to position oneself in the social world. The language of healing is always embedded in larger discursive frames that are conveyed through specific metaphors and narratives. Any given metaphor captures only part of the ways that cultural models are deployed. Every metaphor also has unintended connotations and surplus meanings that influence the ways we think and act. An especially apt or compelling metaphor can take us off in unexpected directions that change the way we see the world and ourselves, for better or for worse. My aim, then, is to uncover how the metaphors produced by patients and clinicians shape the process of clinical interaction, the negotiation of meaning, and the bodily, psychological, and social processes of coping, helping, and healing. This provides a way to look at the embodiment of illness experience and its therapeutic transformations that can illuminate the processes and practice of contemporary psychiatry, psychology, and psychotherapy, as well as the great diversity of symbolic healing systems around the world.

To that end, I offer a *poetics*—not in the narrow sense of a treatise on literary style or form, but in its broadest sense, as a consideration of the aesthetics of language and action through poiesis, the act of making or fashioning with words. This broad use of "poetics" has a venerable tradition that goes back to Aristotle.[23] Here, the term *poetics* is meant to help us keep constantly in mind the fact that ordinary thought and action are shaped by the creative faculties of imagination and largely governed by aesthetic values that make particular constructions or construals of experience especially apt, evocative, rhetorically powerful, and transformative. It also reminds us that the languages of suffering and healing, though they borrow from conventional idioms, are endlessly inventive.

## 4-E Cognitive Science and the Pragmatics of Communication

While this book is concerned with the poetics of experience and its expression in clinical discourse, I approach discourse from a situated, social-pragmatic perspective. This approach emphasizes that discourse is not a self-contained or autonomous domain of linguistic or social process with its own logic, force, or agency, but rather part of social, cultural, and institutional practices that provide individuals with background knowledge, resources, norms, and possibilities for self-fashioning. These resources are deployed through culturally mediated interpersonal interactions in the diverse social contexts or settings in which people collaborate to create and negotiate meaning. Any newly minted meaning must be tried and tested and, when taken up by others, lived out in a social world. Understanding the effectiveness of metaphor in healing therefore must appeal to knowledge about the intentions of actors and the larger social ideologies, norms, and values that inform, energize, and constrain individuals' actions and agendas.

The chapters in this volume weave together phenomenological, cognitive, and social accounts of meaning and sense-making. The framework that brings this together is based on contemporary "4-E" cognitive science, which offers us a picture of perception, thought, and action as bound together in ongoing cycles or loops of sense- and meaning-making.[24] In this view, cognition is *embodied*, *embedded*, *enacted*, and *extended* in ways that make it deeply social and cultural. Embodiment reflects the ways that cognition and imagination emerge developmentally from basic bodily experiences and continue to be elaborated through both internal physiological processes and engagements with the external environment in both its material and symbolic or linguistic dimensions. A rich experimental literature shows the ways in which bodily processes both structure and interrupt or intrude on everyday thinking.[25] These bodily processes involve actions in and on the environment and hence are always embedded in a particular context or niche that provides *affordances* (opportunities for action and perception) and that structures the process of cognition. The world then appears to us full of signs: our local niche is a matrix of affordances for perception and action. These affordances are both *natural*—that is, based on our inborn, physical capacities, and *cultural*—arising from socially patterned possibilities in the humanly designed and constructed environment and its associated scripts and modes of attention.[26]

The realization that action and perception are closely coupled and that the (original, evolutionary) purpose of cognition is to guide adaptive action in specific niches or contexts has led to work on *enactivism* that aims to show how cognition has its origins in modes of action and interaction between the body and the world. Enactivism argues that even complex cognitions that appear to involve internal models or representations involve not only the computational machinery of brain but also action-oriented engagement with the world.[27] Moreover, these actions allow us to extend our thinking through interactions with others in the world, as well as with cultural artifacts and institutions, in ways that dramatically amplify our cognitive capacities.

Our own self-understanding through metaphors and narrative constructions plays a key role both in internal regulation and engagement with our environments, which are largely constituted through the ongoing cooperative social actions of ourselves and others. The language we have available to articulate and express our experience changes the very nature of that experience. This is the case even for seemingly preformed, obdurate experiences of pain and suffering, no less than for the stories we borrow or invent to project ourselves into new and better circumstances. The implication is that an adequate picture of the emergence of illness experience and its transformation through healing practices must lay bare the embodied process of imagination, as well as the social processes of self-construal, social positioning, and active engagement with the cultural affordances that constitute our local worlds and niches.[28] This very general scheme can shed new light on the mechanisms of healing and points toward a way to integrate phenomenology and mechanistic explanation in an ontology and epistemology adequate to address the key questions and concerns of psychiatry.[29] This approach also allows us to situate mental health practices in relationship to broader ecosocial processes of human adaptation, revealing both their potential mechanisms of efficacy and their sometimes unexpected social and political consequences.

## Languages of Suffering and Healing

A central concern of this book is how to understand the process of healing across diverse systems of medicine through the psychophysiological, cognitive, and social-rhetorical effects of metaphor. Although I draw examples from a variety of healing rituals and practices to illustrate this efficacy of metaphor, the emphasis will be on contemporary psychiatry. Perhaps, this emphasis requires some justification beyond the fact that I have been a participant observer in this enterprise and so have a ready source of observations and examples at hand.

Recent decades have seen interesting changes in the models and metaphors at play in psychiatry and other mental health professions. Psychoanalysis and psychodynamic psychotherapy dominated North American psychiatric practice from the 1940s through to the 1970s, but, in recent years, psychotherapy has been on the wane within psychiatry as the profession reconfigures itself as a branch of biomedicine rooted in the neurosciences.[30] This effort reflects the conviction that mental health problems are fundamentally brain disorders and that explanations for the range of psychiatric conditions eventually will be found in neuroscience.[31] Confidence in such neurobiological explanation has persisted despite limited evidence and translation into effective clinical interventions. Psychiatry increasingly focuses on diagnosis and medication prescription, while other mental health practitioners, including clinical and counseling psychologists and social workers, have become the main professional providers of psychotherapy and psychosocial care. They can provide the "talking cure" with less stigma than psychiatrists, who are associated with the treatment of severe mental illness. Of course, these changes in health care and professional roles have also been driven by economic considerations. The pharmaceutical industry is big business, and psychotherapeutic and psychosocial interventions are time and labor intensive. Insofar as psychiatrists command high fees for their time and expertise, limiting their role to diagnosis and drug prescriptions and leaving psychotherapy or psychosocial interventions to other professions may be more cost-effective.

Despite this enormous investment in biological approaches in psychiatry, the number of psychologically oriented practitioners and the availability of psychotherapies is growing globally, through popular media, humanitarian practices in global mental health, and even as a by-product of marketing efforts to promote pharmaceuticals. This has effects on how people understand and talk about themselves and others. Psychosocial counselors and others engaged by nongovernmental organizations in every corner of the world offer new ways of framing human predicaments. Psychotherapeutic idioms and ideas that are conveyed through popular media may work to transform ways of thinking about self and other far beyond the clinical setting. Indeed, through both biological and psychosocial models and metaphors, psychiatry shapes our concepts of self and personhood in diverse social contexts, from the classroom to the courtroom, and from the family to the political arena.[32] Psychiatry, psychology, and psychotherapeutic discourse provide models and metaphors for mind, self, and experience. Laying bare these models and metaphors is essential for understanding the ways we narrate our lives, the logic of reasons and causes, and the corresponding moral modes of experience in health and illness.[33]

Of course, every model or metaphor reveals some facets of reality while hiding others. Consistent with the perspectival nature of metaphoric thinking, the arguments and examples in this book suppose that each of the many different theories and schools of psychotherapy and the myriad forms of symbolic healing have something important to show us. In the 1950s and sixties, therapeutic eclecticism was in bad repute in psychiatric training, equated with a lack of clarity, rigor, or commitment. This criticism was possible because the adherents of some schools, notably psychoanalysts, believed they already had the last and best word on what works in psychotherapy. Other approaches were seen as watered down, inferior, or simply misguided. In recent decades, the critique of eclecticism has been revived but reoriented on the assumption neurobiology alone can provide a solid foundation for a scientific psychiatry.[34]

The other common reason for rejecting eclecticism was the claim that all therapy works by similar underlying mechanisms (e.g., providing positive expectations, mobilizing hope, and improving morale). If so, then much of the variation in therapeutic practice was just window-dressing, an artifact of the struggle for market share, or irrelevant detail, and clinicians were free to adopt a single mode of psychotherapy and fit the patient to it. Unfortunately, patients who did not act in ways that fit the model were then judged "untreatable." In settings where psychodynamic theory was dominant, many patients preoccupied with physical symptoms, from non-Western cultures, or with less formal education, found it difficult to speak the idiom of psychology and were judged "not psychologically minded."[35] If they were offered treatment at all, they were usually referred for supportive counseling or behavior therapy, which were viewed as second-class forms of treatment by these same practitioners.

Times have changed. The embrace of biological treatments for psychosis, mania, depression, and anxiety promoted the view that common mental health problems and even "problems in living" can be traced to underlying neurochemical disorders. This claim has persisted despite mounting evidence that mental health problems involve complex interactions among many brain circuits, as well as interactions with the environment, none of which usually can be reduced to a few neurobiological parameters. In psychotherapy, cognitive-behavioral approaches are in ascendance, buoyed by the reams of research carried out by generations of graduate students in psychology. Within psychiatry, some of psychodynamic theory has been translated into cognitive or neurobiological terms.[36] Outside the mental health professions, psychoanalytic ideas have been adopted by literary theorists glad to curate and contribute to its nuanced language of desire, conflict, and ambivalence.

Nowadays, eclecticism is accepted within psychiatry as the corollary of our limited knowledge about the wide range of problems encompassed by diagnostic nosology. At a deeper level, therapeutic eclecticism and bricolage seem inevitable because processes involving multiple levels of systems (biological, psychological, and social) contribute to human suffering, healing, and recovery. Even with more integrative models, eclecticism will remain necessary given the recognition that all theories are partial or incomplete and hide or distort as much as they reveal and clarify. This perspectivism is urged on us by philosophers of science on epistemological grounds, as well as by social critics concerned with the political use of rhetoric to hide manifest injustices and abuses of power. Describing problems as due to a broken brain, an inadequate childhood, weak will, faulty learning, or poor decisions all have social consequences. The choice of a mode or level of explanation, then, is never purely a technical or scientific decision but one that is inherently moral and political.

## Cultural Logics of Healing and Psychotherapy

The theory and practice of any healing tradition—including the diverse forms of psychotherapy—is drawn from the norms and expectations of a society, restating these as therapeutic goals and guidelines, and aiming to return participants better adapted to some version of the quotidian. In the case of psychotherapy, these practices involve explicit talk about the "psyche." However abstract or technical the psychotherapist's model of psyche and suffering, the rationale for specific practices, and processes of therapeutic change are usually framed in terms of folk psychological models, normative standards of functioning, and everyday ways of narrating and explaining experience. What we take for granted in our theories of healing is just what has become culturally implicit. Psychotherapy, then, cannot help but reinforce some of our cultural blind spots, even if it successfully uncovers and liberates us from others. The cultural embedding, implicit values, and consequences of a therapeutic system can only be appreciated by standing outside its assumptions for a moment to consider alternate ways of thinking about suffering and healing. This attempt to stand outside the received wisdom is the special contribution of the cross-cultural study of healing.

Many cross-cultural studies of symbolic healing have emphasized their universal dimensions: the social power and authority of the healer and the ritual; the imposition of symbolic order on the distress, chaos, and confusion caused by disease; the lifting of morale by fostering positive expectations of cure; and the mobilization of endogenous mechanisms of healing.[37] But it is also possible to use cross-cultural comparison to clarify the distinctive characteristics of Western psychotherapies—by paying close attention to the specific metaphors in which our theories are framed and the practices through which these metaphors are enacted.

In his classic text *Persuasion and Healing* (1961), the social psychiatrist Jerome Frank argued that all successful forms of healing address a common experience of demoralization, working to instill hope, make sense of suffering, and improve morale and so promote a universal human capacity for adaptation.[38] But this general picture of the *common factors* in healing is more a statement of outcome than an account of underlying process and does not go far in explaining either the cultural fit of specific therapies or their potential efficacy. Clearly, raised morale is not the only salient or important outcome of healing. Healers aim not simply to convince the afflicted person and their entourage that they are somehow healed or cured, but equally to help them to understand, accept, or transcend aspects of their predicaments: to show that afflictions have meaning, even if they are terrible; to show how illness can be mastered, controlled, or transformed; or, when neither understanding nor control can be achieved, to show that there is a way to continue with life—in this world or the next.

Subsequent work on common factors in healing has considered a wide range of processes in physiological, psychological, and sociocultural models.[39] At a biological level, these include endogenous processes involved in the regulation of pain and emotional arousal. Psychological processes include changes in cognitive maps or models of the self and the social world that affect attention, symptom attribution, and problem solving. Social mediators include changes in social identity, position, and relationships with others. Although many of these processes are involved in every form of healing, they also have specific effects related to the nature of the problem and its personal and social meanings. These meanings depend on both the individual's history and larger cultural frames that endow healing practices with social power and authority.[40]

In later efforts to refine his original account of nonspecific therapeutic effects, Frank came to recognize the central importance of rhetoric in healing.[41] Rhetoric is concerned with what moves people—with the use of language to transform meanings or conceptual positions along with perceptions, emotions, and moral convictions. Although some accounts of rhetoric emphasize the force of logical argument, recent attention has focused on pragmatics and poetics.[42] The pragmatics of rhetoric include the situated nature of discourse, which mobilizes institutional authority and social power through drama and charisma.[43] The poetics of rhetoric addresses the evocative power of language which works on the imagination to orient, energize, and direct feeling, thought, and action.

This book, then, takes up where Frank and others leave off in their accounts of the nonspecific dimensions of healing, with the role of rhetoric, narrative, and metaphor in symbolic healing.[44] Instead of emphasizing common or nonspecific factors, I consider the diversity of models and mechanisms involved in healing practices around the world. This diversity is also found among the different schools of psychotherapy within the pluralistic societies that we call "Western." Similar diversity is present as well among the range of clients who attempt to follow a particular form of therapy. Each person responds in their own fashion to the expectations and interventions of the clinical encounter. Every sufferer lives their own metaphor in sickness and in health—that is, every person's psychological conflicts and problems in living are constituted by specific metaphoric conceptions of self and other that shape the experience of illness and healing. Each of these personal modes of construal have their own specificity, but they draw on common tropes and master narratives circulating in the cultures and communities to which individuals belong or with which they are in dialogue.

## Conceptual Metaphor Theory and the Scaffolding of Experience

Although metaphor was classically approached as a matter of poetic figures that add color, emotion and rhetorical power to speech, there is a long tradition of seeing metaphor as central to culture and cognition. In *The New Science* (1725), the Enlightenment philosopher Giambatista Vico (1668–1744) argued that the poetic logic of metaphor was essential to the development of thought and language itself.[45] Fredrich Nietzsche recognized the "mobile army" of metaphors as the medium through which we interpret the world and seem to apprehend truth but warned of the danger in mistaking metaphor for reality.[46] Over the last four decades, work in cognitive linguistics has provided empirical evidence for the centrality of metaphor in thought.[47] This work recognizes metaphor as the master trope in meaning-making.[48] In this view, in addition to their obvious aesthetic and rhetorical functions, metaphors provide conceptual structures that organize perception, cognition, emotion, and action.[49]

The general process of conceptual metaphor is thinking of one thing in terms of another. The metaphor "A IS B" is an invitation to think of A (the *target* or *topic*) as if it were a sort of B (the *source* or *vehicle*). More formally, metaphors are mappings of one concept or experience (the *source* or *vehicle*) onto another (the *target* or *topic*). This mapping confers new meaning on the target and, as the term "vehicle" suggests, the cognitive process of metaphor allows us to extend the mapping to derive additional associations or implications. Metaphoric mappings are asymmetrical in that high salience features of the vehicle are applied to the topic.[50] Thus, the metaphor SURGEONS ARE BUTCHERS (which might evoke an image of the surgeon cutting crudely with a scalpel like a cleaver, leaving hunks of meat and a bloody apron) is quite distinct from BUTCHERS ARE SURGEONS (wielding a knife like a scalpel with care and precision)—each metaphor draws on salient features of the vehicle to make latent features of the topic more salient. Although the concept mapping that underlies metaphor is asymmetrical, metaphor comprehension and production involve an interaction between source and target that can alter them both, creating new meaning and salience.[51]

What is salient is, of course, relative to both topic and vehicle, so metaphor comprehension involves a process of exploration to find analogies that fit. The mapping of topic onto vehicle may occur in many small leaps in which features of the topic are translated into the vehicle, moved through the representational space of the vehicle and then translated back to check for coherence within the structure of the topic. This cycle of forward and back-translation is necessary because otherwise a metaphoric extension might quickly become misleading or even uninterpretable by using extraneous or irrelevant aspects of the vehicle to represent the topic (SURGEONS ARE BUTCHERS might be taken to mean that surgeons sell their services by the kilo). To be meaningful, the analogic transformations within metaphor must be widely context dependent at both ends of the metaphoric bridge from topic to vehicle and back. In the way that they function in metaphor, topic and vehicle are best understood not as isolated lexical terms but as conceptual models or structures. Metaphors relate whole structures not just their elements.[52] The translation process inherent to metaphor is a microcosm of the larger process of linguistic translation and many of the successes and failures of translation stem from the challenge of finding comparable metaphors that carry over crucial aspects of conceptual structure and that are not sabotaged by divergent connotations or associations unique to one or the other linguistic tradition or cultural context.[53]

The metaphors we use to make sense of experience can be described as schemas or models based on analogies. Some have argued, therefore, that metaphors are simply loose, deviant, or odd analogies that draw attention to themselves.[54] However, while analogies may provide the initial structure or mapping that prompts a metaphor, metaphors can generate meaning that is not captured by a formal analogy. This occurs because novel metaphors prompt a search for meaning—and the more novel or unexpected the juxtaposition of source and target, the wider and deeper the search for links. This search may involve considering many facets of the source to attach a potentially relevant quality to the target or it may involve constructing images, scenarios, or situations in which the metaphor makes sense (see Figure 1.1).[55]

Metaphors can provide a basis for conceptual elaboration, scaffolding more complex or abstract cognition. Lakoff argues that abstract reasoning "is a matter of two things: (a) reason based on bodily experience, and (b) metaphorical projections from concrete to abstract domains."[56] Analogic representations ("mental models") based on spatial relationships can encode logical properties of the world without invoking propositional logic.[57] Similarly, the logical functions of natural language can emerge from mental representations of abstract "spaces" that are intermediate between language

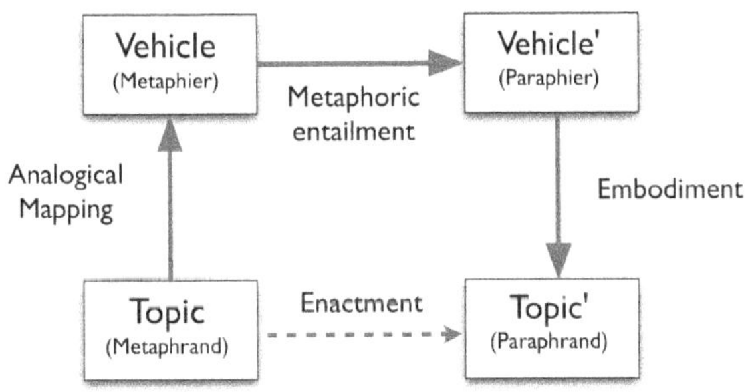


Figure 1.1 The structure of metaphor
Metaphor involves thinking about one thing (a *topic* or *target*) in terms of another (*vehicle* or *source*). Finding the relevant analogies or facets of source and target involves interaction between the two in a context-driven process of search or imaginative construction. Metaphors can build a scaffolding that links developmentally earlier and conceptually simpler bodily experiences to more complex situations, scenes, or scenarios. The terms *metaphier/paraphier* and *metaphrand/paraphrand* are borrowed from Jaynes (1976). In addition to the cognitive effects of analogical mapping, the key to the transformative effects of metaphor lies in the processes that link metaphoric entailment with embodiment and enactment (adapted from Kirmayer, 2011a, Creative Commons).

and the world.[58] Metaphoric phrases are interpreted as instructions for constructing and operating on a mental space to simulate an action perception or relationship between objects or events. This simulation can then be worked with to explore the implications of statements.

At the base of this scaffolding, metaphors provide semantic pointers to meanings grounded in sensory experience and actions.[59] This implies a direct mapping from source onto target. But metaphors typically present multiple facets or dimensions of meaning that point in different (sometimes discordant) directions. Some of these facets are obvious but others may lie dormant, waiting to be activated in surprising ways. The metaphor THE BRAIN IS A COMPUTER, for example, not only provides a rationale for building computational models of the brain; it also implies the brain can be programmed, that it is precise, and that, if burdened with too many tasks, it can get overheated. For someone with little experience with computers, the metaphor may be less evocative, shallow, or simply puzzling.

Many everyday metaphors are part of conventional idioms or expressions that have become the literal name or description of an object or event. Conventional metaphors express tacit knowledge. They may also provide reassurances that we are participating with others in the same language game, the same community or form of life, with its familiar etiquette, idioms, rules, norms, and implicit ontology. The use of a novel metaphor—or of a conventional metaphor in a novel way that reactivates some of the meanings inherent in its etymology or experiential grounding—is an invitation or provocation to rethink some aspect or domain of experience. This is a basic way we generate new ideas, actions, and perceptions that extend the boundaries of culture and convention.

Metaphors emerge from our experiential engagements with the world and, as they are enacted and deployed in that world, they reshape experience. Metaphors can influence physiology and embodied experience, constitute new cognitive structures or mental mechanisms, configure new social arrangements and relationships, and confer new forms of power. Understanding the ways that metaphors work requires the resources of biological, cognitive, and social science. The theory of metaphor can provide a crucial framework for an integrative view of illness and healing for three main reasons.

(1) Metaphors are ubiquitous in cognition and experience, although often disguised by convention as literal statements. A large body of work in cognitive science demonstrates that metaphors are not merely literary figures or ornaments applied after the fact—in moments of poetic exuberance or rhetorical excess—to our conceptual models and experiences.

Instead, metaphors serve to organize categories, concepts, models, and even the structure of modes of reasoning that give rise to both concrete and abstract thought and experience.[60] Metaphoric expressions and concepts are used to frame the technical models of medicine, psychiatry, and psychology, the everyday concepts and categories that constitute our folk psychology and local worlds of meaning, and the most personal and inward or private experiences of illness, symptoms, and suffering.

(2) Metaphors have sensory, affective, and conceptual connotations and hence fuse multiple dimensions of meaning in the same verbal act or cognition. The sensory and affective levels of meaning, as well as many of the conceptual implications, of metaphor are often hidden, particularly when metaphors are taken as literal because they have become conventional or "dead."[61] These hidden or implicit levels of meaning nevertheless can be shown to influence the direction of thought and action and our conviction of what makes sense, is plausible, or self-evidently true. In this way, metaphor contributes to the production of the "natural" world.

(3) Metaphors, whether conventional or novel, are creative, constitutive, and transformative of meaning and experience. Metaphor is not simply a colorful or fanciful representation of what already exists but the presentation and enactment of what is possible or conceivable. The potential meaning may involve resituating experience in a different frame, world, or ontology.[62] A theory of symbolic meaning built on metaphor emphasizes the inventive, evocative, and performative powers of language and imagination, which are central to individuals' efforts to understand and cope with distress, as well as to the symbolic logic and evocative power of healing systems, rituals, and interventions.

(4) The metaphors we use to make sense of experience can be systematized as schemas or models based on analogical mappings. When a metaphor is schematized or systematized, it can become a model of experience but, unlike a formal analogy or explicit mapping, the metaphor need not conform to its initial target domain, and this may lead to divergent meanings. While analogies may provide the basic structure or mapping that prompts metaphor, metaphors have excess or supplementary meaning reflecting the wider or deeper search for associations, correspondences, or connections. This search may involve picking out one or other aspect of the source to attach its quality (or entailment) to the target in a focal way, or it may involve constructing possible worlds or situations in which the extended metaphor makes sense.

When metaphors offer new ways of looking at or "taking hold" of familiar objects or events, they can be viewed as *cognitive tools* or gadgets.[63] New metaphors can be readily fashioned, yielding new tools. In this way, metaphor provides a highly flexible, granular modularity of mind. In a sense, metaphors can function as temporary cognitive modules assembled to do specific types of information processing, regulation or transformation of action and perception. Each metaphor becomes a jury-rigged module that serves the generative/constructive nature of cognition. But metaphors have lives of their own, both cognitively and socially. As a cognitive tool, every metaphor has its own affective resonances, affordances, and limitations that leave marks or traces on the concepts and experiences to which it is applied. Socially, every metaphor provides a particular perspective or way of seeing the world, framing situations, identifying goals, and organizing action for individuals and groups.[64] Crucial to this autonomy and constructive power of metaphors is the extent to which metaphoric meanings can be stabilized and put to use. This stabilization can occur through a metaphor's connection to embodied experience or discourse, its elaboration in narratives that are shared with others, and by its embedding in a web of social practices and institutions. This points to the need to understand metaphor (and its narrative elaborations) in terms of the dynamics of social-ecological contexts.[65]

## Metaphor in Ecosocial Context

The chief problem with putting metaphor at the center of a theory of meaning is that, in metaphoric worlds, anything goes. While individual metaphors bias and constrain our associations, they do so in partial and flexible ways that can be easily subverted or transcended by the production of new metaphors. The coherence of metaphors is like the organization of a tool kit: though they may be carried together in the toolbox, each tool, when taken out, encourages hand and eye to approach a problem in a particular fashion (of course, a tool can be used in unintended ways). While a degree of continuity occurs because each tool must work with the material left by its predecessor, each tool affords new possibilities and allows radical departures. In a similar way, when different metaphors are used to explore a region of experience, we can try to make them fit with each other or take off with a train of associations at an oblique angle. The use of multiple metaphors may yield no overarching coherence, because the polysemy of metaphor imposes no necessary or rigid logical order, unless there is some reason to grant a particular metaphor primacy or centrality and use it to corral, constrain, and hierarchically structure the rest of our cognitive constructions and inventions. In many cases, the central metaphor remains unclear. Instead, we achieve coherence by imposing the formal constraints of logic and the pragmatic constraints of practice. In addition to logical coherence, these constraints may be based on the trajectory of our personal history or biography or the demands of adapting to particular situations, social norms and institutions. Coherence and consistency of meaning then usually come not from within the field of potential metaphors but from the subordination of metaphors to features of the world relevant to specific goals.[66] The goal or use constrains the choice of metaphor even as the metaphor can reframe or modify the goal. In particular, it is grounding in bodily experience on the one hand and the social order on the other that provide constraints and norms and, in so doing, a sense of aptness, epistemic authority, and cognitive or rhetorical efficacy that promotes some metaphors to the status of central, core, or root metaphors that come to dominate our symptom perception, illness narratives, and medical models.

Early bodily experiences provide preconceptual templates for subsequent knowledge and experience.[67] These templates may be what George Lakoff and Mark Johnson call "image-schemas"—that is, combinations of images and propositional knowledge about situations[68]—but they may also involve forms of procedural or embodied knowledge (skills, biases, stances, propensities to respond) that cannot be easily articulated or described. More elaborate metaphors that structure both concepts and the syntax of language may be built on these rudimentary sensorimotor schemas.

Social structures and patterns of interaction shaped by cultural beliefs and practices influence our bodily experiences of the world from their inception.[69] Social practices conjoin disparate bodily experiences in familiar sequences that, however contingent, have the experiential quality of *immediacy*, of occurring in the moment without any mediation, which is easily mistaken for necessity—that is, the sense or conviction that things could not possibly be any other way. These seem to be basic building blocks of experience that cannot depend on the mediation of language and cultural history. Yet, insofar as such experiences are apprehended through a culturally shaped consciousness or habitus and articulated in common language, the basic qualities and elements of bodily experience are never free of culture.

At another level of organization, social models, myths, and ideologies that circulate through many forms of discourse provide narratives that constrain the choice of metaphor. In formal terms, a narrative structure imposes a partial ordering or lattice on experiences and events.[70] The operators that relate one node to the next in the lattice of narrative can be based on implicit metaphors. For example, for English speakers, the passage of time—which is fundamental to narrative structure—is often based on spatial metaphors in which we move forward along a path toward the future (e.g., "I LOOK FORWARD TO TOMORROW"); in parallel, we metaphorize events as entities that move toward us from the future and disappear behind us into the past (e.g., "ALL THINGS MUST PASS"); these structures vary by language and culture, with effects on how we process, perceive, and evaluate events.[71] Metaphors lie at the basis of both such simple narrative structures and the more complex stories that imbue our lives with emotional and historical meaning. But the bridge from metaphor to narrative is not unidirectional: narratives, in turn, may suggest metaphors, and the framework of a familiar narrative allows us to use many disparate, even incompatible metaphors, without obvious incoherence.

The higher order conceptual structure and self-referentiality made possible by narrative practices is key for understanding how metaphors are stabilized and extend their reach into the social world. Narratives come in many shapes and sizes, some concocted for a transitory occasion, others drawn from a common fund of stories that circulate within and between communities. Some of these stories are tentative, the result of casual bricolage, while others are highly valorized, deeply held, and defended. Certain dominant, socially constructed narratives can be called "myths," not in the sense that they are false beliefs or a special genre of story, but in recognition of their function as unquestioned truths and master narratives or frameworks that we use to order and explain vital aspects of our worlds.[72] The classical myths of Greece or India are stories about gods who are human-like actors with intelligible motivations, if sometimes awe-inspiring powers. The more mundane stories invoked in illness narratives describe the motivations, conflicts, and concerns of ordinary human lives. Some of these become exemplary as models for suffering, endurance, and moral personhood. We use these narratives to justify, order, and make sense of our lives and, in so doing, we constitute our selves. In this sense, ordinary narratives draw from cultural templates that are similar to grand myths: they are story-forms that convey central values and concerns. Like classical myths, the origins of the mundane myths provided by secular society remain largely unexamined and unquestioned in everyday life; that taken-for-grantedness is part of their rhetorical power.[73]

There is a triadic relationship between bodily experience, metaphoric constructions, and overarching narratives in the production of meaning-

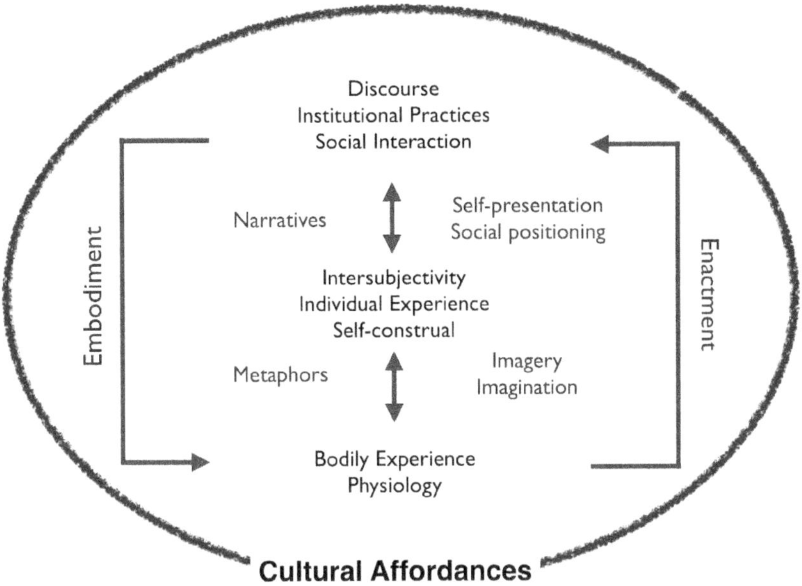


Figure 1.2 Embodiment and enactment in experience
This figure outlines the cyclical processes of embodiment and enactment that mediate experience. There is two-way traffic between bodily processes and individual experience mediated by cognitive processes of metaphor, imagery, and imagination. Similarly, there is traffic between experience and social discourse or institutional practices mediated by interpersonal communication through narratives, self-presentation, and positioning. Embodied experiences give rise to metaphors, which structure and shape individual experience, and to narratives, which are amplified, stabilized, and extended through collective enactments. In turn, discursive practices give rise to new metaphors and modes of embodiment. These cycles of enactment and embodiment occur on multiple timescales: (i) in the historical process of producing culture, novel metaphors become the building blocks of common sense; (ii) over the course of individual development, collective narratives and modes of cooperative enactment structure individual autobiographical narratives and identity; and (iii) in the ongoing improvisations of everyday life, extended metaphors and narratives are tools for self-fashioning and positioning. All of this occurs in a field of cultural affordances provided by local niches and larger social contexts (adapted from Kirmayer & Ramstead, 2017, with permission of MIT Press).

and sense-making. Figure 1.2 depicts the interaction of these processes. Social forces work at all three of these sites (body, metaphor, discourse), though they are most explicit and conspicuous in the process of constructing discursive formations. Exclusive attention to one site gives an incomplete picture of the process of meaning-making and leads to predictable distortions in our picture of the forces that shape experience. Research on embodiment shows how the body undergirds and constrains perception and thought, just as critical anthropology and social constructivism expose the self-confirming realities maintained by political economic structures and ideologies. The study of the role of metaphor in mediating transactions of embodied and socially situated selves offers a way to move beyond some of the limitations of disembodied and apolitical theories of illness experience and healing.

## Some Notes on Method

There are many ways to study metaphor, reflecting both disciplinary interests and the multiple uses of metaphor as linguistic trope, pragmatic speech act, rhetorical device, and conceptual structure.[74] The approach to metaphor analysis in this book is informal and unsystematic but adequate to the task of showing some of the hidden meanings and unintended consequences of our models in medicine and psychiatry. There are three steps to this informal method: tracing and tracking, analysis and critique, and integration. Tracing and tracking explore the uses of a metaphor as well as its origins, applications, and extensions. Critique is based on clarifying the assumptions inherent in the production or use of a metaphor, both implicit and explicit, identifying alternative metaphors for the same domain of interest, and considering the consequences of the use of the metaphor, both deliberate and unintended. Integration aims to identify or invent larger frames or ecologies within which multiple (even contradictory) metaphors can coexist.

While any metaphor easily generates polarities (HARD/SOFT, CONCRETE/ABSTRACT, INSIDE/OUTSIDE), the possible contrasts are endless, and the narrative strands implied by metaphor are always multiple and tangled rather than constituting a simple binary opposition. The goal of analyzing multiple metaphors is not a synthesis that transcends differences but a pluralism that recognizes the unique virtues and limitations of particular metaphors and stays with the generative tensions of difference, contrast, and invention. The methods of metaphor analysis borrow from cognitive poetics and critical discourse analysis.[75] This allows us to uncover and trace some of the connotations or implications of specific metaphors presented as words, images, or actions. Tracing connotations can be done in several ways, each informed by a set of pragmatic concerns.

The most basic metaphors have their roots in sensory analogy. This level of metaphoric meaning can be recognized by considering personal, conventional, and cultural associations to the sensory qualities invoked in describing or expressing an idea. Many basic concepts make direct appeal to these sensory qualities but they are also present in abstract discourse. More elaborate sensory associations are found, for example, in the work of the philosopher Gaston Bachelard, though in his reveries on matter, the passage from common or conventional sensory associations to personal, often idiosyncratic meanings is quick and unannounced.[76] Linguistic research on metaphor often relies on the intuitions of the author as native speaker, but it can also engage more systematically with a corpus of language drawn from particular discursive contexts like books, newspapers, and conversations (increasingly captured through social media). Of course, context shapes discourse, and that includes the medium through which metaphor is conveyed. Some metaphors may reflect the sensory qualities of the medium (speech, written text, electronic media) itself rather than the specific topic, interlocutors, or occasion. And, while one's own associations can be a guide to common experience, they must be tested for generality both within and across cultures. Intuitions about metaphoric meaning must be treated as hypotheses rather than final truths.

Beyond the sensory qualities conveyed by metaphors, there is a layer of meaning associated with affect or emotion. Some of this can be captured through Charles Osgood's device of the *semantic differential*, in which a respondent is asked to rate various words, concepts, or experiences on bipolar scales anchored at each end by semantic opposites (e.g., hot/cold, fast/slow, pleasant/unpleasant).[77] It is easy for people to do this—showing our facility with cross-modal sensory analogies, emotional valences, and metaphoric thinking. Factor analyses of answers to many such scales yield a small set of common dimensions of affective or motivational meaning.[78] We all have the capacity to recognize such simple meaning and can use our bodily and emotional responses to identify some of the affective connotations of a particular metaphor. In effect, our capacity for affective response allows us to unpack some of the potential meaning of the metaphor. However, while some simple or basic emotions may be closely tied to particular bodily states or dispositions to respond, more complex emotions or sentiments depend on specific social scenarios or situations. Interpersonal or intercultural understanding of more specific or fine-grained aspects of emotional meaning then depends on greater levels of shared experience with the kinds of social scenarios, scripts, positions, and predicaments encoded in the emotion.[79] Complex feelings that involve cognition extended over time and space to include personal and collective history and geography will require the same sort of unpacking as abstract concepts.

Everyday affective meaning may be communicated not only through the content and connotations of a metaphor but also (or, in some cases, exclusively) through its paralinguistic expression in voice, tone, and gesture. Listening to the tone and other pragmatic features of a speaker's utterance may yield metaphoric connotations that supplement, contextualize, or even contradict other levels or layers of meaning. This is part of the pragmatics of the use of metaphor to convey irony or sarcasm.

By relating two different domains of experiences, metaphors can generate affective meaning simply by juxtaposition. The activation of two different image-schemas or sets of associations creates a superposition, interaction or blending in which each modifies the other.[80] This can occur without an explicit model, awareness, or understanding of the connection between the domains. To understand the content of a metaphor, we construct an image, action, model, scenario, or story implied by the metaphor. From this image, model, or story, we can then reason analogically to explore the implications of the metaphor. We can return to the initial metaphoric image repeatedly and move out along other arcs of associations. Of course, this kind of cognitive engagement and elaboration works within the metaphor and cannot reveal all of its connotations. To get beyond or behind the assumptions conveyed by the metaphor, we need to compare and contrast the image or story invoked by the metaphor with alternative metaphors. This comparison of alternatives can make it clear why "THE FIGHT AGAINST CANCER," for example, is not the only way to think about the search for a cure, public health efforts, or one's personal struggle.[81] "Fighting" can be contrasted with "taming," "treating," or "controlling" or "living with" in terms of its sensory, affective, and conceptual connotations. This generation of alternatives is a basic way to open up the meaning of metaphor and is especially revealing when metaphors have become entirely conventional and, hence, hard to recognize as such.

Clearly, metaphors are grounded not only in bodily experience but in the social world. Exploring the social and cultural connotations of metaphor then involves reconstructing the scene, setting, or scenario where action and experience unfold. This requires detailed knowledge of cultural particulars. While bodily experience tends to be single if not singular—occurring to you or me in this moment, though experiences of intersubjectivity and intercorporeality are common[82]—social experience is characterized by its multiplicity of voices. The social connotations of metaphor include the invocation of or allusion to these other voices. This *heteroglossia* may involve other voices from history, oral tradition, literature, or communities.[83]

Meanings may lie buried or sedimented in layers of metaphors that link a word to its historical origin and changing contexts of use. Etymological analysis can expose the historical roots of metaphors that are obscure or that have become entirely conventional. This archaeology of metaphor can reveal whole systems of meaning and metaphysics that may have been elided or suppressed by changes in cultural models and ontologies. Some of the historical connotations of a metaphor may be lost, but other connotations may leave traces that can structure whole conceptual domains. There is a rich literature exploring the history of metaphors for mind and psychological functions that provides the undergirding for contemporary academic and folk psychologies and concepts of self and personhood.[84]

All of these layers of meaning coexist with and contribute to the social significance and rhetorical force of any speech act. As shown throughout this book, metaphors are grounded in both bodily and social experience. Thus, metaphoric connotations can be traced inward to bodily, interoceptive, sensorimotor, and experiential roots, and outward to social context and interactions, including both discursive practices and material circumstances. Explicating what seems to be going on in the body and in social interactions clarifies the meaning of metaphors derived from these experiences. This explication builds on insights from phenomenology and mechanistic accounts of the physiology of the body, the dynamics of the social world, the history of individual experience, and collective culture sedimented in language, institutions, and practices.

Metaphor analysis reveals that meaning includes dimensions that are essentially connotative rather simply denotative. These connotations may be received as part of the everyday use of a metaphor, or excavated from its etymological history, but they can also be generated de novo by the new linguistic and social contexts in which the metaphor is deployed. While acquiring new metaphors may begin with *ostension*—pointing to an object or event—and hence depend on a primitive concept of denotation, the things of the world are not logical atoms but scenes, situations, and opportunities for action that, by virtue of how we interact with them, yield many different sorts of experience. While a conventional metaphor like SHE GAVE HIM AN ICY STARE may seem to have a relatively narrow or specific meaning associated with its sensory qualities of coldness, transparency, solidity, and slipperiness, ice can be mined for deeper affective and metonymic meaning. Ice as metaphor can conjure a whole season (winter), a physical state (solid water) or phase transition (freezing, melting, sublimating), and a wide variety of sensations and actions: ice can crack or craze, be shaped into a cube that can be plunked in a glass, crunched between the teeth, skated on, scraped from a car windshield, or carved by a chainsaw into ephemeral sculptures. The word "ice" can generate rich metaphoric connotations drawn from the bodily, social, and abstract consequences of all of these potential modes of interaction. We might say these meanings are latent in the metaphor of ice.

To say that meanings are latent in a metaphor, however, is not to claim that every individual who encounters or uses the metaphor has access to all of those meanings all of the time. The salience of meanings depends on having had particular experiences and background knowledge. Some meanings are available to most people by virtue of the many existential universals of human experience: being born, discovering one's body and becoming self-aware; being dependent on the care of others for comfort and survival; learning and acquiring new skills; experiencing attachment, motivations, and desires like thirst and hunger and emotions like fear and anger; experiencing pain, injury and sickness, and loss; growing old; and facing mortality.[85] Other meanings depend on living in a particular kind of body, a specific social environment or niche, occupying a certain social position or having had certain life experiences.[86] Whatever one's own position and life trajectory, many of the latent meanings are available in the larger social world, distributed among people and places where the metaphors are used and circulate. This means that, whether or not an individual knows, intends, or has access to a particular connotation of a metaphor, that meaning may become important for some participants at some point in the circulation of the metaphor. In a sense, then, the potential meanings travel along with the metaphor, whether or not they are taken up and responded to by anyone, ready to spring to life, provided that the bodily experience and cultural knowledge needed to elaborate their meaning become available.

Systematic study of metaphor shows that there are certain key words or root metaphors that structure larger domains of thought and experience.[87] These key words may be identified by their high frequency of occurrence in speech, by their central role in organizing a conceptual domain, by evidence that they are concrete terms or "logical atoms" that cannot be further decomposed, or through their status as socially authorized truths or certainties. In many cases, however, root metaphors may be hidden or implicit, buried under a complex superstructure of abstraction and habitual use. Such core metaphors form part of our background knowledge—tacit assumptions, habits of thought, and skills we use to take hold of the world. We may find it hard to identify these root metaphors because they are implicit, involving procedural knowledge or ways of doing things that are viewed as natural or inevitable and, sometimes, because bringing them to light might reveal biases or raise issues that threaten or destabilize the status quo.

Metaphors reflect categorical knowledge, but metaphors also allow the creation of new categories.[88] In this way, metaphors populate the world with new entities and, to the extent that these give rise to new ontologies, some philosophers have argued that there is a sense in which metaphors impel the construction of whole new worlds.[89] Metaphors may be taken as literal statements if we view them as initiating the construction of worlds (local or global) in which the metaphoric relation finally obtains because it has recognized or brought into being a new ontology. If metaphors create whole worlds, and if these worlds can only be accessed or inhabited by those who live within a particular regime of metaphors, then it is a small step to the claim that these worlds are incommensurable—that is, there can be no Archimedean point from which to compare them, or, still worse, no easy traffic or exchange between them.[90] In fact, we see constant traffic between disparate metaphoric "worlds" both within and between individuals and communities, with borrowing, blending, and hybridizing, suggesting that any incommensurability we perceive is only as large as the limits of our imagination and ability to create communicative situations of openness, equity, intimacy, and prolonged engagement.[91] Indeed, metaphor itself invites intimacy and enhances our understanding of others' experience.[92] When they challenge or unsettle conventional worldviews, metaphors serve as modes of inquiry that can lead to the recognition of similarity as well as difference. This points to the fundamentally social and political nature of metaphoric constructions and their implicit ontologies.

Indeed, as much as metaphors structure our world, the claim that metaphors create worlds is overstated: metaphors create *worlds of imagination* or possibility, not *this* world, which—in its fullness, complexity, and intransigence—escapes any encompassing metaphor.[93] Metaphors allow us to take hold of the raw materials of the world to fashion shelter, build bridges, and enter into dialogue with others. To do this, we must recognize the material exigencies that lie beyond the metaphoric frame. Metaphor can be enacted in ways that create new structures and processes that transform our world. It provides us with tools to negotiate a larger reality that is, at least potentially, shared with others with whom we enter into relationships of mutual recognition. This results in a hermeneutic circle or cycle in which meaning is co-constructed. On one side of the cycle between imagination and reality, we have the piecemeal constructions of metaphor based on experiences with the world, on the other side, the calling into being of a shared world through narratives and imaginative constructions in which metaphor finds purchase, makes sense, and solicits both serious and playful engagement.

## An Outline of This Volume

Reflecting the way that hermeneutic circles are actually cycles that unfold in time, this book spirals around the central theme of metaphor and healing, first addressing the embodied nature of metaphor, then various models of healing, and finally issues of meaning, truth, and transcendence central to the politics, ethics, and pragmatics of metaphor in individual and social rhetorics of transformation.

Chapter 2 explores the developmental psychology of metaphor and its significance for illness experience. Illness experience is articulated through metaphors that are grounded in—and constrained by—both bodily experience and social interaction. The bodily grounding of metaphor is based on the elaboration of sensorimotor equivalences, as seen early in development in synesthesia and cross-modal analogies. The social grounding of metaphor resides in the pragmatics of language where context and goal are inseparable from meaning. Metaphors allow for inventive play, despite the dual constraints of body and society, by requiring only piecemeal correspondences to the world through ostension. The meaning of metaphors is then to be found not in representation but in *presentation*—modes of action of ways or life. Clinical examples illustrate how a semantics of metaphor can clarify the tensions between the essential irrationality of illness experience and the biomedical presumption of rationality. Notions of embodiment are central to this analysis, but the body itself appears in these reflections in many ways: as the primary locus and vehicle of experience, as our means of engaging with the world, as the material substrate of cognition and action, as footing for the scaffold of metaphoric meaning, and as itself a metaphor.

Chapter 3 illustrates the poetics of illness experience by examining the clinical conversation during a psychiatric assessment of a patient with "psychosomatic" complaints. The narratives presented by patients in clinical contexts are often fragmentary and contradictory, reflecting their ongoing struggle to make sense of inchoate experience and position themselves in ways that elicit care and concern. Metaphors of illness experience open up narrative possibilities, but these may be blocked by the conflicting agendas or cross-purposes of clinician and patient. As a result, in place of an overarching integrative narrative, we find interruption, miscommunication, and mutual subversion of accounts. Focusing on narratives in their pragmatic context, with close attention to the speakers' rhetorical aims, can identify situations of tension and misunderstanding that are common kinds of clinical impasse and that point to structural problems and ideological conflicts in the institutions and practice of biomedical care.

Having looked at meaning construction in the clinical encounter, we then turn to a closer examination of the dynamics of transformation. Healing rituals use metaphoric language and symbolic actions not only to represent experience but also to change it. How do symbols alter social, psychological, and physiological processes? Chapter 4 applies recent work in cognitive neuroscience to explore plausible models for a physiology of metaphor as imaginative enactment. Examples drawn from ethnographic studies of Indigenous healing practices, including shamanism, illustrate how metaphors and images may entrain and transform affliction through parallel processes at the levels of bodily feelings, emotional states, cognitive maps, and mythic narratives.

The narrative construction of the self is the pivot between embodied experience and the social world. The key argument of Chapter 5 is that a theory of meaning adequate to account for the effectiveness of symbolic healing and psychotherapy requires some variant of the three concepts of myth, metaphor, and archetype. Here, *myth* stands for the over-arching narrative and discursive structures of self and society, produced and lent authority by cultural tradition. *Archetype* stands not for preformed ideas or images, but for bodily and existentially given structures in experience that undergird specific images, metaphors, and imaginative constructions. Metaphors then occupy an intermediate realm (as depicted in Figure 1.2), linking overarching narratives or discursive formations and bodily given structures and through imaginative enactments that allow movement in sensory-affective quality space. This multilevel perspective itself constitutes a middle ground between constructivist and realist approaches to meaning that can integrate causal and interpretive models of symbolic healing.

Autobiographical narratives link past, present and future in the service of making sense of the world and anticipating and adapting to its many challenges. Life events and changes to the social world can disrupt existing narratives and demand a reconstructive process that recapitulates elements of the original developmental process through which the narrative self emerges. In Chapter 6, I discuss the representation of memory in narratives of trauma.

The accounts of victims of childhood trauma are contrasted with the testimony of survivors of the Holocaust. These accounts differ strikingly in the contours of the struggle to remember and forget. For the childhood trauma victim, the violence of traumatic events makes them difficult to remember, while, for the Holocaust victim, violence makes events impossible to forget. I argue that that the distinctive qualities of trauma narratives can also be understood as differences in the culturally constructed landscapes of memory that shape the distance and effort required to remember affectively charged and socially defined events. Landscapes of memory draw from implicit models of memory that influence what can be recalled and warranted as accurate. Narratives of trauma, then, involve cultural models and metaphors of personal and historical memory.

The ethics of storytelling has an essential counterpart in the ethics of listening and this involves particular forms of temporality (being present with and in the story) and ways of participating in a cultural community. Chapter 7 explores some ways in which the psychological dynamics of trauma shape the experience of the self and temporality. I distinguish two meta-narratives or concepts of the self in terms of their implicit root metaphors and associated temporalities: the endurance of the *adamantine self*, characterized by its integrity, coherence, autonomy, self-definition, self-determination, and self-control; and the flexibility of the *relational self*, characterized by its fluidity, sensitivity to context, multivocality, interdependence, and responsiveness to others. These two implicit models of the self are associated with different ideologies of the person and forms of social life that shape trauma memory and experience.

The intersubjectivity through which experience emerges involves encounters with others that confront us with difference.[94] Chapter 8 considers the politics and poetics of alterity, of understanding the other when they have experiences or use modes of expression that are radically unfamiliar. Some forms of psychopathology can render people strange and difficult to understand. Communication can lead to empathic understanding, which, in turn, can guide compassionate action. But communication depends on a shared conceptual world. How can language convey meanings that are not shared, that mark a divide between human beings or whole communities? The work of the poet Paul Celan sheds light on the power of language to bridge disparate worlds and on the ethical stance needed when empathy fails. Celan's poetics of alterity have implications for our efforts to understand individuals' illness experience as a grounding for the ethics of the clinical encounter.

Illness itself constitutes a primordial form of otherness that structures the process of healing. Chapter 9 considers the ways the "other" of illness shapes the dynamics of the healer–sufferer relationship through the archetype of the wounded healer. Shamanism and other elementary systems of medicine are built on an ethos that identifies healers' calling, authority, and effectiveness with their own initiatory illness experiences. This chapter argues that the ethos of the wounded-healer provides an underlying affective logic to contemporary medicine, psychiatry, and psychotherapy. Developmental changes during psychiatric training in the relationship of a healer to his wounds are illustrated by a series of dreams. The ethos of the wounded-healer has implications for understanding the epistemic authority of healers, the training of clinicians, and for addressing basic ethical and pragmatic issues in intercultural health care.

The final chapter returns to broader issues of the cultural politics of metaphor, examining the tensions between ethics and aesthetics in illness experience and healing. While the focus on language allows us to mobilize the richness of literature to explore illness experience and healing, in doing so, we may inadvertently downplay the material circumstances that determine health disparities and inequities. Against this apparent opposition, I argue that attention to the aesthetics of language and to the creative functions of imagination and poeisis can help us understand the mechanisms of suffering and affliction and devise forms of healing that better respond to the needs of individuals within and across diverse cultures and contexts.

## Toward a Poetics of Illness and Healing

The epigraphs from Francis Bacon and René Char at the start of this chapter speak to a basic tension in approaching experience through metaphor. Bacon stands for the value of scientific empiricism and objectivity, knowing the world as it really is, apart from our wishes and self-serving distortions or the collective myths and ideologies that hide us from inconvenient truths. The surrealist poet Char reminds us of the deeper layers of meaning sedimented in language as dead metaphors, idioms, forgotten etymologies, and formulaic accounts waiting to be brought back to life by close attention to language, and by the playful, oneiric refiguring of conventional forms of speech in poetic imagery and art. This backcountry of meaning is also part of reality—the reality of the imagination. As Simon Critchley puts it: "Absolute fact is not absolute, in the sense of being absolved from any relation to the imagination; it is simply the *arrière-pays* of the imagination and therefore relative to its power."[95]

Metaphor theory shows how symbols and things—imagination and reality—live in the same world. Medical anthropology, psychology, and psychiatry must steer a course between realism and constructivism, somehow integrating the useful features of both perspectives. Perhaps this is not so quixotic as it first appears. The philosopher Ian Hacking has laid out some of the many meanings of social construction, each associated with different modes of looping between human cognition, action, and the social world.[96] If experience, identity, and the social world emerge from a cyclical process in which we invent and are reinvented by our own metaphors, the opposing arms of the process are then part of a great hermeneutic circle.[97] Metaphor is a site for the social construction of embodied experience. At the same time, metaphors are grounded in bodily experiences that appear to be universals—so metaphor is also shaped by bodily givens and projects them into the social world through physical and symbolic action or enactments. There can be no sharp demarcation then between the bodily given and the socially constructed, since both bodily constraints and social practices shape experience from its inception.

Beyond the microdynamics of symptom experience, work on metaphor has implications for the larger project of understanding the biomedical system of knowledge/power. The metaphors that arise in individuals' struggles to apprehend and make sense of their predicaments borrow from and contribute to the political language of power, resistance, and dissent. Every choice of metaphor lends power to a particular view of the world. We must judge the value of metaphors therefore on ethical, aesthetic, and pragmatic grounds. Certainly, the ability to become aware of metaphor qua metaphor ("*only* a figure of speech") is a valuable corrective to blind acceptance of our current models, to which we owe, in part, the advances of science. Yet, this self-critical awareness always occurs within a skein of unexamined metaphors generated anew with every effort to take hold of the world. There is no end to uncovering the metaphors of the cultural implicit. Instead of naive efforts to replace metaphors with literal descriptions of experience then, we need constant attentiveness to the taken-for-granted language of experience, continued creativity in the invention of metaphors, and steadfast commitment to thinking through their implications.

CHAPTER 2

# *The Body's Insistence on Meaning*

> Don't be the rider who gallops all night
> and never sees the horse that is beneath him.
>
> – Rumi[1]

> The experience of struggling with illness is the experience of the fundamentally metaphorical nature of self: one is, and is not one's body . . . In illness, we grasp how the self approaches the condition of language.
>
> – Jan Zwicky[2]

With language we construct fictions, but not all experience is fictive, subject to the limitless power of imagination to transfigure and invent. Our aching bodies remind us there are at least two orders to experience: the order of the body and the order of the text.[3] In recent decades, scholars in many disciplines have approached the body with renewed respect, and *embodiment* has become a keyword in medical anthropology, sociology, epidemiology, and cognitive science.[4] This recognition of the body seems to be a response to obvious imbalances in many different strands of contemporary Western thought: the long history of dualism in which the activity of the mind is valued over and against the life of the body; a rationalism that ignores the significance of bodily felt meaning and minimizes the ways in which emotions organize thought and action; an emphasis on theoretical knowledge, divorced from skilled and situated know-how; and the postmodern deconstructions of traditions in terms of texts divorced from their embodiment and enactment in communities of practice. Against all of these ways of unmaking the world, the turn toward the body represents a longing for community, for bodily connection and participation in a habitable world of substance and feeling.

Despite the ease with which we make the distinction, there is an inescapable circularity between the order of the body and the order of the text. Past infancy, bodily experience is most conspicuously elaborated and communicated through language. Language, in turn, is grounded in bodily experiences that provide common referents for a lexicon and in the organization of bodily action that provides a basis for syntactic structure.[5] Any attempt to give autonomy to the study of either body or text, divorced from the other order of experience, is epistemologically naive. For how can we say the body is inherently "so," when that knowledge is worked out through language that imposes its own structure on thought and experience? Contrariwise, how can we claim to encompass all possible worlds of meaning in the permutations of language, when bodily pain and suffering upend our orderly lives, and drive us to the most desperate acts?

The healthy body is often silent or "absent" from awareness and makes itself known only in fleeting moments of pain or pleasure, exertion, or sudden release and repose.[6] Symptoms of pain, nausea, vertigo, and other forms of distress, malaise, or sickness place the body insistently in the foreground. As Arthur Kleinman movingly illustrates in his work on illness narratives, the problem of sickness raises two fundamental questions for the sufferer: "Why me?" (the problem of bafflement) and "What can be done?" (the problem of order and control).[7] These are the existential questions of Job, which arise at some point in every life, made personal and immediate by the insistence of bodily suffering. How can meaning and value be sustained when consciousness is constricted, degraded, and defiled by pain?

Searching for a comprehensive framework for medical anthropology, Nancy Scheper-Hughes and Margaret Lock described three realms of the body: the individual body-self of lived experience, approached by phenomenology, but known most directly in the wrenching immediacy of pain; the social body of symbolic representation; and the body-politic of power, domination, and control.[8] In truth, these distinctions point not so much to three bodies as to three types of text produced by scholars.[9] In any real event, the three bodies form a single system, which may be simultaneously riven by conflict and unified by mutual interaction and regulatory processes. Translations between these texts then demands an understanding of the processes that mediate the relationships between body, self, and society: between bodily feeling and social symbolism, *psychophysiology*; between social symbolism and politics, *rhetoric*; and between body-politic and body-self, *sociophysiology* and the dynamics of knowledge/power.

Despite the rhetoric of holism, the epistemological circularity of body and text does not imply the two orders can be readily dissolved into one. Body and text (like body and mind, from which this modern duality is transposed) stand in dialectical relationship to each other. And if the text stands for a hard-won rational order, imposed on thought through the careful composition of writing, the body provides a structure to thought that is, in part, extrarational and disorderly. This extrarational dimension to thought carries important information about emotional, aesthetic, and moral value. The dominant representational theories of meaning employed in medicine, psychiatry, anthropology, and cognitive science have tended to consider only those aspects of thought that conform to the rationality of an ideal, disembodied, mentality. The body and its passions are viewed as disruptions to the flow of logical thought, as momentary aberrations or troublesome forms of deviance to be rationalized, contained, and controlled. Yet in everyday life, bodily experience preempts our rational constructions. Through the pain and suffering that foreshadow its own mortality, the body drives us to seek meaning, to take our words as seriously as our deeds. Ultimately, the body insists that we finalize our temporary mental constructions and commit ourselves to some perspective, path, and version of reality.[10]

Any theory of meaning that hopes to address the experience of illness must give due weight to the primacy of the body not only as an object of thought but as itself a vehicle for thinking, feeling, and acting. The body cannot be contained by a theory of representation—for the body is not the same as the body-image. The body's influence on thought is more *presentation* than representation—given in substance and action rather than in imagination and reflection. How to approach this privileged position of the body without discarding the perspectivism of representational theory is a problem for any serious medical anthropology and person-centered clinical practice.

## Ridding the Body of Poison

> Dr. A is bewildered by the irrational behavior of Mr. Y, a thirty-five-year-old businessman receiving hemodialysis for chronic renal failure. Although Mr. Y has severe anemia, with a dangerously low hemoglobin, he refuses a blood transfusion. Mr. Y explains that he is terrified of receiving other people's blood because it may contain genetic material that carries their personality traits. This could affect his mind and alter his personality. His nephrologist, Dr. A, finds this explanation absurd. He reasons with Mr. Y, trying to impress on him the biomedical facts: "Red blood cells don't contain genetic material. Genes do not transmit personality from one adult to another. Personality is a function of the brain not the

> blood. You are in desperate need of a blood transfusion to avoid a heart attack or stroke." Mr. Y acknowledges this information but remains unconvinced.

The doctor's rational explanation begins with the "facts" of the body revealed by biomedicine and proceeds, with logic and the rhetorical style of clinical authority, to an imperative for action. The patient's rationality is evidenced by his ability to grasp the doctor's argument, acknowledge the premises of biomedicine, and follow the logic to its necessary conclusion. The physician expects that, by argument and education, the patient can be made to accept the real state of affairs and choose the only rational course of action—unless, of course, his capacity for reason is somehow impaired.

The epistemology implicit in the doctor's approach stems from a naive realism: The patient's world is made up of tangible objects (blood, hemoglobin, genes) which, if only he could see clearly, would provide accurate information about how, when, and why to act. Although the physician's vision is mediated by technical instruments (measures of blood chemistry and kidney function), and his residual uncertainty (due to the limitations of current medical knowledge) is shored up by colleagues and canonical texts, he acts as though the world he perceives, through the medium of medical theory and technology, is simply "out there" for all to see. The epistemology of biomedicine is based on the metaphor of vision, in which the eye takes in a replica of an objective world which the brain then represents or mirrors.[11] Technology extends the range of the eye but does not alter its intrinsic objectivity. The mind figures in this picture as the place where information about the world is recorded, organized, and stored. Thus, mental representations are presumed to be more or less isomorphic to reality, encoding facts about the world. This epistemology supports the radical separation of fact and value—where, by *value* I mean both the felt importance and social significance of means and ends.[12] In the tacit epistemology of biomedicine, mental representations are primarily about facts and only secondarily are they deformed or disrupted by idiosyncratic personal or social values.

The physician ignores the way in which medical training and the adoption of a theory embedded in technical language and practices actually create the ordered reality in which he discovers and situates the patient's "real" problems. Within the narrow epistemological framework of biomedicine, the rationality of Mr. Y's view of the world depends entirely on the empirical truth of his beliefs as judged against the standard provided by biomedical theory. Given this occlusion of the reality-creating function of medical theory and practice, it is not surprising that the physician quickly grows impatient with the patient's inability to see what is obviously *there*. Disagreement with medical opinion is prima facie evidence of irrationality. In his frustration, the doctor falls back on clinical authority to resolve, deflect, or ignore the patient's doubt.

The theory of meaning that corresponds to the physician's epistemology subordinates meaning to truth and holds that truth resides in the world. Facts, then, are represented in the mind as explicit conscious propositions whose main property is their truth value. As such, the doctor can provide Mr. Y with factual truths that have unambiguous meaning and that, if complete enough, lead inescapably to certain conclusions. Mr. Y may hold certain false beliefs, which can be challenged and replaced on a piecemeal basis by more accurate information. When this sort of education fails to change the patient's behavior—even though the patient can recite the biomedical facts and seems to follow the doctor's line of reasoning—the physician suspects there is some hidden irrationality or pathology of the patient's mind.[13]

> Dr. A then asks for a psychiatric consultation "to get Mr. Y to do the reasonable thing." In conversation with the psychiatrist, Mr. Y recounts his frightening experiences with childhood hospitalizations for kidney disease. He says he is mistrustful of doctors because of these experiences. When the psychiatrist asks Mr. Y if he is careful about what he puts into his body, like water or food, he smiles with some embarrassment and says: "You understand me very well doctor. I only drink purified spring water and eat only meat with no hormones or additives. You will probably think it is irrational, but I believe it is better for my health." Some days later, when his symptoms become more severe, Mr. Y accepts a blood transfusion, although he is obviously distressed by the situation.

The psychiatrist listens to Mr. Y's self-description for evidence of his conflicts and motivations both conscious and unconscious. The cognitive theories of health psychology recognize that there are many reasons why patients may be conflicted about the meaning of illness and the right course of action.[14] Psychodynamic theory assumes that patients cannot fully describe their predicament as a conscious set of beliefs, that there are hidden conflicts and motivations, and that explicit reasons are always, to some degree, rationalizations. The psychiatrist looks to the patient's history of relationships, and to the twists and turns of the clinical conversation, to reveal the core conflicts that organize the patient's experience. In this case, a sense of physical vulnerability, and a fragile body-boundary that must be vigilantly guarded against pollution by contact or intrusion, are prominent in Mr. Y's thinking. From this the psychiatrist links to other potentially related symptoms, like concerns about diet, which the patient confirms. Extrapolating backward, the psychiatrist searches for historical events that have conditioned Mr. Y's mistrust of doctors and fear of medical treatment. A childhood history of kidney disease led to repeated hospitalizations for investigative procedures. These childhood hospitalizations involved separations from his family, with feelings of abandonment that have shaped his lack of trust in caretaking relationships. These separations have continued: Mr. Y now lives alone in Canada while his wife and child live with his extended family in Europe. He denies any marital difficulty, claiming that this arrangement is due to his efforts to conduct business in Canada. He minimizes the impact this separation has had on his illness. The psychiatrist interprets this denial as further evidence of conflict: Mr. Y has difficulty forming close relationships; he probably feels abandoned but has learned to hide his feelings. His anger and disappointment with family, past and present, are expressed as mistrust of the doctors and nurses whose treatment he disparages and compares unfavorably with the care he has received in Europe. This position allows him to maintain the fiction of positive relationships with others back home while communicating his suffering to the medical caretakers with whom he has vital ongoing relationships.

## The Epistemology of Belief in Biomedicine and Psychiatry

The epistemology implicit in the psychiatrist's approach is a version of *psychological realism.* Human action is distinguished from nonhuman events by meaning, goal-directedness, and intention. Behavior is guided by belief, and so reasons can be causes. Beliefs may not correspond closely to a consensual reality and may be hidden from consciousness. However, the psychiatrist, as a detached observer, can discern the underlying beliefs and goals that govern the patient's behavior. The patient's lifeworld is not made up of material objects but of mental representations associated with emotion. If Mr. Y believes that foreign blood is polluted with microscopic fragments of the donor's personality then this is "psychologically true"—true, that is, for him.

This respect for the autonomy of the psyche coexists uneasily with the materialism of biomedicine and probably accounts for some of the suspicion with which medical practitioners continue to view psychiatry. The psychiatrists' goal, however, is not much different from that of their other medical colleagues—to rationalize the irrational and so induce the patient to accept the authority of medicine in the form of a "clinically necessary" blood transfusion. The psychiatric strategy to accomplish this goal may include showing patients the origins of their idiosyncratic beliefs in details of their personal history. Once these beliefs are situated in this history, it is easier to discount their relevance for rational decision making. But even when its origins are laid bare, the emotional charge that shapes conviction and concern may remain.

A second focus of psychiatry or psychological medicine, then, involves helping patients better express and manage their emotions. This may begin by acknowledging emotions as an understandable response to a predicament. Even in the encouragement to freely express emotion, however, there is the implicit expectation that, once expressed, the intensity of strong emotions will subside and allow the patient to make more rational decisions. There may be limited recognition of the extent to which emotions are a response to an ongoing situation that includes the clinician and their own values, commitments, and emotional stance. Indeed, the epistemology of psychiatry sometimes holds that psychiatrists are able to see patients' minds more clearly than the patients themselves, not only because the clinician is emotionally detached but precisely because, as trained observers, psychiatrists have become aware of the distorting effects of their own emotions and can somehow factor them out of their perceptions.

The theory of meaning that corresponds to this psychiatric epistemology is based on mental representation. These representations are evident in the dramatic monologues and scenarios played out in the theater of the mind.[15] According to psychodynamic theory, however, many of the representations that impart meaning may be hidden from consciousness—never articulated or pushed away from awareness, hived off in the unconscious through an active process of repression. The representations revealed by the patient's actions may be conflictual or distorted and part of the work of psychotherapy is to expose them so that they may be rationally confronted, revised, and brought back into accord with an adaptive stance toward consensual reality. Doing so should "normalize" the patent's illness experience and behavior.

The biomedical perspective emphasizes biological disease to the exclusion of illness experience.[16] Health psychology and psychiatry place illness experience at center stage, but their emphasis on cognitive representations or the ongoing drama in the inner theater of the mind minimizes the importance of the material circumstances of the body and the lifeworld. Both biomedical and psychological perspectives miss crucial dimensions of embodiment: the sensual qualities of bodily experience and social context of the patient's predicament.

### The Phenomenology and Social Meaning of Hemodialysis

Hemodialysis contravenes the healthy order of bodily experience. Patients witness blood leaving their body and traveling through plastic tubing into the hidden depths of the dialysis machine. The machine has nervous habits: clicks and beeps mark the passage of blood through the machine. Once "cleansed" by the machine, the blood returns to the patient's body to be hidden inside once more. Ordinarily, the presence of blood is indicated by a healthy color and turgor to the skin, a steady heart rate and stable blood pressure, a clear-headed ability to perceive and think, and a strong and energetic body, able to stand, move, work, and play without fatigue. During and immediately after dialysis, however, patients often feel exhausted, unsteady on their feet, their thinking clouded; if they stand up abruptly, they may feel faint. When patients experience such complications of dialysis, it may seem as though the machine has somehow altered their blood or incompletely returned it to their body.

Dialysis confronts patients with violations of conventional body boundaries. This transgression of boundaries is paralleled by recurrent dilemmas about the limits of self-control.[17] Patients are expected to passively cooperate with treatment and accept "machine-dependency" while actively participating in managing their illness and maintaining their autonomy in other spheres of life. The regions of the patient's life given over to medical care and those areas that remain independent change dramatically with the fortunes of treatment and the progress of disease. Depending on shifting circumstances that may be obscure to the patient, medical staff may view either acquiescence or independence as signs of rational behavior.

For the patient on hemodialysis, the permeability and transgression of body boundaries parallel recurrent ambiguities about the limits of autonomy and necessary dependence. These issues take on heightened meaning in the context of each individual's history. In the case of Mr. Y, early childhood experiences of unexplained pain made his body a mystery to himself. The surgeons and nurses who treated him caused more pain with knives and needles. He experienced his body as something appropriated by others for study and manipulation. At times, it seemed that others knew his insides more intimately than he did—with their ability to peer inside his body and their arcane knowledge of how the body works. Encouraged to take charge of his own care, he acquired the vocabulary of biomedicine but put it to his own use, emphasizing those elements of his health that were under his direct control. So he became preoccupied with what he put into his body. He posited—and perhaps felt—a direct link between what went in and what came out of his body, and this was dramatically confirmed by the daily consequences of even slight deviations from the strict diet and fluid intake he had to follow on dialysis. He idealized what was natural, organic, and pure—food from the country, untainted by the toxins and pollution of technologized urban life.[18]

There was a further social dimension to Mr. Y's preoccupation with reestablishing the integrity of his body boundary and maintaining the purity of his "insides." Mr. Y was a foreigner, a businessman who had come from Europe to Canada. Like his colonialist forebears, he viewed the locals as less cultured and sophisticated than himself. He felt their crudeness was intrinsic, part of their bodily constitution, and he feared receiving blood from them since this would taint his body and with it his mind. This incipiently racist theme of "blood purity," although it may have been influenced by Mr. Y's childhood traumas, found support in collective representations and discriminatory practices. Mr. Y was not alone in using birthplace, accent, education, and other signs of ethnicity to mark status or conflate historical identity and "blood." Mr. Y's assumed superiority was endorsed by a segment of his community of origin, who inherited colonial attitudes. It was matched by local constructions of identity associated with feelings of inferiority among the formerly colonized. Mr. Y's prejudice served to draw a sharp boundary that separated him from others. It alienated him from his medical caregivers who not only found him difficult to understand but, reacting with moral repugnance, no longer tried to understand his predicament.

## Islands of Reason, Oceans of Desire

In sickness we confront the inchoate. Bodily suffering distorts the landscape of thought, rendering our previous constructions incoherent and incomplete. The study of the essential irrationality of sickness is hampered by the fact that the social sciences adopt many of the same rationalistic values as biomedicine. For medicine the irrational is pathological; for the social sciences the irrational is deviant, erratic, eccentric, or exotic—a source of wildness and excess. Those who sympathize with the deviant offer rational explanations as justification. Those who valorize the irrational emphasize its function as a source of creativity and invention. Whether celebrated or shunned, the dominant theories of the social sciences tend to treat the nonrational aspects of existence as defective and in need of rationalization.[19] This emphasis on rationality and control is a central preoccupation of Western culture, and it permeates our models of the acquisition and use of knowledge, no less than our ethical and aesthetic vision.

The rhetoric of rationality promotes a naive view of conceptual representations as propositions directly accessible to consciousness. This leads to the assumption that people can, quite reasonably, tell us their beliefs. Rationality then inheres in the logical consistency or coherence of beliefs and in the consistent entailment of our actions by our beliefs. Western academic psychology is founded on a similar assumption of rationality: states of mind can be correlated with behavior only if we assume a coherent and stable set of production rules by which intention and belief are translated into action.[20]

A similar view of belief obtains in anthropology. Allan Young[21] characterized the "rational man position" in medical anthropology, which comprises several underlying assumptions about human nature, including: (1) Language and cognition share the same underlying structure. Language allows access to people's beliefs, which can be expressed as explicit statements about the world. Thus, there need be no significant gap between someone's volition and their verbalized intentions. (2) Knowledge and beliefs are (or should be) internally consistent according to some variety of propositional logic. (3) Reasoning is a conscious mental process by which people organize knowledge to provide useful information and guide action. It loosely follows deductive or inductive logic. Other forms of reasoning (e.g., through symbolism or metaphoric elaboration) have only restricted application to dreams, rituals, magic, or expressive culture. (4) Finally, people behave pragmatically on the basis of causal models to attempt to predict and control what is going to happen to them.

Into this neat scheme, the irrational intrudes. Action does not spring directly from belief—at least if belief is understood as explicit propositions. Belief often follows action, manufactured to justify behavior to one's self or to further a strategic self-presentation. Beliefs themselves are situational, inconsistent, and at times incoherent. What coherence belief attains may reside not in logical consistency but in the wholeness of an image or metaphor, in the dynamics of emotion or the persistence of a mood, or arise in the course of turning inconsistent beliefs into action, when a degree of coherence is imposed by the physical constraints of the body and the sequence of actions. Belief then may be better understood as reflecting habits, habitus, or dispositions to respond, which can only be partially captured by explicit propositions, and which are intertwined with particular affects and emotions.[22]

The irrational then can be thought of not simply as the mere absence of rationality, a residual or defective mode of cognition but as a category with its own distinct qualities. Often, the irrational stands for the role of the body in thought: sensuous and emotional. In Michelle Rosaldo's pithy formulation, emotions are "*embodied* thoughts, thoughts seeped with the apprehension that 'I am involved.'"[23] Emotions are a form of thought with their own rationality.[24] They determine not what is logical to do to achieve certain ends but what ends are most pressing in a given situation or social context. The affective significance of words, concepts, and images is not given in their formal relationships with each other but is tied to their human significance. Food and sex, fear and desire, and sickness and health, however much they are elaborated in abstract models, take their urgency and power from their embodied significance in peoples' ways of life.[25] The attempt to model these exigencies of human life as equivalent to any other rationally held proposition ignores their salience, structuring effects on action and experience, and subjectively compelling quality. This failure to recognize the primacy of the irrational is part of a more basic defect of rationalistic semantic models—their lack of attention to the embodied grounding of thought.[26]

While the interpretive methods of psychoanalytic and structuralist theory offered approaches to the irrational, both lacked sufficiently rich concepts of embodiment and so, inevitably, ended in rationalistic reduction. Classical psychoanalysis sought to contain the irrationality of the body within a system of a few correspondences between universal existential themes and supervenient biological drives. The vast array of symbols and forms of expression were reduced to a few core conflicts. Indeed, in one especially narrow account, the psychoanalyst Ernest Jones defined "symbol" as a sign signifying one of a set of universal bodily experiences: birth, death, hunger, sex, aggression, and a few others.[27] By virtue of its signifying one such knot of human passions, the symbol takes on a powerful evocative function that can speak to us across cultures. Psychoanalytic anthropology tended to view culture as a layer of shared beliefs plastered onto the basic biopsychodynamic structure of the human being.[28] On this view, the diversity of cultures reflects variation in surface meanings, while the depths of each individual involve the same processes of psychological conflict. The symbol can be decoded in terms of universal human themes; even religious symbols serve primarily to represent, deflect, and resolve inner conflicts. From the psychoanalytic viewpoint then, there could be only a few possible meanings for any conceivable symbol. In some hands, psychoanalytic explanation reduced the complex variety and multivocality of the patients' bodily experience and expression, with its frequent conscious lacunae, to the arbitrary completeness, rationality, and self-consciousness of the analyst's theory.[29]

Structuralism reduces the body to abstract parts and functions that populate a symbolic order. In Lévi-Strauss's original conception, this order is a mathematical group in which each symbol is related to others through operators that permutate or transform its essential features.[30] A structuralist account finds order in the enormous variety of individual symbolic expressions by explicating the structure of all possible permutations. Substituting form for content, structuralist theory results in a cognitive crystallography in which each symbol is motivated only by logical criteria of coherence, symmetry, and completeness. Yet there is much more at stake in symbolic language and action, as James Fernandez cogently put it:

> symbols are generated out of a need, whether a life wish or a death wish, but there is no real interpretation that is not situational and strategic. To suppose that there is a real or true interpretation that surpasses situation and the primal preoccupations of a given participant is the first strategy by which the inchoate has been approached . . . Judgement in symbolic analysis is much less empirical than moral.[31]

Ultimately, structuralism is limited in its explanatory power because it promotes a separation of abstract meaning and embodied use. For structuralism, the body is a mannequin—a stripped down, inanimate frame on which the vestments of theory can be draped. For psychoanalysis, the body is a primitive, ungoverned engine of desire. In practice, both approaches tend to deal not with the experience and realities of the body itself but with limited images or representations of the body. In substituting the image of the body for the body, of text for performance, and representation for action, both psychoanalysis and structuralism tended to exaggerate the coherence of meaning systems and downplayed the complexity of the body's materiality.

Despite their limitations, both psychoanalytic theory and structuralism identify crucial elements for an embodied theory of meaning. Psychodynamics draws attention to the wellsprings of action, the motive force and power of mattering. Structuralism focuses on the interrelatedness of symbols and the formal structure and coherence of symbolic systems that allows them to encode complex structures of the social world. Only a perspective that encompasses both can hope to provide an adequate approach to the shifting meanings of illness experience. It is a central task of this book to show how a semantics of metaphor can offer us a way into the urgency and inventiveness of language in suffering and healing.

## A Semantics of Metaphor

A metaphor is a mapping of similarities from one domain to another; when these are not already identified, it prompts us to *create* similarities by constructing an image, story, scenario, or world in which connections between topic and vehicle can be found.[32] From this point of view, analogy is one aspect of the metaphoric process but metaphors—involving sensory, affective, and imagery-based reshaping of concepts and experience—convey surplus meanings or connotations that are muted, truncated, or cordoned off in explicit analogies. Whereas simile draws attention to an existing similarity, metaphor can invent a relation where previously none existed. Along with this, unlike most similes or analogies, metaphoric concepts may be implicit or unintentional, used without awareness of or concern for the metaphoric/literal distinction.

Metaphors not only change the way we view a specific topic, they can restructure a whole domain of thought or experience.[33] This occurs because metaphors can use a high salience domain to reinterpret one that is less salient, affectively charged, or clearly organized. A metaphor introduces a new frame through which to view its topic and this is readily generalized to other related topics. Once a metaphoric comparison is made with a specific event, related events can be thought of in terms of parallel metaphors. Even a moment of metaphoric contact between two concepts encourages us to play with structuring whole regions of experience in terms of metaphors borrowed from previously unrelated domains. This process is at the root of everyday creative thinking, as well as many insights in science and other fields.[34]

While metaphors can structure and lend coherence to whole domains of thought,[35] in practice, we are free to pick discordant metaphors to try to get at some "underlying experience." For example, anthropologist Naomi Quinn studied the many different metaphors used by people to describe their marriage—as commitment, mutually beneficial relationship, enduring, project, journey, or even an ice cream cone.[36] In everyday conversation, mixed metaphors are the rule. Their coherence stems not from any key structuring metaphoric concept but from a specific experience, object, or event that can be returned to in perception, memory, or imagination to be repeatedly described from many angles. Similarly, personal autobiographies may employ divergent metaphors in the service of some overarching narrative that attains coherence not from a single root metaphor but from a distinctive sequence, trajectory, or transformation that is only secondarily and incompletely metaphorized in self-depictions.[37]

The sheer variety of metaphors deployed to talk about experiences suggests that metaphors are derivative of or aimed at something deeper and more fundamental. What is the structure of this underlying experience that admits of such infinite and contradictory metaphoric expression? The "real presence" that lies behind our metaphoric constructions includes our experience of embodiment—as Johnson and Lakoff emphasized—but it is also the social body, the presence of others, the palpable bonds and forces we feel with them, and the niches we inhabit together and the terrain we can explore.[38] Social relationships and patterns of interaction, like our experiences with the body and the physical world, can be endlessly mined for new metaphors.

## The Developmental Scaffold of Meaning

The perceptual basis of metaphor is similarity or equivalence. In its crudest form this perceptual equivalence involves synesthesia—equivalences across different sensory modalities.[39] The term synesthesia is used to refer to the experience of one sensory modality in terms of another. Thus, a person may hear a word or number and immediately visualize a specific color, or see a color and experience a particular taste. Such full-blown synesthesia is rare, but simple forms of cross-modal association are common, and most people can easily make reliable correspondences across sensory modalities when asked. A well-known example is the *kiki-bouba* effect presented in Figure 2.1.

Infants readily perceive cross-modal analogies in what may be taken as the earliest form of metaphor.[41] The Russian neuropsychologist Alexander Luria's famous account of S, the mnemonist who claimed to have eidetic recall for many of his childhood experiences, provides evidence for the role of synesthesia in spontaneously organizing perceptual categories. In a stream of imagery and associations recollecting (or imagining) his early experience of the Russian word *zhuk* (beetle), S provides a vivid portrait of the metaphoric world of the infant:

> *A zhuk*—that's a dented piece in the potty ... It's a piece of rye bread ... And in the evening when you turn on the light, that's also *a zhuk*, for the entire room isn't lit up, just a small area, while everything else remains

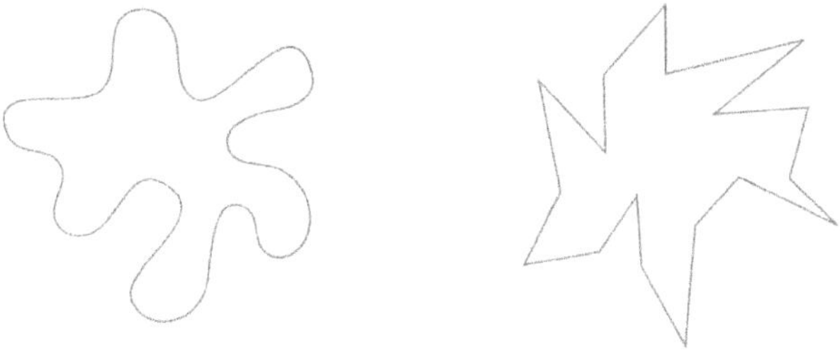


Figure 2.1 Cross-modal analogy: The *kiki-bouba* effect
Which of the two objects would you call *kiki* and which one is *bouba*? Across cultures, people assign the name "*kiki*" with its sharp, hard consonants to the figure on the right and name with softer, rounded sounds to the figure on the left. First described by Wolfgang Köhler as the *takete-maluma* effect, Vilajanur Ramachandran and colleagues renamed it "*kiki-bouba*," showed that it occurs in very different languages like Tamil, and identified brain lesions that interfere with the effect. They argue this provides evidence of cross-modal analogy occurring early in sensory processing. This might provide a scaffolding for more complex cross-modal analogies.[40]

> dark—*a zhuk*. Warts are also *a zhuk* . . . Now I see them sitting me before a mirror. There's noise, laughter. There are my eyes staring at me from the mirror—dark—they're also *a zhuk* . . . Now I'm lying in my crib . . . I hear a shout, noise, threats. Then someone's boiling something in the enamel teakettle. It's my grandmother making coffee. First she drops something red into the kettle, then takes it out—*a zhuk*. A piece of coal—that's also *a zhuk* . . . I see them lighting candles on the Sabbath. A candle is burning in the holder, but some of the tallow hasn't melted yet. The wick flickers and goes out. Then everything turns black. I'm scared, I cry—this is also *a zhuk* . . . And when people are sloppy pouring tea, and the drops miss the pot and land on the plates, that's also *a zhuk*.[42]

As this passage makes clear, the links between disparate perceptual experience are based not only cross-modal sensory analogies but also on affects or emotions. Spontaneous perceptual metaphors become more elaborate as the child grows. A fifteen-month-old child points to his toe, sticking through a hole in his sock and laughingly says "Turtle"; a three-and-a-half-year-old child peers into her mother's curly dark hair and proclaims: "Dark."[43] Such inventive metaphors rest on salient perceptual similarities, elements of which are universal. In adulthood, these similarities are often overshadowed by conventional associations based on socialization (e.g., hair is viewed in terms of its grooming and conformity to standards of attractiveness, which are gendered and tied to racialized identities[44]). In the underlying similarities that arise from perceptual salience, we find one way the body makes its presence known through metaphor.

Metaphors are not only sensory or perceptual, however, they can also be created through action. Enactive metaphors transform an object not by how it is perceived but by how it is used. By eighteen months, children are able to play with objects as if they were something else: a comb becomes a toothbrush; a truck becomes a telephone.[45] Even where there is little or no resemblance between objects, enactive metaphors can transform the meaning of one thing into the other. Such gestural metaphors persist as an important feature of nonverbal communication.[46]

Metaphors arise from symbolic play and the perception of resemblances before they are recognized as anomalous parts of speech, and long before they can be explained.[47] Both perceptual and enactive metaphors are grounded in bodily experience. Without prior perceptual equivalence classes, the infant would have no way to recognize regularities and construct a coherent world. Elementary perceptual similarities arising from the bodily experience are extended through metaphor to yield more complex categorizations of experience. Enactment and metaphoric similarity based on perception are closely related. We can call this *sensorimotor equivalence*: things that look similar and things that can be used the same way are made the same through cycles of perception and action.

Metaphors have affective, as well as sensorimotor, roots. Robert Zajonc provided evidence that affective evaluations or judgments can be made quickly and reliably in the total absence of stimulus recognition.[48] His studies suggested that there are information processing systems associated with emotion that allow rapid judgments of certain qualities of stimuli. These affective qualities supply a metaphoric dimension to words and concepts. Osgood's work with the semantic differential established cross-cultural universals of affective meaning involving dimensions of *evaluation*, *potency*, and *activity* (E-P-A).[49] These dimensions parallel the functioning of adaptive biological systems for approach/avoidance, attention, and arousal, respectively. These fundamental aspects of motivation and emotion can still be discerned in the more complex forms of sentiment that arise from patterns of social interaction. Indeed, some of the structure of interpersonal action can be explained in terms of the social regulation of these dimensions of affective experience.[50]

Developmental studies indicate that metaphor comprehension begins at an early age and is governed not so much by the maturation of specific cognitive skills (such as logical operations or classification) as by the child's fund of knowledge about the world and, hence, about the objects referred to in a metaphor. Until the age of eight or nine, children make many errors in metaphor comprehension because they lack knowledge of the world, particularly of the abstract properties and interrelationships of things. Young children tend to look for sensory similarities between topic and vehicle when a nonsensory, relational similarity is intended.[51] Older children learn to decode metaphors in terms of affective meaning; they are sensitive to the evaluative, potency, and activity dimensions of metaphoric meaning. Finally, as a fund of abstract relational knowledge develops, metaphor comprehension reaches an adult level of sophistication in selected domains. But the ability to understand metaphors continues to depend on knowledge of the specific domains referred to in the metaphor not on a general or abstract thought process.[52]

What sort of semantics can be built on these considerations of the developmental psychology of metaphor? The meaning of words and gestures is grounded in bodily experience. Meaning resides not exclusively in the relationships between concepts (as structuralism would have it) but in their connection to the body and its sensorimotor engagements with the world. Meaning emerges from the capacity to use bodily experience (including socially embodied experience) to think metaphorically.

The enactive nature of early symbolization suggests a metaphor for metaphor: metaphors can be thought of as tools for working with experience. A metaphor expresses something that the body knows how to do, a way of working with or transforming a concept. Of course, tools are pluripotential. Their shape suggests a use to the hand, and for the skilled user calls up a repertoire of moves that can be combined in complex grammars of action, but they also can be used in many ways never intended.[53] Metaphor, as a tool, provides ways of acting on our representations, or of making presentations to others, that transform the conventional representation, unpack new meanings, and open up the situation. This fits with the idea that meaning resides in use: the logic of a metaphor can only be appreciated when we see how it is applied and there are always new uses to which a metaphoric tool can be put. So metaphors cannot be reduced to any fixed analogy, finite diagram, or set of images. Metaphoric meaning is inexhaustible because, like a tool, a metaphor can always be used to fashion something new. The more we know of the world, the further we can extend our metaphors and the more skillfully we can use them to reshape experience.

## The Embodiment of Metaphor

To see the bodily grounding of metaphor in action, let us return to the story of Mr. Y. When Mr. Y expresses his fear of tainted blood and personality invasion, he is using metaphors that structure his experience in terms of contagion. The logic of contagion, one of the laws of primitive magic described by James Frazer in *The Golden Bough* (1890) and again by Marcel Mauss (1902/1972), asserts that "things that have once been in contact with each other may affect each other through a transfer of some of their properties via an invisible 'essence.'"[54] This is not simply a belief or abstract thought. Nor is it the result of conflicts pushed out of consciousness. The contagion metaphor is a consequence of bodily learning built on particular kinds of emotional responsiveness, and it persists as a result of the bodily nature of revulsion and disgust.[55]

Paul Rozin and his colleagues conducted studies that show the operation of the laws of sympathetic magic in everyday life.[56] The law of contagion ("once in contact always in contact") reflects the psychological process of forging metonymic relationships. For example, drinks that have once had contact with a dead, sterilized cockroach are viewed as contaminated and rejected with disgust. Clothing previously worn by a disliked person remains undesirable even when freshly laundered. The law of similarity ("the image equals the object") is illustrated by experiments showing that people are repelled by chocolate fudge shaped like dog feces and are less accurate throwing darts at a picture of someone they like than at a picture of an enemy. In Rozin's studies, the laws of sympathetic magic operate even though people "know better," and they can be activated with a simple shift in symbolic meaning. If you put on a clean shirt and then are told it was last worn by a mass murderer, you may become physically uncomfortable. The affective meaning conveyed by metonym and metaphor transcends the dictates of logic and reason.[57]

Talk of flesh and blood makes our words immediate. This immediacy is a consequence of the developmental history of metaphor. The earliest vehicles for metaphor are bodily sensations and actions.[58] Over time, bodily emotions and sequences of interaction with others in particular social contexts give rise to complex sentiments that provide more elaborate grounds for metaphor. In this way, our complex conceptions are built from elemental bodily experiences by extending a scaffolding of metaphor. It might seem that the elaborate structure that underlies metaphor would make for great distance between abstraction and physical experience. An unfamiliar metaphor may require some time to understand. In some instances, though, metaphors take no longer to process and understand than literal expressions.[59] At the same, bodily sensations and actions make particular metaphors salient and ready-to-hand. Feeling unsteady on our feet, we think in terms of metaphors of balance, equilibrium, and vulnerability to falling.[60] The psychophysiology of metaphor mediates the immediate, closing the gap between the body and socially situated or scripted experience.

The body provides a taken-for-granted infrastructure for everyday thought and feeling. Injury or alteration of the body changes not only the content of thought, but its form. Oliver Sacks described this process after an injury that damaged nerves in his leg, when he tried to move his limb under the guidance of a physiotherapist:

> I felt the effort diffuse uselessly, unfocussed, as it were. I felt that it had no proper point of application or reference. I felt that it wasn't really "trying," wasn't really "willing"—because all "willing" is willing *something*, and it was precisely that something which was missing. Miss Preston had said, at the start of our session, "Tense the quad. I don't need to tell you how." But it was precisely this "how," the very idea, which was missing. I couldn't "think" how to contract the quadriceps anymore. I couldn't "think" how to pull the patella, and I couldn't "think" how to flex the hip. I had the feeling that something had happened, therefore, to the power of my "thinking"—although only with regard to this one single muscle.[61]

A partial loss of sensorimotor function is experienced as a loss of the ability to think certain thoughts. In place of the clarity of willing a movement, Sacks experiences his intention as "diffuse . . . unfocussed . . . without point of application." The loss of nerve connections to his limb causes alterations in sensation that contribute to a more profound sense of disorientation. Touching his own leg, Sacks is horrified to find it losing its sense of reality and substantiality. The sense of disorientation spreads and, ultimately, the integrity of his sense of self is undermined by the alterations in sensation and control of his leg.

Just as bodily changes can immediately affect the metaphoric process of thought, the interactional nature of metaphor ensures that thoughts may be felt in the body. This is illustrated by the experience of Mrs. W, a middle-aged woman in psychotherapy following a hospitalization for a life-threatening episode of self-starvation (anorexia nervosa).[62] During her hospitalization, her husband decided to separate and established a new household without her. She left the hospital to find that she had lost everything she had built with her family over a period of twenty years. She moved into an apartment by herself and came for psychotherapy with chief complaints of depression, chronic pain, and a persistent physical sensation of "floating." She felt this floating first while in hospital after a protracted fast during which she had become emaciated, disoriented, and delusional about her weight. A neurologist suggested that she had suffered nerve damage from nutritional deficiency resulting in a loss of position sense (proprioception) in her legs, and so she could not locate the position of her feet without looking. This type of sensory impairment can result from prolonged deficiency of vitamin $B_{12}$. This explanation, however, could not be confirmed by laboratory tests, including $B_{12}$ levels, as well as muscle and nerve conduction studies.

The floating sensation made it difficult for Mrs. W to walk. With it came what she described as "total body pain." She felt this pain was caused by constantly having to exert effort to keep herself from falling because of "a sensation of the ground shifting." She had to strain downward toward the ground to find it and never felt her feet were solidly planted. Consequently, she was always unsure of taking the next step. She could not count on the ground being there and giving her support to stand confidently and move steadily.

For Mrs. W the ground *had* shifted—and continued to shift—as her family "pulled the rug out from under her" and left her without a leg to stand on. Sacks described a similar widening circle of metaphoric meanings caused by the injury that severed nerves to his leg. Sacks's disorientation resolved slowly as his nerves healed. For Mrs. W, it was the gradual construction of a new life that allowed her to get her feet back on the ground and find her footing. As she felt steadier, her sensations became more those of pain and soreness, of difficulty moving against the resistance of her muscles, rather than the sensation of floating and defying gravity.

Is the floating that Mrs. W reported a literal description of her experience or a metaphor? The variety of conventional metaphors I have used to describe her situation are evidence for the pervasiveness of metaphors relating the security and stability of the person to her physical stance.[63] Floating is thus a natural metaphor for the socially dislocated or detached self. Is this metaphor central or peripheral to Mrs. W's concerns? Clearly, the loss of her family was a more devastating event than her difficulty walking. It is tempting then to emphasize the metaphoric meaning of "floating" in place of its more literal reference to altered proprioception. But this does not mean her symptom is *only* a metaphor. Much is at stake in the alternative interpretations of her symptoms as literal descriptions of raw bodily suffering or as metaphors for social position both for Mrs. W as a patient (e.g., the ontological reality of her symptoms and suffering, its legitimacy and coherence) and for her therapy (i.e., how best to interpret and reframe her distress to help reduce it).

An evaluating psychiatrist referred to her floating sensations as "a bizarre form of depersonalization" and described her as having a "delusional preoccupation with pain . . . She concretizes and this pain is consciously played out for others in her somatic concerns." This emphasis on floating and pain as metaphors for communication and social positioning discounts Mrs. W's own quite plausible construction of the circular links between sensation, attention, and symptom experience. In effect, she could not find her footing and placed each step so consciously and carefully that there was excessive muscle tension and cognitive effort in placing her feet, which exhausted and demoralized her. She tended to avoid going out of her home, and, when she did, the physical act of walking constantly occupied her awareness, closely followed by thoughts about the origins and implications of this symptom. She saw the symptom of floating as a direct physical effect of her fasting, malnutrition, and psychiatric illness; but she also saw it as an indirect consequence of neglect by her primary care physician and her family, who failed to recognize that such a serious problem was emerging and therefore to urge her to get help early enough and to hospitalize her before the damage occurred.[64] For her, this lack of care was part of a larger picture of abandonment.

How does metaphor work in this instance? Tracing the process first from the top down, the loss and disorientation in Mrs. W's life make her think of herself as cut loose from her moorings, floating, and unable to get her feet on the ground. As she focuses on it, this metaphor of being cut off and floating becomes central to her consciousness and structures her experience. This structuring occurs both cognitively, as floating provides an extended metaphor for many aspects of her experience of self and body, but also psychophysiologically, as the metaphor becomes a body-image or autosuggestion and, so, influences motor activity (like the deliberate way she places each foot, feeling for the ground) and the interpretation of sensorimotor feedback, feeling unsteady and unsupported.

A model for how this top-down psychophysiological effect of metaphor might work comes from hypnosis, where an image or a direct verbal suggestion seems to control bodily movement and sensation. Mrs. W's sensation of floating is similar to hypnotic catalepsy, where subjects who are asked to imagine their arm is getting lighter experience the arm floating up without any conscious effort.[65] When this kind of experience is sought after, it can be pleasurable as a form of imaginative play or intriguing phenomenon, but when it comes unbidden and persists, it is an affliction.

The psychiatric perspective fails to grasp the relationship between Mrs. W's symptoms and suffering because it tries to reduce the metaphoric coherence of her symptoms to a single, linear causal sequence in which psychic distress causes physical pain. In so doing, it ignores the circular causality that she herself recognizes. She resists an exclusively psychological or social characterization of her symptoms because she can feel them arise in her body. While "floating" condenses metaphoric meanings about her situation and contributes to her conceptualization of her problems, her distress cannot be reduced to a metaphoric gloss on that situation. Nor, in the form of reduction favored by biomedicine, can her symptoms be reduced to biochemical derangements in peripheral nerves. Her experience and reports of floating are both an index of physical alterations causing sensations that lead to metaphors that are extended to describe a wider domain and, at the same time, a metaphoric depiction of self and predicament that engenders physical sensations, leading to changes in levels of muscle tension, coordination, and locomotion. Giving primacy to one side of this circular loop is not simply a technical choice of intervention or a theoretical preference; it is a moral choice of how to divide up a world bound together by the marriage of body and mind through imaginative enactment.

## Social Embodiments of Mind

In their seminal work on metaphor, Lakoff and Johnson suggested that a small number of image-schemas based on bodily experience of the physical world provide basic metaphors that structure our more abstract models of experience.[66] For example, they propose that our understanding of containment is based on experiences of taking things out of and putting things into physical containers. However, as Quinn pointed out, many of the experiences they offered as basic or foundational, do not seem to be truly simple actions or events.[67] Even casual observation of an infant at play suggests that these early experiences are not simply motor acts but events charged with emotion: the pleasurable anticipation of exploration, vague fears about what is hidden in the shadows, and surprise at an unexpected discovery. In the infant's experience, others usually are present during this process of exploration and their attentive gaze, verbalizations, and emotional reactions color the experience. Even solitary play often has a background of imagined others, a virtual social world based on past experience that imbues private gestures with social meaning.

Thus, metaphors that seem to arise from simple motor acts are themselves rooted in affectively charged motivational schemas. This affect is, in turn, shaped and interpreted by culturally governed interactions with others. If this social shaping of embodiment is present from the start for the image-schemas of even simple motor acts, it is still more significant when extended to emotionally charged concepts like "the experience of the body as a container of blood and sensation."[68]

The bodily experiences that Lakoff and Johnson would place at the base of metaphor, then, are themselves complex social and cultural constructions. Some of this complexity is reintroduced by Lakoff in later work when he considers how part of the structure of metaphoric models may stem not directly from the body but from prototypical social situations or scenarios. For example, metaphoric thought about anger is commonly described in terms of heated fluid under pressure as in idioms like "MY BLOOD WAS BOILING," "HE GOT ME STEAMED UP," "I THOUGHT I WOULD BLOW MY TOP." The metaphoric qualities of heat and pressure come from the bodily experience of autonomic arousal and cardiovascular response central to anger as a motivational state that prepares the body for conflict and communicates one's state of mind or intention to others through tensed muscles and a flushed face. But anger also is anchored in social situations in which there is a sense of attack or injustice by an offending agent who has transgressed and is associated with culturally scripted possibilities for attack, domination, retribution, and revenge.[69] Conventional metaphors are shaped by knowledge of social situations that are culture-specific to a greater degree than bodily experiences or responses.

Due to their physical embodiment and social enactment, metaphors create meaning not only through representation but through presentation. The presentation of metaphor takes two forms: metaphors as cognitive tools that work on our concepts to fashion new meaning (as discussed in the previous section) and metaphors as communicative acts or gestures, constrained by social structure yet giving rise to new patterns of social interaction and modes of discourse.[70] These two faces of metaphor as presentation and representation are linked: our cognitive constructions are derived from experiences in the social world with language, perceptual affordances, and possibilities for action that reflect a cultural history. In turn, we use metaphors to reproduce and maintain cultural models that allow us to participate in meaningful exchanges with others by following rules of relevance, invoking shared understanding of the world and, at times, introducing new images or ways of taking hold of the world that contribute to culture change.

Wittgenstein's concept of the language game is helpful to clarify the sense of metaphoric presentation as social enactment: "[T]he term "language-*game*" is meant to bring into prominence the fact that the speaking of language is part of an activity, or of a form of life."[71] Wittgenstein sees the use of language in any domain as like a game in which there are tacit rules and participants take turns to create a meaningful activity. Meaning resides in use. Learning the meaning of words is equivalent to learning the proper occasions and techniques for their use.[72] This pragmatic view of meaning as use puts presentation before representation and can account for the observation that people often use metaphors without a clear sense of what they point toward. The assumption that the use of a metaphor implies a discrete image or model that lies behind it and that, once that model is identified, it can replace the metaphor has led some ethnographers of healing practices astray.

In fact, language games can give meaning to words for which there are no discrete objects, actions, or events to be represented. As an illustration consider Pascal Boyer's analysis of terms like "mana" (a spiritual life force, energy, or healing power recognized in Melanesian and Polynesian cultures), which play a central role in the conceptual systems of many cultures, yet seem empty—that is, have no apparent content, existing without clear referents, internal structure, or representation.[73] Contrary to earlier ethnographic accounts that viewed mana as a metaphysical substance, Roger Keesing argued that mana is a metaphor for efficacy or potency, indicating that some action or state of affairs has social power and significance.[74] Reifying the metaphor leads to the impression there is a distinct ontology at play. Considering the metaphor of mana from the perspective of enactivism, as a mode of action or attention in relation to particular cultural affordances, leads to a more pragmatic account, without the need to invoke any alternate ontology.[75]

In a sense, mana is pure affective meaning that does not require an image or other kind of representation to be used to think with. Boyer suggests that these sorts of terms are learned by participation in a succession of situations where mana is known to be present. Social practices provide contexts in which it is appropriate to use the "empty" term. Social interaction (including, for example, responding to emotions in the faces and gestures of others at ritual events where mana is immanent or manifested) shapes the meaning of mana as potency. A variety of discourses—from informal gossip, to technical discussions and the expression of expert opinions—supply meaning to the "empty" term not through ostension but through its use.

Clearly, the word "mana" is not a meaningless or "floating" signifier, a null sign, or a wild card, capable of standing in place of anything. It stands only for what is potent or imbued with power. This meaning is produced not at the level of complex cognitions but at an earlier or more basic affective level. As Boyer argues, for "empty" concepts, there is a necessary causal link between the entity referred to and the acquisition of the concept (i.e., one has to have been influenced by mana to understand what the concept means). Mana is not an abstract concept but rather an experiential one. Its "emptiness" lies in the fact that experiential knowledge need not be represented, it can be presented by the body. The experience of potency in ritual settings and human relationships shapes a crude concept of *mana* which can then be elaborated through participation in specific social contexts where rules of ritual action and social interaction are acquired. The nature of power and potency is enlarged through the cognitive elaborations of metaphor that draw on (and reshape) a way of life. In Wittgenstein's terms, then, "empty" concepts derive meaning through participation in language games that teach the rules of usage. Indeed, the ability to use a concept properly encourages in us the illusion that it points to something in the world and has a corresponding mental representation.[76]

The metaphor of language game is employed by Wittgenstein to highlight the rule-governed aspects of social life. But the rules of language games are usually not explicit; the very idea of following a rule is abstracted out of the larger whole that constitutes a form of life that is naturalized, normalized, and taken for granted.[77] The rules of social interaction are not embodied in any one individual; a rule-governed pattern emerges from the fact that each person knows how to play their part and that knowledge often is not declarative and representational, but resides in bodily habitus or dispositions to respond to others and to cultural affordances. Crucially, this embodiment means that the sources of meaning lie not just in an abstract game played by disembodied agents or participants in a larger system but by embodied beings whose materiality engages with the world in ways that inscribe its shape and structure on the body. This materiality then recovers the importance of representation: a body interacting with the world in order to survive necessarily changes in its structure in ways that can be understood as representations of the world.[78]

Metaphor theory points to the dual grounding of knowledge in bodily and social experience and provides an answer to the question of cultural grounding posed by Quinn: "How can knowledge be the construct of individual minds, yet public and shared? If our universal experience of the human body gives rise to universally shared understanding, culturally received models of the world account for the fact that there remains a good deal of understanding that is, at the same time, culturally shared and relative to given cultures."[79] Metaphors embody the situational knowledge that constitutes culture. While conventional metaphors reflect common sense, the idiosyncratic metaphors produced by individuals are contributions to the local cultures and communities in which they participate. Each individual retains the potential to create new meaning from his or her unique perspective that may be taken up by others who find it apt and useful.

The social grounding of metaphor in a way of life is crucial to the development of an ethics, aesthetics, and pragmatics of knowledge. Left to tinker on its own, a metaphor is capable of wild and limitless invention. This inventiveness is constrained by participation in the language games, institutional norms, and cultural practices that constitute a community. While the bodily grounding of metaphors ensures their quality of immediacy, through social interaction a critical or "objective" dimension is introduced into the play of metaphor. Cultural meaning, then, cannot be reduced to metaphors, any more than things can be reduced to words. Culture remains a way of life, possible only by virtue of the existence of others ready to play their roles, participating in social practices underwritten by specific ontologies, modes of knowledge production, and forms of institutional authority.

## Cultural Ontologies of Illness and Healing

Taking culture seriously requires considering the ways in which ontologies arise from specific modes of material and discursive practice. This is illustrated in a paper by Louis Sass and Edgar Alvarez in which they engage with the anthropological debate about ontology through reflections on their ethnographic research with practitioners of an Indigenous healing system.[80] They describe some key concepts of mental or emotional disorders recognized by healers (*curandera*) among the Mexican Indigenous Purépecha people. They explore both the metaphoric meaning and underlying ontology of *locura* (madness), *nervios* (nerves), and *susto* (fright illness). The Purépecha distinguish "good" illnesses that have physical or natural causes and "bad" illnesses that reflect supernatural, magical, or malign effects of witchcraft and spirits. Bad illnesses often have a mental or psychological quality associated with emotionality. Sass and Alvarez invoke Michel Foucault's analysis of epistemes in *The Order of Things* and relate these to different ontologies.[81] Foucault argued that the medieval and Renaissance episteme was grounded in the concept and experience of "similitude" of which four varieties were recognized: (i) *Convenientia* is based on physical proximity (contiguity or metonymy); (ii) *Aemulatio* involves perceptual resemblance (physiognomy or appearance, metaphor); (iii) *Analogy* reflects structural parallels (synecdoche); and (iv) *Sympathy*, which reflects similarity of effect or impact on the person. These forms of similitude provide the epistemic grounding of magical healing in which symbolic actions are thought to lead to a cure. This episteme is experienced not just as a valid, trusted way of knowing but also as an embodied ontology—entities, agents, presences, and facts about the world that one can feel, and experience in self-vindicating cycles of action and perception. Sass and Alvarez suggest that this approach can help ground recent efforts to better appreciate and characterize differences in ontology across cultures by recognizing "their depth, encompassing scope or constituting power." They compare the ontological dimension of human experience to a "mood-like state." In computational models of cognition, this might appear as a Bayesian prior (or expectation) not just in a system of causal modelling/attributions or perceptual templates, but as a broader anticipatory stance and affective ambience.

This is an important shift from viewing an ontology as a set of predicate-like assertions or catalog of what the world consists of or contains (gods, spirits, animals, atoms, quarks) to understanding it as an affective stance that precedes and pervades our engagements with the world. We can take this further. An embodied-enactive perspective would suggest that we experience the world as harboring supernatural entities not only because we observe things moving or acting "on their own" or have feelings of "presence," but also because we engage in practices like prayer, curses, and magical spells that enact an ontology; in effect, there is an implicit ontology that resides in the loop between perception and action. Ontologies, then, may be experienced and enacted through practices. The active inference or predictive processing model suggests that the most basic features of ontologies are the expectations that guide attention, generate sensations of perceptual presence, and govern attributions of agency and constraint. These are embodied experiences that can exist prior to the elaboration of any particular metaphysics. Making these ontologies explicit in healing systems or other cultural domains allows people to talk, theorize, and interpret experience in ways that add an additional linguistic loop to more basic embodied engagements.

## Conclusion

In addition to providing an account of conceptual invention, metaphor theory offers a remedy for the drought of passion in semantics. Individual experience is organized by metaphors whose meaning is not completely accessible to consciousness and is not circumscribed by a rational accounting of associations or beliefs. Metaphor theory shows how our purest, most abstract ideas are products of bodily action and emotion. Unlike psychodynamic theories of meaning, metaphor theory does not assume that conflict lies behind every symbol. Conflict and ambivalence can arise from the dynamics of bodily and affective processes, but there is a depth and breadth of symbolic meaning that arises from the metaphoric elaboration of images and experiences that are themselves unconflicted. The social world provides further ways of extending metaphor to generate symbols that reflect cultural patterns and scenarios. Thus, the multivocality of symbols need not be reduced to a single personal theme. The meaning of illness experience and behavior can be sought not only in personal history but also in the social contexts and ways of life that also serve to ground metaphor.

Of course, talk of the bodily grounding of metaphor often conceals a fundamental evasion, for there are two ways of conceiving of the body as a ground for experience: one phenomenological and the other biological. The phenomenological body appears as salient qualia of experience in introspective accounts. The biological body is studied from the outside as a physical entity, by naturalistic observation and experiment. Neither is an infallible source of truth. Phenomenology may be suspect because it lacks tools for distinguishing between imagination or secondary elaboration and primary experience (e.g., body image vs. bodily sensation). There is ample evidence for the fallibility (and cultural shaping) of introspection.[82] On the other hand, to engage with psychological and experiential phenomena, biology must acknowledge these reality of the subjective, including phenomenological categories and qualia of experience. The best pictures of the body we have come from correlating these two sorts of knowledge. For this reason, we must seek the grounding of metaphor not in disembodied literary texts or in decontextualized phenomenology, but in the sensual qualities of lived experience and our pragmatic engagements with the body as a biological, experiential, and social presence.

CHAPTER 3

# *Broken Narratives*

There is a unique way in which the maker and appreciator of a metaphor are drawn closer to each other.

– Ted Cohen[1]

Language doesn't only build bridges into the world, but also into loneliness.

– Paul Celan[2]

The clinical encounter is a crucial site for the construction of illness meaning. The stories and metaphors that people use to make sense of symptoms and suffering must serve their efforts at self-understanding and adaptation, as well as their negotiation of relationships with others. These personal-cognitive and social-communicative functions of illness experience and expression are in constant interaction and may be mutually reinforcing or misaligned.

In this chapter, I examine the presentation of illness experience in a clinical encounter to show how different narrative possibilities are tendered but not accepted because of cross-purposes between clinician and patient. What exists in place of an overarching co-constructed narrative, or even two side-by-side texts that might comment on each other, is an intercutting heteroglossia and, ultimately, mutual subversion of accounts. This subversion leads to the failure to construct a shared narrative on which joint action can proceed. In offering this example, I hope to show that by focusing on narratives in their discursive context, with attention to rhetorical aims, we can identify situations of flawed reality construction that are among the most common kinds of clinical impasse.[3] These situations of conflict and contestation can reveal structural problems and ideological conflicts in medical care[4]; at the same time, they provide important opportunities for the creation of new meaning.

## The Making and Breaking of Clinical Narratives

The social sciences and humanities of medicine have put increasing emphasis on narrativity in accounts of suffering and healing.[5] The analysis of narrative seems to give us a way to understand how personal and cultural constructions of illness become stabilized, reified, embodied, and enacted through stories told to the self and others. But narratives are not the only constituents of experience. Indeed, in acute illness, narratives are often fragmentary or undeveloped; where narratives are most coherent they also may be formulaic and distant from sufferers' experience. In many cases, prior to narrativization, salient illness experiences are apprehended and extended through metaphors. At times, these metaphors may subvert the project of narrative and come to dominate the sense of self.

For many illness episodes, narrative represents an endpoint not a beginning. In psychotherapy, we try to construct coherent narratives out of symptoms and behaviors that seem to make no sense or else struggle to revise stories that make only hurtful sense. Sufferers are encouraged to discover new narrative possibilities latent in their own metaphors of self and illness. For classical psychoanalysis and other forms of therapy devoted to uncovering historical truth, the goal of therapy is the retelling of hidden (suppressed or repressed) narratives, either as an end in itself (insight is a virtue that confers status on its holder within the psychoanalytic community), or to trade in for a new story, a revisioned account of the self as victim, survivor, and author of its own heroic journey.[6] Work in cognitive and developmental psychology—and on the philosophical underpinnings of psychoanalytic interpretation—has challenged the historical veracity of the accounts produced in psychotherapy and shown how such accounts are shaped by narrative templates given by the theory itself.[7] This self-confirming process, however, does not vitiate the potential therapeutic benefit of such narratives. Indeed, solution-oriented, strategic, and narrative psychotherapies, growing out of the work of Milton Erickson and subsequent generations of family therapists,[8] embraced this circularity, and moved toward story-telling and interpretation ("reframing") as ways to remoralize patients and restore a sense of meaning and coherence that can support new patterns of behavior.[9] Similarly, many cognitive psychotherapists emphasize the basis of psychopathology in self-defeating narratives and seek solutions through constructing new narrative accounts of self and others that can sustain more successful social behavior.[10] For all such constructivist therapies, the goal is to weave the narrative strands of self into a tapestry that is a cognitively useful, socially workable, and rhetorically powerful account.

Through narrative we construct a morally valued and conceptually coherent identity and sense of self.[11] Narrative conventions serve to stabilize and authorize stories, including those that make up personal history, through direct effects on remembering (narrative conventions guide semantic encoding and reconstruction), and through effects on social acceptance (narrative conventions determine what is considered a credible, coherent, complete, interesting, moving, and morally sound story).[12] Through reconstruction, narrative exerts effects that move backward in time to reshape memories to fit current conventions and concerns.[13] This effect can be therapeutic or pernicious according to the psychological, social, and moral consequences of rewriting the past.

A corollary of this synthetic function and malleability of narrative is that identity can become fragmented through ruptures in narrative. These ruptures can occur because of pathologies including discontinuities in attention or memory (e.g., dissociation; see Chapter 6) or cognitive developmental delays that impair the sense of continuity of self.[14] Even where cognition and attention are intact, mundane experiences may undermine our efforts at self-construction. A minimal list of these threats to the narrative coherence of the self would include: intrusions of bodily distress; cognitive dissonance that makes us unable or unwilling to assimilate unpleasant but necessary facts about our self; and a wide range of social constraints or outright sabotage by others with conflicting goals. Narrative reasoning is used to repair these ruptures in the autobiographical construction of the self.[15]

Narratives are important for codifying, representing, and remembering experience, but there are other knowledge structures which may be more common, including action-schemas, image-schemas, metaphors, and other figures of thought and speech. Just as fragments of poetry can be written with no overarching narrative, so can we articulate our suffering without appeal to elaborate stories of origins, motives, obstacles, and change. Instead, we may create metaphors that lack the larger temporal structure of narrative but are no less persistent and powerful. Such fragments of poetic thought may be the building blocks of narrative: moments of evocative and potential meaning, indelible images, irreducible feelings, and intuitions that serve as narrative opportunities or turning points that drive the story onward.

As Ricoeur has shown, metaphor is literary work "in miniature."[16] Metaphors present narrative possibilities and can be extended to create more complex stories. Even the few words of an isolated trope invoke a whole conceptual space or world. Indeed, metaphor involves the blending of two or more different conceptual spaces, which opens up new narrative possibilities.[17] A similar process underlies the creation of meaning in more extended narratives like parables which are structured in terms of core metaphors.[18] At the same time, the meaning of metaphor itself depends on a larger narrative context that may exist prior to or independently of the specific metaphor. This overarching narrative can generate divergent metaphors and block some avenues of metaphoric elaboration while encouraging others. Metaphors then may function as gestures toward a story that is not taken up and completed or as reminders of a story that is already installed and authoritative—even if it remains implicit or untold.

Although the approach to narrative in medical anthropology has borrowed heavily from literary theory, the metaphors of patient and healer as a reader or writer producing texts that are employed in some of this literature may obscure essential features of clinical storytelling. The act of telling one's story—no less than the act of "reading" implicit in diagnosis and clinical or psychotherapeutic interpretation—occurs in a social context radically different from that of the writer carefully composing a text for publication.[19] Everyday stories are more tentative, fragile, inconsistent, and incomplete than a self-consciously constructed text. The sufferer is driven by the need to elicit a helpful response rather than produce a coherent story. Clinicians, as readers, are heavily constrained by their professional role and institutional context, which limit interpretive frames and demand timely action based on an appropriate "technical" reading of the situation.

A more apposite rendering of the clinical situation then would borrow from another field of criticism, that of rhetoric. If we think of rhetoric as the verbal art of persuading others, we see it at work in the clinical conversation and interaction as patient and healer try to influence each other to reach a mutually workable way to continue. Studies of rhetoric suggest that much argument and effort to influence others rests on the poetic and evocative use of language.[20] The task for a discourse poetics of the clinical encounter then, is to understand how patient and clinician co-construct narratives that embody experience, provide rhetorical power, and confirm or challenge larger narrative structures, including both the patient's autobiographical and illness narratives and the textual authority of medicine.[21]

Patients and clinicians are actors engaged in conversation and, although they need each other to tell and enact their stories, they may wrestle with each other to see whose version of the story will be enacted. This wrestling itself can become part of the final version of the story or it may be surpassed or suppressed to arrive at an authoritative account. Once authorized and accepted, a story is retold and so persists, becomes stabilized, and influences future stories. This interactional account of narrative production points to the limitations of literary theory to address what are, for medical anthropology and clinical practice, central questions: the relationships of narrative to bodily experience and to social power.

In so far as it is dialogical, clinical work can scarcely be anything other than a conversation, but not all forms of conversation are therapeutic. And not all therapeutic action is verbal. Much goes on in silence, which may be pregnant with meaning because of context—that is to say, the location of silence within the stream of conversation, relationship, social situation, or other structures of relatedness. An emphasis on what can be said or made explicit may miss how much is communicated through silence. Along with the reliance on the sayable and the doable goes a tendency to downplay the significance of emotion and bodily experience. In losing silence, we lose some imaginal space: the room to maneuver, reflect, and create that communication can foster and protect. This loss of imaginal space—through inattention to what cannot be said but only dreamt or felt—is only one of many problems with overextending the metaphor of conversation, as well as those of discourse, narrative, and text.

## A Fire Inside

The following exchanges are taken from the transcript of an interview of a patient referred to a psychiatric screening clinic. Miss P, a twenty-three-year-old woman, was referred by a general practitioner concerned that her bodily symptoms were related to personal difficulties or stress. The interviewer was an experienced clinical psychiatrist at an academic general hospital psychiatry department. The interview was videotaped originally for teaching purposes, to provide an exemplary clinical evaluation interview in which the basic goal is to make an assessment and referral for psychotherapy or other appropriate treatment.[22] As such, a crucial part of clinician's task was to arrive at a definition or diagnosis of the problem that either identified it as amenable to some of form of psychiatric or psychological treatment or determined that it was unnecessary or not possible to treat the patient's problem within the local mental health care system. For her part, the patient sought to have her troubles understood, explained, and, most importantly, alleviated.

At the start of the interview, just after the psychiatrist has told the patient that the interview will be fifty minutes in duration and that, at the end, he will give her "an idea of what we can do for you," she begins by explaining:

P: OK. I have suddenly, I have been having a tremendous amount of . . . of stomach and heartburn and chest pains. I've been to two gastroenterologists. I've been to St. Elizabeth's Hospital. I've been taking antibiotics. I've had all sorts of X-rays, from gastrostropic to large and small intestine. They have mentioned . . . these gastroenterologists, they've mentioned that it's merely a case of nerves, acidity, anxiety, mainly, that wraps it up. And it's very discomforting, very aggravating. I have this burning sensation within my chest and within my stomach. They've given me all sorts of antibiotics, Ativan, to relax my stomach and etcetera, antibiotics, antacids, all sorts of things, and . . . up until now, up until now, it's been five months, five months and a half, close to six months, absolutely nothing.

T: Six months.

P: More or less, between five to six months, yeah.

T: That sounds miserable.

P: More or less, yes. I go to bed; I wake up in the middle of the night with that burning sensation. It's greatly, greatly centered in my stomach area and within my chest.

T: And there's no ulcer

P: They have found absolutely nothing, absolutely nothing. With all the tests that I've taken, absolutely nothing. I've been to Doctor, Doctor Digby, he had referred me to you, and they have mentioned that "go see a psychiatrist to see if it is a case of nerves." But personally, myself, it is not. Because I feel inside that burning sensation where . . . it's discomforting, very aggravating, very, very aggravating. Now . . .

T: Yes.

P: Can you say, personally, is this a case of nerves?

T: Well, why don't we try to find out more about you and see.

In this opening account, she clearly sets out her dilemma. First, there is a "tremendous amount . . . of stomach and heartburn and chest pains." Two gastroenterologists, numerous diagnostic tests, and treatment with medication all have been to no avail. The doctors now say it is "merely a case of nerves, acidity, anxiety." While that "wraps it up" for the doctors—an ironic comment on the limits of the clinicians' understanding—it leaves her with the burning pain, the aggravation, and "absolutely nothing" by way of satisfactory explanation or treatment. She then throws down the gauntlet: "Can you say, personally, is this a case of nerves?"

She has already given indications that she does not find "nerves" to be a sufficient explanation. So this question is a challenge to the clinician: will he repeat the same reductionistic explanation she has already encountered? By asking him to speak "personally" she seems to ask for his authentic response even as she signals her reluctance to receive yet another expert opinion founded on the authority of medical texts.

The clinician is quickly engaged by the question of whether this is "a case of nerves." Although framed as a technical diagnostic question, at root, this is a problem of social legitimation: of certifying *real* disease versus imaginary or self-inflicted, and humiliating, "nerves." "Nerves" is a common idiom of distress in everyday discourse used to comment on a wide range of personal and social troubles.[23] In the clinical context, the idiom of nerves becomes contested ground since it implies a measure of personal weakness or culpability. By joining in her quest for legitimation through resolving the causal or ontological status of the problem, the clinician has allowed the encounter to focus on a question on which the clinical negotiation will ultimately founder—for while "nerves" for the patient may point outward to social predicaments, for the doctor, talk of "nerves" leads inward to intrapsychic conflict, emotional dysregulation, or personality traits assessed against a normative model of psychological development and functioning.

The patient presents the psychiatrist with two conundrums that challenge his authority on the basis of the failure of the doctors she has already seen: (1) everything has been done to diagnose this problem, but it remains unnamed; and (2) after extensive evaluation and treatment, her symptoms persist. The doctors she has seen have attempted to explain away her problem as excess acid due to nerves. Despite naming it "nerves," the patient can identify no area of tension or anxiety sufficient to account for the symptoms; if it was "merely nerves," then naming the problem and doing something for "nerves" should be sufficient to make the pain disappear. The persistent burning pain, present and irrefutable in her body, challenges the explanations about "nerves" offered by physicians based on textual authority.

After some discussion about her life situation, including the heavy workload of her last semester at school and her part-time housekeeping job, she introduces a problem in her social world that doctors have already linked to her distress: a disappointing love affair with a man, an immigrant from the Middle East, which ended in anger and recriminations. She says she was attracted to him because he was cultured, refined, polite, spoke beautifully, and was intellectually her superior. He was "masterful," but different expectations for heterosexual relationships lead to her being "pushed around." The relationship that was "loving" and "full of everything" at the start became an arena of conflict and misunderstanding. The relationship ended just one month prior to this consultation.

T: You broke up.
P: Sure, I had to, because . . .
T: When was that?
P: Just recently, the month of November. I had to because I was becoming very aggravated and I couldn't take it anymore, I still had the, the sensation within me, now, I really can't pinpoint if this, surely, this did begin in July, but I guess it also was also the cause of my relationship too. I must admit, but not fully, fully. And they have mentioned that, these gastroenterologists have mentioned that all the tension and the aggravation and the anxiety that you have taken from him . . .
T: He was giving you a stomachache. That's, that's the hypothesis.
P: More or less, more or less. I have reached to a conclusion that yes, he did give me what I had inside but why is it still continuing? If . . .
T: OK, that's a good question.
P: Why do I still have the sensation, why do I feel that I have more than a case of nerves. Why . . .

He gave her what she has inside—the burning pain. Now she wants to be "free and liberated," no longer subservient to a man who made increasing demands for acquiescence and obedience. But since she is now free of this confining relationship, why does the burning continue? Working the causal connection backward, she raises one possible explanation: she continues to think of him, so he continues to be present in her.

T: Are you worried about him? Since you've broken with him?
P: To tell you very frankly, there are times where all those very good, and those loving memories flash right by me, but there are plenty times where I have those aggravating moments and those bad mem . . . bad memories that I have flash by me too. Deep in my heart, there is usually, after a relationship, there are little spots in the heart where you still feel that you love him. But I've turned out to be so bitter inside because I guess he made me suffer at the very last minute, the last point, and he's made me very aggravated. Now, I don't know if his aggravation is leading to my stomach and chest pain, burn, pain, that, I'm trying to find out. But there are times that I wake up and I'm crying, that I do feel lonely and very hurt, used.
T: Angry, still?
P: More or less, yes. More or less.

The burning pain is a reminder of her relationship, perhaps a result of ongoing hurt and loneliness, or "bad memories" that lead to anger and "aggravation," but it also a way she remains connected to her boyfriend. She offers what is clearly a sort of psychosomatic explanation, but the clinician fails to explore the epistemological grounds for this connection. Following a common folk and biomedical notion that links anger with stomach acid[24] (and, perhaps, searching for the emotion that is downplayed in her self-presentation), the clinician ignores her mention of crying, feeling lonely and hurt, and picks up on the theme of anger implicit in her mention of "aggravation."

Her family did not approve of the relationship because of differences in ethnicity, religion, and citizenship. The breakup of the relationship coincided with the intensification of her symptoms; they worsened even though the stress of schoolwork was over for the semester and her family responded with solicitous concern—a point that the interviewer, looking for evidence of secondary gain,[25] immediately picks up on.

T: So your symptoms have made your mother fuss over you more.

P: She's very worried, very, very, very worried and more or less, we've reached a point where we're both fed up. I'm . . . I've reached a point where I'm tired, because what's inside of me is very discomforting, like, at the present moment now, I have, I have a lit fireplace inside of me, which is very terrible, very, very discomforting. They've also mentioned that, you know, I produce too much acid inside of me, which, I have my meals, my stomach burns.

T: Does your mother have to make special meals for you?

P: Oh yes.

The burning is a "lit fireplace," a hearth that has become a source of discomfort that goes on and on, tiring both the patient and her mother who must prepare special meals to avoid aggravating her daughter's condition.[26] For the patient this is simple comfort; for the clinician it is evidence of reinforcement of the sick role and, perhaps, of pathological "enmeshment" of mother and daughter.

After discussing her relationship with mother and father, the interviewer turns the conversation back to the relationship with her boyfriend, as someone challenging to her parents' expectations for her. He also reviews her school career, determining that she took longer than average to finish high school. Finally, he asks about her larger social world.

P: To tell you very frankly, I'm very closed and very reserved, I'm very quiet, I'm to myself. There are times where I wake up, there are times at work, if I go out, I'm very closed, I'm very quiet, very lonely inside, very lonely, very depressed . . . I do have a couple of friends but at the present time now, I'm very closed and I'm very reserved because I, inside I feel very hurt, very used. And at work, I just feel like crying because I feel left out. A friend has suggested that it's all in my mind. Is it all in my mind, is it myself?

Again, the ontological question: "Is it all in my mind, is it myself?" If it is all in her mind perhaps it is not real. Here, the reflexive pronoun *myself* implies her ownership of the symptoms and her self as the potential locus of causation, raising the question of agency. Yet there is a pain inside her, in her stomach, and a feeling of sadness "deep inside." The depth of this feeling makes it hard to talk about, understand, and express. She speaks "very frankly" of being "very closed and reserved," challenging the clinician to draw her out.

Telling her story, she has arrived back at a place of loneliness and isolation. Some rupture in her sense of self has occurred: "I saw myself as a young, respectable lady." Something has challenged her self-respect and she has retreated from a relationship that might have led her away from her family of origin, a relationship that, in her choice of boyfriend, already constituted a challenge to her parents' expectations. The relationship did not work out, and she is left with the dilemma of her anger and frustration, which are not only directed at the partner who let her down but, presumably, also at family members who hoped for the relationship to fail and who are now relieved to have her back.

In this clinical conversation, the patient's narrative of self is sketchy and conventional. There is no complicated story about who she is or aspires to be, no obstacles to be mastered, only an effort to reach developmental milestones appropriate for her chronological age (have a boyfriend, get married). This uncomplicated life trajectory—which amounts to a lack of plot—is found also in her recollections of childhood. If this is her habitual style of self-narration, then it is marked by a shallowness or lack of elaboration that suggests a reluctance to engage in self-reflection. If it is a response to the clinical context, then it suggests a lack of trust or a narrow conceptualization of what is appropriate to discuss with a psychiatrist. Although not an either/or, explaining her truncated narrative in terms of her personal characteristics or the nature of the clinical interaction would depend not only in the way she responds to invitations to say more but also on the clinician's own conceptual models, awareness of the social context and its power differentials, and self-reflexivity. In any event, after a few brief mentions of family vacations and meals, she runs out of stories.

P: That's about it, but I've never, my mom has never really told me specifically about my childhood. She told me that I was quite quiet, I wasn't . . .

T: How come your mom has to tell you? How come you can't remember yourself?

P: I never really looked back in my childhood very specifically, you know, point by point, I never really . . .

T: Do you ever think that something was missing in your childhood?

P: No, no, oh no, no, no. As I've reached, now, you know, as a young lady, I'm not missing anything.

The psychiatrist believes he has found gaps in her memory (or willingness to explore it) that indicate psychological defensiveness, and he challenges this to see how well she might engage in a psychotherapeutic conversation oriented toward recollection and reconstruction of her childhood experiences. She resists his effort to elicit dissatisfaction with her childhood and family and emphatically rejects the possibility that something was missing in her childhood. Finally, the clinician uncovers evidence of friction in the family.

T: But what's their . . ., what's your, the reaction of them to your illness?
P: They're blaming me because of this young gentleman that I've been out with.
T: I see, they say it was your fault for making the mistake.
P: Exactly, exactly.
T: I see.
P: They have mentioned that I could have been more brighter, more wiser, more intellectual, more open-minded, but I guess at that time, love was very blind. Love was very blind and I must admit, yes, I did make a very grave, grave mistake, a terrible mistake. That I must endure . . .

"Love was very blind" and led by it she reached an impasse. This appeal to the conventional adage "love is blind" ratifies the authenticity and simplicity of her love and allows her to acknowledge a sense of naiveté but attach it to the common experience of "love" rather than to her self.

Having collected information on the past and present that allows him to understand the problem as a developmental conflict, the psychiatrist makes a "trial interpretation" that emphasizes her dependence on her family and the difficulties in finding a partner as a step toward separating from them. Her reaction to this will indicate her ability to make use of insight-oriented, psychodynamic psychotherapy that would proceed in essentially the same way.

T: Can I suggest to you the following possibility and let's see what you think about it?
P: OK.
T: All your life you've been very close to your mother.
P: Yeah.
T: And, and, in moving outside of that orbit, so to speak, you're kind of unsure of your ground, not quite sure what to look for in a man. Looking for somebody, perhaps, who was older, more sure of himself, could kind of take care of you and perhaps that has something to do with the fact that in the family, you were your mother's special little girl, maybe had less to do with your father and your brothers, and perhaps didn't know men well enough.

P: Exactly, exactly. My parents want to see me married to a nice, respectable gentleman who will take care of me, not have another relationship like I've had that really put me into pain and sorrow. They just want to see me very happy and healthy, that's all. Like any parents want for their children, happiness and health.

The psychiatrist leaves uninterpreted the more provocative notion that the choice of a partner from a different ethnic background might also express some distancing from, opposition to, and anger toward her family.[27] After this first sally, however, she turns away from her anger toward the young man and avoids any potential hostility toward her family. The psychiatrist tries a second interpretation, this time proposing a causal mechanism linking suppressed anger to the burning in the stomach.

T: I think you're very angry.
P: Yes, that I know, yes.
T: And, but the anger has nowhere to go, it's going, it's becoming physical because it's like you can't scream, you can't shout, the anger is kind of all bottled up inside.
P: Bottled up.
T: Yeah.
P: OK, all right.
T: And maybe you've always been like that. To some extent.
P: More or less, yes.
T: Yeah.
P: I'm very to myself. There were times where, I remember when I began to love him, I couldn't tell him, face him, I had to write it on paper. There were many times where I had so many things to tell him, I just bottled it up and he always taught me, "my dear, say it, say it, say it." I guess I just felt afraid and just so unsure not to tell him. I'm, as I've mentioned, I'm very closed and very reserved. I usually don't like to say my feelings, depending what situation and what circumstance, more or less. Yes, I am angry because of this relationship that, you know, I have been through, but I'm mainly, mainly aggravated with what I have inside because it's, like I, as I have mentioned, very discomforting, very, very, very painful.

The psychiatrist introduces the metaphor of anger as a fluid under pressure "bottled up inside." As we have noted earlier, this is a conventional metaphor for anger that has wide currency, probably because it reflects experiential qualities of the sort of bodily arousal that accompanies anger (increased heart rate, blood pressure, pulse pressure, facial flushing).[28] Yet while she understands the experiential basis of this metaphor and agrees that her anger is bottled up inside, she sees it only partially as a result of her loss of relationship, and mainly as a consequence of her frustration with persistent stomach pain. Certainly, she does not view the burning pain as a reflection of half-hidden conflicts over autonomy and dependence within her family.[29]

Trying to increase her motivation for psychotherapy, the interviewer makes pessimistic predictions, amplifying the anger metaphor to drive home his point.

T: I don't think your pain is going to go away until you're over this whole thing psychologically, and you're not . . .
P: So you're saying, more or less, psychologically, this is related to what I have inside of me. So, just, it's really a case of nerves.
T: I would say you're boiling over with rage and hurt, actually.
P: OK.
T: And I think that hasn't, that can be like a burning fire inside.
P: OK, all right. Because my mom has also, and I myself, I was thinking if this was not a case of nerves, I wanted to, like, try another top specialist at the University Medical Center.
T: Well, OK, well, that's a key question right now because . . .
P: OK.
T: . . . we're going to, we're coming to the end of the, of our interview. We have to decide what to recommend.
P: OK, exactly.
T: And if you're still going to be looking for a physical answer, there's no point to see the psychiatrist, is there? But are you sufficiently convinced that this is psychological, that you'd be willing . . .
P: I really cannot say, as . . . what you have explained to me, yes, it is psychological, but I'm also looking for the physical inside of me, because I've also been through a lot of, more or less, internal bleeding, and hemorrhage. I've had, I've broken a vein on the side of my leg, on the left side of my leg . . .

The psychiatrist is hoping for a joint decision ("*we* have to decide what to recommend"). He introduces strongly dualistic thinking (the problem is either psychological *or* physical) then tries to soften it. This "either/or" presents a bifurcation into two potential narratives: one that assimilates her pain to "psychological" issues and the other that treats the pain as evidence of physical injury. Forced to choose, the patient opts for the independence—and hence authenticity and seriousness—of her physical problems. She returns to her bodily affliction by mentioning broken blood vessels on her leg. But the psychiatrist does not see any connection between her leg and her stomach. What is salient for him is not the fact of bleeding or some general feeling of bodily vulnerability but the specific anatomical site of the lesion (which, on her description, sounds minor). The fact that she is raising broader concerns about her body might point to a more pervasive sense of physical vulnerability. There is nothing in the personal history she has shared that would explain this and nothing has been said about the details of her relationship—what kind of sexual activity they may have and or whether there was any violence or abuse. The psychiatrist does not explore this in the interview, and the fact that he is a middle-aged man might make it especially difficult for her to raise any such issues. Instead, he reads her return to bodily complaints as indicating an increase in anxiety and her insistence on a physical dimension to her problem that demands a physical explanation and solution, as emotional defensiveness.

T: Maybe you'd rather not talk about it right now; maybe you're feeling like you're too hurt to even discuss it.
P: Depending on who I'm speaking to. Surely, you know, you're in a very, you know, educational field and I, I have to respond to you. To others, a stranger or someone that, who's going to have a one-to-one correspondence to me, maybe I will, but I don't want to be, at home, my parents and others will bring up his name and himself, there are times where I'm still speaking to my parents, pardon me, to my mom, about him. But I try to close the case as much as I can. Because . . .
T: Yeah, I guess we're suggesting reopening the wound, in a way.
P: But if this is going to reopen the wound, is it really going to . . . ?
T: Sometimes you have to reopen the wounds to make them heal.
P: So true. Very logical. But I don't know if I have a wound inside to be healed, I don't know, I really cannot say if it's going to be healed.
T: Well, I can't give you a guarantee either.
P: Yeah, very true.

Despite all the time they have spent in the interview talking about the social world, she insists her body needs more attention, that her physical health really is at stake. She acknowledges that talking about her difficulties helps her emotionally, but she needs physical help as well. Ironically, despite the fragmented or truncated nature of her story, the patient is more able to acknowledge the situated nature of her speech ("depending on who I'm speaking to"), and the many directions it might take, than is the psychiatrist, who seems determined to follow one line of explanation. The irony grows as she notes that his appeal to the metaphor of reopening wounds is "very logical." Of course, it is not logical but might be rhetorically effective because it is a powerful image supported by the clinician's interpretive authority. However, she expresses her doubt that it is empirically true or able to show her a way forward.

The psychiatrist again presents her with an either/or in the form of a logical implication: if she insists on seeking more medical opinions and investigations of her pain, then she is not ready for psychotherapy. Only when she is ready to give up the search for a physical cure can she begin to focus productively on the psychological dimensions of her problem. She is not convinced that psychological help will eliminate her physical problem, although the psychiatrist thinks it will. He interprets her reluctance to give up the search for physical cure and commit to a purely psychological approach as resistance to dealing with emotional issues.

T: But you're afraid it might even be worse if we get into this. You might end up . . .
P: More or less, yes.
T: We might kind of like . . .
P: Pin . . .
T: . . . blow, blow the fire even hotter.
P: Pin, pin the point on the donkey, more or less.
T: That's a risk, but I guess you'd have to feel that . . .
P: Because that's what . . .
T: Yeah.
P: As you've noticed, I'm looking at a physical side, mainly. I don't know why but I'm just looking at that too.
T: I would suggest the reason you're looking at it is because the other side scares you.
P: Are you telling me that emotionally, I'm a little mixed up?
T: I would say, I would say that you probably have never . . .
P: What do you see me . . .
T: I would say . . .
P: [speaking at the same time] . . . right now at the point?
T: I would see you as a person who has never had the opportunity to think through her emotions very clearly. I don't know if anyone has ever helped you with that.
P: No, no, no, no. That's very true. I've . . . true . . . the emotions that I have are mainly, just, out, unlearned, straightforward, that's all.
T: OK. Anything else you want to ask me before we stop?
P: No, not really.
T: OK. So you're going to give me a ring.
P: More or less, yes, and I will give you, I'll let you know.

In this exchange, the psychiatrist does not pick up on the patient's metaphor ("pin the point on the donkey") but persists with his own ("blowing the fire hotter"). Her allusion to the children's party game ("pin the tail on the donkey"), in which a blindfolded child tries to attach a paper tail to an image of a donkey, may reflect her experience of being unable to determine the nature of her problem and needing help to pin down its meaning. It also might reflect her experience of this dialogue—in which she does not feel seen and is left disoriented or in the dark—and of the psychiatrist, who seems blinded by his own suppositions, insistent on making his point and pinning it on her. Not surprisingly, she does not return for follow-up at this clinic. The psychiatrist has presented her with a Hobson's choice: give up on physical diagnosis and treatment even though I can give you no definite alternative diagnosis and little assurance that psychological treatment will make things better.

While she has offered stretches of narrative about the vicissitudes of a relationship and its unhappy end, about stress and anger causing stomach acidity and burning pain, and about a mother and father reacting to her illness with concern, she presents these as unrelated narrative strands. For his part, the psychiatrist has elicited fragments of historical information and interpreted them in terms of his own preexisting theoretical scheme to construct a competing narrative that integrates the separate strands[30]: she has been overprotected or enmeshed in her family of origin; she chose someone from a markedly different background than her family to try to distance, differentiate, and, ultimately, separate from her mother. This motivation biased her view of men in such a way as to undermine the possibility of finding an appropriate partner. Having had the relationship fail, she is now firmly back in the orbit of her family. She chafes at this dependence, but the effort to preserve self-respect and family harmony makes her unable to name or face that component of her anger that is directed at family members.

The psychiatrist's theory-driven hypothetical narrative provides a larger story in which he inserts and contextualizes her account. He then makes tentative interpretations intended to get her to acknowledge this larger story. She fails to do this, returning to elements of the story that she describes in a disconnected way or as related only through the persistence of the burning pain. Her failure to endorse the connections the psychiatrist has made is then interpreted as evidence of her defensiveness or lack of "psychological mindedness."[31] As a result, he judges her as less appropriate for psychotherapy and gives her a test in the form of a choice that, on the evidence of the preceding interview, she is bound to fail. Her failure to follow through for referral then confirms his hypothesis that she is unable, unwilling, or unready to pursue psychotherapy.

Still, we have to ask why—when she is able to use the psychosomatic schema given to her by the doctors (which is very close to popular explanations of "nerves" and ulcers as responses to stress)—she ultimately rejects the prescription of psychotherapy. Why does this schema of psychosomatic causation not provide a coherent framework for a story that would prompt a search for a psychological cure? There might be crucial parts of the story that have been elided or evaded because they are shameful or embarrassing—like conflicts with the boyfriend over sexuality, physical aggression, or concern about being used by someone eager to gain immigrant status. The conventional psychiatric account of this failure to endorse a narrative of psychosomatic causation rests on the idea that the patient has a personality structure or defensiveness that precludes accepting the evident connections between her emotional conflicts and her bodily distress. A sociological view would understand this failure in terms of the stigma associated with psychosomatic explanation or as a consequence of the extent to which doctor and patient use different communicative codes that reflect their respective social positions and reference communities.

But the structure of the clinical conversation also reveals more basic bodily, personal and cultural reasons for this failure to agree on an explanation. At the level of bodily experience, the failure of the psychological narrative reflects its limitations before the obduracy and insistence of somatic distress. In illness we have the breaking through into consciousness of nonnarrativized, inchoate experience that resists narrative smoothing and containment. At the personal level, the psychiatrist fails to join with the patient in her own self-understanding as an initial step to build trust. At a social level, we see the conflicting interests of doctor and patient who take up each other's metaphors for different ends—to legitimate suffering or to identify psychological conflict. These cross-purposes tear apart the fragile construction of shared experience. Examining this failure to coconstruct a joint narrative, we can begin to catalog the many ways that clinical narratives can be broken.[32]

## Voices in the Clinical Encounter

This account illustrates the many voices or heteroglossia characteristic of all clinical encounters. The doctor and patient are attempting to communicate essential information but their conversation is heavily constrained by the demands of the situation and their efforts to present an appropriate face to each other. Each speaks from a different position, which includes awareness of both the interactional context and its relationship to larger social spheres. Each speaks with the voice of the self but invokes the voices of others. Indeed, we can understand this conversation not simply as an exchange between two conversational partners but as the antiphony of many voices in the wings.

At various moments in the conversation, we have the voice of the body, the voices of medical practitioners (which are both temporal and textual), and muffled voices of the family. Each voice carries a particular form of authority and conviction for the partners in this exchange. These voices should not simply be identified with doctor and patient: both participants invoke (and speak on behalf of) multiple versions of the same voices—both patient and physician draw from medical knowledge and popular understandings of life course and situations. The clinical conversation then occurs as an exchange of metaphors drawn from bodily experience and textual or institutional authority. To authorize an interpretation, each participant in the exchange invokes the authority of the voices of the body (physical experience in its privacy, immediacy, and insistence) and the text (technical knowledge, codified norms, institutional procedures).

Bodily experience reflects both the physiology of the body and physically embodied aspects of the social world. The patient returns consistently to the brute facts of bodily distress. The authoritative voice of her body undercuts the technical authority of the physicians who explain it as "all in her head." The psychiatrist tries to move the focus of the conversation from stomach pain to his areas of expertise: psychological conflict and family interaction. In his attention to her social world, he invites her to let other voices speak through her, but the social body of the family is not present, and its voices remain muted and indistinct.

The clinical conversation also draws from myths or models, overarching narratives that are invested with moral significance and more or less unquestioned truth. Medical authority is part of the mythic world of the patient, as well as the physician. But this authority does different work for each. The patient uses accounts of the authority of medical opinion to try to convince the doctor that her problem is physical and intractable, that her problems with her boyfriend are separate from her problems with her stomach, and that she has no problems with her family. For her, medical authority has created a crisis of legitimation by implying that her problem is rooted in her own psychological conflicts. She must manage this assessment interview to save face. She does this both by ironic comments on the inability of physicians to explain or alleviate her symptoms and by appeals to the authority of her own bodily experience to trump the psychiatrist's psychosomatic explanations.

The psychiatrist has a similar problem of managing the encounter, since the patient's persistent symptoms and rejection of a purely psychological explanation cause him to lose face. He is merely another in a long line of experts who have failed. Her skepticism about his offer of treatment not only devalues his expertise, it challenges his ability to provide a convincing explanation and promote psychotherapy as a solution. In the middle ground, through the play of metaphors and competing narratives, each participant tries to turn the conversation to their advantage—to have his point of view taken up by the other, to validate it against shared and implicit cultural values and norms, and to save face and maintain epistemic authority that is threatened both by the power asymmetries in the relationship and by the recalcitrance of the medical problem. Tentative and shifting metaphors are used to negotiate meaning. Each metaphor delivered into the middle ground can be taken up by other and used for different rhetorical purposes.

This view of clinical conversation as strategic self-presentation—as an effort to protect and promote one's social face or self-depiction—ascribes consciousness and agency to the actors. But conversation presents narrative possibilities, at the level of metaphoric models and figural extensions of which the actors are never fully aware. So, the interaction is more than the fencing of two people with conflicting agendas; it occurs within and against a social and cultural background that no matter how much we wish to acknowledge and empower the autonomy of individual actors—heavily conditions and constrains their vision, rhetoric, and action.[33]

## How to Thicken a Plot

In the clinical encounter, we find narratives that are broken by the intrusions of symptoms, the incomprehensibility of illness, the inattention and discounting of powerful interlocutors (like physicians), or the debilitating effects of illness on creative and integrative cognitive functions. In chronic illness, coherent narratives eventually emerge, but in acute illness, we often have a situation where narratives have not yet been constructed or where multiple tentative accounts coexist and compete. Both the absence of narrative and its plurality raise questions of meaning and authority—questions that are urgent insofar as patient and clinician want a satisfactory end to symptoms and suffering, as well as to their encounter.

Psychodynamic theory argues that gaps in narrative may mask or hide a deeper narrative that is repressed or denied because of its painful substance. But the fractures of narrative may also reflect the inchoate nature of illness represented as islands of reason, fragmentary stories, narrative strands, and, above all, poetic evocation through bursts of figural language. This emphasis on figures and fragments rather than extended narratives reflects a basic view of everyday thinking as rooted in poetic refigurations of the world. When these are not simply repetitions of dominant or normative accounts (sometimes expressed as dead metaphors), they may be tentative, fluid, and fungible, open to challenge and renegotiation in an effort to find common ground.

The structure of narrative itself is built upon a scaffolding of tropes, just as abstract thought is built on a scaffold of sensorimotor and emotional experience. The concept of trajectory provides narrative structures that fit the metaphor of life as a journey of the self through time. The sense of temporal ordering this gives can be contrasted with the metaphor of narrative as *emplotment*, embedding the story in a particular situation, with causes and consequences. In Umberto Eco's distinction,[34] *story* is narrative with linear progression; *plot* involves a larger contextualization, in multiple dimensions, which allows looping back in time and can violate the ordinary, linear, unidirectional temporal account with foreshadowing, flashbacks, and an overall structure that creates new levels of meaning by relating past, present, and future. What plot adds to the linear narrative of story is teleological structure, usually given in terms of human goals and intentions. This turns a narrative in which events simply follow one another by temporal contiguity into a narrative that is organized and driven forward by causality. Emplotment can turn a linear narrative into a tableau, landscape, or mythic structure that stands outside conventional time.

While the causal structure of narrative can take many forms, Tsvetan Todorov distinguishes two broad types: *mythological*, in which the minimal units of causality enter into an immediate relationship with each other; or *ideological*, in which the minimal units of causality do so only by the intermediary of a general law (or model) of which they are illustrations.[35] In Todorov's mythological narrative, the causality is that of the irreducible agency of the *actants* (i.e., the personified actors or, in the case of psychological narratives, mental states), while in ideological narratives, the actants are merely exemplars of laws, mechanisms, or processes of action, relationship, and transformation, whether these be political, sociological, or physical.

Both religious and scientific narratives, including psychiatric explanations, may be either mythological or ideological in Todorov's sense. Much of the process of psychiatric diagnosis and therapeutic interpretation involves efforts to turn the patient's mythic narrative into an ideological account. This turning of myth into ideology serves three functions: (1) it gives a specific kind of coherence to the story based on underlying causal mechanisms; (2) it gives the clinician technical control over the interpretation and continuation of the story in terms of those processes; and (3) it reinforces the reality of the ideological explanation from which it draws its narrative structure and authority. These functions serve to maintain medical authority, but they will be helpful for the patient if: (1) the cognitive and social coherence of the ideological account is somehow superior to the coherence obtained by the mythic narrative, for example, it is more consistent with the patient's self-understanding and commitments or with salient social norms and expectations; (2) the coping strategies or technical control afforded by the ideological narrative can alleviate suffering (e.g., by redirecting attention or reframing the interpretation of symptoms in ways that reduce distress or organize adaptive action); or (3) the overarching ideology and its consequences are valued by the patient and others in their intimate circle or community so that accepting it confers personal meaning, social capital, positioning, and solidarity.[36]

The resources that both patient and clinician use to construct an ideological narrative include epistemologies based on specific root metaphors (e.g., psychic causation; personal, family, and social meanings of bodily distress); conventional narrative forms (e.g., models of everyday social predicaments, developmental challenges, or moral conflicts and conundrums); and professional authority (i.e., the power to discount, suppress, distort, or reinterpret alternative accounts—in the present instance, the physician's power to diagnose and treat).

The reluctance of the patient to have her story subsumed, redirected, or reinterpreted by the clinician is termed "resistance" in psychoanalysis on analogy to political resistance to oppression. In her closing exchanges with the psychiatrist, the patient can be read as suggesting that he is trying to blindly pin his conclusions on her. This leaves her feeling unheard. Perhaps, if this experience had been explored, the metaphor might have opened onto the narrative present, and the interview would have brought the psychiatrist's own metaphoric account into closer alignment with the patient's self-understanding.

The asymmetry in power evident in clinical exchanges like this can be framed as a problem of *epistemic injustice*.[37] The patient's account is suspect, not only because of a lack of technical knowledge, but also more basically because both her symptoms and explanations are treated as "subjective"—shot through with potential hidden motives and conflicts, which, even if they cannot be brought into the open and verified, persist as hypotheticals that cast doubt on her account. The institutional and epistemic authority of the psychiatrist gives him the last word in this encounter.

Notwithstanding the manifestly unequal power of doctor and patient, we ought to recognize the symmetry in this situation, in which the doctor too resists the patient's story and tries to overcome it with his own version in which certain hypothetical explanations derived from a therapeutic ideology count for more than the experiences and events themselves. In this sense, the doctor is arguing both for the metaphorization of the patient's suffering and for the concretization or literalness of his own metaphors; the patient, for her part, insists on the literal nature of her experience but reserves the mobilize the polysemy of metaphor in her own exploration of the illness. To recognize this contest of interpretations leads to a semiotics quite different from that evoked by the metaphor of reader/ text. In the real world of hierarchies and broken symmetries, it is the use of power (not merely of temporal sequence, perspective, or position) that gives authority to texts, behaviors, and experiences.

People do not narrate their experience in a void, even when it appears to be a private soliloquy. The social world is always present virtually and is essential to anchor and enrich the story with shared meaning and confer authority. To have their stories heard and ratified, people must find an appropriate time and place with a receptive audience. If time, place, and audience are not readily available, people may need to strategize and work to clear a space to tell their story and to have it heard, accepted, and taken up by others. Narrators try to control the circumstances in which their stories are presented and, to some degree, how they are interpreted through actions taken before, during, and after the moment of narration. But the telling is an interaction in which the audience also shapes the story—indeed, there is always more than one story and storyteller active at once and each shapes the other in an ongoing exchange or contest. Moreover, once it moves beyond the immediate circumstances of the telling, a story begins to have a life of its own and can be used for the purposes of those who retell it, which may diverge from or flatly contradict the purposes for which it was originally told.

In the clinical vignette in this chapter, the patient is not able to tell her story or have it ratified, but neither is the clinician able to advance his interpretation as the dominant narrative, since she fails to return for treatment. To the extent that the master narratives of psychiatry claim healing efficacy, this failure to follow up on treatment and be cured constitutes a threat to its institutional authority. This threat is neutralized by pathologizing the patient—the psychiatrist decides that she does not come for treatment because she is not psychologically minded or otherwise not yet ready to hear the truth.

But where does this truth come from? Although psychiatry, like the rest of biomedicine, lays ideological claim to a scientific basis for its interpretations of human action, in practice, the meaning of the actions and experiences of an individual patient are always underdetermined by any existing body of scientific knowledge. Some interpretations (diagnoses, explanations) are true by virtue of the coherence of the story judged not so much on grounds of logical consistency but in terms of how it well conforms to the overarching narrative forms of myth or ideology; in this context, specific metaphors serve a subsidiary function, shoring up an argument or advancing the plot.[38] Other clinical interpretations are true by virtue of the evocative force of a single image or metaphor in and of itself. In this case, a poetic fragment creates its own context of meaning and truth through the associations and actions it evokes, and we can speak of *poetic truth*.

The contrast between narrative truth and poetic truth is important for understanding this patient's experience because she can be viewed either as evasive or as putting forward her own version of the truth that centers on a particular trope. Her poetic truth resides in "the burning," which is held like an eternal flame in her chest ("He gave me what I had inside") and, equally, in the epistrophe of her frequent statements "more or less," which mark her doubt and reserve her right to add something more to or take something less from the psychiatrist's authoritative narrative of her affliction.

## Conclusion

As a result of structural and ideological constraints, as well as the intrinsic qualities, of much illness experience, the narratives presented in clinical contexts are often fragmentary and contradictory, taking the form of potential stories or tentative metaphors. In this chapter, we have examined the play of metaphors in one type of clinical encounter, a screening evaluation for a psychiatric clinic, where what is at stake is the very definition of the clinical problem. Analysis of the bodily, psychological, and social embedding of this discourse reveals the ways in which metaphoric constructions are presented by both patient and clinician and either stabilized or subverted on the basis of the differential power and rhetorical skill of the participants. Although there is an effort in the clinical encounter to construct a shared narrative, this often fails when the patient and clinician are at cross-purposes. Narrative accounts of suffering and healing can then be understood not as coherent social constructions received ex cathedra, but as locally produced and contested essays of meaning that require shifts in the conceptual models and relative social position of actors to pursue. Indeed, close examination of the fragmentary stories and tentative co-constructions of meaning in clinical or other social interactions underscores the differences between narratives in conversation and texts. Interactive narrative involves a contest of meanings created through a constant process of rhetorical action and positioning in which each participant can challenge, change, ratify, or ignore the meanings offered by the other.

A focus on metaphor and meaning as collaboratively constructed and contested gives us a way to enter into the making and breaking of narrative in the clinical encounter: attend to what is unfinished, incomplete, and tentative—the myriad forms of "nonnarrative" communication; listen to the voices of others who speak through those who are present; and consider *potential* stories—those that may be latent, hinted at (or assumed) in particular metaphors but not told. To recognize potential stories that are not explicitly told or are elided, we need to supplement empathy and intuition with models or theories that tell us what is expected in a given situation or scenario. Psychological or psychodynamic theories provide one set of such accounts, but knowledge of the social world provides other, largely independent, versions. This knowledge of the social world includes both the taken-for-granted fund of common sense and the uncommon sense of critical theory and reflection.[39]

We are able to understand the meaning of the tropes and narrative forays of both clinician and patient by considering the participants' probable communicative aims or intentions given their social positions and roles in the clinical setting, as well as relevant aspects of their lifeworlds and predicaments. We understand these intentions against a backdrop of information about the larger myths, models, ideologies, and institutions that govern the beliefs and practices of clinician and patient. Attention to these larger frames of meaning is the fundamental shift that a social-cultural or ethnographic perspective brings to what would otherwise be a purely structural, semiotic analysis of the stylistic turns and rhetorical power of discourse. With attention to the power structures, demands, and constraints of the social world on one side and the insistence of bodily experience on the other, we are prepared to explore the evocative power, surplus meaning, and narrative potential implicit in and enacted through clinical discourse.

The physician's aim in the clinical encounter is to respond to the patient's health care needs, but it is also to settle, subdue, or deflect the challenge to clinical authority presented by the patients' competing narrative. This can be done by resolving the problem or by developing a convincing account that locates the symptoms in a biomedical framework. The patient's aim is to find relief, breaking through the obduracy of symptoms and suffering. The problem of efficacy then bridges two systems of embodied meaning. Under what circumstances does the professional's authoritative account contribute to the sufferer's relief? More provocatively, we also can ask what kind of epistemic stance and active listening opens the clinician to better understanding of the patient's predicament—even to new models and metaphors for health and illness. The answers must be sought, not in a structural poetics of discourse but in cognitive and social analysis that traces the models and metaphors used in clinical exchanges both inward to their personal meaning and embodiment and outward into the social world, where they function as part of discursive systems that organize institutions and confer power. Close attention to metaphors in lived experience, social interaction, and cultural performance can yield an account of clinical conversations that goes beyond recognition of the moment-to-moment failures of mutual understanding to engage with the politics and poetics of illness and healing.

CHAPTER 4

# *Animal Powers*

## *Ritual Healing and the Physiology of Metaphor*

> Suppose that a medical journal carried two articles reporting two different cures for scrofula: one by ingestion of chicken soup and the other by a king's touch. Even if the statistical evidence presented for these two cures had equal weight, I think that the medical community (and everyone else) would have very different reactions to the two articles. Regarding chicken soup I think that most people would keep an open mind, reserving judgment until the cure could be confirmed by independent tests. Chicken soup is a complicated mixture of good things, and who knows what effect its contents might have on the mycobacteria that cause scrofula? On the other hand whatever statistical evidence were offered to show that a king's touch helps to cure scrofula, readers would tend to be very skeptical, suspecting a hoax or a meaningless coincidence, because they would see no way that such a cure could ever be explained reductively. How could it matter to a mycobacterium whether the person touching its host was properly crowned and anointed or the eldest son of the previous monarch?
>
> – Steven Weinberg[1]

> In magical healing one indicates to an illness that it should leave the patient. After the description of any such magical cure we'd like to add: if the illness doesn't understand that, then I don't know how one ought to say it.
>
> – Ludwig Wittgenstein[2]

Why does chicken soup seem to be a more plausible agent of healing than the king's touch? The passage above from Nobel Laureate physicist Steven Weinberg reveals a common bias in biomedical explanations of the mechanisms of disease. From the perspective of the physical sciences, the chemistry of chicken soup has more obvious links to the tubercle bacillus than does the symbolic gesture of a human being. But why shouldn't a king's touch be even more healing than chicken soup—at least in a feudal society where its power can inspire, ennoble, and empower the peasant who receives that favored touch?[3] Indeed, Weinberg's intuition is at odds with the way that most of humanity has recognized and responded to symbolic power enshrined in the social order. The ontologies that underwrite cultural worldviews, along with universal modes of analogical or metaphorical thinking, make it seem entirely plausible that a person, substance, place, or ceremony imbued with sacred power should have healing efficacy.

Even from the perspective of contemporary biology, Weinberg's skepticism is unwarranted because it misplaces the causal action in infectious disease, privileging the mycobacterium as the essential cause of infection and the natural target of treatment. But the proximate cause of a disease is not simply the capacity of bacteria to infect a person—it includes the person's immune response. On most occasions when we are exposed to bacteria and viruses, infection is prevented or "fought off" successfully by the body's immunologic lines of defense. Only when the immune system is not up to the task—because it faces an overwhelming challenge or is compromised in some way (e.g., by stress, sleep deprivation or other disruptions)—does an infectious agent take hold and cause disease.

The king's touch, then, need not act directly on the mycobacterium to have antibacterial effect: it can act on the thoughts and feelings of the person who is touched, mediated by the brain, which in turn modulates the immune system. These effects include both "unconditioned" or "hardwired" processes acquired during evolution and more elaborate learned effects that depend on personal experience and cultural meaning.[4] Although touch has physiological effects on infants that do not depend on enculturation, these become linked to other dimensions of interaction with caregivers and context throughout development.[5] The *meaning* of touch is crucial to its impact on adults.[6] A touch by oneself is not the same as the touch of another—which may soothe, tickle, irritate, or excite. Indeed, under ordinary circumstances, it is hard to tickle oneself.[7] The distinction between self and other modulates sensory processes so that even basic sensations may be sensitive to the social meaning of a stimulus.[8] The meanings of touch then involve embodied cognitive processes of attribution and interpretation and social embedding that give rise to symbolic distinctions: *a* king's touch is not at all the same as *the* King's touch.

Beyond these culturally mediated psychophysiological processes, touch has social meanings that can alter the behavior of others toward the person who is touched. The king's touch may confer higher social status, prestige, or protection on the person so marked. Such changes in social status and position may have direct effects on emotional well-being and immune status, as well as indirect effects, if the king's touch results in changes in social esteem, increased wealth, or other material advantage. The effectiveness of the king's touch then depends on its personal and collective meaning and social consequences.

Given all these potential effects of the king's touch, Weinberg's assumption that chicken soup is a more plausible antibiotic agent than a human touch seems to reflect a persistent dualism in biomedicine that views mind and meaning as somehow insubstantial.[9] In effect, we have dematerialized social symbols and relationships—which are in fact quite solidly material in their manifestations and consequences.[10] Words, symbols, and gestures are not immaterial abstractions but modes of intervention in systems constituted by human cognition and social relationships. An account of the healing efficacy of metaphor must rematerialize the social and symbolic world, to reveal the dynamics that constitute both our vulnerability to illness and our resilience. In this chapter, I aim to show how the embodied psychophysiology and social enacted processes of metaphor can take us beyond the mere recognition of the effectiveness of symbols, toward a better appreciation of the mechanisms of action of language, image, and symbol in healing.[11]

## The Efficacy of Ritual Healing

There is a vast anthropological literature on healing rituals in diverse cultures.[12] Much of this work has focused on the aesthetics of performance and explored the parallels between healing practices and larger cultural myths, values, and social structures. Healing rituals have received so much ethnographic attention not only because of their claims for efficacy, but also because of their dramatic and arresting aesthetic qualities. Aesthetics play an important role in healing rituals, making the performance attractive, engaging, compelling, absorbing, or entrancing.[13] The rhetorically skillful, evocative, authoritative, numinous, or awe-inspiring aspects of ritual performance are all strategies for mobilizing symbolic power that has material-social, emotional, and cognitive dimensions. Aesthetic elements of healing rituals portray the predicament of the suffering person and dramatize the transition from affliction to wholeness, health, and harmony.

The form, structure, and sensory aspects of healing rituals can convey specific metaphoric qualities (e.g., vigor, strength, power) that are central to their transformative functions. The power of ritual can be bodily felt in ways that convey a sense of immediacy and conviction that something significant is happening. Depending on the ontology that underwrites them, healing rituals mobilize processes that are understood and experienced not only as bodily or social but also as involving spiritual or transcendent realms.

The opening quotation from Wittgenstein portrays "magical" healing as a process in which the healer "indicates" to the illness that it should leave the sufferer. In making this request or command, the healer acts as if the illness itself has agency—sometimes even, a type of personhood—and can be engaged through language and symbol. This personification of illness is a common trope but may be a literal explanation in systems of medicine that view illness is the intrusion of an "other" that may be an object that can be mechanically extracted or an entity that must placated and appeased or challenged and expelled. We can see this ontology at play in many forms of healing. While the scientific worldview eschews this agentic view of illness along with its ontology of spirits and magic, ascriptions of agency to inanimate or nonhuman entities are common in everyday thinking and constitute important dimensions of illness experience and healing.[14]

Talking to the illness as though it is a responsive conversational partner able to carry out injunctions or commands implies that such speech is a performative act: one only needs to say the word "heal" in the right way to have the healing occur, even though the act of healing is not simply the assertion of a new state but a lengthy process of transformation that needs sustained conditions to unfold and that may involve of the agency of others—the patient, the family or community, and the healer—any of which may be obliquely invoked in talking to the illness or agent of affliction.

Ethnographic studies of healing emphasize the embedding of healing practices in larger cultural systems of meaning, ontologies, and ideologies of the person. These cultural ontologies recognize different types of agency or influence as sources of healing efficacy. In different systems of medicine, spirits, humors, "energies," chemicals, or human relationships may be invoked as active agents or powerful mediators of healing. These ontologies and corresponding forms of agency draw from cultural concepts of the person that shape the categories of affliction and the goals and methods of healing. This rootedness in local ontologies gives healing practices symbolic meaning and believed-in efficacy.

The rich tradition of ethnographic research and theorizing must be tempered by the recognition that there is limited evidence for the efficacy of ritual healing.[15] Indeed, close observation and the few systematic outcome studies suggest that healing rituals often do not work—at least not as advertised or expected.[16] On the other hand, there is ample evidence from the study of placebo effects that symbolic meaning and positive expectations can result in physiological, psychological, and behavioral changes with beneficial outcomes.[17] While the actual effectiveness of many healing practices remains uncertain, therefore, authors have continued to explore the potential efficacy of ritual appealing to nonspecific effects of meaning, expectation, and belief that may be related to placebo responses.[18]

## The Predictive Brain

Recent computational models approach cognition as a process of prediction or active inference.[19] The neural networks of the brain are constantly generating predictions of what will happen next and what needs to happen to meet the survival needs and goals of the person. These predictions are compared with incoming information, and discrepancies lead to deeper processing to produce new predictions or actions that can resolve the discrepancies between expectation and event in ways that are conducive to survival. The basic mechanism of active inference is quite general and applies to the kinds of adaptation needed to maintain the integrity of even simple organisms. Humans have both general and specialized processes of prediction that regulate the internal balance or *homeostasis* of the body's internal physiological milieu, anticipate and adjust to new circumstances (*allostasis*), and guide our interactions with the external environment on which we depend.[20] These include our capacities for metaphor, narrative, and storytelling.[21]

Active inference shows why we mainly see the world as we expect it (overlaying our model on the stream of sensory input) and notice only substantial differences and discrepancies (measured against our expectations, goals, and limits of tolerance) as "surprises" that warrant deeper processing. To re-establish our predicted regime, we can either act on the world (moving or changing it in some way) or update our models, expectations, priors, and predictions.[22] Language provides cognitive and communicative resources to co-construct and navigate the social world. A computational theory of narrative and metaphor would allow us to include the creative function of poeisis in our understanding of the mechanisms of psychological adaptation and psychopathology.[23]

The predictive processing or active inference view of the brain makes expectation central to cognition. It is a short step from this to consider the impact of symbolic interventions (including placebo effects) as reflections of this predictive machinery.[24] A symbol stands for situations that matter to us in some way and we engage with it "as if" it is the thing it stands for. This means that we generate expectations associated with the object or event that the symbol stands for, and that the process of generative modelling uses the same neural substrates as the actual engagements. Seeing a picture of food, we salivate and our pancreas releases insulin in anticipation of eating.[25] Seeing a codeine tablet, we anticipate the relief of pain, and the periaqueductal gray region of the brain releases endorphins, dampening pain experience.[26] These are processes of *biosemiosis*, bodily mediated ecological or ecosocial meaning, that are basic to our adaptive engagement with the world.[27] We share many of these basic mechanisms with other animals. The most basic scaffolding of healing, then, stems from our evolutionary history as animals, mammals, and primates. Human beings, though, are quintessentially symbolic animals and through language and other symbolic media, we vastly extend the reach of our anticipatory and predictive capacities by engaging with cultural affordances, models, and practices.[28]

A classic account of expectancy effects in healing is found in the work of Jerome Frank,[29] who identified four components common to all systems of healing that were part of a "shared assumptive world" between sufferer and healer: theories of affliction with particular ontologies; defined roles for healers that confer healing power, authority, and legitimacy; a designated place and time for healing (often imbued with sacred qualities); and the symbolic action of the healing ritual that aims to transform the status of the sick person. Frank saw positive expectations (based on a "shared assumptive world" and the evocative power of healer, context, and treatment) as reducing "demoralization"—a common dimension of many forms of affliction. In later versions of his theory, he considered how the rhetoric of therapy could influence a diversity of healing processes relevant to specific conditions.[30]

The study of rhetoric takes on new significance in societies with high levels of cultural diversity where Frank's concept of a shared assumptive world is challenged. In contemporary societies, people often participate in systems of healing with little shared experience or understanding of the specific tradition. The efficacy of heterodox traditions must be explained by existential universals of meaning, the persuasive language and status of healers, and the appeal of exotic cultural practices, models, and metaphors for illness and healing.[31] Increasingly, the global circulation of healing practices reflects the power of media and marketing to shape our images of affliction and treatment expectations. But even these culturally tailored efforts at persuasion use images and metaphors that appeal to common embodied experiences and existential predicaments.

## The Structure of Healing

In an influential paper on the effectiveness of symbolic healing, the anthropologist Claude Lévi-Strauss considered how a shamanic ritual could evoke physiological changes.[32] In shamanistic healing, a problem or affliction is transformed from the bodily realm to another ontological domain through ritual action that has a metaphorical structure. Thus, the sufferer's affliction is seen as a problem in the spirit world and action on that plane can set it right. Lévi-Strauss argued that:

> The effectiveness of symbols would consist precisely in this "inductive property," by which formally homologous structures built out of different materials at different levels of life—organic processes, unconscious mind, rational thought—are related to one another. Poetic metaphor provides a familiar example of this inductive process, but as a rule it does not transcend the unconscious level. Thus we note the significance of Rimbaud's intuition that metaphor can change the world.[33]

For Lévi-Strauss, the formal analogy or parallels between the structure of the healing ritual and the patients' experience accounted for the healing transformation. In effect, the patient's experience of bodily affliction was mapped analogically onto a mythic landscape (Figure 4.1). This mapping

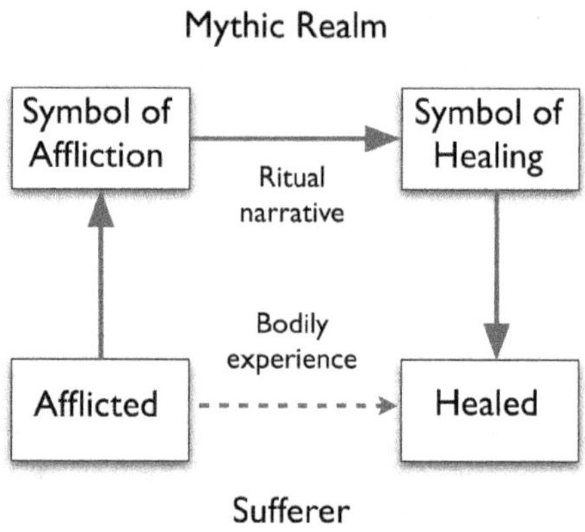


Figure 4.1 The structural logic of healing ritual
The healing ritual maps the sufferer's bodily experience onto a mythic realm where it can be transformed by ritual action that is structured according to a culturally coherent narrative. Transformation at the level of the mythic narrative then works to transform the afflicted person's bodily experience, self-understanding and social identity from sick to healed. Based on Lévi-Strauss (1963). (From Kirmayer, 2011a.)

might occur through divination or other forms of diagnosis before or during the healing ritual, which sometimes involves a metaphorical search to find the cause of the affliction within a mythic landscape. Traversing this mythic landscape through image, metaphor, or narrative conveyed by ritual incantations, the healer or his spirit guide then moves from a place that represents the affliction to one that corresponds to health. This metaphoric movement somehow causes corresponding changes in physiology, attention, cognition, and experience that result in healing. Precisely how this transformation occurs, however, remains unclear. While the analogical structure set up through the healing practice makes the parallel journey of body and myth seem plausible, the mechanisms of this transformation are not specified.[34]

Much of the appeal of Lévi-Strauss's account lies in its formal structure, but this also is its limitation. The process of healing seems under-theorized. In the actual example of Kuna shamans used by Lévi-Strauss, the patient may not understand the arcane language of the healer's incantations; hence, the effectiveness of the ritual must be mediated by nonlinguistic aspects of the healing performance.[35] Nevertheless, the idea that healing involves a transformative process mediated by the evocation of and participation in a mythic or "virtual" world provides a compelling way to understand the formal structure and symbolic logic of healing practices.[36]

Building on the work of Lévi-Strauss, anthropologist James Dow addressed the question of the dynamics of healing with the suggestion that the transformative effects occur by attaching experience to emotionally meaningful symbols.[37] It is the moving quality of emotion itself that ultimately does the psychophysiological or psychological work. Rituals then exert their effects by influencing emotional experience. This fits with observations that healing rituals often are structured like dramatic performances that elicit emotional catharsis.[38] It is also consistent with studies showing that placebo responses may be mediated in part by changes in emotional state.[39]

But the effects of rituals go beyond emotional evocation or regulation. Rituals are *performative* in the sense of bringing into being specific social situations, positions, and relationships, and, as a consequence, new configurations of the person. Performative speech acts are statements that create the social reality or event they name; this occurs, for example, when a justice of the peace pronounces two people "married."[40] Performative rituals or ceremonies work because we agree that the verbal act—when performed by the appropriate authority—transforms the person's social status. Indeed, we define the social status in terms of that verbal act and all that it entails in normative institutional and legal practices. Similarly, physicians are assigned a specific type of social authority to make clinical diagnoses and to prescribe medications or other types of medical treatment. Prescribing a treatment, whether active or placebo, conveys the message "you will get better." Of course, the biomedical intervention is usually not a declarative statement (like a faith healer emphatically saying "You are healed!") but rather an implicit suggestion built into an intervention and its social context, reinforced by statements framed as possibilities ("This should help the pain") or even questions ("Are you starting to feel better yet?"). These forms of indirect or interrogative suggestion have their own pragmatic linguistic, psychological, and social dynamics.

Ultimately, healing rituals, including the techno-scientific practices of biomedicine, are not only performative acts but also emotionally engaging social events in which both healer and patient are active—along with others in their community. As such, healing involves processes of thinking, feeling, and imagining one's way into new modes of action and experience. A more complete account of the effects of symbolic healing will therefore require theories of the psychophysiology of imagination, the social psychology of rhetorical persuasion, and the sociocultural dynamics of enacting forms of relatedness and new ways of being.

Recasting Lévi-Strauss's theory in terms of metaphor, healing processes involve cognitive transformations that have embodied and enactive dimensions. Embodiment involves the ways bodily experience gives rise to particular metaphors and the ways that metaphor can evoke bodily feelings. These are linked through processes of imagination that involve sensorimotor processes. Enactment occurs through the bodily, imaginative, and narrative deployment and extension of the metaphor to draw out its implications or new meanings. Through their engagement with local social structures, norms, and institutions, enactments have transformative effects, carrying the person over into a new social position. In what follows, we will argue that the coupling of bodily and social rhetorical processes through metaphor provides a way to understand the transformative power of such structures (see Figure 4.2).

## A Psychophysiology of Metaphor

Metaphor theory can help us to understand how language and communication influence bodily experiences and, ultimately physiological processes. Metaphor theory grounds abstract conceptualizations and, to a degree, even grammar and logic, in the processes of sensory-affective imagery and

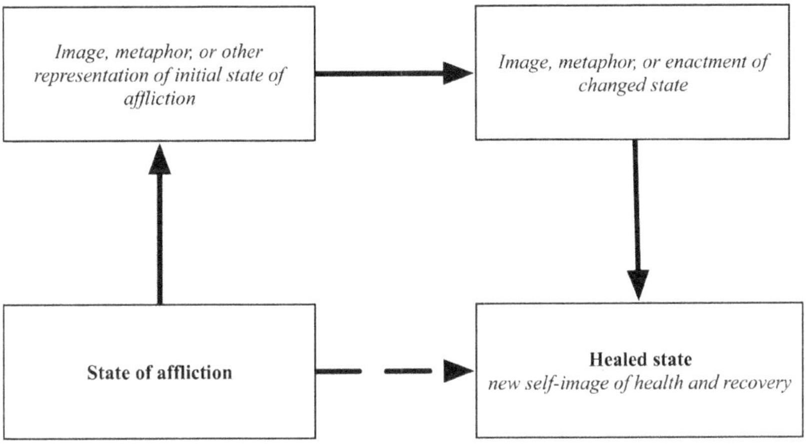


Figure 4.2 Healing performance as metaphoric transformation
In a healing ritual, the sufferer's experience is mapped analogically onto a metaphoric representational space (in literary terms, from metaphoric *topic* to *vehicle*). The initial representation is extended and transformed according to the metaphoric logic and imagery of the ritual. The transformed metaphoric representation is embodied and enacted by the afflicted person. In practice, this occurs as an ongoing cycle of embodiment and enactment throughout the healing ritual and in subsequent re-experiencing, recollection, and narration of the ritual or its expected consequences. The overall structure has been termed a *transformagram* (Hinton & Kirmayer, 2017, p. 11).

bodily action. Skills and concepts that are acquired developmentally through sensorimotor engagements with the world do not lose their connection to bodily action and sensation and using a particular concept may activate the same sensory and action systems through which they were learned.

Imagine now a hierarchy of representational "spaces," only some of which corresponding to spatial arrangements, while most organize other dimensions of meaning and experience.[41] These spaces are representational in the sense that they map aspects of the world onto a medium (the functional systems or networks of the brain) in ways that preserve relationships of contiguity or similarity among these aspects. The lower levels have topological properties corresponding to the sort of processing done by phylogenetically older parts of the nervous system that involve basic sensory, motor, motivational, and emotional (affective) dimensions. The higher levels allow more abstract spatial/temporal representations. Metaphors transform our perceptions and representations by moving them through sensory, affective, imagistic or representational, and more abstract conceptual spaces. According to how this movement occurs within these independent spaces, any communication gives rise to multiple simultaneous meanings. These hierarchically stacked spaces can be viewed as text and subtext, literal and metaphorical layers of meaning in communication and action. The highest levels can loop back in on themselves in self-reference.

We can apply this model of a hierarchy of metaphoric spaces, through which meanings are generated, to the range of symbolic healing practices. Figure 4.3 depicts some of the many processes involved in symbolic healing. In the central column of the figure, these are arranged as a hierarchy of levels of organization, first within the central nervous system (CNS),[42] then on to family and larger social groupings. Each of these levels has its own dynamical processes and corresponding therapeutic interventions. Of course, any actual therapeutic action or communication inevitably affects all of these levels, but they need not always work in concert. Communication occurs on multiple parallel levels, allowing for resonance or reinforcement, conflict, contradiction, and negation. Thus, the same therapeutic act has multiple meanings based on its effects at different levels in this hierarchy. In effect, each level can supply both material mechanisms and metaphoric elaboration to processes at other levels. Theories of healing and psychotherapy usually recognize processes at one or a few levels, while ignoring the role of levels that do not have a privileged place in their ontology.

These levels of organization within a biosocial hierarchy require different languages of description. The activity of the brain is described in terms of neurobiology—which itself includes structural levels from molecules, to cells, synapses (the functional connections between neurons), circuits, and larger networks. The function of these networks is often described in the language of "physiological psychology" or behavioral neurobiology that maintains close links to the vocabulary of everyday folk psychology.

There is a longstanding tradition of contrasting "lower levels" of the brain as corresponding to phylogenetically older, more primitive functions, while higher levels subserve rationality and creativity. In a once popular version of this hierarchy, Paul MacLean proposed a triune model of the brain, stratified phylogenetically, with reptilian, mammalian, and primate layers.[43] While it is not hard to identify behaviors we might characterize as lizard-like compulsivity, warm-blooded furry attachment, or simian ingenuity, contemporary neuroscience has rejected MacLean's zoological garden of the brain, emphasizing the integration of functions

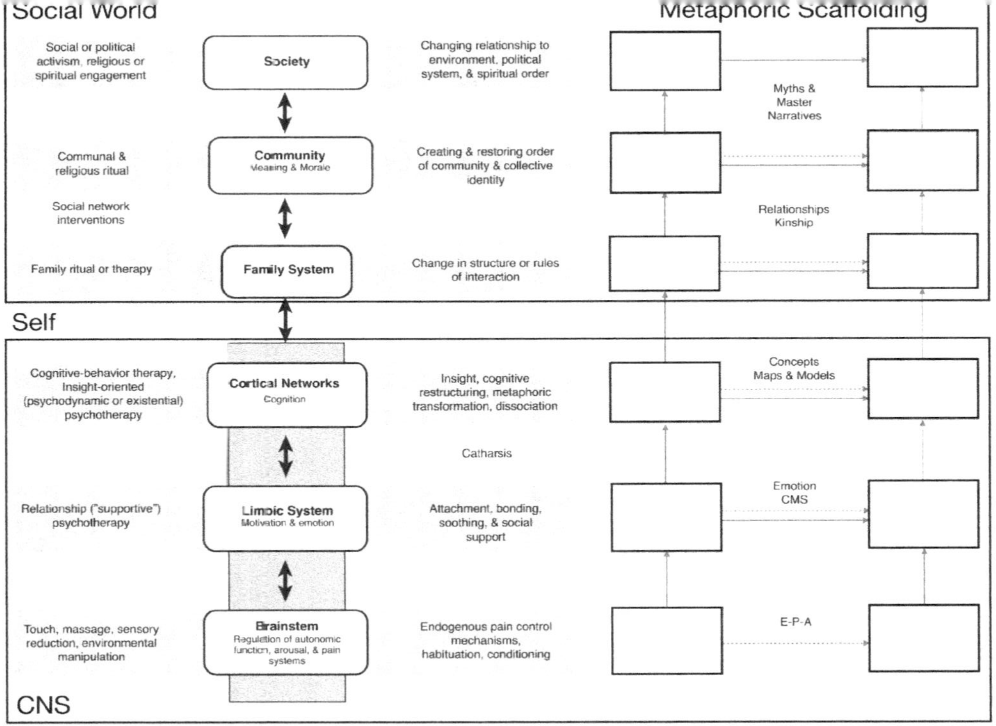


Figure 4.3 A hierarchy of healing processes

Healing or transformational processes can occur at many levels of the constitution of the person, represented schematically here as levels of organization within the brain and in the social world. The self, as a locus of agency and subjectivity, arises through interactions between the body-brain and the social world. On the left are different healing practices and mechanisms that may mediate their effects. On the right is the scaffold of metaphoric meaning built on the same processes that subserve healing. Although particular healing practices may target specific processes—whether explicitly in their own theory or ontology or implicitly as identified from an *etic* perspective—any intervention will have effects at multiple levels. Characterizing these cross-level effects requires knowledge of the dynamics at each level and how they may work together synergistically or in tension to reframe the meaning and modulate the impact of other levels. CNS: Central nervous system; E-P-A: Evaluation, potency, activity; CMS: Central motive states (adapted from Kirmayer, 2015c, p. 649).

across anatomical regions. Nevertheless, there is good evolutionary, cybernetic, and computational sense in thinking of the brain as hierarchically organized in a way that allows the parallel processing of multiple aspects of meaning that may enrich, modify, and sometimes contradict each other.[44]

The lowest level depicted in Figure 4.3 is the brainstem, which includes the brainstem reticular formation which is involved in mechanisms of general arousal, waking or activation.[45] Interventions that work at this level serve to change the overall level of arousal, making the person more or less alert, awake, sensitive, and active in response to any stimulus. Other processes at this level provide a primal sketch of sensory and motivational meaning, corresponding roughly to temperamental differences, drive states, or basic appetites like hunger and thirst.[46] Healing practices that employ touch, massage, some placebo effects, and other phenomena of classical conditioning may work in part at this level by affecting endogenous control systems for arousal, autonomic nervous system function, or pain control.

The second level of the CNS depicted has been called the "limbic system," which includes phylogenetically older structures of the forebrain and diencephalon, characteristic of mammals, that subserve basic processes of motivation, affect, and emotion.[47] These brain systems are implicated in the encoding and decoding of affective meaning, the regulation of emotion, and the dynamics of attachment. This is the domain explored in attachment research and an explicit focus in forms of psychotherapy that emphasize supportive or reparative relationships.[48]

Together, the lower levels of brain processing probably give rise to the three dimensions of affective meaning recovered by Osgood and his colleagues in factorial studies with the semantic differential.[49] When people in diverse cultures are asked to use words metaphorically to rate both concrete and abstract concepts, their responses reveal basic dimensions of *evaluation* (good/bad), *potency* (weak/strong), and *activity* (fast/slow). These rudiments of affective meaning form a metaphoric substratum of language and gesture. In healing rituals, verbal or gestural metaphors confer the affective qualities of the vehicle on the topic and so move us through affective space—whether to experience awe-inspiring power or to find comfort and soothing.[50]

The cerebral cortex adds further levels to this neurobiological hierarchy: the symbolic functions of language and imagery through which self and other are imagined and narrated. Therapeutic action at this level aims to elicit and transform the images and metaphors that mediate experience, the schemas or models that represent the world, and the narrative structures through which the self is enacted. Most cognitive and psychodynamic theory is concerned with this level and its interactions with the other levels of the hierarchy. In psychodynamic theory, the lower levels of organization of the brain are thought to be represented at this level and so can be worked with as though they are cognitive or linguistic structures.[51] Similarly, psychodynamic theory assumes that the higher levels of family and social structure are also represented at the level of cognitive-linguistic function, and that such representations can be made conscious and restructured to conform more adequately to reality. In psychodynamic interpretations, both neurophysiological and social processes are metaphorized as the conflict of internal mental agents. In therapeutic interpretations, a choice of metaphors initially aims to offer a more accurate and encompassing picture of the structure of this inner world. Ultimately, it aims to transform the models of self and other to make the individual able to resolve internal conflict, and achieve better social functioning and, perhaps, some degree of reconciliation with others.

The representations of events and possibilities in memory and imagination may be based on imagery rather than linguistic-propositional processes. Much of what goes on in imagery and affect is difficult to put into words (hence, our respect for the poet's skill in the aptness of metaphor).[52] Modes of healing that use imagery work predominantly with this level of organization, as do efforts to transform cognitive schemas through the elicitation of dominant images and their deliberate modification or substitution with new images that have more positive connotations and adaptive influence on behavior.

Beyond these levels within the CNS, we can distinguish further levels in human biological organization, including the social groupings of family and community or society. In insisting that social structure and process are levels of organization in a biological system, I aim not for a reductionist account, but for the recognition that we are embedded in a single hierarchical system in which each level demands a new vocabulary of description with its own dynamical processes.[53] The brain is the organ of culture, and culture involves particular levels of organization in the systems that constitute, configure, and constrain human beings.

Families and other groups of people living together develop rules of interaction that can give rise to problems that are not reducible to intrapsychic conflicts. Consequently, the unraveling of such interpersonal conflicts may require changes in family structure or the rules of interaction.[54] Family rules are rarely articulated as such. Instead, family members conceive of their group in terms of family myths and metaphors. In healing or psychotherapeutic interventions, a change in metaphor, prescribed by a therapist and subscribed to by even one member of the group, can begin to change the pattern of interaction of the whole system in widespread ways.

Finally, the family unit is embedded in larger social groupings with a collective history and way of life that constitute a community, ethnocultural group, or society. At this sociocultural level of organization, people participate in the construction of institutions and shared symbolic meanings that confer an order that surpasses individual experience. Symbolic healing at this level employs the extended metaphors of secular and religious ritual to create and restore the order of the community and the cosmos and, with it, the sufferer's experience of meaning and morale.[55]

This model is hierarchical in that each level is built on the scaffolding of lower levels. However, this does not imply that the function of higher levels can be reduced to a lower level. Each level has its own emergent dynamics. Certainly, effects at a lower level may be necessary to achieve an impact at higher levels. Thus, an optimal level of arousal may be necessary to form attachments and conduct a satisfying emotional exchange. Attachment or trust in a healing relationship may be necessary for verbal prescriptions to be accepted and assimilated or achieve their evocative power. A self-reflexive awareness of images or concepts of a relationship may be necessary for individuals to attend to a new metaphor for relationships and so change their current mode of family interaction. But the dependence also works the other way; processes at a lower level in the hierarchy may depend on the context created by the higher level: the ideal level of arousal for a particular task depends on how one interacts with others; the quality and stability of an attachment depends on the social and cultural meaning of the relationship.[56]

Despite the mutually constitutive and constraining relationships between levels of organization, each level has a degree of independence. Hence, the model involves multiple parallel processes and therapeutic action or communication can work at each level, to some extent, independently of its impact at other levels. For example, a therapeutic relationship must be minimally soothing to continue, but attachments can form even where the sensory impact of the other is noxious or irritating. Many schools of psychotherapy insist that empathic relatedness can heal even in the absence of accurate insight. Similarly, it is a central tenet of family therapy that change can occur at the level of the family system independently and in advance of changes in individual psychological processes.

Although I have portrayed these levels as distinct to emphasize the parallel nature of sense-making and communication, most modes of healing involve interactions between levels. In practice, every therapeutic action—whether a word, gesture, ritual, or relationship—has effects on all of these levels. There is little evidence to support the claims of particular schools of therapy that a single mechanism like catharsis, insight, reinforcement, or cognitive restructuring alone accounts for the efficacy of its practice. Nor is it very informative to speak of "nonspecific" effects of therapy, like "mobilizing positive expectancies" or "improving morale," since each of these involves specific processes that, while they may remain unacknowledged by a particular theory, are well described in other traditions. The picture of healing offered by each tradition is therefore a limited portrait, that selects certain elements from the wide range of potential processes identified by scientific and comparative methods.

The model of a hierarchy of levels of evocative meaning allows us to recognize the tensions implicit in metaphoric communication as both a potential source of suffering and of healing efficacy. The psychophysiology of metaphor can account for some of the microdynamics of pain and suffering—for example, showing how the quality and intensity of pain can be moderated by imagery or metaphors of distance that bring pain close and in tight focus or move it into the background, to be defused or obscured by other experiences.[57] Again, metaphor can structure the process of attention so that we can become detached from pain by adopting a stance of "just watching."[58] In the case of emotional pain, in addition to influencing self-regulation, metaphor guides the project of self- and social definition through which we may become socially disqualified—viewed as victims and damaged—or carry our afflictions as marks of distinction.[59]

## Animal Powers and the Logic of Shamanism

The study of shamanism can illuminate the ways in which the multiple levels of psychophysiology are evoked and coordinated in healing practices. The term *shamanism*, narrowly construed, refers to healing or problem-solving practices found among hunter peoples whose lives involve a profound interdependence with animals, which are viewed as nonhuman persons. Reflecting this intimate connection to animals, the mythologist Joseph Campbell referred to shamanism as "the way of the animal powers."[60] The livelihood of hunters depended on maintaining appropriate relationships with animals who gave their lives for human sustenance and survival. This was part of a moral economy based on close kinship with animals as nonhuman persons.

From the 1960s onward, shamanism had a popular revival with many finding in its ethos a corrective to the distance and detachment from the natural world characteristic of modern societies.[61] Of course, the experiential and social realities of Indigenous cultures—past or present—should not be confused with the imaginative projections of urban industrialized people longing for "simpler" times. Nevertheless, shamanism recognizes the basic fact that we are animals and can readily connect the bodily aspects of our animal nature to our experiences of wellness, as well as affliction and healing. In fact, it is easy to imagine our way into an animal body and mimic its movements.[62] Many rituals in hunting societies involve people wearing skins or masks and adopting dance movements that re-enact human–animal interactions. Animals stand for ways of being that are potentialities in us not only because of cultural history and imagination but also because of aspects of our embodied experience that reflect deep phylogenetic kinship. Understanding how forms of animal imagery and embodiment work can contribute to our theories of healing. Brave Buffalo, a Teton-Sioux medicine man, had this advice:

> If men would . . . seek what is best to do in order to make themselves worthy of that toward which they are so attracted, they might have dreams which would purify their lives. Let a man decide upon his favorite animal and make a study of it, learning its innocent ways. Let him learn to understand its sounds and motions. The animals want to communicate with man.[63]

The anthropologist Marie-Françoise Guedon described Tshimsian shamanism as a technology of image or metaphor.[64] Each shaman has a number of spirit helpers that take the form of animals or objects (e.g., a rope or a canoe). In healing rituals, the patient's illness is explored and worked on through these symbols. Thus, a canoe may be paddled, tipped over, or even pulled out of the chest of a sufferer. As one shaman told her, "pneumonia I don't know what to do about but a rope that I know all about. So I look for the rope in the patient and work with that—then he gets better." This navigation and working within a metaphoric world is depicted in this story of the Tsimshian shaman "Only-One" (Isaac Tens).

> Only-One, as soon as he arrived at Gitrhahla, saw some of the traps which the Wuda *halaeit* [shaman] had set up for him. He saw, ahead of him as he landed, a huge net. Although it was invisible to all, Only-One was able to see it. He walked around it. Thus he did not become entangled in the net. Then just as he was about to enter the house of the shaman who had invited him, he saw a pit, visible only to *halaeits*. Others could walk over it or on it, and no harm would come to them. But it was different with a *halaeit*, as it was a trap specially made for Only-One. He would have suddenly disappeared

> down this pit and would have been destroyed; as he was on guard, he saw the invisible pit and walked round it.[65]

In this account we see the shaman able to avoid hidden traps that would catch lesser mortals (the net), yet still vulnerable to traps set specifically for shamans with second sight (the pit). The metaphoric world thus confers supernormal knowledge and clarity of vision on the shaman even as it holds its own dangers.

The shaman's vision is rooted in the materiality of everyday experience (knowledge of animal bodies and behavior) and in capacities for imaginative enactment. In hunter societies, people have detailed knowledge of the anatomy of animals and are close observers of their behavior. Thinking with and through animals involves a kind of embodied imagination that calls on this cultural knowledge but also on more basic and often implicit understanding derived from bodily experience, which reflects a shared evolutionary heritage. As mammals, we have modes of experience and imagination that arise from our anatomy, development, and behavioral capacities. Our affinity for, interest in, and dependence on differently bodied creatures then animates the imagination. Shamanism and other practices extend that knowledge in creative ways to move beyond materiality to consider imaginative realms that may be experienced as immanent expressions of an ontology not just of animals and people but also of spirits, who live in the mundane world, but may be visible only to shamans or others with the right knowledge and power.[66]

## Sympathetic Magic: Metaphor, Metonymy, and Synesthesia

Sympathetic magic is perhaps the simplest form of symbolic healing. Stanley Tambiah gives the example of the word-magic of the Trobriand Islanders studied by Bronislaw Malinowski.[67] The Trobrianders used transfer magic to apply the sensory characteristics of one substance to another. Transfer magic is based on analogies between various foods and natural substances and the desirable qualities of a healthy child, a productive garden, a fleet, or a sturdy canoe. These analogies are rooted in cross-modal analogies between sensory phenomena: a loud sound is like a bright light, a tone rising in pitch is like a movement upward. When these cross-modal links are especially strong they may result in synesthesia, in which a sensory stimulus in one modality regularly evokes a response in another modality.[68]

For example, in magic to ensure the prosperity of the village, *leya* (wild ginger) is associated with fierceness and toughness. In using ginger as a symbol, the memory of its smell and taste or liveliness on the tongue evokes affective qualities of high activity and potency. This results in a shift in ritual participants' affective state and, along with that, a change in the way they think about the village. This transformation can occur whether or not the participant is consciously aware of the analogy between ginger and the properties of a lively village.

The figurative logic of transfer magic extends to more complex ritual actions or proscriptions. Pregnant women are forbidden to eat foods that suggest an analogy to the condition of the mother in some respects yet in other ways are antagonistic. Similarly, the objects used in transfer magic are tabooed as foods: in effect, the message is "Don't eat your metaphors" (i.e., don't mistake the figurative for the literal). The careful attention to the metaphoric properties of food among the Trobriand islanders is reinforced by their understanding that the belly is not only the receptacle for food but also the seat of emotion, memory, and understanding. It is thus the storehouse of magical formulae, and, so, food taboos are linked to the efficacy of magic.

The connections between metaphor and sensory qualities are bidirectional. Just as sensations and sensorimotor experiences give rise to metaphors, so too metaphors can elicit sensory experience or change how we process and perceive sensory information. Even the most obdurate sensory experiences have metaphoric mediation and elaboration. Gibbs discusses how metaphor intervenes in the sensory, affective, and cognitive dimensions of the experience of pain.[69] Metaphors may not directly mediate the sensory intensity or "raw feel" of pain, but they certainly influence its evolution over time. Our endurance of pain depends in part on how we describe its sensory qualities and what that description implies in terms of the pain's significance.[70] Pain that is literally or metaphorically framed as injury or disease progression ("THIS PAIN IS KILLING ME") can evoke fear and avoidance that lead to more intense pain and impairments in functioning.[71] Reframing the sensation as a sign of the body protecting or healing itself, as an inevitable aspect of vital processes (like childbirth), physical conditioning ("no pain, no gain"), character development, or as a call to change one's life, can then transform the pain experience.[72]

## Emotion Regulation

As we noted earlier, Dow suggested that the dynamics of emotion can explain the healing effects of symbol and ritual described by Lévi-Strauss.

Emotions are organized patterns of anticipation and dispositions to respond that help us navigate the environment. While some emotions like happiness or fear are associated with basic valences of approach and avoidance, more complex emotion terms are names not for bodily or experiential states but for configurations of social relations unfolding over time. Moral emotions like honor, shame, and guilt are embedded in and regulated by social scripts that assign roles, set norms, and convey expectations to the person which become part of ongoing processes of identifying and managing feelings. Even emotions like fear and anger have local variants that reflect particular concepts of personhood and social relations.[73] As such, complex emotions not only govern (or rationalize) one's interpersonal actions, but also carry expectations about how others will react (or should have reacted) to one's actions.[74] However, not all emotions are future oriented or involve expectations; instead, they speak to a stretch of social interaction including specific antecedents, behaviors, and larger social consequences. Emotions have their own time horizons and may refer to the past (and be situated there as in nostalgia, grief, or shame) or to the future (as in anticipatory joy, fear, or anger). This temporal structure is shaped by metaphors grounded in bodily experiences involving posture, spatial disposition, and movement,[75] as well as in the functioning of sensory systems like olfaction, which has strong links to memory and emotion.[76]

There are many common emotion metaphors found across diverse cultures and languages.[77] Some of these metaphors begin in "physiognomic perception"—seeing the world as like the body, with angry thunderclouds, smiling sunbeams, and placid lakes.[78] Such metaphors represent "low level metaphorical associations between concepts based on experiential correlation."[79] Other metaphors linked to bodily felt states associated with emotions. For example, as we have noted, metaphors linking anger with heat ("HOT HEADED," "BURNING, SIMMERING, OR BOILING WITH RAGE") occur in very different languages and reflect an embodied experience and metonymic connection: anger is commonly associated with flushing and feelings of heat in the face or head that are part of the physiology of anger.[80] In contrast, loneliness, loss of social connection, and isolation may be described as cold.[81] Of course, flushing also occurs with embarrassment or sexual arousal or other forms of excitement. And anger, while built around an adaptive response to threat, is configured and elaborated in diverse ways in different cultures, so that neither the bodily experience nor the meaning of the emotion is precisely the same.[82] Moreover, anger may have very different connotations within and across cultures depending on its larger embedding in interpersonal dynamics and social scripts. In some instances, for example, we might characterize an angry person as cold and distant, or scheming and predatory (the association is with cold-blooded predators).

To the extent that metaphors structure emotional experience and response, changes in metaphors can change emotions. The anthropologist Rebecca Seligman explored the relationship between metaphors and emotion in an ethnographic study of Mexican American adolescents receiving outpatient psychotherapy for a variety of emotional and behavioral problems.[83] She examined the metaphors that adolescents used to make sense of their experience and the ways they responded to the metaphors "prescribed" by the manualized cognitive–behavioral therapy used in that clinical setting. Certain metaphors were presented as explicit interventions intended to reshape patients' emotional control and interpersonal behavior. For example, Seligman describes adolescents' responses to the use of an "EMOTION THERMOMETER" to graphically record the intensity of their feelings. While some youth found the metaphor of intensity easy to map onto the visual analog scale of the thermometer, others protested that the task was difficult and constraining because their feelings fluctuated, were situation dependent, and involved multiple qualities or dimensions. The pancultural metaphor of ANGER IS HEAT was transformed in youths' narratives into a more dynamic account of struggling to contain, manage, and express strong feelings. In some instances, youth rejected the injunction to moderate or reduce emotional intensity, recognizing that strong emotions serve a moral function: anger is a sign of the recognition of injustice, a way to communicate that recognition, and becomes an armature around which an identity as an aggrieved, unfairly treated, and righteous person can be constructed. The instruction to monitor feelings, which is aimed at creating some meta-cognition, distance, and emotional self-regulation may then be perceived as undermining a familiar, socially justified, and legitimate sense of self and moral conviction.

Adolescents found some metaphors apt and readily took them up, while they resisted or refigured other metaphors through acts of poiesis: "Some metaphors may stick, while others may not, depending on what they do for the individual—both intra and interpersonally."[84] What makes a metaphor apt may be its fit with embodied experience, existing models, or overarching narratives that have institutional authority—and, hence, its effectiveness to make sense of or manage feelings both intrapsychically and interpersonally. This interplay between daily experience and culturally salient narratives is evident in accounts of many kinds of symptom experience. For example, acts like self-cutting may exploit aspects of bodily physiology through which injury activates endorphin systems that reduce pain and anxiety.[85] In addition to this physiological response, self-injury is ascribed symbolic meaning—both in the moment and on later experiences with scars—that loops back into its use as a coping strategy and act of communication, identity construction, and social positioning. Through such biolooping, metaphors do not simply describe experience, they reshape it. Emotions, then, are not fixed entities that dictate specific metaphors but embodied and socially situated experiences that are differently constructed in personal and cultural contexts.[86] Part of this construction is mediated by metaphors. Through metaphor, emotions are embodied, embedded, enacted, and encultured in the social world.

## Catharsis and Aesthetic Distance

Many healing practices aim to manage or transform emotions through abreaction or catharsis. Emotional catharsis involves both the imagery-based evocation of emotion and the linguistic framing of the experience to create adequate cognitive "distance" so that the reliving of traumatic experience is not so intense and immediate that it causes a fresh trauma.[87] Distancing may be part of more general processes of metaphoric reframing, but it illustrates the ways in which affective intensity can be moderated by imagery and enactment. Catharsis can then be understood as a transaction between multiple levels of processes that serve emotion regulation governed by metaphors that draw their meaning from both bodily experience and socially prescribed narrative forms. In sociologist Thomas Scheff's analysis, catharsis consists of four phases: "(1) an arrangement of stimuli which is optimally distanced, i.e. which contains a balance of distressful and reassuring stimuli; (2) the participant's response, in which there is a balance between involvement in past distress and present safety; (3) catharsis which is signaled by sobbing with tears, shivering with cold sweat, etc.; and, finally, (4) decrease in tension, increases in mental clarity, and feelings of well-being."[88] These dynamics of emotion regulation can be found in many kinds of ritual and dramatic performance.

A striking example is provided in Edward Schieffelin's account of the *gisaro* ritual of the Kaluli in highland Papua New Guinea.[89] In this ritual, visitors from another village spend time preparing a ritual performance of song and dance that, while formally simple, evokes intense feelings of hunger, loss, and loneliness that make audience members weep. The performance seems to achieve this emotive power by referring to local places and events of great personal significance to specific people in the audience. The performance also has a narrative structure that names specific places and events in a sequence that follows familiar geographic landmarks in local topography. The evocative power of the images builds as the narrative moves through along a virtual path that provides laden with personal memories.

> At Gudesawal I am hungry, I am hungry at the ba: tree there,
> I am hungry at Gudesawal
> At the Masase over there Kalluo; tips are appearing,
> I am hungry

The dancers are costumed with face paint, leaves, and feathers, and when they dance in the torch-lit longhouse, they appear to the audience as birds flapping their wings. When the emotional response of an audience member becomes too intense, they may take a flaming torch and burn the shoulders of the dancer. Although the dancer's shoulders are partially protected by their costumes' epaulets, the scars that result are badges of honour for the performer that mark their aesthetic success.

The power of this ritual performance to evoke strong feelings lies both in its spatial structure and in the experiential grounding of its evocative images. The experiences of hunger and loss target specific audience members for whom the location, names, and feelings are resonant. The pain of hunger and loss is basic to human experience—and, for hunter-gatherers, food and social sustenance are closely intertwined through everyday subsistence activities. "To be hungry, therefore implies more than merely a condition of physical need. It also implies isolation from companionship."[90] Personal histories of relationships, of companionship and loss, hunger and privation, are inscribed in the landscape. For the Kaluli, then, simple place names have great evocative power.

> "When a man lives somewhere for a long time," one informant explained, "his name is in the ground just like you put your name in that book." The subtle changes one sees in the forest regrowth reflect the presence and work of people one has known in the past.[91]

This gives literal meaning to the metaphor of "grounding." This Kaluli cosmology underwrites an ontology in which the sounds of the forest are real presences, the voices of lost loved ones.[92]

Kaluli reality is built on a cosmology in which humans and birds are linked.

> Out hunting with Wanalugo, we heard the plaintive juu-juu-juu of the kalo (a small pigeon). Wanalugo turned to me with a wistful expression and said, "You hear that? It is a little child who is hungry and calling for its mother . . .

> The everyday Kaluli world of gardens, rivers, and forests is coextensive with another, invisible side of reality. The remark that the voice of the kalo is a little child is not merely a metaphor. The kalo may actually be the soul of a child. "Do you see that huge tree?" another man asked one day on the path. "In their [the birds'] world, that is a house. Do you see the birds? To each other, they appear as men." Similarly, houses in our world appear as exceptionally big trees or as river pools to them and we as animals there.[93]

The *gisaro* songs achieve their intensely evocative power through the social significance of the ritual context, the way the performance is structured to mirror local topography, and the anchoring of song, dance, and action in an ontology of human and animal interdependence and co-presence.

Similar interweaving of word and deed, image, and experience, grounded in a local ontology drives the intense affective experience of ritual in shamanistic healing.

> In treating his patient the shaman also offers his audience a performance. What is this performance? Risking a rash generalization on the basis of a few observations, we shall say that it always involves the shaman's enactment of the "call," or the initial crisis which brought him the revelation of his condition. But we must not be deceived by the word performance. The shaman does not limit himself to reproducing or miming certain events. He actually relives them in all their vividness, originality, and violence. And since he returns to his normal state at the end of the séance, we may say, borrowing a key term from psychoanalysis, that he *abreacts*. In psychoanalysis, abreaction refers to the decisive moment in the treatment when the patient intensively relives the initial situation from which his disturbance stems, before he ultimately overcomes it. In this sense, the shaman is a professional abreactor.[94]

In shamanism and forms of healing that employ trance or possession, the performative aspects lie largely with the shaman as a conduit for the spirits. In other forms of healing, the action may be divided between healer and sufferer. Together they choreograph a ritual enactment that evokes and transforms emotion.

The concepts of catharsis and abreaction or emotional release played a key role in the early development of psychoanalysis.[95] The theory of catharsis, with its dramatic re-enactment of traumatic memories and emotional expression is not an empirical discovery of psychological healers but owes its origins directly to the Greek theater. The treatment of Anna O. by Breuer and Sigmund Freud, which formed an essential basis for their development of the cathartic method (described in *Studies on Hysteria* in

1895) occurred in a social context in which there was intense interest in the Aristotelian concept of dramatic catharsis. As the historian Frank Sulloway notes, Jacob Bernays, the uncle of Freud's fiancée at the time had written on catharsis in Greek theater.[96] By 1890, there were more than 140 German-language publications in this area and interest in the salons of Vienna reached "the proportions of a craze."[97] Sulloway suggests that the talented Anna O. might have incorporated her knowledge of catharsis into the "dramatic plot" of illness. The theatrical experience of emotional involvement with catharsis as its culmination then provided the model for psychological abreaction as a method of healing. Of course, the psychological experience may antedate the invention of theater but, even so, the notion of catharsis in dramatic theory provides conceptual structure to understand subsequent emotional experiences. Catharsis, then, becomes a dominant metaphor for a kind of movement through affective space with a crescendo of emotional release followed by calm.

The concept of aesthetic distance is crucial to the cathartic process.[98] The painful experience is relived but with an added awareness that it is not really happening—it is an *as if*; the context has changed, it is only a memory, a dream, or a reverie. A similar experiential distance can be achieved even without the explicit labeling of experience through imagery or bodily enactment. For example, guided by a therapist, a person can recollect or reimagine a traumatic scenario by watching it on a mental movie screen and adjust its intensity by moving the screen closer or further away. Catharsis depends on finding an optimal distance. If the distance is too great, the person may remain unmoved by the image. If the distance is too small, the person may experience emotions that are too intense, and hence, suffer too much pain or even traumatic injury that leads not to relief but to greater distress and subsequent avoidance.

At optimal aesthetic distance, the audience or participant becomes emotionally involved in the drama but with parallel awareness of being an observer. The Kaluli burning of the dancers may represent a point where the ritual becomes underdistant (too intense) for some participants and tension is released through stylized aggressive action. While the act of burning the dancer is a metaphoric expression of this excess of emotion, it is also a shift in bodily and emotional state through enacting the anger and aggression of a physical assault (calibrated or constrained by the ritual script). In the same way, the bodily enactments of ritual, then, may serve to regulate imaginal processes, social interactions, and physical states.

Aesthetic distance is clearly a metaphor for something, but what? In ritual there may be an awareness of artifice, safety, community, or sacredness that renders intense affects manageable, even cathartically pleasurable. This distance may be achieved by the social structuring of the ritual in terms of a designated time and place (the *temenos*) or the use of a metaphor or other figure of speech that signals entry into the realm of ceremony, characterized by seriousness, or into a space of exploration, celebrating playfulness and imagination. The meta-cognition that we are engaged in during ceremony or play sets up competing emotions that may amplify or temper the intensity affect evoked. Aesthetic distance then reflects the stance we take toward experience, the degree of absorption, and the competing thoughts and feelings that may amplify or dilute the intensity of feeling. Both the mode of engagement with experience and our awareness of the process are structured metaphorically.

A similar notion of distance can be applied to understanding pain and suffering in other contexts. Metaphor can be used to explore the micro-dynamics of pain and suffering, to reveal how perceptual distance is controlled by thought and image bringing pain terrifyingly close or sending it comfortably far away. As we have described earlier, metaphor structures the process of attention so that we can become detached from our pain. This may not be simply a matter of distraction but can involve metaphorically mediated regulation of attentional strategies. Here is how the psychiatrist–anthropologist Devon Hinton describes this process for some of the Cambodian refugees with whom he has worked.

> Among Cambodian refugees, for example, there are multiple metaphors that configure the person's attentional focus in ways that increase awareness of the importance of changing attentional focus as an emotion regulation technique. This recognition of the power of attention is central to Buddhist teachings. In Khmer, the word for an attentional object and mood are the same (*arâm*), indicating that mood is determined by the attentional object. Another Cambodian word (*ceut*) has the dual meaning of attentional focus and cognitive-emotional state. One speaks of "cutting the attentional focus" (*gat ceut*) to indicate turning attention from an attentional object, or of "pulling the attentional focus" (*dâceut*), or of "turning the attentional focus" (*beunlâp arâm*). These idioms are based on the metaphoric structure depicted in [Figure 4.4]. This reflects an ethnopsychology and ontology in which emotion and attention are aspects of the same cognitive-bodily-social process.[99]

These metaphors evoke attentional skills that are learned through participation in particular cultural regimes of attention that may include practices like listening to stories, engaging in imaginative play, and participating in ceremonies, meditative practice, and artistic performance.[100]

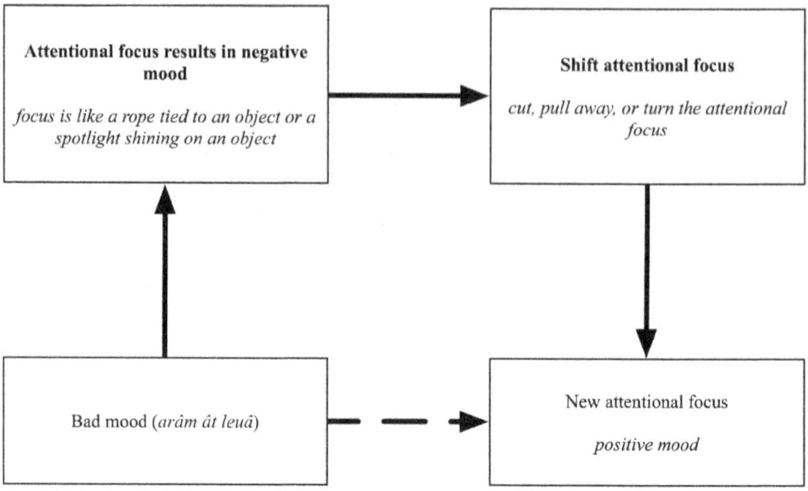


Figure 4.4 Metaphor-mediated shifts of attention in healing
Transformagram of Cambodian healing practice in which "bad mood" is altered by metaphorically prompted shifts in attention (Hinton & Kirmayer, 2017, p.13).

## Embodiment, Morality, Spirituality, and Transcendence

Spatial metaphors in experience go far beyond the notion of aesthetic distance reflecting other facets or dimensions of embodiment. These experiences depend on the particularities of the human body in social and cultural context but they also borrow from our kinship with other beings. The shaman may go down into the darkness of the underworld or fly up into the sky, like a bird, to visit the spirits. In shamanic traditions, the bodies of humans and animals are mutable and interchangeable in imagination. This confluence of being extends beyond animals to encompass other presences. The image of the tree is important in some traditions as a natural symbol that unites the earth and the sky.[101]

Upright posture is a key feature of human embodiment. There is a close link between the vertical dimension of bodily stance and emotional experience. Being UP is generally associated with vitality, health, happiness, and well-being, while being DOWN corresponds to the opposite characteristics.[102] We soar in ecstasy and fall in grief or lamentation. Posture therefore has fundamental meaning as a mode of social communication. We signal our emotional state and our stance toward others in the way that we carry ourselves. This social dimension of posture serves to communicate power, dominance, or submission: standing tall to declare victory over another, bowing in deference, or cowering in submission.

Pain, suffering, and sorrow are dramatically displayed in posture: the depressed person slumps over; the person in pain pulls back and guards themselves. We understand these postures of dejection or abjection not just through a culturally codified language of posture and gesture,[103] but through our ability to embody the feeling by imagining or adopting a similar stance. As Darwin suggested, we share this basic structure of embodied knowing with other animals and we can recognize similar bodily responses to injury, pain, fear, and loss across species.[104] This extends to sharing elements of moral emotions like anger, guilt, and shame.[105] But the particularities of human embodiment and imagination lend additional meaning to bodily stance.

The vertical dimension of stance that conveys our attitude toward experience takes us up the hierarchy of healing processes to engage with the social level which elaborates the domain of morality.

> The "moral," rational self is high, while the "lower" self is associated with the body and bodily functions. This up/down, high/low orientation comes to be correlated with purity versus impurity. The body, with its passions and desires, ties us to that which is dirty, polluted, and impure. The mind, as the seat of reason and will, tries to maintain its purity by rising above and trying to control the body.[106]

Much of our vocabulary for moral strength references bodily stance or position: we carry ourselves high with dignity and righteousness or shrink down in abjection or self-abnegation. We speak of core values, close to our position that we protect and defend, and peripheral issues where we may readily yield to the views of others. Balance metaphors are used to express the search for harmony and a middle way amid conflicting values.[107] Indeed, the very basis of moral action resides in our ability to take a stand and protect a position. Moral authority is embodied as the stance one takes toward the world: leaning forward to engage or shrinking back, standing up to others or giving way, or being morally upright or skulking and devious.

The basic meanings of stance, which contribute to the experience of pain and the logic of morality, also play a vital role in religious iconography, ritual, and practice. What is godly, spiritual, and transcendent usually is located upward beyond our gaze, while the fallen world of human imperfection lies at or beneath our feet. When spiritual traditions elaborate a cosmology, they often use the body as a map and divide or subdivide it along the vertical axis to indicate levels of transcendence of the mundane or earthly world that tends to be associated with the lower half of the body. The human body with its limbs extended represents the totality of the world in its order and symmetry. The body bowed or bent down is in a stressed, uncomfortable, and imperfect state, waiting to be relieved or released. The crucifixion is portrayed in a way that emphasizes the bodily stance of Christ. He may sag on the cross, indicating his mortal aspect, while the high placement of the crucifix in churches emphasizes Christ's spiritual ascendance. The physical arrangement of space structures gaze and posture. The viewer feels both the downward pull of the body in pain and the upward yearning of the spirit for transcendence. The image conveys some of the symbolic meaning of the conjunction of suffering and spiritual transcendence through our own embodied response of looking up at a body that has been both torn down and resurrected.

In many religious traditions, practitioners bow deeply or prostrate themselves to acknowledge, respect, and experience the transcendental power of the divine. While the basic meaning is given in the body's disposition, more complex meanings of prostration come from the religious context of practice, which prescribes specific thoughts and interpretations. In Tibetan Buddhism, for example, practitioners may commit themselves to perform hundreds of thousands of prostrations as a meditative practice.

> The one hundred thousand prostrations are powerful exercises in humility, security, and—done with a spirit of enlightenment in mind—determination. A creative humility emerges by imprinting the awareness of the dangers of unenlightened living and acknowledging that alone you cannot protect yourself from them. A secure comfort emerges by strengthening the connection to the Three Jewels [Buddha, Sangha, and Dharma], considering that they embody freedom from danger, concern for you, and power to protect you from all dangers.[108]

Clearly, although bodily stance presents a basic structure to experience, the meaning of prostration depends crucially on what practitioners think about it and on how others interpret their actions. These cultural meanings imbue the act with significance and shape the work that it does on the body (changing habitus and physical dispositions to respond), in the social world (as a statement of devotion), and in the inner realm as a mode of learning to attend to the world in particular ways.

All of these correspondences suggest ways in which experiences of basic bodily postures or stance scaffold a vocabulary for moral action and experience as well as spiritual elevation or transcendence. These moral and religious metaphors, in turn, govern our bodily actions and dispositions. As a result, our location in space is given added dimensions that reflect our emotional experience, moral position, and social standing. This points toward an understanding of space and place as configured by moral value—a mapping prefigured in the *Sefer Yestirah* ("Book of Creation"), an early Kabbalistic text, which states that there are ten directions to the cosmos: six spatial (up/down, east/west, north/south), two temporal (beginning and end), and the evaluative poles of good and evil.[109] The moral universe, which includes both the mundane realm of physical actions and the ladder of spiritual elevation and development, is mapped onto the human body.[110] In this way, the human body serves both as a site of experiential immediacy and a scaffold for moral meaning and aesthetic engagement in healing ritual.

## Conclusion

I have sketched the outline of a psychophysiology of metaphor that can clarify some of the transformations that occur in healing practices. Multiple processes are in play in every healing ritual or intervention, mediated by different levels of organization in the systems of body, brain, person, and social world. Each level confers specific facets or dimensions of meaning so that any action or communication has multiple layers of meaning, whether or not these are explicitly recognized within the healing system. These levels operate concurrently and can interact in ways that reinforce each other or that move in different, even opposing, directions.

This points the way to a detailed account of how particular healing practices may work not just through common processes of creating hope, positive expectations, and "believed-in" efficacy, but by specific alterations of embodied experience, bodily habitus, attention, and the regulation of multiple cognitive and psychophysiological systems. These changes may be subtle yet create a sense that something is happening and the conviction that one has been changed. But the physiological consequences of embodied and enacted metaphor may also have enduring effects on self-regulatory and social systems that result in beneficial outcomes.

All of this suggests how symbolic action can have healing efficacy through the embodiment and enactment of metaphors. These basic forms of transformation do not depend on language. In most instances, though, these processes are organized and amplified by linguistic constructions. The next chapter extends the discussion to those aspects of healing that depend on the use of language to construct narrative selves and mythic worlds, with new possibilities for self-reflection, understanding, and imaginative invention.

CHAPTER 5

# *Healing Fictions: Narrative Transformations of the Self*

> "I am manipulating," says the Alchemist. "No, you are dreaming," says Novalis. "I am dreaming," says Novalis. "No, you are manipulating." The reason for such a profound duality is that fire is within us and outside us, invisible and dazzling, spirit and smoke.
>
> – Gaston Bachelard[1]

> [The] story the patient tells the doctor at the beginning of his treatment can be the start of the healing process. This raises the question of whether a story might not create the proper climate and favorable conditions for many a recovery, indeed, whether each and every illness might not be curable if it were carried along a river of stories all the way to that river's mouth.
>
> – Walter Benjamin[2]

Psychotherapy involves forms of conversation that clearly differ from the poetic incantations or performative language described in ethnographic accounts of ritual healing. Psychotherapy focuses on explicit talk about the "psyche"—that is, the self and its experiences, internal dynamics, and interpersonal relationships.[3] This talk about the self occurs both within the therapeutic encounter and in its technical framing in particular theories or schools of psychotherapy. While these theories may sometimes lead to surprising insights, most therapeutic conversation involves recounting personal narratives in response to questions that elicit memories, clarify details of events, and explore their emotional impact and implications for the person. Feelings and events may be interpreted in terms of commonsense narratives that constitute a shared folk psychology and rhetoric of motives that explain behavior in terms of goals and intentions.

Telling one's story to someone who listens attentively serves to build interpersonal trust and solidarity. Therapeutic inquiry and interpretation lead to renarration in ways that reorganize and reframe one's story, yielding new insights, hope, and strategies for coping and adaptation. Far from the crises of symbolic death and rebirth depicted in ethnographies of healing rituals, however, the "talking cure" of psychotherapy consist of thousands of small turns that mend, repair, or restore a damaged story or sense of self, locate new possibilities, and carry the sufferer forward into a new situation. Though there is plenty of smoke and sometimes sparks, where in all this talk is the transmuting fire?

In this chapter, I suggest that the narrative elaboration of metaphor is key to this transformative power. We can advance our understanding of the rhetorical power of metaphor by understanding the relationship of narratives of the self to overarching *myths* and experiential *archetypes*. In particular, I want to show how the rhetoric of psychotherapy uses metaphor to first evoke and then bridge the compelling narratives of cultural myths and the bodily felt immediacy of experience. While this approach to the transformative power of language is most obviously applicable to psychotherapy and other "talking cures," which make explicit use of language to reconfigure experience, it captures a discursive level of sense-making that is an important part of all forms of symbolic healing, whether during ritual actions, as part of the prior construction of expectations, or in subsequent interpretation of outcomes.

The metaphors of therapeutic conversation are delivered in narratives that draw from shared knowledge and confer epistemic authority. In focusing on the authority and effectiveness of narratives, we are moving further into the realm of rhetoric. A focus on rhetorical meaning breaks down the distinction between specific and nonspecific, content and process, in psychotherapeutic process. Rhetoric is always specific in that it aims to move a particular audience in a given direction and does this through language, symbols, and performances chosen to fit an audience and context. The nature of the rhetorical process and the corresponding mechanisms of symbolic healing, then, are tied to both content and context of discourse and action. It is not just any meaning that heals, nor simply any metaphor that fits with archetypal or mythic structures, but those meanings and metaphors that offer the sufferer imaginative space and a pragmatic way to continue by carrying meaning from the source of the river to its mouth.

## Narrative Constructions of the Self

A large body of work in philosophy, psychology, and the social sciences has explored the central role of narrative in identity and experience.[4] The self has been viewed as a narrative construction and human psychology rewritten in terms of competing and conflicting stories of the self. This use of the metaphor of narrative sometimes privileges the written text and downplays the origins of narrative in our earliest relationships, in conversation and self-talk, and its elaboration across the lifespan in navigating the social world, engaging in conversation, and positioning oneself in relation to others, as well as in soul searching or soliloquy.

Narratives usually do not begin as text on the page but as stories told to others in conversations and other kinds of situations intended to bring about some action by influencing others. The pragmatic and rhetorical aspects of speech are primary, not secondary, uses of language. Hence, narratives must be understood as *situated*: spoken by someone in a particular social context and position—and responded to by others who also have distinct positions.[5] The meaning of narratives resides in their use, and characterizing that use depends on understanding the social context. The situatedness of narration, the speaker's point of view, interactional context, and pragmatic intent are essential to the construction of meaning and to its impact on behavior and experience. This is so even for the narratives we tell to ourselves in inner monologue (thinking, reflecting, imagining), which always have a virtual community or interlocutor in the wings.

Psychotherapy and other healing practices, then, can be understood in terms of narrative processes that contribute to the ongoing process of construction and reconstruction of the sense of self and social personhood. The narrative construction of the self and personal identity links memories, ongoing experience, and possible futures in an overarching story that includes notions of personal and collective identity. Narratives of the self are based on cultural concepts of the person that convey values, norms, and ideologies. These values may be expressed in narrative templates that can be characterized as dominant or master narratives and discourses.[6] Individuals' narratives are shaped by these dominant discourses both implicitly (through the metaphors, models, and frames made available) and explicitly (through social sanctions for narratives that are viewed as nonnormative, deviant, or defective). When the dominant narratives of a society are consonant with well-being and adaptation, thinking with and living according to them will have psychological and social benefits. However, when the dominant narratives of a culture or community are unrealistic, unhealthy, inaccessible, or disadvantage certain individuals, they may become sources of suffering and affliction.

The master narratives in circulation in a culture or community provide templates for narrating the self in ways that can promote personal transformation and healing. These templates include figures that can be used to organize and transform the self. Figure 5.1 provides a schema of this process in Catholic Charismatic healing in which invoking the image, story, and

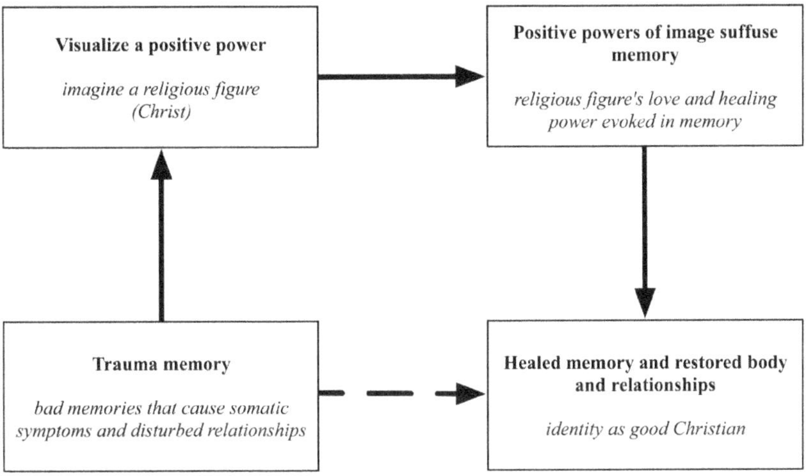


Figure 5.1 Metaphor-mediated shifts in memory and identity
Transformagram in Catholic Charismatic healing practice in which negative autobiographical memories and self-image are altered by imagery and metaphorically mediated shifts in memory and identity (Hinton & Kirmayer, 2017, p.13).

felt-presence of Christ as a loving figure leads to changes in self-image, autobiographical memory, and identity.[7] Imaginative engagement, embodied enactment, and identification promote a positive change in self-image from a demoralized victim to a compassionate Christ-like bearer of burden. The image of Christ is embedded in a larger narrative with many other metaphoric entailments that shape one's attitude toward suffering and affliction.

Healing practices may invoke a narrative or image that has beneficial effects, but the benefit or cost of these effects must be judged both in terms of their cognitive functions for the individual and their social impact. Sometimes these effects are at cross-purposes: what is useful for the person in their internal economy may be problematic socially—or vice versa. Moreover, both individual idiosyncratic stories and collective narratives may result in pathology by providing self-depictions or accounts of the world that lead to maladaptive behavior. In addition to the self-reflection encouraged in psychotherapy, revealing or critiquing the dominant discourse can be a therapeutic intervention because it helps individuals locate sources of oppression, confusion, or constraint and opens up the possibility of rewriting their narratives in ways that are more adaptive.

## Myth, Metaphor, and Archetype

In the hierarchy of symbolic healing processes presented in Chapter 4, the superordinate level is myth or cosmology. Cultural myths and cosmologies are explicitly conveyed through ritual and religious practices, but they undergird everyday life and its implicit ontologies—that is, the tacit understanding of what kind of things, beings, or processes make up the world and, hence, can be invoked to explain illness and promote healing. Placing these forms of narrative at the top of the hierarchy of healing processes in Figure 4.3 is meant to underscore the way in which myths constellate structures larger than the self or family and shape processes of communal and family interaction, as well as individual experience.

By *myth*, I mean not false or foolish beliefs that are widely held, but those narratives that are embraced by a culture and by which a society structures and legitimates itself.[8] For example, in *Myths We Live By*, the philosopher Mary Midgley discusses three connected myths that are foundational to modernity: the *social contract myth* that treats people as fundamentally separate, independent, competing individuals; the *progress myth* that views evolution as having a single, inevitable direction consonant with our current values and aspirations; and the *myth of omnicompetent science*, which holds that the answers to all of life's questions can be found through science.[9] Such pervasive, everyday myths are generally unquestioned stories that authorize societies, social institutions, and forms of life.

What we might call the "great myths" of tradition convey moral, religious, or spiritual truths about sacred or transcendent values. Taking place outside ordinary space and time, the great myths turn sequential stories into timeless moments, cycles, and tableaus, enlarging and ennobling life by linking human experience and institutions to other-than-human agencies—animals, gods, the forces of nature—that are valorized by the cultural worldview or cosmology in which the myth is embedded. Myths thus become the vehicle for the recognition of something larger than ourselves in ways that are consistent with (or, sometimes, in creative tension with) social values and cultural tradition.

The concept of archetypes is central to Jungian psychology but poses difficulties for social scientists and clinicians who recognize the culturally and historically contingent nature of all experience.[10] The term "archetype" implies an elemental and universal quality of experience that seems to stand outside space and time, perhaps because they reflect basic processes of pattern generation and recognition in the nervous system. For our purposes, and consistent with contemporary ideas in cognitive science and cultural anthropology, we can understand archetypes as universal processes of making meaning that give rise to analogous images and narrative structures in diverse human cultures.

Archetypes may reflect aspects of human experience that are universal: certainly, biologically based processes, but equally the existential facts of birth, attachment, desire, illness, suffering, and death. The overarching patterns of behavior and experience that result from imaginative engagement with these existential facts are reflected in each culture's myths, folktales, art, and dreams. The great myths of a culture transcend the narrative of a single life. The basic cultural and panhuman themes of myth and archetype are translated back to a local cultural world and an individual's idiosyncratic psychology through the choice of specific images and stories that condense personal and collective (shared) meaning.[11] The story of any individual life is told within or against the narrative templates of these overarching myths.

Archetypes are experienced as subjectively compelling percepts, images, ideas, or intuitions that seem to be prereflective—present to us before reflection, and necessary or inevitable, rather than arbitrary or invented. Of course, any actual image or experience involves personally, culturally, and historically contingent features. What is archetypal must involve a structure or process that lies behind the many varied versions of an image found across individuals and cultures. At some level of abstraction, the concept of archetypes is quite plausible. For example, gentle finger pressure applied to closed eyes creates visual phosphenes—moiré patterns of rays or checkerboards that reflect the orderly arrangement of neurons in the visual system.[12] Theories of embodiment that ground cognition in basic physical actions also imply an archetypal basis to experience in the structure of the sensorimotor system and bodily constraints.[13] Similarly, our bilateral symmetry and erect stance introduce structures of meaning related to left/right binaries and rudimentary frameworks for elaborating narratives of experiencing and resolving tensions or contradictions through balance, and of moving with or against gravity to fall to the ground or ascend to the sky.

Perhaps the capacity for narrative invention itself reflects a sort of archetypal patterning. Certainly, the basic capacity for storytelling reflects neural structures that subserve language and communication.[14] Other aspects of narrative structure or emplotment also may have a bodily grounding. For example, the temporal dynamics and interaction of motivational systems for attachment, exploration, and aggression could provide templates for familiar narratives of heroic quest, violent confrontation, grievous loss, and reconciliation. Epic quests and heroic victory over adversity reflect our capacity for optimism, hope, and persistence in the face of obstacles to reach distant goals. The obstacles we must negotiate in reaching these goals are in the world—that is, the physical environment and society—but also in ourselves. Tragedy reflects our inner and social limitations, vulnerability, and mortality, but especially the ways in which our reach exceeds our grasp so that we become authors of our own calamities.[15]

Clearly, archetypes do not arise from the brain or body autonomously (i.e., without any contribution from a culturally patterned environment). All human behavior and experience results from interactions between organism and environment. The concept of archetype, then, depends only on acknowledging that, in its interaction with culture, the human body is primed to pick out certain facets of common environmental, social, and existential situations or events (i.e., being born; having a mother, father, siblings, friends, and a mate to whom one is attached; experiencing the limitations of control over events; facing illness, aging, and death). These expectable, recurrent patterns constitute a universal substrate of human experience and imagination. If archetypes reflect potential structures produced by the nervous system in interaction with these expectable situations, they must nevertheless be enabled and given content by specific social experiences. Recurrent or universal patterns in perception may reflect existential universals—inescapable features of our social being—as much as any neurological *anlagen*. What seems bodily given or primordial is also always culturally conditioned and contingent.[16]

I will use *myth* and *archetype* then as a pair of related concepts that each reflect the interaction of body and society. Mythic narratives take shape and authority from social structures and discursive practices that depend on the histories and material arrangements of family, community, and society. Archetypal images take shape and authority from bodily structures and existential realities that emerge in the developmental interactions of body, self, and environment, within the family as well as the larger arenas of society. Although they both reflect the interplay of bodily and social processes, the concepts of myth and archetype are useful for the analysis of symbolism precisely because they can encourage us to consider why certain stories and images have presence, power, and persistence.

## Myth and Metaphor in Psychotherapy

In psychotherapy, as in ordinary conversation, metaphors are embedded in narratives. In healing rituals, the overarching myth can be viewed as a narrative built out of extended metaphors, and the ritual itself as dramatized figures of speech. The study of myth is then the study of a new order of organization, the *narrativization of metaphor*—that is, the imposition of an overarching structure on thought and action. The social ordering of experience encompasses both everyday stories that offer explanations and the authoritative accounts of master narratives or myths.

While scientific models and everyday explanations aim at pragmatic accounts that can guide adaptive action, the narrative structure of myth reflects life trajectories, developmental challenges, conflicts, and predicaments that are of vital concern in particular cultural worlds. The power of myth resides in its ability to give a dramatic structure to experiences that may be disruptive or chaotic. The narrative arc of the myth evokes moments of crisis or confusion that are resolved in acts of creation and destruction that restore order. In the gap between evocation and order, there is time for emotional engagement and confusion, wrestling with chaos and complexity. But the myth is a tale foretold, and, in its totality and circularity, it brings order to this chaos. Myths are captivating because they represent and give order to what Goldie calls "the mess inside."[17] This "mess" reflects not only our inescapable psychological conflicts but equally the inevitable tensions of the social world—which, together, provide the turbulence, contradictions, and absurdities intrinsic to the human condition. Myth acknowledges these contrarieties:

> Myths are made up of actions that include their opposites within themselves. The hero kills the monster, but even as he does so we perceive that the opposite is also true: the monster kills the hero. The hero carries off the princess, yet even as he does we perceive that the opposite is also true: the hero deserts the princess. How can we be sure? The variants tell us. They keep the mythical blood in circulation.[18]

Myth is indispensable because it encompasses the contradictions of human experience, holding them together in the same timeless story or plot, with all its twists and turns. It is characteristic of canonical, established, or foundational myth that, as soon as the story is named or recognized, we know its inevitable end. This may be tragic or heroic—or both—but whatever the trajectory and ultimate ending because the myth has been told and retold, every moment is present at once.[19] In Lévi-Strauss's evocative metaphor, myths are "machines for the suppression of time."[20] By standing outside of time, myth provides a teleology that links goals, desires, actions, and outcomes in looping structures that have both aesthetic and ethical significance.

Recognizing myth and archetype as sources of meaning leads to a pluralistic view of healing practices as grounded in the body and in the authority of overarching discursive practices and traditions. Both are in play in all forms of healing, but in the process of change, much of the action is in the middle realm where metaphor does its work.

## Metaphor and the Technology of Imagination

In Chapter 4, we considered some ways that metaphors may work to transform sensory and affective experience and cognitive or conceptual maps. While in traditional ritual settings specific metaphors are used that have deeply rooted cultural meanings, in psychotherapy, metaphor use often remains tentative, partial, and exploratory; its origins and implications may be unclear or undeclared. How then can these intermediate constructions do the work of healing to become "metaphors we live by"? The examples that follow illustrate three ways: (1) by structuring conceptual domains through the qualitative logic of metaphoric implication; (2) by evoking strong affective associations that change feelings, attitudes and stances toward self and others; and (3) by bridging archetypal and mythic structures to enlarge the sense of self and imbue life with meaning. The examples I have chosen do not present the grand narratives found in dramatic accounts or testimonies of healing. Instead, they show some of the small turns of thought and feeling that metaphor mediates. These are instructive because even dramatic changes may, on closer examination, be found to be composed of these small turns, whether prompted by the therapist or emerging spontaneously in patients' creative efforts at self-understanding.

Here are three examples of the explicit use of metaphor in psychotherapeutic practice by a clinical psychologist:[21]

> A fifty-four-year-old woman, mother of five grown children, now divorced and living alone, was deeply depressed. She likened her experience to a totally black room without a door to get out. Using the total darkness, we agreed that there might be a way out that she could not yet see, but that she had to slowly feel her way around the room at all levels to see what was there.
>
> A twenty-nine-year-old married woman, with no children, was anxious and lacking in self-confidence. She imagined herself falling into a huge pit and couldn't see the bottom. She clung to roots and vines, desperately fearing the fall. We returned to this image over several months and she gradually felt herself getting closer to the bottom and less fearful. When she finally touched bottom, she felt relief and her confidence increased tremendously.

> A thirty-three-year-old woman, married with two children, was afraid that talking about her feelings would be like sinking into a whirlpool from which she could not escape. She was unable to use the image to find a solution until I suggested that therapy was like a rope thrown to her so that, while she experienced the whirlpool, she did not have to go under.

These vignettes illustrate the therapist's willingness to engage with the patient's own metaphor. This openness is motivated in part by empathy but also reflects a strategic choice governed by overarching metaphors of joining, accompanying, and being with. Each metaphor offered by the client or therapist has natural extensions that open up new images of self and other and new possibilities for behavior. These extensions or inventions are credible because they follow from the image and also because they result in a felt experience of transformation of affect and perception. When no transformation from within is forthcoming, the therapist introduces something new: the rope—a metaphor for the therapeutic relationship but not only that, also a *rope* to pull one out of the maelstrom, and an implicit message that there is someone holding the other end. The metaphoric image that describes the problem also provides possibilities for resolution.

The metaphor appears here like the shaman's technology described in Chapter 4, but it is deployed against a different backdrop of shared values and normative narrative structures of individual development. No matter how idiosyncratic a client's metaphors, they can be extended in ways that serve a conventional agenda of adaptation and adjustment to a social world in which expressing one's true feelings, finding a fulfilling job, and renegotiating relationships are all recognized as valuable goals. In this process, the specific metaphors serve to build a shared representation of affective dimensions of the client's predicament, and to convey the quality and intensity of feeling at any given moment in the therapeutic conversation. The metaphors may also contribute to a process of creative search and problem solving that transforms the client's everyday experience beyond the consulting room. But the metaphors admit many interpretations and the therapist's direction of their unfolding reflects personal and culturally grounded moral and aesthetic values.

In an empirical study of the use of metaphor in psychotherapy, Linda McMullen reanalyzed tapes of six cases from the Vanderbilt Psychotherapy Project to count instances of metaphor.[22] She found little evidence that novel figures were more effective than frozen figures or clichés in healing. Successful psychotherapy cases were characterized by repeated well-formed central figures that expressed the client's essential theme or problem, bursts of repeatedly using and elaborating this metaphor, and evidence of some change in this metaphor over time. In contrast, unsuccessful cases used many different metaphors without a clear central self-depiction, did not elaborate the metaphors (i.e., each usage tended to be isolated and remained undeveloped), and did not show any change in metaphors over time. Therapists in unsuccessful cases appeared to have difficulty empathizing with the client as evidenced by a lack of engagement with negative response to the client's own metaphors. For example, a client who referred to himself as "some kind of nut," "a monster," and "the trophy of the rhinoceros you put on your mantle" was responded to by the therapist in terms of the figure of "trying to shock people," indicating the therapist's own discomfort. There were no differences in vividness, uniqueness, or novelty in successful versus unsuccessful cases (as judged by experimenter raters). Indeed, "very few novel figures were found."

Without pre- and postintervention measures or controls, it is unclear whether McMullen's results reflect preexisting characteristics of successful clients or the nature of effective therapy.[23] Moreover, as McMullen notes, the therapists she studied were all psychodynamically oriented and may be less inclined than therapists of other schools to offer metaphors of their own to clients. Nevertheless, the examples above, McMullen's study, and subsequent work by others[24] suggest that the mutative metaphors of psychotherapy need not be wildly inventive, only apt. A conventional metaphor or cliché may be apt when bodily felt conviction or social concern brings it alive. Brought to life, even clichés can be mined for new meaning, but to motivate change and have enduring effects they must mobilize a sense of presence, power, and purpose. This is what myths and archetypal images can provide.

## Myths, Metaphors, and Archetypes of the Self

What makes psychotherapy distinct from other forms of healing is an ontology that recognizes some version of "psyche" or "soul"—grounded in personal experiences of thought, feeling, and imagination in an inner theater of the mind that may be private or at least partly hidden from others. Although the psyche involves experiences that are familiar to others, it is also viewed as having unknown depths. We always approach our being in the world and the inner theater of the mind from a particular perspective, which naturally leads to the view of the self as a locus of experience, action, and perception. The ways that interiority and sense of self are understood and elaborated in everyday life, through giving reasons and accounts of one's experience, aspirations, and frustrations, and self-reflection, constitute our psychology. Beyond the attribution of sensations and actions to our selves, the notion of self is a narrative elaboration of the embodied, situated, and perspectival nature of experience and of our recollection and reconstruction of our own continuity through time. The sense of self, then, is structured as a mirror of the cultural concept of personhood, populated with the content of our experiences and culturally mediated modes of self-understanding and self-depiction.

Psychotherapy works with these narrative structures of self, aiming to identify problematic structures and develop alternate versions that are more adaptive. These new versions of self are latent in the metaphors and narratives with which the self is constructed. While psychotherapy may begin with the narrative clichés and dead metaphors of folk psychology, in the search for a way forward, patient and therapist may discover new narrative possibilities within familiar metaphors.

> A young woman in psychotherapy, asked to visualize early childhood experiences to better understand the origin of her difficulties, sees first a single red brick and then a brick wall. Asked what is behind the wall she states: "Fear." Encouraged to remove one row of bricks at the top to get an image of what lies beyond, she catches a glimpse of a woman in a white dress.[25]

The brick wall here is a conventional expression or dead metaphor ("I hit a brick wall") for the obstacles to recollection and awareness. This metaphoric barrier could be interpreted psychodynamically as reflecting repression, resistance, and defense. This way of speaking replaces the image with a psychological mechanism. Pragmatically, the image serves to communicate to the therapist that the patient does not want the conversation to go any further in that direction. Alternatively, we can recognize that technical terms like repression or resistance are no less metaphorical, and that the image is experienced by the patient as spontaneous. If so, the metaphor is interesting in its own right, organizing the patient's experience in a particular way—which might lead us to say that the repression *is* the brick wall—that is, the image regulates the process of avoidance.[26] Dismantling the wall is lowering the barrier, removing the obstacle to recollection and disclosure. Understood as imaginative enactment, the metaphor and the mental mechanism are one and the same.

In this vignette, the psychotherapist accepts the image of the brick wall as a real barrier in imaginal space. Consequently, the conversation stays with the metaphor: the patient is encouraged to take down just one row of bricks—implying a gradual easing of the barriers to memory. The brick wall structures the process of remembering (much as the metaphor of distance structures the experience of catharsis, as discussed in Chapter 4), so changing the wall modulates that process. Here, metaphor allows not only communication of a predicament and reassuring distance from painful emotion but also space for imaginative play. Respect for the significance of the brick wall affords the patient comfort and confidence in being able to move at her own pace.

Staying with the image invites the patient to take a risk and reveals something hidden and unexpected. The woman in the white dress may be an episodic memory or an improvised construction—white is the conventional color of purity and ideals in the patient's cultural context, of what is morally upright and drenched in light.[27] The image points to an as yet untold story. Just as she saw past the brick wall, the patient's associations allow her to see past the idealization implicit in the fairy tale white dress to the shadows and sorrow of her remembered relationship with her mother. The metaphor then moves toward recollection, emotional reliving and, eventually, renarrating the self.

Psychotherapeutic renarration of the self can center on images that are associated not so much with distinct memories but that capture recurrent states of feeling or being. Such images may arise in dreams or revery and brought to therapy.

> A young man in psychotherapy, prone to sudden feelings of deflation and self-loathing, recounts a dream of riding a spirited white horse along a riverbank. Asked about his associations to the horse, he says: "The only horse I've ever ridden is the twenty-five-cent zoo variety—the tired dusty gray kind that's tied to a stake and just goes round and round in circles."

The memory here is less important than the embodied state it represents. The tired horse is a captive of the circus or a country fair. He is dusty, his energy is spent, and his is back broken by the rides of countless children. He is unable to run wild along the riverbank like the spirited horse of the patient's dream. The dream offers imaginative compensation or escape from the patient's self-described state of demoralization, enervation, and lack of potency and virility. To sustain this vision, to transform the experience associated with the broken horse into that of the spirited stallion, something must be recaptured, but the young man cannot imagine what. To explore a possible path forward, the therapist—in this case a Jungian analyst following the method of amplification—supplies a narrative: the Greek myth of Bellerophon riding Pegasus to slay the chimera.[28] The effect of introducing an explicit mythic narrative into therapy is to point beyond the metaphor of the broken horse to the mythic journey of the hero.[29] This myth animates the patient, valorizing his struggle by linking it to a grand narrative, and provides direction to the search for fresh metaphors and, through metaphor, evokes changes in bodily feeling, habitus, and stance toward his self and the world.

While people and animals provide natural metaphors for the self, the sense of interiority leads to other symbols.

> Mr. R, a middle-aged man, separated from his wife and children, comes to therapy stating he has no feelings, has never had a friend and trusts no one. After several tentative meetings he describes a reverie one day in which he had an image of himself as a series of concentric rings or shells. Asked what is at the center he adds: "In the center is a black stone because I'm a black-hearted bastard." Encouraged to consider whether others can get in or he can get out of these shells, he says, "There is a door, but you have to have the key." Asked whether it is possible for him to open the door from the inside and let someone in, he replies, "I don't know" and adds, "You have to have just the right key to get even a little way inside but once someone does they never leave." He then speaks movingly of the only significant love relationship of his life—a woman he has not seen in many years.

The image of concentric rings or spheres is the form of the celestial spheres in early astronomy and of the mandala, a symbol of the wholeness and plenitude of the self.[30] It conjoins the archetypal experiences of the geometric order produced by the visual system—revealed in phosphenes and found in children's drawings—with the motivational pattern of approach/avoidance or relatedness and detachment. The archetypal roots of this conjunction are alluded to in one of Bachelard's reveries on space: "images of full roundness help us to collect ourselves, permit us to confer an initial constitution on ourselves, and to confirm our being intimately, inside. For when it is experienced from the inside, devoid of all exterior features, being cannot be otherwise than round."[31] Adding multiple shells within the sphere emphasizes the barriers and distance from periphery to center. It is used here to picture the self as inward, away from the social world, and to describe an experience of emptiness, disconnection, or isolation.

The therapist finds Mr. R's metaphor intelligible in sensory, emotional, and relational terms and works with it, asking questions that convey empathy, acceptance, and an invitation for connection. He asks what is at the center of the circles, and Mr. R replies "a black stone," adding a conventional idiom of self-derision: "because I'm a black-hearted bastard." The idiom plays off the qualities of stone synesthetically to assert the sufferer's self-image as dark, negative, hard, cold, and unfeeling.[32] Behind these negative associations, the original image evokes other qualities, not yet acknowledged—the strength, density, and immutability of stone. These qualities of stone make it a natural symbol of the self, of wholeness and resistance to ordinary forces of change. The goal of alchemy was to find the Philosopher's Stone, which could aid any kind of transformation, including that of lead to gold. On some accounts, it could also cure all illness. Alchemy was understood by Jung, Eliade, and others not simply as proto-chemistry but as a practice that aimed at self-transformation.[33]

The metaphor of concentric spheres also evokes the narrative possibilities of myth, including the hero's quest to reach the hidden center of the maze. The therapist's question about whether the shells can be opened from the inside introduces the potential for agency—it implies there are choices to be made about whether to let others alone or reach out to them. This moves the patient to remark: "Once you get inside you never leave." The durability of stone extends to the permanence of relationship once the center has been attained. He is further moved to recollect his only love affair and to re-experience the sense he had of being cherished.

In this conversation, metaphor conveys a basic human experience: the inwardness and privacy of self-awareness. The way the patient elaborates this metaphor provides a model of the self with multiple barriers to relatedness, and harshly negative self-evaluation at its core. The image of the shells presents both a picture of isolation and an opportunity to explore the possibility of relatedness. The metaphor provides archetypal structure to self-experience, communicates a predicament, and invites dialogue and transformation.

## The Playing Fields of Myth

While Jungian analysts have a penchant for archaic myths, ancient Greece is not the only source of mythic narratives. In addition to the rich tapestry of world mythology, new and recycled myths are constantly being produced by both authorized and marginal groups in society. Therapists draw potential healing narratives from myths they have studied or, more often, were unconsciously assimilated through popular culture and psychological theories, and they interpret patients' dreams, reveries, and actions in conformity with these narratives. Only occasionally—mainly in Jungian psychotherapy—are myths explicitly told to patients to valorize their struggle and prime their own narrative ability. More commonly, myths remain implicit and are expressed in conventional wisdom about life events, developmental tasks, and goals. Even when implicit, the structure of myth informs the master narratives that serve as templates for telling a coherent autobiographical story and mapping possibilities for change. When made explicit and imbued institutional authority or sacred meaning, a myth can provide a compelling narrative that affirms the universality of patients' experience, clarifies the nature of their predicament (in its setting and dramatis personae), and suggests ways to resolve the conflict (through its plot).

In secular societies, though, it sometimes seems we no longer have sacred myths, only entertainments and diversions.[34] Of course, we cannot live without stories to give coherence to our lives, but the stories we are inundated with through mass media and social networking are increasingly designed to foster quick consumption.[35] To do the work of healing, stories must be believed in—not in the sense that their truth value is certified by logic or argument but in the sense that they are treated seriously, taken into the imagination and lived with, if only for a time, and socially legitimated and respected. The effectiveness of both secular and sacred myths depends on the dynamics of imagination and conviction.

Literature, popular media, and especially movies provide arenas in which secular myths can be elaborated, reproduced, and, transiently, lived. In some cases, a film not only recounts a myth but reflects on the myth-making process itself. For example, Nicolas Roeg's film *Insignificance* (1985)[36] brings together five figures of American mythic imagination, who are referred to only by their roles or archetypes: *the Ballplayer* (Joe DiMaggio), *the Professor* (Albert Einstein), *the Actress* (Marilyn Monroe), *the Senator* (Joseph McCarthy), and *the Cherokee* (a generic Native American, reduced to working as an elevator operator). Their paths cross one long evening in New York City in 1954 in a series of encounters that confront the tensions and contradictions inherent in our ideals of beauty, strength, knowledge, power, mortality, and timelessness. In the movie, each figure is deliberately portrayed as a stereotype[37]—the inarticulate athlete, the absent-minded genius, the dumb blonde, the venal politician, the dignified Indian—and each is clearly wounded by the projections of others that arise from the position they occupy in the pantheon of popular mythology. As they struggle to transcend the stereotypes they live under, they remind us of the burden we place on those we view as demons or demi-gods, but also of the constriction of our imaginations when we view these figures from only one side. Here the process of making a person into a mythic figure is revealed as corrosive not only to their being but also to our own.[38]

The film *Field of Dreams* (1989)[39] provides apt metaphors for the workings of myth in contemporary North American society. A man in his mid-thirties with a wife, daughter, and a new farm hallucinates a compelling voice that whispers in his cornfield: "If you build it, he will come." He is moved to clear his field and build a baseball diamond. Soon, long-dead baseball players appear on his diamond to resume the game they loved. The hero travels around the country and backward in time to find others who share his ability to dream, and they too draw sustenance from the sight of the ghostly players and even join the game. Sacrificing his own livelihood to pursue this quest, the hero ultimately redeems his dead father, who had put aside his own dream of being a ball player to take up the responsibility of supporting a family. The film ends with father and son playing catch on the diamond. From the air, we see a long line of jewel-like beads of light stretching out to the horizon—a trail of cars bringing other dreamers to the miraculous playing field.

In popular culture, in both secular and religious settings, we can distinguish two ways of engaging with myth—as master narratives or ideologies that shape belief and common sense through everyday practices and as numinous experience or insight obtained through immersive experience in sacred stories. As narrative, myth encodes tacit knowledge of social life, including the taken-for-granted or implicit ontology that undergirds our everyday sense of what is real and present. The authority of such discursive myth, then, stems from its familiarity and the very ordinariness of its narrative. In this view of myth, there is no need for any special mode of mythic consciousness only a social structure that reserves a place for stories that are valorized and that remain unchallenged by critical attitudes and empirical tests.

The second form of engagement with myth depends on participants entering a liminal space and time through a particular kind of attentiveness. This liminality adds to the power of myth to move us, not only because it intensifies our sensory and emotional experience but also because it speaks to our longing for community or transcendence.[40] In the liminal space of myth and ritual, boundaries between self and other may become blurred or dissolve, creating a feeling closeness, union, and *communitas*. In this second mode of participation, myth is not sustained by ordinary argument or conviction. As the philosopher Leszek Kolakowski put it:

> Reference to myth is not knowledge, but an act of total, entrusting acceptance with no sense of need for justification. That is why, if such an acceptance is directed towards a person, it draws that person into a mythic reality. That which Jaspers calls existential communication is a participation in myth, the dwelling of persons in its territory.[41]

This view tries to set myth apart from any technology of persuasion. "Myth cannot be reached by persuasion; persuasion belongs to a different area of interpersonal communication, that is, to an area in which the criteria of the technical resilience of judgments have their force."[42] But this is true only in those contemporary terms in which persuasion is recognized as such and, hence, becomes a technical activity. Persuasion presumes a situation of two people standing apart with different views, power and influence being applied asymmetrically, from one person to the other, across that divide. In contrast, where mutual influence occurs through participation—as may occur in ritual contexts, including the encounter between sufferer and healer—myth is the product of processes of imagination and co-presence that do not depend on power differentials or force of argument.

The distinction between these views of myth as master narrative or as the immersive experience of participation in creative co-presence hinges not only on a distinction between secular and sacred, or mundane and esoteric, but also on views of the process of *mythopoesis*—of fashioning experience through engagement with myth. The narrative view sees this in terms of processes of tacit acceptance, persuasion, and rationalization of the social order. This view leads naturally to a search for hidden interests that maintain the social order.[43] The transcendent view sees myth as sacred revelation or imaginative co-presence that opens the doors of perception to a hitherto unseen world or truth.

In an interesting way, the distinction between modes of mythopoesis parallels the relationship between suggestibility and hypnosis—which suggests the two views of myth are related. Suggestibility, in which the statements of others reshape our experience, is always present as a feature of everyday experience and occurs simply by listening uncritically.[44] The influence of a story or suggestion can be amplified by hypnosis through increased absorption in imagination, decreased critical appraisal, and dissociation of conscious controls. As a state of heightened absorption and imaginative involvement, the ritual of hypnotic trance may be valued for its own sake, as well as for the specific images or enactments that can be evoked. Similarly, mythic consciousness has intrinsic value related to exercising our imaginations, participating in the solidarity of community, and valuing something larger than ourselves. This general value is in addition to the truths of the stories told in specific myths, which themselves may be appreciated both in and out of mythic consciousness. Outside of mythic consciousness, myths may be heard by critical consciousness as fiction or errant history, but they also can be understood as apt metaphors for aspects of the human condition. In the liminal space of mythic consciousness, myths may be experienced as profound insights into the immanent and awe-full actions of the gods or the workings of the cosmos.

The story of *Field of Dreams* hovers at the border between these two forms of mythopoeisis, reflecting the lack of common myth in our time and the devaluing of dreaming and imaginative play as legitimate activities. For those actively engaged with religious ritual or spiritual practices, mythic frameworks that imbue life with meaning and purpose may be ready to hand. For others, the individualistic ethos of North America requires that people to invent their own myths and disguise their ritual enactment as conscientious work or serious play.[45] For many, the secular mythology of baseball, as an emblem of national cultural identity, stands in for religious myths.[46] Even those unmoved by the spectacle respond to the opportunity, created by the field, to find a place to live their dreams. This field of dreams is a version of D. W. Winnicott's transitional space where culture is created through play.[47] In Victor Turner's distinction, it is *liminoid* not liminal—secular not sacred, free play rather than fixed ritual, aleatoric rather than tightly scored.[48]

The *Field* offers secular North Americans a taste of two things we sorely miss: mythic consciousness for its own sake—that is, the opportunity to break out of conventional social roles and mundane reality to dream and play with "antistructure"—and a specific myth of reconciliation—that is, a narrative that brings together alienated or fractured parts of the self—whether in personal history (the lost father, the abandonment of dreams) or cultural predicament (the devaluing of imagination, the loss of enchantment). But the authorized myths of a society have a power beyond playful inventions or entertainment.

> Myths are a source of dangerous intoxication whenever they serve as a defense against anxiety and in that function they demand counteraction. A total taming of the world and a total elimination of otherness may be only an illusion and is not always free of bad faith. Mythological interpretations of the world are capable of helping to remove this otherness to the extent that this is possible, and they are also capable of helping us to understand why this is not possible in full. Myths which perform these two irremovable and irreplaceable functions cannot create a sense of satiety. They always contain within themselves a version of the Myth of the Cave, some variant of the story of paradise lost, a sense of the inability of a harmonious transition from a conditioned to an unconditioned Being.[49]

The social world both enlivens and constrains imagination and, in the process, may harshly treat ways of being that challenge regnant norms and expectations. Through imagination, myth invites back in excluded or abandoned facets of the self or factions of society, animated as figures in a dramatic scenario. Mythic imagination moves from rigid structure, through shadow, conflict, and confusion to order and possibility. Put another way, myths must acknowledge the challenge of the inchoate—not as simply another mythical place (Paradise, Hades, or the Cave) but as an urgent, and enduring predicament and portray a journey that affirms moral order and nourishes the power to dream.[50] As Kolakowski insists, this journey is always unfinished and incomplete and hence myth presents us with an enduring cycle of recreation.

We can now see what constitutes the healing efficacy of great myths: their ability to contain and unite in narrative, ritual action, and sacred space the most disparate themes and deepest contradictions in human experience. These themes take shape through particular histories and cultural traditions but they build on universal human dilemmas. This explains why, although we lack deep familiarity with the pantheons of peoples of other times and places, we can still be moved by their myths. Archaic myths work today just to the extent they are interpreted in ways that tap archetypal structures of desire and concern—like the longing for reconciliation between father and son, dreamer and pragmatist, played out in *Field of Dreams*.[51]

The sacred myths live alongside the secular myths that organize our lives. Both kinds of myths can express moral and social ideals and both shape the narratives of everyday life. Myths also provide rationalizations and legitimation for existing social norms and structures. The social inheritance of cultural norms is facilitated by—indeed, may only be possible within—the framework of mythic narratives that give them an overarching order and authority.[52] This underscores the conservative function of myth.

Kolakowski worries whether a consciousness is possible that acknowledges the social, functional genealogy of myth, yet remains capable of actively participating in myth. But this is like asking whether a consciousness possible which understands the technical and psychological aspects of art or its commerce and is still capable of producing and enjoying art. Kolakowski thinks not because myth requires total (unself-conscious or immersive) participation:

> myth belongs to a different order of spiritual life than participation in myth; it belongs to an area subject essentially to the same criteria as the totality of discursive thought . . . In its verbal realizations myth is an expression of collective experience, and participants in this experience have no obligation to place it in the same order of life in which scientific values function, or to subject them to the rigors of the same criteria of affirming and denying judgments . . . Explained genetically, it [myth] loses its vitality to the extent that mythical consciousness has already succumbed to confusion with technological consciousness—a confusion which is admittedly common

> but neither inescapable nor permanent, but bound to a certain specific cultural formation where technological rapacity, and a cult of the sciences dominates spiritual life. If, for example, religious beliefs are eroded under the influence of religious studies, the cause lies not in the nature of things or in an essential psychological divergence of both of these areas, nor in their logical incompatibility, but in civilizationally defined, suicidal claims of myth to nonmythical legitimacy . . . Thus, while the clash of myth with knowledge about myths is real, it is in each instance civilizationally defined: it is a clash within [or between] certain cultures, rather than within the universal nature of human experience.[53]

For Kolakowski, this clash of cultures is inevitable because myth occupies a transcendental realm and, as such, need not pay heed to technical facts. He thus argues that, for the reasons just adduced, myth cannot help but have an aspect that is turned against the body, since a thoroughgoing materialism would be the death of creative imagination. Here again is the inescapable tension between imagination and reality that makes the mind–body problem a perennial concern.

But this view of myth as necessarily about transcendence hides a fundamentalism. For myths, even when they are transcendental, are not static and must reply to every fact that changes the human condition, the discoveries of science not excepted. The imaginative productions of science are fuel for myth and the tensions and contradictions of a social world fashioned by technology is part of what myth must help us reconcile. The separation of science and myth, techne, and transcendence cannot be sustained for a person or a society open to new knowledge. Reflecting this need, in the last fifty years the literatures of speculative and science fiction have moved from marginal genre to dominant tradition in mainstream entertainment and popular imagination.[54] New technologies offer new metaphors that breed new myths, just as myths authorize the key metaphors they contain.

## Myth, Metaphor, and Narrative Therapy

We have been considering the healing functions of narrative and mythopoiesis in general terms but there are forms of psychotherapy that make storytelling the explicit focus of intervention. Narrative therapies recognize both the origins and solutions for mental health problems may lie with identifying and changing pathogenic stories.[55] The narratives that constitute people's problems and hold their potential solutions have multiple origins. Pathogenic narratives emerge from individuals' past histories, sometimes forced on them by abusive parents and traumatic events, or through more subtle forms of oppression in family regimes, and by formative experiences across the lifespan. In addition to this genealogy, narratives are actively constructed or reconstructed through ongoing efforts to respond to new circumstances and further a particular story of the self. As ongoing constructions, narratives have their own aesthetics and adaptive value and create quandaries that the therapist must appreciate. Of course, narratives stem not just from personal roots but also equally from larger social structures expressed in power relationships, rules, norms, images in the popular media, conventional wisdom, master narratives, and collective myths. The therapists' task, then, is not just to liberate people from problematic or pathogenic narratives caused by their own personal histories or family troubles, nor simply to reconfigure or replace blinkered, faulty, or maladaptive constructions of the self, but also to address the narrative models, discourses, and practices of the larger society that may limit and oppress people.

One form of narrative therapy, developed by Michael White and David Epston, involves countering oppressive narratives by renarrating the self.[56] Inspired by Foucauldian analyses of the intertwining of knowledge and power in discursive formations, they help clients develop externalizing attributions or explanations that situate individuals' problems in the tensions and contradictions of larger social contexts. By laying bare systems of power that oppress clients, externalizing explanations work against the attributional bias of Euro-American psychology that tends to attribute any unusual or deviant behavior to intrinsic characteristics of the person. Externalizing attributions that locate problems in social or environmental factors can avoid some of the pejorative and disabling effects of psychiatric diagnostic labeling and psychodynamic explanation. A second related approach relies on the use of enactments in ritual, writing, and other symbolic expressions. Enacting a new way of looking at or working with a problem or situation can bypass some of the internalized critique and vicious cycles that can maintain symptoms and suffering. Embodiment and enactment work against the tendency in some forms of psychotherapy to focus on the client's inner world to the neglect of real circumstances and predicaments. Embodied or enactive interventions move beyond language to engage more directly with behavior, habitus, and forms of life.

From a sociological viewpoint, there are dilemmas associated with constructing effective therapeutic means in secular societies where there is little shared mythology and few ready-made rituals evocative of both personal and collective values. Psychotherapy itself provides a ritual space for enacting shared values. But with the dethroning of psychoanalytic theory as a source of authoritative truth and the challenge of biological reductionism to meaning-centered therapeutic practice, the resources of myth and ritual available to secular people are limited. Improvised forms of spirituality, which borrow from multiple traditions, are one response to this dilemma.[57]

Our understanding of the dynamics of myth can be advanced by considering the varied experience of people committed to a religious worldview that puts sacred stories at the center of its practice. We alluded to this with the example of Catholic Charismatic healing mentioned earlier in this chapter in which embodiments of the story of Jesus play a key role in personal transformation. Individuals can participate in a mythic story by adopting specific idioms of distress that reference an implicit ontology and sacred order. Another example is provided by "ultra-orthodox" or Haredi communities who practice strict adherence to Jewish law. The role of myth in this community is illustrated in work by the psychiatrist Eliezer Witztum and anthropologist Yehuda Goodman, who developed a model of therapy for ultra-orthodox Jews that draws from Ericksonian hypnotherapy, as well as narrative and strategic therapies.[58] In common with these solution-oriented approaches, their model emphasizes joining with patients by accepting their initial framing of the problem; working within the patients' own metaphors, stories, and worldview to reframe, reattribute, or otherwise transform the problem; and the assumption that working with symbols through imaginal dialogue and ritual enactments can reorganize cognitive schemas, unconscious dynamics, and interpersonal interaction. The narrative–constructivist perspective holds that certain forms of distress arise from stories that people tell themselves and others, so that if these stories are rewritten, symptoms and distress will be alleviated.[59] The aim of narrative therapy, then, is to change cognitive schemas or narratives that are employed by individuals to make sense of experience.

Of course, as Witztum and Goodman note, narratives also circulate among the members of a group, community, culture, or society in ways that serve to construct and validate collective identities and situate individuals within larger social frames. Alluding to anthropologist Gananath Obeyesekere's concept of "the work of culture," they note that "a narrative is a meeting point between the individual and his culture."[60] As a result, narratives are irreducibly social in nature: their sources, durability, and responsiveness to influence depend on cultural, historical, and social interactional processes. These processes may take a distinctive form in some religious or cultural communities. In the case of the Haredi, "the ultra-orthodox are conceived of as a community which strives to close itself off from the polluting influences of the secular modern world by building strong physical and social boundaries between themselves and the modern world."[61]

This is a distinctive sort of social world or subculture and raises questions about how specific Witztum and Goodman's approach is to such communities. Do myth and symbolism function differently in such a strongly bounded or closed-off community than they do in the global agora created by mass media and telecommunications? For individuals raised within such a community and deeply committed to a tradition, sacred stories may retain a power to move that is lost in the sea of competing stories and fragmented traditions that characterizes much of the secular world. Ritual actions may have power and efficacy as a result of their roots in tradition.[62] For the Haredi, embedded in a community that engages in daily ritual and study of foundational religious texts, individual stories—especially those centred on dreams or affliction—are always inscribed within a larger narrative with spiritual meaning.[63]

In their therapeutic interventions, Witztum and Goodman aim to understand symptomatic expressions of distress and "construct a therapeutic narrative plot," consistent with cultural values and practices, that can be introduced, be ritually enacted, and, ultimately, replace a less adaptive or pathogenic narrative. They approach symptom expression through the concept of cultural idioms of distress, introduced by the anthropologist Mark Nichter.[64] Idioms are conventional modes of expression. The concept of a cultural idiom thus highlights the meaning of distress as communication in a particular culture or community context. Talk about bodily distress, for example, can point to or comment on social circumstances that cannot be talked about explicitly. This focus on communication leads naturally to a systemic analysis of symptoms and treatment, as has been developed in the fields of family and strategic therapy.[65]

The term "cultural idiom" also suggests that the expression of distress is formulaic and consistent within a community and readily intelligible to others because it is firmly rooted in cultural codes. While the concept of a cultural idiom implies collective meaning and common currency, some expressions of distress are idiosyncratic to the sufferer or their entourage and require that others decode or interpret symptoms that seem vague, ambiguous, or indeterminate in meaning. The polysemous nature and indeterminate meaning of symptoms serves necessary functions, both to keep open the possibility of improvising new meaning and to reposition the self while hiding some of the more threatening implications of suffering.

In Witztum and Goodman's cases, the patients do not simply use a cultural idiom to convey their predicament in ways that can be understood within their community, but have deviated from the idiom and associated social norms sufficiently to worry others and suggest that they are ill. Their illness narratives are not subsumed by the idiom but reflect challenging experiences that lead to an ongoing search for meaning through the fluid use of multiple metaphors. This multiplicity presents an interpretive challenge. We need to know how and why one story is taken up over another—even when it is unpopular or brings hardship to the storyteller—and how, in the ebb and flow of alternative accounts around an experience of affliction, certain stories get authorized and stabilized or challenged and changed.

In the Haredi cases, supernatural entities and protagonists actively participate in the narratives. "Each of these figures has specific symbolic and narrative characteristics in the Jewish mystical tradition which participate in the construction of the narratives (and of patients' experiences)."[66] These are examples of what Todorov has called "mythic narratives"—using this term technically to refer to narratives in which the causal logic and progression derives not from some overarching ideology but from the agency of the actors within the narrative (in this case the supernatural entities).[67] In one case, for example, the spirit of an injured woman demands an explanation for why she was abandoned. Other spirits demand that the afflicted person bend their will to the spirits' own. Psychotherapists often aims to translate such mythological narratives into ideological ones in which the narrative structure depends on an overarching logic of causality based on psychological truths. Thus, the persecuting spirits might represent unresolved intrapsychic issues or conflicts with significant others in the patient's past or present social world. In contrast, Witztum and Goodman, while forming such psychological hypotheses about the origins of their patients' suffering, try to stay within the mythological narrative in prescribing their interventions. To do this effectively, though, they must understand the patient's narrative in cultural and religious context—not with the same depth and conviction of the patient —but with enough sophistication to make intelligible and intelligent moves within the mythic realm.

How can therapists who do not share religious beliefs with their clients understand the meaning of illness narratives? Witztum and Goodman focus on a few metaphoric qualities of the figures in the mythic narratives (e.g., power, strength, safety, and the ability of certain actions to mark and define boundaries). These they combine with models drawn from psychodynamic theory. "We also conceptualize the case using a developmental model: a traumatic, unresolved, ambivalent or problematic relationship with a 'significant other' (usually the father, or father figure) from the past, interacts with a recent traumatic event (terrorist attack, road accident), or loss (death of a father or close Rabbi)."[68] This leads to an understanding of the structure of the story based on an explicit developmental model and the impact of trauma, which is used to guide the renarration of experience.

The models that guide the therapeutic renarration are not complex, applying a simple, generalized object relations theory. For example, when an angel is identified as connected with guilt, depression, and unresolved grief after a father's sudden death, the goal is to integrate it rather than reject it. Thus through the symbolic strategic maneuver the therapists try to alter the ambivalent relationship with the internalized father figure. Throughout, the interventions address multiple facets of the patient's predicament reflecting their cultural world, personal circumstances, psychiatric diagnosis and psychodynamics. This process of combining different models and metaphors is at the heart of the therapeutic approach and merits closer examination.

Turner and Fauconnier have explored the ways in which different conceptual systems can be blended to give rise to emergent features not fully present or realized in either of the original accounts.[69] This is precisely what Witztum and Goodman are doing, creating a blended narrative that borrows features of the traditional account present in or implied by the patient's original illness narrative with a metaphoric space constructed from a simple psychological model of intrapsychic conflicts, social interaction, and development tasks.

Many of the cases Witztum and Goodman describe involve narratives with obvious spiritual and aesthetic dimensions. For example, in a session employing hypnosis and active imagery, the patient, Abraham, traversed a desert landscape toward a distant oasis:

> the metaphor of moving through the desert towards the distant green spot was crystallized as Abraham, aided by his wife and with the encouragement of his therapists, kept moving in the direction of the "green", despite obstacles and attacks by the Black One and his assistants. As he came closer to the green place Abraham could see that it was a beautiful garden surrounded by high walls and a gate. He also smelled very pleasant aromas from the garden. His expression improved, but then the Black One and his comrades attacked Abraham and tried to throw him into a pit. With the help of the *Zaddik* and the suggestions and encouragement of his therapists

> Abraham cried out "I am not afraid of you! Go away!" He cited verses from Psalms including "He that dwells in the secret place of the Most High shall abide under the shadow of the Almighty. . ." (Psalms 91: 1). Abraham stood up and waved his arms and kicked his legs, as if fighting the demons. Then he informed the therapists that the demons had run away. The therapists instructed Abraham, who was still under hypnosis, to continue his way towards the green place.[70]

In a later session, he had a visionary experience.

> At this point he informed his wife and the therapists that he was entering the lower paradise, that the air smelled like perfume and that he saw two springs of water. He was encouraged to drink and satisfy his thirst. He said that the water was sweet and fresh, and he appeared completely refreshed and reborn . . . Abraham said that the journey to the lower paradise was a great privilege, and that it was like a mystical miracle and that he did not want to return to it.[71]

The garden and the springs of fresh water are natural symbols of purity and the well-tended self.[72] The garden also evokes a more culture-specific set of meanings associated with Eden as paradise that has profound moral and spiritual significance. These moral, spiritual, and aesthetic dimensions make the experience intense and memorable, a source of power and solace, and a convincing mark of therapeutic transformation.

Some of the cases Witztum and Goodman present involve dissociative experiences that are characterized by a loss of agency, in which split-off aspects of the self—experienced as spirits or supernatural figures—afflict the patient. Therapy, therefore, aims at reintegrating the split-off aspects of self and restoring a sense of agency. Shifts of agency (which Witztum and Goodman describe in some instances as a shift from the position of anti-hero to that of hero) occur in many of the cases, usually prompted by prescribing an active role for the patient in a ritual.

Imaginal dialogues with the supernatural figures provide a flexible and dynamic method to encourage the patient to adopt an active stance. "The therapist tries to add new dimensions to the relationships with the figure, usually by encouraging the patient to talk back to the figure as opposed to passively listening to it, and by actively initiating new actions, thus taking more responsibility."[73] There are close parallels here to Jung's technique of *active imagination* in which patients are encouraged to dialogue with imaginal figures and allow the figures a degree of autonomy.[74] This gives voice to aspects of the self that are distinct from the conscious "I" or ego. Some of Witztum and Goodman's patients, however, already experience too much autonomy in their imaginal figures, who intrude in their everyday lives in ways that destabilize their ability to function in social roles and pursue life goals. The goal of the therapeutic interaction then is to bring the imaginal figures back in dialogue with the ego or self to foster healing transformation.

As Witztum and Goodman describe their approach: "The general goal of this kind of therapy is to integrate the patients' symbolic idioms presented at an abstract cosmological level, into a more particular personal and concrete form."[75] They cite Dow's general model for symbolic healing here (discussed in Chapter 4), but their account actually inverts Dow's model, in which the personal experience of the sufferer is attached to more abstract cosmological symbols at which level healing transformations of meaning can occur.[76] For ultra-orthodox patients, the illness may already be framed in specific cultural terms and therapeutic work involves developing a transformative narrative that remains within this mythic framework. A similar approach may be appropriate for people from cultures and communities that de-emphasize the importance of individual biography in favour of narratives that reflect collective stories (whether shared history or myth). Performances of mythic cycles or epics, like the Mahabharata, present the audience with scenarios that mirror the moral conundrums of their lives and provide vicarious resolution of personal conflicts.[77] In contrast, people living in societies shaped by neoliberal values and versions of the person may employ psychological idioms to characterize their dilemmas in terms of conflicting motivations and desires, described in mechanistic or economic terms to be resolved by strategic self-management guided by a calculus of cost and benefit.[78] Of course, even such deracinated neoliberal selves may be remoralized by having their personal experience of suffering attached to larger mythic narratives, which are valorized within the culture. This is the strategy of Jungian psychotherapy and certain forms of narrative or arts-based therapies that could be called mythopoetic.[79]

But what Jungian psychology tries to recuperate from an archaic past, the religious patient experiences as immanent through everyday practice. The sacred stories in which religious patients' suffering is inscribed do not function in the same ways as mundane stories. The storyteller Gioia Timpanelli described this difference:

> Unlike secular stories, which happen in the common perception of time passing, sacred stories are consecrated to truth and teaching and are not attached to our usual perception of cause and effect. Rather, they are stories without time—showing us no-time—so we can experience the world from within and without at the same moment. Even if the stories have a beginning, middle and end, we understand that this form allows the

> communication of the enduring, the *always is*. Thus, we can perceive that they are stories "from that time"; we can hear the sacred story and experience the eternal. Often, these holy stories are memorized, so that nothing is out of place, for stories and words have a real place in the world.[80]

Sacred stories invoke a timeless realm, have a degree of authority and moral weight that transcends individual psychology, and, in consequence, cannot be played with without risking transgression.[81] This puts heavy constraints on the practice of psychotherapy. The seriousness of these stories gives them exceptional power and significance for the sufferer and for those around him.

Working with or within the patient's myth or metaphor is central to strategic therapy and makes intuitive sense to psychotherapists in multicultural settings who must address the grounding of experience in culture. At its most basic, this means using the patient's own imagery and language. While psychotherapy offers patients ways of looking at the world that have implications beyond the presenting problem, interventions that are symptom-focused and framed within the patient's own personal and cultural idioms often have the more modest goal of symptom alleviation. In doing so, they take a stance that seeks only to fix what is broken and not to "raise consciousness" or map out a new way of living. This modesty contributes to the appeal of symptom- or problem-focused treatments for clients and patients from conservative religious or cultural backgrounds who may be suspicious of more broadly based psychotherapy that, in fact, introduces ways of thinking and moral paradigms that may be in more direct conflict with traditional values. The question remains whether these ethical conflicts are being sidestepped or merely deferred. The links between psychology and the yearning for transcendence cannot be entirely effaced by the disenchantments of secular society or the pragmatic approaches of contemporary psychotherapy.

## Conclusion: Crossed Destinies

In Italo Calvino's *The Castle of Crossed Destinies*, the narrator enters a forest where his voice is stilled.[82] He comes upon a castle and enters a great hall. There, around a table, sit a silent host of characters playing a game of cards. On closer inspection, the narrator sees that they are dealing tarot cards. He soon realizes they are telling each other stories through the details of the images on the cards. As each character tells their story and lays down the tarot cards, they fit together with a magic square of intersecting stories at center. Reading in one direction, we find the story of the Courtier, from another, cutting across the same cards, the story of the Knight. Every path through the field of cards yields a new narrative. This same artifice is applied twice in the book: once with the Sforza-Bembo Tarot and idiosyncratic tales and, again, with the Tarot of Marseille and some of the great narratives of Western literature.

The compositional artifice of *The Castle of Crossed Destinies* comes from Calvino's interest in generating narrative possibilities through constraints.[83] But Calvino's narrative method here is not simply a formal combinatorics of words; it has two grounds, each of which is a source of invention and constraint: the images on the cards and the order imposed by making them fit a magic square. The narrative structure moves forward by metaphoric extension or implication based on the "minute particulars" of each image that evoke sensation, feeling, and action in imagination. The images thus provide a determinate but polysemous infrastructure to the narrative; this corresponds to the level of archetypal meaning. To interweave the narratives, though, the author must always have in mind where the next card fits in the square and must search for elements in the card that allow it to play its several roles depending on the path taken through the field of images. This teleological structuring corresponds to myth, insofar as any individual myth itself must take its place in the larger cosmology.[84]

As Calvino's extended metaphor makes clear, however, our destinies are crossed but not determined. The path through the field of cards offers a range of narrative possibilities: it leads the author and the reader to view the next card from a particular narrative angle; but the metaphoric elaboration of the tarot images allows both author and reader to strike out in new directions. The author's artistry creates a seamless fusion of image and intention. Of course, the *Castle* is, after all, a world of literary invention, composed with effort and deliberation, designed to draw attention to its artful construction and playful use of imagination. The cards are like the symbolic materials or resources of language. They are not abstract, logical "atoms" but whole pictures, with an indefinitely large range of correspondences to objects and events in the real world. Each time one of Calvino's constructions escapes the boundaries of its cards, we are reminded that the worlds of literature and imagination are not self-contained. The world of symbols lives in and among the world of things.

CHAPTER 6

# *Landscapes of Memory*

> The colonel returned with a sack used to bring groceries home. He spilled many human ears on the table. They were like dried peach halves. There is no other way to say this. He took one of them in his hands, shook it in our faces, dropped it into a water glass. It came alive there. I am tired of fooling around he said. As for the rights of anyone, tell your people they can go fuck themselves. He swept the ears to the floor with his arm and held the last of his wine in the air. Something for your poetry, no? he said. Some of the ears on the floor caught this scrap of his voice. Some of the ears on the floor were pressed to the ground.
>
> – Carolyn Forché[1]

> A Klee painting named "Angelus Novus" shows an angel looking as though he is about to move away from something he is fixedly contemplating. His eyes are staring, his mouth is open, his wings are spread. This is how one pictures the angel of history. His face is turned toward the past. Where we perceive a chain of events, he sees one single catastrophe which keeps piling wreckage and hurls it in front of his feet. The angel would like to stay, awaken the dead, and make whole what has been smashed. But a storm is blowing in from Paradise; it has got caught in his wings with such a violence that the angel can no longer close them. The storm irresistibly propels him into the future to which his back is turned, while the pile of debris before him grows skyward. This storm is what we call progress.
>
> – Walter Benjamin[2]

The opening passage from Carolyn Forché's prose poem, drawn from her experiences in El Salvador in the late 1970s, confronts us with the terror and absurdity of civil war and mass atrocities.[3] This does not end with a truce or declarations of peace. Living in the aftermath of war, with perpetrators still in power and only a fragile order restored, how can memory contain the horror and the loss? Must survivors turn away from the past in order to move forward? And if silence is required for safety, what becomes of the history needed to provide a moral compass and guide efforts to rebuild a just society? Ears pressed to the ground, can the dead and dismembered hear stories the living are compelled to forget?

In recent years, psychiatric and social science approaches to violence have been dominated by the metaphor of trauma. Trauma experience, the recollection of traumatic memories, and the cultural and biosocial shaping of individual and collective forms of suffering and healing all tend to treat trauma as a given, a starting point that does not require further specification or clarification. But in this work, *trauma* has at least four different meanings: physically wounding violence, which may be an expectable (if never ordinary) aspect of the human condition; violence that has lasting effects on mental health, the prototype of which has become posttraumatic stress disorder (PTSD); states of extremity that break out of all bounds of reason, containment, and control to violently disrupt and destroy the social order; and an open-ended and ever widening set of diverse and shifting events that are linked metaphorically to one of the first three meanings or exemplars. Trauma has become a cultural keyword and a way to talk about suffering that commands attention and demands a moral response.[4]

Massive violence is a *tremendum* that can not only destroy lives but also subvert cosmologies, justifying its unique place in mental health theory and practice. Still, there are subtler, more insidious forms of structural violence that are embedded in routines of the ordinary. Trauma is part of local forms of life and the phenomenology of trauma is shaped by social contexts and relationships. Trauma often is treated as self-evidently basic, as a brute fact that determines its own outcome or else as something that utterly defies description, the disaster that transcends any human capacity to articulate. A common claim is that massive trauma and disaster are ineffable, unutterable, and a radical otherness that cannot be captured or contained by language. In fact, the experience and response to mass violence evokes intense interpretive activity and drives much modern art and literature.[5]

This chapter will consider the ways that trauma experience is embodied, articulated, and enacted in particular places. Understanding the personal, social, and political meanings of trauma in theory and practice requires tracing the systemic loops that link memory, symptom, and response with a landscape of affordances.[6]

## Trauma Narratives and Expressive Writing

The ability to construct a story from fragmentary or fragmenting experiencing confers a sense of coherence, order, and meaning on events. Experimental studies by social psychologist James Pennebaker on expressive writing show the potential benefits of disclosing and narrating traumatic events.[7] Pennebaker found that asking people to write about traumatic experiences caused a temporary increase in distress but longer-term improvements in both physical and emotional health. Subsequent studies suggest that it is not simply reexperiencing but cognitive reframing (thinking differently about feelings and experiences while having them) that makes the therapeutic difference.[8] Health psychology supports the value of giving testimony or disclosing traumas and renarrating terrible events in the presence of an empathic other. But there are many questions that remain about when such recounting is helpful and when it may cause more distress.[9] Answering these questions requires attention to the larger social, cultural, and historical significance of self-narratives.

As discussed in earlier chapters, part of the value of the narrative framing of strong emotion, trauma, and conflict may be related to achieving an optimal distance from painful events that allows emotional catharsis. Narrative expression of emotion also serves many other functions. It is *cartographic*, mapping out a social domain of what matters to us, indicating regions of pleasure, pain, and morally significant feelings. Narratives are also *rhetorical*, conveying our experience to others, convincing them of the seriousness of our predicament, and *performative*, shifting our social position. As a result, any specific narrative of trauma has implications far beyond the creation of psychological coherence or meaning for the individual.

Despite the potential benefits of the disclosure of trauma, there also are social costs. Talk about trauma, and expression of strong emotion, may cause rewounding of the speaker and vicarious traumatization of others. When such talk contravenes social and cultural norms, it may disrupt family and community ties with serious consequences for the individual. We do not know enough about the costs and benefits of disclosure and narration in different social and cultural contexts.[10] For example, in some instances of rape as a weapon of war, women may feel that if they disclose their violation to their kin, they will be carrying out the rapist's intention to demoralize and destroy their communities. In such situations, the pressure to tell their story to a therapist or to testify in a legal setting may threaten their safety. The threat may be partially mitigated when they can control the place and pace of recounting, but many of the consequences of disclosure are beyond the control of the survivor of violence. This points to a larger problem in psychological accounts of the origins and treatment of trauma that ignore the persistent social conditions and political circumstances that may be beyond the ability of the individual, their family, or community to change. Appreciating these conditions requires understanding the social landscapes of trauma, recollection, and survivance for individuals and their communities.

## Trauma Memory as Narrative Embodiment and Enactment

Memory defines the distinctive syndromes of psychological trauma like PTSD, linking current suffering to past events through recollection. But there are many varieties of memory, some of which can be described as images or narrated as stories, others that are embodied dispositions to respond in ways that may reveal a history of violence. Narratives of trauma include personal and collective, informal or improvised, and formal or official versions. These narratives are enacted by individuals as autobiographical stories, identities, symptoms, and rhetorical claims to power and moral authority. They also are part of collective acts of commemoration of shared history that serve the myths and ideologies that define group identities. Both individual and collective identities are realized through discursive practices. Remembering and retelling can therefore serve to reconstruct identity at both individual and communal levels. This is vividly illustrated by ethnographic studies in psychological anthropology.

In his ethnographic research in Vietnam, for example, Heonik Kwon described how the state-instituted "heroic memory" of war in postwar society changed domestic space.[11] Political campaigns substituted the commemoration of heroic war dead for the traditional cult of ancestors. Against this official version, villagers improvised other ways to acknowledge the moral complexity of local history. Everyday acts of commemoration—kneeling and offering incense to the ancestors of the household—were transformed by adding a second gesture, "turning the body to the opposite side to repeat the action towards the street-wandering ghosts."[12] This act recognized persisting wounds associated with the ghosts of those who suffered unjust deaths and whose apparitions remind villagers of their own enduring pain and loss.

In Vietnamese thought, there is a moral economy to death. A violent, unjust death and the memory of its terror can trap the soul in a negative afterlife. In this terrible state, the soul must relive the violent event over and over again. The My Lai villagers with whom Kwon worked mentioned the names of certain older villagers as the most grievous victims of the 1968 massacre, and they belonged to families whose genealogy was decimated by the violence. The decimated family genealogy provoked the strongest sense of injustice and moral indignation in other communities affected by civilian massacres. A grievous death in this context is not only the destruction of innocent lives but also a crisis in the social foundation of commemoration. The dead have an inalienable right to be liberated from their violent history, and the protection of this right depends on the secular institutions of commemoration. Commemoration, then, is a process that supports the moral structures of society and works therapeutically at both individual and collective levels.

Kwon describes the ontology that brings to life the suffering of the dead as a parallel to the psychodynamics of traumatic memory in the survivor, so that we might say, without irony, that the dead *embody* the disavowed, unspeakable, and unresolved experiences of the living. The experience of the dead constitutes a realm of moral imagination, both for individuals and, through the cultural ontology of forms of death and the social regulation of commemorative action, of collective imagination. This, in turn, opens up the possibility of a new form of political action, in which the dead speak back to the living, challenging collective silence and seeking acknowledgment, restitution, and repair. From their position beyond the mundane world, the dead can challenge the oppression of everyday life and the political arrangements that try to suppress or rewrite history.

The interaction of trauma narratives and norms of expression is also evident in the work of Conerly Casey on the experience of those who, as children, witnessed the 1990 Iraqi invasion of Kuwait.[13] For Kuwaitis, psychological distress was highly stigmatized with consequences for family reputation, marriage, and community relations. Bodily distress due to physical illnesses, however, was more socially accepted, especially when the illness was attributed to exposure to war contaminants or other "outside assaults." Indeed, seen as the result of attacks from outside, somatic symptoms became vectors of a specific type of memory with clear moral implications. Many young adults did not believe government reports that attributed prevalent somatic symptoms to stress rather than to the effects of environmental contaminants spread during the war. Psychological explanations for their suffering were not reassuring or empowering and instead might be viewed as evidence of official denial and betrayal. Persistent somatic symptoms spoke back forcefully to this betrayal.

For the young adults who experienced the 1990 Iraqi invasion of Kuwait, the 2003 US war in Iraq was a trigger, elicitor or amplifier of symptoms rooted in past trauma. The amplification of trauma reflected the convergence of past and present memories evoked by the sensorial qualities of experiences and the emotional resonances of specific events and moral predicaments. The wars were associated with strong feelings of betrayal and abandonment. These sentiments had their own power as organizers of memory. Familial, social, and national stories, commemorative events, and topographical reminders, such as bombed-out buildings, all functioned as what Casey terms "emotive institutions," anchoring and eliciting affect. These institutions were both evocative symbols and settings for ritual and commemorative performance. Those who witnessed the Iraqi invasion as children vividly recalled the dangers of Iraqi checkpoints and the destruction of community centers, religious sites, public parks, schoolyards, and marketplaces. Many of the damaged sites were not repaired but marked with plaques describing particular incidents of violence, insuring they retained a place in collective memory. The "post" of posttrauma, then, was an altered landscape, one that was not only scarred but, in some ways, unstable. In Kuwait, the violence left great feelings of uncertainty and many young people had an escape plan, with a passport or visa that would let them leave quickly if needed.

War changed the physical landscape, giving it new affective contours, charged with meaning and populated with memories of dangerous figures. There were many topographical referents to the invasion that inscribed trauma into "Kuwaiti cityscapes." These topographies varied according to individuals' experiences constituting a sort of urban memory theater.[14] The environmental damage visited on the landscape during the war also had a moral meaning and, together, memory and morality shaped bodily experience.[15] The health consequences of violence, then, stemmed not just from the immediate impact of events but also from the ways in which they resituated the self in a landscape of memory and identity.

Landscapes of a different sort figure in work by Orkideh Behrouzan and Michael Fischer on echoes of the revolution and violent conflicts in Iran.[16] The persistence of traumatic memory reflects both its psychobiology and social dynamics, but in the case of the Iranian diasporic community, the impact of historical events was intensified by the regime change and transformation of society in ways that turned exiles' fantasies of return into nightmares. Behrouzan and Fischer describe a "sonic landscape" of echoes of the past that included spaces for expression found on the internet, in dreams, and popular media, after political repression had shut down the agora.[17] They note the difficulties of communication across the generations of the Iranian revolution. Persian cultural and religious traditions of mourning and melancholia valorize grief and the commemoration of loss, but, within Iran, these traditions were appropriated and subverted by the state.[18] Persian cinema has been an important arena of expression and also offers a kind of collective dream work. Films can tell family stories against a backdrop of larger political stories that may be harder and more dangerous to tell.

The weaving of satellite television and the internet into the fabric of Iranian diasporic culture provides new media for the culture of metaphors. Internet blogs mediate communities in which the exchange of accounts of dreams serve as tokens of identity, presence, and solidarity. The dreams and nightmares recounted are remixes: cutting, layering, and blending disparate images and themes drawn from contemporary Persian culture. The use of the internet and engagement with popular psychology also went hand-in-hand. The "rise of the psychiatric self" among Iranians was reflected in psychiatric, psychological, and self-help talk shows that attracted callers from all strata of society, rural as well as urban.[19] Along with this came a shift from the indirection and allusion of poetry to explicitly psychological language. Pop psychological language created a space to name and acknowledge certain personal and collective realities. Work on the self is a political project, and the "traumatic dream work of the present"[20] is both an undercurrent to contemporary community and a site of proto-political discourse that can cut across the generations.

The intergenerational transmission of memory and identity is central to Carol Kidron's work on embodiments of memory in the developmental experiences of children of Holocaust survivors.[21] For many of this second generation, the histories of their parents' suffering were shrouded in "oppressive silence," but Kidron shows how silence itself maintains traces of the past and can constitute a powerful mode of communication and remembrance within the family. She also points to the value of silence as an alternative to the insistent efforts of psychotherapies to promote disclosure, confession, and testimony. Personal memories need not enter the social sphere to have meaning and value; they can remain within the inner world of the individual or the family as private knowledge.

In subsequent work, Kidron has examined memory practices among the children of Cambodian survivors of the Khmer Rouge genocide.[22] In marked contrast to children of Jewish Holocaust survivors, she found that trauma narratives are largely absent in the accounts of the children of Cambodian survivors. Consistent with Buddhist ethical values, survivors and their children were enjoined not to dwell on the past, but to focus on right thought and right action in the present. Culturally prescribed norms and modes of remembering thus shape individual and family efforts to make sense of mass violence. Reconnecting to ancestors, however, requires culturally prescribed modes of managing recollection, which were further complicated in Cambodia by state practices of enshrining the remains of those murdered as sites of commemoration.

When memories circulate in local worlds, they can be taken up by others in ways not intended by their original bearer. Kidron's work with psychotherapy groups in Israel illustrates how transgenerational processes of remembering can be put to political ends.[23] Through direct and indirect means, the state appropriates and regulates personal memory to serve collective identity and stake moral claims. What makes trauma memory special, then, is not just the neurobiology of fear conditioning, but also the way the politics of memory *as* identity determine the narrative templates and metaphors that organize remembering and the interpretation of symptoms. For example, for the children of survivors in Israel, symptoms may become marks of distinction (*srutim* or scars) that identify them not only as bearers of important collective memories but as uniquely resilient.[24]

This political structuring and appropriation of memory is a central theme in ethnographic work by Vincent Crapanzano on the predicament of the children of the Harkis, Muslim Algerians who served the French army.[25] The Harkis faced torture and ostracism in Algeria and incarceration in detention camps in France, suffering "the pathologies of abjection." They have continued to face painful historical memories and a collective "wound," which, as Crapanzano notes, "we all too readily describe as trauma and embed in our psychological understanding."[26]

Like Kidron, Crapanzano is concerned with the transmission of memory across generations, in this instance, shaped by French and Algerian politics. Experiences of betrayal and abandonment served to bind the Harkis into a community of memory, the specific contents of which they were unable to tell their children. Betrayal and abandonment engendered thoughts and feelings particularly liable to be the focus of obsessive ruminations. For the children, who had never heard the details of their fathers' experiences, a shifting, fragmentary, and generic story had to take the place of specific memories. This incompleteness was both a cause of rumination and, ultimately, of dissatisfaction, in that it made it impossible to take the full measure of their parents' suffering or achieve some closure. The lack of detailed narratives led to a vague, generic account of Harki history. The events that were clear, unequivocal, and directly accessible to the second generation were the community's continued lack of recognition. Consequently, many of the younger generation became involved in political activism, lobbying for recognition and compensation for the sacrifices their parents made for France.

The Harkis came to see their predicament as a "fated destiny" and Crapanzano sets his reflections in the larger frame of notions of contingency (as destiny, fate, fortune, or luck). Various ontologies, ethnopsychologies, and systems of religious belief connect contingency to a sociomoral order with assumptions about freedom, risk, responsibility, and blame. Causal explanation assigns moral significance and points toward what must be done in terms of apology and restitution. In accounting for events, *how* and *why* narratives may be quite separate: the how providing mechanistic explanation, the why, moralistic evaluation. And the failure to provide a coherent why itself stands as a sign of the enormity of events: "there are stories whose aim is to call attention to the impossibility of ever answering the ultimate why. They turn impossibility into a rhetorical figure, playing on mystery, the harrowing acknowledgement of the unexplainable."[27] This is the genre of the story of Job and its modern echoes. Indeed, we can build theologies on this experience of the inexplicable.[28]

Unexplained, hard, refractory contingency is both troubling and fascinating—and demands explanatory work on both counts. Literary genres provide strategies for narrative ordering, smoothing, and containment; they specify appropriate whys and wherefores for the apparently contingent or, by giving an explicit place to the noncontingent or accidental—creating a meta-order that contains disorder (e.g., an all-powerful God whose actions are beyond human understanding). Individuals may shift among alternate accounts because any narrative is limited in its ability to contain the chaos and contradiction brought by massive violence.

In the case of the Harkis, the collective story overshadowed any individual's account, which remained unclear in its details and potentially damning if revealed. Hence, the collective obligation to remember hid the individual impossibility of recollection. The collective story surpassed the individual both because this individual story was elided or suppressed and because it was this same collective story that constituted the Harkis as a community and that valorized an otherwise marginal and difficult identity. The narrative became what Crapanzano calls a "frozen story"—a fixed and formulaic account that cannot grow and evolve because it must serve as an historical anchor of collective identity.

## Reconstructing Memory and Identity

In Georges Perec's shattering novel *W, or The Memory of Childhood*, we encounter two interleaved stories.[29] One presents Perec's groping efforts to recall his childhood in wartime France—efforts that result only in a few fragmentary memories immediately picked apart by his own critical footnotes, which correct the many imprecisions and confabulations. What gradually emerges is the story of a childhood lived at the margins of the Holocaust, of a father who dies in the resistance, a mother deported to die in a Nazi camp, and a Jewish boy raised by relatives as Catholic. Throughout, Perec struggles with absence: he fantasizes about a family life that never was, then lapses into a silence in which his mother is never mentioned again. The flat, matter-of-fact tone in which the story is told does not veil his grief but intensifies our awareness of the acuity of his loss.

The second narrative, which alternates chapters with the first throughout the book, is also drawn from childhood reveries, but, after a false start involving the search for a lost child, it becomes the fantasy of "W,"[30] an island nation devoted to the Olympic ideal of athletic competition. Projected forward in the narrator's imagination, the account of life in "W" grows increasingly bizarre and sinister until it converges on a portrait of a Nazi concentration camp.

The two narratives, personal history and fantasy, seem unrelated at first, going past each other like two ships in the night. In the space between them, however, an ominous terror and depth of grief are created that surpass what would be felt from either sentimental recollection or gothic horror tale. In its carefully constructed gaps, Perec's narrative alludes to another untold story. This artful arrangement did not occur to Perec at first; he set out to write a novel developing his adolescent fantasy of W. As each chapter was completed, he published it as a serial in a literary magazine. When the writing led him to descend into a personal pain that was too unmanageable or unknown—particularly in the chapter that describes the methods of reproduction in "W"—Perec broke off the story and reentered psychoanalysis.[31] Later he solved the aesthetic and psychological problem of finding distance from the text by constructing a fiction that affords the reader the experience of complicity in both seeking and hiding from memory.

Reading *W* as autobiography reminds us of the fundamental connection between memory and imagination, retelling and recreating the self. Of course, the narrative based on "pure" fantasy is more seamless and integrated than the autobiographical narrative for which memory offers only snapshots, shadows, and feelings half-acknowledged and half-suppressed. Indeed, the very incompleteness and tentativeness of the autobiographical account attests to its veracity. Stories that are seamless are suspect. Yet more of Perec's predicament—more of his self—is revealed in the fantasy story recovered and reimagined from adolescence, as the transmuted fears of childhood drive the Olympic ideal toward a Nazi world of tortures and humiliations in the name of the athletic superman, impervious to any emotion other than lust for victory.

In Perec's story the greatest terror and loss are presented not in the explicit narrative of *W* but in the gaps between the two narratives, in the frailty and impersistence of memory and the felt absence of mother, family, and a safe world set against the unexpectedly dark journey of fantasy. Perec's fiction, then, serves to introduce the problem of the relation of narrative to remembering and forgetting and to that special type of forgetting—unexpected and precipitous—that is called "dissociation." As the child of parents who perished (and who was himself sent away from Paris to hide with relatives in a rural village), Perec's memoir points to this kind of divide through the metafictional strategy of alternating fragmentary recollection with explicitly imaginative construction.

Accounts of victims of childhood trauma differ strikingly from the testimony of survivors of the Holocaust in the contours of the struggle to remember and forget. For the childhood trauma victim, the violence of traumatic events renders events difficult to remember while for the Holocaust victim violence renders events ineradicable. Whatever the epidemiology of responses to trauma, what accounts for this stereotypical difference in cultural representations of the two types of trauma narrative?

Survivors of the Holocaust are usually depicted as overwhelmed by memories and unwilling to recount their tale for fear of the pain it will reevoke. Their problem is not the limits of memory but of language—the inadequacy of ordinary words to express all they have witnessed. The Holocaust presents an incomprehensible catastrophe that undermines the very possibility of coherent narrative.[32] In contrast, adults with a history of childhood abuse are often depicted as initially unaware of their traumatic experiences as memories. They suffer from dissociative disorders like depersonalization, psychogenic amnesia, or, in severe cases, dissociative identity disorder.[33] They evince their traumatic past through symptoms, including physical and emotional pain, numbing, self-injury, substance abuse, lapses of memory, and changes of identity.[34] In both cases, symptoms are explained by trauma. However, for the Holocaust survivor, the public nature of the overarching story blocks the process of forgetting. The reaction is one of being overwhelmed and then responding by numbing, detachment, or suppression so that one's story sits forever at the edges of consciousness to be worked around or told in fragments. For the survivor of childhood abuse, whose story is often private, the response to overwhelming trauma can be a form of mental escape by resolute partition of memory, self, and experience. There is no narrative of trauma then, no memory—only symptoms and signs that can be read as an outline of absence.

This difference may be understood as a consequence of mechanisms of memory stemming from different psychological defenses or from specific psychiatric disorders (PTSD versus dissociative amnesia). This view treats trauma narratives as direct outcomes of psychobiological mechanisms of memory. In what follows, however, I suggest that the distinctive qualities of trauma narratives can also be understood as differences in the culturally constructed *landscape of memory*: the metaphoric terrain that shapes the distance and effort required to remember affectively charged and socially defined events that initially may be vague, impressionistic, or simply absent from memory. Landscapes of memory are given shape by the personal and social significance of specific memories but also draw from *meta-memory*—implicit models of memory which influence what can be recalled and cited as veridical. Narratives of trauma may be understood then as cultural constructions of personal and historical memory.

## Meta-Memory: Cultural Models of Remembering and Forgetting

The concept of memory collects a family of diverse processes in a single category by conflating the stories we tell about our past with the many ways in which we are changed by experience, only some of which rely on this narrative capacity to remember and recollect. Cognitive theories of memory view it as something stored like an object in a particular place in the brain so that retrieval is a process of searching the neural archive for that object.[35] Popular conceptions of memory make several assumptions not born out by experimental studies. In one common metaphor, memories are "snapshots," laid down at the time of experience through a process of registration. They persist unchanged throughout our lives to be recalled when we look for them, like opening a photo album. If certain memories remain hidden or difficult to retrieve, it is only because we are looking in the wrong place or, as we grow older, because of the accumulated clutter that must be cleared away. On this view, memories may fade like photographs and this too can limit the vividness of recollection.

Research contradicts this naive view of memory.[36] Memory is not a photographic record of experience; it is a roadway full of potholes, badly in need of repair, worked on day and night by revisionist crews. What is registered is highly selective and thoroughly transformed by interpretation and semantic encoding at the moment of experience and on later recollection. What can be recalled is limited and routinely reconstructed to fit models of what might have—*must* have—happened. When encouraged to flesh it out, we readily engage in imaginative elaboration and confabulation and, once we have done this, the original memory may be lost forever within the animated story we have (re)constructed.[37] Memories go through processes of repeated retrieval and reconsolidation that can alter their content and associated emotion.[38]

Naive theories of memory also assume that memories are "time-stamped," and therefore offer themselves up in sequence. This sequence then provides a temporal structure for narrative. Each memory carries with it instructions for how to insert it into a larger narrative (like a piece of a puzzle with instructions on its back). Research suggests, however, that memory for the timing of events is not usually tied to images of the events themselves.[39] Instead, the process typically works in the other direction: narrative structure supplies the temporal sequence of memory.

Similar processes of reconstruction, governed by different narrative templates, give rise to other aspects of memory. Memories are not stamped with their source, so that it is easy to forget where or how we learned something ("source amnesia") and to misremember inventions as actual events, constructing images to fit our knowledge and belief.[40] To take a trivial example, many people who recall themselves swimming report seeing an image of their whole body as if from poolside or the air. Clearly, an imaginative construction based on experiences of seeing others has been substituted for a veridical memory.

There are, of course, many forms of memory. The dominant cultural prototype of memory is declarative: we are able to describe what we know (semantic memory) and what we have experienced (episodic memory). The emphasis on declarative memory as the exemplar follows from our models of consciousness as representation. But we do not always have pictures for memories: often we have knowledge, skills, or dispositions to act, which are represented by an image only after the fact. We are unable to remember the details of most of what we have lived through, although these events have surely formed us. There is much that we commemorate through our accent, posture, habits of gesture, and thought—things we may be unaware of and forever unable to describe except in vague, abstract, or secondhand terms. These forms of nondeclarative or implicit memory have been called "procedural" because they involve skills or ways of responding to situations that may be acquired and accessed without consciousness awareness.[41]

All forms of memory show great plasticity. The effects of imagination on reconstruction and recall are pervasive.[42] The tendency to underestimate this—and so to treat ordinary memory as veridical recall—probably reflects a more general tendency in contemporary Western culture to underestimate (and pathologize) the role of imagination in normal psychological development.[43] If memory is not simply a snapshot of the past (as folk theory assumes), then how memories get stored and recalled may be less crucial to whether they are perceived as authentic than what authorizes and stabilizes memories so that they become *my* memory or *the* memory of an event.

Folk models of memory govern what we try to remember, what we expect others to be able to remember, what we deem a "real" memory and how we compose memories through narrative. Some types of events are meant to be easily remembered and others are not. Societies have a range of institutions, calendars, rituals, and practices to serve collective remembering.[44] These may also anchor and rehearse personal memory even as they serve to distort and change it to conform to cultural templates and expectations.

Psychotherapy can provide an important site for the work of memory. The experience of insight sought in psychodynamic psychotherapy is closely allied to the recovery of personal historical memory. In psychotherapy, the impress of past events is revealed in two ways: first, through the historical recall of declarative memory, in which events and feelings are recollected and described explicitly. The historical accounts produced in therapy are now widely recognized as narrative reconstructions.[45] Opinion differs, however, on the extent to which this reconstruction is based on episodic memory (i.e., recollecting factual details of scenes and events) or semantic memory that recovers only abstract knowledge and meanings. In either case, reconstruction exerts a mutative effect on the past—supplying missing details in images of episodic memory and imputing meanings to events that may not have been present or salient when the event occurred.[46]

A second dimension to personal history is revealed in the way we react rather than recollect. Psychodynamic theory allows much of our behavior to be interpreted as symptoms and signs that are residues of repressed memories, kept out of awareness by unconscious mechanisms of defense. Psychodynamically oriented clinicians have claimed that, after long intervals of amnesia, repressed memories may be activated by idiosyncratic associations and more or less vividly recalled.[47] Claims of amnesia for traumatic memory were challenged by skeptics who noted the lack of empirical evidence.[48] The resultant "memory wars" reached a peak in the 1990s, when opposing camps produced evidence of the individual and societal harms arising from the widespread endorsement or rejection of the existence of repressed traumatic memory.[49] Subsequent research has provided little evidence for repression as a general psychological mechanism. There is more evidence of the role of suppression and dissociation in memory lapses or lacunae, and for the potential belated traumatic effects of reinterpreting memories of childhood experiences as transgressive, but not for claims that traumatic memories tend to be especially fragmented and easy to repress or forget compared to other memories.[50] The broad implication is that how we think about memory can affect our experience of trauma and its consequences.[51]

The context of retelling is crucial to the nature of memory. There are many possible situations of retelling, ranging from parenthetical remarks inserted into a conversation with one's doctor to explain bodily scars,[52] to the reflective soliloquys of psychotherapy, courtroom depositions, or videotaped testimonies to be stored in official archives as a bulwark against future tyranny.[53] Indeed, even where public retelling does not—and may never—occur, there is a "virtual context," a potential social space of retelling that influences even private reconstructions of memory. Recollection and recall are always socially situated.

## Holocaust Narratives: Speaking the Unspeakable

The challenge of speaking the unspeakable is central to the dilemma of Holocaust survivors. Accounts of the Holocaust in literature and film use aesthetic devices to frame and contain the chaos that surrounds the experience. The struggle to give narrative form to inchoate experience is revealed in studies of Holocaust testimonies collected by interview and recorded on videotape for posterity.[54] In these testimonies, the speaker does not have the same opportunities for careful composition and editing after the fact that characterize literary accounts.[55] Consequently, studies of oral testimony emphasize the emotional difficulties of retelling and the profound effect of living with memories that subvert everyday constructions of the self.

In a study of trauma-related memory, Lawrence Langer provides a searching analysis of some of the 1,400 testimonies in the Fortunoff Video Archives for Holocaust Testimonies at Yale University.[56] He organizes his discussion around the different processes of recollection he sees at work in the testimonies. Each form involves some disruption or violation of the normal social context and conditions for recollection and shows the link of memory to some affective process or pathology. If memories are narrative reconstructions, in this view, each form of reconstruction (or failure of reconstruction) is governed by an underlying affective predicament or paradox that has intrapsychic, bodily, and socio-political elements. The predicament that governs the retelling is revealed by strong emotions associated with ruptures in the narrative. Take, for example, what Langer calls "humiliated memory":

> If anguished memory may be seen as discontent in search of a form, humiliated memory recalls an utter distress that shatters all molds designed to contain a unified and irreproachable image of the self. Its voice represents pure misery, even decades after the events that it narrates. Neither time nor amnesia soothes its gnawing. After hearing its testimony, we are less prone to dismiss as exaggeration the insistence by many surviving victims that the humiliations they endured in the camps were often worse than death. The details uncovered by humiliated memory dispute the claim still advanced by many commentators that the invincible spirit provided an armor invulnerable to Nazi assaults against the self.[57]
>
> Like what I have called deep and anguished memory, humiliated memory is an especially intense form of uncompensating recall. Instead of restoring a sense of power or control over a disabling past (one of the presumed goals of therapy —and perhaps of history too), it achieves the reverse, reanimating the governing impotence of the worst moments in a distinctly non-therapeutic way.[58]

In his metaphors, Langer puts affect before memory. Emotion is foregrounded in the struggle to recollect. But emotions may also be hidden or suppressed. When affect is put behind memory, hidden or obscured, we have to see various approaches to avoid painful recollection.

> Numerous strategies are available to individuals who wish to escape the burden of a vexatious past: forget, repress, ignore, deny, or simply falsify the facts. For reasons difficult to ascertain, what I have called humiliated memory seems immune to these forms of evasion.[59]

Langer invokes a range of methods by which memory may be evaded or occluded; yet "dissociate" is absent from this list, as it has been from many literary and clinical accounts of Holocaust experience and pathology. Whereas Holocaust survivors might be expected to suffer from severe dissociation, they are described instead as suffering from painful recollections, anxiety or numbing, and emotional disconnection.[60] Despite this absence, oral testimonies give striking examples of derealization, depersonalization, duality of consciousness, and disturbed memory in symptomatic narratives that closely resemble—yet remain distinct from—dissociation.

Asked if she lives with Auschwitz inside her, survivor Charlotte Delbo replies:

> No—I live beside it. Auschwitz is there, fixed and unchangeable, but wrapped in the impervious skin of memory that segregates itself from the present "me." Unlike the snake's skin, the skin of memory doesn't renew itself . . . I have the feeling . . . that the "self" who was in the camp isn't me, isn't the person who is here opposite you. No, it's too unbelievable. And everything that happened to this other "self," the one from Auschwitz, doesn't touch me now, doesn't concern me, so distinct are deep memory [*mémoire profond*] and common memory [*mémoire ordinaire*].[61]

Here Delbo describes depersonalization, derealization, and a doubling of identity that, in another context, would surely be characterized as dissociative, yet her own awareness of this predicament prevents the label from being attached. The metaphors of doubling and self-estrangement break up the narrative representation of self; but the effect is conscious and self-reflective and so does not result in amnesia.

This same doubling or duality occurs in many of the narratives Langer discusses. He suggests that the distinction between deep memory and common (ordinary) memory helps to explain the two strands found in Holocaust narratives, in which intense bodily experiences of reliving and narrative descriptions of the self from a more detached vantage point interfere with one another. Even the sense of multiple voices within the person, characteristic of the most extreme form of dissociation, dissociative identity disorder, is approximated in the accounts of some Holocaust survivors: "As we listen to the shifting idioms of the multiple voices emerging from the same person, we are present at the birth of a self that is made permanently provisional as a result of fragmentary excavations that never coalesce into a single, recognizable monument to the past."[62] The self is only whole (or undiminished) when it is allowed a coherent field of moral action. The doubling and disjunction between self at the time of trauma (e.g., life in a concentration camp) and the present shows the difficulty in linking the narratives, and, as a result, the coexistence of two selves, which are linked to distinct places and times, but coexist in the continuity of private pain and collective memory.

## Landscapes of Memory

In the face of such stark examples of altered identity, depersonalization, derealization, and intense motivation to forget, we have to ask why

Holocaust narratives emphasize recollection while the literature on the consequences of child abuse placed so much emphasis on amnesia. To some degree, the two types of narrative reflect different forms of pathology: PTSD characterized by intrusions, and dissociative disorders characterized by gaps. Could there be a difference in the prevalence of each pathology in different traumatic situations?

From a psychological point of view, what differentiates these narratives are differences in modes of attention and self-awareness. The two situations also differ markedly in the degrees, types, and duration of trauma. Up to a certain level of severity or duration of trauma, individuals might respond one way and then switch to another pattern of response. For example, the literature on childhood trauma claims that single traumatic events usually result in clear recollections and associated fears while prolonged and repeated traumas may lead the person to develop more elaborate strategies of repression and dissociation.[63]

It might be argued that Holocaust and childhood trauma accounts differ because the trauma occurred at different ages. The traumas of the Holocaust were visited on all age groups, but most of the testimonies we have are of survivors who were adolescents or adults at the time of the violence. When childhood Holocaust survivors are interviewed, some do indeed display difficulty in recollection.[64] But if coherent memories are never recovered, is this dissociative amnesia or simply the failure to register memories in a socially accessible, adult form common to all childhood experience?[65] The tendency in some work to use the same leading questions and techniques of imaginative elaboration now common in reconstructing childhood abuse memories further clouds the issue.[66]

While it is tempting to attribute differences between the literatures of childhood sexual abuse and Holocaust survivors to differences in the actual prevalence of experiences, available evidence is insufficient to support this conclusion. In the case of the Holocaust, as with survivors of childhood abuse, we do not know how many experienced dissociation during or after their traumatic experiences but recovered and never sought help. An epidemiological survey might find similar levels of intrusive recollections and dissociative amnesias in both populations. Certainly, there are many individuals who recount their childhood abuse without dissociation.[67] And there may be Holocaust survivors who have dissociated aspects of their experience and whose stories, therefore, have not been told. In fact, intrusions and amnestic gaps often coexist in the same individual. The distinction between prototypical narratives, then, may not reflect actual differences in psychopathology but rather differing expectations for recollection and different contexts for retelling.

This points toward a social explanation for the difference in prototypical narratives. The situation of the Holocaust survivor differs strikingly from the usual accounts of adult victims of childhood abuse. While Holocaust stories involve bearing witness to what is widely, if not universally recognized as a human catastrophe, personal stories of abuse are revelatory, shameful, and damaging to the individual and family. In the case of childhood abuse, it is precisely the distinctive qualities of the socially constructed relationship to the past that foster dissociation.[68]

In situations where telling and even thinking are forbidden, where individuals are utterly alone (in prison, or the isolation of an abusive family), they still may construct a virtual space where their story can be narrated.[69] When this virtual space is imagined as a social landscape, memory remains accessible. When the costs of recollection seem catastrophic for self or others, memory may be sequestered in a virtual (mental) space that closes in on itself through the conviction that no telling will ever be possible. Dissociation is the sequestration of memory in a virtual space shaped by the social demand—and personal decision—to remain silent, or to speak the unspeakable only with a voice one can disown.[70]

The historical circumstances of Holocaust survivors gave them little opportunity to dissociate. Instead, they felt compelled to tell their stories.[71] After liberation, survivors were witnesses to an epochal catastrophe. However, survivors soon learned to be selective in their retelling—lest they meet with incomprehension or others recoiling and avoiding them. They found themselves in what Langer calls a position of "moral quarantine," their stories too corrosive to the moral order. In this situation, the management of memory becomes more difficult. Survivors found they could not tell their stories again until a public literature of the Holocaust became more available, beginning in the 1960s with the publication of Raul Hilberg's *The Destruction of the European Jews*. In the decades that followed, there were increasing numbers of Holocaust accounts, movies, monuments, and public commemorations.[72] Each collective act of remembering made it more possible for individuals to recollect and tell their personal stories, while also privileging or imposing particular narrative forms.

There is a crucial distinction between the social space in which the trauma occurred and the contemporary space in which it is (or is not) recollected. In the case of the dissociative disorder patient and the Holocaust victim, the difference is between a public space of solidarity and private space of shame. Trauma shared by a whole community creates a potential public space for retelling. If a community agrees that certain traumatic events occurred and interweaves this fact into its identity, then collective memory survives and individual memory can find a place (albeit transformed) within that landscape. If a family or a community decides that a trauma did not happen, then it vanishes from collective memory and the possibility for individual memory is severely strained.

A public space of trauma provides a consensual reality and collective memory through which the fragments of personal memory can be reconstructed, assembled, and displayed with a tacit assumption of validity. A private space of trauma places the victim in a predicament, since the validation of suffering depends on recovering enough memory to make it real for others but this memory can be retrieved only by reliving or representing the place of victimization. Of course, this experience of reliving may be vigorously resisted by survivor and audience alike.

While "moral quarantine" makes Holocaust witnesses cautious in their accounts, they can afford to be reticent, since the underlying horror of their tale goes without saying. We are willing to listen to survivors tell their broken stories, and relive their stories as symptoms, because we recognize the magnitude of what they have suffered. We do not see their failure to surpass their traumas and move on as a consequence of personal weakness but as evidence of the inhuman force of the evil they have endured.

Survivors of child abuse cannot count on the same public recognition of their trauma without recounting details. When others minimize, trivialize, or normalize the violence they have experienced by putting it on a continuum with other forms of privation, they may experience a sense of invalidation akin to that felt by survivors of the Holocaust when they hear of those who deny its reality. There is a need to have the extremity of the rupture with ordinary experience acknowledged by others. This acknowledgment offers a path back from estrangement to human fellowship and community.

## Sites of Rupture, Resistance, and Repair

Trauma creates ruptures in memory and experience that can make people strangers to themselves and others. Working through the self-estrangement and social ruptures requires spaces that allow the flexibility to reconfigure identity and renegotiate roles. But trauma also calls for ways of challenging and resisting the oppressive structures that cause, maintain and, inevitably, follow mass violence.

Table 6.1 summarizes some of common sites of rupture, resistance, and repair in communal responses in the aftermath of mass violence. These

Table 6.1 *Sites of rupture, resistance, and repair in the aftermath of mass violence*

| Realms of Experience | Descriptive Languages | Injuries or Ruptures | Idioms of Distress | Sites of Resistance & Repair |
|---|---|---|---|---|
| Body | Physiological | Incurable wounds and scars | Symptoms & syndromes | Medical care, clinical encounter |
| Self/Person | Psychological | Fragmented self, emptiness, madness | Personal memory, internal conflict | Psychotherapy, dreams, fantasy |
| Interpersonal relationships | Moral | Capricious evil, inhumanity, loss of trust | Wrongdoing, revenge, redress | Family, communal activities, internet communities |
| Communal/ Political | Justice/ Human Rights | Unjust social order, absence of safety | Collective memory, history, speaking truth to power | Court, *gacaca,* TRC |
| Spirit world | Religious | Damaged cosmology | Grievously injured spirits, witchcraft | Shrine, cemetery, ritual space |

include clinical settings that focus on physical illness or emotional distress, but also everyday interpersonal situations, and more formal arenas like courts or communal hearings for conflict resolution that directly address moral and political issues, religious places, and practices that engage with a spiritual or transcendent order. These spaces, realms, and registers serve to reestablish and reaffirm the coherence of the social order, rebuilding trust between individuals and groups, but they may also provide opportunities for survivors of mass violence to challenge cultural forms or dominant narratives, and push back against constraints. They allow this resistance partly because they partially escape surveillance and control by powerful interests that would enforce a single ideological account of events; by allowing circulation of these warded off ideas and experiences, they also help keep memory alive.

The realms of experience reflect locations and local ontologies, that is, notions of what the world is made up of including: bodies, persons, relationships, families, clans, communities, nations, peoples, and spirits. However, these ontologies need not involve elaborate or explicit metaphysical systems, theories, or beliefs. They may be engaged through tacit knowledge or intuitions and situated social practices or institutional routines tied to particular contexts and cultural affordances. Each of these entities or kinds of being has its own ideas of order and disorder, as well as its own dynamics that can give rise to violent ruptures and injuries that cause damage to individuals, manifested as symptoms and afflictions, and to the social fabric, resulting in forms of social suffering. Each sort of impact is associated with particular idioms of distress, through which suffering can be elaborated and communicated. And each has its own prescribed practices for the production of narratives, recollection of memories, and participation in discourse that can express predicaments, make knowledge claims, and mobilize resistance, resilience, and repair.

In each culture or community, there are individuals and institutions warranted to speak the appropriate languages, diagnose conditions of suffering or disorder, and intervene in ways that may help the sufferer and maintain the larger social order. Each person makes use of available cultural idioms to articulate their own suffering. The observed cultural idioms of distress are the result of interactions of biology, individual agency, and discursive forms that are socially mediated and constrained.

Within the socially created and prescribed sites for engaging and talking about these levels or aspects of experience, people can take part in conversations, rituals, or negotiations without explicitly knowing or subscribing to an ontology. All that is needed is a commitment to follow the discursive forms and norms. Transformations of experience occur through the exercise of imaginative capacities, the performative functions of language that conjures things into being by saying, and the responses of others who agree to follow the corresponding social script.

The multiple levels or domains engaged at each site are linked through both material and discursive processes. Although the effects of violence may be seen or felt in distinctive ways at each level, mass violence affects all of these sites, disrupting the order of each level, as well as the coordination or coherence across levels. These realms of experience are embedded in local social practices and cultural systems of meaning. The importance of these systems is evident in ethnographic studies of reconciliation processes, which show the "contradictory logics" at work.[73] The grand narratives of reconciliation taken from religious myths and exemplars, like Archbishop Desmond Tutu's invocation of Christian forgiveness in the South African Truth and Reconciliation Commission (TRC),[74] meet the vagaries of human frailty on the ground. This can be understood both in terms of the complexities of human motivation, the lasting traces of violence in memory and emotion, the situated, place-based dynamics of identity and social positioning, and the dynamics of communities and larger social systems.

This is illustrated by the ethnographic work of Christopher Taylor, who described the dilemmas surrounding the use of village-level courts or *gacaca* in postgenocide Rwanda. The *gacaca*, originally used to adjudicate minor disputes, were pressed into service to deal with larger ruptures following the genocide. Many felt that the only way the culture of impunity could be surpassed would be through reprisals of sufficient magnitude to balance the past aggression. The *gacaca* were invoked to try to avoid such retributive escalation.

Taylor notes that some traditional forms of justice in Africa have adhered to what has been called restorative justice as a way to manage the desire for vengeance by focusing on compensating the wronged party rather than punishing the guilty. Restorative justice is an alternative to retributive justice that works to maintain reciprocity and social homeostasis. In the aftermath of violent ruptures, it can work to repair the political structures and relationships that weave the fabric of communal life. The *gacaca* involved a hybrid of retributive and restorative justice. It could sentence people convicted of serious crimes, but those who made full and open confessions of less serious transgressions could be required to compensate their victims, symbolically or otherwise.

In all of the *gacaca* sessions that Taylor observed in 2005, the accused and other witnesses obviously lied. It is no surprise that people deal with this volatile and dangerous situation by evasion and dissimulation. Yet, in his later observations of *gacaca* in 2009, Taylor found victims who stated that attending these hearings had helped them manage troubling symptoms of *guhahamuka*, feelings of tightness in the chest and shortness of breath associated with intense fear. In effect, the *gacaca* provided a site for in vivo exposure therapy for some survivors. Other survivors chose not to attend *gacaca* for precisely the same reason—to avoid reexperiencing unbearable memories. The *gacaca* also prompted migration to cities and emigration by those eager to avoid village justice. A community survey of Rwandans in 2006 found high levels of distress among *gacaca* witnesses and no evidence that levels of depression or PTSD were lower in communities where *gacaca* had operated for somewhat longer periods, casting doubt on the mental health benefits of trauma testimony in this setting.[75] Though opinions differ on the ethnic and political biases inherent in the process, by eliciting confessions and apologies, demanding restitution, and meting out punishments, the *gacaca* served to reassert a moral order. At the very least, conjoining restorative and retributive justice advanced a process of moral education: vengeance killing diminished, the death penalty was abolished, and a sense of belonging to a nonethnic nation was strengthened in some communities.

Beyond the local social ecology, the postconflict predicaments of survivors of mass violence reflect not just their preconflict positions and trajectories or the brute effects of violence, but also preexisting and persistent structural inequalities and injustices that have global origins.[76] The consequences of mass violence, then, must be understood in the context of the enduring forms of economic inequity and the influence of agencies and institutions that seek not only to maintain their power but also to capitalize on catastrophe through mobile capital and strategic maneuvering.[77]

## Historical Trauma and Reconciliation

The last century brought a terrible burden of catastrophes—so that we could say, with the philosopher Maurice Blanchot, that we were all living after the disaster—but for many the disaster is ongoing with war, oppression, and the onrushing catastrophe of climate change.[78] Past and present are intertwined and historical memory kindles new conflagrations. What captures the backward gaze of Benjamin's angel of history, invoked in the passage quoted at the start of this chapter, is not nostalgia for a past Eden, celebration of a heroic past, or a romantic rebellion against the progress of modernity, but absolute horror at the growing pile of human debris left behind. The angel is an otherworldly being, a messenger from beyond, but also an embodiment of our longing for redemption. While the storm from Paradise pushes us forward, compassion would have us turn back, standing against the wind, to retrieve, remember, and restore what has been lost.

Witnessing, remembering, and recounting the history and experience of mass violence depend on the dynamics of memory itself, which, as we have discussed, includes embodied, psychological, and social processes. Indeed, there are many kinds of memory reflecting the diverse systems in brain, body, and society that are marked, changed, transformed, or even created by events and that can be said to hold traces, records or representations. Despite this rich and varied archive, memory is often fragmentary, unstable, and incomplete. Narrative accounts are always reconstructions and undergo smoothing and restructuring to fit narrative templates. Traumatic memories do persist and some of this is due to the indelibility of fear conditioning—ensuring that once burned twice shy—but there are other mechanisms that work to keep trauma memories alive.[79] The obdurate, persistent parts of traumatic memory have multiple roots: physical scars that inscribe history on the body in ways that are, at once, indexical, metonymic, and metaphorical; classical conditioning that results in automatic or reflexive responses that may be hard to extinguish; autobiographical narratives that sustain identity and self-presentation; social norms and institutions that govern collective acts of remembering; moral commitments that we struggle to honor and uphold; and myths and ideologies that set the boundaries of what we defend as sacred and inviolable.

Remembering, therefore, involves not only the neurobiology of memory but also the dynamics of family and community, individual and collective constructions of identity, the geography of memorial landscapes, and the political uses of events. Collective memory is a function not just of the witness and the storyteller but of the audiences that participate in the memory's performance and transmission. These audiences (real or imagined, present in the flesh or virtual) are central to the moral significance of remembering. Forgiving and forgetting are regulated by and sustain specific moral regimes where they may be the object of struggle and contestation.

The recent effort in Canada to address the history of oppression of Indigenous Peoples illustrates this moral struggle. From 1869 to the 1980s, the Canadian government mandated a system of residential schools for Indigenous children, run by the churches, with the express purpose of forced assimilation.[80] About 150,000 children went through these schools, where, in addition to harsh suppression of their language, cultural and spiritual traditions, and painful separations from their families, many experienced physical and sexual abuse. On June 11, 2008, the prime minister of Canada stood in the House of Commons to make a formal statement of apology to former students of the Indian Residential Schools. He faced the leaders of Indigenous nations and others who stood in the gallery and there were crowds gathered on Parliament Hill for this event. The media carried stories of Residential School experiences. With the apology came the announcement of further efforts at restorative justice: compensation payments for Residential School survivors and a TRC.[81]

A cynical observer might see all of this as the government's attempt to contain the threat represented by the many lawsuits pending over the harm caused by the Residential Schools. Clearly, the government wanted a resolution in order to "turn the page." However, at a societal level, the act of apology provided basic recognition that raised the possibility for a new relationship. The testimony collected through the TRC will find its way into history books, museums and other places where the work of collective memory and commemoration can continue. Even the initial recognition had immediate effects that went beyond political rhetoric. At a meeting of our research network for Indigenous mental health research soon after the official apology, an Indigenous scholar told the story of returning to her rural community and encountering nuns from a nearby institution that had previously evaded or denied the history of the Indian Residential Schools, who now came to her in tears with personal apologies, ready for a new kind of conversation.

Yet newspapers that day also carried a photograph of residential school survivor Geronimo Henry's clenched fist, tattooed with "M R.S. #48 survivor" and quoted his comment that this was "just a bunch of words"—too little and too late to help the many whose lives were destroyed.[82] Those who insist on remembering the violence or who cannot escape it play a crucial role in our moral economy. They bear the burden of historical memory that can spur others to continue to strive for justice. The labor of memory is essential to building a just society. Remembering works against the "institutionalized forgetfulness" or collective amnesia welcomed, or deliberately engineered, by those in power. Acts of commemoration are essential to recognize and learn from the suffering of the other. The challenge is how to do this without rewounding and igniting a cycle of violence driven by the desire for retribution.

TRCs can be ritualized performances that record suffering and assert lofty values without engaging the lived experience of suffering and the dilemmas of postconflict coexistence. To understand paths to reconciliation, we need to look more locally at how people actually manage the day-to-day encounters, the upwellings of grief and anger, and the paroxysms of mistrust and paranoid fear that are part of the legacy of mass violence. An apology is a step toward a new sort of relationship and when it concerns collective violence, toward a new relationship between communities. Forms of expiation and restitution must follow. Forgiveness may be yet another step in this process, but it does not turn the page. It is simply another chapter in an unfolding story in which each participant reshapes the other's narrative.

For Indigenous Peoples in the Americas, the concepts of historical trauma, loss and grief have become popular ways to understand the origins of contemporary forms of social suffering.[83] Historical trauma is a way of configuring cultural memory, linking the story of each individual to the collective wounds of a people. The narrative of historical trauma situates individual and collective suffering in social and historical context. It serves to reduce individual blame and directs attention to source of injustices in social and political events. In so doing, it organizes and motivates action to redress past wrongs. However, by framing individuals as victims, it may reinforce a sense of being damaged and create feelings of fragility and entitlement. Linking the consequences of this historical violence to current psychiatric illness (e.g., "Residential School Syndrome") is a way to lend immediacy to arguments for restitution but risks obscuring individuals' predicaments with larger political agendas and deflecting attention from ongoing structural violence and inequities.[84]

Understanding the structure and limits of trauma narratives is important in both political and psychotherapeutic contexts. Recounting history is essential for accountability. The practice of *testimonio* developed in Chile to aid political prisoners who were survivors of organized violence and torture suggests the essential political and human rights work of telling the story of atrocities can have a therapeutic effect as well.[85] The therapist's act of bearing witness provides a social context that allows the story to cohere both because of the effect of receiving another's empathic attention and because it is a step toward a broader solidarity grounded in the acknowledgment of history.

For trauma stories to function as personal and collective history, there must be public places for them to be told, acknowledged, and retold. The political recognition of collective identity and history can help create this place for individuals to tell their stories. Individuals' stories, in turn, can serve as testimony to ground collective history and call for further moral and political response. Countervailing political forces can make certain stories hard to imagine and tell to others. Despite the difficulty of understanding and articulating the experience of mass violence, survivors continue to wrestle with the angels of history. In standing with them, we hope to regain some essential human truth and sustainable community.

## Conclusion

Trauma narratives are rhetorical forms that emerge from the effort to bridge or anneal sundered parts of the self and the social world. Traumatic memories are imaginatively reconstructed along narrative lines guided by bodily experience and cultural models of memory and self. This chapter has contrasted two types of trauma narrative: that of the Holocaust survivor whose suffering springs from ineradicable memories and the victim of childhood abuse who suffers from amnesia and struggles to regain contested memory to reclaim and rebuild an unsettled self. Although these and other trauma narratives are often conflated, there are theoretical and empirical grounds for them at the level of the social and cultural shaping of landscapes of memory. These landscapes provide spaces and place that allow for recollection, recognition, and the solidarity that comes from bearing witness to each other's lives.

When that recognition fails, survivors may experience forms of suffering that reflect the lack of solidarity with others. The social world can fail to bear witness for many reasons. Even reparative accounts of the terrible things that happen to people (violations, traumas, losses) may be warded off because of their capacity to create vicarious fear and pain and because they constitute a threat to current social and political arrangements. Psychotherapy aims to help individuals get unstuck by bearing witness to their suffering. To be most effective it must also support their efforts to be heard beyond the consulting room, in a community or local world.[86]

Contemporary social movements empowering "trauma victims" are part of this process—they enable recollection by providing therapist and client with a shared belief system and expectations, and a context in which the work of remembering can occur. The social movement creates and validates narrative forms through self-help groups, media presentations, and shifts in public attitudes and juridical practices. Of course, the reconstruction of memory in terms of victimhood may alienate families and communities, oversimplify problems with complex origins, and, ultimately, disempower those it aims to help by institutionalizing the position of victim. The alternate metaphor of survivor recognizes that the experience of trauma presents a possibility for renewal and moral authority as a bearer of personal and historical memory.

The injunction "never forget" made with regard to the Holocaust points to the danger that even so extreme a rupture of experience can be forgotten, suppressed or mythologized until unrecognizable.[87] The moral order requires memory—and memory, in turn, demands coherent narrative forms. Martin Amis's novel *Time's Arrow* is a striking illustration of the links between narrative, memory, and morality.[88] The entire novel is written from the point of view of an unnamed consciousness inhabiting the body of a doctor moving backward in time from the moment of his death toward his birth. As the story unfolds, we see this strange reversal begin to undo the self-willed amnesia by which he has lived his life: emigrating, changing his name, and forging a new identity, all to hide from his terrible past as a Nazi doctor. Eventually he is forced to confront his past, returning to the crematorium where he consigned the disabled to death. Flakes of ash and curls of smoke coalesce and spiral downward into the smokestack of the crematorium to settle and thicken, reconstituting bodies which are pulled from the ovens like loaves of bread. Entropy is reversed, chaos stuffed back into its box. But this moment of restoration is fleeting, for time continues to move relentlessly backward carrying the Nazi doctor toward the undoing of his own birth and conception. Amis creates a counterclock world that is inhuman and absurd. The novel is a form of sadistic revenge exacted on the Nazi doctor, forced to live his life in a grotesque devolution toward nothingness. Time reversal turns moral choice into inevitability, creating a world where moral action is impossible.

Amis's book drives home the impossibility of moral life under circumstances where history is denied. The moral function of memory is to compel us to confront what we—and all around us—wish to leave behind. This depends on the constraints of social and cultural worlds to provide narrative forms, places, and times where the self can be narrated. This process of narration binds past, present, and future in an arc that makes sense of our history and aspirations. In the next chapter, we continue our discussion of trauma, focusing on the temporal ordering and time-binding effects of narrative.

CHAPTER 7

# *The Texture of Time*

Time is a fluid medium for the culture of metaphors.

– Vladimir Nabokov[1]

Time and its grief are a patience burning in the depth of the night,
where every word is a cold star, the sun of its being yet to come.

– Juan Gelman[2]

## Introduction

Trauma and its legacy through time raise profound questions about the relationship of narrative and self. Torture, state-organized violence, and genocide tear apart the fabric of consensual reality. This extends beyond the social world. Survivors may report a sense of altered temporality, alienation, and self-estrangement that renders strange the tacit and taken-for-granted dimensions of experience. Even witnesses at many removes from the scene of violence may experience vicarious pain and confusion that draw them into moments of frozen time. This kind of disruptive experience can occur through loss and dislocation, as well as through the experience or threat of physical violence. Forced migration that fragments families, leaving loved ones in peril, and propels the migrant toward an uncertain future also constitutes a profound challenge to the integrity of self, the solidarity of community, and hope for a viable future.

While the predicament of forced migration poses many unique challenges, it also captures something essential about the human condition. The refugee's efforts to articulate and maintain a stable and socially effective sense of self and identity, despite the loss of home and the encounter with radically unfamiliar and improvised environments, reveals the extent to which the self is an ongoing achievement that depends on active interaction with others. The interaction continues throughout life through participation in a local niche and larger networks or community. This embedding in a local world is never seamless; there are always tensions between imagination and reality, desire and possibility, that remind us of the contingent nature of belonging. Our sense of being at home, rooted in a familiar place, or moving through a landscape filled with reminders of personal biography and collective history is always in tension with its counterstory: the experience of being different, alienated, cast out, lost in a world that is unknown, and facing unpredictable challenges and demands. This state of exile recurs in myths of heroic voyages and transformation, but also occurs in more ordinary form in ordinary developmental trajectories that take us beyond our natal home, neighborhood, and community into a larger world in which our status may be uncertain. The identities we enact in our local social niches must be translated into some more universal currency to allow us this mobility, just as unfamiliar environments must be assimilated into the known, as we master new skills of self-fashioning and self-presentation. In this light, the experience of the refugee is paradigmatic of the "bare human," stripped of social roles, uniforms, and insignia, forced to explore, navigate, and domesticate an unfamiliar, even hostile world, in order to remake a sense of home and community.

In this chapter, I explore some ways in which the experience of refugees and of survivors of mass violence that has destroyed whole communities reveals the dynamics of self-constitution. The bridge between these realms of the social and the psychological is the narrative construction of the self. Narrative serves to organize the self as subject and agent, and to locate the self in space and time. There is a constant circulation between the narrative fashioning of the self, as a social act or interaction, and the experience of interiority. This circulation occurs on many different timescales: on the developmental scale of a lifetime, in the emotional ebb and flow of significant life events, and in the fine-grained structure of moments of experience. These different timescales each contribute to the texture of experience. The analysis of metaphor can help us to understand how the social world enters into and mediates the immediate. The temporal dimensions of narrative are crucial for this—not only to construct and consolidate our senses of memory and identity and of future possibility, but also for the quality of moment-to-moment experience.

## Narrative and the Self through Time

Much work in cognitive psychology, anthropology, and philosophy shows the importance of narrative for controlling the direction of cognition, reframing experience, and constructing an autobiographical self with a sense of personal and historical continuity through time.[3] The narrative self is constituted in and through stories told to oneself in private soliloquy and to others in intimate dialogue, everyday negotiation, and public performance. Narratives serve cognition and communication. Developmental psychology suggests that the social–communicative function is primary and that we learn to narrate our experience in relationship to others.[4] Self-narratives, then, must be understood as dialogical and discursive practices situated in particular social contexts or forms of life. These modes of narration are internalized as self-talk and become part of our capacity for deliberation and reflection.[5]

Narratives of the self have both private and public functions. They order the inner world of the self, creating a sense of coherence and point of view from which to describe and think about the world. They locate the person in place and time along a life trajectory and in relation to family, community, and larger social institutions. Narratives of the self also serve rhetorical purposes—providing us with a story or biography that constitutes our social personhood as something meaningful to and valued by others. Drawing from cultural models, this biography takes the form of a myth of origins and salient episodes of personal transformation, strung along a temporal trajectory, structured by causal theories that invoke culturally meaningful agencies and explanations.[6] This biography is unfinished and anticipates future chapters; biographical narratives are subjunctive and can create self-continuity and engender hope or despair based on the projection of the arc of the self into the future.

Narratives of the self are constrained by cultural ideologies that provide templates, prototypes, and meta-narratives of what it is to be a person and how the self should function.[7] Everyday moral judgments are conditioned by these cultural meta-narratives. In Euro-American folk psychology, we can contrast two such meta-narratives or views of the self. What we might call the *adamantine self* involves a view of the self as a solid and enduring over time and circumstance. In the United States, this takes the form of the *rugged individual* characterized by independence, autonomy, self-definition, self-determination, and self-control.[8] An alternate view, which we can call *relational, dialogical*, or *transactional*, sees the self as constituted by relationships with others and characterized by interdependence, heteronomy, multivocality, and responsiveness to context, including especially responsibilities and obligations to others.[9] This relational view is commonly attributed to people in "non-Western" societies but coexists with more individualistic notions in the West as well.[10] Versions of these two views of the self are at play in everyday thinking about life trajectories, and shape how we view people who have suffered wrenching disruptions and transformations of their worlds through violence, dislocation, and loss.

Clinical psychology and psychiatry, though, are largely based on an individualistic concept of the self that assumes that there is some inviolable essence to the person, a monological self, constant over time, that may be hidden, silenced, or suppressed by others, or more subtly, by the efforts of that same self to conform to some oppressive image or ideal. Psychotherapy, then, provides a protected space for patients to find and liberate their true or authentic self and give it voice and presence in the social world.[11]

Although the adamantine self fits the Western cultural ideal of rugged individualism, it is something of a fiction. Individuals are not the sole authors of their stories and do not (usually *cannot*) hew close to a self-prescribed version of an ideal self. Close scrutiny of everyday self-narratives reveals their improvised, stitched-together, and often tattered state, with many gaps, inconsistencies, and contradictions that are only partially covered over by formulaic accounts or post hoc rationalizations. High levels of coherence in self-narratives are rarely achieved outside of the deliberate process of constructing a formal autobiography or else, ironically, among people who are content to replace the complexity of their own biography with a generic version that fits the norms of a master narrative.

In practice, self-narratives are mutable and shift as they are told and retold in different settings. Indeed, this is part of their usefulness—they are not simply accounts of past experiences and events that can be accessed when needed to respond to current exigencies, but serve as frameworks for thinking about the trajectory of the self through time. As such, self-narratives are frequently rewritten in subtle ways to reduce dissonance and to conform to our current situations, values, and commitments and enable us to move toward future goals. Major life events may lead us to rewrite whole chapters of our autobiography to justify a particular course of action or rationalize outcomes that were unforeseen. Memories, in turn, are shaped by these narratives, so that potential ruptures can be integrated into a meaningful story.

From early childhood, we learn to narrate our experience in particular ways.[12] This narrative practice reflects local cultural theories of self and personhood. Cultural ideologies, values, and concepts of personhood guide the social practices of narrating the self as a monological and enduring whole or as a flexible, situational responsive being, located at the intersection of multiple relationships. The implications of these different modes of self-narration are illustrated by the experience of refugees, who face violence, loss, and the challenge of negotiating a new identity in the places where they find asylum. While trauma seems like the most obdurate of experiences, as discussed in Chapter 6, it is shaped by the contexts of retelling and the way the self and its narratives are conceived and received by others. The consequences of violence and loss, therefore, cannot be appreciated without some understanding of the politics of trauma and the ongoing predicament of those living with the many ambiguities and contradictions of forced migration.

## The Refugee's Predicament

Refugee status is granted to people who have fled desperate situations involving persecution, violence, and threats to life. Physical and psychological trauma are thus at the center of the legal definition of the category of refugee and psychiatry often plays a legitimating role by documenting the impact of violence. Although much of the focus in psychiatry has been on symptoms that can be directly attributed to exposure to violence, the subsequent life contexts of survivors are key determinants of the quality and course of their illness experience. A wealth of epidemiological and ethnographic research documents the impact on refugee health and well-being of the migration journey itself, which is often prolonged and uncertain, and for those who escape interminable internment in refugee camps, the eventual context of resettlement.

This is illustrated by the work of anthropologist Nadia El-Shaarawi, who explored the predicament of Iraqi refugees in Egypt.[13] They linked their health and well-being not so much to traumatic experiences in Iraq but to the difficulties of life in Egypt and, especially, to uncertainties and anxieties about their future. The symptom of tiredness ("*ta'abana*") emerged in many of her interviews and was described as a deep and overwhelming sense of physical exhaustion that was attributed to stressful life circumstances. Other common symptoms included a mix of anxiety and depression, which were traced to experiences of torture and other violence endured before fleeing Iraq and to their ongoing predicament as exiles in Egypt. They called this complex condition "*hala nufsia*," a "psychological situation," reflecting the centrality of loss, fear, and demoralization in their lives, but also, perhaps, their sense of being suspended in time because of the difficulty of moving forward with life projects.

Those who survive mass violence may face internal displacement or forced migration. The ability to find safe haven and embark on future-oriented projects is essential for the well-being of survivors. In a longitudinal study of

Southeast Asian refugees to Canada, the social psychiatrist Morton Beiser and colleagues found that time orientation was an important predictor of well-being.[14] Those who were forward looking, focused on building a new life and on the future, had better mental health on follow-up ten years after their resettlement in Canada. In contrast, those who were preoccupied with the past, with a pervasive sense of nostalgia and longing for what they had lost, were more likely to suffer from depression over time.

Refugees' relationship to time is shaped by their status after migration as well as by how they view the whole trajectory of displacement and relocation. The distinction between voluntary and forced migration is often blurred. People may migrate for multiple reasons, with varying degrees of pressure, and this may change along their trajectory. Maintaining a sense of agency, of having made a deliberate choice to move, and investing in a future project centered on self, family, or children can mitigate the sense of dislocation and loss. The different stances individuals take toward migration affect their subsequent mental health; but these stances are determined as much by the reception in the receiving society as they are by any characteristics of the individual.[15]

The psychologist Gadi BenEzer provides an illuminating account of some of these dynamics in his ethnographic study of the migration of Ethiopian Jews to Israel.[16] The community kept its history and traditions alive for millennia in exile. Prophecies told of an eventual return to Yerussalem. From 1977 to 1985, over 20,000 people attempted to make their way on foot from Ethiopia to Israel. About one in five lost their life on the journey. In a late phase, the secret "Operation Moses" by the Israeli military airlifted 7,000 Jews who had made it to Sudan. While the journey involved great violence and the loss of thousands of lives, it was seen within the migrating community as the fulfillment of a centuries-old prophecy of return. Israeli society, in contrast, framed the migration as the rescue of a downtrodden people and minimized or ignored the agency of the migrants and their community. The story of exiles finally returning home mirrored the larger narrative of the return of diasporic Jews that validated the state.[17] Reestablished in Israel, the newcomers faced the challenge of integration into a society whose institutional norms and practices have been shaped by a European Jewish elite, with significant institutional racism directed toward them.[18]

The study of refugee experience reveals the importance of temporality on multiple timescales: the long durée of human migration, historical narratives of exile and the promise of return, the months or years of displacement, and the daily challenge of making sense of life with an uncertain future. For those urgently seeking asylum, uncertainty and delays in the refugee status determination process are major causes of suffering.[19] If asylum is granted, they may come to see themselves as immigrants building a new life as part of growing diasporic communities. But if longing for what they have lost persists, they may come to see themselves as exiles, perennial strangers in a strange land. Even when it is possible to forge a new life, if the place of exile is viewed only as a temporary waystation, then life may be lived in a provisional way, waiting for the time of return. When politics, war, genocide, or other forms of catastrophe make return impossible, those who have no possibility of permanent residence and citizenship or of return may be left feeling they belong nowhere. The liminal states of waiting and unbelonging may contribute to suffering because they suspend life projects that could otherwise be absorbing and that could provide some answer to the ruptures in identity and losses resulting from past violence, migration, and resettlement. Here again, temporality is central to the process of adaptation. Understanding how stories, metaphors, and embodiment shape the experience of time is crucial to making sense of the impact of the ruptures of trauma and forced migration and the ways they can be bridged or healed.

## Time's Texture or Tincture

My title for this chapter is borrowed from *Ada*, one of the most sensual of Vladimir Nabokov's novels, which is at root a novel of longing for a lost place and time, set in a fictional world that blends the Russia of his childhood with the United States of his adult life in exile. In *Ada*, the novel's hero, the psychiatrist–metaphysician Van Veen, produces a treatise, *The Texture of Time*, setting the sensuality of lived time against the strictures of clock time:

> I delight sensually in Time, in its stuff and spread, in the fall of its folds, in the very impalpability of its grayish gauze, in the coolness of its continuum. I wish to do something about it; to indulge in a simulacrum of possession. I am aware that all who have tried to reach the charmed castle have got lost in obscurity or have bogged down in Space. I am also aware that Time is a fluid medium for the culture of metaphors.[20]

Texture implies a tactile quality achieved by metaphor or synesthesia in the imaginative evocation of the sensual qualities of the world.[21] Through aesthetic absorption, Van Veen tries to step outside the serial order of time, to regain what has been lost through accident and entropic decay:

> The Past, then, is a constant accumulation of images. It can be easily contemplated and listened to, tested and tasted at random, so that it ceases to mean the orderly alternation of linked events that it does in the large theoretical sense. It is now a generous chaos out of which the genius of total recall can pick anything he pleases . . .[22]

Here, the serial order of narrative order gives way to the lyric exploration of imagery through the eidetic memory of "total recall."

Nabokov seems to be the very opposite of the survivor of trauma in his freedom to savor memory, drawing out each image and recollection to enlarge and sustain its pleasure. His goal is to obliterate time and space through the simultaneity of imagery; throughout *Ada*, he plays with parallels and permutations, synesthetic condensations, and other devices, so that time is folded in on itself to bring distant moments together.[23] This alteration in temporal experience happens to the reader subliminally through the resonance in imagination of moments of vivid sensation imbued with meaning by their place in the larger tapestry of the text. The collapse of time and space in sensual memory had an added metaphysical meaning for Nabokov, who hoped that such recollection and reexperiencing could reveal traces of others lost to us, and so allow us to transcend our mortality.[24]

But Nabokov was not a flaneur, an idle loiterer in the corridors or arcades of time; despite his privileged background, something more urgent and serious is at play in his novels, for it is the relentless time of mortality, loss, and decay that he is trying to resist more than any punch-clock of bureaucratic order. Nabokov's autobiographical memoir, *Speak, Memory*, begins with an image from childhood of his father being thrown into the air on a makeshift trampoline by the peasants of his estate, who were celebrating his help and support to their families; in a cinematic dissolve, this image transforms into one of his father lying in a coffin, dead in midlife from an assassin's errant bullet.[25] Just where we meet literature at its most sensual, we find memories of traumatic experience amid or underneath the wordplay, revealing the author's passion and purpose.

While literary texts create aesthetic effects through deliberate play with time, the unfolding of time in personal narratives is rarely so conscious or contrived. Where then does it come from? Not from the authorial self, cloistered in her study, but from embodied experience and the flow of social interaction: inhabiting a cultural world, participating in daily routines and cultural practices, traversing a landscape occupied by others and by material and institutional facts—a landscape that is both resolutely "other" and familiar because it is constructed by selves in motion in a world cross-cut by the high tension wires of power and politics.

## Memory and Temporality

Nabokov's ability to slow time to a stop and dwell within a moment as a form of sensual pleasure and aesthetic practice is central to poiesis, but it comes unbidden to those who suffer from grievous loss or riveting memories of horror. This is nowhere more evident than in the testimonies of Holocaust survivors. Reflecting on the presence of temporal dislocations in Holocaust narratives, Langer contrasts the *chronological time* of history or personal biography, which moves along a sequence of events, with the *durational time* of experience, in which one dwells within a moment or a memory as though it were a bubble, sealed off from the progression of time in the social world.[26] The more intense and absorbing an experience, the more time closes in on itself so that duration becomes more salient than progression.[27]

In his analysis of Holocaust testimonies, Langer finds different forms of recollection—that he names *deep memory*, *anguished memory*, *humiliated memory*, *tainted memory*, and *unheroic memory*—are all associated with durational experience of time. The names of these forms of memory point to sociomoral predicaments. Each form is distinctive in that it involves some intense emotion that disrupts or violates the psychological and social conditions for "ordinary" memory, which is expected to be evoked and subside punctually in response to the needs of the moment. In the forced recollection of trauma, pain, and loss, the sufferer is forced to dwell within a memory whose duration is itself a source of suffering.

For Holocaust survivors, the link between trauma, emotion, and the experience of durational time was forged in the extraordinary experience of the camps. Beyond the limit of emotional intensity, the routinized horror of the camps caused a sort of psychic numbing or anesthesia in which impressions were dulled, attention narrowed, and consciousness limited, so that, in psychiatrist–survivor Leo Eitinger's words:

> the area of interest . . . reduced to primitive self preservation, the mere battle for existence, represented by a bowl of soup and a crust of bread. Neither the outer world, the course of the war, nor the fate of others appeared to have meaning in the daily life of the prisoners. Everything seemed unreal, as in a nightmare. The reality confronting the individual after the liberation was therefore very painful, and apart from the somatically improved situation, it was almost worse than the dream from which they had just awakened. They became suddenly aware of the full weight of their isolation, the lack of purpose and meaning in their life.[28]

These conditions of extremity left their impress on the dynamics of memory and temporal experience, amplifying and distorting the ordinary experience of duration. When the recollection of a painful experience persists, drawn out not by intentional lingering but by the eruption of strong emotion, the flow of time may be arrested. Langer insists that we recognize and treat this collapse or involution of the usual trajectory of time not as a deliberate strategy but as the lasting trace of violence: inevitable, inescapable, and tragic in its arc, horrific in its reliving.

The ability to become deeply absorbed in the moment and experience the slowing down of time involves embodied processes of attention. In the experience of durational time described by Langer, memory and bodily experience form a closed loop, so that the person may be cut off from the world in a kind of dissociative state for a timeless moment. When the focus of attention is on more positive memories or experiences in the world, we may experience duration as rapid and enjoyable—associated with aesthetic pleasure or a sense of flow.[29] Ordinarily, durational time is inscribed within chronological time—all we begin with are moments of experience, no matter how miserable or delicious, but these are given order and additional meaning through narrative, arranged in a sequence like beads on a string or situated along a trajectory in a higher dimensional plot. In the extremities of agony or ecstasy, though, durational time breaks free of the larger order of chronology that links us to the resources of the past and the possibilities of the future.

Trauma theorists have argued that this extremity of experience results in a unique form of memory, but as suggested in Chapter 6, the distinctive quality of remembering in Holocaust narratives and other accounts of extreme violence can also be understood as a consequence of the absence of ordinary contexts of renarration so that memories are relived in the absence of dialogue or exchange with others. The interlocutors whose presence would introduce a more ordinary sense of time, turn away in fear, or are avoided by the survivor in an effort to protect them from the corrosive effects of recollections. The fragmentation of narrative then comes not only from the narrow focus of attention and constriction of time in the traumatic moment, or from ongoing efforts to ward off painful affect, but also from the absence of others in the social world, able and willing to help to weave memory and experience into a coherent story.

In the case of the death camps, the regime of violence went far beyond any concept of discrete traumatic events to constitute a machine for the destruction of identity and consciousness. The far limit of this dismemberment and dissolution was inhabited by the *Muselmann*, the living dead of the camps whose experience of time was slowed to nothing.[30]

The analogy that comes to mind is of the death of a star, collapsing in on itself, to result in a black hole from which no light can be emitted.[31]

Langer's approach to the forms of traumatic memory reifies them as emotional states or predicaments, which the survivor is condemned to experience. The claim that a form of temporal experience is forced on survivors by the dynamics of trauma challenges the logic of the adamantine self, which would have us imagine a perduring center of self-direction that insures we are always free to choose what to remember and forget or at least to choose our attitude toward memories.[32] In ordinary experience, of course, we can easily become lost in reveries, thoughts, or feelings evoked accidentally and against our best intentions, even though such absorption can also occur in response to conscious effort. And within the broad domain of what is considered "accident," we recognize certain motivated but unconscious acts that serve personal needs and agendas. This suggests that we have varying degrees of choice about whether and how to dwell on terrible memories.

In her work on Holocaust trauma, Carol Kidron approaches trauma memory as an embodied experience that is prereflexive and often unwilled and undesired.[33] For example, she describes one mother's Proustian moment at the kitchen sink, smelling potato peelings, placing them in her mouth, and being catapulted back to a mode of existence in which potato peels were the only sustenance. When her daughter asks what she is eating, the mother says, "This is what we have to eat." The Holocaust survivor, like Billy Pilgrim in Kurt Vonnegut's *Slaughterhouse-Five*, has come unstuck in time.[34] This temporal dislocation is part of the depersonalization and derealization that can occur during or after traumatic experience. When it recurs during later recollection such dislocation may last not just for the moment that a memory is evoked by particular cues (peeling potatoes at the sink), but can take the form of a persistent mood, even without episodic content. Kidron speaks of the "dark cloud" conveying the memory of the Shoah. This vague but powerful sense of the presence of memory can occur in parallel with moments of clear recollection and formal acts of remembrance in Jewish ritual life, as when participants in the Passover Seder are told to remember the Exodus from Egypt as though "it happened to you," inscribing cultural memory in personal identity.[35] The extent to which this ritual retelling of a story is experienced as in the moment—as affirmation of collective identity, imaginative identification, or mythopoetic reverie—reflects both the expectations that come with the performance of myth and the individual's own desire and capacity for aesthetic absorption.[36]

Just as ceremony can prescribe recollection as part of the ritual enactment of mythic time, other forms of remembering take their temporality from specific social cues and contexts. Revisiting a childhood place or even looking at an album of photographs invites reminiscences about past times that may become present when others who shared that history fall back into old modes of interaction. Shifts in temporal experience need not be explicitly prescribed—they can arise from embodied and attentional processes with their own temporality. For example, while sitting outside their psychotherapists' office, waiting for a regularly scheduled session, patients may experience a slowing down of the ordinary experience of time as their thoughts return to the conversation of previous sessions.[37] During the session, they may recount memories as happening somewhere "over there," contained, and distant. Alternatively, they may evoke the place and time of past events and dwell within feelings "from the past" as if reliving them in the present. These modes of experiencing can make emotions accessible in ways that allow insight, but they also may intensify suffering and impede working through past events.

Temporality is central to the experience of pain and suffering. Many forms of pain can be endured if they have a clear purpose and end. Pain of indefinite duration is the most fearsome and subverts strategies for containment and survival. Pain framed by massive loss of social ties threatens the most fundamental structures of the self. But it is still possible to hold on to a virtual world in imagination, secreted within the most desperate circumstances.[38] This virtual world creates its own temporal structure and trajectories within its horizon. When this virtual world is torn apart, the self is finally dismembered by destroying the conditions necessary for imagination. This was the situation for the *Muselmänner*, whose obtundation likely reflected not only the neurological effects of prolonged starvation and illness but also the psychological effects of pervasive helplessness and the destruction of the social conditions of community and solidarity needed to maintain a sense of hope. For those who returned from this "limit experience," some lasting wound remains.

In his analysis of the testimonies in the Fortunoff Video Archives, Langer finds that the experience of durational time blocks survivors' efforts to move beyond recollection and heal their traumatic wounds:

> The notion that a Holocaust survivor—I suspect one might say this of any atrocity survivor—can generalize his or her personal suffering and move beyond the role of victim derives from an unfamiliarity with how durational time assails the memory of a witness. That is why I believe all attempts to investigate the effects of atrocity on a group or a community must begin

> with the narratives of individual victims, and especially with moments of durational time . . . which mock the very idea of traumas that can be healed.[39]

This temporal rupture and failure to heal, Langer argues, has marked the lives of many who have been held up as exemplars of the healing power of creative work; he cites the example of Primo Levi, who, despite a life of literary productivity and artistic success, succumbed to depression and suicide,[40] an end that Langer found presaged in Levi's writing. In his reflections on the Holocaust, Levi never claimed any heroism, triumph, or transcendence of the suffering of the death camps; instead, his writing revealed an irremediable split.

> Chronological time allowed Levi, through the chance of survival, to free himself from this paralysis and to rejoin the human community as a productive chemist and a successful writer. But durational time plunged him back into the chaos of his Auschwitz past, where even forty years after the event he was still exploring the meaning of shame and judgment, and that gray zone where man's vaunted moral self had lost its dignity and never found a way to reclaim it.[41]

In grappling with Holocaust memory, Levi insisted on staying with the murky gray zones of human compromise and collusion, the drastic trade-offs required to survive in situations of extremity.[42] The very fact of his testimony seemed to stand for the persistence of the adamantine self through the violent dismantling of identity and debasement of consciousness. But he insisted that there was nothing remarkable about being a survivor beyond the fact of existence, no mark of resilience, or resourcefulness that distinguished the drowned and the saved. Levi returned from a world of utter senselessness, a world where the person was reduced to states of minimal consciousness through the crushing regime of the camp or the forced march through winter where death began with shoes.[43] This submersion in senselessness left indelible scars: "It was reported that when Primo Levi was wheeled into the operating room for prostate surgery a few months before his death, he rolled up his sleeve and pointed to the number tattooed on his arm saying, 'That is my disease.'"[44] For Levi, the tattoo was a wound, which became a metaphor for the belatedness of his post-Holocaust existence. Nothing could erase the marks on his body; indeed, his tattoo was at once an affliction and an archival record of unspeakable violence.

Compare Levi's insistence about the writing on his body with the words of German–Swedish–Jewish poet Nelly Sachs, writing from her place of exile in Stockholm: "My metaphors are my wounds. Only through that is my work to be understood."[45] Here Sachs insists that language carries the wounds of the body. Together, Levi and Sachs describe a circle from body to metaphor and back: wound gives rise to story and story reopens wound. This is the temporal loop that Holocaust survivors may regularly revisit—and in which they can become caught. The self-sustaining properties of this loop justify a view of the survivor as suffering from an ineradicable wound that disrupts the flow of time.

## Embodiment and Temporal Experience

The body has many rhythms that contribute to our sense of time and ability to judge duration: neurophysiological processes that create sudden changes in experience in fractions of a second; heartbeat and respiration that cycle on the order of seconds; diurnal rhythms of sleep and wakefulness on the order of hours; monthly cycles of menstruation; yearly cycles related to length of day; and longer-term changes of growth and development. Awareness of these processes creates a sense of the passage of time on multiple scales.[46] Individuals who are more aware of their heartbeat, for example, can better judge intervals of seconds.[47] This awareness depends on how and where we direct our attention and on the cognitive resources devoted to marking time. Attention training, as in meditative practice, for example, can alter the sense of temporal duration.[48]

This bodily grounding of temporality can be modified by cognitive load. If we have much to do or think about, time seems to go by quickly; with little to do or tedium, time slows down. Socially configured temporalities and associated regimes of attention modify the ways we orient ourselves and the pace we expect. The ways we metaphorically conceptualize time also shape this embodied experience. As mentioned in Chapter 1, for English speakers, the structure and passage of time usually are framed in terms of spatial metaphors, with the future in front of us and the past trailing behind.[49] This metaphor seems to follow from the embodied experience of moving forward as we engage the world and carry out actions. For Mandarin Chinese speakers, however, time may be metaphorically thought of in terms of a vertical axis in which future events are up, while the past is down. These different spatial metaphors may influence the ways that people process temporal information.

Embodiment shapes not only present experience but also our sense of past and future. Remembering occurs in and through embodied processes of imagination and enactment, bringing the body into configurations that re-enact previous scenarios. The body also orients itself toward the proximate future in modes of attention and anticipation. This can be shaped by thoughts and feelings of apprehension, fear, hope, or pleasure directed to the immediate future. Narratives can extend our experience of time in long arcs that reach back far into the past and forward into the future, binding them together in a coherent and compelling story. The experience of periods of weeks, months, and years is mediated by narratives that build the arcs of personal history and autobiography. Beyond this scale of an individual's lifetime, historical memory allows us to think about the distant past and incorporate transgenerational or collective memories into our sense of embodied identity, self, and personhood.

## Enduring Duration: Pain, Loss, and Grief

Pain, loss, and grief impose their own temporality on experience, reflecting embodied processes, which narrative framing can moderate but not efface. Pain systems likely evolved as a mechanism to detect and remember danger and to promote withdrawal and avoidance to allow healing from injury or illness.[50] Pain organizes both the immediate and intermediate term response to injury. Initially, pain provokes reflexive pulling back or guarding of the affected part of the body and action to stop the inciting event; if persistent, pain slows us down, forcing us to leave the fray to recover. During the period of recovery, pain maintains the immobility needed for tissue repair. Throughout, pain binds memory to strong affect, ensuring that we learn to avoid whatever has caused us injury.

When pain persists, it becomes a problem in its own right, as it influences every aspect of bodily and emotional life, intruding on relationships, narrowing consciousness, and upending our usual hierarchy of values and activities. Once pain is planted in memory, it can exert effects even when not present, as something to anticipate, fear, and avoid. The suffering of pain is closely related to the apprehension, belief, or conviction that it will persist indefinitely—an experience of temporality that is partly given by pain itself (intrinsic to its phenomenology, in the sense that the experience of pain slows the flow of time) and partly a result of the meanings attached to the pain.

The experience and effects of pain then are both preverbal—built into conditioned bodily responses that make us grimace or flinch in anticipation—and mediated by language, connected through metaphor and narrative to larger social meanings. Through the organization of memory and multiple forms of learning, pain forges links between the immediate noxiousness of an event and the longer-term organization of behavioral repertoires and the patterns of self-description and interaction that comprise personal identity. Pain also contributes to the organization of the social world, which comes to be seen in terms of our history of injury and the potential for future suffering. Religious ritual and rites of initiation make deliberate use of pain to heighten the memory and meaning of events that mark changes or transitions in identity.[51]

The emotional distress associated with separation, loss, or rejection shares some of the same brain circuitry as bodily pain.[52] Describing such feelings as pain, then, may be based not on metaphor but sensory commonality. Grief, the emotional response to loss, involves both bodily aching and altered sense of self and of time.[53] Grieving, the working through of loss, involves processes of reappraisal, reorganizing, and rearranging one's thinking about self, identity, and the story of one's life.

Grief is not a punctual emotion but involves persistent and recurrent feelings of sadness and longing, along with a shifting mix of other emotions, including anger, fear, and other culturally distinctive sentiments related to particular social scenarios that are evoked by thoughts and memories of times together and apart.[54] Grieving involves a kind of preoccupation with loss and rumination that colors, overlays, or preempts everyday engagements. Along with the withdrawal and disengagement from everyday life, comes a slowing down, and thickening or viscosity of time. Writing of her experience after the death of her adult son, the philosopher–poet Denise Riley describes how time became pure, almost unbearable duration: "inhabiting the drift of time is a mutable perception; one which can stop, leaving you breathing but stranded, stock still."[55]

Although intense grief stops the flow of time, the process of grieving has its own temporal arc that serves adaptive functions, through a kind emotional "working through" that eventually allows the bereaved to reconnect and invest in other relationships. The work of mourning is a process of reappraisal and reorganization that involves reconfiguring one's identity, place, and projects. This is driven by both the difficult emotions and pragmatic consequences of the loss, but these depend, in turn, on larger cultural narratives of the meaning of different types of loss, their expected course, and outcome. The dependence of grieving on a larger narrative frame is evident in situations of ambiguous loss, like the kind experienced by the wives of soldiers missing in action, when uncertainty about the fate of their loved one stalls the process of grieving and blocks its resolution through adopting a new identity and reengaging in a future-oriented life plan.[56]

Grief occurs not just with loss of loved ones but with loss of body parts or changes in function, social roles, and place. Homesickness may be a kind of grief "in miniature" experienced even by those who choose to move to a new place.[57] The migrant must deal both with the emotional impact of separation from a familiar environment and network of attachments and the specific demands of learning to navigate a novel environment in which their identity is framed in a new way, and in which they face challenges related not only to loss of their usual relationships, but to the demands of a new identity, role, or niche. The changes in one's life situation affect time orientation, both because the loss of familiar cultural anchors and affordances increases cognitive load and because the new status, social position, and niche impose unfamiliar rhythms and routines.

People differ in the ways they are rooted to place and time through familiar roles and routines, and some people are accustomed to a high degree of flux. Cosmopolitans who define their identity in terms of mobility and carry key parts of their niche with them (e.g., laptop, cell phone, list of contacts) may have an easier time with the process of relocation, but this is also conditioned by a sense of transiency or temporariness that limits the extent to which they come to rely on local connections and affordances.[58] Diasporic communities living in exile or repeated migration may develop forms of portable community that confer some degree of protection against uprooting. The converse can be seen in the predicament of Indigenous Peoples who grieve the loss of land that defines their identities when it is radically altered by development or, increasingly, by climate change.[59]

Although the pain of losing loved ones is grounded in basic emotional processes of attachment and loss, the experience of grieving varies across cultures. Most cultures have formal mourning rituals and, along with that, expectations for how long it should take to work through a loss and become reengaged in everyday life—usually with an identity that is changed in some way that integrates the loss (e.g., becoming a widow or widower). Of course, this change in social status does not mean that the sense of loss disappears; grieving may be a long, even lifelong process, and many cues may reevoke the sense of loss and absence.[60] Grief has its own bodily dynamics that may not fit cultural expectations, creating tensions and contradictions. The normative prescriptions of culture may not fit the complexities of individuals' experience—though people may struggle valiantly to live up to cultural expectations and suffer added pain or shame when they fail.[61]

The relationship between the bodily given temporality of grieving and the culturally prescribed time course of mourning is mediated by processes

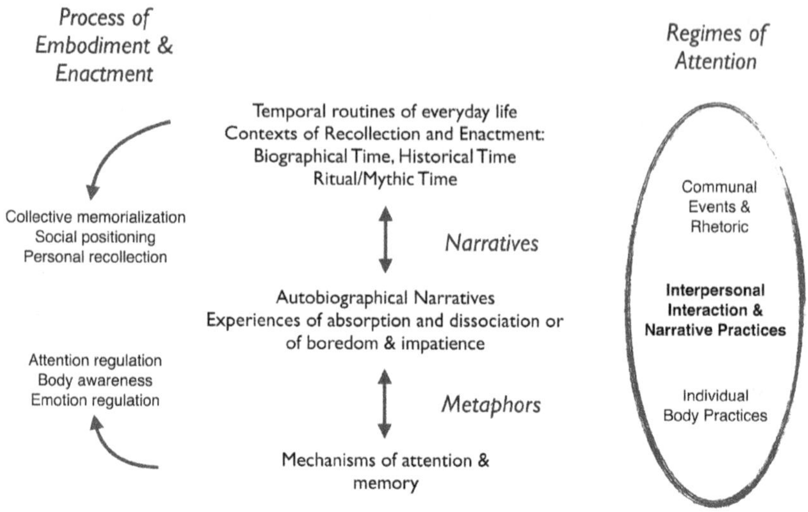


Figure 7.1 The metaphoric mediation of temporal experience
The experience of time has both embodied and narrative sources. The experience of duration is influenced by bodily processes that shape attention guided by cultural contexts and affordances. Narratives can bind longer stretches of time together in a causal sequence or other form. These narratives are part of collective commemorative practices, as well as autobiographical constructions of the self.

of embodiment and enactment. Metaphoric and narrative constructions of temporal experience can modulate the processes that subserve our experience of duration (Figure 7.1). The way we narrate loss to ourselves or others may cause aspects of grief to endure or subside. These effects of models and metaphors occur not only through direct reflections on time and temporality, but through the way we deploy our attention.[62] Becoming absorbed in the process of narration itself can provide distance or distraction from the interoceptive cues that mark the passage of time. Culturally prescribed ways of engaging with the predicament of loss can change the nature of the experience and its outcomes. Various forms of mourning rituals and grief therapy make deliberate use of metaphors to help the bereaved find sense and meaning in loss and reengage in their lives.[63]

## Memory and Mindfulness

Our experience of duration is constructed both within the moment and after the fact and, so, is dependent on memory. This extends to the experience of pain and other forms of suffering and affliction. Pain and memory are linked in multiple ways: pain evokes and cements memory, and memory, in turn, can reevoke pain or even generate new pain when the meaning of past events is revised. The temporal qualities of pain that lead to suffering then depend on many of the same social processes that govern remembering and forgetting. We tend to forget pains that had good outcomes and ruminate about pains that mark some moral violation or unaccepted loss. We may dwell on and prolong pains that allow us to hold on to a valued past. The social processes that underlie memory also may work to keep pain alive because it serves collective identity.

Our sense of duration is also tied to the ways in which we deploy attention. In states of deep absorption or reverie we may be unaware of the passage of time.[64] Attention in turn may be regulated by social actions and by explicit efforts to train the mind, for example, through meditative practice. I recall my own brief experience with Vipassana meditation at a weeklong retreat at the Insight Meditation Society in Barre, Massachusetts.[65] As I sat immobile for an hour, my knees began to ache terribly. Time seemed to be passing interminably slowly and I did not think I could sit still for another second. I had vivid images of jumping up and running from the meditation hall in disgrace. I had been instructed to keep coming back to simply watching my experience without judging. When my attention was drawn to the pain, I repeated to myself, "pain, pain, pain..." as the meditation teacher had suggested. Suddenly, my experience was radically transformed. The pain in my knees was still there—I could have described its sensory qualities in great detail, summoning many of the adjectives of the McGill Pain Questionnaire—but instead of crowding in on me, the pain fell back to become just a phenomenon I was watching. Sensation was separated from emotional response. A metaphorical space opened up between the observing "I" and the sensory object of pain. And with this space came a sense of distance or detachment from the pain so that it lost its "in your face" urgency, unbearable intensity, and harrying quality. There was no pressure or hurry to move, no concern that pain would go on building in intensity forever. In its place was a sense of timelessness and spaciousness.

This is not unlike the experience reported by many patients in hypnosis and even the effect of opiate analgesics like morphine. With hypnotic suggestion, it is possible to experience elements of the same experiences achieved through meditation. The clinical use of hypnosis for pain control, for example, allows people to experience themselves as separate from their pain, just watching it.[66] Hypnosis can modify the subjective experience of the passage of time and so prolong a pleasurable state of relaxation or allow us to remember a pain as fleeting and less consequential.[67]

The fundamental difference between hypnotic pain control and meditation is the meaning drawn from the experience. Hypnosis usually is presented as a technique devoid of larger moral meaning, though it is framed in terms of personal development within a system of values centered on self-direction, self-mastery, and self-control. From a Buddhist perspective, the aim of meditation is soteriological, becoming free from the endless cycle of birth, suffering, and death. The change in pain experience in response to meditation, then, is valued not simply as an instance of self-control but as a demonstration of the illusory nature of the self.[68] Arguably, these meanings are not intrinsic to the experience of meditation but derive from the larger context in which the practice occurs, which shapes both bodily experience and the way that it is interpreted.

Religion aims to help us transcend suffering or gives it transcendental meaning. This is achieved through specific practices (prayer, meditation, ritual acts of asceticism, purification, and devotion) oriented toward a realm of the eternal presented in religious canons, myths, and texts. There is a parallel between the timeless present of myth and the unending time of pain. Pain presents itself as a fundamentally moral and religious problem, not only because its urgency preempts our other agendas, but also because it calls for the supervenient presence sought after through contemplative practice and mystical experience.

## A Poetics of Survival

The image of dwelling within an experience of memory, grief, or pain—so that the flow of time slows or stops as one is caught in an endless loop—offers both a picture of a certain type of problem and points to its potential transformation. How can the experience of time and the process of recollection be altered to free someone from the suffering of arrested time or unbearable duration?

In trauma, the mutability of memory conferred by narrative may be challenged by the obduracy of trauma as wound or affliction. The limited power of narrative to transform trauma reflects the magnitude of the originary event. When survivors speak of guilt, rage, or despair, their emotions are understood to be only a shadow of the past; the scale and scope of their suffering, past and present, far exceeds what can be told in mere words.

> All such accounts are based on the attempt to give comprehensible, communicable form to memories that for survivors live on as the negation of comprehensible and communicable form. Set against those memories, all such accounts are attempts to "make a story" of what is "not a story."[69]

To struggle to give shape to one's suffering is still to experience or hope for human connection; however, as the extremity of the situation builds in survivors' accounts:

> narrative unfolding stops, and instead of a plot's trajectory through foreground and background, we hear a staccato of snapshot images, each present and surrounding. While this way of recounting is, like the story mode, also a mediating form, it is as though memories start to retell themselves at these times. Crowding in at a faster pace than the recounter can speak them . . .[70]

The image here is of narration breaking down because narrative is an insufficient container or organizer for traumatic memory which rushes in to disrupt any orderly temporal progression.[71] Narrative provides order both in its linear unfolding in speech or text and the trajectories of the story it tells. But narrative is not only a conveyor of structure, order, and holding; it can also create crevasses, ruptures, and deep wells of emptiness or nonbeing. Elie Wiesel and other survivors spoke of having died during the Holocaust yet continuing to live[72]: Charlotte Delbo described this experience of dying while alive as a recurrent event.

> The skin covering the memory of Auschwitz . . . is tough: Sometimes, however, it bursts, and gives back its contents. In a dream, the will is powerless. And in these dreams, there I see myself again, me, yes me, just as I know I was: scarcely able to stand . . . pierced with cold, filthy, gaunt, and the pain is so unbearable, so exactly the pain I suffered there, that I feel it again physically, I feel it again through my whole body, which becomes a block of pain, and I feel death seizing me, I feel myself die. Fortunately, in my anguish, I cry out. The cry awakens me, and I emerge from the nightmare, exhausted. It takes days for everything to return to normal, for memory to be "refilled" and for the skin of memory to mend itself. I become myself again, the one you know, who can speak to you of Auschwitz without showing any sign of distress or emotion.[73]

This experience of being lost in the past is part of posttrauma experience for many survivors.

> As contrary as it is to our usual logic and experience, this simultaneity of being and not-being should be understood literally. The copresence of ongoing death and ongoing life—without resolution or higher synthesis—is, for survivors, embodied reality.[74]

In the face of this breakdown of narrative coherence, the psychologist Henry Greenspan describes the therapeutic value of having Holocaust survivors tell their stories.[75] This recounting aims to break the silence that has overtaken survivors and that, in a way, has rendered them symptomatic. Psychotherapy provides a social context that allows the story to cohere both through the emotional holding of empathic attention and because it invokes the tacit dimension of shared (or public) history. Even fragments can be read as a story if a larger narrative context is supplied by an audience primed by history. Narration in public settings for archival or political purposes may have some of the same benefits but makes the essential process of emotion regulation more difficult. The perennial danger when stories are recounted for political purpose is that they become generic and the ongoing effort to make sense of one's life is subordinated to the social role of providing testimony, preserving historical memory, and advancing claims for justice and restitution.[76]

A public narrative context for survivors' experience was established over several decades as the history of the Holocaust was popularized through mass media.[77] However, there are fundamental disjunctions between the heroic and aestheticized views of the Holocaust in movies and literature and the experiences of survivors. Dramatic accounts of war and genocide can be framed in ways that make them less disruptive and the viewer retains a measure of control. The story occurs elsewhere and elsewhen and usually comes with its own comforting interpretation, partitioning of good and evil and resolution. So the viewer must inevitably fail to fully grasp the breach of trust and shattering of the human and cosmic orders that is central to survivors' experience. This failure of imagination marks all later attempts to meet survivors on a common ground and condemns them to face the persistent and defensive incredulity, unwillingness, or inability of others to bear witness.

The most pervasive damage to the self in the camps occurred from the lack of recognition and systematic negation of the individual's subjectivity, agency, and integrity with regard to their most profound ties—to self, family, and community, even to the idea of a comprehensible, if manifestly unjust, world. This violation may be revisited and compounded in the aftermath when others fail to grasp the dimensions of the catastrophe. Even violence that is not of genocidal proportions may be hard for others to comprehend. In a study of the cases rejected by the refugee tribunal that determines the fate of asylum seekers coming to Canada, cultural psychiatrist Cécile Rousseau and colleagues identified moments of incredulity and denial that reflected the inability of the tribunal members to imagine or accept a refugee claimants' account. Survivors of torture have described the disbelief they encountered when presenting their story to the Immigration and Refugee Board as more agonizing than the torture itself.[78]

The failure of imagination here is not only in apprehending the magnitude of violence, nor even recognizing foreign histories, geographies and ways of life, but fundamentally about the nature of the self and memory. The refugee tribunal appeals to a juridical view of truth and memory that is underwritten by the myth of the adamantine self. The self holds within it the record of all it has experienced, and the honest person recounts this consistently and completely. From the perspective of the relational self, however, memory is a communal construction that depends on the willingness of the audience to witness what the witness has to tell. As Richard Sennett argues, extending Maurice Halbwachs's analysis of collective memory:

> Remembering well requires reopening wounds in a particular way, one which people cannot do by themselves; remembering well requires a social structure in which people can address others across the boundaries of difference. This is the liberal hope for collective memory.[79]

This is the hope that is denied when empathy and imagination fail to recognize our shared humanity and extend community to receive the survivor of genocide or the person seeking refuge. To restore the self fractured by such fundamental denials of humanity requires the empathic presence of a community (which may be embodied for a time in the presence of one person) that does not turn away from the face of the other.[80] True witnessing requires imagination, emotional presence, unflinching honesty, and clarity of speech. Given our capacity to evade, distort, and forget whatever challenges dominant narratives, we must work hard to use language to locate, retrieve, and preserve personal and historical truth.

## The Politics of Memory

Stories are containers and conveyors of moral truth across time and serve to call into being and transmit whole systems of ethics and praxis. When we tell our own story, we take our place in a particular moral universe. Every narrative told to another presents multiple levels of commitment: to continue one's story in a certain way; to occupy a specific social position; to take a stance; and to enter into certain forms of relationship with others.

The political questions, therefore, become: What stories are preserved? What stories can be told? And what contexts are available for telling, retelling, remembering and participating with others to construct a durable community?

Our repertoire of stories depends crucially on the integrity of collective memory. In traditional societies, stories are held by elders and storytelling is a fundamental activity that welds the generations together in an unbroken arc. The accelerating pace of posttraditional societies leaves a constricted and ambivalent place for elders in general, let alone those with scars or persistent wounds and difficult stories to tell—stories that lead even professional helpers to recoil or marshal technical strategies to contain and deflect.

> [T]he survivors were reproached for their unwillingness to forget. The world seemed to forget that many prisoners' will to survive was based on their determination to let the world know ... A conflict emerged between doctors, who had as their therapeutic goal to make their patients let go of past sufferings, and patients determined not to forget. Again, the patient-survivor is made to feel guilty. He is dismissed as either "untreatable" or stubborn, even hopeless. The psychiatrist's theory and "therapeutic aim" remain undisturbed; the patient suffers.[81]

Stories of violence, though they may be frozen in memory, locked in the body, and quarantined by society, are carried along by survivors who live within a world of constant change. As survivors age they build new lives, have families, and find fulfillment in the continuity of work and relationships, but this continuity exists in tension with recurrent reminders of rupture and loss.

> [T]he daily life of many survivors is characterized by isolation: they are refugees, old people, survivors of a period nearly everybody else wants to forget. The latter have more than enough to think about. For the former it is more than enough to worry about, more than enough to not be listened to, to not be understood, to be distrusted and misjudged, and they fall into despair and depression ...
>
> With the passage of time health deteriorates, strength is reduced, and mental capacities dwindle. Traumatic experiences return with reinforced strength. Survivors are of course in need of help for all their somatic ailments but still more for their psychological isolation, their feeling of having lost their anchorage in the world and in humanity.[82]

This anchorage can only be found in dialogical relationship with others unafraid to live in history, as well as imaginative possibility.

## Conclusion

Temporal experience is not simply a feature of individual, embodied awareness or human narrative capacities, but is also a product of relationships with others and with the environment. These relationships change as we age and the arcs of our lives become part of a weave with others that creates a sense of community and continuity or else unravels into frayed and frail strands.

The complexity of both individual and collective acts of remembering is redoubled by the effects of mass media representation of individuals and groups, so that people now work to position themselves not only in a local world but in relation to global frameworks over which they have little or no control. TV projects the global system onto the scale of the local—indeed, it can bypass the local, and even the family, to colonize individuals' imagination. The global is brought into the living room, but in a highly selective way that serves interests distant and detached from those of the consumer of images. While, through electronic media and networks, people seem to have greater access to personal and collective histories and can recover or reinvent narratives of identity that preserve, honor and revitalize diverse traditions, the processes of recollection are heavily constrained and easily co-opted.

> My claim is that people do not remember well because the modern economy does not encourage it. Defence lies not in repression of the past but in narratives which empower the remembering subject, and this private empowerment is an act in which people can collectively collude. Durkheim's and Halbwach's liberal dream has been defeated by the denials of time in the economy and, perversely, by the freedom of the narrating subject.[83]
>
> The sociological problem of collective memory is how to compose a body of critical voices that will de-centre one another.[84]

An answer to the economic and political corruption of collective memory may lie in the dialectic between the adamantine and relational self, and the forms of life that allow each way of being to coexist. Those who hold memory inviolable and insist on their voices being heard are crucial to this decentering. But every memory calls forth a form of community that can only thrive with relationality.

The adamantine self can be critiqued as a fiction, as acultural, asocial, and self-deluding—but it is also the place from which the individual can take a stand against the tsunami of lies, self-interested promotion, and domination of others that has come with the mediatized hyperconnectivity and moral disconnection of the contemporary world. The steadfastness of the adamantine self as moral stance can support the urgent work of remembering needed to provide a place for the disavowed and forgotten.

The relational self too can be critiqued as a fiction born of conformity, collusion, and false consciousness, in which individuals suppress their voices for an illusory sameness and feigned solidarity. But this is to deny the centrality of relationships with others from whom we receive basic sustenance, with whom we co-construct shelter, and from whom we receive news of worlds we cannot otherwise know.

Respecting the partial truths offered by metaphors of adamantine and relational selves allows forms of dialogue that are personal and transcendental, rooted in communal tradition and responsive to the ethical demand presented by the face of the other. The ethics of storytelling has its necessary counterpart in the ethics of listening, of witnessing and taking part in the creation of community through copresence. Narratives and metaphors of the self, no matter how novel, are not freestanding structures but must participate in forms of community, with a sense of place and history that lend texture, layers, depth, and breadth to the immediacy of experience. Intermediate structures like religious institutions are places where local stories are held, and the capacities to listen and to speak are learned and practiced. The ethics of these intermediate levels of social organization then becomes crucial for the preservation of collective memory.[85] With the right ethical stance, they can also be places where listening and learning extend the reach of compassion.

CHAPTER 8

# *Poetics of Alterity*

> Reading poetry is an act of reciprocity, and one of the great tasks of lyric is to bring us into right relationship to each other . . . The lyric poem is a highly concentrated and passionate form of communication between strangers.
>
> – Edward Hirsch[1]

> The poem wants to reach an Other, it needs this Other, it needs an Over-against. It seeks it out, speaks toward it.
>
> For the poem making toward an Other, each thing, each human being is a form of this Other.
>
> – Paul Celan[2]

## Introduction

Other people confront us with experiences that may be radically unfamiliar, strange, and unsettling. This sense of otherness may be compounded by illness, trauma, and cultural difference. With empathy and imagination, it is possible to gain an understanding of another's experience, get a glimpse of their perspective, and build a picture of their predicament. The imaginative spaces and places conjured by stories offer us a way into another's lifeworld—even when that world is profoundly different from our own due to cultural background, personal history, or extremity of experience. In long-term psychotherapy, patient and clinician may coconstruct an elaborate house of shared stories. Similarly, ethnographers who live in a community for a long time come to know something of the fund of collective memory, master narratives, and cultural affordances through which individuals elaborate their unique experiences. However, the detailed narratives collected in clinical ethnography and prized in literary pathographies contrast with the often fragmentary and ambiguous accounts offered by patients who are suffering from acute illness or who have afflictions that undermine their self-narrative. To capture the range of expressive uses of language a broader concept than story or narrative is needed. Lyric poetry, with its emphasis on images and metaphors, may correspond more closely to the fragmentary, condensed, but evocative language of the clinical encounter. This raises questions about how we make sense of metaphors grounded in distinctive or divergent life experience.

This chapter explores the problem of otherness in clinical practice and everyday life. We will consider several kinds of otherness or alterity, associated with bodily affliction, "madness," trauma, social position, and cultural difference. We will approach the possibility of bridging the ruptures created by alterity through the practice of *poeisis*, the fashioning of imaginative worlds with language. We will draw in particular from the writing and reflections of the poets Paul Celan and Édouard Glissant. Celan offers an especially illuminating way to approach the dilemmas of alterity because of his own experiences of profound estrangement from others—and his conviction that language could build a bridge that would allow authentic communication across the divide of world-shattering violence. Celan's effort to work out an explicit poetics of alterity has much to teach us about the dilemmas of the clinical encounter. Glissant, a poet–philosopher who explicitly focused on the politics and poetics of creolization as a response to the history of colonial violence and emerging world of large-scale intermixing, points to a way forward through the capacity of lyric to create aesthetic meaning and order out of the chaos of global turbulence and confluence.

## Othering and Alterity

*Alterity* is a term for the fact and the experience of the unfamiliar, the un-family-like, the disturbing and unpredictable. At its most extreme, this sense of otherness gives rise to feelings of the uncanny or horror at the inhuman. The opposite of alterity is *ipseity*, sameness, belonging, the sense of the familiar, which is rooted developmentally in the experiences of family life and community. The estrangement of alterity is fundamentally interpersonal because, from our earliest experience, we rely on others for sustenance, comfort, and support and, in so doing, come to associate the familiar with a secure base in which we feel most at home and where we are most ourselves. The disturbing sense of the unfamiliar other as profoundly different therefore challenges our sense of comfort in and reliance on sameness. This sameness is also at the root of our own identity constructed as a seamless autobiographical narrative or continuous life trajectory. We build this narrative with the participation of others, with raw materials provided by cultural templates for life stories and salient events, so there is always already a socially shared basis to our sense of self and individuality.

Of course, beneath the comforting blanket woven of shared stories and affirmations of belonging, there are constant moments of difference and distance that reveal us as separate from those we call family and friends, with attendant feelings of being alone with our interiority and opacity to others. Moreover, just as it is possible to feel estranged from others in our family and community—when we find our temperament, sensibility, or values markedly at odds with them—so, too, we can come to feel estranged from our self. This self-estrangement can occur at moments of abrupt change or discontinuity in our lives, for example, in the extremity of limit experiences of psychosis or religious revelation, but it is also a commonplace in the course of individual development, arising from the very facts of embodiment, and the inevitable experience of illness and affliction.

## The Body as Other

The persistent dualism of mind and body in both biomedicine and broader popular culture can be traced to the contrast between the mobility of imagination and the material constraints of the body.[3] We discover ourselves through interaction with others—each of us embodied—but also through the exploration of our own bodies and the experience of needs and desires that arise from the body and the realization that we can transform desire into action and, at least transiently, satisfaction. The impression that desire originates somewhere deep inside (the mind, soul, or spirit) to be expressed through the body is an illusion because we need our bodies to think *with* and *through* desire, and to discover the possibilities and priorities for action. But so too is the idea that the body presents us with desires already fully formed as particular drives or hungers. Enactivist cognitive science teaches us that we learn to articulate desire through action. When the body is doing its job, it engages the world through rolling cycles of perception and action. These, in turn, participate in embodied processes of imagination.

Illness, aging, and mortality each confront us with the body as other: something separate from our wishes, resistant to our plans, clumsy, flailing, and failing, a source of disruptive sensations like pain, nausea, vertigo, itching, restlessness, or torpor from which we wish to escape.[4] This desire for escape is central to our sense of having a self that is distinct from the body and, arguably, drives the fantasies of disembodied immortality that populate religious mythology and contemporary science fiction.

The silent body may be taken for granted or imagined in ways that reflect personal history and cultural models of personhood, but its anatomy and physiology exert constant influence on cognition outside awareness. The pleasurable and enabling body is a friend and a delight; the painful (irritable, nauseous, dizzy) body is an unwelcome stranger or opponent that can become familiar over time and integrated into an altered sense of self as damaged, disabled, or suffering recurrent disruption. Chapter 2 presented several examples of such bodily estrangement. In Oliver Sacks's account of losing sensation in his injured leg, he described a radical disorientation that affected not only his feeling of bodily integrity but his sense of agency. Mrs. W was tormented by sensations of floating, which prevented her from walking steadily, planting each step firmly on the ground, and this reflected a broader sense of having lost the foundation of her life. Mr. Y struggled with the experience of dialysis—watching his blood leave his body and travel through a machine—and deeply feared the prospect of a blood transfusion as an invasion by something wholly other (containing the substance of another's personality) that would alter his identity.[5]

The philosopher Jean-Luc Nancy has written of his own experience of receiving a heart transplantation as "the intruder" (*l'intrus*) within his body—on which his life depends completely.[6] This experience presented him with a "life that not only lives on but that still lives properly, within the three-fold grip of the stranger/the foreign: that of the decision [to receive a transplant], the organ, and of the transplant's effects."[7] Alterity then stems from the material facts of the afflicted body and its tissues, his conscious recognition of the heart as having belonged to someone else, and the bodily, physiological, and social consequences of transplantation—including all of the medications taken to suppress the immune system to prevent rejection of the organ, which have their own bodily effects and provide a constant reminder of the tenuous nature of bodily integrity. The biomedical intervention and the underlying process of immune recognition and (potential rejection) are conflated in his analysis: "Medical practice thus renders the graftee a stranger to himself: stranger, that is, to his immune system's identity—which is something like his physiological signature."[8] Accepting that he is foreign to himself is not a tenable way to proceed and does not offer him any reconciliation with the other in his body. "Strangeness and strangerness become ordinary everyday occurrences."[9] Through all his subsequent medical complications and afflictions, he endures but "emerges from this adventure lost."[10]

Indeed, "the 'I' end/ends up being no more than a tenuous thread—from pain to pain, strangeness to strangeness"[11] and he must build a sense of continuity of identity on this procession of insult, injury, and loss, incorporating the radically other.

> I am the illness and the medical intervention. I am the cancerous cell and the grafted organ. I am the immuno-depressive agents and their palliatives. I am the bits of wire that held together my sternum, and I am the injection site permanently stitched in below my clavicle, just as I was already the screws in my hip and this plate in my groin. I am becoming like a science-fiction android, or the living-dead, as my youngest son said to me one day.[12]

Bodily estrangement need not arise from pathology. As children we all undergo profound changes in our embodiment over the course of development and, when not explained away as "growing pains," these may be experienced as perplexing and self-alienating. The bodily changes of puberty, in particular, are often challenging, and, however welcome, entail an ongoing process of adjustment and reincorporation. For people with gender dysphoria, this settling into a sexual body may be impeded. In some cases, people become aware early on that there is a discrepancy between their body and their gender and, with increasing social recognition of this dilemma, space has opened up for trans* identities and for biomedical interventions to reconcile the experience of gender with physical embodiment.[13] Afforded the opportunity to transform their bodies to better fit their gender identity, some describe this as a kind of "coming home."[14] Of course, this newfound alignment and comfort with the body also depends on the availability of communal space to live out one's gender, and this is requires changing social norms. Embodied gender may be a persistent structure from which one can never fully extricate oneself,[15] but trans* activists and theorists argue for a more fluid concept of embodiment that will allow us to realize new kinds of sensuality, sexuality, and aesthetics.[16]

Moments of bodily estrangement can arise from even small shifts or disruptions in sensorimotor coordination. In experimental settings, it is possible to create out-of-body experiences, illusions of ownership of a rubber hand, or of not owning part of one's body, through altering the synchrony between actions and observations.[17] This kind of experiment suggests that our sense of bodily integrity and self-sameness is not something settled once and for all in early development but is constantly being revised and maintained through sensorimotor feedback loops. This is what allows us to rapidly integrate sensory or motor prostheses into our sense of bodily self. The initial strangeness of having metal or plastic mechanical parts quickly gives way to having a natural extension of the body through these feedback loops. But there are top-down cognitive evaluations and interpersonal responses that can modulate or interrupt that process of sensorimotor integration so that a sense of strangeness persists or recurs.[18]

These examples of the malleability of our sense of self reveal the constant process of creating and surpassing alterity in the construction of bodily identity, integrity, and self-sameness. Illness, injury, and affliction may confront us with more obdurate experiences of otherness that become persistent preoccupations and prevent the body from ever being taken for granted. That foregrounding of the body as an object that resists, confounds or confutes our subjectivity is in itself a problem that may drive people to seek help.

## Facing the Other: Empathy and Alterity

> The nakedness of the face is not a figure of speech.
>
> – Emannuel Levinas[19]

In early development, we are confronted with otherness in the presence of those on whom we depend and who we come to understand have their own perspectives and experiences. This sense of the other comes not only from the difference between touching and being touched or between actions we initiate and those that arise from the actions of others, but also from the early recognition of others as having their own agency and subjectivity. Infants can track the gaze of others and soon learn to infer that some objects or events are important because they are the focus of the other's attention. This is the basis of what has been called infant's "theory of mind," which allows them to recognize the intentionality of others and use this information to identify objects of interest in the environment as well as to learn modes of engagement, stances, and skills through modeling and mimicry. This learning occurs within regimes of attention that mark out socially and culturally significant environmental affordances.[20] This organization of attention serves enculturation and is coupled with emotional or affective valence marking events as beneficial or harmful, pleasurable or distressing, or relevant to particular motives, goals, and concerns.

The expression of emotion is at the center of evolutionary accounts of facial function and experience. The face is a powerful medium for the communication of emotion including pain, fear, anger, or disgust, as well as pleasure, interest, and affiliation. Facial expression can go beyond the basic valences of approach and avoidance expressed through stance or posture to convey nuances of feeling, multiple layered meanings, and rapidly changing dynamics. As well, the distinctive features of the face—and the voice, which emerges from and is synchronized with the movement of the face—are important ways that we recognize others as distinct individuals.[21] The face is thus a basic vehicle for organizing interpersonal relationships and, by extension, the social world.[22]

The face is both a transmitter and receiver of emotion: a transmitter because it reflects our experience and broadcasts it to others—not only for them to read and reflect on, but more palpably, viscerally, and immediately, as a display that evokes emotions, so that our expressions are mirrored in the faces of others, just as their emotions are implanted in our own being. The face (along with the voice) plays a key role in emotional interaction because we involuntarily mimic our interactional partner's facial expressions, which can induce corresponding emotional states.[23] Our reading and response to the face of others is usually rapid and can occur without conscious awareness. Even brief presentations of another's face showing emotions of happiness or sadness can evoke similar feelings in a viewer.[24]

Interpersonal interaction usually involves a constant exchange of facial signals. When infants interact with a caregiver who deliberately keeps their face still for a period of time, they may exhibit distress, try to elicit a response, and eventually disengage.[25] The still-face paradigm has been used to probe the dynamics of emotional absence or separation and recovery after reunion.[26] Individuals with facial paralysis may be perceived by others not as neutral but as exhibiting negative emotion because of the violation of the expectation for a responsive face.[27] Even partial paralysis, like a Bell's palsy that results in lopsided facial expressions, can affect interpersonal interaction. The effects extend to the affected person's own sense of self.

Infants engage in imitation of the faces of adults looking at them.[28] Over the course of early development, this imitation and mirroring serves to establish a repertoire of expressions that have social meaning and provides a foundation for knowing the feelings of others and abstracting from that to develop a theory of mind.[29] Following the gaze of others establishes the focus of their attention (as distinct from our own),[30] and watching (and automatically mirroring) their facial expression gives us a sense of what they think and feel about what they are watching. A particularly powerful element of this interaction occurs when the gaze of the other is directed toward oneself. We then see ourselves mirrored in the face of the other and come to know ourselves as social beings. This process of self-definition is reciprocal, occurring in ongoing loops during early development and continuing throughout our lives. As a result, "A face is not only an expression of a self available for others to read, but to some extent the self is constituted in the face and developed, and experienced, in the interaction between faces."[31] Through reading the faces of others, we learn the emotional meaning of social events, including our own actions. The face of the other is the stage on which we watch the play of emotions that give flesh to abstract concepts of personhood implicit in the moral order.[32]

Even the experience of our own body is mediated by exchanges with the faces of others. One thinks of the child who injures themselves and then looks at the parent to determine how they should respond.[33] If the parent appears anxious or distressed, the child begins to cry. In contrast, a parent's apparent indifference may convey an implicit instruction for the child to suppress, deny, or dissociate awareness of their pain. The child comes to know their own bodily and emotional vulnerability (and the socially appropriate response) through the parent's face. Though we can learn to use the face to dissimulate, we must first learn the code by accurate mirroring of others. Through their reporting back to us what our face reveals we learn to be self-consistent or begin to recognize our own contradictions and akrasias.

Facial expression is a prime indicator of another's pain and suffering. If facial expressions are masked or faked, we have difficulty discriminating real suffering from play-acting. Indeed, when people are asked to pretend they are in pain (or those in pain are asked to pretend that they are not) trained clinicians cannot accurately identify those who are in pain and those who are merely play-acting.[34]

Because the face reveals our feelings and responses to others, it is the primordial site of our own social presence and identity. The other is most present and compelling for us in their facial expression, which communicates both their individuality and the immediacy of their own experience. This primacy and directness of the face led the philosopher Emmanuel Levinas to give it a privileged moral status, referring to "that bit of absolutely decent skin that is the face."[35] For Levinas, the face is not simply a metaphor for our social relatedness but the vehicle for alterity. The face is always the face of someone. Hence, it is socially situated and morally compelling. Levinas views recognition of and responsibility for the other as "the essential, primary and fundamental structure of subjectivity."[36] For this reason, "access to the face is straightaway ethical."[37] What Levinas refers to as "the epiphany of the face of the other" provides the origin and ground of ethical concern.[38] If the other's face presents us with this imperative, the big ethical question is why we so often turn away.

In health care settings, we often fail to allow ourselves to experience the pain of others; instead, we turn away and ignore their faces. In large part, this may be due to our inability to tolerate vicarious pain and accept our own powerlessness to alleviate the suffering of others. These are the most obvious explanations for the unsettling finding that health professionals tend to minimize and deny the pain of patients. For example, an ethnographic study on an orthopedic surgery ward for children found that nurses tended to dismiss patients' pain by viewing their complaints as evidence of childish dependency, histrionics, and self-indulgence.[39] Children were enjoined to suppress and deny their pain to be "good patients" and, when they did not respond to such expectations, were sometimes threatened with reprisals. Parents who attempted to convey their child's distress to nurses saw these strategies of discounting, dismissal, and denial directed toward them as well. Throughout, the child's unique experience was subordinated to a generic model of stages of recovery, so that when their experience did not accord with the nurses' expectations children could be told: "you can't be feeling that"—their most fundamental experience effaced by medical routine.[40]

The face is the first site of empathy: the ability to feel something akin to what another feels.[41] And the failure to empathize with someone in pain is generally recognized as a moral failing. Feeling for others as suffering beings makes possible moral action. But empathy goes beyond sympathetic pain to imaginatively reconstruct the Other's world of experience, a process that involves not only apprehending their point of view, or way of facing the world, but also their position in it.

Empathy can be decomposed into several distinct components: (1) vicarious emotion (e.g., feeling grief because another has facial expressions that evoke that response in oneself either directly or through unintentional mirroring of the other's facial expression); (2) analogical associations to the other's experience (e.g., thinking of one's own losses to evoke a grief that parallels the other's emotion); (3) imaginative reconstruction of the position of another through imagery or story (e.g., imagining in detail what it would be like to lose a parent); and (4) placing oneself in an analogous position to the other (e.g., in the face of someone who experienced early loss, acting as if one's own mother had died when one was young). These basic bodily and cognitive–emotional actions are not static one-off responses but must be sustained over time. Thus, empathy further requires: (5) regulation of one's own personal associations to stay on track with those most pertinent to mirroring the other (e.g., truncating or discarding idiosyncratic divergent trains of associations); and, especially, (6) tolerating negative affect and discomfort and regulating its intensity to be able to continue to track the other person. Excess "empathy" leads to distancing from feelings that are too intense or to appropriating the other's experience, mistaking it for one's own, and, ultimately, occluding it with one's own thoughts and feelings. Hence, empathy itself can be a vehicle not for recognizing sameness but for producing alterity when faced with Other's, who are seen to present a threat.

## Ghostly Others

Trauma is associated with a wide variety of symptoms, some of which have been portrayed as specific to violence but most of which occur in many contexts. Symptoms may arise from physiological perturbations and become stabilized as persistent disorders through several mechanisms: the ongoing effect of unrelenting external stressors; physiological final common pathways involving altered neural regulatory systems; and vicious circles in which the symptom is amplified by feedback, either through psychophysiological loops within the person or social–interactional loops involving interpersonal processes. The psychological responses to violence include not only the fears, anxieties, and avoidance behaviors characteristic of posttraumatic stress disorder (PTSD) but also panic, anger, grief, and demoralization.[42] When violence is perpetrated by those we previously trusted and depended on, it results in the added trauma of betrayal, which can occur at different levels including family, institutional authority, community, and nation.

Among the symptoms and experiences viewed as distinctive to trauma and its aftermath are feelings of horror and the uncanny. Reflecting on his experiences working in Aceh, Indonesia, where he co-led an International Organization for Migration (IOM) program to identify and treat trauma after the tsunami, Byron Good described his own experiences of the uncanny.[43] The tsunami that took so many lives also swept aside the longstanding military conflict, ushering in a postconflict era. However, the apparent calm was haunted by ghosts of the past.

Living with ghosts and specters is more than a metaphor for the anxieties associated with both public and private space in a regime where so much of historical memory has been suppressed. The "eerie moments when the ghosts of violence refuse to be quiet" that Good describes point to the survivors' experience not simply of intrusive thoughts but of entities or beings. The notion of spirits and specters depends on a cultural ontology, but the ease with which we can be led to an ontology of ghosts and spirits—which need not be uncanny (they can be friendly and familiar)—reflects our cognitive capacity to attribute agency and to personify such agents as human like ourselves.[44]

For Freud, the uncanny (*unheimlich*) arises from something secretly familiar but repressed, which returns to consciousness in shadowy form.[45] It is not some intrinsic strangeness or tenuousness of memories, but their active repression that makes them return as phantoms and apparitions. The effort to make what is intolerable vanish from memory gives rise to the troubling portents that lurk about and visit in dreams or moments of crisis and disruption.

The ghosts of mass violence reflect the horror and incongruity of the original events and their echoes in feelings of dislocation, depersonalization, and derealization. Ethologists and comparative psychologists might argue, in contrast to Freud, that it is some essential strangeness, incongruity, and indeterminacy, defined against evolutionary ecological norms and expectations that make certain events intrinsically horrible and haunting. Intense experiences of the uncanny can be provoked by images of damaged or distorted bodily integrity.[46] But this sense of strangeness also can occur in response to images that do not represent injury or death.[47] The violent and grotesque are only two of many routes to the uncanny. In the settings Good described, perhaps the most direct source of feelings of the uncanny was the history of political repression that produced categories of the unspeakable and the transgressive that continued to configure social spaces in ways that created intimations of great danger. The eerie or uncanny could then come from social predicaments like meeting one's former torturer in a café or living one's daily life beside a neighbor who killed one's father.[48]

In most instances, the uncanny is a fleeting feeling that subsides over time with familiarity. Images of horror and incongruity can lose their emotional shock value with prolonged or repeated exposure. But there is much in the nature of mass violence that prevents this process of habituation or familiarization. In particular, mass violence can disrupt the moral, ontological, and symbolic order that creates and protects the spaces in which exposure can occur safely. Citing Derrida, Good suggests that when ontologies are ruptured they give rise to "hauntologies."[49] Apparitions continue to hover at the margins of awareness, in the frightening imagery of ghosts and nightmares, and can be self-perpetuating as they prompt fears that circulate through gossip and mass media, maintaining high levels of anxiety within a community.

In these situations, activities like art and psychotherapy can work to reestablish a sense of safety. They do this by creating a frame for activities that are marked as play or "as if" and ensuring the presence of an other who is committed to the vulnerable person's safety. Good recounts a dramatic performance by Indonesian artist Butet Kartaredjasa to illustrate how theater can provide a transitional space where the audience can watch the actor play with the ghosts of violence—exerting some control over their comings and goings by regulating aesthetic distance. The ghosts can be invoked and invited onstage, because this is a play, and in a playful, comic, or elegiac mode, the ghosts' threat—to remember their sundered lives, naming names, places, events—is aestheticized, muted, and controlled.[50]

Good describes the suffering associated with the conventional symptoms of PTSD and the value of psychiatric treatment with medication, psychosocial support, and counseling. It seems a bitter irony, though, that it was only by eliding details about the perpetrators of political violence that government support and funding could be secured to treat some of the aftermath of the violence. The tsunami provided a politically neutral catastrophe on which to focus attention.[51] And the individual treatment interventions many received did not provide a place for basic processes of recognition, restitution, and reconciliation. The ghosts of the past, then, must follow the scripts given them by the powers that be. They can express their resistance in symptoms, intrusive memories, and performances in designated places that are framed as "just play."

The anthropologist Robert Lemelson has also traced the legacy of violence in Indonesia into the world of ghosts.[52] In ethnographic film and essays, he has presented the case of "Nyoman," a Balinese man who lives with the repeated intrusions of apparitions that he calls "shadows" (in Indonesian, *bayangan*). Nyoman describes himself as living in two worlds: that of his community and the realm of the spirits. Nyoman traces his illness back to 1965, when he witnessed the massacre of fellow villagers during the mass violence. His subsequent problems with anxiety and social withdrawal began after this terrifying experience, which weakened his "life force" (Balinese, *bayu*), with persistent symptoms of feeling his heart beating rapidly, and a sensation of "inner pressure" weighing down his body. He had other symptoms typical of PTSD, including being jumpy and easily startled, and frequent nightmares with images of people being butchered. He avoided social gatherings and public places and stopped participating in community work projects.

Another layer was added to his suffering with the death of a newborn child some years later. In addition to ordinary expressions of grief, he experienced an intensification of his social anxiety and avoidance and began to have more unusual experiences with auditory and visual hallucinations. He began seeing small, black figures, which he believed to be spirits known as the *wong samar*, which are widely recognized in Bali as potential causes of illness or emotional problems. In Balinese cosmology, many different sorts of spirits and ghosts are believed to inhabit rivers, graveyards, ravines, and trees. If they are offended, these spirits can cause illness and emotional or interpersonal problems.

Although the spirits occupy a different realm, their ability to cause illness depends on conditions in the social world. When political changes occurred in Indonesia in 2002, and it became more possible to speak of the conflicts of the past, the spirits returned and began asking Nyoman to join the Communist Party. To protect himself from these subversive spirits, Nyoman took to wearing a military camouflage jacket and helmet, which he believed constituted an effective barrier to spirits trying to enter his body. Antipsychotic medication also helped to reduce his hallucinations and other symptoms.

Lemelson's detailed account of Nyoman's symptoms illustrates how cultural ontologies shape the phenomenology of psychopathology. Symptomatology is cognitively mediated through interpretive processes, but it is also shaped by social practices that reference specific levels or domains of experience and that constitute various sorts of spirit beings as real and important for social order and well-being. The spirit realm parallels the mundane world but affords greater fluidity and possibilities for transformation through metaphoric constructions and symbolic action. Nyoman found a truce with the *wong samar* by symbolically renouncing his former political affiliations.

Individuals' efforts to make meaning of trauma draw from cultural models, but mass violence can undermine these structures and resources. In ethnographic research in Sri Lanka, the anthropologist Alexandra Pillen explored the ways in which violence that is extreme in its savagery, scale, and scope can attack not only individuals' sense of coherence but also the collective forms of order embedded in and expressed through cultural and religious cosmologies. There are plenty of frightening images of demons, death, and aggression in Sinhalese mythology, but they usually follow familiar scripts.[53] The cosmological order implicit in such scripts was challenged by the deliberately transgressive nature of the political violence. In Sri Lanka, "images of displaced spirits and a cosmology damaged by war go hand in hand with representations of dehumanization and inhuman people."[54] The spirits of the Sinhala Buddhist pantheon fled in terror from the chaotic violence of the civil war. For some Sinhalese, youth who committed atrocities and senseless violence that transgresses all social mores became "spirit-like people," who lacked full human personhood, and were frightening to both humans and spirits.[55] Even the unsocialized spirits or demons that cause illness were horrified by these other than humans and "shivered away" from them. The violence of war then transcended the ordinary forms of evil that were understood and managed through relationships with the spirit world. Pillen notes other examples of such fracturing of cosmologies in the violence in Peru, Uganda, Cambodia, and the famine in North Korea.

Pillen suggests that the subsequent acts of mockery and disruptions of healing rituals by youth may reflect efforts by these youth to reenter the social order, finding a place for the limit experiences they have endured as perpetrators and witnesses to extreme violence, and, so, to become human again. Pillen also discusses the role of the artist in reconstructing a shattered cosmology, reassembling its elements, beginning with the most personal reflections, giving them form and materiality and bringing them into the social sphere, even into confrontation with the forces that would seek to fracture and abscond with the world or remake it in their own violent image. Art provides unique modalities to order and contain the chaotic and inexpressible through silence, nonsense, and new forms of representation. Ethnographic interviewing itself is also a kind of intervention, in which empathy, active listening, and bearing witness create opportunities to recollect, make meaning of senseless violence, and articulate a coherent narrative. However, in searching for coherence, thick description, and articulate informants, ethnographers may downplay experiences that are shallow, empty, and incoherent or simply inchoate. Pillen speaks to the importance of fractured narratives both as expressions of injury and early attempts at the reconstruction of meaning that must follow disaster. "A cultural formation of temporary non-sense needs to be carefully observed as a cultural moment the entire community goes through."[56] She suggests that rather than emphasizing empathic connection as a direct route to emotional meaning, sensitivity to language can open up new possibilities to apprehend the struggle to make sense of a fractured reality. Rhetoric and poetics, in particular, offer tools for exploring the pragmatics of meaning-making at the precipice of madness.

Mass violence and genocide have recognized as catastrophes that transcend our powers of expression.[57] Yet narratives can provide the framework and emplotment we need to understand something of the radical alterity inherent in the experience of disaster. The evocative power of lyric can present still more of the unreconstructed, raw, inchoate aspect of memory and experience. Can we rebuild cosmology, then, not by asserting the grand sweep of a totalizing narrative—that may contain the seeds of a future round of mutually assured destruction—but through the more fragile, tentative, essays of lyric that invite us into a relation of trust, intimacy, and connection with another consciousness or way of being?

## Making Sense of Madness

The otherness or alterity that is simply part of the human condition is compounded in psychiatry by the clinical encounter with people who have suffered exceptionally violent and traumatic life experiences that are difficult and disturbing to confront. It is redoubled by the nature of psychopathology itself, which not only exposes people to what Karl Jaspers called the "limit situations" of psychosis[58] but which may alter individuals' psychological processes in ways that make them hard to understand or follow. This sets obstacles in the way of empathy and solidarity. Psychiatry aims to reach across this divide to meet the suffering patient with understanding and empathy despite the strangeness of their experience. This empathy may be as slight as an intimation of their pain or it may follow the contours of the other's experience closely. Clinicians achieve this closer mapping of patients' experience through familiarity with their lifeworlds, supplemented by technical models of the nature of psychopathology.[59] The technical model, while not directly translatable into the texture of lived experience, gives a sketch of how the mind works in pathological states or conditions and so allows the clinician to identify patterns that cannot be adequately intuited or empathically felt. When the technical model is shared with the patient it becomes a basis for a common experience of looking at the illness, objectified as mechanisms, from the outside.

The psychiatrist–anthropologist Robert Barrett addressed the issue of understanding others when their experience is radically altered in a review essay of the book *Madness and Modernism* by Louis Sass.[60] Sass offered a rich phenomenology of schizophrenia drawing out the parallels between psychotic experience and the explorations of extremity and liminality in modernist art. According to Sass, conventional theories of schizophrenia are based on ideas of deficiency and degeneracy or on excess. In contrast, Sass sought a theory that would fully engage the particularity of schizophrenic experience. Faced with the diversity of experience among people with schizophrenia, Sass appealed to some overarching characteristics similar to those invoked by Jaspers. Here is how Barrett described this move.

> However diverse they are, argues Jaspers, people with schizophrenia have the following features in common: they are strange, they are enigmatic, they are alien, they are bizarre. They are unknowable. You cannot empathize with them. Their symptoms lie beyond the realm of human meaning, beyond the possibility of human interpretation. They are, not to put too fine a word on it, "ununderstandable."[61]

Asserting the unintelligibility of schizophrenia leaves us free to focus on mechanism rather than experience. Schizophrenic symptoms become important not as a window into the person's suffering and coping but only as indices of disease, markers of the type and severity of the person's psychopathology. This is the path taken by contemporary psychiatry, exemplified by the nosological system of the *Diagnostic and Statistical Manual* of the American Psychiatric Association, which is less interested in the form and content of symptoms of schizophrenia as lived experience than in their value as diagnostic indicators of a specific disorder.[62]

In his book, Sass treated the person with schizophrenia as identical to their illness for rhetorical purposes.[63] He used the term "schizophrenic" as a noun rather than an adjective and, in doing so, equated the person with the illness, as often happens in everyday medical discourse. Clinicians metonymically conflate the patient and the symptom, illness ("a diabetic") or body part ("the gallbladder in bed 2") as pragmatic shorthand, but it also reflects an underlying reductive or essentialist assumption that diseases can be treated with limited attention to the particularities of individuals and contexts. The metonym may also provide some emotional distance from patients' experiences that might otherwise be threatening to the clinician. Substituting the more accurate locution "the person with schizophrenia," not only distinguishes the person from their illness, rescuing their ordinary human identity, it encourages us to think of the space between the person and the illness as a place where specific attitudes and strategies of coping can be deployed, to live with, confront, contain, and transform the challenging and disorienting experiences of illness.[64]

Barrett was sympathetic to Sass's aim of bringing schizophrenia back into "the community of human understanding" by finding something "just as bizarre" to compare it to—namely, modern art. Sass described both the prodrome of schizophrenia and essence of modernism as characterized by a "detached hyperconsciousness." This was expressed in modernist visual art and poetry in a preoccupation with the properties of visual media and with language itself. However, Barrett found some of the analogies made by Sass between the experience of schizophrenia and modernist art in all its self-conscious striving to be strained and overly aestheticized. As a remedy, Barrett suggested that we shift the focus to precisely the social and institutional uses of disease labels to better understand their political and interpersonal uses and consequences. In place of Sass's use of modern art as a source of tropes and images that could shed light on the experience of psychosis, Barrett suggested that "an alternative strategy might be to identify the metaphors that people with schizophrenia use to make sense of their illness."[65] He noted that people draw on a wide range of metaphors from religion, science, popular culture, myth, and their personal biography:

> They make sense of their experience by means of tropes which, though not mundane, are sufficiently conventional that they provide a bridge to connect that person with the everyday world, rendering bizarre experiences at least partly plausible .... Understanding people with schizophrenia may better be pursued by studying how they themselves forge a connection with (but maintain a discreet distance from) the cultural mainstream.[66]

Barrett called for close attention to the metaphors used by patients to track their own understanding of their illness both in terms of its phenomenology and its discursive functions. In the decades following his essay, several studies have explored the metaphors people use to understand their own psychopathological experiences, including work by contributors to an important volume that Barrett edited with Janis Jenkins.[67] Barrett's call to examine the tropes for bizarre experiences leads us directly to a concern with the poetics of alterity.

## Celan's Poetics of Alterity

Although metaphors can be used to make the strange intelligible, metaphoric language can also make the familiar strange. Lyric poetry plays this both ways, using familiar phrases or idioms to anchor experiences and fresh metaphors to evoke vivid images that unseat and uproot the taken-for-granted constructions of conventional language. This duality allows us some intimation of the conjunction of the strange and the familiar that is basic to experience but difficult to capture in ordinary language too stolidly anchored in the narrative conventions of common sense.

This unsettling is strikingly illustrated in the work of the essential post-Holocaust poet Paul Celan.[68] As a Jew who lost his family in the Shoah, Celan endured exile from his home (Czernowitz in Bukovina) and estrangement from the language of his mother (German); yet he remained committed to working with and through the German language to fashion poems of loss and longing that called for an ethical response of attentiveness to the other. Celan's work provides an instructive example to think through the evocative power of language, recognize its dependence on a commitment to listen closely, and realize its limits to achieve shared understanding and connection.

Throughout his adult life, Celan struggled with the alienation brought on by the traumatic rupture of his world. He suffered recurrent bouts of depression and paranoia that damaged even his closest relationships, endured repeated hospitalizations with little therapeutic benefit, and died by suicide in 1970. Despite depression and despair, he continued to hold out the hope that writing could bring some human connection that would move beyond his estrangement from self and other. In his own poetics, worked out in two essays written as acceptance speeches for literary prizes, Celan saw the writer as engaged in constant striving toward the other but also insisted on the obduracy of the strange and ineffable that can only be expressed in silence.[69]

It is instructive to consider how Celan used the medium of poetry to communicate limit experiences. His most famous—though, in light of his later work, least representative—poem, "Todesfuge" ("Deathfugue"), is as strong an example of the poetic evocation of emotion as one can imagine. Written in Celan's youth soon after the death of his parents at the hands of the Nazis, the poem begins:

> Schwarze Milch der Fruehe wir trinken sie abends
> wir trinken sie mittags und morgens wir trinken sie nachts
> wir trinken und trinken
> wir schaufeln ein Grab in den Lueften da liegt man nicht eng
>
> Black milk of daybreak we drink it at evening
> we drink it at midday and morning we drink it at night
> we drink and we drink
> we shovel a grave in the air where you won't lie too cramped[70]

Here *black* stands in stark contradiction to both *milk* and *daybreak*: in a single sensory metaphor, BLACK MILK OF DAYBREAK inverts and negates both the nourishment of mothers' milk and the hopeful light of dawn. This double negation of the possibility of family and future captures the relentless horror of genocide. As the stanza progresses, another level of horror is revealed in the way the narrators are forced to actively participate in their own annihilation, drinking and shoveling, shoveling and drinking, as they work at gunpoint, to dig their own mass grave in the air—a self-erasure and oblivion that is countered only by the sheer intensity of the music of the poem itself and the human presence of its speaking.

Our understanding of this poem draws first from bodily grounded metaphors that have universal appeal and from a music that is immediately intelligible. But unpacking its meaning also requires an awareness of history and context. In terms of cognitive poetics, then, part of the meaning of this text is accessible by tracing the words down to their embodied ground, but part of the meaning is only attained by following the language upward and outward into the larger social world to encounter others in all their uniqueness, presence, and opacity.[71]

Celan's later poems foregrounded that opacity by juxtaposing technical words that required wide reading in the natural sciences, philosophy, Jewish mysticism, and other sources to grasp their metaphoric meaning, as well as neologisms that wrought startling new effects with the German language.[72] He continued to use a vocabulary grounded in sensory experiences but constructed words that would negate that sensation, suggesting that some connection to the world was blocked, denied, or subverted.[73]

Celan's later poetry became increasingly compressed and elliptical, which rendered it difficult to understand and still more difficult to translate. However, Celan was affronted by descriptions of his poetry as "hermetic."[74] Far from making his message inaccessible or arcane, the concision, density, and fractures of his writing were an essential part of his poetics that grappled with the limits of language to say the unsayable.[75] Celan's deliberate use of language was not only a way to command the concentrated attention essential to all poetry, but an effort to come to terms with the magnitude of loss that shattered his world.

In Celan's later poems, metaphor was made to work in especially complex ways, with multiple layers or levels playing off against each other. It is useful to distinguish at least five different levels of meaning in Celan's work, which are present in all language, whether or not they are used intentionally for aesthetic or communicative purposes. As illustrated in the stanza from "Todesfuge" quoted above, a first level involves basic sensory, affective, symbolic meaning, much of which is available even in translation, as long as it points to objects and events that are common or universal in human experience (darkness, milk, daybreak, digging, death, and air). The felt and conceptual meaning of these metaphors is grounded in shared bodily experience and is quickly intelligible to the listener. A second level becomes available only by tracing the connotations of words to their cultural and historical origins; that is to say, it is sedimented in them through their etymology. A third level resides in the current social contexts of language use: local idioms, technical practices, and conventions (grave digging, *luftmenschen*, the smoke from the chimneys of Nazi crematoria). This leads to a fourth, personal or more idiosyncratic level of meaning based on the individual's biography and developmental history. Finally, like most poets, Celan made use of the materiality of words as objects, fashioning puns and other self-conscious forms of word play based on sound and shape. Each of these levels is inherently polysemous, drawing from cultural universals, existential givens, the particularities of a local world, and an individual's history. Identifying these disparate source domains and sorting out the corresponding meanings of words is often not possible to do with confidence since, in the life of the poet and in the practice of poiesis, they remain thoroughly entangled. The listeners or readers and their own communities then participate in creating new versions of the poem through their interpretive efforts.

## Alterity, Language, and Community

Poets are distinguished by their intense investment in language in its essential materiality, both of sound and the world of objects it invokes. Language, then, is not only a vehicle of expression but also a bedrock of identity and authentic presence that can survive even the worst violence against persons and preserve within itself the possibility of renewed community. For Celan in exile, stripped of all that was familiar:

> Only one thing remained reachable, close and secure amid all losses: language. Yes, language. In spite of everything, it remained secure against loss. But it had to go through its own lack of answers, through terrifying silence. Through the thousand darknesses of murderous speech. It went through. It gave me no words for what was happening, but went through it. Went through and could resurface, "enriched" by it all.[76]

Poetry begins and ends as embodied language, anchored in bodily experience and sensuality, including the feeling of words in the mouth, their sound, and relation to breath.[77] This bodily expression unfolds in a social world that gives meaning to speech and gesture. Although, for most poets, the poem gestates in solitude, emerging from an interior process of heightened sensitivity to the personal resonances of words and images, it usually ends as a missive spoken or sent out to some real or imagined other. For most poets, this presence of the other as a potential reader of the poem is a crucial motive for the creative process and shapes the form and content of the poem. Celan explicitly recognized and emphasized the dialogical nature of the poem, but spoke of this as an effort more than a realized fact.

> A poem, being an instance of language, hence essentially dialogue, may be a letter in a bottle thrown out to sea with the—surely not always strong—hope that it may somehow wash up somewhere, perhaps on a shoreline of the heart. In this way, too, poems are en route: they are headed toward.
>
> Toward what? Toward something open, inhabitable, an approachable you, perhaps, an approachable reality.
>
> Such realities are, I think, at stake in a poem.[78]

Clearly, despite the great concision of his poems, Celan understood himself to be reaching toward some other—some kindred person lost like his family, but also, perhaps, the uncanny other responsible for the destruction of his world. The difficulty of the poem reflects the difficulty of the feelings it subtends and calls forth from the reader an intensity of engagement with language that can create a kind of intimacy.

Celan's effort to encompass and respond to this radical otherness is described with painstaking care in a speech he titled "The Meridian," given in Germany on the occasion of receiving a literary prize: "the poem has always hoped . . . to speak on behalf of the *strange*—no I can no longer use this word here—*on behalf of the other*, who knows, perhaps of an *altogether other*."[79] In this talk, Celan faces the altogether other of the perpetrators and bystanders of the murders of his family and his people, to whom he, as Jew, was also altogether other.[80] He comes to them as a survivor, as someone who has endured, and whose work therefore necessarily speaks of endurance.

> The poem holds its ground on its own margin. In order to endure, it constantly calls and pulls itself back from an "already-no-more" into a "still-here."
>
> The poem intends another, needs this other, needs an opposite. It goes toward it, bespeaks it.
>
> For the poem, everything and everybody is a figure of this other toward which it is heading.
>
> [. . .]
>
> The poem becomes conversation—often desperate conversation.[81]

Speaking his mother tongue and the language of his vocation as poet, Celan addresses a German audience that is at once familiar, yet also profoundly other. He calls out to them to become aware of his otherness and theirs as a ground for meeting and conversation.[82] In its self-conscious locutions, backtracking, and corrections, though, Celan's speech shows his struggle to find the precise words to describe the predicament of alterity, as if to ask, "Is any language reliable enough to build a bridge between such utter strangers?" Celan invites his audience to join him beyond the familiarity of a common language in a place of encounter with radical otherness.

Despite growing recognition in Germany, and the inclusion of his Holocaust poem "Todesfugue" in school textbooks, Celan remained ill at ease with and mistrustful of his German audience. Yet, in part because of the deep connection with the language that made him a poet, he was forced to struggle with that unseen audience, both intimate and knowing and unutterably cold and alien. The implication of the audience in this struggle to give words to experience becomes still clearer in contrasting the "Meridian" with a speech given not long afterward to the Hebrew Writers' Association in Jerusalem.

> Here in your inner and outer landscape, I find much of the compulsion toward truth, much of the self-evidence, much of the world-open uniqueness of great poetry. And I believe I have encountered the calm and confident resolution to hold on to what is human.[83]

The difference between the two audiences—representing two imagined communities, one imbued with the qualities of home, evoking feelings of warm reception, identification, and incorporation, and the other of distance and strangeness, alienation and the uncanny—is apparent in Celan's text and reflects his struggle to use poetry as a way to affirm identity and continuity in the aftermath of world-shattering violence.

Celan's poetics takes us beyond the common encounter of self and other, or even of victim and perpetrator, to the centrality of language in the effort to (re)construct a viable, ethical, and hospitable place to dwell. Words have direction; they reach toward someone to make contact and call forth a response. The response often is not something new but something forgotten. In a sense, then, every poem is both greeting and invocation. As Phillipe Lacoue-Labarthe says of Celan's writing: "What the poem indicates and shows, what it moves toward, is its source."[84] The poem offers simultaneously the unique perspective of an individual and the common heritage of a community as the place of embodied identity and the source of collective stories. In Celan's case, this was a community destroyed by genocide, and his poems reveal the absent community through their images of solitude and yearning.[85]

## Authenticity and the Other

An "urge to reach some other obsessed Celan, some *du* (which is 'thou' or 'you')—the word occurs in [four hundred] of his poems . . . which come to us terse and compelled, seeking a listener, an other, seeking recognition."[86] Celan's poems often address an absent "you" or call the reader closer to listen to their saying. They use language that is close to embodied experience.

> Now I am a person who likes simple words. It is true, I had realized before this journey that there was much evil and injustice in the world I had now left, but I had believed I could shake the foundations if I called things by their proper names.[87]

The claim that the poem calls things by their proper names is at once an ethical, aesthetic, and epistemological claim. "Proper names" are experientially weighted and, insofar as this is so, they are authentic language. Such words speak truth to violence, following experience to its roots, to call for an authentic response from the other. Celan insisted on truth as something that demanded precise language but that ultimately depended on the way words were used by a speaker committed to the integrity of the search and the effort to engage the other.

> This language, not withstanding its inalienable complexity of expression, is concerned with precision. It does not transfigure or render "poetical"; it names, it posits, it tries to measure the area of the given and the possible. True, this is never the working of language itself, language as such, but always of an "I" who speaks from the particular angle of reflection which is his existence and who is concerned with outlines and orientation. Reality is not simply there, it must be searched and won.[88]

For Celan, the resolute attentiveness and precision of language in writing (or reading) a poem is fundamentally ethical. The purpose of this precision and integrity of language is to make possible the very condition of human community, the real presence of the other.[89]

> Craft means handiwork, a matter of hands. And these hands must belong to one person, i.e. a unique, mortal soul searching for its way with its voice and its dumbness. Only truthful hands write true poems. I cannot see any basic difference between a handshake and a poem.[90]

Language here is key to authentic human connection, symbolized by a handshake with its bodily presence and nonverbal message that can signal either open greeting and solidarity or the diffidence and absence of someone who is simply "going through the motions." Integrity resides in taking responsibility for one's personal history and acknowledging one's current stance or position.

Authenticity, in the sense expressed in the maxim "To thine own self be true," depends on a process of being free from coercion, able to think and speak one's own mind, along with a commitment to follow one's own truth. As an interpersonal stance, authenticity must be lived with others, and if it is to be something more than a platform for self-aggrandizing individualism, it must rest on a dialogical ethic. Authenticity, then, resides in the serious effort to understand (and be understood by) the other, the honesty to acknowledge when we have failed, the commitment to recognize the other as a vulnerable human being despite that failure, and the renewed effort to strive for understanding. It demands our openness to show where we are in this cycle and to reveal something of the anger, exhaustion, and self-doubt that come with our inevitably limited understanding of self and other.[91]

Consider this stanza from a poem written in 1969 when Celan was in and out of the psychiatric hospital, living apart from his wife and son.[92]

I stand
up from the shatter of
madness
and watch my hand
trace the one
single
circle

After the shattering experience of madness, the poet stands and traces a single circle, a symbol of both the fullness of the plenum and the emptiness of the void. The circle is singular, suggesting its individuality, uniqueness, and the solitude of the speaker. Celan is outside, separated from his loved ones by death and madness, shattered but able to stand again to seek (or remember the trace of) some measure of wholeness. The circle stands for containment, symmetry, completeness, and connection.[93] As the translator Ian Fairley[94] notes, the circle in this poem is related to the *meridian* that is the central figure in Celan's speech on acceptance of the Büchner Prize for Literature. The circle's circumference arcs out and away toward the other but always returns; like the poet himself, it is always underway, in a cycle of reaching toward others and receiving their response, in a hermeneutic circle in which both poet and listener participate. "The poet stands in mindful relation to a circle—which can be conceived, I suggest, as the circle of circumstance—and in internally distant relation to himself, as if returned to a circuit of self-estrangement and self-recognition."[95] All that it contains within its circumference is marked off from what it excludes. The circle creates an inside and outside and the poem is ambiguous: does the circle contain or exclude the self? The poem, too, has a circumference, though its location depends on the relationship between poet and listener. The tracing of the circle stands for the poem's construction as the trace of an inner circle of experience into which the other is invited to stand with the poet. "The poem's standing toward its circumstance is a matter of bearing another in mind."[96]

The imagery of the lyric poem commands our attention and through that attentiveness we have the opportunity to stand with the poem and with the poet for whom it speaks.[97] For Celan, every poem is spoken by someone, an "I," who asks that we listen. Celan's poetics points toward an ethic of authenticity founded on the effort to be present with and for the other: standing with them in solidarity, acknowledging the distance and difference of perspective, and remaining committed to the possibility of communication despite the sometimes vast gulf in experience. The difficulty of understanding a poem is no greater than the difficulty of standing with a person.

## Language and the Geopolitics of Othering

> My mouth shall be the mouth of those calamities that have no mouth, my voice the freedom of those who break down in the prison holes of despair.
>
> – Aimé Césaire[98]

Celan lived and wrote within a European context in which the most extreme ruptures occurred against a backdrop of shared language, history, and tradition. Even when this shared history was denigrated or denied by revisionists who sought to elevate themselves by eliding, erasing, or annihilating others, this history—inscribed in institutions, landscapes, and language itself—formed a tacit ground of mutual understanding. In the prelude to the Shoah, this shared history was the target of propaganda that aimed to exaggerate difference, create sharp divisions, and dehumanize the other to lay the ground for genocide. Recognition and respect for others in their difference and distinctiveness, and for the specificity of their languages, are then essential steps toward restitution and repair.

World history is replete with the accounts of explorers and adventurers, missionaries, and traders who encountered others with whom they shared no language or culture and who were seen therefore as radically other. European colonialism provides grim demonstrations of the ease with which other peoples can be devalued, dehumanized, exploited, and exterminated.[99] Postcolonial theory has emphasized the ways in which colonizing powers framed the Indigenous Peoples they met as other and "less than" to justify their domination and destruction.[100] *Othering* in this history is a form of violence that dehumanizes people, generally in the service of subjugation and exploitation.

In the colonial context, Indigenous Peoples were viewed as primitive, uncivilized people without history. The land they occupied was *terra nullius* and could be taken over with little negotiation or recompense. In the same way, the millions of people bought and sold as slaves and transported across the Atlantic Ocean to serve the colonial plantation system were viewed as other in ways that justified their violent subjugation.

The psychology of colonization has explored how this structural violence and devaluing of the other was internalized as self-alienation. Frantz Fanon described this dynamic as he walked the streets of Paris and was singled out as an object of fear in ways that made him view himself as other.[101] Relief from self-alienation comes at the cost not only of wearing a white mask but also of identifying with it. Anticolonial struggles have worked to counter this othering and dehumanization, asserting the primacy and power of original peoples and the autonomy and political agency of all those oppressed by structures of domination. This unfinished transformation has occurred in political institutions, cultural narratives, and individual psychology. These changes have been enacted through human rights declarations and legislation, but they are driven by shifts in the stories we tell about who we are and how we view the other.[102]

Stories allow us some access to the world of the other but making sense of any story requires shared background knowledge. No matter how universal or generic, this language is always grounded in local worlds of experience. One of the effects of colonialism was to displace local languages, subordinating them to a language and literature that expresses the values of the colonizing power, suppresses the history of its violence, and ensures its supremacy.[103] French and English colonialism in the Africa and the Caribbean installed education systems that taught students that their own traditions were inferior to those of European capitals where great literature originates. Poets and writers then strove to speak the language of

Shakespeare or Molière, disavowing their own roots. Colonized subjects became fluent in a language that was at once their own and other.

Postcolonial theorists have examined the dilemmas of anchoring identity in the language of the colonizer and of the marginalization of Indigenous languages or creoles.[104] The Martiniquan poet and philosopher Édouard Glissant challenged the denigration of creoles arguing that, despite power inequities in the collision of languages, creolization represented a fundamental source of creativity, vigor, and invention in language.

> I call creolization the meeting, interference, shock, harmonies and disharmonies between the cultures of the world . . . [it] has the following characteristics: the lightning speed of interaction among its elements; the "awareness of awareness" thus provoked in us; the reevaluation of the various elements brought into contact (for creolization has no presupposed scale of values); unforeseeable results. Creolization is not a simple cross breeding that would produce easily anticipated results.[105]

Creolization implies something more than simple intermixing or "hybridization"—at least in the biological sense of that metaphor, since hybrid organisms may be vigorous but sterile. The creole form is something novel that is viable in its own right, a new venture, an innovative grammar of thought and action, and a well of human possibilities from which to draw.

Identity may be conceived of as a narrative of personal history or biography, as an act of social positioning, and as the ongoing experience of self and social personhood. Creolization has a different significance for each of these aspects of identity. In personal history, the existence of creoles serves to create the solidity of tradition out of crossed and confluent streams, valorizing the hybrid, mongrel, and mestizo as its own valid and vigorous form. In some cases, this may mark the emergence of a new ethnocultural group, while, in others, it may clear a space for more transitory constructions of identity and community to suit a specific moment and particular purposes. In terms of social positioning, creolization serves to create new roles and forms of power outside the usual frames dictated by cultural traditions.

At the level of the experience of self and personhood, creoles shape the sensory, affective, and aesthetic landscapes that individuals inhabit. Creolization provides a place to root the fecundity of imagination in the unique particulars of a life lived at the crossroads of diverse peoples and traditions. As Glissant insists, poetic and evocative language and images emerge from the idiosyncratic features of local history, geography, and experience that are sedimented in creolized identities and cultural selves.

Knowing something of that history allows us to begin to understand the other but also demands our engagement in an ethics of recognition, responsiveness, and care.

## Conclusion

The clinical encounter confronts us with "otherness" in many ways: the uniqueness of each individual's experience of suffering, the inhumanness of disease and disability, and the uncanniness of bodies disfigured by affliction. In some types of psychiatric illness, these ubiquitous forms of otherness are compounded by changes in ways of thinking and acting that may make the person seem both alien and alienating.

In medicine, these various forms of otherness are tamed and transformed. The idiosyncrasies of individual experience are reduced to signs and symptoms of disease and the strangeness of disease is translated into familiar pathophysiological mechanisms that call forth a technical response. This technical response may override any attempt to empathize with the patient's predicament. When a quick cure is possible, this lack of empathy may not be a problem. For patients facing mortal illness, significant disability, or persistent symptoms, however, empathic understanding is a crucial element of the clinical encounter. The erosion of empathy in clinical practice through one-sided emphasis on the diagnostic and therapeutic technology of biomedicine accounts for much dissatisfaction with contemporary health care services and is a continuing concern in medical education. Work in narrative medicine has tried to counteract this tendency to displace the lifeworld of the patient by providing a pedagogy of empathic understanding through literature.[106] While much of this work appeals to story, lyric poetry offers another mode or medium for articulating illness experience that may be closer to the emotionally charged, confused, and confusing efforts of patients to make sense of acute illness experiences that do not fit cultural models or templates.

In earlier chapters, I have tried to show some ways in which languages of suffering involve metaphoric constructions that are often fragmentary, tentative, and contradictory. Understanding and responding to this language demands a poetics of illness experience. A medical ethics attentive to the lyric construction of the self in health and illness would supplement narrative-based ethics in several ways. It would increase interest in the personal and social impact of fragmentary, metaphorical, and imagistic constructions of experience, which may be transitory yet powerful ways of configuring the self in relation to symptoms and suffering. In contrast to the temporal structure of narrative, which typically lays out the causal path from past events through current experience to future prospects, lyric poetry tends to emphasize simultaneity, evoking a moment of consciousness. These temporary constructions may be stabilized by psychological and social interactional processes and so come to dominate experience, even without an authorizing or overarching cultural model or narrative. Attention to lyric also helps us recognize the rootedness of individuals' language in personal histories that involve limit experiences that strain the capacity of metaphor to capture and convey. Lyric returns us to the dialogical process in which the speaker and listener coconstruct a shared system of meaning.

Reading or writing poetry moves us toward greater intimacy and engagement with the presence of the other. A poem is the trace of a moment of knowing achieved through the construction of an aesthetic object that can bring the listener into an intense confrontation with the language of the other in all its urgency and conviction. Lyric compels us to acknowledge the limits of knowability of the other. This recognition of limits urges on us an ethics of alterity that begins with a stance of respect toward the other as a vulnerable being who demands our attention and responsiveness.[107]

While the halting efforts of patients to articulate their experience in clinical settings usually do not involve the same deliberate process that allows the poet to fashion an aesthetic object, they use the same faculties of language and imagination to reach the other and call forth an empathic response. Illness narratives and clinical conversations, no matter how brief, ask to be received with the same attentiveness we give to a poem. In so doing, we contribute to a form of community and a kind of medicine that can sustain and respect the voice of each individual in all its human strangeness.

CHAPTER 9

# *Asklepian Dreams*

> A man falls sick, does not eat, becomes "a house of dreams," weeps, has convulsions. He is treated for years, all his wealth is eaten up by the practitioners. He is but skin and bones. His death is daily expected. But then he becomes able to detect hidden things and after a purification ceremony he is a medicine man and well again.
>
> – Edward Ackerknecht[1]

> The wounder heals.
>
> – Oracle of Apollo[2]

Accounts of the efficacy of healing practices appeal to universal psychobiological processes, the dynamics of interpersonal relationships and social positioning, and cultural systems of meaning. Each healing tradition has its own explanations of how and why healing works that are tied to cultural ontologies, cosmologies, and concepts of the person. These provide specific models and metaphors for the healer, who may be thought of variously as a technician, professional, educator, and advocate or a spiritual advisor, guide, intermediary, or guru. Clearly, each of these models and metaphors convey different expectations for sufferer and healer and for the process of healing, including protocols, rituals, sources of authority, interpersonal dynamics, sociomoral implications, and even concepts of health and recovery.

The aim of this chapter is to explore the origins of healing authority and its experiential grounding. Miriam Siegler and Humphry Osmond used the term "Aesculapian authority" to refer to the unique authority of the physician as healer.[3] They suggest that this authority has three sources or dimensions: special knowledge, the moral imperative to relieve suffering and prevent death, and the charismatic effect of viewing the power to heal as a kind of magic. Sociological accounts of authority usually refer to institutional power. This power may be built into social structure and maintained by governmental, legal, or professional regulations, norms, and routines, but it is usually also rationalized and naturalized by cultural ontologies and ideology. Following Jerome Frank,[4] we can conjecture that the authority of a healing practice resides in the local form of its universal features: an authorizing myth (rooted in a shared ontology or assumptive world), the institutional authority of the healer, the site of the ritual, and the healing practice—which I have argued involves metaphors that engage and transform bodily experience and imagination. In this chapter, I will suggest that, in addition to the appeal to shared symbols and institutions, there is a metaphoric logic in the relation between wounding and healing that is an existential given. Recognition of this logic can inform an ethics of care.

There are many potential institutional sources of healing authority. Biomedicine emphasizes technical training, formal certification, and grounding practice in scientific evidence. In all systems of medicine, healers may gain authority not only from their training or apprenticeship but also from their social position in a web of relationships, institutions, and practices. Perhaps the most basic source of healing authority, though, is the healer's own experience of illness. Many elementary systems of medicine, particularly shamanism, emphasize the connection of healers' afflictions to their therapeutic power.[5] There is an intuitive logic in the idea that someone who has been sick and survived possesses intimate knowledge of the nature of illness and its cure.[6] Shamans' initiatory illness is both a call to their vocation and part of the process that transforms them into a person of power. As the psychiatrist and anthropologist Horacio Fabrega observed:

> Occurrences of disease play an important role in creating the healing hierarchy. It is as though experience with disease and more specifically being threatened by it and consequently winning the struggle against the elemental forces in disease (forces which are personified as other beings) gives the individual a special awareness of what disease signifies. This encounter allows him a communicational access to those beings and ultimately to the power to control them. Experiences with disease seem to constitute tangible evidence that an individual has been identified with supernatural beings which, in turn, make him capable of curing disease supernaturally.[7]

What distinguishes those who are transformed by their illness into healers from those who are simply laid low, depleted, and disabled or, equally, from those who, when they recover, turn away from illness, feeling no inclination to adopt the identity of healer? The passage quoted from Fabrega above suggests one possibility: healers-to-be are simply stronger or more resilient than others, taking an active role in their own self-healing and having the capacity and determination to continue working with the illness of others after their own recovery. For a time, anthropological studies of shamanism took the contrary position, emphasizing the shaman's own persistent psychopathology.[8] With more careful recent studies, this view has lost credibility as a general explanation.[9] Shamans and other traditional healers are neither consistently sicker nor healthier than others of comparable background and resources.[10] Many of the shamanic experiences attributed to psychosis (e.g., visual and auditory hallucinations) are now understood as imaginative or dissociative experiences that can occur in the absence of psychopathology. Persistent psychoses are usually incompatible with the complex social relationships the healer must negotiate to be successful. However, if we put aside the serious forms of psychotic pathology mistakenly linked to shamanism, the intuition that healers' fascination with and commitment to the healing arts are related to their own persistent psychological wounds bears closer examination. Indeed, there is evidence that the choice of a career in medicine, as well as the choice of a specific medical specialty, are shaped by encounters with illness in oneself and one's family.[11]

The nature of healers' relationships to their own wounds influences the structure and dynamics of healing. The cultural psychiatrist Raymond Prince suggested that much symbolic healing relies on endogenous mechanisms in the patient.[12] The task of the healer, then, is to activate dormant or malfunctioning mechanisms of healing and resilience in the patient (which may be personified as an "inner healer"). Patients may project their own healing capacity onto the clinician. If healers accept this projection uncritically, they may strengthen their sense of power but risk pathologizing the patient. This polarization characterizes many of the interactions seen in contemporary biomedical settings, where the clinician represents health, wholeness, competence, and rationality, and the patient is a passive recipient of treatments directed to their broken body, brain, or psyche. In this scheme, patient and clinician have fixed roles that each helps to maintain through an asymmetrical relationship. However, alternative relational structures are possible. In particular, healers can acknowledge their own wounds and also recognize the patient as a healer. This may help patients to acknowledge their wounds but also their strengths and resilience.

In this chapter, I argue that healers' relationships to their own wounds not only convey symbolic power but can evoke specific psychological and interpersonal dynamics that may contribute to the effectiveness of treatment. The nature of this relationship also has important ethical implications. Even in biomedicine, which claims to be underwritten by scientific evidence and where technology dominates practice, practitioners' own experiences of affliction contribute to their power and authority. When clinicians acknowledge their own woundedness, they need not defensively deny the reflections of that affliction in their patients. Further, the willingness to remain in contact with parts of the self that are wounded or in pain allows the healer to engage the patient on this empathic ground. Ultimately, patients' own healing resources may be evoked by their recognition of the healer's vulnerability. This can open the door to healing transformations where none seemed possible. Healers' acknowledgment of their own vulnerability can also foster a redistribution and sharing of power crucial to an ethics of care.[13]

## The Structure of the Clinical Encounter

Like all skilled practice, the healing encounter is organized hierarchically. The constituent elements are actions governed by explicit protocols and procedures that may be learned and carried out more or less consciously by following scripts or rules. In the case of training in psychotherapy, this is the stuff of treatment manuals, guidelines, and rules of thumb. Of course, such conscious efforts at technique are never more than fractions of the ongoing verbal and nonverbal interaction between patient and psychotherapist. Even when the interaction is deliberately slowed down or constrained by limiting the topics of conversation, too much is going on to be consciously controlled. Much action follows from models or metaphors that are learned implicitly and have both procedural implications and affective connotations. One of the goals of the metaphor analysis of therapeutic discourse is to lay bare these implicit structures.

However, in psychotherapy, as in any conversation or social situation, there are always unexpected events and "gaps" that deviate from the script or fall outside the reach of a particular metaphor. These gaps must be bridged by improvisations that draw from the available cognitive and contextual resources or affordances, but also from the therapist's own personality, attitudes, thoughts and feelings, bodily habitus, and habitual modes of self-presentation. The psychotherapist's personally motivated and technically guided actions are embedded in larger social and cultural systems of meaning. These can be described at many levels corresponding to the personal, communal, and institutional organization of training and practice, which may involve many cross-cutting or contradictory goals and agendas. Every healer also participates in a community's *ethos*—its affective, aesthetic, and moral climate—which provides overarching values that guide the selection of technique, the healer's attitudes, and give specific meaning to words and gestures. The abstraction of ethos provides us with a way of considering the origin and consequences of practices in terms of affective climate, aesthetic values, and sociomoral commitments.[14]

In the clinical encounter, then, the patient and healer interact on three different levels, each of which contributes to the cognitive, relational, and wider social dynamics of healing: (i) the technical level of deliberate speech acts and gestures learned as part of a formal healing practice; (ii) the level of bodily presence, personality, individual style, and idiosyncrasy in which spontaneity, improvisation, and invention lead to exchanges that reflect both conscious and nonconscious plans and possibilities[15]; and (iii) the level of ethos—overarching patterns of affective and aesthetic meaning and value that both healer and patient participate in as part of the evolving structure of the culturally prescribed healing relationship.

An overarching ethos provides images and expectations that contribute to the interactional process between patient and healer and may be constellated in ways that open up new possibilities or ways forward. For example, a patient in the middle phase of long-term psychotherapy recounted the following dream.

> I am with my therapist in his office but there is a third person there, an older woman. She has white hair and is serene yet powerful. Her presence makes me feel secure. She is different from my therapist though, somehow, she seems to be his ally. I feel it is really her who is doing the therapy.

While conscious and personal elements of the therapeutic relationship are important in understanding this dream, the patient maintained that this image of a powerful old woman was quite unfamiliar to her in waking life. There was no one in her childhood history full of abuse and neglect to connect with this profound feeling of comfort. The dream presence drew from a common fund of cultural knowledge, expressed in an image of the *Wise Old Woman*.[16] To the extent this dream arose from—and was reported at a particular moment—in the evolving therapy, it can be viewed as imaginative co-construction constellated by the relationship between patient and physician.[17] The dynamics of the clinical interaction can evoke compensatory or transformative images that allow patient and healer to go beyond their personal wounds or limits of imagination. Figure 9.1 depicts the structure of this intersubjective process.

While expressed in conventional cultural tropes found in myth and fairy tales, the numinous quality of the dream for the patient conveyed a sense of profound meaning—invoking something beyond her personal history and memories. This is the kind of experience that prompted Jung to develop the idea of archetypes, and the corresponding projections by patient and clinician have been called *archetypal transference* and *countertransference*, respectively.[18] What makes an image archetypal is the recognition that it emerges not from idiosyncratic individual or cultural associations but from an existential predicament intrinsic to the human condition.

As discussed in Chapter 5, much of the confusion and unease surrounding Jung's uses of the terms *archetype* and *collective unconscious* can be resolved by locating the collective not in the deepest layers of the psyche but in the social and cultural surround. The emergent level of organization that we call "culture" creates images that transcend our personal history

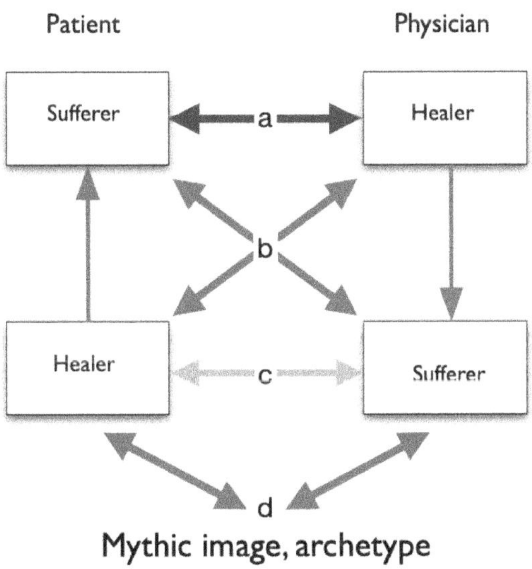


Figure 9.1 Constellation of the wounded-healer in the clinical encounter
The wounded-healer archetype reflects the structure and dynamics of the healing relationship. (a) The patient is explicitly identified with the sufferer and the clinician with the healer. However, each has their own experience as sufferer and healer that allows identification with the other (b) and reciprocal relationships (c). Together these constellate a relational structure that can evoke the image and function of the wounded healer.

and requires its own language of archetypal images and mythological stories. Myths, folktales, fairy tales, and dreams are progressively more local or personalized versions of culturally informed responses to the questions posed by our existential predicaments.

The concepts of myth and archetype are useful in thinking about the relational structure of psychotherapy and other forms of healing practice. When all the distortions of transference are recognized, interpreted and reintegrated, there remains a level of implicit structure which shapes the relationship between patient and healer. Every clinical encounter draws from a range of culture-specific roles and patterns of interaction, which to some extent can be understood as local variations on more universal or archetypal themes. The archetypal image of the Wise Old Woman draws from existential universals related to the accumulation of experience with age, the gendered nature of woman's knowing, and the traditional association of wisdom with elders who are culture bearers. This configuration varies with culturally shaped attitudes to aging, gender roles, and knowledge but recurs across very diverse cultures and historical contexts. The feelings and fantasies evoked by and condensed in the image constitute a cultural or collective level of imagination that is nevertheless historically contingent. Nonshared historical experience will lead to divergent images and associations.

The historical aspects of relationships between ethnocultural groups also can give rise to what has been termed *ethnocultural transference* and *countertransference.*[19] Just as personal countertransference can provide useful information, revealing the therapist's own biases and conflicts that may impede treatment, so too cultural countertransference sheds light on the larger social contexts that shape the clinician–patient relationship. Given their different social positions, how well does the clinician understand the patient's predicament? What structural inequities are reenacted in the clinical encounter? Does the clinician from a dominant group feel historical guilt toward a minority patient who has suffered racism, colonialism, or oppression?[20] Is the clinician unable—or too quick—to link patients' suffering to these social injustices? Does the minoritized clinician feel disqualified in ways that undermine their confidence and effectiveness?

Any healing relationship is embedded in historical particulars of the relationships between peoples and places that precede the development of a therapeutic "working alliance." But there are also relational patterns and possibilities that transcend any local history, pointing toward more universal or archetypal themes. The image of the wounded-healer is one such archetypal pattern that can be discerned in both elementary systems of medicine and the religious healing of the cults of Asklepios in ancient Greece. Given the historical roots of Western medicine in ancient Greece, it instructive to consider this version of the myth of the wounded-healer.

## The Myth of Asklepios

In Greek mythology, the image of the healer or physician (*iatros*) appears in many forms but the most important of these is Asklepios (Latinized as Aesculapius). Asklepios may have been an historical figure who in successive transmissions of oral tradition became first a hero and then a demigod. Functioning cults of Asklepios with ritual healing practices existed until the third century AD, when they were supplanted by Christian institutions.[21] Central to the healing rites of purification and incubation were the widely known stories of the life of the great physician.[22]

> The father of Asklepios was the great god Apollo whose gifts included healing, mantic vision and a piercing rationality. His mother was Coronis. The story is told that while Coronis was already pregnant with Apollo's child she enjoyed a liaison with the youth Ischys who had caught her fancy. Apollo was enraged when he discovered this infidelity and he had Coronis summarily killed by his sister Artemis. As she lay on the funeral pyre, flames already rising about her, Apollo had a change of heart and turned to Hermes who cut the still living child from his dead mother's womb. Apollo named the child Asklepios and took him to the cave of Chiron, the centaur, to be raised.
>
> Chiron was a son of Kronos and foremost among the centaurs—a race of demigods, half-man, half-horse, who dwelt on the mountain Pelion. With his animal body, Chiron was viewed as a dark god and his cave was an entrance to the underworld. Renowned for his knowledge of medicine, hunting and music, Chiron taught these arts to Asklepios. Chiron had been struck by an arrow, meant for someone else, and suffered an incurable wound from which he drew his healing power. Chiron was, like Apollo, able to restore eyesight to the blind.
>
> Athene gave Asklepios two vials of blood from the Gorgon Medusa's jugular veins. With the blood drawn from her left side, Asklepios could raise the dead and with the blood from her right he could destroy life instantly. Asklepios became a famous healer. Once, however, he dared to use the Medusa's blood to restore life to a slain warrior. This hubris so angered Zeus that he struck Asklepios down with a lightning bolt.
>
> Later, Zeus too, had second thoughts and raised Asklepios from the dead to join the pantheon of gods. His sons became great healers as well. One of

> them, Machaon, was also wounded by an arrow meant for another man as he tended to the injured on the battlefield.[23]

The hero Asklepios is born of both human and divine parentage just at the moment that the family romance is torn asunder by infidelity and rageful vengeance. Hermes—trickster, messenger, and guide of souls to the underworld—acts as midwife, to deliver the infant from his mother's womb when she is burning to death.[24] The connection to transgression—through infidelity, the intercourse of gods and mortals, and the intercession of Hermes, the prototypical hermeneut—reminds us of the common origin story of the healer. Physicians are often called to their profession by some confrontation with illness and mortality. Psychotherapists may be drawn to their vocation by their awareness of the painful undercurrents of family life and efforts to master conflict.[25] This experience of the underlife of the family can give rise to a hermeneutics of suspicion in which there is the sense that there is meaning hidden behind people's actions—and if only that hidden meaning could be understood, the world (the family) could be set right.[26]

Asklepios learns the art of healing from the centaur Chiron: not his biological father but a mentor or spiritual father who joins together in his body both human and animal realms. The human realm aspires to be Apollonian: abstract, lucid, and filled with light and reason. The animal realm is chthonic: dark, muscular, virile, and connected to the Earth as to sweat and semen. The myth moves back and forth between the celestial world of Apollo and the chthonian world of Chiron and the Gorgon.

The image of Chiron hints at the incorporation of shamanic tradition in Greek mythology.[27] In hunting societies, shamans acquire their healing power from animal spirits.[28] Chiron embodies the dual nature of healing: the Apollonian intellect that orders and illuminates through language, reason, and technical precision; and the visceral intuition and animal intelligence that reaches into the shrouded recesses of the body to probe and work with torn and bloody flesh. The result is a quintessentially human combination of *praxis* and *logos*, treating with the hands and with words. Indeed, "Chiron" comes from the Greek root meaning "working by hand, producing a handcraft or art," which also gives us the English word "surgeon." The practitioner of healing arts comes to understand that they, like their patients, join the realms of animal and human. Chiron's darkness, his connection to the underworld, gives him access to knowledge of the unknown.

Chiron is wounded and his wound is incurable. This theme recurs throughout the story. Asklepios is struck down by lightning for aspiring to raise the dead. Machaon, his son, is wounded in battle even as he strives to heal others. With few exceptions, the Greek myths portray the healer with their own formative and persistent wounds. In mythic thought, healing power and woundedness are inseparable.

> Wounding and being wounded are the dark premises of healing; it is they that make the profession possible and indeed a necessity for human existence. For this existence may—among other possibilities—be conceived as that of a wounding and vulnerable being who can also heal, while the animal is merely wounding and vulnerable. But it is only man's wounds that can be healed, not man himself. Machaon wounds and heals, but in essence he is incurable. Eurypylos, the underworld ruler "with the wide gate", engulfs him forever. The warrior surgeon dies of his wounds. But in the cult of his tomb he lives on, attaining to the existence of the Greek gods, wounding and vulnerable, healing and susceptible of being healed.[29]

Participation in the process of wounding and healing holds great danger for mortals. Identifying with these powerful forces, healers can become "inflated," filled with the delusion that it is *they* who do the healing and not some supraindividual or transpersonal process acting through them. This was Asklepios's error in his hubris of restoring the dead to life. He acted as though the power was his to be used as he saw fit. For this inflation he suffered the inevitable deflation, in this case, the swift justice of Zeus. The risk for the healer who identifies personally with the healing process is more than arrogance; it is a kind of death of consciousness: the loss of awareness of one's own limitedness and, hence, a loss of ordinary human identity and moral intelligence.

For all the reasons adduced in this chapter, healers may be assigned an elevated or numinous status. Despite the crises of trust that have undermined the authority of many professions, physicians are still seen as having god-like qualities.[30] Perhaps it was easier to avoid this inflation in ancient Greece, where sickness and healing were both seen as actions of the gods, clearly independent of the individual's wishes and limited power.

> Classical man saw sickness as the effect of a divine action. Thus a clear form of homeopathy, the divine sickness being cast out by the divine remedy (*similia similibus curantur*) was practiced in the clinics of antiquity. When sickness is vested with such dignity, it has the inestimable advantage that it can be vested with a healing power. The *divina afflictio* then contains its own diagnosis, therapy and prognosis, provided of course that the right attitude is adopted. The right attitude was made possible by the cult, which simply

> consisted in leaving the entire act of healing to the divine physician: *He* was the sickness *and* the remedy. These two conceptions were identical. Because he was the sickness, he himself was afflicted (wounded or perhaps persecuted like Asclepius or Trophonius), and because he was the divine patient he also knew the way to healing. To such a god the oracle of Apollo applies: "He who wounds also heals."[31]

The myth ends with renewal: Asklepios is restored to life as a god. The experience of identification with the healing process and so, of inflation, is inescapable. Indeed, it is a necessary part of the healing process. For a time, healer and patient are lost together in the symbolic reality of their relationship. In this liminal space, on the edge of awareness, in myth, dream, and reverie, the images of gods and goddesses do their work of healing and illumination.

Cults of Asklepios flourished throughout the Greco-Roman world. Important temples existed at Epidavros, Athens, and Kos.[32] Historians suggest that "[t]he cult appealed strongly to the rising individualism of the fourth and ensuing centuries since it provided a close personal relationship with the divine and could evoke a fervid personal devotion ... seldom found in the formal State religion."[33] In actual practice, the sick came to the temples for healing through the process of *incubation*. After rites of purification, and offerings to Apollo and Asklepios, incubation involved staying within a sacred central region of the temple grounds, the *abaton*, often constructed as a labyrinth sunken into the ground. There the afflicted person slept or tranced to experience healing dreams or visions.[34] Healing was done directly by the god Asklepios, who might appear in dreams as a fair youth touching one's wounds or a snake or dog licking them. Asklepios was depicted in statues as either young or old but often accompanied by a staff with a single serpent twined around it. The snake is a natural symbol of renewal because it sheds its skin periodically to rejuvenate itself. The snake is also a reminder of the lowliest, of that which crawls along the ground in contact with the earth. Beneath the temples were labyrinths where live snakes were kept.

In contemporary psychological terms, we might say that the process of incubation relied on the sufferer's own unconscious to provide the healing images and experiences.[35] The god Asklepios represents the "inner healer" who could be invoked without the direct mediation of a worldly healer. Priest attendants assisted with the rituals of purification and the interpretation of the dreams and, in some temples, it was the priests themselves who had the dreams, magically acting through them to diagnose and treat the sufferer's illness. The *temenos* (sacred place) adjacent to the healing temple provided a space where individuals could petition and become receptive to the divine healer, whether encountered directly in dreams or reverie or, indirectly, through the mediation of the priest. In a like manner, we can think of the relationship between healer and sufferer in contemporary psychotherapy as occurring in a place that is located within or adjacent to institutions that confer authority and healing power on the interaction, or as creating an intersubjective and imaginative *temenos* where healing imagery can be evoked and be allowed to do its work.

## Jung's Journey to *The Red Book*

The archetypal image of the "wounded physician" was invoked by Jung to argue for the importance of training analysis to help therapists come to terms with their own psychological difficulties.[36] This grew out of his own experiences of affliction and was reflected in his whole approach to individual development and psychotherapy.

Jung is a seminal figure in the study of the psychology of imagination. The theory and practice he elaborated around his own work with imaginal presences provides many ideas that are "good to think with." Jungian psychology claims to be phenomenological in that it stays close to the form and context of experience in its modes of exploration and explanation.[37] Experience is not secondary to or eclipsed by mechanistic or processual models. Clinically, this is seen in a willingness to engage with the details of an individual's experience, to explore their quality, context, and texture as intrinsically meaningful.

Jungian hermeneutics allows for a broad, open-ended approach to meaning. This hermeneutic approach was at the center of Jung's rupture with Freud. In *Symbols of Transformation*, Jung argued that the search for meaning was more basic than sexuality as a motive force and logic in human experience.[38] This led to a nonreductive approach to interpretation in which symbols do not simply stand in for repressed sexual conflicts. In Jung's view, *symbols stand for themselves* in the sense that they are already the most condensed expression of a structure of meaning. The elaboration of personally or clinically relevant meaning then requires staying close to the image in the interpretive process. Images as symbols in the Jungian sense are irreducible in that (i) they bring together varied elements in a specific configuration that is more than the sum of its parts; and (ii) they are generative (performative or presentational rather than simply representational), providing tools for thinking with, possibilities for imaginative construction and exploration, and confronting us with moral predicaments.[39]

Jung called the method of interpretation that these assumptions led to *amplification*, governed by the logic of "as well as" rather than "nothing but." Amplification heaps association upon association, image upon image, in widening circles that connect individuals' experience to a larger archaeology of imagination found in myth and dream across time and culture. This nonreductive approach to elaborating meaning is congenial to those who approach psychological development, creativity, as well as religious or spiritual practice, as paths toward perennial existential or transpersonal truths.

The final crucial step in Jung's thought carries this hermeneutics over into an ethics, aesthetics, and practice he termed "the symbolic life." This involves not simply a valorization of imagination, but the recognition of images as centers of psychic activity, with their own agency. This means taking fantasy, reveries, and dreams seriously.[40] Jung described this as a process of "active imagination," in which one confronts images as real presences. Granting autonomy to imaginative processes provides a way to break out of the confines of a personally or culturally constricted version of the self. Engaging imaginary entities in serious, consequential dialogue becomes a strategy for increasing self-awareness, enlarging the self, and encountering the patterns of coherence Jung termed the *Self*, capitalizing the word to distinguish it as an archetype of wholeness that exceeds the personal self.

The origin of this orientation and technique lies in Jung's own experience of affliction and healing. In 1913, Freud and Jung broke with each other after an intense relationship over several years. Overtly, this was precipitated by theoretical disagreements but clearly it had deeper personal, social, and cultural roots. Freud's authoritarianism and commitment to defending his doctrine offended Jung. In the father–son relationship they constellated, Jung could not tolerate Freud's rigidity and unwillingness to see Jung individuate and surpass him. All of this was complicated by a larger socio-political context in which Freud hoped that Jung, as a non-Jew, would be the heir who would bring wider acceptance to his work.

Against the backdrop of rising international tensions, this break precipitated a crisis for Jung. From 1913 to 1914, he withdrew from many activities and began an intensive process of exploring the imagery that had erupted in his dreams and fantasy. He deliberately invited visionary experiences and adopted an attitude of taking the images, beings, and felt presences that appeared seriously and engaging them in dialogue. Although at many points in this process, he feared he might be losing his mind, he felt he had no choice but to continue. The outcome was a series of extended dialogues with imaginative figures that included a neo-gnostic text (*Seven Sermons to the Dead*), dictated to Jung by visionary figures, and many arresting images capturing his personal mythology. He recorded all of these visions, reveries, and imaginative excursions in notebooks and later transcribed and elaborated them in calligraphic text and images. He painted a series of vivid watercolors that captured the imagery, dreams, and fantasies of his journey, as well as intricate designs or mandalas that provided a kind of aesthetic organization and integration of the play of opposites that had emerged in his reveries. He assembled these images and text into a large leatherbound tome he called *The Red Book*.[41] His reflections on this self-transformative process became the basis for much of his later theoretical work and therapeutic practice.

Although Jung's crisis has sometimes been characterized as a psychotic episode, there is little evidence this is the case. The self-reflexivity that he maintained through this process marks it as distinct from psychotic afflictions in which the person's grounding in consensual reality is disrupted. No doubt, these experiences also influenced his ontology—he came to declare his deep conviction in the presence of the divine and in a realm of experience beyond the mundane world, yet he retained a thoroughly psychological view of the transformative process he termed "individuation."[42]

## Dreams and Initiation

A central tenet of Jungian or archetypal psychology holds that the meaning of an image lies in its detail and configuration.[43] To explore the ethos of the wounded-healer more deeply, then, we must attend to the minute particulars of the images of wounding and healing. In what follows, I will present a sequence of my own dreams, all of which occurred during my internship and residency training in psychiatry and some of which occurred while I was a patient in Jungian psychotherapy.[44] The dreams span a period of about two years. I have chosen them from a much larger number of dreams solely on the criterion that they were successive dreams in which explicit images of wounding and healing appeared. Between the occurrences of each of these dreams were many others that dealt with different themes. Each dream is framed by a brief interpretation that moves from my personal associations at the time to larger cultural resonances related to the archetype of the wounded-healer. The style of interpretation follows Jung's method of amplification in which multiple personal and collective associations are brought together like the corolla of a flower.[45]

When I sought psychotherapy, my conscious goals were mostly didactic: to learn more about therapy from the inside as an essential part of my professional training. My therapist responded to this explicit agenda by saying that he had an additional goal for me: he hoped that I would learn what it is to be a patient. This struck a chord in terms of my concern for equity and presented a challenge in its invitation to let myself be more vulnerable, acknowledge my woundedness, and undergo a healing process. The first dream I present here occurred after several months of therapy and soon after beginning to work on an inpatient psychiatric ward:

> **Dream 1**: I am sanding wood in my old bedroom in my parents' home, explaining to M and my mother when to use fresh sandpaper. I get two bad splinters in my hands, one in each thumb. The splinters are completely beneath the skin so I can't remove them. They are only faintly visible as gray spots below the surface.
>
> I go downstairs to look for a sharp needle to remove them. The splinters begin to move themselves, under the internal pressure of the flesh. As they move they cut clear through the surface of my right hand, separating thenar eminence from palm, but the splinter is still not visible.
>
> M is sitting to my left playing with some black cats. He does not help me although I think that he could.
>
> My mother finds large ring forceps and tries to pluck the splinter, I caution her to wait—they're still moving by themselves. But it is too late. She severs some fascia and the right thumb is left hanging loosely by the side of the dissected palm. I knew that, had we just endured patiently, the splinters would have worked themselves out.
>
> I can see the splinters clearly now. They are almost out. All the damage to the hand has been along fascial planes so it will be possible to repair.

Working with one's hands to build something is also working on the self—we use the abrasive experiences of life to create our finished form. But this work is never entirely under our control: while the surface is being worn smooth, we may be wounded. A sharp splinter, like the arrow that wounds Chiron and Machaon, cuts beneath the surface adaptation to expose raw flesh. The splinters cause wounds to the hands, with which we shape the world giving materiality to imagination.

Chiron, we have noted, means "works by hand." In Greek religion, hands (*cheires*) and divine powers were linked.[46] Much healing occurs by touch, not only by the surgeon's cutting and sewing, or the manipulation and massage of physiotherapy and bodywork, but also the gentle touch of solace. In magical therapy, the combination of word and touch (*praxis* and *logos*) is essential.[47] Statues of Asklepios and other Greek healing figures were often gilded just on their hands and fingers.[48]

Once the splinters have entered they work inside to open the wound. The shadowy figure of M—a brash and abrasive schoolmate who was outcast by his friends, and who later had a psychotic disorder—is unwilling to help with the healing. Instead, he plays with black cats, domestic animals with a diffident relationship to humans, linked in folklore with witches.[49] This image suggests that, while an active part of the psyche could take action to heal (or heal through taking action), it is too caught up in fascination with the introverted, dark, nonhuman realm to be of any help.[50]

My mother tries to deliver me from my wounds with forceps. This image reminded me of the same type of forceps I had used in the emergency room a few weeks earlier to deliver a fifteen-year-old girl of the remaining "products of conception" after a spontaneous abortion. During this typical "sink-or-swim" internship experience of learning to use my hands, the girl cried and kept pleading, "Please don't tell my mother." The mother in the dream tries to get rid of the splinter prematurely, rather than allowing a natural process to occur, in which I can learn about my wounds as they transform.

Something in me has been aborted; there is "dead wood" in my hands. But these forceps are not the right instruments to deliver me of my wound, particularly when wielded by my mother. My wounds must work their way out on their own, moving along fascial planes, following a path found in the anatomical structure of the hands. There is a clear sense of the danger of aggressive help itself, which can cause iatrogenic illness, and the value of letting things "work themselves out." This recalls a central meaning of the term "patient"—the willingness or necessity to suffer and endure, rather than evading or escaping from the problem with a quick fix.[51]

Perhaps my mother does help, paradoxically, by making my wounds worse, tearing them right open. Their ghastliness forces an eye-opening awareness that something has been injured. In the end, much has been laid bare, the wounding agent is revealed, and it is possible to see that the exposed tissues are intact, each muscle held in its fascial bundle, so that healing will be possible. Working in medicine, with disease, with the roughest materials of the world, it is impossible not to get splinters. This wounding is a kind of initiation—a descent into darkness that can lead to transformation and rebirth.[52] The ring forceps point to this conjunction between uncovering wounds and being born.

The next dream occurred one month later and moves deeper into regions of woundedness using images influenced by the setting of a psychiatric ward where only the most dangerous and incapacitated patients were hospitalized and treated.

> **Dream 2**: A large stone building, an orphanage or hospital run by a religious order. I am with an older friend visiting the facility in mid-winter. As we go through the central gate, we pass a sign that says: "Terminal Radiation Unit"—apparently a place where children with cancer are treated.
>
> I find my friend engaged in an illicit conversation with a young boy who is not sick and could leave the orphanage–hospital. But the Order never lets anyone leave.
>
> We start to climb stairs to visit floor after floor of dormitories. The interior is prison-like. The barred windows are opaque with dirt. With fright we see so many sick and deformed children. Dirty, crippled, and defective children are thrown like rags about the crowded room.
>
> We climb further. The children are supposed to be healthier on the higher levels. The guided tour is catching up with us and we fear we may be in trouble for our unauthorized exploration. Suddenly, the first child we met comes running up the stairwell after us. He seems to be healthy, only lame from stiffness and lack of exercise. He wants to leave with us, to be free. We decide to smuggle him out.
>
> Down to the ground level where, in the twilight, the Order's guards are swinging red and white lamps. We slip out unseen during a changing of the guard and run into a heavily wooded area. I leave the child to hide and go back to misdirect the searching parties that have already formed.
>
> I lead the soldiers in the wrong direction and then run ahead to join the child. We make our way out through a hole in the old stone wall to find ourselves outside on a snow-covered country road. We are free! The beautiful light of winter twilight is about us as we walk back to the entrance gate of the orphanage. It is there we will meet my partner and take the bus back to the outside world. We disguise the boy as my son or younger brother. What a powerful child he is!

The orphanage–hospital run by a strict, authoritarian religious order reminded me of the general hospital where I was doing my training. The Terminal Radiation Unit was the psychiatric ward where incurable wounds were given noxious treatments in the hope of palliation. Going deeper into this heavily guarded abode, we uncover a stunning amount of damaged human life. The wounded, deformed, or dead child could be taken to stand for the injured, stunted, and undeveloped in myself. The healthy child is natural a symbol of rebirth, youth, playfulness, and the light and promise of a new day.[53] But these children have been cast aside. Some terrible defects or injuries have set them back from life. Or is it that they are orphans, deprived of parental care and abandoned? There was nothing obvious in my own life to explain this image; at a personal level, it seemed a dramatization of subtler wounds. Of course, no family life is ideal; even in the most benign family, there are aspects of each child to which a parent cannot respond and that languish, orphaned, or disowned. Often it is the child's own efforts to please and to fit in that lead to self-estrangement, abandoning aspects of the self that do not meet the expectations of parents or the wider social world and constructing a "false self" in its stead.[54]

There is some sense in the dream that these children really don't have to be hospitalized. They are kept there by a repressive Order, leading the dreamer to wonder if they could be freed. Something freeing does occur: my double and I are able to help a child escape. This escape is the child's own idea and it is with his strength and determination that we are able to carry out the rescue. There was a marvelous feeling in the dream—and in the retelling—when we escape from the dark underworld through a cave-like opening in the stone wall, to be reborn into the light. Emerging from Chiron's cave, we experience the magic of early winter evening when the air seems charged with electricity and the pristine snow reflects the light.

Work in psychiatric settings involves intense interaction with people whose suffering evokes the wounded aspects of the clinician's own self. This sometimes leads clinicians to distance themselves in self-protection. If we align with patients through empathy and advocacy, we face the danger of overidentification with their wounds.

> **Dream 3**: I return from vacation to work on the psychiatric ward dressed in jeans and torn clothes. My hair is tremendously long, wild and knotted like a Rastafarian's dreadlocks. I have a dark tan. It seems people at work are afraid of me. My outpatient C has relapsed and been admitted to the ward.

Making contact with my wounds means that a neat suit and combed hair may no longer be sufficient to mask the darkness and chaos inside. In this dream, there is the first hint of the problem of growing into the professional role of the physician. Here the dreamer identifies more with the psychotic patient than with the physician. My patient, C, a young man with schizophrenia, whom I worked with in psychotherapy, had been an honors philosophy student. He spent our sessions teaching me about the philosophy of Wittgenstein and R. D. Laing's theories of psychopathology.[55] He once he told me, "My mind is dissolving and someday I will have no choice but to kill myself." One year after abruptly leaving therapy, he jumped off a bridge. At times, I saw him as a mad version of myself—at once more intelligent, eloquent, and tortured. He often seemed to me to be more alive and intellectually acute than those of us who tried treat his madness. My identification with him in the dream is expressed through cultural otherness—I appear as a Rastafarian with dreadlocks and dark skin. The psychologically alienated and the culturally alien are easily exchanged in the symbolism of wildness and social exclusion.

The next dream shows a significant shift in the image of self-as-healer. The *persona* (a term used in Jung psychology for socially presented self, borrowed from the Latin for mask or role) of the physician is still worn dubiously but there is a struggle to make it legitimately my own.

> **Dream 4**: I have a sore on my lip. I think it is herpes and I go to an emergency room to get some ether on a cotton swab to cure it. The nurses won't recognize me as a physician despite all the cards and credentials I show them. They treat me as though I'm malingering and say that since the sore is black it probably isn't herpes anyway.

My wound is black and on the skin for everyone to see. What is more, it may be herpes—a wound that is recurrent and incurable. Although I try to identify myself as a physician, the nurses will not acknowledge this. When medical students work in clinical settings, they are closely supervised and, in some settings, wear a short white coat distinct from the full-length lab coats worn by residents and staff physicians.[56] Much as short and long pants distinguish boys from men, the length of the white coat marks the medical student as a tyro. The transition from medical student to intern involves acquiring a new identity and status. This status is conferred by others on the health care setting, especially nurses. As an intern, I often felt that my sense of being a doctor came not from some intrinsic identity, felt inside but, rather, soaked in from the outside through the expectations of nurses, patients, and colleagues that I act the socially prescribed role. In the dream, this identity is fragile and contested as the nurses challenge my credibility as a healer.

If I am not yet the physician who can heal his own wounds, the wound is also not what I think it is. It is not herpes, nor is it an illness that can treated with a narcotizing ether. It is a black mark, ineradicable and prominent for all to see on the lips that speak to others, take in nourishment, and express affection.

> **Dream 5**: I am on the TV show *Saturday Night Live* performing in a sketch with John Belushi in which I cut the shirt sleeve off his right arm with a razor blade. After we are off-stage I hear someone say: "John's been hurt." I rush to see him and find that in cutting off his shirt I have hacked up his arm. I'm aghast but John reassures me: "It's OK man, it's all in the work. You gotta be

> professional." He embraces me warmly. He is solid and strong and I feel proud to be associated with such a courageous troupe of performers—even though I'm only a guest.

John Belushi, the comedian and trickster figure who made humor of excess, later died of a drug overdose.[57] His TV sketches and movies celebrated adolescent exuberance and provided cathartic experiences for me and my friends during medical school. On television, Belushi often played the role of a crazed samurai warrior—incoherent, barely contained, and enthusiastically wielding his slashing blade. In this dream, his wild energy and manic intensity are matched by personal strength and an ethos of professionalism that allows a place for wounding in performance.

In the Greek myths, Kerenyi notes, "warriors and physicians are one person, they express a unity."[58] Frightening as it seems, the aggressive and destructive side of the healer's power must be accepted before that power can be freely wielded for good. Recall that Asklepios received in the Gorgon's blood a medicine that could kill or cure. This dual quality is not a contrived opposition but a natural conjunction, part of the logic inherent in the Greek term "*pharmakon*" (which can mean both remedy and poison) and in the principle of homeopathy, in which small (to vanishing) amounts of a toxic substance may be viewed as curative. In the relational contexts of psychiatry and psychotherapy, this serves as a metaphor for the doubled-edged effects of interpretation: at once opening up possibilities and constraining patients' self-understanding and autonomy. Attending to the potential violence of interpretation is a crucial step toward "doing no harm." In the context of biomedicine, though, it is not simply a question of accepting our own aggression—the scalpel wounds no matter how benevolent our intentions. "Iatrogenic" means "physician created," and it applies everywhere to both sickness and health. Any medicine strong enough to cure is also sufficient to kill.

Medicine affords the healer the power to wound but also allows the possibility of choosing to be passive before the natural forces of sickness, suffering, and death. In a culture and profession in which self-esteem and social status are founded on active, instrumental control of the environment, acceptance and even yielding to the inevitability of suffering and mortality may be the most difficult aspects to integrate into the persona of the healer.

> **Dream 6:** I am called to do an emergency psychiatric consultation by a family practice intern. He is caring for a poor Black woman and her

> newborn baby and wants me to certify her insane so that he can take the baby away for proper care.
>
> We arrive at some ramshackle brick tenements. In the bedroom now, with cracked plaster walls and a bare light bulb, an emaciated Black woman lies sprawled on the bed, half-covered by a white sheet. On a radiator next to her is a pale blue premature infant loosely wrapped in cloth. I can't tell if it is still alive but feel it hasn't long to live. I turn to the woman feeling at least we can save her. She tells us with slurred speech to leave her alone. A bearded Black man beside her in bed curses at us to get out.
>
> I step outside to speak with the intern. He seems all light and pale while I feel partly dark. The darkness in me seems to be the knowledge that we may be unable to do anything for these people. They live in their own world we cannot fully understand or intervene in.

In this dream, the professional role or persona of the psychiatrist is worn more easily. The power to certify someone insane and involuntarily commit them is psychiatry's scalpel, cutting the person away from family and home and limiting their freedom. But the work of psychiatry takes us from the stainless-steel and scrubbed white tile of the emergency room, into the dusty, broken-down tenements of the dispossessed. Inside we find a starving Black couple and a dying newborn infant. As Eldridge Cleaver argued in *Soul on Ice*, in North America, for white men, the image of the Black man has come to symbolize the body.[59] The premature child dying amid poverty and neglect speaks to the pervasive social wounding of racism, so starkly visible in the United States.[60] The dream ends with a kind of resignation and abandonment. The structural violence associated with racism cannot be solved by simply adopting a healing attitude toward individuals. Even empathy is challenged by the radical alterity created by living in a regime of systemic racism.

Here again there is a shift in attitude toward the wound: in the dream, I feel dark myself, touched by the blackness of the race wound, and this blackness confers a new sense of wisdom, compassion, and authority grounded in recognizing the limits of medicine. This contrasts with the intern who is pale and light and who believes that through the rationality of medicine everything can be fixed. Somehow my awareness of the parts we cannot understand and that continue to suffer and die gives me a feeling of being more substantial and "down-to-earth." This is not just a recognition of the larger political problems that require something beyond medicine—through advocacy and activism—but also an essential humility about the limits of empathy.[61]

As I awoke from this dream, I found myself thinking of the mind–body problem, a philosophical puzzle central to medicine, and had a sense that I now better understood why this problem had long engaged me.

> the sources constantly emphasize that Asklepios cares for *soma* and *psyche*, both body and mind—"body and soul" is the corresponding Christian term; and second, bodily sickness and psychic defect were for the ancient world an inseparable unity. The saying *mens sana in corpore sano*, which is misunderstood today, is a later formulation of this idea.[62]

The duality of mind and body expresses a tension between rationality, intellect, limitlessness, and light on the one hand and irrationality, emotion, limitedness, and darkness on the other.[63] Intellect and imagination allow us to escape for a moment from the implacable reality of suffering and mortality. In its physicality and mortality, the body pulls mind back into the world of sensation, pain and pleasure, desire and despair. Worldviews that seek to dissolve mind-into-body (materialism) or body-into-mind (idealism) deny a persisting pragmatic and ethical tension between limitless imagination and the finitude of mortality, between what we can control and what exceeds our grasp. The experiences that underlie our naive concepts of mind and body present us with a problem of reconciling opposites or polarities whose outcome can be an enlarged sense of self, in the developmental process Jung called *individuation*.

In the last dream of this series, from my third year of residency training, the function of the wounded-healer is graphically depicted.

> **Dream 7:** I am making bedside rounds on a psychiatric consultation service in the hospital in Sacramento. I join a medical student at the bed of a patient, a young man with lymphoma who has been very depressed. He has gone for X-rays, so the student presents his case to me. He says that he has worked with this young man by allowing him to see the student's own pain. The young man has gotten much better. I'm pleased and explain to the student: "What you did is really beautiful. You see, by being willing to expose your wounds to him you helped him to mobilize his own resources to help you. In healing you, he became better." The medical student replies: "Don't get me wrong, I didn't tell him my problems. Actually, I just shared some of my poetry with him." I say, "Of course, you wouldn't want to burden him with everything—just let him in enough to feel his equal in you." In gratitude for this work, the patient has given the student three gifts: a feather, a pen and a small box. I feel proud and a little envious of my student.
>
> Later, it is near midnight, and we are walking outside the hospital. I meet my patient E outside a theater waiting for a film. We are pleased to see each other but it feels awkward to meet this way. She is with her friends. I ask

> what's playing and she says, "*The Miracle Worker.*" I realize it's in black and white and I've seen it before, so I decide to go home. She says with concern: "Yeah, you should get some sleep—aren't you on-call tomorrow?" I realize then that I'm on staff at the hospital and have a lot of responsibility. I say good-bye warmly and walk off into the slushy winter street (Sacramento has become Montreal). I lose one shoe in the slush and walk in my socks for a while before going back to get it. I wake up feeling poignant, tender, and replete.

In this dream, my naive student works with a young man who is dying of cancer. The student is receptive to his own wounds, and this allows the patient to heal the healer. The student is anxious to clarify that he does not intend to burden the patient with his personal wounds. It is his poetry—his creative search for meaning, feeling, and aesthetic awareness—that he shares with the patient. The patient's depression lifts as he mobilizes his own strength to help the student. He expresses his gratitude to the student with gifts of a feather, a pen, and a small box.

At the time of this dream, I was engrossed in reading *Black Elk Speaks*, the autobiography of a Lakota medicine man.[64] In it, Black Elk tells of his initiation, of the sickness and the visions that brought the spirit helpers who made him a healer. To use the power of his visions, Black Elk had to perform parts of them for others to see. In the ceremonial depiction of his visions, he wore a single eagle feather hanging from the left side of his body. A sign of courage in battle for Native Americans, the feather is a natural symbol of flight, of the voyage the shaman must make—liberated from the weight of the body—to the spirit realm. There he achieves clairvoyance and can divine our earthly afflictions.

The second gift is a pen, an ordinary instrument of writing. In our culture, one way to perform our vision for others to see is through the written word. This narrative of our journey as healers may be crucial to the creation of both a personal attitude and a social environment receptive to the spirit of our work. As Black Elk says of the ceremony he performed to enact part of his vision and honor the spirits that had helped him survive:

> it was only after the ceremony … that I had the power to practice as a medicine man, curing sick people, and many I cured with the power that came through me. Of course it was not I who cured. It was the power from the outer world, and the vision and ceremonies had only made me like a hole through which the power could come to the two-leggeds. If I thought that I was doing it myself, the hole would close up and no power could come through. Then everything I could do would be foolish. There were other

> parts of my vision I still had to perform before I could use the power that was in those parts.[65]

In most societies, the healer is also a conveyor of traditional wisdom. In shamanistic healing, this was usually an oral tradition, performed through ritual and storytelling. Throughout Western history, the physician has been a philosopher and teacher, as well as a practitioner.[66] Today, physicians transmit the scientific tradition that has largely supplanted religion as the tacit ground of faith, contributing to the social presence and power of medical knowledge by writing scientific publications. An enactment of sacred myth, however, goes beyond the secular transmission of knowledge both in the risk it entails for the performer and in the potential impact on an audience that is invited to participate in the mystery.[67]

The third gift is a small, hinged box, covered in beadwork and lined with black velvet. Clearly, it is a place to store something precious. Equally, it is a hermetic space where those small experiences of greatest value can be hidden from sight. Some aspects of the healer's visions must be publicly performed to become shared symbols in the social world, but it is vital that some part of the vision be kept secret to retain its power. Black Elk tells his biographer that he had never told anyone *all* of his vision. When he finally did, near the end of his life, he said: "It has made me very sad to do this at last . . . for I know I have given away my power when I have given away my vision."[68] Just as the pen is a gift of expressiveness, the box is an image of containment, a reminder that what is most valuable must be protected and saved for the future.

In front of the theater, I meet my patient. We are on equal ground, both waiting in line to see *The Miracle Worker*. The longing for miraculous cure is shared by patient and healer. But this story of the healer's miraculous power is in black and white: in some ways the opposites are united (or at least coexist) but the inflated image of the healer's omnipotence lacks color compared to the living experience of relationship. The world, with its many shadows, is fatiguing, leaving the healer tired and vulnerable. My patient nurtures me, gently encouraging me to return home to rest and restore myself. As I leave, my shoe comes off in the snow. I am humbled, soaked to the skin, almost directly in contact with the earth now. The shoe is of part our civilized clothing that insulates us from the impact of the Earth, weather, and the elements. Getting snow in one's boots is a common discomfort in Montreal winters and a reminder of the supervenience of nature over the humanly constructed. But this experience is not simply a dismantling of any remaining hubris. As Moses is commanded by

God to remove his shoes when he is on hallowed ground, so the ordinary city street becomes sacred when we no longer hold ourselves apart from the world. In stocking feet in winter, as though wounded in the foot like Oedipus, I am without possession, protection, or claim to any territory. I do not dominate my body, the city, or the Earth and its elements—they simply pass through me, rising like water up through the wick of my socks. Hobbling along with only one shoe, it is impossible to become inflated: the wet foot is a constant reminder of the incomplete and unfinished nature of the healer's confrontation with the affliction that grounds him.

## From Ethos to Ethics: Initiation and Transformation

I have presented a series of dreams that occurred during a time of initiation, the first years of residency training in psychiatry. Despite the emphasis on scientific knowledge in biomedicine, medical training also functions as a *rite de passage* or initiation, transforming the identity and social role of the person who is to become a healer. In the central importance of initiation, the psychological underpinnings of the training of physicians today still resembles that of their shamanic forbears in hunter-gatherer societies. William Reed reviews the process of shamanic initiation from the shaman's perspective and emphasizes its transformative function:

> Profound initiatory upheaval is not a response to maladaptation nor to stage of life; instead it represents a particular spirit's need for actualization through a human partner ... Initiation, the spontaneous occurrence of death-rebirth imagery with its attendant illness, is the first act in a lifelong subjective relationship to a specific spiritual principle or agency called the "helping spirit;" ... The ego's hegemony is overturned by the helping spirit on the occasion of its first manifestation. Living in close quarters with death is the ineluctable demand of the ally upon the shaman *for the rest of his life* ... Although the human subject of all this upheaval has no choice in the matter, his consolation prize is power. He is not better, more kindly, or more accepting but simply more powerful, though the choice to do good or evil is not fully his to make.[69]

In the dreams presented here we can follow the process of initiation as it affects both the healer's attitude toward his own inner wounds and his professional relationship to the wounds of others.

Looking at the process of initiation in terms of inner process and outward social role, we can identify several steps in the development of the wounded-healer.

(1) The role of the healer is foreign at first. People are drawn to the practice of medicine or psychotherapy through concern about the suffering of others and, sometimes, after experiences as the family confidante, fixer, caretaker, or go-between. Initially, the healer is unaware of or reluctant to confront his own woundedness. He consciously seeks to identify with the power of healing and sees himself as quite different from those he helps.

(2) The exposure to the intense suffering of others during apprenticeship or clinical training rewounds healers-to-be along the fault lines created by their own history of personal conflicts and affliction. The apprentice healer identifies with patients through their shared wounds. This identification may contribute to the apprentice's worry about performing the role of healer, aware of the burden of expectations and struggling with a sense of being seen as an imposter. The healer may be overwhelmed by shadow and darkness and identify himself entirely with his own wounds. He loses sight of being a healer and sees himself as a patient, and, what is more, one who is incurably wounded. He looks outside himself for the cure.

(3) Accepting this wound, the "inner healer" is evoked. Forced to find resources within, the student begins to assume the healer role. The sufferer-as-healer appears at first in a tentative way, doubtful of his legitimacy or limited in his power. He may still hope for the limitless power of the hero to rescue him from his unfinished state. This is the stage where many stop, content to work with a configuration in which the healer's active stance addresses the wounds of both patient and self.

(4) Having acknowledged his inner wound, the healer accepts the patient's own healing capacity as an equal participant in the healing process. This entails the healer's continued recognition of his own vulnerability, so that the patient can both wound and heal the physician. Realizing the wounded can only ever be partly healed, the healer-in-the-sufferer develops his power by remaining in contact with his inner wounds. He descends again and again to the underworld of suffering and affliction. He comes to see this process as a way to continue.

The ethos of the wounded-healer implies that the process of initiation as a healer must foster the development of the healer's relationship to his own wounds. This sequence of development, in which the healer-as-patient opens a channel between his own wounds and inner healer, allows a parallel development to occur in his identity, role, and functioning in the social world. In the context of professional training, this developmental model requires a setting that makes it safe for students to discuss their own emotional vulnerability and the resonance of patients' stories with their own wounds and conflicts. Over the decades since I wrote the first version of this chapter, I have presented this material many times to trainees in an effort to clear a space to begin working with our respective vulnerabilities. Always I have faced the apprehension that such personal disclosure risks a loss of authority or credibility with colleagues. Still it has seemed essential to me to find a way to acknowledge our commonality with all who suffer.

What are the implications of the ethos of the wounded-healer for the clinician–patient relationship? If the wounded side of the healer is devalued or denied, then the clinical encounter will be limited and distorted. Although this is most obvious in the practice of psychotherapy, the same issues arise in every area of medicine, since the relationship between healer and sufferer contributes to the efficacy of every clinical intervention, and the relationship remains the central arena for clinical and ethical decision-making. Indeed, some of the deficiencies of contemporary biomedical institutions in providing humane care can be attributed to failures to acknowledge and support the ethos of the wounded-healer.

The image of the wounded-healer suggests the importance of acknowledging the sufferer and healer in both patient and physician. The failure of the initiatory process may leave patient and healer caught in a lopsided ethos in which one or another of these functions within the participants is suppressed. Let us briefly consider some consequences of each type of failure in turn.

The suppression or denial of the healer in the patient results in a consistent pathologizing of experience. The patient is viewed as the passive recipient of treatment. On this view, the patients' only role is "compliance"—if they take their medicine or follow the prescribed regimen, they will get better despite their pathology. This view is most common in surgery and internal medicine, where it models the effects of interventions—at least if we ignore the importance of wound healing and the role of the immune system in infectious disease. Biological psychiatry often adopts a similar view in its approach to psychopharmacology. The low rates of treatment adherence in medicine and psychiatry may be directly related to a failure to enlist the patient's own active stance as a healer or ally in the treatment.

Even psychologically oriented practitioners may ignore the patient's healer, particularly if they are reluctant to acknowledge their own limitations. The psychoanalyst Harold Searles wrote sensitively about the patient's need to have his own efforts to heal his psychotherapist acknowledged:

> At the moment, it is fair to say that psychoanalytic literature is written with the assumption that the analyst is healthy and therefore does not need help from the patient, who is ill and is therefore in need of psychological help from, and unable to give such help to, the analyst. My own training analysis was a highly classical one and I emerged from it markedly less ill than I had been at the beginning; but it is a source of lasting pain to me that the analyst, like each of my parents long before, maintained a high degree of unacknowledgement of my genuine desire to be helpful to him . . . I have found over and over that stalemates in treatment, when explored sufficiently, involve the analyst's receiving currently a kind a therapeutic support from the patient of which both patient and analyst have been unconscious.[70]

Less often, the sickness in the patient is denied. Some versions of the antipsychiatry critique of the 1960s argued that mental illness is something foisted on patients by their families and practitioners,[71] or else that people do not have illnesses, only "problems in living."[72] We find this denial in biomedicine as well, when patients' diseases have been treated yet their suffering remains: patients are then viewed as hypochondriacal or malingering.[73] The illness has not been truly seen, or if glimpsed, invalidated as "imaginary" and so the true locus of the wound is never acknowledged. At times, the "holistic health" movement approaches this form of denial when it implies that positive thinking or careful lifestyle choices can vanquish any illness.

Frequently, we deny the wounds of the physician who is portrayed as omniscient, omnipotent, unsullied, and invincible. This idealization contributes to the power disparity in the doctor–patient relationship.[74] The patient is the passive recipient of help poured from the overfull vessel of the healer. Doctors' denial of their own wounds leads them to lifestyles that may be self-destructive in their one-sided pursuit of power or prestige. Some psychotherapists need to be around patients sicker than themselves in order to minimize or evade recognition of their own wounds. In this way, institutions evolve that serve to reinforce the illusion of health in their caretakers, sometimes at the expense of the continued illness of their patients.

Finally, we have witnessed the most peculiar distortion of the wounded-healer ethos: the eclipse of the healer in the physician. In the 1970s, the self-help movement, Ivan Illich, and other critics of Asklepian authority challenged the "cultural iatrogenesis" brought about by our dependency on medical institutions and sought to reign in the authority of the professional healer. Recent decades have seen the progressive commodification of healing through managed care in which physicians become "cost centers" and the slow process of healing through relationship and symbolic transformation is pushed aside by economic rationalization. Genetic engineering holds out the promise of curing disease through biological techniques that do not require the physician to ever meet their patient. Artificial intelligence promises chatbots that can provide psychotherapy on a large scale.[75] Throughout, the deemphasis of the relational dimension of medical practice in favor of a technologized and impersonal "armamentarium" supports an ethos of the physician as "body mechanic" and psychotherapist as disembodied expert system.[76] The effort to reduce human error leads to a medicine based on algorithms that, in the end, may be better administered by computers than through a fallible human presence.

There is, of course, another way forward, founded on human presence that continues alongside the technics of mastery that occupy biomedicine. For many, medicine is still a calling. And beyond the deformations of professional training, we each inevitably confront our woundedness in meeting the other in their states of suffering. Arthur Kleinman's moving account of his journey as a husband, carer for his wife during her devastating illness, and as scholar of social suffering and healing, reveals the essential work of caring as a path to soul.[77] Through caring for others, we are remade as moral beings. Through witnessing their pain, we are confronted with the human condition, but through our commitments to care, still more through acts of caring—even through our struggles and failures—we are humbled, wounded, and made more human.

## Conclusion

> A bough of fruit falls from the sun on your dark garment
> The great roots of night
> grow suddenly from your soul,
> and the things that hide in you come out again
>
> – Pablo Neruda[78]

With the exponential growth in biomedical knowledge, practitioners may be compelled to give less attention to the experiential dimensions of wounding and healing. Focusing on technical aspects of medicine, we may lose sight of the ethical encounter with suffering and mortality that was the original mandate of medicine.[79] Confronted with threatening and disruptive experiences of suffering, madness, and death, the medical profession turns toward "technique" to routinize the clinical encounter and hive off the dark and inchoate regions of life that sickness reveals.

The alternative to this lopsided view of the clinical encounter involves recognizing the inevitability of sickness and healing in both patient and physician.[80] This allows a redistribution of power that is especially urgent in intercultural work, where the disparities between patient and clinician may be aggravated by uprooting, migration, marginality, racism, and historical conflicts between peoples. In intercultural encounters, clinicians often experience vulnerability, confusion, and powerlessness. They may feel inadequate, incompetent, and dull—and be vicariously traumatized by patients' stories of suffering. The ability to deal with these threats to the self, and (re)wounding, without retaliation or appropriation of the healing function, depends on integrating the image of the wounded-healer, not just cognitively but in the stance toward one's own vulnerability and clinical authority.

The ethos of wounded-healer stands for the possibility of meeting in a space that acknowledges human vulnerability as well as the transformative power of symbolic action. If we meet patients on an equal footing, together we can create a place where a personally and culturally meaningful process of healing can be coconstructed and enacted. As Marie-Louise von Franz wrote of Jung's own psychotherapeutic work:

> Hermes, the god of peacemakers, dominated Jung's ... way of dealing with his patients. He had no interest in "training" or "educating" a patient according to any kind of method. Instead he always tried to help him find peace with himself by mediating the messages sent by the patient's own unconscious. He felt that his was the role of obstetrician, so to speak, or midwife, assisting in bringing into the light of day a natural inner process, the process of coming into one's self ... The physician is thus truly a *hermeneut*, an interpreter who translates the symbolic dream-letters the patient receives out of his own psychic depths during the night. In this respect, Jung's work resembled that of the old shamans and medicine men ... The shaman or medicine man also seeks with his own means (trance, oracles, etc.) to learn what the "spirits", that is, the activated unconscious or certain complexes, want from the person who is suffering, so that they can be propitiated through appropriate rituals ... or driven away if the spirits are alien to the personality. The shaman is able to do this because, during his initiation ordeal, he himself has struggled with the spirit-world, the unconscious, and has come to terms with it; so he has learned to understand the language of spirits and animals. As Mircea Eliade points out, the shaman himself does not heal; he mediates the healing confrontation of the patient with the divine powers.[81]

This language of gods, spirits, and divine powers points to an awareness of currents of experience beyond the purely personal.[82] Connection to this deeper ground means we do not work alone but with the richness of the archetypes of the unconscious as our ally. But for this to happen the psychotherapist must reexperience the wounds of initiation. With each new patient, we are brought down again into fresh regions of darkness. Complacency is a sure sign we have ceased to grow and our link with the depths is broken.

> No analysis is capable of banishing all unconsciousness forever. The analyst must go on learning endlessly, and never forget that each new case brings new problems to light and thus gives rise to unconscious assumptions that have never before been constellated. We could say, without too much exaggeration, that a good half of every treatment that probes at all deeply consists in the doctor's examining himself, for only what he can put right in himself can he hope to put right in the patient. It is no less, either, if he feels that the patient is hitting him, or even scoring off him: it is his own hurt that gives the measure of his power to heal. This, and nothing else, is the meaning of the Greek myth of the wounded physician.[83]

The fact that healers must revisit their own wounds again and again is, after all, no more than the human condition: illness, suffering, and death leave their marks on us all. What privileges the healer's knowledge and position may be expertise and institutional authority, but it is the willingness to confront this woundedness that allows ethical integrity. In the symbolic logic of healing, the healer's own wounds become sources of wisdom when they are confronted rather than denied. To accept the power of the healing archetypes that work through us, we must turn inward, into our own darkness, and experience confusion until "the great roots of night grow" and the things that hide in us come out again.

CHAPTER 10

# *Epilogue: Ethics, Aesthetics, and Poiesis*

> His prey has no flavour because it is under the curse of aesthetics.
>
> – Hans Blumenberg[1]

> At the still point of the turning world, the job of the artist is not to resolve or beautify, but to hold complexities, to see and make clear.
>
> – Toi Derricotte[2]

## Introduction

In this epilogue, I consider the ethical implications of the focus on aesthetics and poiesis in illness experience and healing. There is legitimate concern that aestheticizing experience can evade or elide the material realities of people's lives by creating a burnished image that minimizes or valorizes suffering, downplaying the limitations of language and imagination to address the coarseness, difficulty, pain, brutality, and injustice of affliction. A fascination with the aesthetics of language and metaphor, then, becomes an obstacle to recognizing and responding to the human predicament and the urgent call presented by the face of the other.

Against this, I have argued that the metaphors we use to take hold of the world and transform experience are crucial to coping, adaptation, and healing. Poiesis, then, is not solely the province of the poet, but part of everyday engagements with affliction. The aesthetic impulse is at the heart of making sense of experience and transmuting suffering. Poiesis offers order, connection, community, playfulness, and possibility in the face of our finitude. Attention to the metaphors through which we make sense of the world can reveal the biases that create and maintain inequities. A critical poetics of healing and health care theory, rhetoric, and practice can contribute to efforts to improve our institutions and achieve greater equity not only by recognizing and respecting difference and diversity but also by engaging with the minute particulars of each individual's experience.

## Metaphor and Biosemiotics

Metaphor theory traces the origins of the metaphoric "as if" to the sensory and perceptual capacities of the body and our physical interactions with the world. Our conceptual models and abstract systems of thought are built on a scaffolding of metaphors that are grounded in more basic sensory experiences and sensorimotor actions in everyday situations, relationships and events that are affectively charged and culturally meaningful.

In human development, the earliest metaphors draw from cross-modal sensory qualities that can appear in vision (bright and dark, angular and round), sound (loud and soft, high and low, pulsing and steady), touch, visceral interoception, and proprioception. These experiences give rise to images that can be juxtaposed, combined, and transformed in ways that extend our perception and modes of responding to the world. Imagery and sensory experience are fertile sources of metaphors, but the generative power of metaphor allows us to go beyond embodied experience to conjure imaginative realms and situations. Our recognition of this imaginative capacity guides our awareness of images and metaphors as such—that is, as analogies, versions, or possibilities rather than the thing itself.[3]

Biosemiosis insists that our symbol systems have their roots in the world—indeed, the capacity for constructing and inventing symbols is central to our modes of adaptation. Far from being an arbitrary collection of signs, the study of metaphor reveals that language emerges from and is intrinsic to our engagement with the natural world. Metaphor, then, presents us with this paradox: it is at once deeply rooted in our most basic bodily experiences and physical interactions with the world and endlessly inventive, a fount of new images, ideas, and insights. How can this be? The answer lies in our use of metaphor as a toolkit to take hold of the world and transform objects, experiences and events in novel ways. Of course, the world we engage is not just 'natural' or given but already socially constructed, shaped by human cultural history and replete with perceptual affordances and imaginative possibilities rooted in language.

We introduced the concepts of myth and archetype to unpack the process of symbolization in metaphor (Figure 10.1). These categories are idealizations that mislead insofar as they imply we can separate the bodily and discursive processes that contribute to imaginative elaboration or unfolding. For any

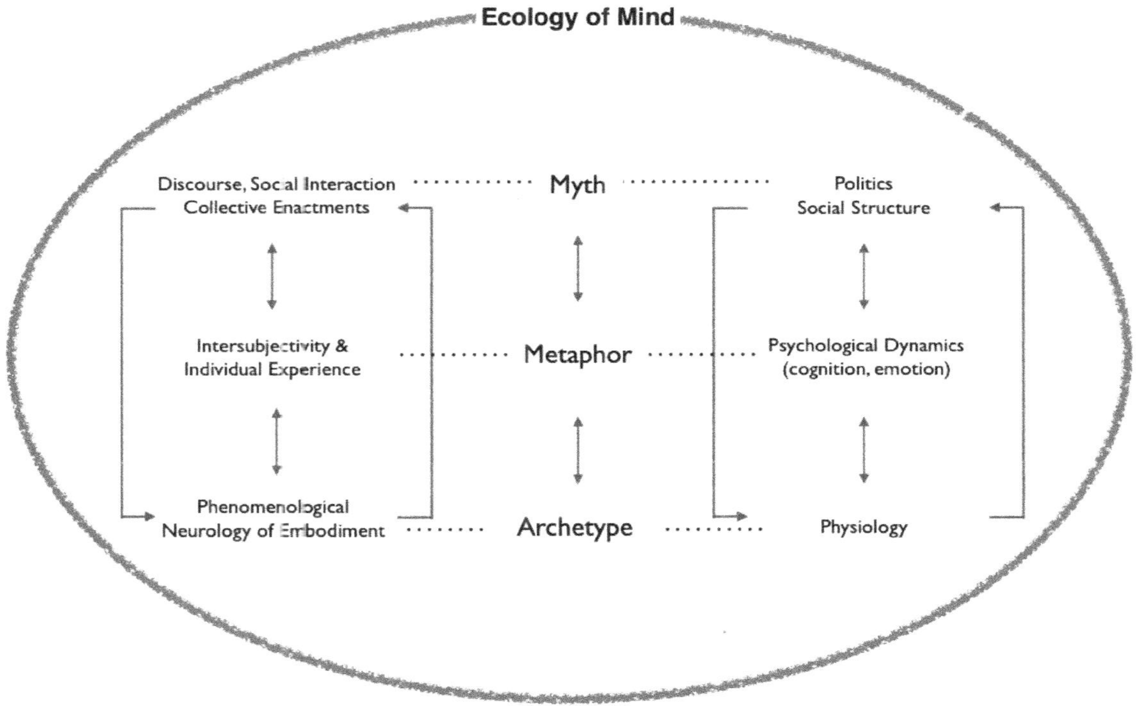


Figure 10.1 Hermeneutic cycles in the ecology of mind
Hermeneutic cycles of myth, metaphor, and archetype constitute an ecology of mind. The left side of the figure outlines sites of meaning-making, the right side corresponding languages of description and explanation. Beyond providing a map with placeholders for the key sites and processes of meaning making, the diagram points toward a view that replaces the search for an ontology of essences with a system of hermeneutical cycles of organism–environment interaction: from sensorimotor loops of action and sensation, to cognitive loops of prediction and surprise, to social loops of narration and response. The loops are not independent but temporally and spatially nested across biographical, developmental, cultural-historical, and coevolutionary scales, each of which arises from engagements with environments constituted by other people, social institutions, languages and practices. The aesthetics of imagination involves all of these levels, through processes of recollection and gestures of possibility or protention, maps and metaphors, and overarching stories of past, present, and future that are embodied and enacted.

individual, these processes are thoroughly entwined. Yet they have their own dynamics that involve interactions between bodies as bodies and discourses as discursive formations. In this many-layered dynamical system of hermeneutic circles and cycles, metaphor occupies a middle ground. Attention to metaphor as mediating body and discourse, myth and archetype, allows us to consider the given in the constructed and the constructed beyond the given. Both body and discourse are crucial to the process of human sense-making or semiosis.

Metaphoric thought reflects modes of bodily and linguistic interactions with an environment that is at once human and nonhuman, social and material, and cultural and natural. We can move beyond these dichotomies by recognizing that human nature is fundamentally biocultural, so that our co-constructed worlds of myth, ritual, and story live in and through nature itself. We relate to the world through the media of language and imagination which afford us the capacity to change the world in ways that suit our emotional, ethical and aesthetic values. Aesthetics, then, reflect a quintessentially human form of engagement with the world.[4] The unity of nature and of humankind with and within nature is ultimately not ontological but aesthetic and political—that is, arising from the ways in which we apprehend and appreciate the world and inhabit it through culture, history, and community.

## Metaphors of Mental Health and Illness

Every choice of metaphor draws from and points toward a form of life. The critique of metaphors, which begins with an appreciation of the qualities they confer on experience, the ways they make us think and feel, then moves out into the social world to identify ways that systems and structures are configured, rationalized, and maintained. This general framework for thinking about the impact of metaphors provides us with a way to explore the language we use to describe mental health and illness. It suggests that, in the process of finding apt metaphors, we are not simply homing in on the correct description, but putting into play imaginative possibilities that have cognitive, affective, social, and ontological implications. These implications need not be consonant or coordinated and often may be at cross-purposes. We can employ specific metaphors for one set of purposes and be unaware of or only discover belatedly the unintended consequences of our language.

Our metaphors for mental illness start with an ontological distinction ("mental" versus "physical") and center on depictions of troubled and troubling behavior that transgresses social norms and that is vexing for the afflicted person and others around them and that assign them to particular social positions. Consider, for example, the ways that we describe people with mental disorders, as *mentally ill*, *disturbed*, *crazy*, or *mad*, and those in health care settings as *patients*, *clients*, *consumers*, or *service users*.

*Patient* comes from the Latin "*patiens*"—one who suffers—from "*patior*," to suffer or to bear, and shares roots with patience, *patientia*, the quality of being willing and able to bear adversities calmly. *Patient* has connotations of endurance, waiting for help, and needing the care (and tolerance) of others, and encapsulates a moral economy of emotion regulation. While some have criticized this as consigning the person to an enforced passivity, it also recognizes the fundamental character of afflictions, which demand that the person slow down, take stock, and devote time to healing. Pain and fatigue move us in this direction and the healer's ability to recognize and support this withdrawal and inward turn—in patients, as well as themselves—may be a basic element of care and a step on the path to healing.

*Client*, from Latin *cliens*, in late Middle English denoted a person under the protection or patronage of another, and now takes as its implicit model the relationship of a person to a lawyer or other professional. *Consumer*, one who consumes a commodity, has an explicitly commercial connotation. *Service user* invokes administrative and economic capitation and its associated social regulation.

Each term implies a kind of problem and situates the sufferer in a particular type of moral, political, and economic relationship to a healing practice and its institutions. The client–therapist metaphor conditions the relationship that ensues. It sets us on a certain footing, which may be modified or corrected over time to conform to the exigencies of the relationship, but that may also exert a pull or undertow that influences the dynamics and direction of that relationship. It may even lead the participants to feel that their interaction is not conforming to its implicit (metaphoric) model, as well as to the norms (implicit or explicit) it invokes.

When people seek to distance themselves from the stigmatizing effects of psychiatry, they may adopt metaphoric descriptions of themselves as "survivors" or "ex-patients."[5] The *psychiatric survivor* is defined not as having suffered through an illness but as having endured its institutional treatment. *Ex*-patients are no longer willing to patiently suffer or submit to illness. These labels have direct effects on how people with mental health problems understand themselves, internalize stereotypes, experience stigma, and navigate a social world that responds to these labels in institutional and everyday encounters. People can also appropriate derogatory labels ("mad," "crazy") and infuse them with new meaning and connotations to assert their right to recognition and self-definition and advance political changes needed for equity and justice. The recovery movement has attempted to change the vocabulary of psychiatry to open up space for greater agency, self-determination, and self-esteem.[6] But it has done this largely through metaphors that reinforce a neoliberal version of the self as autonomous and driven to accumulate and achieve.[7] Other critical approaches to psychiatry imagine other kinds of community.[8]

## Metaphor, Trauma and Ceremony

Throughout this book, we have insisted that the imaginative freedom provided by metaphor must always be set against the material, structural, and political realities of the body and the social world. This is especially clear when we consider the ways in which the language of trauma, which has its origins in physical wounding and healing, has been extended to describe the enduring impacts of exposure to violence, terror, and life-threatening events. Current conceptions of historical trauma employed by Indigenous Peoples in the Americas, provide an important example of how the metaphor of trauma can be expanded for personal, communal, and political reasons.[9] Framing the long history of the violence of European colonialism, oppression, marginalization, and exclusion that has plagued Indigenous Peoples in terms of historical trauma, loss, and grief draws attention to the violence and locates the causes of current mental health problems in these past events. This serves a vital political function in consciousness raising, advocacy, and moral accountability and allows both for better self-understanding and counternarratives to those that locate pathology in individuals or communities rather than in larger struggles of power and domination. As important as this naming of the roots of violence is for advancing self-determination, it also inevitably simplifies the tangle of ongoing issues that maintain structural disadvantage, as well as social and individual suffering.

The concept of historical trauma is clearly not a model but a metaphor that is readily extended to a wide range of experiences and events. To become a model, the metaphor has to be unpacked, its analogical mappings specified and delimited. There are many ways in which historical violence might act across generations—but most of these imply a transformation of the original experience that results in new features and dynamics.

Most work on historical trauma is rooted in the narratives of people who recall their own suffering and privation and the effects it had on their lives. Of course, this recollection is shaped by the available narratives. Efforts to explore the links of historical trauma to individual psychological outcomes have looked at correlations between past exposures in individuals or their parents and grandparents and current or lifetime measures of distress. This leaves the connection subject to recall biases and narrative framing.

The sociologist Les Whitbeck developed a questionnaire that aimed to measure the lived experience of historical trauma and its impacts on mental health.[10] The questions ask people how they feel in certain situations, what they recall, and whether they link it to historical events. The questions imply that people live the metaphors of historical trauma, grief and loss as situated experiences, memory practices, modes of self-construal, and identities that position them in specific ways. The metaphor of historical trauma, then, is part of loops of perceiving and acting in and on the world in ways that become reifying or self-vindicating, and that can serve both to reveal and hide forms of structural violence not recognized in current versions of collective history. To make sense of these accounts of the impact of historical trauma and the shifts in identity and experience they engender, we need a critical approach to narrative identity and self-presentation. This critique must trace the links between the personal and political through the middle ground of forms of social life.

These forms of life reside in families, communities, institutions, and wider society. They are enacted through everyday norms and practices that can be thrown into relief by following specific protocols. Across Canada, many First Nations have adapted the ceremony of the *talking circle*, originally a method of decision-making, consensus building, and conflict resolution, to promote individual and collective healing.[11] Participants sit in a circle and pass a talking stick, feather, or other ceremonial object that designates the holder as the speaker. Each person in turn speaks for as long as they need to. They are enjoined to speak "from the heart," that is to say, with honesty and genuine feeling. After each person has said what they wish, they pass the talking stick to the next person. The circle may go round several times until everyone has had their say.

This protocol interrupts the usual back and forth of group conversation driven by individuals' verbal assertiveness and reactivity. Instead, people must sit patiently, listen closely, and wait their turn. The consequences of this proccss arc manyfold: individuals practicc patience, emotion regula tion, and allowing their thoughts to evolve in response to each person's reflections. The form of the circle levels out hierarchies and ensures that each person is allotted time according to their self-defined need.

Talking circles have been a key element in processes of restorative justice in response to domestic violence and abuse, as well as other kinds of interpersonal and social conflict.[12] The circles aim to rebuild connections and a sense of belonging within families and communities that would otherwise be torn apart by the responses of a corrections system that gives little attention to culture or context. The healing effects of this protocol stem from the group process of the ceremony and the values or ethos it enacts. Although described as "leaderless," the circle is usually organized by an Elder, healer, or helper who may introduce the process with stories and other teachings that convey the rationale for the protocol, create a sense of safety, and elicit a receptive frame of mind. And, as Cree Elder and psychologist Joseph Couture suggested, the larger cultural and spiritual value system invoked by ceremony also provides a healing order:

> Truly, healing circles never are leaderless. The "smoke" of whatever smudge is used—the sweet grass, sage, cedar, grey-willow fungus—makes manifest the fullness of Spirit presence, filling the circle space, fully, equally touching and embracing all participants, within and without.[13]

While talking circles and other ceremonial practices depend for their full effects on ongoing relationships with shared values in a specific social and cultural context, they can have beneficial effects even in situations where there is no kinship or community among participants and little shared culture. Simply participating in the ceremony with an open mind and heart results in an increase in authenticity and relatedness among participants.[14] This speaks to the power of particular kinds of ceremonial enactment to create possibilities for mutual understanding and connection. Here ceremony becomes a micropolitics that introduces an aesthetics of the sacred into the quotidian. The effects of this kind of intervention must be tracked outward into the larger society to understand the consequences for justice and coexistence.

## Poeisis and Healing

Healing practices use metaphors to construct narratives that frame, contain and transform experience in ways that have personal meaning and social currency. This narrativizing occurs in everyday conversation, clinical communication, and in a wide variety of oral and written forms of storytelling. Narration may heal by allowing symbolic closure, bringing a sense of completeness or coherent emplotment to the fragmented and chaotic elements of illness experience.[15] It may transform the meaning of experience by conferring metaphorical qualities or blending representational spaces.[16] It may build solidarity with others through shared accounts of suffering in socially understandable and valorized terms.[17] Finally, narration may open up new possibilities, subjunctivizing predicaments viewed as fixed and unchangeable.[18]

In addition to these broad effects, the order created by narrative suggests a special value of textuality: writing and reading let us create more complex or higher-order structures that give meaning and coherence to fleeting, ambiguous, and disturbing experiences.[19] Reading an account of someone's illness or healing experience can shift our relationship to our self, changing our self-awareness, the ways we narrate experience, the imaginative worlds we inhabit, and the fictional company we keep.

Reading a story can provide catharsis as one is moved through a narrative landscape that mirrors one's own experience in important respects, but at an optimal aesthetic distance (underdistant and we are rewounded, overdistant and the text is flat and unevocative) created by the use of aesthetic devices that are rooted both in the metaphorical structure of representations and in particular cultural modes of performance.[20] In portrayals of violence or trauma, aesthetic distance not only protects us from rewounding, while allowing us to be energized and moved, it also opens up space for reflection, self-reflexivity, and critique.

Other aesthetic forms, including visual arts and music, share many of the same functions as language arts but have their own unique features that arise from the medium, its sensory qualities, modes of bodily engagement, temporality, and cultural history. Visual art in particular builds on similarity or mimesis while introducing novel perspectives that have the structure of metaphor: the visual image is not the thing it represents but a metaphor that invites new ways of looking. Visual imagery, too, can be a vehicle for healing.[21] Similarly, music—which may have mimetic qualities related to the aural environments we inhabit and the rhythms of our bodies, can also evoke emotions through its contours, and other images and thoughts related to its more extended form.

In 2014, at the age of twenty-six, Jon Henrik Fjällgren took part in Sweden's version of *Got Talent*, a televised competition for musicians and entertainers. He won the competition with his performance of a *joik*, a traditional Sami musical form associated with shamanism.[22] His *joik* was dedicated to his friend Daniel, who died in adolescence. Daniel's *joik*, sung in Sami with only a few words, which most present could not understand, moved the judges and the audience to tears. The way the form of the song, its plaintive tone, dynamic turns, and soaring melody, powerfully conveyed grief and longing, provides a clear demonstration of the emotional power of music even when its genre is unfamiliar and lyrics obscure.[23]

Fjällgren's use of the traditional musical form, wearing Sami costume, and his explicit self-identification as a traditional reindeer herder, made his win significant for the Sami people and he became a kind of culture hero. This recognition was particularly striking in view of his heritage: as a child he was adopted from an orphanage in Cali, Colombia, by a Sami family and he experienced bullying throughout his childhood due to his dark skin and foreign origin. His success through a cultural art form transformed his social identity and he went on to produce more music and to win an elected position in the Sami parliament of Sweden in 2021. An artistic expression of grief through a form that validated tradition served both personal and collective healing.

## Art and Poiesis: Vision, Mimesis, and Transcendence

The healing efficacy of art may stem from its form, message, or content, ways of enlivening the body and enriching the social world, or through meta-messages about flexibility, imagination, playfulness, creativity, and transgression.[24] Some of these effects may be incidental to art as a medium or activity and could be achieved in other ways. Other healing processes rely on the modality and media of art for their power and transformative effects. In addition to the explicit and metaphoric content of images, art provides objects of attention that allow both artist and beholder to learn to read and experience the body and the world in new ways.

Art making can provide creative avenues for individual therapeutic exploration, growth, and transformation and for collective mental health promotion and conflict resolution. Art may provide raw material for various forms of therapy. Reflection on art can yield important insights. Art provides tools for the exploration or amplification of personal themes or issues that can then worked with in ways that follow from the particular school of therapy. But art making can also constitute a means of therapeutic transformation in its own right, with the impetus and trajectory coming from within the process itself.

The artist's ability to create a semblance of reality in painting, literature, or other media through imagery and narrative conventions is termed mimesis in aesthetic theory.[25] Through mimesis, an image or story becomes a mirror of our own world or a window onto another that, however fabulous, seems real. But mimesis is always an act of interpretation even when it veils its choices and strategies, creating the illusion of presence and worldedness.[26] If we take this mimetic capacity seriously, we have to interrogate our own imagination not as a window on the world but as an engine of invention. To do this is to confront the images, figures, and feelings that emerge and allow them the space to unfold, make their presence felt, and discover their significance—while recognizing all the while their contingency and fictiveness.

The philosopher Simon Critchley makes this clear when he describes the twofold task of poetry:

> 1. Poetry permits us to see fiction as fiction, to see the fictiveness or contingency of the world. It reveals the idea of order which we imaginatively impose on reality. Plainly stated, the world is what you make of it. The fact of the world is a *factum*: a deed, an act, an artifice. Such is what we might call the *critical* task of poetry . . .
> 2. However, the second task of poetry is to give ". . . to life the supreme fictions without which we are unable to conceive of it." Beyond the critical function described above, we might describe this as the therapeutic task of poetry. Namely, poetry is one of the enlargements of life.[27]

This enlargement is not only a matter of populating the imagination with images and stories that are good to think with and that reveal the hidden costs and consequences of our current constructions; it can also offer novel visions of the world that might be realized as new forms of life.

Visionary experience poses fundamental questions with ethical, epistemic and aesthetic dimensions. Vision is a common metaphor for direct knowing: light reveals and darkness conceals.[28] In Plato's famous allegory of the cave, humanity is imprisoned within a cave and condemned to mistake the shadows on its walls for reality.[29] The lack of direct vision stands for the mediated and imperfect nature of human understanding of the world. Reduced to looking at shadows, we are unable to discern reality. For Plato, poets were part of the problem, since they offer us only flights of imagination that excite the emotions. "The heart of Plato's case against the poets is that, when it comes to a choice between truth and beauty, they are too ready to sacrifice truth. The heart of the poets' case is that beauty is its own truth."[30]

For the poet and visionary, the products of imagination are every bit as real and significant as the objects of the mundane world. William Blake, who has become the exemplary visionary artist, insisted on this in a famous declaration:

> I assert for myself that I do not behold the outward creation, and that to me it is hindrance and not action. "What!" it will be questioned, "when the sun rises do you not see a round disc of fire somewhat like a guinea?" Oh! No, no! I see an innumerable company of the heavenly host, crying "Holy, holy, holy is the lord God Almighty!" I question not my corporeal eye any more than I would question a window concerning a sight. I look through it and not with it.[31]

For Blake, imaginative vision is the source of energy and "eternal delight." Visionary experiences played a central role in his art, both as subject and method. One night the spirit of his brother came to him and taught him the method of engraving his poems on copper.[32]

> I know that our deceased friends are more really with us than when they are apparent to our mortal part. Thirteen years ago I lost a brother and with his spirit I converse daily and hourly in the spirit, and see him in remembrance in the region of my imagination. I hear his advice, and even now write from his dictates. Forgive me for expressing to you my enthusiasm, which I wish all to partake of, since it is to me a source of immortal joy, even in this world. May you continue to be so more and more, and be more and more persuaded, that every mortal loss is an immortal gain. The ruins of time build mansions in eternity.[33]

It seems likely that Blake engaged with imaginative imagery with a concentration, seriousness, and commitment that suffused and sustained its reality. Blake contrasted the images of his visionary experiences with the allegorical depictions of figures in other works of art:

> Blake's strong sense that his symbolic figures were the living persons of a cosmogonic drama gave them a solid flesh that no other personifications of the period possessed. Words alone could not have expressed the authentic particularities of Blake's vision. For words alone had too often abjectly served reason and enforced the life-denying generalizations of neoclassical culture—those "Mountains & Valleys, which are not Real, in a Land of Abstraction where Spectres of the Dead wander."[34]

Though Blake was clear that his visions were not the same as ordinary perception and should not be mistaken for such, he was described as mad by some of his contemporaries, and this characterization has persisted. The misinterpretation of visionary experience as madness reflects a misunderstanding and devaluing of imagination. Imagination is assigned to reverie, recreation, and artistic practice and is epistemically suspect. Still, there many spiritual or religious practices in which one learns to access and enter into dialogue with a presence understood as divine.[35] More prosaically, people may experience internal voices or presences that serve as companions that enrich their lives. For example, Samuel Veissière described the practice of tulpamancy, in which members of an online community guide each other in developing inner beings that may comment on and participate in their lives.[36] The distinction between serious spiritual practice, playful exploration, and pathological fragmentation of identity may be one of intensity or duration (how much time is devoted to the interior other) and quality (what is the nature of our relationship to the imagined other). This depends on the autonomy of imaginal activity, the commitment with which it is engaged, and the ways its insistence and disruptive effects are handled.[37]

As W. B. Yeats insisted, "The profound sanity of [Blake's] inspiration is proved by his never having, no matter how great the contrast between himself and the blind men and women about him, pronounced himself to be chosen and set apart among men."[38] According to, Yeats:

> [Blake] had learned from Jacob Boehme and from old alchemist writers that imagination was the first emanation of divinity, "the body of God," "the Divine members," and he drew the deduction, which they did not draw, that the imaginative arts were therefore the greatest of Divine revelations, and that the sympathy with all living things, sinful and righteous alike, which the imaginative arts awaken, is that forgiveness of sin commanded by Christ.[39]

The intensity of Blake's search and the passion of his insistence on idiosyncratic vision reflected both the politics of reception of his heterodox ideas, and his location within the class society of Britain.[40] Although viewed as mad by some during his lifetime and after, many have recognized in Blake a way of being that connects to the wellsprings of human vitality, creativity, and healing through active engagement with imagination.[41]

## Sacred Texts and Poiesis

It is not only imagery but also text that can stir the imagination and offer spiritual insight. Our engagement with texts can open a path to transcendence. Religious or mystical texts aim not to heal a bodily affliction or bring order to a confused mind, but to speak to the suffering intrinsic to the human condition. Such texts are honored as repositories of sacred wisdom, bearing traces of the divine, or as ladders to scale to achieve transcendence. Through the techniques of meditative practice, the text becomes a source of enactive metaphors to reconfigure the self. The essential element is not the modality but the attitude taken toward experience.

Meditative practices fall into two broad approaches, cultivating either intense concentration or freely moving awareness, though as they are developed these paths converge.[42] Within each tradition, readers may approach the text in different ways: as a recipe or procedure for practices that train the mind; as a map or conceptual model of experiences to be sought and recognized; and, finally, as a window onto or link with a higher reality, in which the text itself may be understood as sacred materiality. Although a particular system of mysticism may privilege one of these levels, all three may coexist in any given practice.

Buddhism is replete with texts that provide explicit instructions for meditation, and that describe the states of mind and world-pictures that arise at various stages in the practice. There is a close connection between bodily healing and the spiritual healing achieved through meditation and study of the scriptures. The aim is to realize the wisdom pointed to in the text in one's own experience. The meditator who reads Buddhist texts for advice on how to practice eventually puts the book aside and explores the structure of consciousness in order to dispel the illusions of the self that are the root cause of suffering.

Some forms of meditation involve visualizing deities and in so doing, the description becomes an embodied reality. For example, in the meditative practices centered on *Bhaisajyaguru* (Tibetan, *Sangye Menla*), the medicine or healing Buddha, one visualizes the Buddha in his lapis lazuli radiance.[43] The Buddha's radiance can cure the three poisons of desire, hatred, and delusion, but:

> [T]o become healed, one must do more than construct an image (either physically or mentally); the image must come alive with the spirit force of the Buddha and merge with the viewer. When one's own body becomes the Tathagata's body, and when one's own mind merges with the Divine mind, then the most profound healing can take place.[44]

Visualization involves embodied experience but is also a socially (textually) guided activity. The image occupies a space that is neither strictly inner nor outer, revealing the way in which mind constructs the world, only to cut through to a transcendent truth.

In Jewish mysticism, the idea of reading for spiritual transformation is central to the encounter with the sacred texts of the Torah. The many versions of Kabbalah offer a great variety of meditative approaches based on reading the Torah as spiritual allegory, map of the supernal realm, and encounter with the divine.[45] At the center of the mystics' reverence for the text is the image of the Torah as a book written by God with black fire on white fire. This act of inscription creates the world and the text in one fiery flourish. "For the Kabbalah, in fact, each term of the Bible, in each of its occurrences is used absolutely. All words in the lexicon are the names of spiritual spheres and, through their mediation, the names given to the diverse attributes of God."[46] "God is not only the author of the written Torah: He is also the substratum of the written letters."[47] This attitude allows us to read without attention to or concern about what is outside the text, since the whole world is to be found there. The order of text *is* the order of the world. Hence, apprehending that order allows one's own fragmentation and disorder to be restructured and reformed.

The reader who meditates on the text may work with worldly meaning or with the text itself. From a psychological perspective, in both cases there is a restructuring of consciousness, of the mobility of awareness, and the representations of self and other through both the content and the medium of the text. From a cultural-ecosocial point of view, contemplative practices situate the person in a community of like-minded practitioners who share a conviction about the truth and value of this path. From a viewpoint within the tradition, what happens is transcendental, a step toward an elevated meaning that carries us beyond merely human and contingent constructions.

Buddhism, Jewish mysticism, and many other paths to transcendence are available to those who seek refuge in their traditions. But amid the welter of secular books and texts that paper our lives, other forms of *lectio spiritualis* are still possible: spiritually informed reading of sacred texts can be replaced by sacral readings of secular texts. These sources of spiritual medicine often come with no instructions for reading or practice but contain the possibility of self-transformation in the incandescence of the text.

Among the many forms of text–mysticism alive and at hand in the contemporary world, two continue to be especially potent: the gnostic exuberance of Blake, who offers the illuminated text as a world system packed with minute particulars to populate the imagination and, in stark contrast, the spare poetics of Paul Celan, in which concision, inwardness, and fragmentation force the reader toward an aching stillness, longing, and intimation of the unreachable other. Blake's prophetic books call for a type of reading that allows us to feel the tensions of opposites contained within a mythic system filled to bursting. With Celan, we read the presence of absence, the density of language held compact within a fragment of stone, as we are called to confront the shards of a shattered world.[48] These two very different ways of exploring the possibility of transcendence—presenting its epiphanies and its elusiveness—invite an intensity of aesthetic absorption that works against the banal forms of reading we use to simply pass the time.[49] Sacred reading moves us from the empty time of mindless routine and consumption into the timeless realm of self-transcendence.

## Poetics of Relation, Dislocation, and Survivance

The promise of transcendence as an ultimate form of healing may seem to be an evasion of the ongoing violence and inequities of the world. We live in a time when the use of metaphors in political rhetoric that aims to dehumanize and destroy is rampant and threatens to dismantle the hard-won gains of global civil society. Myth, metaphor, and poeisis can serve violence and exclusion, as well as recognition and solidarity.[50] What would allow us to move beyond the violent rhetoric of othering and exclusion? The question raises issues of ethics, aesthetics, and politics and invites us to consider the work of poets who have wrestled with finding language that can bridge divides by going deeply into local, personal, and idiosyncratic language to uncover the possibilities for recognition, connection, and creative coexistence.

Edouard Glissant has written of a poetics of relation animated by the experience of the Caribbean archipelago with its history of colonization, genocide, the Middle Passage, enslavement, and liberation.[51] This history is seen not simply as one of violence, destruction, grief, and loss but also as creative rupture and hybridization that lend depth to experience. Glissant's poetics of relation invites us to consider the difference between the heroic individual (like Robinson Crusoe) stranded by shipwreck and the slave, uprooted, dehumanized as chattel, transported through liminality, and cast into a world defined by subservience, oppression, exploitation, and the constant threat of annihilation—who survives to fashion creolized language, poetry and music on the shores of an archipelago. This vision provides a counter to the rhetorics of domination that rationalized the violence of colonialism, enslavement, and genocide. It celebrates the multiplicity and new forms of relatedness that emerge from the collision of cultures.

> *The non-hierarchical multiplicity of languages leads irreversibly to new langages.*
>
> The phenomena of creolization at work in our world concern not only the diversity of times experienced by communities which may or may not be in contact, but also the interchange of the written and spoken languages. Beyond these languages, the imagination (or imaginations) of human communities could inspire *langages*, or archipelagos of *langages*, which would be the equivalent of the infinite variation of our relations. Languages is the ever-shattered crucible of my unity. *Langage* would the open field of my Relation.[52]

Glissant makes a distinction between language, as explicit grammar, and *langage*, as the capacity for language and its realization in literature and conversation. His concern is with the possibilities for dialogue with the whole of the world that would allow both opacity[53] (the acknowledgment of alterity) and discovery (the experience of connection), and with those experiences of situated language that reflect a creolization of indigenous and cosmopolitan ways of being. In *Poetics of Diversity*, Glissant writes:

> In the encounter of the world's cultures, it is necessary that we have the imaginary force to conceive all of those cultures as exercising at one and the same time an action that unifies and an action that liberates diversity. This is why I reclaim, for all of us, the right to opacity ... Today, the right to opacity would be the most evident sign of non-barbarism.[54]

The aesthetic appreciation of difference and diversity, then, is tempered by respect for opacity, the unknown in the other, that allows the other to simply be, without pushing, probing, normative judgments, or contestation. Opacity here is both respect for interiority and the protection of boundaries that make possible that interiority as a space of creative imagination. This has universal significance but is an especially urgent ethical imperative in political situations where people have been subject to relentless surveillance and denied agency.

A complementary poetics is offered by Meena Alexander, who aims to capture crucial dimensions of the experience of those who migrate, whether by choice or under duress, acquiring new, imposed, or improvised identities, and who may come to constitute a diasporic community or live in exile.[55] We need poems that speak to these experiences but also reflections on the nature of poiesis from these diverse life positions and trajectories to make sense of our current predicament, understand each other, and imagine ways forward.

In our work on cultural consultation, we have tried in some small way to use this process of poeisis, using culturally grounded language to make the clinical encounter a place for mutual recognition, advocacy, and responsiveness.[56] In this work, attention to metaphor is a path to recognizing difference, grasping essential cultural meanings in context, building an alliance, and co-constructing solutions. This work confronts us everywhere with hybridity and with the effort to find metaphors that are not just consonant with particular cultural histories but can also serve as bridges between traditions and new forms of identity and community.

## Aesthetic Awareness and the Politics of Metaphor

A recurrent tension in both aesthetic debates and political rhetoric is whether truth and insight are best achieved through clarity and simplicity or by embracing complexity, obscurity, and confusion. Clarity is crucial to find common ground and space for meaningful critique. But a clear vision of the world must recognize its own partiality, entanglements, and limitations in the face of the world's prodigious complexity. Clarity is not an endpoint that is ever fully achievable, but something to which we are always en route. To stay the course, we must be aware of how easy it is to get lost.

Many years ago, on my way to a poetry retreat, I sat on a bus beside a young woman who appeared deeply vexed. She explained that the source of her consternation and confusion was that a week earlier, while attending a storytelling workshop, she had fallen into a story and now could not get out. Those around her on the bus took this to be a metaphor for an experience of deep aesthetic engagement or imaginative play, but it soon became apparent that this was not a playful experience but a serious quandary. She was stuck inside a story, not of her own making, that impeded her ability to be in the present and engage with the flow of everyday life activities. Over the next few days at the retreat, she had difficulty participating in the program and during an art workshop became engrossed in wrapping her arm in plaster cast material, oblivious to the social context and requests to move on to the next activity. The coordinators of the retreat worried that she was "out of touch with reality" and wondered whether she should be brought to a hospital for emergency psychiatric evaluation.

Is this an example of excessive absorption characteristic of dissociative disorders or a symptom of psychosis? Or is it simply an intense version of the kind of absorption common in listening to stories? Ordinarily we expect people to be able to tell the difference between a story and reality and to know when storytelling time is over. Telling the difference between metaphors or stories and reality is a basic skill for navigating the world. Becoming aware of our poetic constructions is central to the ways we engage with art—adding a layer of self-reflection and aesthetic appreciation to our feelings of pleasure associated with mimetic fulfillment of our desires.

If so, how does getting lost in a story differ from our usual mode of engagement with dominant or master narratives of myth and ideology? Is the difference the inability to distinguish between the state of absorption and the state of clarity and detachment? Or, if our participation in stories requires no special mental state or commitment beyond listening closely, does the difficulty lie in our forgetting the source and losing the ability to think outside the story's box? In everyday life, we constantly engage with stories and the social-cultural world is largely constructed of interlocking narratives. To make sense of them we must inhabit them. Waking up to the fact that we are caught within the story (caught in the net of the alien or the comfort of the familiar) is what allows us to question the received wisdom.

Getting lost in a story involves absorption, an attentional process, and imagination, an engagement with the possible world implied by the text. It does not take much to evoke a sense of place and time and engage us in a way that is vividly present. Even a brief narrative evocation of a person or situation creates a sense of space, time, and presence. In his novel *Man in the Dark*,[57] Paul Auster simply sketches the predicament of a man in a hole, unable to extricate himself, and, as he adds details, suddenly we are *there*—image becomes reality, even though its artifice is on display, compelling a visceral engagement with the text. The same power of conjuring worlds occurs repeatedly in Italo Calvino's *If on a Winter's Night a Traveller*,[58] which begins by describing the reader's situation ("You are about to begin reading Italo Calvino's new novel . . .") and then invites us into a chain of nested narratives, each of which is suddenly broken off at the end of a chapter to be replaced in the next chapter by a new narrative that takes off from within a book just mentioned in the previous narrative strand. We follow along, through multiple interruptions and stories within stories, adopting new positions and personas, inhabiting worlds within worlds. These texts create an oscillation between participation and self-aware distance through the larger narrative that moves between mimesis and self-reference. The oscillation reveals both our powerful attraction to immersive engagement through imagination and our capacity for self-reflection. The very fact of interruption and the ease of reengagement shows us something about how stories work, not as part of a single grand narrative, but as "presence machines" that readily evoke a sense of real presences and, always beyond that, the horizon of a whole world. This worlding does not require elaborate detail, only a rough sketch and, in the case of speculative fiction, it can even introduce strange, and impossible situations that we inhabit like a dream. What Auster calls "the mechanics of reality"[59] provides the grounds for worlding even when details are not supplied by the narrative sketch or metaphor. These mechanics or dynamics are part of our bodies and brains, our existential predicaments, and the cultural worlds we inhabit, whose histories are sedimented in language. Our ability to recognize these dynamics depends on self-reflexivity that may be limited by the immersive push and pull of rhetoric that serve political ideologies.[60]

The counter to Plato's argument that poets simply present a shadowy or distorted picture of reality and, in so doing, distance us from truth, is that much of human reality is constituted by the representations we create. These are not arbitrary or disposable but serve to orient and coordinate our actions and allow us to construct niches and social forms within the material world that are the vehicles for human truth, invention, and adaptation. So, the distinction between a truth, whether materially instantiated in the world or transcendentally present in the mind of God, and representation as humanly constructed, fungible, and misleading pictures of the world that are no better than shadows on the walls of cave, is itself a profound misrepresentation of human being in the world. Rather than dispensing with poetics to get at the hard truth, we need a poetic naturalism that breaks down the sharp distinction between representation and reality by recognizing that we are language animals.[61] The worlds we inhabit are cooperatively built and constitute systems of signs and symbols with their own dynamics that depend on social structure, institutions and forms of life. The human adaptive niche is woven of matter and representation, story and history, grounded metaphor and imaginative possibility. As Paul Auster observed, metaphor provides us with a second nature as precious as the first:

> For what does it mean to look at something, a real object in the real world, an animal, for example, and say that it is something other than what it is? It is to say that each thing leads a double life, at once in the world and in our minds, and that to deny either one of these lives is to kill the thing in both its lives at once. . . Both are enchantments, both the real and the imaginary, and each exists by virtue of the other.[62]

Some of the mystification, confusion, or confinement of living under a myth can be lifted when we develop the capacity to see the myth as myth and metaphor as metaphor. This need not result in a loss of our ability to participate in the myth when it offers wisdom or an aesthetically pleasing way of life, but it insists on the ethical urgency of cultivating a duality of awareness: present and participating in the myth, while cultivating our sense of its artifice, origins, and limitations. This duality of awareness offers us another kind of truth and perhaps a deeper aesthetic pleasure. The rainbow is no less wondrous for learning something of its mechanism; the physics, history, and cultural symbolism all add layers to its meaning.[63]

We began this book by suggesting that attention to metaphor can open two paths: one toward the critique of regnant structures and identities and their rhetorics of justification and promotion and another toward the mutative power of symbols of transformation. We can now see how aesthetics are central to both of these paths. The coherence, aptness, and attractiveness of particular images or tropes no less than their stickiness, insistence, and ability to colonize the imagination is central to their propagation and capture of hearts and minds. And the ways that metaphors open onto other possible worlds, selves, or courses of action serves their mutative power as vehicles of healing transformation—or as traps that lead to foundering, rupture, and dissolution.

Is an aesthetic ideal then a recognition or an achievement? Are we presented with a world that includes its terminus ad quem (point of arrival) or do we construct a ladder toward unknown possibilities with only temporary signposts along the way? The idea of scaffolding implies the possibility of climbing upward but not a necessary end. It is up to us to imagine our ideals and discover to what extent they are realizable and whether and how they actually result in the kinds of lives and worlds we imagine or hope for—or, inevitably, have unexpected, unintended, and unwanted consequences. This working through of consequences brings together ethics, aesthetics, and politics.

Coexistence means we must listen to and engage with others. When we listen to the world, though, we sometimes hear only echoes: the world seems to mirror our desire or taunts us with distorted echoes of our own voice. What transforms such *echopoetics* into *ecopoetics* is our recognition of other voices in the world that present the unexpected and unimagined. This engagement can reanimate and repopulate our imagination with new metaphors and perspectives in surprising and unanticipated ways. The poet–philosopher Jan Zwicky has offered a lyric philosophy that highlights this process of poetic refiguration as the basic way we encounter the world and come to recognize our selves.[64] Lyric philosophy taken into the world becomes lyric ecology, an approach that holds the promise of bridging the nature/culture divide by insisting on the ecological embedding of poiesis.

## Conclusion

The human condition is one of recurrent wounding and healing, fracture and annealing, and loss and restoration over the span of a lifetime and across generations. Healing happens through natural processes of reconstruction and repair, and also through the ways that we narrate the self, its goals and direction. We do this by imaginative enactments that generate new possibilities, configurations of the self, and modes of inhabiting the world.

Metaphor is the medium of imagination—the tool we use to take hold of the world and invent new realities. Imaginative invention is playful, aesthetically rewarding, and demonstrably powerful—yet it also poses dangers. Sober minds regard the excesses of imagination with concern. Since the Enlightenment imagination has become a debased currency, shouldered aside by the clarity, precision, and promise of scientific reason. Imagination is valued as a source of creativity or kind of recreation, but must be tamed, contained, harnessed, and controlled to contribute to the more deliberate and deliberative processes of self-construction.

The emphasis on metaphor and poetics throughout this book stems in part from recognition of the central role of aesthetics in the articulation of illness experience and the process of healing. Many traditions valorize suffering and healing as paths to the character development, wisdom, and moral or spiritual attainment and celebrate this process in art and ritual. There is reason for concern, though, that exclusive focus on the aesthetics of illness may lead us to ignore the structural violence that produces and maintains inequities and obscure the multilevel dynamics of power involved in change. Appreciating the limits of aesthetic analysis provides a crucial counterbalance to this valorization. At the same time, attention to the aesthetics of illness experience and healing can allow us to recognize new ways of thinking, feeling, and imagining that allow us to work toward change. Aesthetic analysis then does not rob experience of its material reality or sensual qualities but allows us to feel its presence, savor its taste and texture, and appreciate its transformative power that can be wielded in ways that are both creative and destructive.

Aesthetic engagement involves modes of attentiveness, ways of knowing, and respect for the texture of experience that can work against its commodification. Image and metaphor have an experiential presence like one of Marianne Moore's real toads in an imaginary garden.[65] Moore encouraged poets to be "literalists of the imagination" (a phrase used by Yeats to characterize Blake)—recognizing that our experience of reality depends on imagination. Attention to the aesthetic dimensions of illness experience need not undermine our ability to feel and respond to the most serious exigencies of health and illness. To the contrary, aesthetic attention can energize, inform, and direct the imagination in ways essential for empathy, understanding, and compassionate action.

Attending to the metaphors of ordinary speech can allow us to challenge the taken-for-granted or formulaic interpretations of experience that constitute the *status quo* and open up new imaginative possibilities and ways of being. We can recognize the implicit connotations of extant metaphors by deliberate substitution of an alternative metaphor. For example, we may shift from a hermeneutics of *suspicion* to one of *trust*[66]; from emotions as disruptive, irrational, and "out-of-control" to emotions as ways of knowing, moral intuition, intelligence, perspicacity, and insistence[67]; from *understanding* as reducing something to its components to *overstanding* as grasping its larger situated meaning[68]; from a *broken brain* to an *ecology of mind*.[69] The fact that it is easy to make such shifts that point to new truths reflects the reality that metaphorical thinking is inherently perspectival and always yields partial truths that both reveal and conceal. The play of metaphors—their poetic production, exploration, and critique—is essential to the growth of knowledge. Cultivating forms of life conducive to this play is essential to human survival, healing, and flourishing.

# *Notes*

## Preface

1. Blake, 1975.
2. Quoted in Gussow, 2000.
3. See for example: Barker, 2013; Cox & Theilgaard, 1997; Siegelman, 1993; Stott et al., 2010; Törneke, 2017. For discussions of the use of metaphor in medical communication more broadly see: Bleakley, 2017; Fuks, 2021.
4. "Romanticism tells us that reason would have had nothing to do—that we would have had nothing to think about—had imagination not been at work. Pragmatism tells us that imagination should not be allowed to interfere with reason's activities. Once an activity of reason becomes a social practice, such as mathematics, experimental science, or constitutional jurisprudence, it becomes self-regulating, and should be granted autonomy. It is one thing for an imaginative genius to suggest that we might play a different game, but quite another to disrupt the game presently being played by making illegal moves" (Rorty, 2016, pp. 45–46).

## Chapter 1: Into the Backcountry

1. Bacon, 2000.
2. René Char in a letter to Jonathan Griffin (Caws & Griffin, 1976, p. xxx).
3. An influential view of metaphors as models was introduced by the philosopher Max Black (1962, 1993) and elaborated by Hesse (1966, 2017) to approach scientific thinking as a process of metaphoric redescription. Subsequent work in conceptual metaphor theory has shown the ubiquity of metaphor and the ways it undergirds everyday cognition (Gibbs, 2008; Lakoff & Johnson, 1980), as well as scientific reasoning, creativity, and model building (Boyd, 1979). For a temperate view of the role and limitations of metaphor in science see: "Dry truth and real knowledge: Epistemologies of metaphor and metaphors of epistemology," in Haack, 2000.
4. Lee & Kirmayer, 2020.

5. Choudhury, McKinney, & Kirmayer, 2015.
6. Groesbeck, 1975.
7. Kirmayer, 1990.
8. Niezen, 2017; Truth & Reconciliation Commission, 2015.
9. Lee, Kirmayer & Groleau, 2010; Lee, 2016.
10. Patten, 2015; Syed & Jacob, 2024. The metaphor of chemical imbalance likely has persisted despite its misrepresentation of neurobiological theory and evidence because it suits the need for simple intuitive explanations with the "ring of science" in clinical negotiation of illness meaning and pharmaceutical advertising (Ang, Horowitz, Moncrieff, 2022). Balance provides a natural experience that motivates metaphors in many areas including physiology, economics, politics, and morality (Thagard, 2022).
11. The hypnotherapist Milton Erickson framed the unconscious as a storehouse of knowledge and wisdom that could be mobilized through hypnotic trance, reverie, or suggestion, including the deliberate use of metaphoric reframing (Kirmayer, 1988b). Jungian psychology also views the unconscious as operating in ways that constitute an inner healer that offers images and insights through dreams and reveries that are compensatory to the person's conscious attitude (Groesbeck, 1975; Jung, 1967). The metaphor of an inner healer underwrites some current approaches to the therapeutic use of psychedelics (Peil et al., 2024).
12. Stott et al., 2010; Stoddard & Afari, 2014. Attitudes toward the therapeutic use of metaphor vary across schools of psychotherapy as do the use of specific metaphors like DEPTH-SURFACE (central to psychodynamic psychotherapies) and therapeutic TOOLS or EXPERIMENTS (central to cognitive behavioral therapy (CBT; Malkomsen et al., 2022). Patients may use similar metaphors (Malkomsen et al., 2021). Over time, patients' metaphors may come to align with those of their therapist, though they may resist or reject metaphors that are not apposite (Seligman, 2023).
13. This was the thrust of Susan Sontag's (1978) critique of the uses of metaphors in describing illness. The notion that we can somehow entirely dispense with metaphor, however, is misguided.
14. Barfield, 1973, p. 63.
15. For estimates of the frequency of metaphors see: Bowdle & Gentner, 2005, and Cameron, 2008.
16. Gibbs, 1994.
17. Styron, 1992, p. 50. For a detailed analysis of Styron's metaphors for depression, see: Schoenman et al. (2004). They counted 671 metaphors for depression in the book, which are internally consistent and describe depression being DOWN, BLACK, INWARD, and AWAY (FROM LIFE). Recovery is described in contrasting terms as UP, LIGHT, OUTWARD, and

TOWARD. Similar metaphors of darkness and heaviness can be found in both historical and current accounts (Radden, 2009). Other work based on lived experience describes the frequent use of metaphors of helplessness and being trapped: "Many people suffering from depression describe it as a prison they cannot escape: "*Depression is like a hole. You are stuck in the hole. You can't get out*" (personal communication). The metaphors used (e.g., a hole, a fog, an endless tunnel) equally express the sense of violent constraint and impotence: "*Lost in a really thick fog, you can't find your way out, you have no direction or energy. It weighs you down, and you can't work it out*"."(Fusar-Poli et al., 2023, p. 356, italics in original).

18. This the dominant approach in biological psychiatry (Patten, 2015) and is commonly used by patients in treatment and their families (Coll-Florit et al., 2021). But the metaphors used vary across cultures (Pritzker, 2007) and with the particular facet of experience or conundrum with which the person is grappling (Choudhury et al., 2015).
19. Crucially, the common experiential metaphors for depression of blackness, heaviness, and inwardness can also yield contrary meanings. In the Renaissance, melancholia—as state and temperament—was linked to philosophical contemplation, depth, and creativity in the work of Marsilio Ficino (1433–1499), reflected in the image of Durer's *Melencolia* (1514), and later taken up by Robert Burton (1577–1640) in *The Anatomy of Melancholy* (Klibansky, Panofsky & Saxl, 2019). Jung (2014) found analogies in the alchemical concept of *nigredo,* which he viewed as the first stage of the transformative process that leads from a descent into darkness, through the dissolution of old structures, chaos, and confusion, to eventual wholeness and rebirth.
20. Following a common convention, metaphors that are the focus of discussion will be presented in small caps. Key metaphors and technical concepts are indexed so that readers can readily locate their definitions and uses in the text.
21. Von Neumann (1958) made the analogy, which is both useful and misleading. The accuracy of the analogy depends on our concept of *computer* (Richards & Lillicrap, 2022). If we define a computer broadly as any device or entity that can do computations, then the brain is literally a computer. If we define computer more narrowly in terms of specific kinds of functional organization or architecture, or as a general-purpose device in which hardware (substrate) and software (program) are distinct, then the metaphor is misleading: the functional architecture of the brain does not mirror that of the digital computer and computational processes regularly involve changes in the structure of the brain. The functioning of the brain is grounded in sensorimotor processes and analog mechanisms that depend on physiology, embodiment, and the environmental embedding of neurodevelopment, learning, and adaptation (see: Brette, 2022; Reynolds, 2022). If the mind is

conceptualized as software, then cognitive therapy aims to reprogram the mind. The recognition of brain plasticity also leads to the use of metaphors of "reprogramming the brain" to explain therapeutic interventions.

22. Martin, 2010; Rose & Abi-Rached, 2013; Vidal & Ortega, 2020.
23. Whalley, 1997. Ricoeur (1977) traces the implications of Aristotle's thinking about metaphor in both the *Poetics* and *Rhetoric*. While Aristotle contrasted *poeisis* (fashioning objects outside the self) with *praxis* (ethical action or fashioning the self) (Shusterman, 2006), we will be concerned throughout with poeisis *as* praxis.
24. Overviews of recent work in 4-E cognitive science can be found in: Gallagher (2023a) and Newen, De Bruin, & Gallagher (2018). On embodiment see: Gallagher, 2006; Gibbs, 2005; Shapiro, 2010; Varela, Thompson, & Rosch, 1991; enactivism (Chemero, 2011; Gallagher, 2018; Hutto & Myin, 2012; 2017); embedded or situated mind (Robbins & Aydede, 2009); and extended mind (Clark, 2008). Others have argued for the recognizing "emotive" (or affective) as another key dimension, and Mark Johnson (2017) added "exapted" to this list to emphasize how in human evolutionary history abilities that emerged for one reason have taken on new functions in response to novel, humanly constructed, contexts. All of these elaborations share a concern with understanding human cognition not as disembodied computations but as something that people do in and through their bodies in social contexts inhabited by other people who participate in the process of cognition. We have elaborated on this idea in an account of cognition as "thinking through other minds" (Veissière et al., 2020).
25. Gibbs, 2005; Shapiro, 2010.
26. Ramstead, Veissière, & Kirmayer, 2016.
27. Chemero, 2011; Gallagher, 2017; Hutto & Myin, 2012, 2017. In its more radical versions, enactivism aims to show that complex cognition does not require representations. This suggests that we think of symbols (and metaphors) in pragmatic terms as forms of social action. Wagner (1986) develops a notion of symbols as nonrepresentational by emphasizing their social meaning as affordances for perception and practice.
28. Ramstead, Veissière, & Kirmayer, 2016; Kirmayer & Ramstead, 2017; Veissière et al., 2020. On positioning see: Davies & Harré, 1990; Harré & Van Langenhove, 1991.
29. Berrios & Markova, 2015; De Haan, 2020; Kirmayer, 2015c; Kirmayer & Ramstead, 2017.
30. In his ethnographic study of psychiatric training in the 1970s, the sociologist Donald Light (1980) described this dominant position of psychoanalysis just before its displacement by biological psychiatry; thirty years later, Luhrmann (2011) described a changed scene; while exposure to psychodynamics was still

part of psychiatrists' training, it has lost much of its institutional authority. This decline in importance has continued.

31. See, for example, the 2005 editorial in *JAMA* by the then leader of the US National Institute of Mental Health and his Canadian counterpart, which depicted psychiatry as "clinical neuroscience" and saw a bright future in novel diagnostic techniques based in brain imaging and neurogenetics (Insel & Quirion, 2005). This heralded a major shift in the focus on mental health research in the United States away from clinically derived diagnostic categories (described in the American Psychiatric Association's Diagnostic and Statistical Manuals) and toward neurobiological processes in a concerted search for the substrates of mental disorder. For a critique of this emphasis on neurobiological explanations, see: Kirmayer & Crafa, 2014. This shift away from social and psychological explanations of disorders actually began with the so-called "decade of the brain" from 1990 to 1999 (Jones & Mendel, 1999). Tanya Luhrmann (2011) chronicled the decline of psychodynamic psychiatry and its replacement by a thoroughly biologized account of human beings empty of interiority. In many psychiatric training programs, time devoted to learning neuroscience has displaced exposure to various forms of therapeutic intervention including psychotherapy, family therapy, and social interventions. Of course, this change in the focus of training both reflects and contributes to changes in practice and influences who is attracted to the profession.
32. While religion has long played a central role in the cultural configuration of the self (Allen, 2018; Dumont, 1982; Marsella, Devos, & Hsu, 1985; Roland, 1988; Taylor, 1989), individualistic notions of personhood derived from the psychological disciplines have become pervasive in Western cultures and increasingly globalized through mass media presentations of melodramas, "reality TV," talk shows, and self-help advice (see: Bellah et al., 1985; Cushman, 1995; Illouz, 2008; Rose, 1998).
33. Kleinman, 1999.
34. The psychiatrist Nassir Ghaemi (2010) leveled a similar critique of unprincipled eclecticism at the "biopsychosocial model" in psychiatry. His argument seems to be based on the tacit assumption that neurobiology alone can provide a scientific explanation of the mechanisms of psychopathology. For clinical practice, he thinks this scientific psychiatry should be supplemented by phenomenology to allow the clinician an empathetic understanding of the quality of patients' suffering and predicament. Strangely, he points to William Osler's prepsychological medical humanism as an alternative to psychology and social sciences. Absent from Ghaemi's account is any systematic engagement with scientific research on cognitive

and social processes as central to the mechanisms of mental health problems and their treatment.

35. This notion is built into the psychosomatic concept of *alexithymia* (Kirmayer, 1987).
36. See for example: Cieri, 2023; Holmes, 2020; Solms, 2019.
37. Frank, 1973; Kirmayer, 2004; Kleinman, 1980, 1998a; Prince, 1980, 1982.
38. See Young (1988) for an analysis of Frank's construct of demoralization and Alarcón and Frank (2011) for its impact on psychiatry and psychotherapy.
39. For discussions of common factors in healing and psychotherapy see: Cuijpers, Reijnders, & Huibers, 2019; Draguns, 1975; Hinton & Kirmayer, 2017; Kirmayer, 2004; Kleinman & Sung, 1979; Kohrt et al., 2020; Mulder, Murray, & Rucklage, 2017; Prince, 1980; Wampold & Imel, 2015. In the psychotherapy literature, the list of common factors varies with the level of abstraction and effort to capture elements considered crucial within particular schools of therapy but generally includes: (1) hope and expectations for positive change through the therapeutic intervention; (2) an emotionally charged bond with the therapist (or the institution) that conveys empathic recognition, concern, caring and encouragement and imbues the therapeutic conversation with personal significance; (3) a circumscribed, protected place and time that allows the development of trust, a confiding relationship, and self-disclosure; (4) explanations for symptoms and suffering that make sense to the patient and others in their local world. This may invoke an existing cultural ontology or introduce new ways of thinking (e.g., psychological models of the person); (5) a symbolic reframing or transformation of patients' self-understanding or view of their predicament. This may be framed as "insight" into the true nature of the self and relationships with others; and (6) a set of procedures, practices and ritual enactments that that lead to beneficial outcomes in day-to-day functioning. Within this general framework specific interventions may target modes of self-construal, emotion regulation, interpersonal interaction or other cognitive and social processes foregrounded by particular approaches. Chapter 4 revisits these common factors through a hierarchical systems model of healing practices.
40. As discussed in later chapters, these meanings derive both from embodied experience and overarching narratives or myths that confer shared meaning and expectations for healing and recovery. The literature on cultural adaptations of psychotherapy suggests that the consonance or fit of a treatment intervention with these authorizing myths is associated with greater efficacy (Benish, Quintana, & Wampold, 2011).
41. Frank & Frank, 1993. This shift was influenced by the work of Glaser (1980) and Spillane (1987).
42. Perelman, 1982; Phelan, 2017.

43. Amossy, 2001. In comments on an earlier version of this chapter, Omri Moses notes the tensions between rhetoric and poetics: "Rhetoric is much more associated with logos and ethos (and the dominant forms of rationality entailed in them). This is true even if we think of the alignment of rhetorical traditions with pragmatic and pragmatist discourses. Poetics is concerned with the novel (Heideggerian poiesis), the emergent, and the unknown—and it is often thought to give voice to alternative forms of rationality . . . The tensions between rhetoric and poetics also trace a fault line between narrative and metaphor as ways of organizing illness experience, where narrative (especially causal rather than paratactical narrative) is associated with the possibility of explanatory closure, and metaphor expresses what is emergent, open, fragmentary, and thus aligned with poetic traditions" (OM, personal communication, July 23, 2019). As discussed in Chapter 2, this aspect of poetics is important in the clinical context because patients' metaphors serve as windows into an illness experience that is less rationalized, measured, and medically authorized. For both developmental and cognitive reasons, metaphors can capture aspects of our embodiment and feeling that would be lost (or lose their salience and coherence) if we were to characterize experience and beliefs in terms of minimal semantic propositions. Instead, poetics opens onto the coherence and generativity of metaphors, images, and sensually or affectively charged language.
44. Although originally intended to mark a distinction with biomedical processes of healing, the term "symbolic healing" is best applied not so much to a specific kind of healing practice as to that aspect of healing that depends on the meaning of the practice to participants (including, patient, healer, and others). Symbolic or meaning-based effects are an important aspect of every kind of healing, even those that involve processes that do not depend on participants' awareness, interpretation, or other explicit meaning-centered responses (Moerman, 2002). These may involve conditioned learning or other modes of responding to the affordances presented by an intervention (Annoni & Blease, 2018).
45. Bergin & Fisch, 1970; Verene, 1981.
46. Hinman, 1982. Early on, Nietzsche favored the energy of metaphor over lifeless concepts, but he arrived at a more nuanced view of the interplay of metaphor and concept (Kofman, 1993).
47. Lakoff & Johnson, 1980; Gibbs, 1994; Kövecses, 2010.
48. This view of metaphor as the master trope goes back to Aristotle (for discussion of this history and its long reach, see: Derrida, 1974; Eco, 1983). The various forms of analogy, including simile, synecdoche, metonym, and metaphor can be grouped under the broad heading of metaphor. Though the

distinctions among different types of tropes are important in more fine-grained analyses of linguistic meaning, metaphor is central to conceptual structure. On cultural comparative grounds, Friedrich (1986) argues against the use of metaphor as the master trope, even in its more limited and literal application to linguistic figures: "The omnium gatherum use of metaphor reflects Aristotle, more recent theory, and some ethnic, historical, and personal biases. Even in its narrow meaning the role of metaphor varies enormously between poems, poets, poetic traditions, and cultures; the salience of metaphor as trope is low, for example, in some American Indian traditions" (p. 30). He suggests the value of keeping metaphor separate from irony, parallelism, gist, riddle, and metonymy in linguistic analysis and offers his own rough taxonomy of tropes: imagistic, modal, analogical, formal-constructional, expansion-condensation (p. 29). He goes on to note, though, that "within any such scheme a given trope will have to be cross-classified because each trope, while partly independent, also partly interdepends with other tropes." This leads us back to the argument for the validity of naming a master trope that governs this network of interrelationships—and from Aristotle through Vico, to current literary theory, metaphor has generally held this privileged position. While Friedrich believes that processes of analogy and association are more psychologically fundamental, much current work in cognitive science gives primacy to metaphor as a more exploratory way of bringing disparate concepts together.

49. Gibbs, 2017; Kövecses, 2020.
50. Ortony, 1979.
51. Black, 1962, 1993; Sternberg & Nigro, 1983.
52. Metaphor theory, thus, captures the essential insight of structuralism that meaning resides in networks of relationships without structuralism's excessive demand for symmetry.
53. Among its diverse uses, TRANSLATION provides a metaphor for metaphor (Guldin, 2016), but the mechanisms of metaphor are crucial to understanding the process of both conceptual and linguistic translation. Translation of poetry (and other forms of verbal art) are further complicated by the materiality of language as sound (or image on the page) that conveys parallel associations that enrich meaning and aesthetic experience (Hofstadter, 1997).
54. For a discussion of the metaphor–analogy relationship, see: Gentner et al., 2001.
55. Metaphors may be based on images (in any sensory modality) that may lead to both imagistic and linguistic elaboration. They may also begin as linguistic constructions that provoke a search for images or scenarios to make sense of

the juxtaposed words. The grounding of language in early sensory experience makes some links to images inbuilt or "automatic" (Barsalou, 2008). A focus on metaphor reminds us that imagination is not only about imagery but equally about the evocative powers of language (Ricouer, 1977).

56. Lakoff, 1987, p. 275. To this I would add (c) critical selection and elimination of metaphoric implications by a (scientific) community.
57. Johnson-Laird, 1983.
58. Fauconnier, 1997.
59. The idea of semantic pointers allows for multiple types of meaning-laden content in cognition (Blouw et al., 2016). This can be instantiated in particular computational architectures of the brain (Eliasmith, 2013) that are consistent with grounded theories of cognition (Barsalou, 2020), which imply the cultural specificity of specific images and concepts (Barsalou, 2023; Kemmerer, 2019, 2023). For a discussion of metaphoric meaning in terms of semantic pointers, see: Thagard, 2022.
60. Gibbs, 2008; Lakoff & Johnson, 1980; Ortony, 1993.
61. Gibbs, 1994; Johnson, 1987; Lakoff, 1987.
62. Indurkhya, 2007.
63. Heyes, 2019.
64. Schön, 1979.
65. Gibbs, 2019. For an ecological approach to understanding narrative in healing dynamics, see: Stromberg, 2023.
66. This problem of the indeterminacy of metaphor is quite general. For the use of metaphorical reasoning in physics and the operation of constraints related both to empirical measurement and existing theory, see, for example, Dunbar, 2009; Krieger, 2012.
67. Crovitz, 1970; Johnson, 1987; Williams, Huang, & Bargh, 2009.
68. Lakoff & Johnson, 1980; Oakley, 2007.
69. Quinn, 1991; Kövecses, 2015; Yu, 2008.
70. "Narrative may be a cognitive instrument of a specific type, one 'invented' for the decipherment of details of the real that take on their meaning only when linked in a series, enchained in a manner that allows one to detect that 'someone passed this way'" (Brooks, 2022, p. 17).
71. For Chinese speakers, time may be structured vertically; Boroditsky, 2011, 2018; Thibodeau & Boroditsky, 2011; Traugott, 1985.
72. "Myths are usually stories about something that cannot be explained through logical reasoning—origins, for instance, or the meaning of death. Story may be a necessary part of our cognitive interaction with the world because its mode of explaining takes place within time, and humans are time-bound in a way that they are not place-bound. Story is the *logic* of explanations and

meanings that unfold in time, the logic of those who are mortal" (Brooks, 2022, p. 13, italics in original).

While there is a tradition of framing modernity as the abandonment of myth for a disenchanted view of the world, or its partial replacement by novels, fiction, and stories that lack the authority or intensity of mythopoetic imagination (see for example: Blumenberg, 1985; Cassirer, 1946), there are ways in which much of the power of myth persists in popular imagination as well as sacred traditions (Coupe, 2009; Schremp & Hansen, 2002; Sebeok, 1965; Segal, 2020).

73. Perhaps precisely because these myths mirror our lives: "The forms of mythical invention reflect, not the objective character of things, but the forms of human practices" (Cassirer, 1946, p. 41). However, we do have a pantheon of god-like figures in popular culture to whom we ascribe magical powers and hence find their all-too-human flaws all the more fascinating. See Chapter 5, "The Playing Fields of Myth."
74. Cameron & Low, 1999; Gibbs, 2008.
75. Musolff, 2012.
76. Bachelard, 1964, 1969, 1971, 1983, 1987; McAllester Jones, 1991.
77. Osgood, 1964; Osgood, 1981.
78. Osgood, May, & Miron, 1975.
79. Reddy, 2001.
80. The notion of blending conceptual spaces is developed in Fauconnier & Turner, 1998, 2008.
81. For the pervasive influence of war metaphors in medicine, see: Bleakley, 2017, Fuks, 2021, and Wohlman, 2022.
82. Csordas, 2008.
83. The notion of heteroglossia in literature was introduced by Bakhtin (2010). In everyday conversation, heteroglossia involves not only explicit quotation or borrowing from different voices but the use of language that sediments multiple perspectives and strands of history.
84. See, for example: Onians, 1951; Jaynes, 1976; Snell, 1982; Gentner & Grudin, 1985; Leary, 1994; Barrett, 2017; Gabriel, 2023.
85. Brown, 2004; Norenzayan & Heine, 2005.
86. Interestingly, older adults may be better at understanding novel metaphors because life experience has enriched their capacity to make conceptual combinations (Ichien et al., 2024). The authors describe this ability to make conceptual combinations as a form of "crystallized intelligence" and distinguish it from the construction of analogies, which involves a "fluid intelligence" that younger adults may be better at and that may diminish with aging.

87. Lakoff and Johnson (1980) provide many examples of core metaphors that structure multiple concepts, models or domains of thought. The notion of root, key or core metaphor has been explored by Pepper (1935, 1982) in metaphysics and Williams (1976) in cultural criticism. Ortner (1973) argued this provides a useful way to approach the analysis of cultural "key symbols" in ethnography, linking social practices, scenarios, and the cognitive structures of thought. Since many metaphors are produced on the fly in response to particular contextual cues and demands, or as "throwaway" attempts to characterize an experience, establishing that a specific metaphor is root, core, or key for an individual requires determining the organizational role in plays in larger structures of thought and behavior and its recurrence across time and context. Identifying a metaphor as key in cultural practices may appeal to the ways in which it is sedimented in language, discourse, disciplinary traditions, and institutional structures. Blumenberg (2020) uses the term "absolute metaphors" for metaphors that are fundamental to philosophical language in the sense that they cannot be reduced to a discrete list of concepts or logical expressions and serve the generative process through which new concepts emerge. By insisting on the metaphoric nature of such absolutes he offers a way into the historical and conceptual roots of philosophical frameworks and styles of argument (Adams, 1991).
88. Glucksberg & Keysar, 1990.
89. Goodman, 1978; Levin, 1988; Overing, 1990. Recent work in anthropology and sociology has advocated for an ontological turn in which cultural systems are recognized as constituting fundamentally different realities (both experiential worlds and material orders) in which humans and other beings are deeply intertwined in ways that are not adequately captured by the usual divides of culture and biology (Descola, 2013; Kohn, 2015; Latour, 2013; Viveiros de Castro, 2004). Taking cultural ontologies seriously requires considering the ways in which ontologies arise from specific modes of material and discursive practice (Hacking, 2002; Pickering, 2017).
90. Rorty, 1979; Povinelli, 2001.
91. Attention to the conditions for this kind of metaphoric engagement and mutual understanding adds a crucial dimension to communicative ethics (Habermas, 1990) and links it not only to the nature of community but to the histories sedimented in language.
92. Cohen, 1978; for experimental evidence, see: Bowes & Katz, 2015.
93. Where am I standing when I say "*this* world"? Here with you! We live in one world though it provides many different niches, each with a distinct set of perceptual affordances. The deictic power of language allows us to point to aspects of our perceptual niche or *umwelt*, whether externally realized or

simply imagined and, in so doing, invites others to construct a model, map, or imaginal space that can be shared and coinhabited (Rubba, 1996).

94. "Intersubjectivity is the very condition of human speech: subjectivity is not conceivable without it. And it is the situation of speech that summons up the other distinctions of language: deictic markers (here, there) and temporal adjectives (yesterday, in the future). Verb tenses themselves, our distinctions of past, future, conditional (and refinements like the past conditional, the subjunctive, and so forth) are established in reference to the moment of speaking, what we call 'the present'" (Brooks, 2022, p. 97).
95. Critchley, 2005, p. 54. A version of this tension lies behind the epochal debate between the philosophers Ernst Cassirer and Martin Heidegger at Davos in 1929 (Gordon, 2010). While framed as a debate about the meaning of Kant's philosophical work and the essential question "What is man?" Cassirer and Heidegger set out sharply contrasting visions. For Cassirer, humans are characterized by our creative capacity to fashion new worlds of meaning through symbolic forms. Heidegger argued that what is most essential about humans is our finitude and "thrownness" into the world, which confronts us with a fundamental existential predicament. With hindsight, these contrasting visions cannot be viewed as an either/or—both are essential dimensions of the human condition and of any inclusive framework for ethics and politics. The challenge is to specify how the inventiveness of imagination and symbolic forms of culture work with and against the constraints of our being—which are not only existentially given but also socially constructed and historically contingent—to allow us to create new forms of identity and community.
96. Hacking, 1995a, 1995b, 1999, 2002, 2004. Hacking refers to loops that depend in part on biological responses of the body as "bio-looping." See: Seligman, 2014, 2018.
97. Bateson, 1972.

## Chapter 2: The Body's Insistence on Meaning

1. Bly, 1986.
2. Zwicky, 2003, p. 35.
3. This distinction, a version of mind-body dualism, is made in Berger (1987). "Text" here can be taken broadly, not just as written text but oral narrative or use of language to organize and express experience. Language as cognition and communication is more basic, developmentally prior, and immediate than text as such and is deeply woven into bodily experience (Di Paolo, Cuffari, & De Jaegher, 2018). The composition of formal texts adds layers of order to the more improvised and transitory exchanges of everyday speech. Texts can

circulate widely and are used in ways that add institutional and epistemic authority and hence are crucial to understand the social construction and negotiation of illness experience. Blumenberg (1997, p. 86) observes that the metaphor of the world as a book that can be read or deciphered is pervasive in Western history.

4. See: Johnson, 1987; Lakoff, 1987; Levin, 1985; O'Neill, 1985; Rochberg-Halton, 1986; Scarry, 1985; Turner, 1984; Welton, 1998; Krieger, 2005.
5. See: Barsalou, 2008; Crovitz, 1970; Glenberg & Kashak, 2003; Howell, Jankowicz, & Becker, 2005; Kemmerer, 2006; Lakoff & Johnson, 1977; Vowles, 1970.
6. Lederer, 1990.
7. Kleinman, 1988a.
8. Scheper-Hughes and Lock (1987). Examples of studies focused on each of these three bodies can be found in the work of Elaine Scarry (1985), Mary Douglas (1973), and Bryan Turner (1984), respectively.
9. And a fourth, semiotically distinct bodily realm is side-stepped: the body of biology is not entirely subsumed by the three categories of Scheper-Hughes and Lock. Compare: (a) feeling sick; (b) being treated as sick by others; (c) being told you are sick by a doctor; and (d) finding your temperature elevated on a thermometer. Each has a different epistemology. The last event is neither strictly bodily felt, social-symbolic nor political, but *indexical*—demonstrably linked to the body's physical condition (cf. Mounin, 1985). This points toward a semiotic analysis of the unique value of scientific methods of inquiry into the body's biological, cognitive, and social functions and dysfunctions.
10. There is a parallel here to the study of action systems in cognitive science. Ambiguity and ambivalence in thought are resolved by the need to take action and, indeed, the action system resolves what may continue to be ambiguous at some level of cognition and representation. Thus, embodiment is crucial to being able to make up one's mind (Shallice, 1978; Clark, 1997). To the extent that survival depends on taking appropriate action, the body insists that we make sense of the world. For humans, these actions involve organizing cooperative actions with others building on cultural knowledge and institutions, and so basic sense-making extends to wider realms of culturally and historically grounded linguistic meaning.
11. Rorty, 1979. Foucault (1975) describes this visual epistemology in the rise of the clinico-anatomical method in biomedicine. For the roots and implications of this metaphor for knowledge in philosophy see: Levin, 1993.
12. Clearly, value resides not only in felt significance but in reasoned principles supported by logical argument or the weight of evidence, and also in conventional practices accepted by a historical community. However, values

that are initially experienced as extrinsic are internalized as bodily felt convictions through participation in a way of life. The language of values (both moral and aesthetic) is replete with metaphors not only of vision but of gut feelings that convey conviction.

13. The doctor's judgment of irrationality, then, rests on the patient's failure to accept the tenets of biomedicine (beliefs); to articulate a sensible priority among his goals (personal survival versus avoiding genetic pollution); and, finally, to restrain his emotional reaction to his predicament. These distinct aspects of irrationality may be given different weight by individuals practicing within the same cultural framework.
14. Leventhal et al., 1992.
15. McDougall, 2013. For a review of the wide use of theater metaphors to capture the dynamics of the unconscious see: Karbelnig, 2020.
16. Kleinman, 1988a; Mishler, 1984. In routine medical practice, illness experience is viewed as mainly in terms of the challenge of seeing through the patient's story to get an accurate history and account of current symptoms which function as indicators or indices of disease. Biotechnology increasingly replaces patients' stories with more reliable measures of physiological parameters and imaging, moving the everyday practice of medicine away from any grounding in patients' experience and prompting compensatory efforts to development person-centered or narrative medicine and psychiatry (Charon, 2008; Charon et al., 2017; Greenhalgh, & Hurwitz, 1999; Hamkins, 2013; Kirmayer et al., 2023; Lewis, 2011).
17. Alexander, 1981.
18. Herzlich (1973) describes this symbolic link between health and the countryside in France. This focus on purity and association of nature and wildness with vitality and health, and of urban life with pollution, risk, and vulnerability is at the center of many health food practices (see: Coker, 2004; Veissière & Gibbs-Braco, 2016).
19. Sperber, 1985.
20. Heil, 1986.
21. Young, 1981, 1982.
22. In a sense, then, beliefs are practices. In this they are no different than other forms of practical reasoning in which "cognitive structures are not forms of consciousness but *dispositions of the body*" (Bourdieu, 1998, p. 54). Beliefs differ from other forms of embodied dispositions because they participate in language games of faith, commitment, and conviction that have epistemic, social, and moral meaning.
23. Rosaldo, 1984, p. 143.
24. Nussbaum, 2003.

25. For discussions of the role of embodiment and emotion in moral thinking, see: Damasio, 1994; Johnson, 1993.
26. A theory of embodied thought can also address the formal limitations of semantic network models of cognition, which do not take sufficient note of the role of reference or denotation in meaning (Johnson-Laird et al., 1984).
27. Jones, 1967.
28. Spiro, 1982.
29. Sperber, 1974; Gellner, 1985.
30. For an account of the central importance of the mathematical concepts of symmetry, groups, and operators in Lévi-Strauss's structuralism, see: Almeida, 1990.
31. Fernandez, 1982, pp. 19–20
32. Glucksberg & Keysar, 1990.
33. Kelly & Keil, 1987.
34. Kevin Dunbar (1997) has shown how this sort of metaphoric borrowing from distant domains is central to scientific creativity. For recent reviews, see: Dunbar & Fugelsing, 2005; Sanchez-Ruiz et al., 2013.
35. Gibbs 1992.
36. Quinn, 1982, 1991; Quinn & Holland, 1987.
37. Bruner, 1990.
38. Steiner (1990) discusses the importance of this experience of real presence to counter the arbitrariness and indeterminacy of meaning that arises from relentless deconstruction. Insofar as the sense of real presences stems from the encounter with something larger than or beyond our individual self, it may convey a feeling of self-transcendence that is articulated in religious traditions, though, on this social interpretation and contra Steiner, it need not imply any transcendent god or metaphysics.
39. Baron-Cohen & Harrison, 1997; Ramachandran et al., 2020.
40. Köhler, 1929; Ramachandran et al., 2020.
41. Wagner et al., 1981.
42. Luria, 1968, p. 84.
43. Winner et al., 1979.
44. See: Joseph-Salisbury & Connelly, 2018; Lashley 2020; Obeyesekere, 1981.
45. Winner et al., 1979; Winner, 1988.
46. Cienki & Muller, 2008; Cuffari, 2012; Cooperrider & Goldin-Meadow, 2017.
47. Vosniadou & Ortony, 1983; Winner, 1988.
48. Zajonc, 1980, 1984.
49. Osgood et al., 1975.
50. Heise, 1985.
51. Winner, 1988, p. 36.

52. Metaphor understanding involves a dynamic interplay of embodied experiences and knowledge derived from specific cultural contexts (Gibbs, 2017; Kovecses, 2020). Individuals continue to accumulate knowledge and skills over their lifespan that allow them to make sense of novel metaphors. This knowledge may be organized in terms of schemas based on particular cultural niches, situations and scenarios as well as specialized domains of knowledge acquired vicariously or through lived experience.
53. Sudnow (1993) provides an account of learning to play jazz piano that shows how the "hand" acquires a gestural vocabulary and grammatical rules that create the musical form.
54. Rozin, Millman, & Nemeroff, 1986, p. 703.
55. Curtis, 2013.
56. Rozin et al., 1986, 1990.
57. Indeed, recognizing the systematic nature of these judgments, we might as well speak of an "affect logic," as Allan Young (1995) has suggested.
58. Johnson, 1987.
59. Winner, 1988, p. 125.
60. Gibbs et al., 1994; Thagard, 2022.
61. Sacks, 1982, pp. 43–44, italics in original. See Stone, 2012, for a different take on the nature of his injury and its significance.
62. This vignette is based on clinical notes and discussions with the patient and is presented with her permission. Details have been changed to protect confidentiality.
63. This link is evident in the phenomenological accounts of stance and standing in Straus (1966) and Levinas (2003a) and in experimental work by Gibbs et al. (1994).
64. These interpretations come directly from Mrs. W, who read an earlier version of this passage and added her own insights.
65. The phenomenon of hypnotic catalepsy—in which a limb floats effortlessly, without conscious will or control—receives two types of explanation in the hypnosis literature: as a misattribution or as a dissociation of control (Lynn, Rhue, & Weekes, 1990). In the first explanation, the phenomenon is essentially attributional, having to do with how movement is explained, that is, whether it is attributed to self or other. In the second explanation, some distinctive change in cognitive control processes is posited: the cataleptic limb is controlled not by a simple motor action plan with feedback from the muscles confirming the execution of the willed movement; instead, it is engendered as an indirect consequence of communication from others or another aspect of the self that is less closely allied or fused with a central willing agency (Kirmayer et al., 2020). Thus, an image may evoke certain unintentional responses: thinking of a balloon

attached to a limb may cause an arm to rise with the feeling that this is happening automatically. For the misattribution theorist, the movement occurs voluntarily but we misattribute it to some effect of the image of the balloon. For the dissociationist, the image itself is the proximate cause of the levitation. The dissociation model allows for a second type of automaticity in which verbal suggestions or statements may also set in motion motor (and, we might add, autonomic or visceral) effects without conscious control. In the dissociationist view, then, the experience of involuntariness is not a misattribution, but a consequence of special control mechanisms or an altered hierarchy of control in which action occurs without an immediate or direct link to explicit intention (Hilgard, 1977). A hybrid account would locate the regulation of control in loops that include cognitive-attributional processes that are influenced by cultural scripts (Seligman & Kirmayer, 2008).

66. Lakoff & Johnson, 1980. For discussion of image-schemas see: Lakoff 1987; Johnson, 1987; Hampe & Grady, 2005. Suggestions for the neural grounding of image-schemas can be found in Dodge & Lakoff (2005).
67. Quinn, 1991.
68. For an illustration of the role of culture in shaping such elemental body experiences, consider the permeable boundaries of the Hindu body-self (Bharati, 1985), which make the worries of Mr. Y. seem eminently sane and sensible.
69. Lakoff, 1987, pp. 397ff; Kövecses, 2003; Hollan, 1988. Note, though, that we also speak of "cold anger"—and this too likely has a physiological basis, whether related to the interplay of fear or autonomic rebound or, perhaps, the way in which angry behavior without the physiological concomitants of anger evident on the face may be viewed as particularly threatening, because it implies either very intense self-restraint (that could break) or calculatedness (that could be malevolent).
70. Fernandez, 1986.
71. Wittgenstein, 1958 I: para. 23.
72. "The whole point of this emphasis on technique is to help us get rid of the common impression that language is like a mirror, and that whenever a sentence has meaning there is something, a proposition corresponding to it. Using language is exercising a technique .... W. tried to explain by the analogy with a map. In a map, squares may represent houses and lines may represent streets, and this now may be explained to a child. This is a house and this is a street. 'Now it's as though everything on the map represents something,' W. said, but 'representing is not represented on the map.' The map we may say represents. That it is a map involves that the map is used in a certain way. Its use is what makes it a map. In the same way it is the use of a sentence which makes it intelligible" (Bouwsma, 1986, pp. 23–24).

Wittgenstein's focus on technique or use in place of representation owes much to earlier concepts of "imageless thought" in German academic psychology (Bartley, 1985, pp. 128ff; but see Bloor, 1983, pp. 14ff).

73. Boyer, 1986.
74. Keesing et al., 1989.
75. Kirmayer & Ramstead, 2017; Ramstead, Veissière, & Kirmayer, 2016. Ernst Cassirer anticipates this view in his reflections on mana as an example of mythico-religious thought:

    "It is not a matter of "what," but of "how"; not the object of attention, but the sort of attention directed to it, is the crucial factor here. Mana and its several equivalents do not denote a single, definite predicate; but in all of them we find it peculiar and consistent *form of predication.* This predication may indeed be designated as the primeval mythico-religious predication, since it expresses the spiritual "crisis" whereby the holy is divided from the profane, and set apart from the sphere of the ordinary, in a religious sense indifferent, reality. By this process is division the object of religious experience may really be said to be brought into existence, and the realm in which it moves to be first established" (Cassirer, 1946, p. 66).
76. "'But surely you can see ... ?' That is just the characteristic expression of someone who is under the compulsion of a rule" (Wittgenstein, 1958, p. 86e). This seems to me to lay the ground for a more satisfying account than Sperber's (1985) somewhat opaque notion of "semi-propositional representations." By insisting on a representational model of knowledge, Sperber is forced to classify representations that fail to identify a unique verifiable proposition as "semi-propositional." A view of metaphor as presentation or enactment suggests that rules of usage, bodily, and rhetorical skills may be embodied dispositions to respond or ways of acting that are neither propositional nor imagistic in structure. Action systems based on procedural knowledge do not require mental representations to generate complex sequences of behavior.
77. This naturalization occurs tacitly through development and enculturation and provides a comfortable skin for social presence and scaffolding for action: "one of the privileges associated with the fact of being born in a game is that one can avoid cynicism since one has a feel for the game ... To the reduction of conscious calculation, I oppose the relationship of ontological complicity between the habitus and the field. Between agents and the social world there is a relationship of infraconscious, infralinguistic complicity" (Bourdieu, 1998, p. 79).
78. There has been a vigorous debate between proponents of radical enactivism, who eschew the reliance on the concept representations in characterizing basic processes of cognition (Hutto & Myin, 2012. 2017), and others who seek

a rapprochement with the broader field of cognitive science in which both action (presentation) and representation play key roles in cognition (Barsalou, 2016; Constant et al., 2021; Ramstead et al., 2021; Williams, 2018). The radical enactivist account is useful because it clarifies how many processes—including the early developmental steps that scaffold more complex cognition—might begin without detailed representations of the world. However, the position I outline here recognizes that organisms are shaped to respond adaptively to the environment in ways that necessarily make them (or their adaptive circuitry) constitute a representation of relevant parts of the world (Veissière et al., 2019). This representation is not just an external description of a reciprocity between organism and environment but a functional capacity of the organism to internally model and anticipate the environment and to work on that internal model in ways that have consequences for subsequent cognition and action. These models may be multimodal, employing various subsystems associated with particular sensory modalities as well as motor systems. In the case of humans, this representative capacity is dramatically elaborated through imagination which allows us to represent novel possibilities and configurations of the world and work toward their realization (Asma, 2017; Dor, 2017).

79. Quinn & Holland, 1987.
80. Sass & Alvarez, 2023.
81. Foucault, 2005.
82. On the fallibility of introspection, see: Dennett 1991; Schwitzgebel 2011; on cultural determinants of introspection, see: Nisbett & Wilson, 1977.

## Chapter 3: Broken Narratives

1. Cohen, 1978, p. 8.
2. Felstiner, 1995, p. 16.
3. The concept of flawed reality construction is developed by Hubert (1984) in a discussion on chronic pain.
4. Waitzkin & Britt, 1993.
5. Frank, 2013; Good, 1993; Kleinman, 1988b; for a critique of this emphasis on narrative, see: Woods, 2011.
6. Spence, 1982; Schafer, 1992.
7. There is by now a voluminous critique of the epistemological basis and empirical truth of psychoanalytic interpretation; most of these arguments apply to the range of psychodynamic psychotherapies. The classic philosophical treatment is Grünbaum (1984); for a summary and peer commentary, see: Grünbaum, 1986. Macmillan (1997) undertook a wide-ranging review that revealed the shaky empirical basis of psychoanalytic theory, and Paris (2019) provided a recent stock-taking

of the evidence for clinical applications. Over the years, there have been many efforts to recast psychoanalytic theory in terms of contemporary neuroscience (e.g., Pribram, 1986; Fotopoulu, Pfaff, & Conway, 2012; Hopkins, 2019; Solms, 2020). In some instances, these take as givens various psychoanalytic theories and propose plausible neural substrates; more critically, some authors use neuroscience to interrogate psychoanalytic assumptions. Although approaches vary, in general, these accounts tend to elide the multiple social and psychological processes that configure neural mechanisms to give rise complex behavior or phenomenology.

8. Kirmayer, 1988a.
9. Lieblich, McAdams, & Josselson 2004.
10. Neimeyer & Mahoney, 1995.
11. Linde, 1993. See also: Bruner, 1990, 2003; Freeman, 2015; Kerby, 1991; McAdams, 1991. "Identity is a life story—an internalized narrative integration of past, present, and anticipated future which provides lives with a sense of unity of purpose" (McAdams, 1989, p. 161). Explicit, self-conscious links occur between different stages of a person's life—indeed, such links define the stages—and their absence may signal developmental problems to a clinical ear tuned to conventional life narratives.
12. McAdams, 2006.
13. Bartlett, 1932; Neisser, 1994; Young, 1995.
14. Chandler & Lalonde, 1995.
15. Habermas & Köber, 2014, 2015.
16. Ricoeur, 1977.
17. Lakoff, 1993; Fauconnier & Turner, 1998.
18. Turner, 1996.
19. Bal (2017) describes some of the many technical strategies and devices used in novels and other kinds of literary texts to control the reader's attention, point of view, and degree of immersion to achieve aesthetic effects including the sense of mimesis (mirroring reality), temporality (location in past, present or future, duration and trajectory), familiarity and empathetic identification, distancing, strangeness, alterity, and reflexivity.
20. Perelman, 1982; Phelan, 2017.
21. For compelling examples of such poetics, see: Capps & Ochs, 1995; Stromberg, 2023.
22. The patient gave informed consent for the use of this tape for teaching and research purposes. The transcription follows Mishler's (1984) conventions. Although essentially a verbatim transcript, details have been changed to protect patient anonymity. Her knowledge that it would be viewed by others undoubtedly colored the interview and made her more guarded. Some of her equivocation and reluctance to discuss personal matters may

well reflect this special circumstance. A transcript gives only a very partial sense of what is communicated in the actual interview. There are many idiosyncrasies in the patient's use of language. She speaks in a hushed and solemn voice; she tries to use an elevated vocabulary but at times makes malapropisms; she frequently answers simple yes or no questions with "more or less . . . more or less." Many of these odd locutions also can be understood in the light of information that comes out later in the interview. She is the daughter of immigrants from Italy, the first in her family to attend college. Her father worked as a janitor, while her mother cleans houses of middle-class people. Her speech style expresses her preoccupation with social status and a conscious effort to elevate herself through more cultivated diction. Her qualified agreement "more or less" may reflect this effort at refined speech (or simply direct a translation from the Italian idiom *più o meno*), but it also allows her to give only partial assent to statements she does not accept, without open confrontation of the interviewers' clinical authority.

23. Low, 1994.
24. Biomedical theory recognizes links between stress and emotion distress, for example, between anxiety and symptoms of gastroesophageal reflux or "heartburn" (Fass et al., 2020). In clinical studies, there may be little or no increase in acid in the esophagus but patients appear sensitive to visceral sensations, and this sensitivity can be increased by acute stress (Bradley et al., 1993; Fass et al., 2008). In English-language idioms, the links between anger and the digestive system can be traced to Galenic humoral medicine:

    "Feelings of anger are said to be affected by and, in turn, affect, the stomach, liver and spleen. Hence, *splenetic* (from *spleen*) came to mean 'extremely angry or annoyed', someone who becomes angry easily came to be referred to as *bilious* (which has the primary meaning of 'feeling as though you are going to vomit food from your stomach'), somebody who is 'in an angry and unpleasant mood' is described as *dyspeptic* (originally, 'affected by indigestion'). *Acrimony* is linked etymologically to 'acid', perhaps stomach acid, and when we are angry we say we are *fed up* (as though we have eaten too much food) or that we *have had a bellyful* or are *sick to the stomach*. At the definition for *gorge* a strong link is made between feeling physically sick and feeling angry: 'if someone's gorge rises, they feel sick or angry'" (Nicholls, 2004).

    Idioms linking anger and gastrointestinal symptoms are found across diverse cultures (Keys et al., 2012; Ogarkova & Soriano, 2014; Ots, 1990; Yu, 1995), likely reflecting both cultural diffusion and an experiential link between bodily symptoms with emotional distress.

25. *Secondary gain* refers to benefits that accrue to the patient as a result of illness and which, therefore, may be motivations for or reinforcers of symptoms and the sick role. In practice, the assessment of secondary gain depends on circumstantial evidence such as the lack of fit of symptoms with physiological models or the patient's style of clinical self-presentation (Kirmayer, 1988a, 1994a).
26. In his reflections on the symbolism of fire, Bachelard (1964) notes that fire can be a source of intense pain and destruction and a vehicle for transformation. When confined and controlled within a hearth, it becomes a source of comfort and sustenance. The imagery of fire runs as a subtext throughout this conversation.
27. Cf. Paris & Guzder, 1989.
28. Lakoff, 1987; Hollan, 1988; Kövecses, 2003.
29. Although anger may be a moral emotion, elicited in situations that are experienced as unfair, injust, or devaluing, locating anger inside the individual (rather in interpersonal or intersubjective space) makes it a problem for the person to manage. Being "beside oneself with rage" is an English language idiom that describes the experience of doubling and displacing the self in response to strong negative emotion (a similar expression is used for other strong emotions including fear and joy). Hofstra (2022) describes this externalization of anger by a patient with brain injury and in the R. L. Stevenson story *The Strange Case of Dr Jekyll and Mr Hyde*. The perceived irrationality of anger (or other strong emotion) makes it foreign to the rational, self-controlled, self-contained, or self-possessed person and prompts this metaphoric displacement.
30. This account of the clinician's implicit narrative is based on later informal conversations with him.
31. "Psychological mindedness" was held to be a prerequisite to engage in psychodynamically oriented psychotherapy (Coltart, 1988).
32. Reflecting on this case study (based on the version in Kirmayer, 2000), in the context of a larger discussion of poetry in medicine, Bleakley and Neilson (2022) raise questions about how to listen to and interpret such symptoms in the clinical encounter. They note: "Poetry is not a therapy here, but embodied as the psychological rupture experienced as phantom pain, for metaphors are writ large on and within the body, where a carnal hermeneutics serves to examine and interpret or give meaning to such expressions. And they speak. Psychiatry, of course, is the twin use of the literal pharmacy and the poetry pharmacy, where minds make symptoms out of metaphors and metaphors make meaning out of symptoms" (p. 182).
33. Bourdieu (1998) argues that "[f]or a symbolic exchange to function two parties must have identical categories of perception and appreciation"

(p. 100). But symbolic action between participants who come from different social positions or cultural backgrounds may involve complementary categories that can be made to fit together in some way such that each ratifies, reinforces, or extends the other. Moreover, symbolic interaction can also occur with a sense of conflict, contestation, or dancing at the precipice. In fact, even in exchanges that operate with a shared set of categories, goals, and horizons, there is always some measure of talking past each other. When this becomes the predominant affect, interaction breaks down with feelings of misunderstanding, rejection, or abandonment.

34. Eco, 1994, pp. 33–34.
35. Todorov, 1981, pp. 43ff. Todorov's use of "mythological" and "ideological" here is meant to draw attention to particular types of narrative construction. This is a narrower use than is common in philosophical and social science literature where "myth" and "ideology" name forms of knowledge that are characterized by particular epistemic stances, social norms, and structures of power rather than narrative genres.
36. Stromberg (1990) illustrates how a religious conversion experiences can lead to beneficial transformations in identity, providing an ideological language to create meaning for life problems or afflictions.
37. Fricker, 2007. A growing literature examines the failures of clinical communication in terms of epistemic injustice, which may include the discounting of patient subjectivity, knowledge, self-understanding, and authority, as well as lack of awareness of the larger social contexts of suffering. See: Carel & Kidd, 2014; Crichton, Carel, & Kidd, 2017; Fricker, 2017; Peet, 2017; Pohlhaus, 2012.
38. Spence, 1982.
39. Critical theory and reflection can allow us to see beyond the common sense of everyday practice, as well as dominant myths and ideologies, to consider the structures of inequality and oppression (Crehan, 2016).

## Chapter 4: Animal Powers

1. Weinberg, 1992, p. 63.
2. Wittgenstein, 1979, p. 6.
3. Bloch, 1989. One reason for Weinberg's intuition lies in the ways in which metaphoric entailment differs for events and substances (Kövecses, 2010, p. 103). The king's touch is a transient event with no transfer of substances (though our bodies may exchange substances including microflora and pheromones that have biological consequences), while chicken soup is a nutritious substance taken into the body. Making the argument for the efficacy of the king's touch then requires revealing invisible mechanisms of

mediation between symbolic events and physiological outcomes. As we shall see, the intuition or conviction that power can be conferred through touch has deeper roots and is reflected in images of the divine physician Asklepios healing by touch of a gilded finger (see Chapter 9).

4. Research in psychoneuroimmunology demonstrates the effects of learning and experience on immune function and related health outcomes (Ader, Cohen, & Felten, 1995; Hadamitzky et al., 2020; Kiecolt-Glaser & Glaser, 1995; Madison et al., 2024).
5. See, for example: Cascio et al., 2019; Feldman et al., 2010.
6. There is a large and growing literature on the cognitive, emotional and physiological effects of touch and its mediation. See, for example: Saarinen et al., 2021; Saunders et al., 2018; von Mohr et al., 2017.
7. Weiskrantz et al., 1971.
8. The sense of agency (i.e., that I am the one initiating the action) alters the sensory experience. In effect, the prediction that I am about to touch myself cancels out the signal that something ticklish is happening (Blakemore et al., 2000). Various psychiatric disorders (e.g., schizophrenia), personality traits (schizotypal), and experimental manipulations (lengthening the time and displacing the location between action and sensation) can influence this process of sensorimotor cancellation, so that individuals can tickle themselves (Leavens & Bard, 2016; Lemaitre, Luyat, & Lefargue, 2016).
9. For evidence of this dualism, see: Miresco & Kirmayer, 2006; Perricone & Ahn, 2023.
10. I cannot resist pointing to another obvious cultural and political aspect to Weinberg's example. As a mainstay of Jewish home cooking, chicken soup represents the sort of remedy available to the marginalized peasant, who is not likely to have access to the king. It is explicitly within the ironic, hierarchy-disdaining culture of Eastern European Jewry, of which the diaspora still bears traces, that Bubbie's (Yiddish for "grandma's") soup might be viewed as more powerful than the king's touch. Indeed, it is Bubbie's special touch in preparing the soup that makes it so effective. So, beyond the appeal to chemistry, we have a cultural politics of the subaltern.
11. Of course, the effectiveness of healing also has to do with social arrangements, institutions, and roles that precede and go far beyond the moments of the ritual encounter. And the power of language may not always reside in its physiological or psychological meaning, but in its social function as a prescriptive or performative act (Littlewood & Dein, 1995). In this chapter and the next, however, I focus on the ways that metaphoric and narrative structures may directly contribute to the cognitive and social process.

12. Csordas, 2022; Csordas & Lewton, 1998; Laderman & Rosenman, 2016; Sax et al., 2010; Shore, 2023.
13. The etymology of the word "empathy," from the German *Einfühlung*, stems from this experience of aesthetic absorption. See Chapter 8.
14. For a discussion of potential mechanisms of agency and ontology see: Kirmayer, Gómez-Carrillo et al., 2020; for dilemmas of ascribing agency in psychological medicine, see: Kirmayer & Gómez-Carrillo, 2019.
15. Nortje et al., 2016; van der Watt et al., 2018.
16. For example, in a study of healing by Chinese shamans (*dang-ki*) in Singapore, we found that some of the people resorting to this form of syncretic healing tradition did not have strong beliefs or expectations in the treatment; they sought out the healer with some tentative hope or open-minded interest to see if it might work (Lee, Kirmayer, & Groleau, 2010). People sought evidence during and after the healing that something significant had happened, noticing changes in bodily sensations or other signs. In many cases, the healing did not work quite as expected. While some people then gave up on the healer, many preserved their hope and commitment by identifying another change in symptoms or life events that they interpreted as a positive sign of efficacy. In this way, they could preserve and strengthen a belief in the healer's efficacy. The pragmatic, tentative, subjunctivizing ("What if it works?") stance, the active search for evidence of effectiveness, and the shifting criteria for positive outcome seen in this ethnographic study are probably not unique to this cultural context but are features of help-seeking in many contemporary settings and healing systems, including biomedicine.
17. Benedetti, 2020; Harrington, 1997; Moerman, 2002; White et al., 1985.
18. Frank, 1961; Kohrt et al., 2020; Moerman, 2002; van der Watt et al., 2018; Waldram, 2000. For the distinction between potential and effective meaning in healing practices, see: McCreery, 1979.
19. Clark, 2015; Parr, Pezzulo, & Friston, 2022.
20. Sterling, 2012; Schulkin & Sterling, 2019.
21. Metaphors and their narrative elaboration serve both cognitive and interpersonal functions that can be modeled in terms of processes of active inference, in which linguistic processes serve a broad adaptive function of predicting the future or imagining possible situations we can anticipate or avoid through action (Bouizegarene et al., 2024).
22. In the Bayesian computational modeling of active inference, priors are the expected values of a predicted outcome before any new information (Parr et al., 2022); priors can be revised based on information, or higher-order changes in expectation. Cultural contexts and practices can install higher

order priors through explicit communication and implicit learning (Veissière et al., 2019).

23. Resources for developing a neural or computational theory of conceptual metaphor can be found in earlier work on computational modeling of linguistic metaphor (Kintsch, 2000), neurobiological research on language and metaphor (Beaty et al., 2017; Desai, 2022; Feldman, 2008; Lakoff, 2008, 2014), semantic pointer theory (Eliasmith, 2013; Thagard, 2022), as well as recent predictive processing or active inference approaches (Bouizegarene et al., 2020). While the active inference approach provides a generic version of cognitive structure, the neural theory of metaphor invokes specific brain structures and processes that reflect evolutionary, developmental, and cultural history. Hence, the associations generated by metaphor are not arbitrary but reflect: (i) sensory similarities or cross-modal links through synesthesia; (ii) assessments of affective meaning that extend Osgood's E-P-A (Osgood, May, & Miron, 1975) to other culturally grounded, neurally constructed dimensions of affect and emotion (Barrett, 2017); and (iii) topographic connections associated with the structure of neural representations of action and perception. Cultural scripts and scenarios forge additional links. The key point is that metaphoric associations are not arbitrary but rooted in the structure of the nervous system, learning histories, and modes of engagement with the socially constructed worlds we inhabit.

24. Ongaro & Ward, 2017; Ongaro & Kaptchuk, 2019; but see: Arandia & DiPaolo, 2021, 2022. Of course, the abstract notion of expectation in the Bayesian statistics of predictive processing is not the same as the human experience of expectation, which is the outcome of embodied emotional and social meanings related to a stance toward and anticipation of the future. Statistical expectancy in specific brain systems is presumably a building block of the psychological process of expectation, which takes on its subjective quality and specific meaning in relation to larger systemic processes that include brain, body, and context. Experiences of expectation or anticipation are embedded in a personal history and social context that creates a particular stance toward the immediate and longer-term future that is folded into individuals' expectations. To capture this, a predictive processing model would require deep and wide hierarchical structure and dynamic engagement with a social world with particular cultural affordances and associated action repertoires (Ramstead et al., 2016; Veissière et al., 2019).

25. There are many other anticipatory physiological responses involving visceral and endocrine systems (Power & Schulkin, 2008).

26. The specific mechanism of placebo analgesia depends on the conditioned associations or expectations associated with the medication and differs for different medications. For example, aspirin-related placebo analgesia is mediated by prostaglandins, while the analgesic effect of placebos that are perceived as opiates, like codeine, is mediated by the endogenous opioid systems (endorphins). See: Benedetti, 2020; Benedetti, Frisaldi, & Shaibani, 2022. Moreover, pain experience itself has sensory, affective and cognitive dimensions that may be differentially affect by medications as well as learning, emotion, or other psychological processes (Melzack & Casey, 1968).
27. Biosemiotics, which approaches systems of signs, meaning and interpretation as fundamental biological phenomena, traces its origins to Charles Peirce in philosophy and to Jakob von Uexküll in ethology (Barbieri, 2009). More recently, there has been a renewed engagement with the humanities to understand the distinctive features of human culture (Cobley, 2016; Favareau et al., 2017).
28. This recognition is central to Cassirer's (2021) philosophy of symbolic forms:

> As a "philosophical anthropology," the philosophy of symbolic forms articulates a normative image of the human being as a symbolic animal that does not level down the human into a homogenous mode of being. This conception of the symbolic animal serves as the basis for a symbolic humanism that is not based on liberal subjectivity. To this end, the philosophy of symbolic forms provides an intersubjective ethical project that points the way to an open cosmopolitanism that is not based on a Eurocentric conception of either the human being or culture. (Gordon in Cassirer, 2021, p. xix)

29. Frank, 1961. This seminal work went through several editions (1973, Frank & Frank, 1993), culminating in a version, coauthored with his daughter, that emphasized the important of rhetoric in healing (Frank & Frank, 1993).
30. Frank & Frank, 1993.
31. See: Kaptchuk & Eisenberg, 1998.
32. Lévi-Strauss, 1963: "The effectiveness of symbols" published in *Structural Anthropology*, a collection of his classic papers.
33. Lévi-Strauss, 1963, p. 21–22.
34. Lévi-Strauss's comment in the quoted text that poetic metaphor does not transcend the "unconscious level" seems to imply a lack of awareness on the part of the person deploying the metaphor. This could arise because the metaphoric space is taken as ontologically real (hence, the transformation is not metaphorical), or because the metaphor is implicit, formulaic, or conventional. Because healers generally must subscribe to an ontology that warrants their practice, whatever their notions of the poetics of language, they are not likely to view the realms invoked in ritual as purely "metaphorical." "Metaphor" is an ambivalent metaphor for the ontology of healing transformations.

This was very evident in my conversations with the Indigenous scholar Joseph Couture who, when I described his account of healing as metaphorical, insisted that it was "not a metaphor" (interview with Joseph Couture, May 2000). His collected papers, published posthumously, were titled by his editors "A Metaphoric Mind" (Couture, McGowan, & Couture, 2013).

35. See: Sherzer, 1983; Laderman, 1987.
36. Kapferer & Papigny, 2005.
37. Dow, 1986.
38. Scheff, 1979.
39. Flaten et al., 2011; Geers et al., 2021.
40. Austin, 1975. Bourdieu (1991) critiques Austin's notion of the performative function of words, insisting on the social nature of power that precedes words and gives them their authority. He emphasizes the social force of naming and labeling, or, we might add, of metaphorical interpretation, qualification, redescription, adumbration, and reframing of situations: "The power of words is nothing other than the delegated power of the spokesperson, and his speech—that is, the substance of his discourse and, inseparably, his way of speaking—is no more than a testimony, and one among others, of the guarantee of delegation which is vested in him" (p. 107). He further notes that "efforts to find, in the specifically linguistic logic of different forms of argumentation, rhetoric and style, the source of their symbolic efficacy are destined to fail as long as they do not establish the relationship between the properties of discourses, the properties of the person who pronounces them and the properties of the institution which authorizes him to pronounce them" (p. 110). While identifying essential elements of authority, this sociological view sidesteps the dimensions of embodied authority and conviction that a theory of metaphor can address.
41. While there is robust evidence for topographic mapping in somatosensory and visual cortex, other brain mappings may be more abstract (Bokeria et al., 2021; Whittington et al., 2022). The representational spaces that the brain provides may be unimodal or multimodal, and they reflect what is ecologically and socially important to us. Although for evolutionary-developmental reasons, there is conservation of phylogenetically older structures in the brain, and hierarchical structure in computation, the levels of processing may employ diverse circuits and distributed systems, assembled developmentally, culturally, or even "on-the-fly" in response to particular contexts for specific purposes (Karmiloff-Smith, 2015; Sirois et al., 2008).
42. Here the "CNS" might better stand for what Hebb (1955) called the "conceptual nervous system" for several reasons. First, brain function

depends in myriad ways on the body. Through the peripheral nervous system—including autonomic and spinal sensorimotor systems, the neural networks of the gut, the vascular, endocrine and immune systems, and many other bodily systems—brain and body are interdependent and work together to regulate organism states, not only to maintain internal homeostasis but also to anticipate and respond to external environmental demands. Second, the ongoing engagements of the brain with the world through our sensorimotor activity mean that brain functions extend into and are, to some degree, constituted by the (humanly constructed) social environment. Brain function then cannot be characterized without considering the culturally shaped contexts of neurodevelopment and everyday life (which include the ways we conceptualize the brain itself).

43. MacLean (1949, 1980) built on earlier anatomical and functional studies of the limbic system as the seat of mammalian emotions and his account has been enormously popular in psychology. Indeed, it fits with the recurrent portrait of human conflict as a struggle to master our animal nature found in many religious and moral texts as well as in Freud's *Civilization and Its Discontents* (1930/2010). For a critique based on the misleading evolutionary genealogy of brain architecture in MacLean's account see: Cesario et al., 2020. For a better-grounded evolutionary account, see: Panksepp & Biven, 2012. For the link to gendered views of psychosomatic disorders, see: Wilson, 2004.
44. Simon, 1969. Briefly, complex structures must be built from simpler building blocks over time, both phylogenetically in evolution, and ontogenetically in development. Moreover, there are organizational efficiencies possible with hierarchical structure that cannot be achieved with a flat network. This hierarchical view does not mean that basic building blocks are more fundamental except in the sense that for evolutionary, developmental and organizational purposes, they must be laid down first and hence constrain later elaborations of brain architecture. However, brain plasticity, rewiring, long-distance connections, and efferent loops can reorganize this basic architecture in ways that alter or upend any simple hierarchical structure. For a discussion of the various meanings and uses of hierarchy in biology, see: Gómez-Carrillo & Kirmayer, 2023.
45. Jones, 2020.
46. Any such correspondences between neurology and experience are rough because the vocabulary of experience cuts across the natural levels of organization suggested by anatomy (Riss, 1968).
47. Panksepp, 2004. Contemporary neuroscience has moved beyond the account of a distinctive "emotional" or mammalian brain, located in the limbic system to recognize multiple systems with specific functions that involve vertical integration across multiple anatomical structures (Rolls,

2015; Janacek et al., 2022; Kamali et al., 2023). Emotions, then, are not located in one region but assembled, over the course of development, from functional brain systems, embodied modes of responding, and culturally meaningful social situations, scenarios, or predicaments (Barrett, 2013, 2017). Words for emotion name not simply basic bodily or brain states but social scripts which include prescribed modes of action and response. These scripts implicate others as well as the self and hence cannot be described without given a broader account of cultural context (Gendron & Barrett, 2018; Mesquita, 2022).

48. Bowlby, 1988; Holmes, 2020; Jones, 1983.
49. Osgood, 1964; Osgood, May, & Miron, 1975.
50. Fernandez, 1986, pp. 40ff.
51. This is one way of understanding Jacques Lacan's (2001) famous dictum that the unconscious is structured like a language, which may include the oneiric logic of image, metaphor, and blended stories. Of course, this a way of defining the unconscious makes it a subset of the much larger domain of the "nonconscious" that may include many other nonlinguistic kinds of structures that do not follow a recognizable grammar.
52. This also points to what is wrong with purely cognitive accounts of emotion that aim to reduce ineffable feelings entirely to explicit networks of verbal meanings or propositions. There is something residual that arises from the embodied and experientially grounded nature of affect.
53. Hinde, 1989; Prosser, 1970. See also: Kirmayer, Worthman, & Kitayama, 2020.
54. The notion of families as dynamical systems (Cox & Paley, 1997) goes beyond the rule metaphor though it can include linguistic or symbolic processes that are governed by explicit rules. In some respect the use of the term "rules" is unfortunate, since no single participant may, in fact, have a representation of "the" rules. The rules of interaction, abstracted by the observer, emerge from each person's response to others who are themselves responding to earlier transactions. The patterns that emerge can be described by rules after the fact although what each participant had access to was only some idiosyncratic and context-dependent feelings or notions about the others. Hence, the metaphor of rules, like that of games, employed by family therapists, attributes a misleading agency to individuals who are themselves embedded in a systemic process larger than themselves. To put it another way, the repetitive interactional patterns of families are games only in the Kafkaesque sense in which each member is the pawn of some extrahuman extrarational order (and so, seemingly, irrational).
55. Turner, 1974.

56. The notion that causality and constraint work in both directions across the hierarchy in biological systems is a key aspect of the principle of biological relativity advanced by the physiologist Denis Noble (2012, 2016).
57. Finke, 1989.
58. Adopting an attitude of "just watching" experience is a key instruction in *vipassana* or insight meditation that can result in changes in pain experience (Goldstein, 2017). See Chapter 7. Hinton and Kirmayer (2017) present examples of metaphoric alterations of attention in ritual and healing practices.
59. Gaines & Farmer, 1986. See also: Kidron, Kotliar, & Kirmayer, 2019.
60. Campbell, 1984. The classical account of shamanism among the Siberian Tungu is Shirokogoroff (1935). Vitebsky (2001) provides a concise overview. Evidence for the early emergence of shamanistic practices can be found in paleolithic cave art (e.g., Chauvet et al., 2016). Eliade (1964) used the term shamanism to cover a much broader range of traditions, including many forms of religious practice that involve spirit travel to another realm. Other scholars of religion have used the term shamanism to describe practices that use trance to access other levels or realms of experience, including making contact with the divine (e.g., Garb, 2011).
61. Harner, 1980, 2012. See, for example: Balzer, 1996; Itzhak, 2015; Wallis, 2003; Ripinsky-Naxon, 1993. Mayer (2008) discusses the appeal of shamanism as a "modern myth"; Kowalewski (2019), von Stuckrad (2023), and others link it to efforts to address the epistemic injustices of colonialism that suppressed Indigenous Peoples' traditions and, most recently, to the need for an ethos that could avert the impending climate catastrophe whether by adopting an ecologically informed epistemology, recognizing the sentience and rights of nonhuman beings, or resacralizing nature.
62. Leder, 2012.
63. Brave Buffalo, Teton Sioux, quoted in: Densmore, 1981, p. 172.
64. Personal communication, March 1982. See: Guedon, 1984.
65. Barbeau, 1958, p. 79.
66. Sahlins (2022) documents the historical and cross-cultural ubiquity of this mode of perception and corresponding animistic ontology in which other than human beings (plants, animals, spirits) have agency, subjectivity, and varying kinds of identity and presence as nonhuman persons.
67. Tambiah, 1968.
68. Baron-Cohen & Harrison, 1997; Maurer et al., 2020; Ramachandran et al., 2020; Ward & Simner, 2020. Hsu (2021) explores some ways that an embodied understanding of color synaesthesia (e.g., the association of green with specific sounds and smells) may account for the metaphoric

logic (and presumed efficacy) of particular treatments in completely unrelated medical systems.

69. Gibbs, 2023. The McGill Pain Questionnaire (Melzack, 2005) provides a large vocabulary of English pain descriptors—including *drilling, gnawing, wrenching, scalding, splitting, freezing, torturing, lancinating, rasping*—many of which are metaphors based on sensations associated with particular actions or events.
70. Munday et al., 2022; Stilwell & Stilwell, 2024.
71. Löfvander & Furhoff, 1996.
72. Bueño-Gomez, 2017.
73. Briggs, 1971; Rosaldo, 1980. What makes these moral emotions is precisely their importance in recognizing and responding to social norms and values.
74. In this sense, expectation is not so much a specific emotion as a label for the temporal frame of all future-oriented emotions or cognitive evaluations. We may have positive or negative expectations, fearful apprehension or pleasurable anticipation—all of which function as different types of expectancy that may have corresponding "placebo" effects. Expectation may be best described, following Wilce and Price (2003), as a meta-level phenomenon in the hierarchy of semiotic levels they describe as relevant to emotion.
75. Alverson, 1994.
76. Ibarrretxe-Antuñano, 1999.
77. Kövecses, 2003.
78. Marks, 1996
79. Grady, 1999, p. 24
80. Matsuki, 1995; Kövecses, 2003; Wilkowski et al., 2009; Yu, 1995.
81. IJzerman et al., 2012.
82. Barrett, 2017.
83. Seligman, 2023.
84. Seligman, 2023, p. 821.
85. Kirmayer & Carroll, 1987; Kirmayer, 2008a.
86. Barrett, 2017.
87. Scheff, 1979.
88. Scheff, 1979, p. 66.
89. Schieffelin, 1979.
90. Schieffelin, 1976, p. 71.
91. Schieffelin, 1976, p. 44.
92. See also Feld (2012), who describes the profound connections between sound and memory, absence and presence in Kaluli experience.
93. Schieffelin, 1976, p. 96.
94. Lévi-Strauss, 1963, p. 180–181.

95. Jackson, 1994.
96. Joseph Breuer & Sigmund Freud, *Studien über Hysterie* (1895). See: Sulloway, 1979, p. 56; For a discussion of the many distortions and misrepresentations in Breuer and Freud's case study, see: Ellenberger, 1972; Borch-Jacobsen, 2014.
97. Sulloway, 1979, p. 57.
98. Scheff, 1979.
99. Hinton & Kirmayer, 2017, p. 11. For further discussion of Cambodian metaphors for attentional processes, see: Hinton et al., 2016.
100. For a discussion of regimes of attention, see: Ramstead et al., 2016.
101. Sandner & Wong, 2013. In Norse mythology, Yggdrasil, the world tree or axis mundi, sending its roots deep into the ground and its branches to the stars, unites the nine worlds. This element of Norse mythology may have been drawn from Sami cosmology and hence be linked to an older shamanistic tradition (Von Schnurbein, 2003). For an account of an early nineteenth-century Sami shaman's practice involving a sacred tree, see: Bergman & Östlund, 2022. The tree is also a central image in other traditions, including medieval Kabbalistic texts where it is used in cosmographic maps intended as objects of meditation and illumination (Chajes, 2022). In his remarkable novel *The Overstory*, Richard Powers (2018) explores the archetypal symbolism and social imaginary of the tree as sentient being and moral imperative.
102. Lakoff & Johnson, 1980. Desjarlais (1992) describes the vitality embodied in the stance of a Yolmo young man in Nepal.
103. Barasch, 1976.
104. Darwin, 1965 (orig. 1872); Hess & Thibault, 2009; for a critique see: Barrett, 2013.
105. LaCapra, 2018. This emotional kinship not only makes animals "good to think with," providing natural metaphors for our own experience but, more fundamentally, demands that we recognize their agency, subjectivity, and suffering as part of any moral system.
106. Johnson, 1993, p. 51.
107. Gibbs, 2017; Thagard, 2022.
108. Thurman, 1995, p. 40.
109. Kaplan, 1993. For visual representations, see: Chajes, 2022.
110. Scholem, 1961.

## Chapter 5: Healing Fictions: Narrative Transformations of the Self

1. Bachelard, 1964, p. 55.
2. Benjamin, 2002, p. 33 (orig. 1935).

3. Shamdasani (2017) traces the origins of the term *psychotherapy* and its role in bringing together diverse historical practices under one rubric.
4. See, for example: Bruner, 2003; Kerby, 1991; Ricoeur, 1991; Sarbin, 1986; Schechtman, 2007. The notion of a narrative self has been critiqued by Strawson (2004), who argues for a nonnarrative basis of the self and offers his own experience as evidence. Gallagher (2000) and Zahavi (2017) have argued on phenomenological grounds for a prelinguistic, embodied minimal self that constitutes subjectivity and that is elaborated and extended later through language and social interaction. However, even the minimal self of an infant emerges through social interactions (Kyselo, 2016; Stern, 2018). Taken together, these arguments suggest multiple facets, components, or kinds of self that exist in dynamic relation to each other, woven together by embodied cognitive processes, developmental experiences, cultural models, and ongoing interactions with others. Versions of this ecumenical approach can be found in Neisser (1994) and in Gallagher's (2023b) "pattern theory" of the self.
5. Phelan, 2017.
6. The idea of cultural master narratives has been developed by McLean and colleagues (McLean & Syed, 2015; McLean et al., 2018), who understand these dominant stories as templates that can be used to organize personal identity narratives in ways that conform, transform, or rebel against normative structures. The tensions and creative possibilities between personal and master narratives—and the creative possibilities and challenge of fashioning an alternative or counter narrative—are grist for the mill of psychotherapeutic conversation.
7. Csordas, 1983, 1997.
8. This use of "myth" is common in many accounts (Midgley, 2011), but acknowledges that some myths may have an extramundane authority and an experiential numinosity that renders them especially powerful, convincing, and—when delivered as part of a ceremony, ritual, or rite de passage—potentially transformative of identity (Coupe, 2009). The question of whether the Enlightenment, modernity, science, and secularism have undermined and displaced the power of myth or simply transformed it, has been the focus of intense philosophical debate (e.g., Blumenberg, 1985; Cassirer, 1946; Schrempp & Hansen, 2002; Sebeok, 1965).
9. Midgley, 2011.
10. The critique of the concept of archetypes stems in part from concerns about its use to promote stereotypes or view phenomena as natural and inevitable, whereas, in fact, they are historically contingent and culturally variable. Some of the discomfort with the term stems from essentialized notions of identity and "the collective unconscious" (cf. Abramovitch & Kirmayer, 2003; Goodwyn, 2010). Jung sometimes wrote of this in ways that reproduced

antisemitic and other racist tropes. More recent work aims to show how archetypal structures might emerge out of interactions of evolutionarily shaped neurobiological substrates in interaction with cultural–historical contexts (Hunt, 2012; Roesler, 2012; Vaughn Becker & Neuberg, 2019; Oatley, 2019). Although it is easy to see patterns in sensory systems that are elaborated into actual percepts, there may also be proto-narrative structures in affective or other systems that are then elaborated in particular kinds of stories (Green, Fitzgerald, & Moore, 2019). However, any actual image or story will involve culturally and historically contingent social settings, scenarios, and scripts, through the which the rudimentary narrative structure is elaborated. My use of archetype then differs substantially from Jung's in two respects: (i) explicitly recognizing the existential, social and cultural-historical origins of many "givens" in experience; and (ii) not viewing the archetypes as inherently (necessarily) numinous. Contemporary cognitive science views the experiential given as emergent through interactions of body and the culturally shaped environmental affordances (Ramstead et al., 2016; Wilkinson & Chemero, 2024). The experience of awe or numinosity, in my view, stems from the coordination of archetype and myth through emotionally resonant metaphor. This gives rise to the powerful feeling that "It all fits together," charged with specific affective valence. It remains that calling something "archetypal" may be a rhetorical move that serves mainly to say it is emotionally powerful or "primal" in some aesthetic sense, and blocks further thinking about context, process, and contingency.

Despite its rejection by anthropologists and psychologists, the notion of archetypes has been used by many phenomenologists and literary critics, notably the philosopher Gaston Bachelard (McAllester Jones, 1991):

> Bachelard explains his refusal to account for images in terms of organic impulses by his lack of medical knowledge, alleging that this prevents him from going to the same depths as psychoanalysis. The real reason is that he wants to seize the specific originality of the symbol without reducing it to its causes. That is why he favors the Jungian concept of "archetype," which offers the advantage of including symbolism in the unconscious. Strictly speaking, an archetype is not an image. For Jung, it is psychic energy spontaneously condensing the results of organic and ancestral experiences into images; it can be designated as the paradigm of a series of images. When Bachelard uses any such psychoanalytical concept, he limits his investigation to the present life of images; he disregards the historical and anthropological background of archetypes and attempts instead an "archaeology of the human soul" (Bachelard, 1987, p. xxxviii).

However, Bachelard's (1964, 1969, 1971, 1983) own reveries on the elements of fire, water, air, and space move back and forth between associations with a fair claim to universality and those that are profoundly idiosyncratic, tied to his personal history and culture. This points to a further critique of the notion of archetype: in any given instance, it may be impossible to sort out the universal and the particular, the individual and the collective. As a result, appeals to the archetypal may serve to obscure the cultural and historical origins of myths and symbols, sidestep the biographical basis of personal material, and evade responsibility for one's ideological choices and commitments.

11. Obeyesekere, 1981.
12. Oster, 1970. This phenomenon was recognized in antiquity and was taken as evidence that the eyes produce light (Grüsser & Hanger, 1990). Current understanding related this to transduction of pressure-induced sheer by the retina, with interference patterns occurring at higher levels of neural processing. Such *entoptic* phenomena can occur with migraine, hypnagogic stage of sleep, and other common circumstances and have been proposed as an origin for some of the geometric figures found in Upper Paleolithic rock art (Lewis-Williams, 2004).
13. Gallagher, 2006; Gibbs, 2005; Goodwyn, 2024; Johnson, 1987.
14. Armstrong, 2020.
15. Critchley, 2019. Tragedy goes far beyond the simple facts of grief and loss, to include a mythic narrative or cosmological frame that confronts us with our mortality and limitations.
16. This view of archetype is, in fact, quite close to one of Jung's usages. In Jungian psychotherapy, work with archetypes may involve both exploring personal associations and "amplification" by invoking cultural meanings and elaborations. For Jung, the fact of the widespread recurrence of certain images (the Great Mother, the Hero, the Wise Old Man) provides evidence for archetypal patterns. The images themselves do not, however, constitute the archetype; they only point toward the archetypal process that, being a contentless pattern or propensity, is itself ineffable. The notion of archetype applies to the psyche as a whole, which is organized in terms of the interplay of phenomenologically recognizable agencies, that can be characterized as *persona* (mask or social role), *shadow* (disavowed aspects of the self), *anima* (soul, or, for men, feminine aspects of the psyche), and the overarching integrative structure of *Self* (with a capital S), which includes all of these facets, and, hence, is distinct from the ego or everyday self with whom one is identified. See Samuels (1985) for a lucid discussion of notions of archetype in Jungian psychology.
17. Goldie, 2012. Referring to our inner complexity and contradiction as a "mess" betrays a certain discomfort with matter and thought out of place: irrationality disturbs the comfortable order of rationality—an aesthetic preference for disembodied intellect that is also gendered (Lloyd, 2002).
18. Calasso, 1993, p. 281. Here is how Calasso (1993, p. 242) describes the expression of this recognition of opposites in Greek mythology:

> So what did these Greek gods want of men? What they certainly did not require was that we behave one way rather than another. They were as ready to defend the

> unique actions of a favorite as to condemn the just actions of someone they disliked. So what did they want? To be recognized. Every recognition is an awareness of form. Hence in our enfeebled modern vocabulary we might say that the way they imposed themselves was first and foremost aesthetic. But in a sense of the word which, with time, has been lost: the aesthetic of a mesh of powers concentrated in a figure, a body, a voice.

Calasso goes on to argue that we can see this function of myth influencing the novels that have largely replace myth in our time.

> But let's imagine that all the variants of a certain myth have been lost, erased by some invisible hand. Would the myth still be the same? Here one arrives at the hairline distinction between myth and every other kind of narrative. Even without its variants, the myth includes its opposite. How do we know? The knowledge intrinsic in the novel tells us so. The novel, a narrative deprived of variants, attempts to recover them by making the single text to which it is entrusted more dense, more detailed. Thus the action of the novel tends, as though toward its paradise, to the inclusion of its opposite, something the myth possesses as of right. (p. 281)

19. To some extent this is true of all story-like narratives, but when they are presented orally for the first time, we must wait to find out how things end, experiencing a prolonged period of anticipation and confusion. When stories are written, we can skip ahead to discover how things turn out and reread to discover the foreshadowing and cross-references that were hidden in the text. When stories become familiar through repetition (or because they reference well known templates), they acquire the temporality of myth. This can be used for dramatic effect as, for example, in Rita Dove's (2017) play *The Darker Face of the Earth*, which frames a story of the violence of plantation enslavement as myth, drawing elements of its staging from Greek theater.
20. Lévi-Strauss, 1969, p. 16.
21. I am indebted to Dr. Jacqueline Carroll for the first three case examples. Details have been changed to protect client confidentiality.
22. McMullen (1989). McMullen counted instances of metaphors other than completely conventional idioms (i.e., she ignored common everyday figures of speech with no special significance to the case; figures unrelated to the therapy theme; figures that were frequently used by clients and therapists in general unless they were specifically related to the specific therapy theme). Ignoring so much dialogue may mitigate her conclusions.
23. Antecedent client characteristics that might determine both effective use of metaphor and good therapeutic outcome include (McMullen, 1989: pp. 221ff): (1) more cohesive self-image reflected in more consistent use of figurative language; (2) better self-understanding reflected in more well-formed figures; (3) better ability to express self and emotion in words (hence more apt use of metaphor); (4) willingness to reveal and express emotions through metaphors that present the self in a more intimate light;

and (5) ability to work through problems by staying within a productive metaphor.

24. For a review, see: McMullen & Tay, 2023.
25. These vignettes come from my own and colleagues' psychotherapy practices. Identifying details have been changed or omitted to protect confidentiality.
26. For a discussion of the metaphor of resistance and alternate approaches that emphasize metaphors of joining with the patient's perspective, see: Kirmayer, 1990.
27. Sherman & Clore, 2009. The color symbolism of white, black, and red appears in many fairytales and conveys gender norms as well as messages about purity and danger (Da Silva, 2007; Douglas, 1973; von Franz, 1972). The doctor's white coat trades on this association with purity, cleanliness, and the laboratory setting of science (Blumhagen, 1979). For the symbolism of "white" and its appropriation by racial ideologies, see Jablonski, 2004; For evidence for cross-cultural commonalities, see: Tham et al., 2020.
28. Graves, 1960.
29. Norman, 1990.
30. Jung, 1969. In many religious and spiritual traditions, including Neoplatonism and Kabbalah (Chajes, 2022), concentric circles represent images of wholeness and cosmic order, linking center and periphery through intermediate layers or levels. Hsu (1971) uses concentric circles to map cultural differences in boundaries of self and other.
31. Bachelard, 1969, p. 234.
32. It is worth noting that while coldness, hardness, and lack of feeling may be natural metaphorical associations to the image of a stone, it is also possible for imagination to take such grounded experiences in new directions. The poet Charles Simic, for example, reimagines a stone in startling ways in several of his poems (Simic, 2013, p. 15). Like the prose poems of Francis Ponge (2008) and Bachelard's reveries, the process of imagining with objects discovers endless possibilities in what is familiar and seemingly mundane.
33. On the Philosopher's Stone in alchemy, see: Eamon, 2000; Knapp, 2000; on the cultural history and archetypal logic of alchemy, see: Eliade, 1978; Pagel, 1948; von Franz, 1979. "The 'medicine of metals' is a common name of the Philosopher's stone. It evidently derives its meaning form the alleged power of the stone to transmute sick (e.g., base) metals into precious ones" (Scholem, 2006, p. 69). For Jung, as a symbol of wholeness, the Philosopher's Stone represents the outcome of the union of opposites (Jung, 2014).
34. Lévi-Strauss (1978, p. 45) suggests that novels appeared as a literary form in Western history just as mythical thought was passing into the background. Novels supply narratives that take the place of myth but, by the very fact of their explicit human authorship, they imply the

possibility of self-authorship—which, in the absence of canonical myth, becomes necessity. However, this is a task most of us are ill-equipped for; hence, the enthusiasm for "pop" psychology and psychotherapy as forms of ghost-writing one's autobiography as mythic journey within a specific genre.

35. Han, 2024.
36. Based on the play by Terry Johnson originally performed at the Royal Court Theatre in London in 1982. See: Izod, 1992.
37. This stepping back from the numinous qualities that each mythic figure points toward, to consider their mundane incarnation, reminds us that the imaginative functions and consequences of archetypes and stereotypes are quite different. An archetype is a many-sided, powerfully evocative, and generative image not reducible to the static configuration of a few attributes that constitutes a stereotype. The stereotype is a flattening or hollowing out of an archetype, that turns the imaginative energy and generativity of archetypes and qualities they invoke (wisdom, beauty, skill, compassion) into two-dimensional cardboard cutouts. The contrast of archetype and stereotype confronts us with the difficulty of realizing our ideals and aspirations.
38. In secular society, famous people are our surrogate gods and the projections we impose on them can lead to *inflation* (the term that Jungians use for the process of identifying with an archetype) with disastrous consequences for those who achieve fame. Famous people embody our aspirations but "fame is a religion in which the famous are guiltily burdened with being a replacement for rather than an avenue to God" (Richard Combs, Review of *Insignificance, Monthly Film Bulletin 52,* August 1985, p. 236, quoted in Izod, 1992). Izod (1992) provides a Jungian exegesis and appreciation of the film. He quotes from an interview with Roeg: "There's a marvellously enigmatic phrase of Einstein's, which I read somewhere. He was looking up at the night sky, looking into the blackness, and he suddenly said, 'Something is moving'. We must have a sense of something greater than ourselves, we must have a sense of wonder and awe about ourselves .... That's what I like about the title of the piece: the idea that the world, society, has very little sense of a mystical movement of things. What it means is not that 'it's all insignificant', but that nothing has more significance than anything else" (Nicolas Roeg interviewed by Combs, "Relatively Speaking," p. 238, quoted in Izod, 1992, pp. 155–156).
39. Directed by Phil Alden Robinson, based on the novel *Shoeless Joe* by the Canadian writer W. P. Kinsella (1982).
40. Turner (1969, 1974) discusses this function of liminality in ritual as a path to feelings of collective belonging, togetherness, or *communitas*.
41. Kolakowski, 1989, p. 45.
42. Kolakowski, 1989, p. 7.

43. As Bourdieu (1990) puts it:

> To grasp the mythopoeic act as the constituting moment, through myth understood as the constituted reality, does not mean, as idealists suppose, looking in consciousness for the universal categories of what Cassirer calls a "mythopoeic subjectivity" or, in Levi-Straus's terms, the "fundamental structures of the human mind," which are supposed to govern all the empirical configurations realized regardless of social conditions. Rather, it means reconstructing the socially constituted system of inseparably cognitive and evaluative structures that organizes perception of the world and action in the world in accordance with the objective structures of a given state of the social world (p. 95).

44. See Oakley et al., 2021.
45. Han (2020) describes the displacement of ritual enactment by individual consumption and play.
46. Robert Coover's novel *The Universal Baseball Association* (1971) invites the reader into the world of Henry Waugh, a man devoting his life to running an imaginary baseball league in his head—constructing his own mythic world with its own metaphysical reality—which offers him an escape from his mundane existence as an accountant. In his creation and dominion over this imaginary world, he is a (minor) god at play (Berman, 1978).
47. Winnicott, 1971. "Transitional objects and transitional phenomena belong to the realm of illusion which is at the basis of initiation of experience . . . this intermediate area of experience, unchallenged in respect of its belonging to internal or external (shared) reality, constitutes the greater part of the infants' experience, and throughout life is retained in the intense experiencing that belongs to the arts and to religion and to imaginative living, and to creative scientific work" (Winnicott, 2018, p. 242).
    For a discussion of the importance of play, see: Nachmanovitch, 1991.
48. Turner, 1969, 1974, 1982. The emotional impact of the film reveals the relationship between myth and bodily-felt meaning. For example, the precise moment that I began to cry when first watching this film was when one of the players, a doctor, was about to cross the line from the world of the baseball diamond to that of the spectators in the bleachers to rescue his granddaughter who was choking. I knew intuitively (felt in my body) that crossing the line from the field to the bleachers would mean that he would sacrifice his (heroic) identity and immortality as a player in the mythic world of baseball for the mundane temporality and mortality of his role as a healer; in so doing, he conformed to the larger myth of the wounded-healer (see Chapter 9). This personally evocative moment reflected my own associations, the larger meaning of the mythic scenario, and the bodily felt significance of liminality and loss.
49. Kolakowski, 1989, p. 105.
50. Hillman, 1979.

51. In the film, the baseball diamond becomes a *temenos*, a sacred place of healing (Aden, 1994). And this is not just a conceit of the movie: the field in rural Iowa where the film was shot became a tourist attraction and, for some, a place of pilgrimage (Mandell, 2002). The actor who played the protagonist's father, who is brought back to life as ballplayer to fulfill his unrequited dream, described how he was often approached by people who had seen the film and were overcome with emotion, recalling their own father–son stories, dreams, and dilemmas (Brown, 2014).
52. Kolakowski, 1989, p. 115.
53. Kolakowski, 1989, p. 120.
54. Atwood, 2011; Ball, 2022; Disch, 2000.
55. White & Epston, 1990; Lewis, 2011; Kirmayer et al., 2023.
56. White & Epston, 1990; see also Combs & Freedman, 2012.
57. Dein, 2005.
58. Witztum & Goodman, 1999a, b. For Erickson, see: Rossi, 1980 and Kirmayer, 1988b. For strategic and narrative therapies: Rabkin, 1977; White & Epston, 1990.
59. Neimeyer & Mahoney, 1995.
60. Obeyesekere, 1991; Witztum & Goodman, 1999a, p. 423.
61. Witztum & Goodman, 2004, p. 139.
62. Littlewood & Dein, 1995.
63. The stories and teachings also have obvious moral and psychological meaning and so may provide a way to think about human conflicts and desires that can serve both social regulation and mystical teaching (Garb, 2016).
64. Nichter, 1981. Witztum and Goodman view cultural idioms as less institutionalized and developed than culture-bound syndromes, but there are more fundamental differences between idioms and syndromes in that idioms are essentially aspects of the pragmatics of communication (Lewis-Fernández & Kirmayer, 2019; Nichter, 2010, 2022).
65. Guttman, 2014; Watzlawick, Beavin, & Jackson, 1967.
66. Witztum & Goodman, 1999a, p. 419.
67. Todorov, 1981.
68. Witztum & Goodman, 1999a, p. 419.
69. Turner, 1996; Fauconnier & Turner, 1998, 2008.
70. Witztum & Goodman, 1991a, p. 411–412.
71. Witztum & Goodman, 1991a, p. 412.
72. Harrison, 2008. Of course, gardens are constructed by human activity. Hence, "natural" does not mean ready-made or pregiven but rather apposite and ready-to-hand.
73. Witztum & Goodman, 1999a, p. 428.
74. Hannah, 1981; Watkins, 1986. See Chapter 9.

75. Witztum & Goodman, 1999a, p. 426.
76. Dow, 1986.
77. Arora & Ananthanarayanan, 2022.
78. For discussions of the impacts of this neoliberal view of the person on the management of emotions, psychotherapy, and self-help practices, see: Ahmed, 2013; Cushman, 2018; Ilouz, 2008; Foster, 2016; Rimke, 2020; Rodriguez-López, 2023.
79. See for example Silverman, 2020. When tailored to American culture, myths become individualized and the quest is for something that allows one to realize one's personal goals (Feinstein & Krippner, 1997).
80. Timpanelli, 1993, p. 94.
81. Exploring these boundaries is one function of the arts in contemporary society (Hyde, 1998).
82. Calvino, 1977.
83. Calvino was a member of Oulipo, the *Ouvroir de littérature potentielle*, a group of writers (including Georges Perec and Raymond Queneau) and mathematicians who explored the use of combinatorics, symmetries, and formal constraints in generating literature (see: Becker, 2012).
84. It is instructive to compare Calvino's imaginative engagement with the tarot cards with the arrangement of materials in the Warburg Library of Cultural History (Johnson, 2012). In the 1920s, pursing his interest in a "science of culture," the historian Aby Warburg assembled an archive of some 350,000 books organized by subject according to his division of human history into the categories of Action, Orientation, Word, and Image. Rather than being a memory palace that simply provided a scheme to efficiently store and retrieve information (Yates, 2013), the library was intended to be a tool for thought, with the arrangement of materials designed to reveal meaningful connections across a vast cultural–historical arc, tracing "the afterlife of antiquity." The library influenced the work of Cassirer (2021, original 1923–1929) on symbolic forms and later Blumenberg (1985) on myth and metaphor (Wimmer, 2017). "It would not be misleading to describe *The Philosophy of Symbolic Forms* as an attempt to provide the Warburg Library with a transcendental foundation" (Peter Gordon, quoted in Cassirer, 2021, p. ix)

    > Warburg, as director of the library, had initially used the rubric "Orientation" to reflect the fact that the world is for us far from self-explanatory. We come into the world largely helpless, without instincts, and also, crucially, without bearings. Our basic need to orient ourselves in thought and action, in our entire relationship with the world, gives rise to what we call culture. This was already the point of departure for Kantian philosophy. Not only was this view expressly shared by Cassirer, but it represents the true foundation of his major work, still in its early stages. Under the rubric of Orientation, Warburg's library variously included works of superstition, magic, religion, and science – considered central cultural products of our fundamental human need for orientation (Ellenberger, 2021, p. 129).

The archive also included a photographic collection of 450,000 photographs of paintings, sculptures, prints and drawings. Warburg created montages of images according to his intuitions about links across time and space (Johnson, 2012).

> Warburg's collection is founded on the idea of a continuous cultural non-simultaneity of the simultaneous, in which a great variety of approaches from a great variety of sources influence and also contradict one another. At the same time, his taxonomic system is based on the conviction that there is something like an unconscious cultural memory that lurks behind the various epochs and the objects of their scholars' attention, with significant though subtle effect (Ellenberger, 2021, p. 130).

Though Warburg aimed for something other than a machine for generating fiction, the library's arrangement seems no less fanciful than Calvino's matrix of tarot cards—necessarily so, because the conceptual space of cultural history cannot be captured by a few categories and new contexts or conjunctions can generate new dimensions of meaning.

## Chapter 6: Landscapes of Memory

1. Forché, 1994, p. 15.
2. Benjamin, 1968.
3. Forché (2019) describes her experiences in a recent autobiographical account.
4. Fassin & Rechtman, 2009; Kirmayer, Lemelson, & Barad, 2007; Leys, 2000; Young, 1995.
5. Indeed, for Lyotard (1992), the unique function of modern art is precisely to bear witness to the inexpressible and this requires new expressive forms. In visual art, one thinks immediately of the work of Anselm Kiefer (Kiefer & Dermutz, 2019; Lauterwein, 2007); in poetry, Paul Celan (Felstiner, 2001); in narrative art, W. G. Sebald's novels that limn lost memory (Sebald, 1996, 2001); or Daša Drndić's (2012) novel *Trieste*, which breaks into a list of the names of 9,000 Italian Jews whose lives were lost in the Shoah. These works face the challenge of using images less violent than the historical record to convey something of the meaning and magnitude of the event. The ethical responsibility they bear is to refuse any false closure that betrays history, to honor the specificity of lost lives by naming names (Margalit, 2002), and support the never-ending process of mourning, restitution and repair.
6. Casey (2001, 2013) provides a phenomenological analysis of how we come to embody the past through movement in space/place and in relation to others. Through repeated interactions with particular environments or landscapes, affective and visceral experiences become deeply embedded or sedimented in memory and habits. Our embodied memories of place have a reciprocal relationship with our sense of self, space, and time. The memories of past

places can resurface to haunt our present experiences. This is a dynamic process involving interactions with environments mediated by our bodily, metaphoric and narrative modes of engagement but it also depends crucially on cultural meaning. The cultural affordances of a place or space must be learned (Ramstead et al., 2016). In an ethnographic study of a halfway house for Indigenous offenders, Brass (2008) illustrates how a place-based therapeutic program may be experienced very differently by participants with different backgrounds, identities and social positions.

7. Pennebaker, 2012, 2018.
8. Pennebaker & Smyth, 2016.
9. Gerger et al., 2022; Guo, 2023; Knowles, Wearing, & Campos, 2011; Lu & Stanton, 2010.
10. Ahmed, 2024; Henry, 2010.
11. Kwon, 2008, 2015.
12. Kwon, 2015, p. 49.
13. Casey, 2015, 2018.
14. Yates (2013) describes the memory theaters of Renaissance that enabled prodigious feats of memory through the imaginative organization of space.
15. This inscription of history into landscape may be especially resonant for Indigenous Peoples who define their sense of self and personhood in explicit relation to the physical environment (Basso, 1996). Whitbeck and colleagues (2004) have shown how specific memories and symptoms associated with historical trauma may be felt at particular places. In our own work on resilience among Indigenous Peoples, the Mohawk of Kahnewake speak of the painful memories associated with the creation of the St. Lawrence Seaway (Kirmayer et al., 2011). Long after the historical events of colonization, symbols and signs of collective trauma are present in the landscape as vivid reminders of structural violence and ongoing discrimination.
16. Behrouzan & Fischer, 2015.
17. Gordon Sheppard (2006) illustrates the evocative power of such sonic landscapes or soundscapes in his remarkable documentary novel on the suicide of modernist writer Hubert Aquin.
18. Good & Good, 1988.
19. See Mianji and Kirmayer (2020, 2022, 2023) for discussion of some of the multiple strands of this counterdiscourse to the biological psychiatry that dominates Iran's mental health care system.
20. The quoted phrase appears in an earlier, unpublished version of Behrouzan and Fischer's chapter.
21. Kidron, 2009, 2015.
22. Kidron, 2012, 2018, 2020.

23. Kidron, 2004.
24. Kidron, Kotliar, & Kirmayer, 2019.
25. Crapanzano, 2015.
26. Crapanzano, 2015, p. 157.
27. Crapanzano, 2015, p. 160–161.
28. Mosès, 2009.
29. Perec, 1988. Like Calvino, Perec was a member of Oulipo and a master of writing built on self-imposed constraints, like a detective novel (*La Disparition,* 1969) written entirely without the letter "e"—translated in English as *A Void* (Perec, 2005)—a playful circumlocution of more profound loss that was a recurrent theme in Perec's work (Bellos, 2010; Leak, 2019; Wadhera, 2019).
30. The pronunciation in French is "double V."
31. See Lejeune (1993) and Bellos (2010) for an account of Perec's struggles in writing *W.*
32. Funkenstein, 1993.
33. Kihlstrom, 2005.
34. Herman, 1992; Terr, 1994.
35. Roediger, 1980.
36. Neisser, 1994; Schacter, 1999, 2022; Craik & Jacoby, 2023.
37. Bartlett, 1932; Loftus, 1993. Two apparent challenges to this view of memory as patchy and vulnerable to distortion through reconstruction are so-called "flashbulb" memories and individuals with highly superior autobiographical memory (HSAM). Flashbulb memories are vivid, long-lasting memories of the circumstances surrounding an unusual, surprising, consequential, and emotionally arousing event (Hirst & Phelps, 2016). They are a type of autobiographical memory and likely do not involve different mechanisms from other forms of memory. Despite their vivid quality, flashbulb memories are prone to distortion over time, just like other types of autobiographical memories (Craik & Jacoby, 2023). Individuals with HSAM are able to recall copious details of personal life events, sometimes back to early childhood, when asked about specific dates (Talbot et al., 2024). This suggests that the memory registration process can include a lot of information about events but for most people, this decays or becomes inaccessible over time. Individuals with HSAM appear to differ in the strength of the processes of memory consolidation and retrieval, as indicated by intense activation of brain networks involved in personal memory. However, they are still vulnerable to the reconstructive errors found in experimental studies of "false memories" (Patihis et al., 2013).
38. Elsey, Van Ast, & Kindt, 2018; Schwabe, Nader, & Pruessner, 2014. This provides a rationale for the treatment of PTSD by eliciting memories and

altering the reconsolidation process through medications that dampen the sympathetic nervous system response so that the memory is stored with less strong emotion attached to it (e.g., Astill Wright et al., 2021; Brunet et al., 2018; Ecker & Vaz, 2022).

39. Friedman, 1993.
40. Belli & Loftus, 1994; Laurence & Perry, 1983.
41. For evidence in support of the procedural/declarative distinction, see: Ullman, 2004.
42. This is the major lesson of work on the "enhancement" of memory by hypnosis. Hypnosis encourages imaginative elaboration and confabulation, increasing the number of details recalled but not their accuracy (Orne et al., 1988). These effects of hypnosis make its forensic use to enhance memory extremely dangerous and such applications have been widely prohibited.
43. Watkins, 1986.
44. Connerton, 1989; Halbwachs, 1992; Zerubavel, 2003.
45. Spence, 1982.
46. Lewis, 1995.
47. Terr, 1994.
48. Holmes, 1990; Loftus, 1993; Pope & Hudson, 1995.
49. Crews, 1995; Otgaar, Howe, & Patihis, 2022; Lynn et al., 2023; Craik & Jacoby, 2023.
50. McNally, 2024.
51. Brewin, 2020.
52. Young, 1989.
53. Langer, 1991.
54. Greenspan, 1992; Langer, 1991.
55. Young, 1988.
56. Langer, 1991.
57. Langer, 1991, p. 77.
58. Langer, 1991, p. 84.
59. Langer, 1991, p. 96.
60. Eitinger, 1980; Krystal, 1988; Kuch & Cox, 1992; Niederland, 1968; Tillman, Nash, & Lerner, 1994.
61. Langer, 1991, p. 5. Delbo again: "When I speak to you of Auschwitz, my words don't come from deep memory; they come, so to speak, from external memory [mémoire externe], intellectual memory, reflective memory" (Delbo, 2014, p. xx). And Langer continues, "Refining the opposition between deep and common memory, she develops a parallel distinction between what we might call 'thinking memory' and what she labels 'sense memory' ('*mémoire des sens*')." This distinction recalls that of declarative (descriptive, semantic) versus procedural (episodic, bodily) memory. Pain

(*sens*) has made memory itself an object to be dissected. But *mémoire des sens* is also "memory of meanings," putting the body at the center of meaning as articulate witness to the past even in its mute survival.

62. Langer, 1991, p. 161.
63. Terr, 1994.
64. Kestenberg & Fogelman, 1994; Stein, 1993.
65. Lewis, 1995; White & Pillemer, 1979.
66. Cf. Kestenberg & Fogelman, 1994, p. xiii, 6–12.
67. McNally, 2003, 2024.
68. André Stein (1993, pp. 226ff) tells his own story of forgetting a memory of being raped yet recalling all the surrounding memories of his time in hiding as a child during the Holocaust. It was more difficult to recollect the shameful personal memory of this sexual assault than the terrors and suffering shared with his older sister. Only when his sister, on her deathbed, revealed this never-spoken-of traumatic event did his memories return.
69. Richard Powers (2000) describes this virtuality of memory as a survival strategy in his novel *Ploughing the Dark*.
70. Familial abuse presents the child with the added problem of integrating contradictory images of the aggressing parent as also loving and kind and of the nonaggressing parent as failing to protect and colluding with abuse. Dissociation provides a strategy for managing the intense dissonance created by this contradiction.
71. "Whatever the specific purposes, many survivors recall a period immediately after liberation when they were simply compelled to speak about what they had witnessed and survived" (Greenspan, 1992, p. 147).
72. Aarons & Lassner, 2020; Young, 1988, 1993.
73. Avruch, 2010.
74. Shore, 2016.
75. Brounéus, 2010; later assessments suggest some more positive impact: Caparos et al., 2020.
76. Farmer, 2004.
77. Klein, 2007.
78. Blanchot, 1986.
79. McNally, 2003.
80. Milloy, 1999.
81. Brant Castellano, Archibald, & DeGagné, 2008.
82. *The Globe and Mail*, June 12, 2008, p. A1.
83. Brave Heart & Debruyn, 1998; Brave Heart et al., 2011.
84. The logic of historical trauma and its rhetorical uses are discussed in Kirmayer, Gone, and Moses (2014); Gone, 2023.
85. Aron, 1992.

86. In a recent discussion of the political dimensions of trauma, Herman (2023) acknowledges the importance of distinctive social processes in reparation and recovery.
87. Judt, 1992; Vidal-Naquet, 1992.
88. Amis, 1991.

## Chapter 7: The Texture of Time

1. Nabokov, 1969, p. 571.
2. Gelman, 1997, p. 151.
3. Bruner, 2004; Freeman, 2015; Habermas & Köber, 2015; Kerby, 1991; McAdams, 2018; Ricoeur, 1991; Schechtman, 2007.
4. Fivush & Haden, 2003; Nelson, 2003.
5. Vygotsky, 1980.
6. Howard, 1991.
7. Cultural exemplars may be used as templates, prototypes and meta-narratives to develop an individual biography and sense of self. Used as templates, exemplars are modified by replacing elements of a generic story with the particulars of an individual's life; prototypes are salient stories used to reason analogically about one's own life; to create a meta-narrative, some quality of the exemplar is abstracted out as a key principle, metaphoric quality, or mythic structure to which the individual's biography must then conform.
8. Cushman, 1990; Greene, 2008; Sampson, 1977. In the United States, a version of this rugged individualism can be traced to frontier experience (Bazzi et al., 2020). Although not a common trope, the adjective "adamantine" is used to characterize the moral integrity of Thomas More in John Bolt's (1960) play *A Man for All Seasons*. For a discussion of the some of the dilemmas of this image of constancy and rectitude, see: Casey (2008).
9. Hermans, 2001. This relational self is a mainstay in the literatures of cross-cultural psychology and psychological anthropology, which generally contrast the Western (Euro-American) individualistic self with more interdependent, collectivistic, communal selves (Marsella, Devos, & Hsu, 1985; see also Sullivan, 2014). Marriott (1976; see also Bharati, 1985; Sax, 2002) referred to the Hindu version of this self as a "dividual" rather than an individual, emphasizing the ways in which boundaries are experienced as permeable and the person as naturally divided into bits that may be shared—even transmitted to others, through breath or bodily contact in sweat, saliva, or other bodily fluids. In a very different vein, Bauman (2007, 2013; Bauman & Leoncini, 2018) has written extensively about the *liquid self* as characteristic of contemporary global society. Here liquidity refers not so much to the mobility of capital in neoliberal global economy, but to the instability,

changeableness, and impersistence of the self, which results in a search for solidity, sometimes found in identity politics or in efforts to inscribe identity on the flesh. The metaphor of liquid invokes feelings of excessive mutability, of flowing into any available space to fit the form. This might confer extreme flexibility or adaptability but also presents a challenging and often disturbing lack of intrinsic form.

10. Marsella, Devos, & Hsu, 1985.
11. Although framed as liberatory and celebrating individual autonomy, the rhetoric of authenticity often serves the values of contemporary neoliberal capitalism (Foster, 2016; Rose, 1998).
12. Fivush, 2022; Fivush & Haden, 2003; Hutto, 2012.
13. El Shaarawi, 2015.
14. Beiser & Hyman, 1997; Beiser, 1999, 2009.
15. Porter, 2007.
16. BenEzer, 2003, 2007.
17. Kaplan, 2005.
18. Despite greater integration, these dynamics continue to the present and are entangled with racialized distinctions between Ashkenazim (from Europe) and Mirzrahim (from other Middle Eastern or Asian countries; see: Shoshana, 2020).
19. Silove, Steel, & Watters, 2000.
20. Nabokov, 1969, p. 571.
21. Nabokov himself had frequent synesthetic experiences, which are reflected both in his accounts of characters' sensoria and the sensual qualities of his prose (Boyd, 1985; 1991).
22. Nabokov, 1969, p. 581.
23. Boyd, 1985.
24. Boyd, 2001.
25. Nabokov, 1966; Boyd, 1991.
26. Langer, 1991, 1995, 1998. This parallels distinctions in the phenomenological literature (going back to Husserl) between lived-time (internal, subjective) and the world-time of nature. But lived time is not only durational; it may include experiences of instantaneity, fragmented or punctuated time that can be stretched out or annealed by particular modes of attention and social practices, including the experience of daily social rhythms and routines (which may be influenced by bodily processes and clock-time), and the narrative time of situational, autobiographical, and historical chronologies (Ricoeur, 1988). Bachelard (2013) suggests that lyric poetry is especially able to draw experiences of an instant in ways that create a sense of duration.

27. This phenomenon of absorption is an important link between the psychology of aesthetic experience and the dynamics of traumatic memory (Benson, 1993).
28. Eitinger, 1998, pp. 768–769.
29. Nakamura & Csikszentmihalyi, 2014.
30. Agamben, 1999.
31. The metaphor is irresistible. In January 1987, the Italian journal *La Stampa* published an article on Holocaust denial by Levi titled "Buco nero di Auschwitz" ("The Black Hole of Auschwitz") (Anissimov, 1998, p. 394). Levi ended his personal anthology of texts with an excerpt from an article by physicist Kip Thorne on black holes; he titled the chapter "We Are Alone" (Levi, 2000, p. 214).
32. The link between temporal experience and kinds of selves comes from the ways in which persistence and mutability are constructed. Thus, the adamantine self is supposed to remain solid and endure without change, while the relational self responds to the exigencies of the current context, and the liquid self is always in flux, with no still point. Of course, while the adamantine self portrays the person as something solid and immovable, the reality of human existence is constant change. Persistence in nonequilibrium systems such as ourselves is a consequence of dynamics.
33. Kidron, 2009, 2015.
34. Vonnegut, 1969. The feeling of being unmoored in time is a common feature of depersonalization, in which people may have find it difficult to discriminate past, present, and future, or to project themselves into the future (Ferroni et al., 2024).
35. Gubkin, 2007.
36. Benson, 1993. The individual propensity to become absorbed interacts with culturally prescribed modes of attention. For example, those who observe the Sabbath as a ritual, may experience an altered sense of time that comes from putting aside the daily rhythms of the week, deliberately slowing down, and engaging in religious study, prayer, or contemplation (Shulevitz, 2011). In Jewish mysticism, the ritual time of the Sabbath undoes the exile (Idel, 2004).
37. Without this process of recollection, some patients may experience a lack of continuity in therapy. This was the dilemma of poet Anne Sexton in her psychotherapy with psychiatrist–psychologist Martin Orne, and they hit on the idea of audio recording their sessions and having her review the previous week's conversation just before each meeting (Middlebrook, 1992).
38. Frankl, 1985.
39. Langer, 1998, p. 69.
40. Anissimov, 1998; Wood, 2020.
41. Langer, 1998, pp. 32–33.

42. Levi, 1988.
43. Levi wrote of shoes as a matter of life and death for those facing long forced marches:

> And do not think that shoes form a factor of secondary importance in the life of the Lager. Death begins with the shoes; for most of us, they show themselves to be instruments of torture, which after a few hours of marching cause painful sores which become fatally infected (Levi, 1996, pp. 34–35).

Oster (2020) describes how shoes became metonym and metaphor for those lost in the Shoah.

44. Langer, 1998, p. 42.
45. Celan & Sachs, 1995.
46. Wittmann, 2016; Wittmann, Jokic, & Pfeifer, 2019.
47. Meissner & Wittman, 2011.
48. Wittmann, 2016.
49. Boroditsky, 2011, 2018; Thibodeau & Boroditsky, 2011; Traugott, 1985
50. Bolles & Fanselow, 1980; Woolf & Salter, 2000.
51. Morinis, 1985; Glucklich, 2001.
52. Eisenberger, 2012; Eslinger et al., 2021.
53. Ratcliffe, 2023.
54. There is debate in the emotion literature on how to view enduring mood states. Ekman (1999) and others defined emotions as brief reactions because they are seen as transient states used to reorient behavior. Frijda (2017) argued that emotional episodes are states of action readiness that can persist over longer periods of time and people can experience them as unbroken engagements (albeit waxing and waning in intensity) as commonly seen with jealousy, anger, and sadness. It seems clear that emotions can persist and recur through the dynamics of self-regulatory loops, which may include metaphoric or narrative framing of experiences in ways that reevoke the emotion. Both the scenarios that elicit emotion and its temporal contours reflect cultural scripts or models that are learned in specific social contexts (Barrett, 2017; Mesquita, 2022).
55. Riley, 2019, p. 33.

> Your altered temporality is not to do with any kind of taking thought. It's prior to that, and supremely indifferent to lament and to cogitation alike. Instead it feels foundational: to do with the entire structuring nature of cognition. Such an unexpected vanishing smashes through your usual cognitive assumption that objects and people will continue to exist and reappear. The person who says, "I keep expecting to hear his key in the door any moment" isn't merely falling back on a well-worn trope. She's issuing a factual report. Once so ferociously shaken up, cognition can't readily regroup its forces to reassemble with its old anticipation intact. The entire stance inside which you'd previously lived is changed. Not by any disfiguring melancholia on your part or even by simple reflective sadness, but by an

upheaval of that pre-conscious topography through which your old apprehension of the world had once quietly moved (Riley, 2019, pp. 59–60).

56. Boss, 1999.
57. Stroebe, Schut, & Nauta, 2016.
58. Appiah, 2017.
59. Cunsolo & Landman, 2017.
60. Fuchs, 2018.
61. Alessandri, 2023; Kenny et al., 2019; Ratcliffe, 2023; Wikan, 1990.
62. Chafe, 1994.
63. Nadeau, 2006; Sas & Coman, 2016.
64. Benson, 1993, 2001; Wittmann, 2016.
65. Goldstein, 2017.
66. Hilgard & Hilgard, 2013.
67. Naish, 2014.
68. In packaging and promoting meditation as a self-care intervention in medical settings, the soteriological aims have been downplayed, while the practical, instrumental functions in self-control become the selling point (Kirmayer, 2015d).
69. Greenspan, 1992, p. 145.

> Leon, the survivor who contributed the idea of "making a story" of what is "not a story," . . . [recalled] returning to a ghetto that had been liquidated only hours before . . . : "the scene coming back from the arms factory into the ghetto. And the grayness of the morning. And those dozens of bodies wherever you turned . . .
>
> You're supposed to react! You're supposed to run up! And race! Yell! Scream! Utter! Emote! Show anything about it! Anything whether it is— . . .
>
> Entering the ghetto in a dead silence. Those columns marching in . . . Maybe a poet can evoke something approaching it, but even sound would be out of place. There's no sound actually, There is no sound. It would have to be a silent poem" (Greenspan, 1992, 145–146).

Just so—the poet Paul Celan used shards of metaphor and silence to display and, in moments, transcend the limits of narrative (see Chapter 8).

70. Greenspan, 1992, p. 149.
71. Here is how Eitinger (1998, p. 774) describes it:

> Just as the future seems impossible to the survivor so too the past seems impossible to return to. In the attempt to resurrect an empathic tie, the survivor turns to prewar memories, for that is the "only place he knows of where a whole hale world exists." Yet this attempt at self-healing through remembering will be seriously compromised in the survivor by the fact that neither selective remembrance nor selective repression works after massive psychic trauma. No matter how persistent the attempt at recapture, that benevolent past will always be associated with the circumstances of its destruction and loss. This is because the enormity of the evil overburdens and outweighs the ego's reservoir of positive imagery and prevents the separation of positive from negative images. The event, therefore, not only retroactively affects the past, but it proactively contaminates all previous and subsequent events,

compromising the healing ability of post-traumatic experience. The imagery of genocide remains indelible, unassimilated, and paralyzing: it continuously intrudes upon the survivor's thoughts.

72. Langer, 1991, pp. 6–7.
73. Langer, 1991, pp. 6–7.
74. Greenspan, 1992, p. 148.
75. Greenspan, 1992.
76. Greenspan, 2010, 2019.
77. Shandler, 1999.
78. The most basic violence is that of turning away in the face of the other's vulnerability:

> Chaim Guri's film The Eighty-First Blow portrays a man who narrates the story of his sufferings in the camps only to hear his audience say: "All this cannot be true, it could not have happened. You must have made it up." This denial by the listener inflicts, according to the film, the ultimately fateful blow, beyond the eighty that a man, in Jewish tradition can sustain and survive. The absence of an empathic listener, or more radically, the absence of an addressable other, an other who can hear the anguish of one's memories and thus recognize their realness, annihilates the story and destroys the survivor once again.
>
> Fearful of this mortal eighty-first blow, of another devastating betrayal and failure of empathy, many survivors choose silence and isolation and stop trying to connect to a life that seems so impossible to live. Intense experiences and feelings need to be avoided because the individual is so helpless to deal with them (Laub & Allard, 1998, p. 804).

79. Sennett, 1998, p. 22.
80. Levinas, 1985.
81. Eitinger, 1998, p. 774.
82. Eitinger, 1998, p. 778.
83. Sennett, 1998, p. 25.
84. Sennett, 1998, p. 20.
85. Sacks, 1997.

## Chapter 8: Poetics of Alterity

1. Hirsch, 1999, p. 4.
2. Felstiner, 2001, p. 409.
3. Kirmayer, 1988a; Lambek, 1998.
4. Levinas, 2003a.
5. The metaphoric contrast between the machine (inanimate, hard, cold) and the body (animate, soft, warm, vulnerable) exists alongside the biomedical view of the body as itself an elaborate machine (Osherson & Amarasingham, 1981).
6. Nancy, 2000.

7. Nancy, 2000, p. 28/8.
8. Nancy, 2000, p. 31/9.
9. Nancy, 2000, p. 33/9.
10. Nancy, 2000, p. 39/11.
11. Nancy, 2000, p. 12.
12. Nancy, 2000, pp. 42–43/13.
13. Halberstam, 2017.
14. Goetz & Arcomano, 2023.
15. Here is how Jack Halberstam, a professor of gender studies and literature who is also transgender, puts it:

    > The concept of being without a gender, however, is whimsical at best, since there are few ways to interact with other human beings without begin identified with some kind of gendered embodiment. The concept of "agender," then, names a wish to be outside of gender norms rather than the real experience of being so (Halberstam, 2017, p. 9–10).

    It remains to be seen whether changes in culture and technology will move this from whimsical wish to lived reality.
16. Speculative fiction has explored alternate forms of embodiment, both biological and artificial in ways that reflect the politics of identity in each generation. See, for example: Butler, 2012; LeGuin, 1969; Newitz, 2017—each of which offer versions of gender fluidity and diversity.
17. Kammers et al., 2009; Kannape et al., 2019.
18. Given intact cognitive machinery, we readily reincorporate ourselves, making prostheses into parts of our body, integrating new modes of self-presentation and being in the world. However, in many instances people fail to fully adjust to these bodily changes. It is instructive then to consider possible reasons for this failure. Obstacles to integration might include: intrinsic properties of the foreign part and its coupling to the body that cause constant reminders of otherness (e.g., unpredictable asynchrony, pain, impairment of function); failures in the integrative machinery of sensorimotor habituation (difficulties in regulating the loops between action, sensation, and intention); and gaps in the narrative reconstruction of the self because of a preexisting dissonant or subsequent self-alienating story. Each of these kinds of obstacle could come from within the individual or from the actions of others (e.g., by reacting to the anomaly in ways that elicit distress [stigmatizing or avoiding]; focusing on the alien part in ways that increase self-consciousness; and undermining or rejecting the narrative of an integrated self).
19. Levinas, 1998, p. 10.
20. Ramstead, Veissière, & Kirmayer, 2016.
21. Cole, 1999.

22. The logic of facial expression as emotional presence and identity is revealed in the play of the mask. The mask is an antiface: it cloaks the face to provide a stylized expression that changes little (except with changing light and shadow or accompanying gestures) across situations thus freezing the temporal dynamics of feeling. (The fixed mask is also a death mask, a dead face—a primal source of fear for primates; cf. Hebb, 1946.) This accentuates the meaning of a single facial expression by rendering it as something divorced from ongoing interaction. The mask hides the true face behind a static caricature, which may be shocking or amusing in its very stasis or exaggeration and distortion. The mask codifies and represents feeling at one remove from individual experience; it replaces individuality with collectivity, idiosyncrasy with cultural convention, and so serves to make emotional responses more abstract and formulaic. Thus, the mask allows us aesthetic distance so that we can modulate the intensity of our emotions in response to the other (Scheff, 1979). So it is that the surgeon's mask or the blank face of the clinician maintaining therapeutic "neutrality," protecting them from the intensity of their own emotional response to the other. But the mask adds its own freight of strangeness and alienation. In healing ceremonies, masks can make the gods or spirits present in ways that are powerful and uncanny (Napier, 1986).
23. Levenson, Ekman, & Friesen, 1990; Zajonc, 1984. It remains unclear, however, whether the facial mimicry accounts for emotional contagion or whether contagion also depends on other cognitive and perceptual process (Hatfield et al., 2014; Hess, 2021).
24. Wild, Erb, & Bartels, 2001. It comes as no surprise then to learn that the human brain has specialized systems concerned with recognizing faces and decoding facial expression (Damasio et al., 1990). Face perception involves several regions of cortex including an area in the fusiform gyrus that is selectively responsive to faces (Adolphs, 2002; Kanwisher et al., 1997). While the recognition of faces involves circuitry in the fusiform gyrus, the identification of the familiarity of a person (based on their face or voice) involves activity in posterior cingulate and retrosplenial cortex (Shah et al., 2001). The amygdala, which is involved in fear conditioning, receives inputs from the cortical areas involved in recognition of faces and facial expressions. These connections allow a rapid response to facial expressions; brief presentations of fearful faces may activate the amygdala even in the absence of awareness of the stimulus. Very likely, this provides part of the basis for the common phenomenon of emotional contagion in which feelings spread from one person to another simply by exposure to their face (Hatfield, Cacciopo, & Rapson, 1994). When the source of anxiety is

misattributed, this process of emotional contagion may give rise to epidemics of bodily distress and disability (Bartholomew & Sirois, 2001).

25. Tronick et al., 1978.
26. Mesman et al., 2009.
27. Cole, 1999.
28. Meltzoff & Moore, 1977.
29. Gopnick, 1993.
30. Baron-Cohen, 1995.
31. Cole, 1999, p. 316.
32. Interestingly, blind people may show the same facial expressions of emotion as the sighted but may have difficulty deliberately producing these expressions—reflecting the neurobiological difference between "automatic" and voluntary expressions of emotion (Valente et al., 2018). Blind infants must use other modalities to determine caretaker affect and attention (Bigelow, 2003) and show delays in developing understanding of others' perspectives (Roch-Levecq, 2006). Infants of blind parents still watch their faces for emotion cues but learn to rely on other information to determine the focus of joint attention (Senju et al., 2013)
33. The example is drawn from my informal observations. There is limited research on children's pain behavior and adults' responses in everyday nonclinical settings. See: Goubert et al., 2008; Hadjistavropoulos et al., 2011; Noel et al., 2018.
34. Poole & Craig, 1992.
35. Levinas, 1998, p. 32
36. Levinas, 1985, p. 95.
37. Levinas, 1985, p. 85.
38. This underwrites the widespread moral language of honor and duty to others that is couched in metaphors of the maintenance or loss of face. To save face is to maintain social standing, moral presence, and social capital; to lose face is to endure the pain of shame, dishonour, and social marginalization.
39. Byrne, Morton, & Salmon, 2001.
40. Mara Buchbinder (2015) has explored the ambiguities of pain explanation in pediatric settings, where the suffering of children poses a constant, almost intolerable demand on clinicians to manage their own emotional response.
41. Cole, 2001; Decety & Holvoet, 2021; Drimalla et al., 2019.
42. Afana et al., 2010; Hinton et al., 2009, 2013; Hinton & Kirmayer, 2017; Silove et al., 2009.
43. Good, 2015. Rahimi (2021) provides an extended discussion of haunting presences that are not only generated by trauma and its aftermath but part of everyday life, the inescapable shadow of the subjunctive nature of sense perception and meaning-making.

44. Epley, Waytz, & Cacciоppo, 2007.
45. Freud, 2003 (orig. 1919).
46. As mentioned, Hebb (1946) described the terror of chimpanzees when they saw a plaster death mask of another chimpanzee.
47. Artificial intelligence researchers who construct humanoid robots describe the "uncanny valley," the place along the continuum of similitude where plastic faces are creepy because they are close but not-quite human (Seyama & Nagayama, 2007). Something is being violated in these simulacra, some essential aspect of the human cleaved off, distorted, or reversed in a way that unsettles.
48. This is powerfully presented Robert Lemelson's film *40 Years of Silence: An Indonesian Tragedy* (2009), when the Balinese anthropologist Degung Santikarma confronts the neighbor who killed his father. Inappropriate affect and the effort to normalize or valorize violence also can give rise to the uncanny as displayed in Joshua Oppenheimer's film *The Act of Killing* (2012) in which the perpetrators of mass violence in Indonesia reenact their acts of torture and murder for the camera.
49. Good, 2015; see also: Good, 2019; Good, Chiovinda, & Rahimi, 2022.
50. See: Winet, 2010.
51. Of course, most catastrophes have their greatest effects on those already vulnerable due to structural violence (e.g., economic inequity, substandard housing, precarious living conditions) and political marginalization or oppression, so even "natural" catastrophes are never truly politically neutral (Farmer, 2004; Kirmayer et al., 2010).
52. Lemelson, 2014; Lemelson & Suryani, 2006; on the film *Shadows and Illuminations*, see Chapter 5 in Lemelson & Tucker, 2017; for a broader discussion of ethnographic film in research, see: Lemelson & Tucker, 2021. For more on the Balinese context and the memory of trauma, see: Dwyer & Santikarma, 2007; Lemelson, Kirmayer, & Barad, 2007.
53. Kapferer & Papigny, 2005.
54. Kirmayer, 2015a, p. 402; Pillen, 2015.
55. People invoke different metaphors of dehumanization depending on cultural contexts, for example, as animals (subhuman) or as machines (nonhuman) (Haslam et al., 2007; Haslam, 2019), but as the Sinhalese examples suggest, this list is not exhaustive and the metaphors can be blended and extended in novel ways.
56. Pillen, 2015, p. 10. We can recognize different cultural forms of emptiness and senselessness—distinguishing gibberish, craziness, wildness, ineffability, speechlessness, and nothingness. For example, Celan's poem "Tübingen, Jänner," a meditation on Holderlein's madness, ends with the nonsense words, "Pallaksch, pallaksch" (Celan & Hamburger, 2002). Celan's poem

moves from hermetic imagery toward stuttering, stammering, and babbling. Since the time of Plato, madness has been a privileged point of entry into understanding the uniqueness of poetry compared to other modes of speaking, but the breakdown in language with Holderlein's madness also speaks to the larger breakdown of language in the wake of the Holocaust (Weineck, 1999, p. 263). The barbarians are those who babble—and in the wake of the barbarians, babble is all that is left to us. Madness is a kind of visitation of the Divine that leads the poet to speak in tongues, a kind of fluent babble. Words have immediate sensual qualities, which Celan keeps negating, dissolving, or surpassing (Burnside, 2006). In this way, he speaks to (and instantiates) the predicament of *poesis* through language that has lost its communal ground or had it undermined and disfigured, rendered uncanny by the violence of the other who admits no other. Emptiness can be deadness like Agamben's (1999) description of the *Muselmänn* of the death camps, located beyond empathy with that racialized epithet, the emptiness of the blank canvas, or the alchemists' *nigredo*, calling forth creativity out of darkness, or even the emptiness of the clear mind of the meditator realizing the co-constructed nature of experience (von Franz, 1980).

57. Blanchot, 1986.
58. Mundt, 2014.
59. Kirmayer, 2015b.
60. Barrett, 1998. See: Sass, 1992.
61. Barrett, 1998, p. 469.
62. American Psychiatric Association, 2022. See: Andreasen, 2007.
63. See quotes in Barrett, 1998, p. 473.
64. Sass is well aware of the problems with this locution but hopes to humanize the person with schizophrenia by drawing attention to the unique ways that the illness constitutes a particular form of selfhood which has its own value. He points out that detaching the person from the illness ("the person with schizophrenia"), ignores the extent to which schizophrenia is an affliction *of* the self (i.e., that transforms the very nature of the self), and further, that such politically correct language is no guarantee against stigmatization and does nothing to challenge our tendency to view the illness itself as entirely negative. See: Sass, 1998, 2007.
65. Barrett, 1998, p. 484.
66. Barrett, 1998, p. 485. Corin (2007) wrote about other dimensions of such distancing as a social and spatial strategy for living with schizophrenia she termed *positive withdrawal.*
67. Jenkins, & Barrett, 2004. See also: Demjen et al., 2019; Mould, Oades, & Crowe, 2010; Qiu, Tay, & Watson, 2024.

68. Felstiner (1995). Referring to Celan as a post-Holocaust poet, of course, recalls Theodor Adorno's famous statement to the effect that writing poetry after Auschwitz is barbaric—a statement he later retracted. Adorno reconsidered the impossibility of lyric art in the light of Celan's work precisely because of the seriousness with which Celan wrestled with the problem of the impurity and limits of language. Celan used absence in his poems to limn the unsayable and the poem itself as an object of attention to call forth a reflective silence.
69. Celan, 1986. See also: Felstiner, 2001.
70. Felstiner, 2001, p. 31. In a remarkable feat of translation, Felstiner gradually reintroduces the German text back into his English version, so that by the end of the poem one can hear some of the sound and rhythm of the original and the poet's reappropriation of his mother tongue. Noting that one can never really own or appropriate a language—since it is necessarily created and sustained by a community, it has a life of its own and always precedes, prods and follows us—Derrida describes Celan's relationship to German as "a hand-to-hand bodily struggle" (2005, p. 99).
71. The opposite of opacity is transparency.

    > We also say of some people that they are transparent to us. It is, however, important as regards this observation that one human being can be a complete enigma to another. We learn this when we come into a strange country with entirely strange traditions; and, what is more, even given a mastery of the country's language. We do not understand the people ... We cannot find ourselves in them (Wittgenstein, 1958, part II, p. 223, but with Cohen's [2008] retranslation of the last sentence [*Wir können nicht in sie finden*]).

    Opacity, then, is a condition of recognition of the other as such. Instead of assimilating them to our selves ("finding ourselves in them"), we feel their otherness and must respond with openness and respect, tolerating not knowing and trusting to the unfolding of the encounter. This alterity is especially clear in intercultural encounters (Kirmayer, 2008b; Kirmayer, 2013; Strand, 2024).
72. Tobias, 2006.
73. "Rather than relying upon adjectives of disabled sensory function such as blind, dead or numb, the dialectic of senselessness in Celan works by naming the sensory faculty of the organ of sense perception – sight/eye, hearing/ear, touch/skin – or an instance of what is sensed, thereby generating a sense impression, before adding the negative postpositional particle '-less', which performs a cancelling function" (Burnside, 2006, p. 146). The dynamic of evocation/revocation reenacts the world building and dismantling of the German language used to engineer genocide.
74. Celan angrily broke off his relationship with translator Michael Hamburger when he mistakenly assumed that Hamburger was the author of an

anonymous review in the *Times Literary Supplement* that referred to his poetry as "hermetic" (Celan & Hamburger, 2002).

75. Celan used the spatial arrangement of words on the page, neologisms, idiosyncratic punctuation, and even nonsense language to great expressive effect. See: Weineck, 1999.
76. Celan, 1986, p. 34.
77. Hall, 1978; Pinsky, 1998.
78. Celan, 1986, pp. 34–35.
79. Celan, 1986, p. 48. Celan made hundreds of pages of notes in preparation for this speech. Celan heard the geographic term *meridian* used to describe "spiritual coordinate points connecting like-minded people" from his friend the poet Nelly Sachs (Lyon, 2006, p. 140).
80. It is instructive to compare Celan's careful choice of words here in *The Meridian*, an attempt to find a light-compass for the soul before a German audience in 1961, with his briefer words of homecoming to the Hebrew Writer's Union in Tel Aviv in 1969, just before his death (see: Celan, 1986). Before the German audience he spoke of "an altogether other" as the test case of tolerance of difference.
81. Celan, 1986, pp. 49–50.
82. The image of Medusa, introduced in a text by Bruchner (the artist after whom the literary prize was named), recurs in Celan's essay not as a terrifying witch-hag, but as standing for the artist's efforts to capture and memorialize others by turning them to stone. Standing before his German audience, Celan invokes this awe-inspiring power, but his text is shadowed by the risk of the audience's incomprehension and stony reception.
83. Celan, 1986, pp. 57–58.
84. Lacoue-Labarthe, 1986, p. 18.
85. Lacoue-Labarthe, 1986, p. 100.
86. Felstiner, 1995, p. 16.
87. Celan, 1986, p. 4.
88. Celan, 1986, p. 16.
89. Levinas, 1985, 2003b.
90. Celan, 1986, pp. 16, 26. "Beginning in 1952 and for the rest of his life, in letters to his wife Celan repeatedly used the words *truth* and *true*. From their context there it is clear that he did not use the term to mean a transcendental or higher value. For him it meant openness, candor, sincerity, genuineness or, in negative terms, the opposite of deceitfulness, falsehood, insincerity, dishonesty, meretriciousness, shallowness" (Lyon, 2006, p. 17).
91. Authenticity might be set against the irony of humor and displacement, the virtues of the trickster, who, from a god's-eye view (present in the telling of

the myth), is authentically true to the unpredictability and caprice of nature, but to others, confined to the mundane plane of existence, seems full of guile and insincerity. Those who tire of authenticity, or see it as impossible attainment and self-delusion, may adopt the trickster's stance of ironic detachment, self-reflexive humor, and worldly recognition of the wish to be seen as virtuous when we are merely pursuing our desires. Celan must be counted among those for whom too much was at stake to adopt an ironic or trickster stance in his writing.

92. Celan & Fairley, 2007, p. xvi.
93. Recall the image of the self as concentric spheres in Chapter 5.
94. Celan & Fairley, 2007, p. xvi.
95. Celan & Fairley, 2007, p. xvi.
96. Celan & Fairley, 2007, p. xvii.
97. Pajevic (2001) discusses the importance of the metaphor of STAND (*Stehen*) in Celan to convey notions of resistance, constancy, insistence and existence associated with an ethics of uprightness and solidarity.
98. Césaire, 2001, p. 14.
99. Lindqvist, 2021.
100. Allard-Tremblay & Coburn, 2023; Bragato & Gordon, 2017; Haslam, 2019; Yancy, 2008.
101. "Look, a Negro! . . . Maman, see the Negro! I'm frightened!" (Fanon, 1967, p. 112).
102. Hunt (2007) argues that shifts in empathy and moral language spurred by the reading of novels contributed to the invention of human rights.
103. Trouillot, 2015.
104. As a Jew from the Maghreb who, through the legacy of colonialism, spoke neither Arabic nor Ladino, Jacques Derrida inherited this struggle (Salmon, 2020). In an extensive footnote that holds the crux (or at least the part that is not essentially confessional) of his essay "Monolingualism of the Other" (1998), on the problem of reappropriating language for those who speak a language that originally and ultimately belongs to an other (e.g., the language of the colonizer), Derrida uses the examples of the relationships to language found in Franz Rosensweig, Hannah Arendt, and Emmanuel Levinas to consider a typology of linguistic identities.

    In Derrida's account, Rosensweig had a complex relationship to three languages, German, Yiddish, and Hebrew: the official language of the state; the quotidian language of mother, family, and the ethnic in-group; and the sacred language of prayer and transcendence. According to Derrida, for Rosenzweig, the Jews' essential language is the prophetic language of the Bible; when in exile, however, they must speak the language of their hosts, and while they may appropriate and adapt it, it is never truly theirs; in a more radical sense, the holy language of Hebrew is not fully theirs except in prayer or prophecy, since (prior to the State of Israel) it does not function as a quotidian language. For its part, Yiddish is the language of creolization and compromise.

For Arendt, German was the mother tongue and fused the quotidian and intimate with the high culture of philosophy. Forgetting or forgoing the mother tongue was thus an act of repression made necessary for some for survival after Auschwitz, but this occurred at the cost of amputating some essential cultural organ of identity.

Levinas declared "the essence of language is friendship and hospitality" (Levinas, 1979, p. 305) Thus, he lived as a guest in the "hospitable space" of the French language and made no fetish of his mother tongue. If the essence of language is expression, then no language had an inherent primacy and superiority—although clearly other, older languages stood as historically prior and hence fundamental media of expression: for philosophy, Greek, and for liturgy, Hebrew.

105. Glissant, 1997.
106. Charon, 2001; 2008, Charon et al., 2017; Kirmayer et al., 2023.
107. This ethics of alterity is central to the work of Levinas (1979, 1985, 1998, 2003b). See: Tauber, 1999; Clifton-Soderstrom, 2003.

## Chapter 9: Asklepian Dreams

1. Ackerknecht, 1943, pp. 43–44.
2. See: Sexson, 1982.
3. Siegler & Osmond, 1973.
4. Frank, 1961.
5. For accounts of shamanism, see: Ackerknecht, 1943; Atkinson, 1992; Eliade, 1964, Hultkrantz, 1992; Vitebsky, 2001. Hahn (1985) discusses physicians' accounts of their own illness experience that reveal varied personal and institutional stances. As he notes, "Among the ethnomedicines of the world, Biomedicine is distinguished by its insularity from the subject, or rather the object of its work. In contrast, anthropological review shows various ways in which patienthood, suffering, and therapy are reflexively incorporated within healing practices in other societies, rather than being kept apart" (p. 97).
6. This same logic lends authority to those with lived experience of mental health problems and underwrites the dynamics of many types of peer support, mutual aid, and self-help groups—though the wounded helper may not be

viewed as a healer but rather a fellow traveler, witness, and friend (Jackson, 2001).

7. Fabrega, 1979, p. 181.
8. Silverman, 1967.
9. Atkinson, 1992; Vitebsky, 2001.
10. Cramer, 1980; Lee & Kirmayer, 2023; but see: Luhrmann, Dulin, & Dzokoto, 2023.
11. Frank & Paris, 1987; Paris & Frank, 1983.
12. Prince, 1976, 1980. Though interested very broadly in the cultural roots of healing, Prince studied indigenous healing in Nigeria in the 1950s and edited an issue of the journal *Ethos* devoted to studies linking the efficacy of shamanic practice to modulation of endogenous opioid systems in the brain (Prince, 1982).
13. There is, of course, another approach to the problem of the healer's wounds that emphasizes the danger associated with unacknowledged and unresolved affliction. In this view, the wounded-healer is a threat to patients because his own affliction impairs his ability to function in a healing mode and may lead him to abuse his power. This literature considers problems of physician "burn out," substance use and addiction, as well as narcissism or other personality disorders. In addition to advocating for professional regulation and treatment of impaired clinicians, these concerns underwrite a larger concern with abuses of power in psychiatry, clinical psychology, and psychotherapy (Cvetovac & Adame, 2017; Ivey & Partington, 2014; Zerubavel & Wright, 2012).
14. In the context of biomedicine, ethos is partly shared through the wider cultural understanding of the institution of medicine but also conveyed through what has been called "the hidden curriculum" in training (Hafferty, 1998; Martimianakis et al., 2015).
15. This includes reactions that might be interpreted as countertransference in psychodynamic theory but that may simply represent appropriate feelings and responses to the patient in context (Spensley & Blacker, 1976).
16. See: De Rose, 2017; Weaver, 2001.
17. There is a lot going on in this use of the metaphor "constellate," which is common in Jungian or archetypal psychology. In effect, the relationship between therapist and patient itself constitutes a microsocial structure with affective qualities that gives rise to particular images. Like the constellations of astronomy, this is a pattern imposed on separate objects to organize them in terms of an image drawn from cultural knowledge or a mythic narrative. *Constellation*, then, has a dual temporality—an immediacy of perceptual affordances and a pattern brought into being by the imaginative gaze.

18. The terms are used by C. Jess Groesbeck (1975, 1978, 1980), who trained as both a Freudian and Jungian analyst and also wrote about shamanism as a model for healing (Groesbeck, 1989).
19. Comas-Diaz & Jacobsen, 1991.
20. Adams, 2019.
21. Edelstein & Edelstein, 1998; Majno, 1975.
22. This account of the myth paraphrases Graves (1960), Kerenyi (1968), and Meier (1967, 1989), who refer to the primary sources. For alternative versions see Gantz (1993); Edelstein and Edelstein (1998) collect all the relevant texts.
23. In later versions of the myth, Asklepios had five daughters: Aceso, Iase (or Laso), the healer, Panacea, with the power of universal healing through herbs, Aglaea, and Hygieia (who personified health) (Grimal, 1986).
24. Kerenyi, 1996; Doty, 1978. As trickster, Hermes is not only an interpreter but also a creator or inventor of culture and meaning (Hyde, 1998). In the Homeric Hymns, his comic irreverence and wile disarm Apollo (Boer, 1970). Hermes's connection to the underworld unnerves some medical commentators, who feel this is somehow antithetical to medicine which should be associated only with the one truth of rationality, light, and life (e.g., Wilcox & Witham, 2003). They see Asklepios as "the blameless physician," in contrast to Hermes, who is full of guile and culpability. Yet the ability to descend into darkness unscathed makes Hermes the guide of souls, not simply conveying mortals to their death, but also into fertile chaos and confusion—and back (Lopez-Pedraza, 2003). Hermes had *metis*—intuition, creativity, and inventiveness (Paris, 1990). The capacity to traverse or transgress boundaries is essential to his inventiveness. Hermetic healing, then, differs from Apollonian healing in that it involves ambiguity, darkness, trickery, polysemy, playfulness, and improvisation—all in the service of finding a balance among many potential meanings and possibilities rather than seeking one great truth. In contrast to the Apollonian authority signified by the doctor's white coat, Hermes might be depicted in checkered black and white, or as a clown in motley. The concern that such hermetic healing is problematic because it celebrates polysemy and ambiguity may result in hermeneutic injustice when it undercuts the process of poiesis and poetic truth.
25. Frank & Paris, 1987; Paris & Frank, 1983.
26. Ricouer (1970) discusses the centrality of this hermeneutics of suspicion in Freud as well as Nietzsche and Marx arguing that all three practiced "a method of interpretation which assumes that the literal or surface-level meaning of a text is an effort to conceal the political interests which are served by the text. The purpose of interpretation is to strip off the concealment, unmasking those interests" (p. 33). In psychoanalysis, this is

evident in the way that negation may be interpreted as secret or denied assent, so that saying "no" is viewed as really "yes." As Jay Haley (1969) argued, this interpretive strategy may be profoundly unsettling and disempowering unless and until patients are able to assert the primacy of their own voice and self-understanding. Orange (2011) discusses the clinical (and ethical) value of an alternate hermeneutics of trust, which serves a different kind of politics.

27. Dodds, 1951; Burkert, 1985.
28. Vitebsky, 2001. See Chapter 5.
29. Kerenyi, 1968, pp. 76–77.
30. Goranson et al., 2020.
31. Meier, 1967, p. 5.
32. Tomlinson, 1983. Wickkiser (2008) presents a very useful description of the cult of Asklepios in the context of Greek medicine based on textual sources as well as archaeological evidence.
33. Hammond & Scullard, 1970, p. 129.
34. Here is how Burkert (1985) describes the ritual context of incubation:

> The most oppressive crisis for the individual is illness. Many different gods or heroes are capable of sending illness in their wrath. Yet a special power to send and to banish sickness belongs of old to Apollo, the god of pestilence and healing, who is nearly identical with the healing song, the paean. The well preserved temple of Bassae testifies to the help of Apollo Epikourios in the plague epidemic about 430 BC. Later Apollo's son Asklepios proved his competence, particularly in dealing with the troubles of the individual, and thus overshadowed other healing gods and heroes. Nevertheless, even incubation in his sanctuary, embellished by many legends of Epidauros, is moulded upon the rhythm of sacrifice. First there is a three-day period of purity with abstinence from sexual intercourse, goat meat, cheese, and other items. Then preliminary offerings are due: garlanded with bay the sick person sacrifices an animal to Apollo, as well as cakes garlanded with olive twigs to various other gods. Next follows the sacrifice of a piglet to Asklepios on his altar, with an accompanying gift in money. Before the incubation in the evening three cakes are to be offered, two in the open air to Tyche and Mnemosyne, Success and Recollection, and one in the sleeping chamber to Themis, Right Order. The sick person keeps on his laurel wreath during incubation and then leaves it behind on his bed. Whoever has been restored to health renders his thanks to the god, as does the victor in a contest or the sailor rescued from the perils of the sea (p. 267).

35. Meier, 1967, 1989.
36. Jackson, 2001.
37. Brooke, 2015.
38. Jung, 1967; Ellenberger, 1970.
39. Following Wagner (1986), we could extend this autonomy of symbols into the social world, where they produce meaning through their use in practices.
40. This "taking fantasy seriously" is both an epistemic and moral stance, but it also reflects imaginative capacities that may vary across individuals in relation to personality traits of openness, absorption, and fantasy proneness (see: Benson, 1993; Lynn & Rhue, 1988).

41. A facsimile edition of *The Red Book* presents Jung's calligraphic manuscript reporting dreams and imaginative reveries along with transformative images, a translation of the text, and extensive editorial notes by historian Sonu Shamdasani (Jung, 2009).
42. This is evident in Jung's comments on neognostic and other spiritualist traditions. As Shamdasani (1998, p. 82) notes: "In 1918 Jung stated that 'development of reactivated contents of the unconscious' at the end of the last century represented by mesmerism and spiritualism led to Anthroposophy and Theosophy on the one hand, and on the other laid the foundations for French psychopathology and especially the school of hypnotism. It was from the latter that analytical psychology emerged. He contended that it: 'seeks to grasp scientifically the phenomena of the unconscious—the same apparitions which the theosophical-gnostic sects made accessible to the simple-minded in the form of portentous mysteries.'" The visionary encounter is suffused with numinous power and the participant risks inflation, mistaking the power of myth, image, and archetype for his own. This is where psychology comes to the rescue with its deflationary account of transcendental experience as a manifestation of the human psyche: "as Jung understood it, the critical psychological task was to overcome the experience of godlikeness, and precisely not to set oneself up as a psychoanalytic prophet or world-redeemer" (Shamdasani, 1998, p. 51).
43. *Archetypal psychology* is the term used by James Hillman (1975, 1983) for an approach that privileges the autonomy of symbols, fantasy, and imagination. This Jungian approach to symbols owes much to Hegel's aesthetics and contrasts with the views of Cassirer (2021), who emphasized the cultural historical roots of all symbols (Pietikainen, 1998), or with pragmatism which would locate meaning and aesthetic value in embodied experience and social use (Johnson, 2018; Shusterman, 2006). Some middle ground can be found through the recognition that meaning always emerges from the interplay of biological, social, and existential universals and cultural particulars. The meaning of an image or symbol must be unpacked in relation to its uses in and implications for people with unique histories in specific social situations or predicaments.
44. The use of oneself as case material in psychiatry is fraught with difficulty, not only because one is liable to accusations of narcissism or exhibitionism but also, more importantly, because one's self-understanding is always limited, and the use of self-generated and self-selected data to support one's own theories is both circular and suspect. These charges—and the persistent stigma of mental illness—make clinicians reluctant to reveal much about their own difficulties and to present their own "case" only obliquely in fragments or heavily disguised as the story of someone else (as Freud

apparently did on multiple occasions). My goal in presenting my own dreams here is explicitly pedagogical—to illustrate a developmental process and to model the value of clinicians acknowledging their own woundedness. I have found this type of sharing helpful in training psychiatric residents and psychotherapists, but it requires close attention to context and ongoing dialogue to ensure the message is clear and to acknowledge one's limitations and blindspots.

45. See: Jung, 1984; von Franz & Boa, 1988; Whitmont & Perera, 1989.
46. Kerenyi, 1968.
47. The embodied experience of language links words and touch: "Wounds that cannot be cured may be healed by narrative catharsis and 'carnal working through,' that is by 'word-touch'" (Kearney, 2018, p. 21).
48. Meier, 1967.
49. Sax, 2009. The domestic cat's relative independence (compared to dogs) creates the impression it is only partly tamed and still bears traces of its feral origins, contributing to our sense of its agency and alterity. In Meso-American traditions, the jaguar was a key symbol of spiritual power that figured in shamanic rites (Prechtel, 1998; Saunders, 2013; Stone, 2012).
50. The female witch provides a complementary archetype to that of the Wise Old Woman. In a sense, she is another facet of the maternal feminine—gone wrong (Jung, 1969; von Franz, 1972, 2017). Often depicted as a crone, she is a danger to humans because of her appeal to our appetites: sweets for children, sexual desire for adults, power for all. As a projection of the patriarchy, she embodies masculine vulnerability and anxieties (Hudson & Jacot, 1991; Kirmayer, 1992c). Historically, accusations of witchcraft served as effective ways to subjugate women and channel broader anxieties (Ben-Yehuda, 1980). Rhetorically, the practice continues in contemporary politics (Lim, 2009), testament to the enduring significance of this image. Naturally, the witch can be reappropriated as an image and possibility for spiritual and worldly power (Bovenschen et al., 1978; Luhrmann, 1991, 2001).
51. Needleman, 1985.
52. von Franz, 1975.
53. "[T]he 'child' distinguishes itself by deeds which point to the conquest of the dark" (Jung, 1969, p. 167). For the dilemma of overidentification with the child, see: von Franz, 1981.
54. Miller, 2008. The idea of a true self that persists despite the creation of a false self built in response to parental and communal expectations has a long history in Western traditions (Anscombe, 1989; Baumeister, 2019; Jongman-Sereno & Leary, 2019). Here TRUE SELF and FALSE SELF are metaphors for the way contradictions between individual desire or proclivities and social demands may be organized, experienced, and lived out. Authenticity, then,

means expressing one's true self or feelings. The dynamics of experiencing a false self reflect cultural concepts of the person and the social latitude given to articulating and expressing contradictory facets of identity. In cultures where responding appropriately to situations means maintaining harmonious relationships these dynamics take different form (Hwang & Chang, 2009; Puett & Gross-Low, 2016; Tu, 1985; Vanini & Williams, 2016).

55. Laing, 1965, 1990. See: Crossley, 1998. I wrote more about this patient in a chapter on insight in psychosis (Kirmayer, Corin, & Jarvis, 2004).
56. The white coat was adopted in the late nineteenth century by physicians who sought to distinguish themselves from the black robes associated with death and align themselves with laboratory science (Blumhagen, 1979).
57. Woodward, 2012.
58. Kerenyi, 1968.
59. Cleaver, 1969.
60. Adams, 2019. In the health care system where I worked at this time, there was a clear sense of the stratification and structural violence of race and class: the county hospital treated people who could not afford a private hospital or HMO.
61. See Kirmayer (2008b, 2015b) for discussions of the limits of empathy.
62. Meier, 1967, p. xv.
63. Kirmayer, 1988a.
64. Neihardt, 1979 (original publication 1932). DeMallie (1985) presents transcripts of the interviews on which the book was based. See Powers (1990) for a discussion of the origins of this account which cannot be taken as a simple transmission of traditional Amerindian tradition since it incorporates much of Black Elk's own Christian evangelical efforts in addition to Neihardt's own concerns. See Deloria (2009) for a comparison of Jungian and Lakota views that finds many affinities but points out the problems that arise from Jung's use of the trope of "the primitive," even when it is valorized as connected to some original knowledge or profound truth.
65. Neidhardt, 1979, pp. 204–205.
66. Lieber, 1979; Needleman, 1985.
67. Kolakowski, 1989.
68. Neidhardt, 1979, p. 128.
69. Reed, 1978, pp. 47–48.
70. Searles, 1975, p. 382.
71. Crossley, 1998.
72. Szasz, 1961. Szasz went on to espouse libertarian and reactionary politics (Goldstein, 1980). The broad-strokes critiques of antipsychiatry have given way to a different approach that appropriates the language of affliction ("mad" or "crazy") and uses it to assert the voice and epistemic authority of

people with lived experience of mental disorders (Arnaud & Gagné-Julien-, 2024; Reaume, 2021).

73. See Kirmayer, 1988a, for an extended discussion of this predicament and a forthcoming companion volume, *Unraveling the World-Knot: Mind Body Problems in Clinical Context.*
74. Guggenbühl-Craig, 1971, pp. 92ff.
75. Fiske, Henningsen, & Buyx, 2019.
76. Bayles, 1978.
77. Kleinman, 2019.
78. Neruda, 1969, p. 11.
79. Needleman, 1985.
80. Groesbeck & Taylor, 1977; Guggenbühl-Craig, 1971.
81. von Franz, 1975.
82. Calasso, 2001.
83. Jung, quoted in Hochheimer, 1969. Recognition of this necessary vulnerability of the healer led Jung to propose the idea of a training analysis during the early days of the International Psychoanalytic Society and to a concern with countertransference as a source of both positive and negative therapeutic effects (Sedgwick, 2016).

## Chapter 10: Epilogue: Ethics, Aesthetics, and Poiesis

1. Blumenberg, 2018, p. 18.
2. Derricotte, 1997, p. ix.
3. Kennedy, 2008.
4. Johnson, 2018. Shusterman (2006) provides an overview of the historical uses of the concept of "the aesthetic" as the result of the cultivation of particular human faculties, sensibilities (e.g., "taste"), and cultural conventions.
5. Braslow, 2013.
6. Woods, Hart, & Spandler, 2022.
7. Adeponle, Whitley, & Kirmayer, 2012.
8. Robcis, 2021.
9. Kirmayer, Gone, & Moses, 2014; Gone, 2023.
10. Whitbeck et al., 2004; Armenta et al., 2016.
11. Several types of circles are commonly discussed in the literature on Indigenous mental health (Kirmayer, Simpson, & Cargo, 2003): *talking circles*, in which people speak openly and listen to others' stories to begin to become aware of issues affecting the person and the community at large; *sharing circles*, in which a high degree of trust is established and people express painful emotions and are supported by others in the circle; *healing circles*, in which people work through memories of painful experiences; and *spiritual circles*, in which people

share their experiences of spirituality as a source of comfort and guidance. These protocols differ somewhat in their goals and in the types of narratives and level of disclosure they call for, but there is much overlap, and each can serve healing processes at both individual and collective levels.

12. Ross, 1996, 2014. In restorative justice, *sentencing circles* may be used to assess and reintegrate offenders who might otherwise be handled entirely within the mainstream legal and corrections system. An important example of the process was developed by the First Nations community of Hollow Water (Couture, 2001; Couture et al., 2001).
13. Couture, McGowan, & Couture, 2013, p. 284. Smudging is a purification ceremony that uses the smoke of sweetgrass or other sacred plants to cleanse body, mind, and place.
14. See: Comas-Díaz & Jacobsen, 2024; Mehl-Madrona & Mainguy, 2014; Williams & Vannini, 2016.
15. Mattingly, 1994; see also Herzfeld, 1986.
16. Sweetser, 2000; Fauconnier & Turner, 2008.
17. Frank, 2013; Kleinman, 1988b.
18. Good, 1993.
19. Schechtman, 2024.
20. Scheff, 1979; Laderman & Rosenman, 2016.
21. This is vividly illustrated in the work of artist Gilah Yelin Hirsch (Stein, 2023).
22. On the revitalization of joik as a cultural art form and emblem of collective identity, see: Aubinet, 2022; Hilder, 2012. Fjällgren's performance at his audition for the TV program can be viewed at: https://www.youtube.com/watch?v=i-T1ZhRmTzM. Videos of subsequent performances have also been posted and comments from listeners across the globe attest to the emotional power of the music. (See, for example: https://www.youtube.com/watch?v=s3cnqkXSdG8.)
23. The form of the song has similarities to other genres of lament, including Karelian lament in Finland (Silvonen & Stepanova, 2019), which may have borrowed elements from the joik tradition (Tolbert, 2007; Wilce, 2017). For discussions of how music can convey emotional meaning across cultures, see: Juslin, 2013; McCrae, 2021.
24. For art and the social world see: Hyde, 1983; for art as creative transgression and culture making, see: Hyde, 1998; on art as play, see: Nachmanovitch, 1991. For a discussion of flexibility in the efficacy and aesthetics of ritual healing, see: Hinton & Kirmayer, 2017.
25. Auerbach, 1953.
26. Hayot, 2012.
27. Critchley, 2005, p. 58–59. The quote is from Stevens, 2011.

28. Blumenberg, 2020. Unpacking the significance of the metaphors that constitute our ways of knowing is central to Blumenberg's (2010) work. Following the cultural, historical, and etymological trail of our metaphoric models of the world and constructions of experience reveals their recursive and self-sustaining structure (Koerner, 1993), as well as the underlying ontological assumptions and aesthetic aspirations, which are manifested in myth-making (Adams, 1991; Nicholls, 2015). This points to the potential for a phenomenology that is fully engaged with the history of ideas and the politics of imagination (Ifergan, 2015; Kirke, 2018).
29. Plato, 1961, Book VII, 741–752 (514a–520a).
30. Coetzee & Kurtz, 2015.
31. Gilchrist, 1969, p. 200. Jacob Bronowski claimed that Blake experienced "eidetic images," that is, his images were equivalent to visual percepts, but here Blake seems clear about the difference.
32. Lister, 1975.
33. William Blake, Letter to William Hayley, dated May 6, 1800, cited in Keynes, 1980.
34. Hagstrum, 1964, p. 20.
35. Luhrmann, 2020.
36. Veissière, 2016.
37. Allowing a place for imagery, reverie, and visionary experience is central to archetypal psychology. "The autonomy of fantasy is the soul's last refuge of dignity" (Hillman, 1975, p. 39). For more on imaginal dialogues and the ontology of imagination in Jungian psychology, see: Hillman, 1983; Avens, 1980; Hannah, 1981.
38. Yeats, 1910, pp. xii–xiii (original 1893).
39. Yeats, 1961, p. 112 ("William Blake and the imagination," original 1897).
40. Ackroyd, 1996; Thompson, 1994.
41. For a Jungian perspective on Blake's visionary experience, see: Singer, 2000.
42. See Goleman, 1977.
43. In a Tibetan thangka showing the Healing Buddha as the Master of Remedies, he is depicted at the center of the medicinal City of Irresistible Beauty. To the south is the Piercing Mountain where plants with hot and sharp qualities grow, including pomegranate, pepper, and cinnamon. These are effective in curing illnesses caused by cold. To the north, we find Snow Mountain, with cooling medicines, including white sandalwood, camphor, eaglewood, gentian, and licorice. To the east, on Fragrant Mountain, are the many varieties of myrobalan fruit, one of which is a panacea. On Malaya Mountain, to the west, are found the six primary ingredients of Tibetan medicine (nutmeg, clove, cardamom, saffron, bamboo pith, and cubeb), in addition to healing rocks and minerals (Avedon, 1998, 74–75).

44. Birnbaum, 1979, p. 107.
45. Scholem, 1961.
46. Rojtman, 1998, p. 136
47. Idel, 2002, p. 76.
48. Celan, 2020. "Aesthetics thus demands hiddenness and rewards it, ethics demands disclosure and punishes hiddenness" (Celan & Joris, 2017, p. 405).
49. Benson, 1993.
50. Indeed, those who valorize myth, aesthetics, and poeisis as paths to ultimate knowledge or gnosis may be especially vulnerable to the rhetoric of fascism with its inhuman ideals and profound failures of empathy. One thinks first of Heidegger (Wolin, 2022), but less catastrophic versions can be found in the personal histories of Jung, Eliade, and Campbell (Ellwood, 1999). Of course, there may be no direct connection: others have been guided by a poetic sensibility toward an astute and compassionate stance at times of political turmoil. And many others have fallen into the madness of genocide without any special sensitivity or responsiveness to the aesthetics of language. Still, it is worth considering what links there may be between a mentality that puts poetics at the center of thought, and the vulnerability to kinds of philosophical idealism that readily embrace (or fail to inoculate against) political extremism and inhumanity. As Levinas (1985, 1998) argued, explicit commitment to the ethical imperative to recognize and care for the other may be an essential bulwark against such violence.
51. Glissant, 1997. As Drabinski puts it, for Glissant:

    > Caribbeanness is *tout-monde*, not as an aesthetic or ethical idea or ideal, but as a direct description of the material histories and memories of the archipelago. Contact is beginning, however violent, and the aftermath is the ambivalent mixture of unthinkable sadness and world-changing depth of meaningfulness (Drabinski, 2019, p. ix).

52. Glissant, 2020b, p. 68.
53. "Opacity names both how and why meaning and cultural production were historically hidden from the colonizer in acts of resistance, whether in the linguistic and cultural cases of creole and pidgin (pace Césaire and Fanon) or, in more complex operations, the development of Afro-Caribbean identities outside the limits of the colonial gaze" (Drabinski, 2019, p. 16).
54. Glissant, 2020b.
55. Alexander, 2009.
56. Kirmayer, Guzder, & Rousseau, 2014.
57. Auster, 2008.
58. Calvino, 1981.
59. Auster, 2013, p. 137. Hayot (2012) speaks of the *physics* of worldedness.

60. Taussig (2018) explores how this tension between mimesis and alterity has served colonialism but also provides opportunities for resistance and revelation.
61. The philosophical history of the "language animal" metaphor is explored by Charles Taylor (2016). I borrow "poetic naturalism" from Sean Carroll (2017), who gives us "the big picture" of the physicists' view of the world but allows that human understanding of that world is necessarily mediated by metaphors. He notes: "The poet Muriel Rukeyser once wrote, 'The universe is made of stories, not atoms.' That is absolutely correct. There is more to the world than what happens; there are the ways we make sense of it by telling its story. The vocabulary we use is not handed to us from outside; it's ultimately a matter of our choice" (p. 19). While Carroll embraces metaphor as a tool for knowing, he nevertheless assumes that all of the dynamics of human lives that appear to be shaped by stories ultimately can be given an account in terms of basic physics. There are reasons to think, however, that the ways we make sense of the world become part of its dynamics. Human systems involve emergent dynamics related to our coevolutionary history in which language and culture allow us to construct imaginary realms, explore counterfactual worlds and possible scenarios, and bind together experiences across long stretches of time to create new causal paths or connections. To capture these dynamics, a physical account must include the historically contingent paths and social structures that have led to our languages and cultural practices.
62. Auster, 1988, p. 153.
63. The physicist Richard Feynman observed that knowing about how the refraction of light gives rise to a rainbow does not lessen aesthetic appreciation but increases it, adding layers of meaning (Mlodinow, 2011)—this is in every way analogous to how knowledge of an aesthetic tradition in music, painting or other arts can enrich and intensify aesthetic experience.

> The beauty of images is situated in front of things, that of ideas behind them. So that the first sort of beauty ceases to astonish us as soon as we have reached the things themselves, but the second is something that we understand only when we have passed beyond them (Bloom, 2019, p. 496).

64. Zwicky, 2014; Dickinson & Goulet, 2010. Again, Cassirer saw this path.

> What poetry expresses is neither the mythic word-picture of gods and daemons, nor the logical truth of abstract determinations and relations. The world of poetry stands apart from both, as a world of illusion and fantasy—but it is just in this mode of illusion that the realm of pure feeling can find utterance, and can therewith attain its full and concrete actualization. Word and mythic image, which once confronted the human mind as hard realistic powers, have now cast off all reality and effectuality; they have become a light, bright ether in which the spirit can move without let or hindrance. This liberation is achieved not because the mind throws aside the sensuous forms of word and image, but in that it uses them both his organs of its own, and thereby recognizes them for what they really are: forms of its own self-revelation (Cassirer, 1946, p. 99).

65. Significantly, Moore borrowed this image from Williams Carlos Williams in a poem about the interiority of someone reflecting on a car crash (Lourdeaux, 1982)—and used it to insist on the immediacy and presence that images must have to render language poetic.
66. Orange, 2011.
67. Otis, 2019; Rosaldo, 1980.
68. Hickling, 2021.
69. Kirmayer, 2015b.

# *References*


Abramovitch, H., & Kirmayer, L. J. (2003). The relevance of Jungian psychology for cultural psychiatry. *Transcultural Psychiatry*, *40*(2), 155–163.

Ackerknecht, E. H. (1943). Psychopathology, primitive medicine and primitive culture. *Bulletin of the History of Medicine*, *14*(1), 30–67.

Ackroyd, P. (1996). *Blake*. Random House.

Adams, D. (1991). Metaphors for mankind: The development of Hans Blumenberg's anthropological metaphorology. *Journal of the History of Ideas*, *52*(1), 152–166.

Adams, M. V. (2019). *The multicultural imagination: "Race," color, and the unconscious*. Routledge.

Aden, R. C. (1994). Back to the garden: Therapeutic place metaphor in *Field of dreams*. *Southern Journal of Communication*, *59*(4), 307–317.

Adeponle, A., Whitley, R., & Kirmayer, L. J. (2012). Cultural contexts and constructions of recovery. In A. Rudnick (Ed.), *Recovery of people with mental illness: Philosophical and related perspectives* (pp. 109–132). Oxford University Press.

Ader, R., Cohen, N., & Felten, D. (1995). Psychoneuroimmunology: Interactions between the nervous system and the immune system. *The Lancet*, *345*, 99–103.

Adolphs, R. (2002). Recognizing emotion from facial expressions: psychological and neurological mechanisms. *Behavioral and Cognitive Neuroscience Reviews*, *1*(1), 21–62.

Afana, A.-H., Pedersen, D., Rønsbo, H., & Kirmayer, L. J. (2010). "Endurance is to be shown at the first blow": Social representations and reactions to traumatic experiences in the Gaza strip. *Traumatology*, *16*(4), 73–84.

Agamben, G. (1999). *Remnants of Auschwitz: The witness and the archive*. MIT Press.

Ahmed, S. (2013). *The cultural politics of emotion*. Routledge.

Ahmed, A. (2024). Disclosure imperatives and women's subjectivities in an emergent culture of sexual trauma testimony. *Ethos*, *52*(4), 431–448. https://doi.org/10.1111/etho.12442

Alarcón, R. D., & Frank, J. B. (Eds.). (2011). *The psychotherapy of hope: The legacy of persuasion and healing*. Johns Hopkins University Press.

Alessandri, M. (2023). *Night vision: Seeing ourselves through dark moods*. Princeton University Press.

Alexander, L. (1981). The double-bind between dialysis patients and their health practitioners. In L. Eisenberg & A. Kleinman (Eds.), *The relevance of social science for medicine* (pp. 307–329). Kluwer.

Alexander, M. (2009). *Poetics of dislocation*. University of Michigan Press.

Allen, D. B. (Ed.). (2018). *Culture and self: Philosophical and religious perspectives, East and West*. Routledge.

Allard-Tremblay, Y., & Coburn, E. (2023). The flying heads of settler colonialism; or the ideological erasures of indigenous peoples in political theorizing. *Political Studies*, *71*(2), 359–378.

Almeida, M. W. de Barbarosa (1990). Symmetry and entropy: Mathematical metaphors in the work of Levi-Strauss. *Current Anthropology*, *31*(4), 367–385.

Alverson, H. (1994). *Semantics and experience: Universal metaphors of time in English, Mandarin, Hindi, and Sesotho*. Johns Hopkins University Press.

American Psychiatric Association. (2022). *Diagnostic and statistical manual, edition 5 text revision (DSM-5-TR)*. American Psychiatric Association.

Amis, M. (1991). *Time's arrow or the nature of the offence*. Penguin Books.

Amossy, R. (2001). Ethos at the crossroads of disciplines: Rhetoric, pragmatics, sociology. *Poetics Today*, *22*(1), 1–23.

Andreasen, N. C. (2007). DSM and the death of phenomenology in America: An example of unintended consequences. *Schizophrenia Bulletin*, *33*(1), 108–112.

Ang, B., Horowitz, M., & Moncrieff, J. (2022). Is the chemical imbalance an "urban legend"? An exploration of the status of the serotonin theory of depression in the scientific literature. *SSM-Mental Health*, *2*, 100098.

Anissimov, M. (1998). *Primo Levi: The tragedy of an optimist*. Overlook Press.

Annoni, M., & Blease, C. (2018). A critical (and cautiously optimistic) appraisal of Moerman's "meaning response." *Perspectives in Biology and Medicine*, *61*(3), 379–387.

Anscombe, R. (1989). The myth of the true self. *Psychiatry*, *52*: 209–217.

Appiah, K. A. (2017). *Cosmopolitanisms*. New York University Press.

Arandia, I. R., & Di Paolo, E. A. (2021). Placebo from an enactive perspective. *Frontiers in Psychology*, *12*, 1884.

Arandia, I. R., & Di Paolo, E. A. (2022). On symptom perception, placebo effects, and the Bayesian brain. *Pain*, *163*(4), 660118.

Armenta, B. E., Whitbeck, L. B., & Habecker, P. N. (2016). The Historical Loss Scale: Longitudinal measurement equivalence and prospective links to anxiety among North American Indigenous adolescents. *Cultural Diversity and Ethnic Minority Psychology*, 22(1), 1–10.

Armstrong, P. B. (2020). *Stories and the brain: The neuroscience of narrative*. Johns Hopkins University Press.

Arnaud, S., & Gagné-Julien, A. M. (2024). The new self-advocacy activism in psychiatry: Toward a scientific turn. *Philosophical Psychology*, 37(8), 2623–2646.

Aron, A. (1992). *Testimonio*, a bridge between psychotherapy and sociotherapy *Women & Therapy*, *13*(3), 173–189.

Arora, K., & Ananthanarayanan, R. (2022). Healing through the Mahabharata. In C. Holmwood, S. Jennings, & S. Jacksties (Eds.), *Routledge international handbook of therapeutic stories and storytelling* (pp. 101–110). Routledge.

Asma, S. T. (2017). *The evolution of imagination*. University of Chicago Press.

Astill Wright, L., Horstmann, L., Holmes, E. A., & Bisson, J. I. (2021). Consolidation/reconsolidation therapies for the prevention and treatment of PTSD and re-experiencing: A systematic review and meta-analysis. *Translational Psychiatry*, *11*(1), 453.

Atkinson, J. M. (1992). Shamanisms today. *Annual Review of Anthropology*, *21*, 307–330.

Atwood, M. (2011). *In other worlds: SF and the human imagination*. Anchor.

Aubinet, S. (2022). *Why Sámi Sing: Knowing through melodies in northern Norway*. Routledge.

Auerbach, E. (1953). *Mimesis: The representation of reality in Western literature*. Princeton University Press.

Auster, P. (1988). *The invention of solitude*. Penguin Books.

Auster, P. (2008). *Man in the dark: A novel*. Henry Holt and Company.

Auster, P. (2013). *Conversations with Paul Auster*. University Press of Mississippi.

Austin, J. L. (1975). *How to do things with words*. Oxford University Press.

Avedon, J. F. (1998). *The Buddha's art of healing: Tibetan paintings rediscovered*. Rizzoli International Publications.

Avens, R. (1980). *Imagination is reality: Western nirvana in Jung, Hillman, Barfield, and Cassirer*. Spring.

Avruch, K. (2010). Truth and reconciliation commissions: Problems in transitional justice and the reconstruction of identity. *Transcultural Psychiatry*, *47*(1), 33–49.

Bachelard, G. (1964). *The psychoanalysis of fire*. Beacon Press.

Bachelard, G. (1969). *The poetics of space* (M. Jolas, Trans.). Beacon Press.

Bachelard, G. (1971). *The poetics of reverie: Childhood, language, and the cosmos*. Beacon Press.

Bachelard, G. (1983). *Water and dreams: An essay on the imagination of matter*. Dallas Institute of Humanities and Culture.

Bachelard, G. (1987). *On poetic imagination and reverie: Selections from Gaston Bachelard* Spring Publications.

Bachelard, G. (2013). *Intuition of the instant*. Northwestern University Press.

Bacon, F. (2000/1620). *The new organon*. Cambridge University Press.

Bakhtin, M. M. (2010). *The dialogic imagination: Four essays*. University of Texas Press.

Bal, M. (2017). *Narratology: Introduction to the theory of narrative*. University of Toronto Press.

Ball, P. (2022). *The modern myths: Adventures in the machinery of the popular imagination*. University of Chicago Press.

Balzer, M. M. (1996). Flights of the sacred: Symbolism and theory in Siberian shamanism. *American Anthropologist*, *98*(2), 305–318.

Barasch, M. (1976). *Gestures of despair in medieval and early Renaissance art.* New York University Press.

Barbeau, M. (1958). *Medicine-men on the North Pacific coast.* King's Printer.

Barbieri, M. (2009). A short history of biosemiotics. *Biosemiotics, 2*(2), 221–245.

Barfield, O. (1973). *Poetic diction: A study in meaning.* Wesleyan University Press.

Barker, P. (2013). *Using metaphors in psychotherapy.* Routledge.

Baron-Cohen, S. (1995). *Mindblindness: An essay on autism and theory of mind.* MIT Press.

Baron-Cohen, S., & Harrison, J. E. (Eds.). (1997). *Synaesthesia: Classic and contemporary readings.* Blackwell.

Barrett, L. F. (2013). Psychological construction: The Darwinian approach to the science of emotion. *Emotion Review, 5*(4), 379–389.

Barrett, L. F. (2017). *How emotions are made: The secret life of the brain.* Houghton Mifflin Harcourt.

Barrett R. J. (1998). The "schizophrenic" and the liminal persona in modern society. *Culture, Medicine and Psychiatry, 22*, 465–494.

Barsalou, L. W. (2008). Grounded cognition. *Annual Review of Psychology, 59*, 617–645.

Barsalou, L. W. (2010). Grounded cognition: Past, present, and future. *Topics in Cognitive Science, 2*(4), 716–724.

Barsalou, L. W. (2016). Processes that mediate stimuli and responses make human action possible. In A. K. Engel, K. J. Friston, & D. Kragic (Eds.), *The pragmatic turn: Toward action-oriented views in cognitive science* (pp. 81–99). MIT Press.

Barsalou, L. W. (2020). Challenges and opportunities for grounding cognition. *Journal of Cognition, 3*(1), 1–24.

Barsalou, L. W. (2023). Implications of grounded cognition for conceptual processing across cultures. *Topics in Cognitive Science, 15*, 648–656.

Bartholomew, R. E., & Sirois, F. (2001). Occupational mass psychogenic illness: A transcultural perspective. *Transcultural Psychiatry, 38*(1), 495–524.

Bartlett, F. C. (1932). *Remembering.* Cambridge University Press.

Bartley, W. W., III (1985). *Wittgenstein* (2nd ed.). Open Court.

Bartrop, R. W., Luckhurst, E., Lazarus, L., Kiloh, L. G., & Penny, R. (1977). Depressed lymphocyte function after bereavement. *The Lancet*, 834–836.

Basso, K. H. (1996). *Wisdom sits in places: Landscape and language among the Western Apache.* University of New Mexico Press.

Bateson, G. (1972). *Steps to an ecology of mind.* Ballantine Books.

Bauman, Z. (2007). *Liquid times: Living in an age of uncertainty.* Polity Press.

Bauman, Z. (2013). *Culture in a liquid modern world.* John Wiley & Sons.

Bauman, Z., & Leoncini, T. (2018). *Born liquid.* John Wiley & Sons.

Baumeister, R. F. (2019). Stalking the true self through the jungles of authenticity: Problems, contradictions, inconsistencies, disturbing findings—And a possible way forward. *Review of General Psychology, 23*(1), 143–154.

Bayles, M. D. (1978). Physicians as body mechanics. In J. W. Davis, B. Hoffmaster, & S. Shorten (Eds.), *Contemporary issues in biomedical ethics* (pp. 167–177). Humana Press.

Bazzi, S., Fiszbein, M., & Gebresilasse, M. (2020). Frontier culture: The roots and persistence of "rugged individualism" in the United States. *Econometrica, 88*(6), 2329–2368.

Becker, D. L. (2012). *Many subtle channels: in praise of potential literature*. Harvard University Press.

Behrouzan, O., & Fischer, M. M. J. (2015). Behaves like a rooster and cries like a (four-eyed) canine: The politics and poetics of depression and psychiatry in Iran. In A. Hinton & D. Hinton (Eds.), *Genocide and mass violence: Memory, symptom, and recovery* (pp. 105–135). Cambridge University Press.

Beiser, M. (1999). *Strangers at the gate: The "boat people's" first ten years in Canada*. University of Toronto Press.

Beiser, M. (2009). Resettling refugees and safeguarding their mental health: Lessons learned from the Canadian Refugee Resettlement Project. *Transcultural Psychiatry, 46*(4), 539–583.

Beiser, M., & Hyman, I. (1997). Refugees' time perspective and mental health. *American Journal of Psychiatry, 154*(7), 996–1002.

Bellah, R. N., Madsen, R., Sullivan, W. M., Swidler, A., & Tipton, S. M. (1985). *Habits of the heart: Individualism and commitment in American life*. University of California Press.

Belli, R. F., & Loftus, E. F. (1994). Recovered memories of childhood abuse: A source monitoring perspective. In S. J. Lynn & J. W. Rhue (Eds.), *Dissociation: Clinical and theoretical perspectives* (pp. 415–433). Guilford Press.

Bellos, D. (2010). *Georges Perec: A life in words*. Random House.

Benedetti, F. (2020). *Placebo effects: Understanding the mechanisms in health and disease*. Oxford University Press.

Benedetti, F., Frisaldi, E., & Shaibani, A. (2022). Thirty years of neuroscientific investigation of placebo and nocebo: the interesting, the good, and the bad. *Annual Review of Pharmacology and Toxicology, 62*, 323–340.

BenEzer, G. (2003). *The Ethiopian Jewish exodus: Narratives of the journey*. Routledge.

BenEzer, G. (2007). Trauma, culture, and myth: Narratives of the Ethiopian Jewish exodus. In L. J. Kirmayer, R. Lemelson, & M. Barad (Eds.), *Understanding trauma: Integrating biological, clinical, and cultural perspectives* (pp. 382–403). Cambridge University Press.

Benish, S. G., Quintana, S., & Wampold, B. E. (2011). Culturally adapted psychotherapy and the legitimacy of myth: a direct-comparison meta-analysis. *Journal of Counseling Psychology, 58*(3), 279–289.

Benjamin, W. (1968). *Illuminations: Essays and reflections*. Schocken Books.

Benjamin, W. (2002). *The storyteller*. NYRB Press.

Benson, C. (1993). *The absorbed self: Pragmatism, psychology and aesthetic experience*. Harvester Wheatsheaf.

Ben-Yehuda, N. (1980). The European witch craze of the 14th to 17th centuries: A sociologist's perspective. *American Journal of Sociology*, 86(1), 1–31.

Berger, B. M. (1995). *An essay on culture: Symbolic structure and social structure*. University of California.

Berger, H., Jr. (1987). Bodies and texts. *Representations, 17*, 144–166.

Bergin, T. G., & Fisch, M. H. (Eds.). (1970). *The new science of Giambattista Vico*. Cornell University Press.

Bergman, I., & Östlund, L. (2022). A sacred tree in the boreal forest: A narrative about a Sami shaman, her tree, and the forest landscape. *Human Ecology, 50*(6), 1023–1033.

Berman, N. (1978). Coover's "Universal Baseball Association": Play as personalized myth. *Modern Fiction Studies, 24*(2), 209–222.

Berrios, G. E., & Marková, I. S. (2015). Toward a new epistemology of psychiatry. In L. J. Kirmayer, R. Lemelson, & C. A. Cummings (Eds.), *Re-visioning psychiatry: Cultural phenomenology, critical neuroscience, and global mental health* (pp. 41–64). Cambridge University Press.

Bharati, A. (1985). The self in Hindu thought and action. In A. J. Marsella, G. DeVos, & F. L. K. Hsu (Eds.), *Culture and self: Asian and Western perspectives* (pp. 185–230). Tavistock Publications.

Bhugra, D., Ventriglio, A., Till, A., & Malhi, G. (2015). Colour, culture and placebo response. *International Journal of Social Psychiatry, 61*(6), 615–617.

Bigelow, A. E. (2003). The development of joint attention in blind infants. *Development and psychopathology, 15*(2), 259–275.

Birnbaum, R. (1979). *The healing Buddha*. Shambhala

Black, M. (1962). *Models and metaphors*. Cornell University Press.

Black, M. (1993). More about metaphor. In A. Ortony (Ed.), *Metaphor and thought* (2nd ed., pp 19–41). Cambridge University Press.

Blake, W. (1975). *The marriage of heaven and hell*. Oxford University Press.

Blakemore, S.-J., Smith, J., Steel, R., Johnstone, E. C., & Frith, C. D. (2000). The perception of self-produced sensory stimuli in patients with auditory hallucinations and passivity experiences: Evidence for a breakdown in self- monitoring. *Psychological Medicine, 30*, 1131–1139.

Blanchot, M. (1986). *The writing of the disaster* [*L'ecriture du désastre*]. (A. Smock, Trans.). University of Nebraska Press.

Bleakley, A. (2017). *Thinking with metaphors in medicine: The state of the art*. Taylor & Francis.

Bleakley, A., & Neilson, S. (2022). *Poetry in the clinic: Towards a lyrical medicine*. Routledge

Bloch, M. (1989). *The royal touch: Monarchy and Miracles in Medieval France and England* (J. E. Anderson, Trans.). Dorset Press.

Bloom, H. (2019). *Possessed by memory: The inward light of criticism*. Vintage.

Bloor, D. (1983). *Wittgenstein: A social theory of knowledge*. MacMillan.

Blouw, P., Solodkin, E., Thagard, P., & Eliasmith, C. (2016). Concepts as semantic pointers: A framework and computational model. *Cognitive Science, 40*(5), 1128–1162.

Blumenberg, H. (1985). *Work on myth* (R. M. Wallace, Trans.). MIT Press.

Blumenberg, H. (1997). *Shipwreck with spectator: Paradigm of a metaphor for existence*. MIT Press.

Blumenberg, H. (2010). *Paradigms for a metaphorology*. Cornell University Press.

Blumenberg, H. (2018). *Lions*. Seagull Books London Limited.

Blumenberg, H. (2020). *History, metaphors, fables: A Hans Blumenberg reader*. Cornell University Press.

Blumhagen, D. W. (1979). The doctor's white coat: The image of the physician in modern America. *Annals of Internal Medicine*, *91*, 111–116.

Bly, R. (1986). *When grapes turn to wine: Versions of Rumi*. Yellow Moon Press.

Boer, C. (1970). *The Homeric hymns*. Swallow Press.

Bokeria, L., Henson, R. N., & Mok, R. M. (2021). Map-like representations of an abstract conceptual space in the human brain. *Frontiers in Human Neuroscience*, *15*, 620056.

Bolles, R. C., & Fanselow, M. S. (1980). A perceptual-defensive-recuperative model of fear and pain. *Behavioral and Brain Sciences*, *3*(2), 291–301.

Bolt, R. (1960). *A man for all seasons*. Heinemann Educational Books.

Borch-Jacobsen, M. (2014). *Remembering Anna O.: A century of mystification*. Routledge.

Boroditsky, L. (2011). How languages construct time. In S. Dehaene & E. Brannon (Eds.), *Space, time and number in the brain: Searching for the foundations of mathematical thought* (pp. 333–341). Academic Press.

Boroditsky, L. (2018). Language and the construction of time through space. *Trends in Neurosciences*, *41*(10), 651–653.

Boss, P. (1999). *Ambiguous loss: Learning to live with unresolved grief*. Harvard University Press.

Bouizegarene, N., Ramstead, M. J., Constant, A., Friston, K. J., & Kirmayer, L. J. (2024). Narrative as active inference: An integrative account of cognitive and social functions in adaptation. *Frontiers in Psychology*, *15*, 1345480.

Bourdieu, P. (1990). *The logic of practice*. Stanford University Press.

Bourdieu, P. (1991). *Language and symbolic power*. Harvard University Press.

Bourdieu, P. (1998). *Practical reason: On the theory of action*. Stanford University Press.

Bovenschen, S., Blackwell, J., Moore, J., & Weckmueller, B. (1978). The contemporary witch, the historical witch and the witch myth: The witch, subject of the appropriation of nature and object of the domination of nature. *New German Critique* (15), 83–119.

Bouwsma, O. K (1986). *Wittgenstein: Conversations 1949–1951*. Hackett Publishing Co.

Bowdle, B. F., & Gentner, D. (2005). The career of metaphor. *Psychological Review*, *112*(1), 193.

Bowes, A., & Katz, A. (2015). Metaphor creates intimacy and temporarily enhances theory of mind. *Memory & Cognition*, *43*, 953–963.

Bowlby, J. (1988). *A secure base: Parent-child attachment and healthy human development*. Basic Books.

Boyd, R. (1979). What is "metaphor" a metaphor for? In A. Ortony (Ed.), *Metaphor and thought* (pp. 481–533). Cambridge University Press.

Boyd, B. (1985). *Nabokov's Ada: The place of consciousness*. Ardis.

Boyd, B. (1991). *Vladimir Nabokov: The American years*. Princeton University Press.

Boyd, B. (2001). *Nabokov's "Pale Fire": The magic of artistic discovery*. Princeton University Press.

Boyd, R. (1993). Metaphor and theory change: What is metaphor a metaphor for? In A. Ortony (Ed.), *Metaphor and thought* (2nd ed.) (pp. 481–532). Cambridge University Press.

Boyer, P. (1986). The "empty" concepts of traditional thinking: a semantic and pragmatic description. *Man*, 21, 50–64.

Bradley, L. A., Richter, J. E., Pulliam, T. J., Haile, J. M., Scarinci, I. C., Schan, C. A., . . . & Salley, A. N. (1993). The relationship between stress and symptoms of gastroesophageal reflux: The influence of psychological factors. *American Journal of Gastroenterology*, *88*(1): 11–18.

Bragato, F. F., & Gordon, L. R. (2017). Dehumanization and selective violation of human rights under the logic of coloniality. In F. F. Bragato & L. R. Gordon (Eds.), *Geopolitics and decolonization: Perspectives from the Global South* (pp. 13–30). Rowman & Littlefield.

Brant Castellano, M., Archibald, L., & DeGagné, M. (Eds.). (2008). *From truth to reconciliation: Transforming the legacy of residential schools*. Aboriginal Healing Foundation.

Braslow, J. T. (2013). The manufacture of recovery. *Annual Review of Clinical Psychology*, 9, 781–809.

Brass, G. M. (2008). Respecting the medicines: Narrating an Aboriginal identity. In L. J. Kirmayer & G. G. Valaskakis (Eds.), *Healing traditions: The mental health of Aboriginal peoples in Canada* (pp. 355–380). University of British Columbia Press.

Brave Heart, M. Y. H., & DeBruyn, L. M. (1998). The American Indian holocaust: Healing historical unresolved grief. *American Indian and Alaska Native Mental Health Research 8*(2), 56–78.

Brave Heart, M. Y. H., Chase, J., Elkins, J., & Altschul, D. (2011). Historical trauma among Indigenous peoples of the Americas: Concepts, research, and clinical considerations. *Journal of Psychoactive Drugs*, *43*(4), 282–290.

Brette, R. (2022). Brains as computers: Metaphor, analogy, theory or fact?. *Frontiers in Ecology and Evolution*, 10, 878729.

Brewin, C. R. (2020). Tilting at windmills: Why attacks on repression are misguided. *Perspectives on Psychological Science*, 1745691620927674.

Briggs, J. L. (1971). *Never in anger: Portrait of an Eskimo family*. Harvard University Press.

Brooke, R. (2015). *Jung and phenomenology*. Routledge.

Brooks, P. (2022). *Seduced by story: The use and abuse of narrative*. NYRB Press.

Brounéus, K. (2010). The trauma of truth telling: Effects of witnessing in the Rwandan gacaca courts on psychological health. *Journal of Conflict Resolution*, *54*(3), 408–437.

Brown, D. (2014). *If you build it . . . : A book about fathers, fate and Field of dreams* Elsie Jean Books.

Brown, D. E. (2004). Human universals, human nature and human culture. *Daedalus, 133*(4), 47–54.

Bruner, J. S. (1990). *Acts of meaning*. Harvard University Press.

Bruner, J. S. (2003). *Making stories: Law, literature, life*. Harvard University Press.

Bruner, J. S. (2004). The narrative creation of self. In L. E. Angus & J. McLeod (Eds.), *The handbook of narrative and psychotherapy: Practice, theory, and research* (pp. 3–14). Sage.

Brunet, A., Saumier, D., Liu, A., Streiner, D. L., Tremblay, J., & Pitman, R. K. (2018). Reduction of PTSD symptoms with pre-reactivation propranolol therapy: A randomized controlled trial. *American Journal of Psychiatry, 175*(5), 427–433.

Buchbinder, M. (2015). *All in your head: Making sense of pediatric pain*. University of California Press.

Bueno-Gómez, N. (2017). Conceptualizing suffering and pain. *Philosophy, Ethics, and Humanities in Medicine, 12*, 1–11.

Burkert, W. (1985). *Greek religion*. Basil Blackwell.

Burnside, S. (2006). Senselessness in Paul Celan's *Mohn und Gedächtns. German Life and Letters, 59*(1), 140–150.

Butler, O. E. (2012). *Lilith's brood: The complete Xenogenesis Trilogy*. Open Road Media.

Byrne, A., Morton, J., & Salmon, P. (2001). Defending against patients' pain: A qualitative analysis of nurses' responses to children's postoperative pain. *Journal of Psychosomatic Research*, 50, 69–76.

Calasso, R. (1993). *The marriage of Cadmus and harmony*. Alfred A. Knopf.

Calasso, R. (2001). *Literature and the gods*. Alfred A. Knopf.

Calvino, I. (1977). *The castle of crossed destinies*. Harcourt Brace Jovanovich.

Calvino, I. (1981). *If on a winter's night a traveler*. Houghton Mifflin Harcourt.

Cameron, L. (2008). Metaphor and talk. In R. W. Gibbs, Jr. (Ed.), *The Cambridge handbook of metaphor and thought* (pp. 197–211). Cambridge University Press.

Cameron, L., & Low, G. (1999). *Researching and applying metaphor*. Cambridge University Press.

Campbell, J. (1984). *The way of the animal powers* (*Historical atlas of world mythology*, Vol. 1). Times Books.

Caparos, S., Rutembesa, E., Habimana, E., & Blanchette, I. (2020). The psychological correlates of transitional justice in Rwanda: A long-term assessment. *Psychological Trauma: Theory, Research, Practice, and Policy, 12*(7), 774–784. https://doi.org/10.1037/tra0000583.

Capps, L., & Ochs, E. (1995). *Constructing panic: The discourse of agoraphobia*. Harvard University Press.

Caravà, M. (2024). Norm-induced forgetting: When social norms induce us to forget. *Philosophical Psychology*, 1–23.

Carel, H., & Kidd, I. J. (2014). Epistemic injustice in healthcare: a philosophical analysis. *Medicine, Health Care and Philosophy, 17*(4), 529–540.

Carroll, S. (2017). *The big picture: On the origins of life, meaning, and the universe itself.* Penguin.

Cascio, C. J., Moore, D., & McGlone, F. (2019). Social touch and human development. *Developmental Cognitive Neuroscience*, *35*, 5–11.
Casey, C. (2015). Remembering and ill health in post-invasion Kuwait: Topographies, collaborations, mediations. In A. Hinton & D. Hinton (Eds.), *Genocide and mass violence: Memory, symptom and recovery* (pp. 83–104). Cambridge University Press.
Casey, C. (2018). Sensory politics and war: Affective anchoring and vitality in Nigeria and Kuwait. In C. Straus & J. R. Friedman (Eds.), *Political sentiments and social movements* (pp. 147–174). Palgrave Macmillan.
Casey, E. (2013). *The fate of place: A philosophical history*. University of California Press.
Casey, E. S. (2001). Between geography and philosophy: what does it mean to be in the place-world? *Annals of the American Association of Geographers*, *94*(1), 683–693.
Casey, J. (2008). Ethics in *A man for all seasons*. *Teaching Ethics*, *9*(1), 43–54.
Cassirer, E. (1946). *Language and myth*. Courier Corporation.
Cassirer, E. (2021). *The philosophy of symbolic forms*. Routledge.
Caws, M. A., & Griffin, J. (Eds.). (1976). *Poems of René Char*. Princeton University Press.
Celan, P. (1986). *Collected Prose* (R. Waldrop, Trans.). Sheep Meadow Press.
Celan, P. (2020). *Microliths they are, little stones: Posthumous prose*. (P. Joris, Trans.). Contra Mundum Press.
Celan, P., & Celan-Lestrange, G. (2001). *Correspondance*. Seuil.
Celan, P., & Fairley, I. (2007). *Snow part = Schneepart by Paul Celan*. Sheep Meadow Press.
Celan, P., & Hamburger, M. (2002). *Poems of Paul Celan*. Persea Books.
Celan, P., & Joris, P. (2017). From "Microliths." *Poetry*, *209*(4): 405–410.
Césaire, A. (2001). *Notebook of a return to the native land* (C. Eshleman & A. Smith, Trans.). Wesleyan University Press.
Cesario, J., Johnson, D. J., & Eisthen, H. L. (2020). Your brain is not an onion with a tiny reptile inside. *Current Directions in Psychological Science*, *29*(3), 255–260.
Chafe, W. (1994). *Discourse, consciousness, and time: The flow and displacement of conscious experience in speaking and writing*. University of Chicago Press.
Chajes, J. H. (2022). *The Kabbalistic tree*. Penn State University Press.
Chandler, M. J., & Lalonde, C. E. (1995). The problem of self-continuity in the context of rapid personal and cultural change. In A. Oosterwegel & R. A. Wickland (Eds.), *The self in European and North American culture: Development and processes* (pp. 45–63). Springer.
Charon, R. (2001). The patient-physician relationship. Narrative medicine: A model for empathy, reflection, profession, and trust. *Journal of the American Medical Association*, *286*(15), 1897–1902.
Charon, R. (2008). *Narrative medicine: Honoring the stories of illness*. Oxford University Press.

Charon, R., Dasgupta, S., Hermann, N., Irvine, C., Colon, E. R., Spencer, D., & Spiegel, M. (Eds.). (2017). *The principles and practice of narrative medicine*. Oxford University Press.

Chauvet, J.-M., Deschamps, E. B., & Hilaire, C. (1996). *Dawn of art: The Chauvet cave*. Thames & Hudson.

Chemero, A. (2011). *Radical embodied cognitive science*. MIT press.

Choudhury, S., McKinney, K. A., & Kirmayer, L. J. (2015). "Learning how to deal with feelings differently": Psychotropic medications as vehicles of socialization in adolescence. *Social Science & Medicine, 143*, 311–319.

Cienki, A., & Müller, C. (2008). Metaphor, gesture, and thought. In R. W. Gibbs Jr. (Ed.), *The Cambridge handbook of metaphor and thought* (pp. 483–501). Cambridge University Press.

Cieri, F., Carhart-Harris, R. L., Mathys, C., Turnbull, O., & Solms, M. (2023). Frontiers in psychodynamic neuroscience. *Frontiers in Human Neuroscience, 17*, 1170480.

Clark, A. (1997). *Being there: Putting brain, body, and world together again*. MIT Press.

Clark, A. (2008). *Supersizing the mind: Embodiment, action, and cognitive extension*. Oxford University Press.

Clark, A. (2015). *Surfing uncertainty: Prediction, action, and the embodied mind*. Oxford University Press.

Cleaver, E. (1969). *Soul on ice*. Bantam Books.

Clifton-Soderstrom, M. (2003). Levinas and the patient as other: The ethical foundation of medicine. *Journal of Medicine and Philosophy, 28*(4), 447–460.

Cobley, P. (2016). *Cultural implications of biosemiotics*. Springer.

Coetzee, J. M., & Kurtz, A. (2015). *The good story: Exchanges on truth, fiction and psychotherapy*. Random House.

Cohen, T. (1978). Metaphor and the cultivation of intimacy. *Critical Inquiry, 5* (1), 3–12.

Cohen, T. (2008). *Thinking of others: On the talent for metaphor*. Princeton University Press.

Coker, E. M. (2004). "Traveling pains": Embodied metaphors of suffering among Southern Sudanese refugees in Cairo. *Culture, Medicine and Psychiatry, 28*(1), 15–39.

Cole, J. (1999). *About face*. MIT Press.

Cole, J. (2001). Empathy needs a face. *Journal of Consciousness Studies, 8*(5–6), 51–68.

Coll-Florit, M., Climent, S., Sanfilippo, M., & Hernández-Encuentra, E. (2021). Metaphors of depression: Studying first person accounts of life with depression published in blogs. *Metaphor and Symbol, 36*(1), 1–19.

Coltart, N. E. (1988). The assessment of psychological-mindedness in the diagnostic interview. *The British Journal of Psychiatry, 153*(6), 819–820.

Comas-Diaz, L., & Jacobsen, F. M. (1991). Ethnocultural transference and countertransference in the therapeutic dyad. *American Journal of Orthopsychiatry, 61*(3), 392–402.

Comas-Díaz, L., & Jacobsen, F. M. (2024). Decolonial psychotherapy: Joining the circle, healing the wound. In L. Comas-Díaz, H. Y. Adames, & N. Y. Chavez-Dueñas (Eds.), *Decolonial psychology: Toward anticolonial theories, research, training, and practice* (pp. 295–320). American Psychological Association. https://doi.org/10.1037/0000376-013.

Combs, G., & Freedman, J. (2012). Narrative, poststructuralism, and social justice: Current practices in narrative therapy. *The Counseling Psychologist, 40*(7), 1033–1060.

Connerton, P. (1989). *How societies remember*. Cambridge University Press.

Constant, A., Badcock, P., Friston, K., & Kirmayer, L. J. (2022). Integrating evolutionary, cultural, and computational psychiatry: A multilevel systemic approach. *Frontiers in Psychiatry, 13*, 763380. https://doi.org/10.3389/fpsyt.2022.763380.

Constant, A., Clark, A., & Friston, K. J. (2021). Representation wars: Enacting an armistice through active inference. *Frontiers in Psychology, 11*, 598733.

Cooperrider, K., & Goldin-Meadow, S. (2017). When gesture becomes analogy. *Topics in Cognitive Science, 9*(3), 719–737.

Coover, R. (1971). *The Universal Baseball Association, Inc., J. Henry Waugh, prop.* Plume Books.

Corin, E. (2007). The "other" of culture in psychosis. In J. G. Biehl, B. Good, & A. Kleinman (Eds.), *Subjectivity: Ethnographic investigations* (pp. 273–314). University of California Press.

Coupe, L. (2009). *Myth*. Routledge.

Couture, J. E. (2001). Comments on Hollow Water community healing. In L. J. Kirmayer, M. E. MacDonald, & G. Brass (Eds.), *The mental health of Indigenous peoples* (pp. 173–176). Institute of Community & Family Psychiatry.

Couture, J. E., McGowan, V. M., & Couture, R. (2013). *A metaphoric mind: Selected writings of Joseph Couture*. Athabasca University Press.

Couture, J., Parker, T., Couture, R., & Laboucane, P. (2001). *A cost-benefit analysis of Hollow Water's community holistic circle healing process*. Aboriginal Corrections Policy Unit, Solicitor General of Canada. http://www.sgc.gc.ca/EPub/AboCor/eAPC2001/eAPC2001.

Cox, M., & Theilgaard, A. (1997). *Mutative metaphors in psychotherapy: The Aeolian mode*. Jessica Kingsley.

Cox, M. J., & Paley, B. (1997). Families as systems. *Annual Review of Psychology, 48* (1), 243–267.

Cramer, M. (1980). Psychopathology and shamanism in rural Mexico: A case study of spirit possession. *British Journal of Medical Psychology, 53*, 67–73.

Crapanzano, V. (2015). Half-disciplined chaos: Thoughts on destiny, contingency, story, and trauma. In A. Hinton & D. Hinton (Eds.), *Genocide and mass violence: Memory, symptom and recovery* (pp. 157–173). Cambridge University Press.

Craik, F., & Jacoby, L. (2023). *Memory*. MIT Press.

Crehan, K. (2016). *Gramsci's common sense: Inequality and its narratives*. Duke University Press.

Crews, F. (1995). *The memory wars: Freud's legacy in dispute*. New York Review Books Press.

Critchley, S. (2005). *Things merely are: Philosophy in the poetry of Wallace Stevens*. Routledge.

Critchley, S. (2019). *Tragedy, the Greeks, and us*. Pantheon.

Crichton, P., Carel, H., & Kidd, I. J. (2017). Epistemic injustice in psychiatry. *BJPsych Bulletin*, *41*(2), 65–70.

Crossley, N. (1998). R. D. Laing and the British anti-psychiatry movement: A socio-historical analysis. *Social Science and Medicine*, *47*(7), 877–889.

Crovitz, H. (1970). *Galton's walk: Methods for the analysis of thinking, intelligence, and creativity*. Harper & Row.

Csordas, T. J. (1983). The rhetoric of transformation in ritual healing. *Culture, Medicine and Psychiatry*, *7*(4), 333–375.

Csordas, T. J. (1990). Embodiment as a paradigm for anthropology. *Ethos*, *18* (1), 5–47.

Csordas, T. J. (1997). *The sacred self: A cultural phenomenology of charismatic healing*. University of California Press.

Csordas, T. J. (2008). Intersubjectivity and intercorporeality. *Subjectivity*, *22*, 110–121.

Csordas, T. J. (2022). The challenge of Indigenous healing for global mental health. *Transcultural Psychiatry*, *60*(3), 443–456.

Csordas, T. J., & Lewton, E. (1998). Practice, performance, and experience in ritual healing. *Transcultural Psychiatry*, *35*(4), 435–512.

Cuffari, E. (2012). Gestural sense-making: Hand gestures as intersubjective linguistic enactments. *Phenomenology and the Cognitive Sciences*, *11*, 599–622.

Cuijpers, P., Reijnders, M., & Huibers, M. J. (2019). The role of common factors in psychotherapy outcomes. *Annual Review of Clinical Psychology*, *15*(1), 207–231.

Curtis, V. (2013). *Don't look, don't touch: The science behind revulsion*. Oxford University Press.

Cunsolo, A., & Landman, K. (Eds.). (2017). *Mourning nature: Hope at the heart of ecological loss and grief*. McGill-Queen's Press.

Cushman, P. (1990). Why the self is empty: Toward a historically situated psychology. *American Psychologist*, *45*(5), 599–611.

Cushman, P. (1995). *Constructing the self, constructing America: A cultural history of psychotherapy*. Cambridge University Press.

Cushman, P. (2018). *Travels with the self: Interpreting psychology as cultural history*. Routledge.

Cvetovac, M. E., & Adame, A. L. (2017). The wounded therapist: Understanding the relationship between personal suffering and clinical practice. *The Humanistic Psychologist*, *45*(4), 348–366.

Da Silva, F. V. (2007). Red as blood, white as snow, black as crow: Chromatic symbolism of womanhood in fairy tales. *Marvels & Tales, 21*(2), 240–252.
Damasio, A. R. (1994). *Descartes' error: Emotion, reason, and the human brain.* G. P. Putnam's Sons.
Damasio, A. R., Tranel, D., & Damasio, H. (1990). Face agnosia and the neural substrates of memory. *Annual Review of Neuroscience, 13*, 89–110.
Darwin, C. (1965). *The expression of the emotions in man and animals.* University of Chicago Press. (Original work published 1872).
Davies, B., & Harré, R. (1990). Positioning: The discursive production of selves. *Journal for the Theory of Social Behaviour, 20*(1), 43–63.
De Haan, S. (2020). An enactive approach to psychiatry. *Philosophy, Psychiatry, & Psychology, 27*(1), 3–25.
De Rose, P. L. (2017). Wise old man/woman: Various motifs. In J. Garry & H. El-Shamy (Eds.), *Archetypes and motifs in folklore and literature: A handbook* (pp. 342–345). Routledge.
Decety, J., & Holvoet, C. (2021). The emergence of empathy: A developmental neuroscience perspective. *Developmental Review*, 62, 100999.
Dein, S. (2005). Spirituality, psychiatry and participation: A cultural analysis. *Transcultural Psychiatry, 42*(4), 526–544.
Delbo, C. (2014). *Auschwitz and after.* Yale University Press.
Deloria, V. (2009). *CG Jung and the Sioux traditions: Dreams, visions, nature and the primitive.* Spring Journal.
DeMallie, R. (Ed.). (1985). *The sixth grandfather: Black Elk's teachings given to John G. Neihardt.* University of Nebraska Press.
Demjén, Z., Marszalek, A., Semino, E., & Varese, F. (2019). Metaphor framing and distress in lived-experience accounts of voice-hearing. *Psychosis, 11*(1), 16–27.
Denham, A. (2015). Ethical estrangement: Pictures, poetry, and epistemic value. In J. Gibson (Ed.), *The philosophy of poetry* (pp. 183–204). Oxford University Press.
Dennett, D. C. (1991). *Consciousness explained.* Little, Brown & Company
Densmore, F. (1981). *Teton Sioux music.* Government Printing Office.
Derricotte, T. (1997). *Tender.* University of Pittsburgh Press.
Derrida, J. (1974). White mythology: Metaphor in the text of philosophy. *New Literary History, 6*(1), 5–74.
Derrida, J. (1998). *Monolingualism of the other, or, the prosthesis of origin.* Stanford University Press.
Derrida, J. (2005). *Sovereignties in question: The poetics of Paul Celan.* Fordham University Press.
Desai, R. H. (2022). Are metaphors embodied? The neural evidence. *Psychological Research, 86*(8), 2417–2433. https://doi.org/10.1007/s00426-021-01604-4.
Descola, P. (2013). *Beyond nature and culture.* University of Chicago Press.
Desjarlais, R. (1992). *Body and emotion: The aesthetics of illness and healing in the Nepal Himalayas.* University of Pennsylvania Press.
Di Paolo, E. A., Cuffari, E. C., & De Jaegher, H. (2018). *Linguistic bodies: The continuity between life and language.* MIT Press.

Dickinson, M., & Goulet, C. (Eds.). (2010). *Lyric ecology: An appreciation of the work of Jan Zwicky*. Cormorant Books.

Disch, T. M. (2000). *The dreams our stuff is made of: How science fiction conquered the world*. Simon and Schuster.

Dodds, E. R. (1951). *The Greeks and the irrational*. University of California Press.

Dodge, E., & Lakoff, G. (2005). Image schemas: From linguistic analysis to neural grounding. In B. Hampe & J. E. Grady (Eds.), *From perception to meaning: Image schemas in cognitive linguistics* (pp. 57–91). Walter de Gruyter.

Dor, D. (2015). *The instruction of imagination: Language as a social communication technology*. Oxford University Press.

Doty, W. G. (1978). Hermes guide of souls. *Journal of Analytic Psychology*, *23*(4), 358–365.

Douglas, M. (1973). *Natural symbols: Explorations in cosmology*. Barrie and Jenkins.

Dove, R. (2017). *The darker face of the Earth*. Bloomsbury Publishing.

Dow, J. (1986). Universal aspects of symbolic healing: A theoretical synthesis. *American Anthropologist*, *88*, 56–69.

Dow, J. W. (2021). Central and North Mexican shamans. In B. R. Huber & A. R. Sandstrom (Eds.), *Mesoamerican healers* (pp. 66–94). University of Texas Press.

Dowden, K. (2002). *The uses of Greek mythology*. Routledge.

Drabinski, J. E. (2019). *Glissant and the middle passage: Philosophy, beginning, abyss*. University of Minnesota Press.

Draguns, J. G. (1975). Resocialization into culture: The complexities of taking a worldwide view of psychotherapy. In R. W. Brislin, S. Bochner, & W. J. Lonner (Eds.), *Cross-cultural perspectives on learning* (pp. 273–289). Sage.

Drimalla, H., Landwehr, N., Hess, U., & Dziobek, I. (2019). From face to face: The contribution of facial mimicry to cognitive and emotional empathy. *Cognition and Emotion*, *33*(8), 1672–1686.

Drndić, D. (2012). *Trieste*. MacLehose Press.

Dumont, L. (1982). A modified view of our origins: The Christian beginnings of modern individualism. *Religion*, *12*(1), 1–27.

Dunbar, K. (1997). How scientists think: On-line creativity and conceptual change in science. In T. B. Ward, S. M. Smith, & J. Vaid (Eds.), *Creative thought: An investigation of conceptual structures and processes* (pp. 461–493). American Psychological Association.

Dunbar, K. N. (2009). The biology of physics: What the brain reveals about our understanding of the physical world. *American Institute of Physics Conference Proceedings*, *1179*(1), 15–18.

Dunbar, K., & Fugelsang, J. (2005). Scientific thinking and reasoning. In K. J. Holyoak & R. G. Morrison (Eds.), *The Cambridge handbook of thinking and reasoning* (pp. 705–725). Cambridge University Press.

Dwyer, L., & Santikarma, D. (2007). Posttraumatic politics: Violence, memory, and biomedical discourse in Bali. In L. J. Kirmayer, R. Lemelson, & M. Barad (Eds.), *Understanding trauma: Integrating biological, clinical, and cultural perspectives* (pp. 403–432). Cambridge University Press.

Eagle, M. N. (1984). *Recent developments in psychoanalysis: A critical evaluation.* Harvard University Press.

Eamon, W. (2000). Alchemy in popular culture: Leonardo Fioravanti and the search for the Philosopher's Stone. *Early Science and Medicine*, *5*(2), 196–213.

Ecker, B., & Vaz, A. (2022). Memory reconsolidation and the crisis of mechanism in psychotherapy. *New Ideas in Psychology*, *66*, 100945.

Eco, U. (1983). The scandal of metaphor: Metaphorology and semiotics. *Poetics Today*, *4*(2), 217–225.

Eco, U. (1994). *Six walks in the fictional woods.* Harvard University Press.

Edelstein, E. J., & Edelstein, L. (1998). *Asclepius: Collection and interpretation of the testimonies.* Johns Hopkins University Press.

Eilenberger, W. (2021). *Time of the magicians: Wittgenstein, Benjamin, Cassirer, Heidegger, and the decade that reinvented philosophy.* Penguin.

Eisenberger, N. I. (2012). The pain of social disconnection: examining the shared neural underpinnings of physical and social pain. *Nature Reviews Neuroscience*, *13*(6), 421–434.

Eitinger, L. (1980). The concentration camp syndrome and its late sequelae. In J. Dimsdale (Ed.), *Survivors, victims and perpetrators.* Hemisphere.

Eitinger, L. (1998). Holocaust survivors in past and present. In M. Berenbaum & A. J. Peck (Eds.), *The Holocaust and history: The known, the unknown, the disputed, and the reexamined* (pp. 767–784). Indiana University Press.

Ekman, P. (1999). Basic emotions. In T. Dalgleish & M. Power (Eds.), *Handbook of cognition and emotion* (pp. 45–60). John Wiley & Sons.

Eliade, M. (1964). *Shamanism: Archaic techniques of ecstasy.* Princeton University Press.

Eliade, M. (1978). *The forge and the crucible: The origins and structure of alchemy.* University of Chicago Press.

Eliasmith, C. (2013). *How to build a brain: A neural architecture for biological cognition.* Oxford University Press.

Ellenberger, H. F. (1970). *The discovery of the unconscious: The history and evolution of dynamic psychiatry.* Basic Books.

Ellenberger, H. F. (1972). The story of "Anna O": A critical review with new data. *Journal of the History of the Behavioral Sciences*, *8*(3), 267–279.

Ellwood, R. (1999). *The politics of myth: A study of CG Jung, Mircea Eliade, and Joseph Campbell.* SUNY Press.

El-Shaarawi, N. (2015). Living an uncertain future: Temporality, uncertainty, and well-being among Iraqi refugees in Egypt. *Social Analysis*, *59*(1), 38–56.

Elsey, J. W., Van Ast, V. A., & Kindt, M. (2018). Human memory reconsolidation: A guiding framework and critical review of the evidence. *Psychological Bulletin*, *144*(8), 797–748.

Epley, N., Waytz, A., & Cacioppo, J. T. (2007). On seeing human: A three-factor theory of anthropomorphism. *Psychological Review*, *114*(4), 864.

Eslinger, P. J., Anders, S., Ballarini, T., Boutros, S., Krach, S., Mayer, A. V., . . . & Zahn, R. (2021). The neuroscience of social feelings: Mechanisms of adaptive social functioning. *Neuroscience & Biobehavioral Reviews*, *128*, 592–620.

Fabrega, H. (1979). Elementary systems of medicine. *Culture, Medicine and Psychiatry, 3*(2), 167–198.
Fanon, F. (1967). *Black skin, white masks*. Grove Press.
Farmer, P. (2004). An anthropology of structural violence. *Current Anthropology, 45*(3), 305–325.
Fass, R., Naliboff, B. D., Fass, S. S., Peleg, N., Wendel, C., Malagon, I. B., & Mayer, E. A. (2008). The effect of auditory stress on perception of intraesophageal acid in patients with gastroesophageal reflux disease. *Gastroenterology, 134*(3), 696–705.
Fass, R., Zerbib, F., & Gyawali, C. P. (2020). AGA clinical practice update on functional heartburn: expert review. *Gastroenterology, 158*(8), 2286–2293.
Fassin, D., & Rechtman, R. (2009). *The empire of trauma: An inquiry into the condition of victimhood*. Princeton University Press.
Fauconnier, G. (1997). *Mappings in thought and language*. Cambridge University Press.
Fauconnier, G., & Turner, M. (1998). Conceptual integration networks. *Cognitive Science, 22*(2), 133–187.
Fauconnier, G., & Turner, M. (2008). *The way we think: Conceptual blending and the mind's hidden complexities*. Basic Books.
Favareau, D., Kull, K., Ostdiek, G., Maran, T., Westling, L., Cobley, P., . . . & Wheeler, W. (2017). How can the study of the humanities inform the study of biosemiotics? *Biosemiotics, 10*, 9–31.
Feinstein, D., & Krippner, S. (1997). *The mythic path: Discovering the guiding stories of your past—creating a vision of your future*. G. P. Putnam's Sons.
Feld, S. (2012). *Sound and sentiment: Weeping, birds, poetics, and song in Kaluli expression*. University of Pennsylvania Press.
Feldman, J. (2008). *From molecule to metaphor: A neural theory of language*. MIT Press.
Feldman, R., Singer, M., & Zagoory, O. (2010). Touch attenuates infants' physiological reactivity to stress. *Developmental Science, 13*(2), 271–278.
Felstiner, J. (1995). *Paul Celan: Poet, survivor, Jew*. Yale University Press.
Felstiner, J. (2001). *Selected poems and prose of Paul Celan*. W. W. Norton.
Fernandez, J. W. (1982). The dark at the bottom of the stairs: The inchoate in symbolic inquiry and some strategies for coping with it. In J. Maquet (Ed.), O*n symbols in anthropology: Essays in honor of Harry Hoijer* (pp. 13–43). Undena Publications.
Fernandez, J. W. (1986). *Persuasions and performances: The play of tropes in culture*. Indiana University Press.
Ferroni, F., Arcuri, E., Ardizzi, M., Chinchella, N., Gallese, V., & Ciaunica, A. (2024). Lost in time and space? Multisensory processing of peripersonal space and time perception in people with frequent experiences of depersonalisation. *Quarterly Journal of Experimental Psychology*, 17470218241261645.
Fewell, D. N., Phillips, G. A., & Sherwood, Y. (2008). *Representing the irreparable: The Shoah, the Bible, and the art of Samuel Bak*. Pucker Gallery.
Finke, R. A. (1989). *Principles of mental imagery*. MIT Press.

Fiske, A., Henningsen, P., & Buyx, A. (2019). Your robot therapist will see you now: Ethical implications of embodied artificial intelligence in psychiatry, psychology, and psychotherapy. *Journal of Medical Internet Research*, *21*(5), e13216.

Fivush, R. (2022). *Autobiographical memory and narrative in childhood*. Cambridge University Press.

Fivush, R., & Haden, C. A. (Eds.). (2003). *Autobiographical memory and the construction of a narrative self: Developmental and cultural perspectives*. Psychology Press.

Flaten, M. A., Aslaksen, P. M., Lyby, P. S., & Bjørkedal, E. (2011). The relation of emotions to placebo responses. *Philosophical Transactions of the Royal Society B: Biological Sciences*, *366*(1572), 1818–1827.

Forché, C. (1994). *The angel of history*. HarperCollins Publishers.

Forché, C. (2019). *What you have heard is true*. Random House.

Foster, R. (2016). Therapeutic culture, authenticity and neo-liberalism. *History of the Human Sciences*, *29*(1), 99–116.

Fotopoulou, A., Pfaff, D., & Conway, M. A. (Eds.). (2012). *From the couch to the lab: Trends in psychodynamic neuroscience*. Oxford University Press.

Foucault, M. (1975). *The birth of the clinic: An archeology of medical knowledge*. Vintage Books.

Foucault, M. (2005). *The order of things*. Routledge.

Frank, A. W. (2013). *The wounded storyteller: Body, illness and ethics*. University of Chicago Press.

Frank, H., & Paris, J. (1987). Psychological factors in the choice of psychiatry as a career. *Canadian Journal of Psychiatry*, *32*, 118–122.

Frank, J. D. (1961). *Persuasion and healing: A comprehensive study of psychotherapy*. Johns Hopkins University Press.

Frank, J. D. (1973). *Persuasion and healing* (Rev. ed.). Johns Hopkins University Press.

Frank, J. D. (1995). Psychotherapy as rhetoric: Some implications. *Clinical Psychology-Science and Practice*, *2*(1), 90–93.

Frank, J. D., & Frank, J. B. (1993). *Persuasion and healing: A comparative study of psychotherapy*. Johns Hopkins University Press.

Frankl, V. E. (1985). *Man's search for meaning*. Simon and Schuster.

Frazer, J. G. (1890/1959). *The new golden bough: A study in magic and religion*. Macmillan.

Freeman, M. (2015). *Rewriting the self: History, memory, narrative*. Routledge.

Freud, S. (2003). *The standard edition of the complete psychological works of Sigmund Freud* (Vol. 17). Hogarth Press.

Freud, S. (2010). *Civilization and its discontents* (1930). W. W. Norton.

Fricker, M. (2007). *Epistemic injustice: Power and the ethics of knowing*. Oxford University Press.

Fricker, M. (2017). Evolving concepts of epistemic injustice. In I. J. Kidd, J. Medina, & G. Pohlhaus (Eds.), *The Routledge handbook of epistemic injustice* (pp. 53–60). Routledge.

Friedman, W. J. (1993). Memory for the time of past events. *Psychological Bulletin, 113*(1), 44–66.

Friedrich, P. (1986). *The language parallax: Linguistic relativism and poetic indeterminacy*. University of Texas Press.

Frijda, N. H. (2017). *The laws of emotion*. Psychology Press.

Fuchs, T. (2018). Presence in absence: The ambiguous phenomenology of grief. *Phenomenology and the Cognitive Sciences, 17*(1), 43–63.

Fuks, A. (2021). *The language of medicine*. Oxford University Press.

Funkenstein, A. (1993). The incomprehensible catastrophe. In R. Josselson & A. Lieblich (Eds.), *The narrative study of lives* (pp. 21–29). Sage.

Fusar-Poli, P., Estradé, A., Stanghellini, G., Esposito, C. M., Rosfort, R., Mancini, M., … & Maj, M. (2023). The lived experience of depression: A bottom-up review co-written by experts by experience and academics. *World Psychiatry, 22*(3), 352–365.

Gabriel, R. (2023). Epistemic cultural constraints on the uses of psychology. *New Ideas in Psychology, 68*, 100986.

Gaines, A. D., & Farmer, P. E. (1986). Visible saints: Social cynosures and dysphoria in the Mediterranean tradition. *Culture, Medicine and Psychiatry, 10* (1), 295–330.

Gallagher, S. (2000). Philosophical conceptions of the self: Implications for cognitive science. *Trends in Cognitive Sciences, 4*(1), 14–21. https://doi.org/10.1016/s1364-6613(99)01417-5

Gallagher, S. (2006). *How the body shapes the mind*. Clarendon Press.

Gallagher, S. (2017). *Enactivist interventions: Rethinking the mind*. Oxford University Press.

Gallagher, S. (2023a). *Embodied and enactive approaches to cognition*. Cambridge University Press.

Gallagher, S. (2023b). *The self and its disorders*. Oxford University Press.

Gantz, T. (1993). *Early Greek myth: A guide to literary and artistic sources*. Johns Hopkins University Press.

Garb, J. (2011). *Shamanic trance in modern Kabbalah*. University of Chicago Press.

Garb, J. (2016). *Yearnings of the soul: Psychological thought in modern Kabbalah*. University of Chicago Press.

Geary, J. (2011). *I is an other*. HarperCollins.

Geers, A. L., Faasse, K., Guevarra, D. A., Clemens, K. S., Helfer, S. G., & Colagiuri, B. (2021). Affect and emotions in placebo and nocebo effects: What do we know so far? *Social and Personality Psychology Compass, 15*(1), e12575.

Gellner, E. (1985). *The psychoanalytic movement: The cunning of unreason*. Paladin.

Gelman, J. (1997). *Unthinkable tenderness: Selected poems*. University of California Press.

Gendron, M., & Barrett, L. F. (2018). Emotion perception as conceptual synchrony. *Emotion Review, 10*(2), 101–110.

Gentner, D., & Grudin, J. (1985). The evolution of mental metaphors in psychology: A 90-year retrospective. *American Psychologist, 40*(2), 181–192.

Gentner, D., Holyoak, K. J., & Kokinov, B. N. (Eds.). (2001). *The analogical mind: Perspectives from cognitive science*. MIT Press.

Gergen, K., & Davis, K. (1985). *The social construction of the person*. Springer-Verlag.

Gerger, H., Werner, C. P., Gaab, J., & Cuijpers, P. (2022). Comparative efficacy and acceptability of expressive writing treatments compared with psychotherapy, other writing treatments, and waiting list control for adult trauma survivors: A systematic review and network meta-analysis. *Psychological Medicine*, 52(15), 3484–3496.

Ghaemi, S. N. (2010). *The rise and fall of the biopsychosocial model: Reconciling art and science in psychiatry*. Johns Hopkins University Press.

Gibbs Jr., R. W. (1992). Categorization and metaphor understanding. *Psychological Review*, *99*(3), 572–577.

Gibbs Jr., R. W. (1994). *The poetics of mind: Figurative thought, language, and understanding*. Cambridge University Press.

Gibbs Jr., R. W. (2005). *Embodiment and cognitive science*. Cambridge University Press.

Gibbs Jr., R. W. (Ed.). (2008). *The Cambridge handbook of metaphor and thought*. Cambridge University Press.

Gibbs, R. W. (2017). *Metaphor wars*. Cambridge University Press.

Gibbs Jr., R. W. (2019). Metaphor as dynamical–ecological performance. *Metaphor and Symbol*, *34*(1), 33–44.

Gibbs Jr., R. W. (2023). How metaphors shape the particularities of illness and healing experiences. *Transcultural Psychiatry*, *60*(5), 770–780. https://doi.org/10.1177/1363461520965424

Gibbs Jr., R. W., Beitel, D. A., Harrington, M., & Sanders, P. E. (1994). Taking a stand on the meanings of stand: Bodily experience as motivation for polysemy. *Journal of Semantics*, *11*(4), 231–251.

Gilchrist, A. (1969). *The life of William Blake*. Phaeton Press.

Glaser, S. R. (1980). Rhetoric and psychotherapy. In M. J. Mahoney (Ed.), *Psychotherapy process: Current issues and future directions* (pp. 313–333). Springer US.

Glenberg, A. M., & Kaschak, M. P. (2003). The body's contribution to language. In B. H. Ross (Ed.), *Psychology of learning and motivation* (Vol. 43, pp. 93–126). Academic Press.

Glissant, E. (1997). *Poetics of relation* (B. Wing, Trans.). University of Michigan Press.

Glissant, E. (2020a). *Introduction to a poetics of diversity* (C. Britton, Trans.). Liverpool University Press

Glissant, E. (2020b). *Treatise on the whole-world* (C. Britton, Trans.). Liverpool University Press

Glucklich, A. (2001). *Sacred pain: Hurting the body for the sake of the soul*. Oxford University Press.

Glucksberg, S., & B. Keysar, B. (1990). Understanding metaphorical comparisons: Beyond similarity. *Psychological Review*, *97*(1), 3–18.

Goetz, T. G., & Arcomano, A. C. (2023). "Coming home to my body": A qualitative exploration of gender-affirming care-seeking and mental health. *Journal of Gay & Lesbian Mental Health*, *27*(4), 380–400.

Goldie, P. (2012). *The mess inside: Narrative, emotion, and the mind.* Oxford University Press.

Goldstein, J. (2017). *The experience of insight: A simple and direct guide to Buddhist meditation*. Shambhala Publications.

Goldstein, M. S. (1980). The politics of Thomas Szasz: A sociological view. *Social Problems*, *27*(5): 570–583.

Goleman, D. (1977). *The varieties of the meditative experience.* Irvington Publishers.

Gómez-Carrillo, A., & Kirmayer, L. J. (2023). A cultural-ecosocial systems view for psychiatry. *Frontiers in Psychiatry*, *14*, 486.

Gone, J. P. (2023). Indigenous historical trauma: Alter-Native explanations for mental health inequities. *Dædalus*, *152*(4), 130–150.

Good, B. J. (1993). *Medicine, rationality and experience: An anthropological perspective.* Cambridge University Press.

Good, B. J. (2015). Haunted by Aceh: Specters of violence in post-Suharto Indonesia. In A. Hinton & D. Hinton (Eds.), *Genocide and mass violence: Memory, symptom, and recovery* (pp. 58–82). Cambridge University Press.

Good, B. J. (2019). Hauntology: Theorizing the spectral in psychological anthropology. *Ethos*, 47(4), 411–426.

Good, B. J., Chiovenda, A., & Rahimi, S. (2022). The anthropology of being haunted: On the emergence of an anthropological hauntology. *Annual Review of Anthropology*, *51*, 437–453.

Good, B. J., Good, M. J. D. V., Togan, I., Ilbars, Z., Güvener, A., & Gelişen, I. (1994). In the subjunctive mode: epilepsy narratives in Turkey. *Social Science & Medicine*, *38*(6), 835–842.

Good, M. J. D., & Good, B. J. (1988). Ritual, the state, and the transformation of emotional discourse in Iranian society. *Culture, Medicine and Psychiatry*, *12*(1), 43–63.

Goodman, N. (1978). *Ways of worldmaking*. Hackett Publishing.

Goodwyn, E. (2010). Approaching archetypes: Reconsidering innateness. *Journal of Analytical Psychology*, *55*(4), 502–521.

Goodwyn, E. D. (2016). *Healing symbols in psychotherapy: A ritual approach.* Routledge.

Goodwyn, E. (2024). The human body is the collective unconscious: Archetypal images as innate embodied metaphors. *Journal of Analytical Psychology*, *69*(3), 411–433.

Gopnik, A. (1993). How we know our minds: The illusion of first-person knowledge of intentionality. *Behavioral and Brain Sciences*, *16*(1), 1–14.

Goranson, A., Sheeran, P., Katz, J., & Gray, K. (2020). Doctors are seen as godlike: Moral typecasting in medicine. *Social Science & Medicine*, *258*, 113008.

Gordon, P. E. (2010). *Continental divide: Heidegger, Cassirer, Davos*. Harvard University Press.

Goubert, L., Vervoort, T., Sullivan, M. J., Verhoeven, K., & Crombez, G. (2008). Parental emotional responses to their child's pain: The role of dispositional empathy and catastrophizing about their child's pain. *The Journal of Pain*, *9*(3), 272–279.

Grady, J. (1999). A typology of motivation for conceptual metaphor. In G. J. Steen & R. W. Gibbs Jr. (Eds.), *Metaphor in cognitive linguistics* (pp. 79–100). John Benjamins.

Graves, R. (1960). *The Greek myths*. Penguin.

Green, M. C., Fitzgerald, K., & Moore, M. M. (2019). Archetypes and narrative processes. *Psychological Inquiry*, *30*(2), 99–102.

Greene, T. W. (2008). Three ideologies of individualism: Toward assimilating a theory of individualisms and their consequences. *Critical Sociology*, *34*(1), 117–137.

Greenhalgh, T., & Hurwitz, B. (Eds.). (1999). *Narrative based medicine: Dialogue and discourse in clinical practice*. BMJ Books.

Greenspan, H. (1992). Lives as texts: Symptoms as modes of recounting in the life histories of Holocaust survivors. In G. C. Rosenwald & R. L. Ochberg (Eds.), *Storied lives: The cultural politics of self-understanding* (pp. 145–164). Yale University Press.

Greenspan, H. (2010). *On listening to Holocaust survivors: Beyond testimony*. Paragon House.

Greenspan, H. (2019). The humanities of contingency: Interviewing and teaching beyond "Testimony" with Holocaust survivors. *The Oral History Review*, *46*(2), 360–379.

Grimal, P. (1986). *The dictionary of classical mythology*. Basil Blackwell.

Groesbeck, C. J. (1975). The archetypal image of the wounded healer. *Journal of Analytical Psychology*, *20*(2), 122–145.

Groesbeck, C. J. (1978). Psychological types in the analysis of transference. *Journal of Analytical Psychology*, *23*(1), 23–52.

Groesbeck, C. J. (1980). The analyst's myth: Freud and Jung as each other's analyst. *Quadrant*, *13*(1), 28–55.

Groesbeck, C. J. (1989). C.G. Jung and the shaman's vision. *Journal of Analytical Psychology*, *34*(3), 255–275.

Groesbeck, C. J., & Taylor, B. (1977). The psychiatrist as wounded physician. *The American Journal of Psychoanalysis*, *37*(2), 131–139.

Grünbaum, A. (1984). *The foundations of psychoanalysis: A philosophical critique*. University of California Press.

Grünbaum, A. (1986). Précis of the foundations of psychoanalysis: A philosophical critique. *Behavioral and Brain Sciences*, *9*(2), 217–284.

Grüsser, O. J., & Hagner, M. (1990). On the history of deformation phosphenes and the idea of internal light generated in the eye for the purpose of vision. *Documenta Ophthalmologica*, *74*, 57–85.

Gubkin, L. (2007). *You shall tell your children: Holocaust memory in American Passover ritual*. Rutgers University Press.

Guedon, M. F. (1984). Tsimshian shamanic images. In M. Seguin (Ed.), *The Tsimshian: Images of the past, views for the present* (pp. 174–211). University of British Columbia Press.

Guggenbühl-Craig, A. (1971). *Power in the helping professions.* Spring Publications.

Guldin, R. (2015). *Translation as metaphor.* Routledge.

Guo, L. (2023). Find a resting place for your emotions and make it yours: A meta-analysis of expressive writing interventions among Asian populations. *Cognitive Therapy and Research, 47*(6), 936–957.

Gussow, M. (2000, September 23). Yehuda Amichai, poet who turned Israel's experience in verse, dies at 76. *New York Times*, A14.

Guttman, H. A. (2014). Systems theory, cybernetics, and epistemology. In A. S. Gurman & D. P. Kniskern (Eds.), *Handbook of family therapy* (pp. 41–62). Routledge.

Haack, S. (2000). *Manifesto of a passionate moderate: Unfashionable essays.* University of Chicago Press.

Habermas, J. (1990). *Moral consciousness and communicative action.* MIT Press.

Habermas, T., & Köber, C. (2014). Autobiographical reasoning is constitutive for narrative identity: The role of the life story for personal continuity. In K. C. McLean & M. Syed (Eds.), *The Oxford handbook of identity development.* Oxford University Press.

Habermas, T., & Köber, C. (2015). Autobiographical reasoning in life narratives buffers the effect of biographical disruptions on the sense of self-continuity. *Memory, 23*(5), 664–674.

Hacking, I. (1995a). The looping effect of human kinds. In D. Sperber, D. Premack, & A. J. Premack (Eds.), *Causal cognition: A multidisciplinary debate* (pp. 351–383). Oxford University Press.

Hacking, I. (1995b). *Rewriting the soul.* Princeton University Press.

Hacking, I. (1999). *The social construction of what?* Harvard University Press.

Hacking, I. (2002). *Historical ontology.* Harvard University Press.

Hacking, I. (2004). Between Michel Foucault and Erving Goffman: Between discourse in the abstract and face-to-face interaction. *Economy and Society, 33* (3), 277–302.

Hadamitzky, M., Lückemann, L., Pacheco-López, G., & Schedlowski, M. (2020). Pavlovian conditioning of immunological and neuroendocrine functions. *Physiological Reviews, 100*(1), 357–405.

Hadjistavropoulos, T., Craig, K. D., Duck, S., Cano, A., Goubert, L., Jackson, P. L., . . . & Fitzgerald, T. D. (2011). A biopsychosocial formulation of pain communication. *Psychological Bulletin, 137*(6), 910–939.

Hafferty, F. W. (1998). Beyond curriculum reform: Confronting medicine's hidden curriculum. *Academic Medicine, 73*(4), 403–407.

Hagstrum, J. H. (1964). *William Blake: Poet and painter: An introduction to the illuminated verse.* University of Chicago Press.

Hahn, R. A. (1985). Between two worlds: Physicians as patients. *Medical Anthropology Quarterly* 16, 87–98.

Halberstam, J. (2017). *Trans*: A quick and quirky account of gender variability.* University of California Press.

Halbwachs, M. (1992). *On collective memory.* University of Chicago Press.

Haley, J. (1969). *The power tactics of Jesus Christ and other essays.* Grossman.

Hall, D. (1978). *Goatfoot milktongue twinbird: Interviews, essays, and notes on poetry, 1970–76.* University of Michigan Press.

Hamburger, M. (1989). *Poems of Paul Celan.* Persea Books.

Hamburger, M. (1996). *The truth of poetry.* Anvil Press Poetry.

Hamkins, S. (2013). *The art of narrative psychiatry: Stories of strength and meaning.* Oxford University Press.

Hammond, N. G., & Scullard, H. H. (Eds.). (1970). *The Oxford classical dictionary* (2nd ed.). Oxford University Press.

Hampe, B., & Grady, J. E. (Eds.). (2005). *From perception to meaning: Image schemas in cognitive linguistics.* Walter de Gruyter.

Han, B. C. (2020). *The disappearance of rituals: A topology of the present.* John Wiley & Sons.

Han, B. C. (2024). *The crisis of narration.* John Wiley & Sons.

Hannah, B. (1981). *Encounters with the soul: Active imagination as developed by CG Jung.* Sigo Press.

Harner, M. (1980). *The way of the shaman.* Bantam.

Harner, M. (2012). My path in shamanism. *International Journal of Transpersonal Studies, 31*(2), 80–90.

Harré, R., & Van Langenhove, L. (1991). Varieties of positioning. *Journal for the Theory of Social Behavior 21*(4), 393–407.

Harrington, A. (Ed.). (1997). *The placebo effect: An interdisciplinary exploration.* Harvard University Press.

Harrison, R. P. (2008). *Gardens: An essay on the human condition.* University of Chicago Press.

Haslam, N. (2019). The many roles of dehumanization in genocide. In L. S. Newman (Ed.), *Confronting humanity at its worst: Social psychological perspectives on genocide* (pp. 119–139). Oxford University Press.

Haslam, N., Loughnana, S., Reynolds, C., & Wilson, S. (2007). Dehumanization: A new perspective. *Social and Personality Psychology Compass, 1*(1), 409–422.

Hatfield, E., Bensman, L., Thornton, P. D., & Rapson, R. L. (2014). New perspectives on emotional contagion: A review of classic and recent research on facial mimicry and contagion. *Interpersona: An International Journal on Personal Relationships*, 8(2), 159–179.

Hatfield, E., Cacioppo, J. T., & Rapson, R. L. (1994). *Emotional contagion.* Cambridge University Press.

Hayot, E. (2012). *On literary worlds.* Oxford University Press.

Hebb, D. O. (1946). On the nature of fear. *Psychological Review, 53*, 259–276.

Hebb, D. O. (1955). Drives and the CNS (conceptual nervous system). *Psychological Review, 62*(4), 243–254.

Heil, J. (1986). Does psychology presuppose rationality? *Journal for the Theory of Social Behaviour 6*(1), 77–87.

Heise, D. (1985). Affect control theory: Respecification, estimation and tests of the formal model. *Journal of Mathematical Sociology 11*, 191–222.

Henry, N. (2010). The impossibility of bearing witness: Wartime rape and the promise of justice. *Violence Against Women, 16*(10), 1098–1119.

Herman, J. (2023). *Truth and repair: How trauma survivors envision justice.* Hachette UK.

Herman, J. L. (1992). *Trauma and recovery.* Harvard University Press

Hermans, H. J. (2001). The dialogical self: Toward a theory of personal and cultural positioning. *Culture & Psychology, 7*(3), 243–281.

Herzfeld, M. (1986). Closure as cure: Tropes in the exploration of bodily and social disorder. *Current Anthropology 27*(2), 107–112.

Herzlich, C. (1973). *Health and illness: A social-psychological analysis.* Academic Press.

Hess, U. (2021). Who to whom and why: The social nature of emotional mimicry. *Psychophysiology, 58*(1), e13675.

Hess, U., & Thibault, P. (2009). Darwin and emotion expression. *American Psychologist, 64*(2), 120–128.

Hesse, M. (1966). *Models and analogies in science.* Notre Dame University Press.

Hesse, M. (2017). Models and analogies. In W. H. Newton-Smith (Ed.), *A companion to the philosophy of science* (pp. 299–307). Wiley.

Heyes, C. (2019). Précis of cognitive gadgets: The cultural evolution of thinking. *Behavioral and Brain Sciences, 42*, e169. https://doi.org/10.1017/S0140525X18002145

Hickling, F. W. (2021). *Decolonization of psychiatry in Jamaica: Madnificent irations.* Springer Nature.

Hilder, T. R. (2012). Repatriation, revival and transmission: The politics of a Sámi musical heritage. *Ethnomusicology Forum, 21*(2), 161–179.

Hilgard, E. R. (1977). *Divided consciousness: Multiple controls in human thought and action.* Academic Press.

Hilgard, E. R., & Hilgard, J. R. (2013). *Hypnosis in the relief of pain.* Routledge.

Hilberg, R. (1961). *The destruction of the European Jews.* Quadrangle Books.

Hillman, J. (1975). *Re-visioning psychology.* Harper & Row.

Hillman, J. (1979). *The dream and the underworld.* Harper & Row.

Hillman, J. (1983). *Archetypal psychology.* Spring Publications.

Hinde, R. A. (1989). Relations between levels of complexity in the behavioral sciences. *The Journal of Nervous and Mental Disease, 177*(11), 655–667.

Hinman, L. M. (1982). Nietzsche, metaphor, and truth. *Philosophy and Phenomenological Research, 43*(2), 179–199.

Hinton, D. E., Barlow, D. H., Reis, R., & de Jong, J. (2016). A transcultural model of the centrality of "thinking a lot" in psychopathologies across the globe and the process of localization: A Cambodian refugee example. *Culture, Medicine, and Psychiatry, 40*, 570–619.

Hinton, D. E., Field, N. P., Nickerson, A., Bryant, R., & Simon, N. (2013). Dreams of the dead among Cambodian refugees: Frequency, phenomenology, and relationship to complicated grief and PTSD. *Death Studies, 37*(8), 750–767.

Hinton, D. E., & Kirmayer, L. J. (2017). The flexibility hypothesis of healing. *Culture, Medicine, and Psychiatry*, *41*(1), 3–34.

Hinton, D. E., Rasmussen, A., Nou, L., Pollack, M. H., & Good, M. J. (2009). Anger, PTSD, and the nuclear family: A study of Cambodian refugees. *Social Science and Medicine*, *69*, 1387–1394.

Hirsch, E. (1999). *How to read a poem: And fall in love with poetry*. Harcourt Brace & Co.

Hirshfield, J. (1997). *Nine gates: Entering the mind of poetry*. HarperCollins.

Hirst, W., & Phelps, E. A. (2016). Flashbulb memories. *Current Directions in Psychological Science*, *25*(1), 36–41.

Hobson, R. F. (1985). *Forms of feeling: The heart of psychotherapy*. Tavistock Publications.

Hochheimer, W. (1969). *The psychotherapy of C. G. Jung*. Putnam.

Hofstadter, D. R. (1997). *Le Ton beau de Marot: In Praise of the music of language*. Basic Books.

Hofstra, J. (2022). Beside oneself with rage: The doubled self as metaphor in a narrative of brain injury with emotional dysregulation. *Journal of Medical Humanities*, *42*: 131–146.

Hollan, D. (1988). Staying "cool" in Toraja: Informal strategies for the management of anger and hostility in a nonviolent society. *Ethos*, *16*, 52–72.

Holmes, D. S. (1990). The evidence for repression: An examination of 60 years of research. In J. L. Singer (Ed.), *Repression and dissociation: Implications for personality theory, psychopathology, and health* (pp. 85–102). University of Chicago Press.

Holmes, J. (2020). *The brain has a mind of its own: Attachment, neurobiology, and the new science of psychotherapy*. Confer.

Hopkins, J. (2019). Psychoanalysis and neuroscience. In R. G. T. Gipps & M. Lacewing (Eds.), *The Oxford handbook of philosophy and psychoanalysis* (pp. 377–406). Oxford University Press.

Howard, G. S. (1991). Culture tales: A narrative approach to thinking, cross-cultural psychology, and psychotherapy. *American Psychologist*, *46*(3), 187–197.

Hsu, E. (2021). The healing green, cultural synaesthesia and triangular comparativism. *Ethnos*, *86*(2), 295–308.

Hsu, F. L. (1971). Psychosocial homeostasis and *jen*: Conceptual tools for advancing psychological anthropology. *American Anthropologist*, *73*(1), 23–44.

Hubert, R. A. (1984). The acultural dimensions of chronic pain: Flawed reality construction and the problem of meaning. *Social Problems*, *31*, 365–378.

Hudson, L., & Jacot, B. (1991). *The way men think: Intellect, intimacy and the erotic imagination*. Yale University Press.

Hultkrantz, A. (1992). *Shamanic healing and ritual drama: Health and medicine in Native North American religious traditions*. Crossroad.

Hunt, H. T. (2012). A collective unconscious reconsidered: Jung's archetypal imagination in the light of contemporary psychology and social science. *Journal of Analytical Psychology*, *57*(1), 76–98.

Hunt, L. (2007). *Inventing human rights: A history*. W. W. Norton.
Hutto, D. D. (2012). *Folk psychological narratives: The sociocultural basis of understanding reasons*. MIT Press.
Hutto, D. D., & Myin, E. (2012). *Radicalizing enactivism: Basic minds without content*. MIT Press.
Hutto, D. D., & Myin, E. (2017). *Evolving enactivism: Basic minds meet content*. MIT Press.
Hwang, K. K., & Chang, J. (2009). Self-cultivation: Culturally sensitive psychotherapies in Confucian societies. *The Counseling Psychologist, 37*(7), 1010–1032.
Hyde, L. (1983). *The gift: Creativity and the artist in the modern world*. Vintage.
Hyde, L. (1998). *Trickster makes this world: Mischief, myth, and art*. Farrar, Strauss & Giroux.
Ibarrretxe-Antuñano, I. (1999). Metaphorical mappings in the sense of smell. In R. W. Gibbs, Jr. & G. J. Steen (Eds.), *Metaphor in cognitive linguistics* (pp. 29–45). John Benjamins.
Ichien, N., Stamenković, D., Whatley, M. C., Castel, A. D., & Holyoak, K. J. (2024). Advancing with age: Older adults excel in comprehension of novel metaphors. *Psychology and Aging*. Advance online publication. https://doi.org/10.1037/pag0000836
Idel, M. (2002). *Absorbing perfections: Kabbalah and interpretation*. Yale University Press.
Idel, M. (2004). Sabbath: On concepts of time in Jewish Mysticism. In J. Blidstein (Ed.), *Sabbath: Idea, history, reality* (pp. 57–93). Ben Gurion University.
Ifergan, P. (2015). Hans Blumenberg's philosophical project: Metaphorology as anthropology. *Continental Philosophy Review, 48*(3), 359–377.
IJzerman, H., Galluci, M., Pouw, W. T. J. L., Weißgerber, S. C., Van Doesum, N. J., & Williams, K. D. (2012). Cold-blooded loneliness: Social exclusion leads to lower skin temperatures. *Acta Psychologica, 140*, 283–288.
Illouz, E. (2008). *Saving the modern soul: Therapy, emotions, and the culture of self-help*. University of California Press.
Indurkhya, B. (2007). Rationality and reasoning with metaphors. *New Ideas in Psychology, 25*(1), 16–36.
Insel, T. R., & Quirion, R. (2005). Psychiatry as a clinical neuroscience discipline. *Journal of the American Medical Association, 294*(17), 2221–2224.
Itzhak, N. (2015). Making selves and meeting others in neo-shamanic healing. *Ethos, 43*(3), 286–310.
Ivey, G., & Partington, T. (2014). Psychological woundedness and its evaluation in applications for clinical psychology training. *Clinical Psychology & Psychotherapy, 21*(2), 166–177.
Izod, J. (1992). *Films of Nicholas Roeg: Myth and mind*. Springer.
Jackson, S. W. (1994). Catharsis and abreaction in the history of psychological healing. *Psychiatric Clinics of North America, 17*(3), 471–491.
Jackson, S. W. (2001). The wounded healer. *Bulletin of the History of Medicine, 75* (1), 1–36.

Janacsek, K., Evans, T. M., Kiss, M., Shah, L., Blumenfeld, H., & Ullman, M. T. (2022). Subcortical cognition: The fruit below the rind. *Annual Review of Neuroscience*, *45*, 361–386.

Jaynes, J. (1976). *The origin of consciousness in the breakdown of the bicameral mind*. Houghton Mifflin.

Jenkins, J. J., & Barrett, R. J. (Eds.). (2004). *Schizophrenia, culture and subjectivity: The edge of experience*. Cambridge University Press.

Johnson, C. D. (2012). *Memory, metaphor, and Aby Warburg's atlas of images*. Cornell University Press.

Johnson, M. (1987). *The body in the mind: The bodily basis of reason and imagination*. University of Chicago Press.

Johnson, M. (1993). *Moral imagination: Implications of cognitive science for ethics*. University of Chicago Press.

Johnson, M. (2017). *Embodied mind, meaning, and reason: How our bodies give rise to understanding*. University of Chicago Press.

Johnson, M. (2018). *The aesthetics of meaning and thought: The bodily roots of philosophy, morality and art*. University of Chicago Press.

Johnson-Laird, P. N. (1983). *Mental models: Towards a cognitive science of language, inference, and consciousness*. Harvard University Press.

Johnson-Laird, P. N., Herrmann, D. J. and Chaffin, R. (1984). Only connections: A critique of semantic networks. *Psychological Bulletin*, *96*(2), 292–315.

Jones, B. A. (1983). Healing factors of psychiatry in light of attachment theory. *American Journal of Psychotherapy*, *37*(2), 235–244.

Jones, B. E. (2020). Arousal and sleep circuits. *Neuropsychopharmacology*, *45* (1), 6–20.

Jones, E. (1967). *Papers on psycho-analysis*. Beacon Press.

Jones, E. G., & Mendell, L. M. (1999). Assessing the decade of the brain. *Science*, *284*(5415), 739–739.

Jongman-Sereno, K. P., & Leary, M. R. (2019). The enigma of being yourself: A critical examination of the concept of authenticity. *Review of General Psychology*, *23*(1), 133–142.

Joris P (1998). Celan/Heidegger: Translation at the Mountain of Death. http://wings.buffalo.edu/epc/authors/joris/todtnauberg.html

Joseph-Salisbury, R., & Connelly, L. (2018). "If your hair is relaxed, white people are relaxed. If your hair is nappy, they're not happy": Black hair as a site of "post-racial" social control in English schools. *Social Sciences*, *7*(11), 219.

Judt, T. (1992). The past is another country: Myth and memory in postwar Europe. *Dædalus*, *121*(4), 83–118.

Jung, C. G. (1966). *The practice of psychotherapy*. Princeton University Press.

Jung, C. G. (1967). *Symbols of transformation*. Princeton University Press. (Original work published in 1912).

Jung, C. G. (1969). *The archetypes and the collective unconscious* (2nd ed.). Princeton University Press.

Jung, C. G. (1984). *Dream analysis: Notes of the seminar given in 1928–1930*. Princeton University Press.

Jung, C. G. (2009). *The red book: Liber novus*. W. W. Norton.

Jung, C. G. (2014). *Alchemical studies*. Routledge.

Juslin, P. N. (2013). What does music express? Basic emotions and beyond. *Frontiers in Psychology*, *4*, 596.

Kakar, S. (1991). *Shamans, mystics and doctors: A psychological inquiry into India and its healing traditions*. University of Chicago Press.

Kamali, A., Milosavljevic, S., Gandhi, A., Lano, K. R., Shobeiri, P., Sherbaf, F. G., ... & Hasan, K. M. (2023). The cortico-limbo-thalamo-cortical circuits: An update to the original Papez circuit of the human limbic system. *Brain Topography*, *36*(3), 371–389.

Kammers, M. P., de Vignemont, F., Verhagen, L., & Dijkerman, H. C. (2009). The rubber hand illusion in action. *Neuropsychologia*, *47*(1), 204–211.

Kannape, O. A., Smith, E. J., Moseley, P., Roy, M. P., & Lenggenhager, B. (2019). Experimentally induced limb-disownership in mixed reality. *Neuropsychologia*, 124, 161–170.

Kanwisher, N., McDermott, J., & Chun, M. M. (1997). The fusiform face area: A module in human extrastriate cortex specialized for face perception. *The Journal of Neuroscience*, *17*(11), 4302–4311.

Kapferer, B., & Papigny, G. (2005). *Tovil: Exorcism & healing rites*. Viator Publications.

Kaplan, A. (1993). *Sefer Yetsirah (The book of creation)*. Samuel Weiser.

Kaplan, S. (2005). Tama Galut Etiopiya: The Ethiopian exile is over. *Diaspora: A Journal of Transnational Studies*, *14*(2), 381–396.

Kaptchuk, T. J., & Eisenberg, D. M. (1998). The persuasive appeal of alternative medicine. *Annals of Internal Medicine*, *129*(12), 1061–1065.

Karbelnig, A. M. (2020). The theater of the unconscious mind. *Psychoanalytic Psychology*, *37*(4), 273–281.

Karmiloff-Smith, A. (2015). An alternative to domain-general or domain-specific frameworks for theorizing about human evolution and ontogenesis. *AIMS Neuroscience*, *2*(2), 91–104.

Kearney, R. (2017). *On Paul Ricoeur: The owl of Minerva*. Routledge.

Kearney, R. (2018). The hermeneutics of wounds. In B. W. Becker, J. P. Manoussakis, & D. M. Goodman (Eds.), *Unconscious incarnations: Psychoanalytic and philosophical perspectives on the body* (pp. 21–42). Routledge.

Keesing, R. M., Davis, R. D., De Ruijter, A., Fernandez, J. W., Fishman, J. A., Guidieri, R., ... & Shaw, R. D. (1989). Exotic readings of cultural texts [and comments and reply]. *Current Anthropology*, *30*(4), 459–479.

Kelly, M. H., & Keil, F. C. (1987). Metaphor comprehension and knowledge of semantic domains. *Metaphor and Symbol*, *2*(1), 33–51.

Kemmerer, D. (2006). Action verbs, argument structure constructions, and the mirror neuron system. In M. A. Arbib (Ed.), *Action to language via the mirror neuron system* (pp. 347–373). Cambridge University Press.

Kemmerer, D. (2019). *Concepts in the brain: The view from cross-linguistic diversity*. Oxford University Press.

Kemmerer, D. (2023). Grounded cognition entails linguistic relativity: A neglected implication of a major semantic theory. *Topics in Cognitive Science, 15*(4), 615–647.
Kennedy, J. M. (2008). Metaphor and art. In R. W. Gibbs Jr. (Ed.), *The Cambridge handbook of metaphor and thought* (pp. 447–461). Cambridge University Press.
Kenny, K., Broom, A., Kirby, E., & Ridge, D. (2019). In one's own time: Contesting the temporality and linearity of bereavement. *Health, 23*(1), 58–75.
Kerby, A. P. (1991). *Narrative and the self.* Indiana University Press.
Kerenyi, K. (1968). *Asklepios, archetypal image of the physician's existence.* Princeton University Press.
Kerényi, K. (1996). *Hermes, guide of souls.* Spring Publications.
Kestenberg, J., & Fogelman, E. (Eds.). (1994). *Children during the Nazi reign.* Praeger
Keynes, G. (Ed.). (1980). *The letters of William Blake: With related documents.* Clarendon Press.
Keys, H. M., Kaiser, B. N., Kohrt, B. A., Khoury, N. M., & Brewster, A. R. T. (2012). Idioms of distress, ethnopsychology, and the clinical encounter in Haiti's Central Plateau. *Social Science & Medicine, 75*(3), 555–564.
Kidron, C. A. (2004). Surviving a distant past: A case study of the cultural construction of trauma descendant identity. *Ethos, 31*(4), 513–544.
Kidron, C. A. (2009). Toward an ethnography of silence: The lived presence of the past in the everyday life of Holocaust trauma survivors and their descendants in Israel. *Current Anthropology, 50*(1), 5–27.
Kidron, C. A. (2012). Alterity and the particular limits of universalism: Comparing Jewish-Israeli Holocaust and Canadian-Cambodian genocide legacies. *Current Anthropology, 53*(6), 723–754.
Kidron, C. A. (2015). Embodying the distant past: Holocaust descendant narratives of the lived presence of the genocidal past. In A. Hinton & D. Hinton (Eds.), *Genocide and mass violence: Memory, symptom, and recovery* (pp. 137–156). Cambridge University Press.
Kidron, C. A. (2018). Resurrecting discontinued bonds: A comparative study of Israeli Holocaust and Cambodian genocide trauma descendant relations with the genocide dead. *Ethos, 46*(2), 230–253.
Kidron, C. A. (2020). The "perfect failure" of communal genocide commemoration in Cambodia: Productive friction or "bone business"? *Current Anthropology, 61*(3), 304–334.
Kidron, C. A., Kotliar, D. M., & Kirmayer, L. J. (2019). Transmitted trauma as badge of honor: Phenomenological accounts of Holocaust descendant resilient vulnerability. *Social Science & Medicine, 239*, 112524.
Kiecolt-Glaser, J. K., & Glaser, R. (1995). Psychoneuroimmunology and health consequences: Data and shared mechanisms. *Psychosomatic Medicine, 57*, 269–274.
Kiefer, A., & Dermutz, K. (2019). *Anselm Kiefer in conversation with Klaus Dermutz.* Seagull Books.

Kihlstrom, J. F. (2005). Dissociative disorders. *Annual Review of Clinical Psychology*, *1*(1), 227–253.
Kinsella, W. P. (1982). *Shoeless Joe*. Ballantine Books.
Kintsch, W. (2000). Metaphor comprehension: A computational theory. *Psychonomic Bulletin & Review*, *7*(2), 257–266. https://doi.org/10.3758/BF03212981
Kirke, X. (2018). *Hans Blumenberg: Myth and significance in modern politics*. Springer.
Kirmayer, L. J. (1987). Languages of suffering and healing: Iaia as a social and cultural process. *Transcultural Psychiatric Research Review 24*, 120–136.
Kirmayer, L. J. (1988a). Mind and body as metaphors: Hidden values in biomedicine. In M. Lock & D. Gordon (Eds.), *Biomedicine examined* (pp. 57–92). Kluwer.
Kirmayer, L. J. (1988b). Word magic and the rhetoric of commonsense: Erickson's metaphors for mind. *International Journal of Clinical and Experimental Hypnosis*, *36*(3), 157–172.
Kirmayer, L. J. (1990). Resistance, reactance and reluctance to change: A cognitive attributional approach to strategic interventions. *Journal of Cognitive Psychotherapy*, *4*(2), 83–104.
Kirmayer, L. J. (1992a). The body's insistence on meaning: Metaphor as presentation and representation in illness experience. *Medical Anthropology Quarterly*, *6* (4), 323–346.
Kirmayer, L. J. (1992b). Social constructions of hypnosis. *International Journal of Clinical and Experimental Hypnosis 40*(4), 276–300.
Kirmayer, L. J. (1992c). From the witches' hammer to the Oedipus complex: Castration anxiety in Western society. *Transcultural Psychiatric Research Review*, *29*(2), 133–158.
Kirmayer, L. J. (1993a). Healing and the invention of metaphor: The effectiveness of symbols revisited. *Culture, Medicine and Psychiatry*, *17*(2), 161–195.
Kirmayer, L. J. (1993b). La folie de la métaphore. *Anthropologie et Societés*, *17*(1–2), 43–55.
Kirmayer, L. J. (1994a). Improvisation and authority in illness meaning. *Culture Medicine and Psychiatry*, *18*(2), 183–214.
Kirmayer, L. J. (1994b). Pacing the void: Social and cultural dimensions of dissociation. In D. Spiegel (Ed.), *Dissociation: Culture, mind and body* (pp. 91–122). American Psychiatric Press.
Kirmayer, L. J. (1996). Landscapes of memory. In P. Antze & M. Lambek (Eds.), *Tense past: Cultural essays in trauma and memory* (pp. 173–198). Routledge.
Kirmayer, L. J. (1999). Myth and ritual in psychotherapy. *Transcultural Psychiatry*, *36*(4), 451–460.
Kirmayer, L. J. (2000). Broken narratives: Clinical encounters and the poetics of illness experience. In C. Mattingly & L. Garro (Eds.), *Narrative and the cultural construction of illness and healing* (pp. 153–180). University of California Press
Kirmayer, L. J. (2003a). Reflections on embodiment. In J. Wilce (Ed.), *Social and cultural lives of immune systems* (pp. 282–302). Routledge.

Kirmayer, L. J. (2003b). Asklepian dreams: The ethos of the wounded-healer in the clinical encounter. *Transcultural Psychiatry, 40*(2), 248–277.
Kirmayer, L. J. (2004). The cultural diversity of healing: Meaning, metaphor and mechanism. *British Medical Bulletin, 69*(1), 33–48.
Kirmayer, L. J. (2006). Toward a medicine of the imagination. *New Literary History, 37*(3), 583–605.
Kirmayer, L. J. (2007a). On the cultural mediation of pain In S. Coakley & K. K. Shelemay (Eds.), *Pain and its transformations: The interface of biology and culture* (pp. 363–401). Harvard University Press.
Kirmayer, L. J. (2007b). Psychotherapy and the cultural concept of the person. *Transcultural psychiatry, 44*(2), 232–257.
Kirmayer, L. J. (2007c). Celan's poetics of alterity: Lyric and the understanding of illness experience in medical ethics. *Monash Bioethics Review, 26*(4), 21–35.
Kirmayer, L. J. (2008a). Culture and the metaphoric mediation of pain. *Transcultural Psychiatry, 45*(2), 318–338.
Kirmayer, L. J. (2008b). Empathy and alterity in cultural psychiatry. *Ethos, 36*(4), 457–474.
Kirmayer, L. J. (2011a). Unpacking the placebo response: Insights from ethnographic studies of healing. *The Journal of Mind-Body Regulation, 1*(3), 112–124.
Kirmayer, L. J. (2011b). Defining and delimiting trauma-related dissociation: A view from cultural psychiatry. *Journal of Trauma & Dissociation, 12*(4), 465–468.
Kirmayer, L. J. (2013). Embracing uncertainty as a path to competence: Cultural safety, empathy, and alterity in clinical training. *Culture, Medicine, and Psychiatry, 37*, 365–372.
Kirmayer, L. J. (2014). Medicines of the imagination: Cultural phenomenology, medical pluralism and the persistence of mind-body dualism. In H. Naraindas, J. Quack, & W. Sax (Eds.), *Asymmetrical Conversations* (pp. 26–55). Berghahn.
Kirmayer, L. J. (2015a). Wrestling with the angels of history: Memory, symptom intervention. In A. Hinton & D. Hinton (Eds.), *Genocide and mass violence: Memory, symptom, and recovery* (pp. 388–420). Cambridge University Press.
Kirmayer, L. J. (2015b). Empathy and alterity in psychiatry. In L. J. Kirmayer, R. Lemeson, & C. A. Cummings (Eds.), *Re-visioning psychiatry: Cultural phenomenology, critical neuroscience and global mental health* (pp. 141–167). Cambridge University Press.
Kirmayer, L. J. (2015c). Re-visioning psychiatry: Toward an ecology of mind in health and illness. In L. J. Kirmayer, R. Lemeson, & C. A. Cummings (Eds.), *Re-visioning psychiatry: Cultural phenomenology, critical neuroscience and global mental health* (pp. 622–660). Cambridge University Press.
Kirmayer, L. J. (2015d). Mindfulness in cultural context. *Transcultural Psychiatry, 52*(4), 447–469.
Kirmayer, L. J. (2023). Cultural poetics of illness and healing. *Transcultural Psychiatry, 60*(4), 753–769.
Kirmayer, L. J., Brass, G. M., & Valaskakis, G. G. (2009). Conclusion: Healing/invention/tradition. In L. J. Kirmayer & G. G. Valaskakis (Eds.), *Healing*

*traditions: The mental health of Aboriginal peoples in Canada* (pp. 440–472). University of British Columbia Press.

Kirmayer, L. J., & Carroll, J. (1987). A neurobiological hypothesis on the nature of chronic self-mutilation. *Integrative Psychiatry, 5*, 212–213.

Kirmayer, L. J., Corin, E., & Jarvis, G. E. (2004). Inside knowledge: Cultural constructions of insight in psychosis. In X. Amador & A. David (Eds.), *Insight and psychosis: Awareness of illness in schizophrenia and related disorders* (pp 197–229). Oxford University Press.

Kirmayer, L. J., & Crafa, D. (2014). What kind of science for psychiatry? *Frontiers in Human Neuroscience, 8*, 435.

Kirmayer, L. J., Dandeneau, S., Marshall, E., Phillips, M. L., & Williamson, K. J. (2011). Rethinking resilience from Indigenous perspectives. *Canadian Journal of Psychiatry, 56*(2), 84–91.

Kirmayer, L. J., & Gómez-Carrillo, A. (2019). Agency, embodiment and enactment in psychosomatic theory and practice. *Medical Humanities, 45*(2), 169–182.

Kirmayer, L. J., Gómez-Carrillo, A., Sukhanova, E., & Garrido, E. (2023). Narrative medicine. In J. E. Mezzich, W. J. Appleyard, P. Glare, J. Snaedal, & R. Wilson (Eds.), *Textbook of person-centered medicine* (pp. 235–255). Springer.

Kirmayer, L. J., Gone, J. P., & Moses, J. (2014). Rethinking historical trauma. *Transcultural Psychiatry, 51*(3), 299–319.

Kirmayer, L. J., Guzder, J., & Rousseau, C. (Eds.). (2014). *Cultural consultation: Encountering the other in mental health care.* Springer.

Kirmayer, L. J., Kienzler, H., Hamid Afana, A., & Pedersen, D. (2010). Trauma and disasters in social and cultural context. In C. Morgan & D. Bhugra (Eds.), *Principles of social psychiatry* (pp. 155–177). Oxford University Press.

Kirmayer, L. J., Gómez-Carrillo, A., Langlois-Thérien, T., Ramstead, M.J.D., & Gold, I. (2020). Culture, self and agency: An ecosocial view. In L. J. Kirmayer, C. Worthman, S. Kitayama, R. Lemelson, & C. A. Cummings (Eds.), *Culture, mind and brain: Emerging concepts, models, applications* (pp. 244–271). Cambridge University Press.

Kirmayer, L. J., & Ramstead, M. J. (2017). Embodiment and enactment in cultural psychiatry. In C. Durt, C. Tewes, & T. Fuchs (Eds.), *Embodiment, enaction, and culture: Investigating the constitution of the shared world* (pp. 397–422). MIT Press.

Kirmayer, L. J., & Santhanam, R. (2001). The anthropology of hysteria. In P. Halligan, C. Bass, & J. C. Marshall (Eds.), *Contemporary approaches to the study of hysteria: Clinical and theoretical perspectives* (pp. 251–270). Oxford University Press.

Kirmayer, L., Simpson, C., & Cargo, M. (2003). Healing traditions: Culture, community and mental health promotion with Canadian Aboriginal peoples. *Australasian Psychiatry, 11*(suppl. 1), S15–S23.

Kirmayer, L. J., Worthman, C., & Kitayama, S. (2020). Introduction: Co-constructing culture, mind and brain. In L. J. Kirmayer, C. Worthman,

S. Kitayama, R. Lemelson, & C. A. Cummings (Eds.), *Culture, mind and brain: Emerging concepts, models, applications* (pp. 1–49). Cambridge University Press.

Klein, N. (2007). *The shock doctrine: The rise of disaster capitalism*. Metropolitan Books/Henry Holt.

Kleinman, A. (1980). *Patients and healers in the context of culture*. University of California Press.

Kleinman, A. (1988a). *Rethinking psychiatry*. Simon and Schuster.

Kleinman, A. (1988b). *The illness narratives: Suffering, healing, and the human condition*. Basic Books.

Kleinman, A. (1999). Experience and its moral modes: Culture, human conditions, and disorder. In G. B. Peterson (Ed.), *The Tanner lectures on human values* (Vol. 20, pp. 355–420). University of Utah Press.

Kleinman, A. (2019). *The soul of care: The moral education of a husband and a doctor*. Penguin.

Kleinman, A., & Sung, L. H. (1979). Why do Indigenous practitioners successfully heal? *Social Science & Medicine. Part B: Medical Anthropology*, *13*(1), 7–26.

Klibansky, R., Panofsky, E., & Saxl, F. (2019). *Saturn and melancholy: Studies in the history of natural philosophy, religion, and art*. McGill-Queen's Press.

Knapp, P. A. (2000). The work of alchemy. *Journal of Medieval and Early Modern Studies*, *30*(3), 575–599.

Koerner, J. L. (1993). Ideas about the thing, not the thing itself: Hans Blumenberg's style. *History of the Human Sciences*, *6*(4), 1–10.

Kofman, S. (1993). *Nietzsche and metaphor*. Standford University Press.

Knowles, E. D., Wearing, J. R., & Campos, B. (2011). Culture and the health benefits of expressive writing. *Social Psychological and Personality Science*, *2*(4), 408–415.

Köhler, W. (1970). *Gestalt psychology: An introduction to new concepts in modern psychology*. Liveright.

Kohn, E. (2015). Anthropology of ontologies. *Annual Review of Anthropology*, *44*, 311–327.

Kohrt, B. A., Ottman, K., Panter-Brick, C., Konner, M., & Patel, V. (2020). Why we heal: The evolution of psychological healing and implications for global mental health. *Clinical Psychology Review*, *82*, 101920.

Kolakowski, L. (1989). *The presence of myth*. University of Chicago Press.

Kövecses, Z. (2003). *Metaphor and emotion: Language, culture, and body in human feeling*. Cambridge University Press.

Kövecses, Z. (2010). *Metaphor: A practical introduction*. Oxford University Press.

Kövecses, Z. (2015). *Where metaphors come from: Reconsidering context in metaphor*. Oxford University Press.

Kövecses, Z. (2020). *Extended conceptual metaphor theory*. Cambridge University Press.

Kowalewski, D. (2019). The shamanic renaissance: What is going on? *Journal of Humanistic Psychology*, *59*(2), 170–184.

Krieger, M. H. (2012). *Doing physics: How physicists take hold of the world*. Indiana University Press.

Krieger, N. (2005). Embodiment: A conceptual glossary for epidemiology. *Journal of Epidemiology and Community Health, 59*(5), 350.

Krystal, H. (1988). *Integration and self-healing: Affect, trauma, alexithymia*. Analytic Press.

Kuch, K., & Cox, B. J. (1992). Symptoms of PTSD in 124 survivors of the Holocaust. *American Journal of Psychiatry*, 149, 337–340.

Kwon, H. (2008). *Ghosts of war in Vietnam*. Cambridge University Press.

Kwon. H. (2015). The Vietnam War traumas. In A. Hinton & D. Hinton (Eds.), *Genocide and mass violence: Memory, symptom, and recovery* (pp. 45–57). Cambridge University Press.

Kyselo, M. (2016). The minimal self needs a social update. *Philosophical Psychology, 29*(7), 1057–1065.

Lacan, J. (2001). *Ecrits: A selection*. Routledge.

LaCapra, D. (2018). *Understanding others: Peoples, animals, pasts*. Cornell University Press.

Lacoue-Labarthe, P. (1986). *Poetry as experience*. Stanford University Press.

Laderman, C. (1987). The ambiguity of symbols in the structure of healing. *Social Science & Medicine, 24*(4), 293–301.

Laderman, C., & Roseman, M. (Eds.). (2016). *The performance of healing*. Routledge.

Laing, R. D. (1965). *The divided self* (2nd ed.). Penguin.

Laing, R. D. (1990). *The politics of experience and the bird of paradise*. Penguin UK.

Lakoff, G. (1987). *Women, fire and dangerous things*. University of Chicago Press.

Lakoff, G. (1993). The contemporary theory of metaphor. In A. Ortony (Ed.), *Metaphor and thought* (2nd ed.) (pp. 202–251). Cambridge University Press.

Lakoff, G. (2008). The neural theory of metaphor. In R. W. Gibbs, Jr. (Ed.), *The Cambridge handbook of metaphor and thought* (pp. 17–38). Cambridge University Press.

Lakoff, G. (2014). Mapping the brain's metaphor circuitry: Metaphorical thought in everyday reason. *Frontiers in Human Neuroscience, 8*, Article 958. https://doi.org/10.3389/fnhum.2014.00958

Lakoff, G., & Johnson, M. (1980). *Metaphors we live by*. University of Chicago Press.

Lambek, M. (1998). Body and mind in mind, body and mind in body: Some anthropological interventions in a long conversation. In M. Lambek & A. Srathern (Eds.), *Bodies and persons: Comparative perspectives from Africa and Melanesia* (pp. 103–126). Cambridge University Press.

Langer, L. L. (1991). *Holocaust testimonials: The ruins of memory*. Yale University Press.

Langer, L. L. (1995). *Admitting the Holocaust: Collected essays*. Oxford University Press.

Langer, L. L. (1998). *Preempting the Holocaust*. Yale University Press.

Lashley, M. (2020). The importance of hair in the identity of Black people. *Nouvelles pratiques sociales, 31*(2), 206–227.

Latour, B. (2013). *An inquiry into modes of existence*. Harvard University Press.

Laub, D., & Allard, M. (1998). History, memory, and truth: Defining the place of the survivor. In M. Berenbaum & A. J. Peck (Eds.), *The Holocaust and history: The known, the unknown, the disputed, and the reexamined* (pp. 799–812). Indiana University Press.

Laurence, J.-R., & Perry, C. (1983). Hypnotically created memory among highly hypnotizable subjects. *Science*, *222*, 523–524.

Lauterwein, A. (2007). *Anselm Kiefer/Paul Celan: Myth, mourning and memory*. Thames & Hudson.

Leak, A. (2019). The mapping of loss. In C. Forsdick, A. Leak, & R. Phillips (Eds.), *George Perec's geographies: Material, performative and textual spaces* (pp. 17–29). London UCL Press.

Leary, D. E. (Ed.). (1994). *Metaphors in the history of psychology*. Cambridge University Press.

Leavens, D. A., & Bard, K. A. (2016). Tickling. *Current Biology*, *26*(3), R91–R93.

Leder, D. (1990). *The absent body*. University of Chicago Press.

Leder, D. (2012). Embodying otherness: Shape-shifting and the natural world. *Environmental Philosophy*, *9*(2), 123–142.

Lee, B. O., (2016). Transformation in *dang-ki* healing: The embodied self and perceived legitimacy. *Culture, Medicine, and Psychiatry*, *40*, 422–449.

Lee, B. O., & Kirmayer, L. J. (2020). *Dang-ki* healing: An embodied, relational healing practice in Singapore. *Transcultural Psychiatry*, *57*(6), 786–800.

Lee, B. O., & Kirmayer, L. J. (2023). Spirit mediumship and mental health: Therapeutic self-transformation among *dang-kis* in Singapore. *Culture, Medicine and Psychiatry*, *47*, 271–300.

Lee, B. O., Kirmayer, L. J., & Groleau, D. (2010). Therapeutic processes and perceived helpfulness of *dang-ki* (Chinese shamanism) from the symbolic healing perspective. *Culture, Medicine and Psychiatry*, *35*(1), 56–105.

Leguin, U. K. (1969). *The left hand of darkness*. Ace Books.

Lejeune, P. (1993). W or the memory of childhood. *Review of Contemporary Fiction* 13(1), 88–97.

Lemaitre, A. L., Luyat, M., & Lafargue, G. (2016). Individuals with pronounced schizotypal traits are particularly successful in tickling themselves. *Consciousness and Cognition*, *41*, 64–71.

Lemelson, R. (2014). "The spirits enter me to force me to be a communist": Political embodiment, idioms of distress, spirit possession, and thought disorder in Bali. In A. Hinton & D. Hinton (Eds.), *Genocide and mass violence: Memory, symptom, and recovery* (pp. 175–194). Rutgers University Press.

Lemelson, R., Kirmayer, L. J., & Barad, M. (2007). Trauma in context: Integrating biological, clinical and cultural perspectives. In L. J. Kirmayer, R. Lemelson, & M. Barad (Eds.), *Understanding trauma: Integrating biological, clinical, and cultural perspectives* (pp. 451–474). Cambridge University Press.

Lemelson, R., & Suryani, L. K. (2006). The spirits, *ngeb*, and the social suppression of memory: A complex clinical case from Bali: Clinical case study. *Culture, Medicine and Psychiatry*, *30*, 389–413.

Lemelson, R., & Tucker, A. (2017). *Afflictions: Steps toward a visual psychological anthropology*. Springer.

Lemelson, R., & Tucker, A. (2021). *Widening the frame with visual psychological anthropology: Perspectives on trauma, gendered violence, and stigma in Indonesia*. Springer Nature.

Levenson, R. W., Ekman, P., & Friesen, W. V. (1990). Voluntary facial action generates emotion-specific autonomic nervous system activity. *Psychophysiology*, *27*(4), 363–384.

Leventhal, H., Diefenbach, M., & Leventhal, E. A. (1992). Illness cognition: Using common sense to understand treatment adherence and affect cognition interactions. *Cognitive Therapy and Research*, *16*, 143–163.

Levi, P. (1988). *The drowned and the saved*. Penguin Books.

Levi, P. (1996). *Survival in Auschwitz*. Simon & Schuster.

Levi, P. (2001). *The search for roots: A personal anthology*. Penguin Books.

Lévi-Strauss, C. (1963). *Structural anthropology*. Basic Books.

Lévi-Strauss, C. (1969). *The raw and the cooked: Introduction to a science of mythology*. HarperCollins.

Lévi-Strauss, C. (1978). *Myth and meaning*. Schocken Books.

Lévi-Strauss, C. (1988). *The way of the masks*. Douglas & McIntyre.

Levin, D. M. (1985). *The body's recollection of being: Phenomenological psychology and the deconstruction of nihilism*. Routledge & Kegan Paul.

Levin, D. M. (Ed.). (1993). *Modernity and the hegemony of vision*. University of California Press.

Levin, S. R. (1988). *Metaphoric worlds: Conceptions of a romantic nature*. Yale University Press.

Levinas, E. (1979). *Totality and infinity*. Duquesne University Press.

Levinas, E. (1985). *Ethics and infinity*. Duquesne University Press.

Levinas, E. (1998). *Entre nous: On thinking-of-the-other*. Columbia University Press.

Levinas, E. (2003a). *On escape*. Stanford University Press.

Levinas, E. (2003b). *Humanism of the other*. University of Illinois Press.

Lewis, B. (2011). *Narrative psychiatry: How stories can shape clinical practice*. Johns Hopkins University Press.

Lewis, M. (1995). Memory and psychoanalysis: A new look at infantile amnesia and transference. *Journal of the American Academy of Child Psychiatry 34*(4), 405–417.

Lewis-Fernández, R., & Kirmayer, L. J. (2019). Cultural concepts of distress and psychiatric disorders: Understanding symptom experience and expression in context. *Transcultural Psychiatry*, *56*(4), 786–803.

Lewis-Williams, J. D. (2004). Neuropsychology and Upper Palaeolithic art: Observations on the progress of altered states of consciousness. *Cambridge Archaeological Journal*, *14*(1), 107–111.

Leys, R. (2000). *Trauma: A genealogy*. University of Chicago Press.

Lieber, E. (1979). Galen: physician as philosopher, Mamonides: philosopher as physician. *Bulletin of the History of Medicine*, *53*, 268–285.

Lieblich, A. E., McAdams, D. P., & Josselson, R. E. (2004). *Healing plots: The narrative basis of psychotherapy*. American Psychological Association.

Light, D. (1980). *Becoming psychiatrists: The professional transformation of self.* W. W. Norton.

Lim, E. T. (2009). Gendered metaphors of women in power: The case of Hillary Clinton as madonna, unruly woman, bitch and witch. In K. Ahrens (Ed.), *Politics, gender and conceptual metaphors* (pp. 254–269). Palgrave Macmillan.

Linde, C. (1993). *Life stories: The creation of coherence*. Oxford University Press.

Lindqvist, S. (2021). *Exterminate all the brutes*. Granta Books.

Lister, R. (1975). *Infernal methods: A study of William Blake's art techniques*. Bell.

Littlewood, R., & Dein, S. (1995). The effectiveness of words: Religion and healing among the Lubavitch of Stamford Hill. *Culture, Medicine and Psychiatry*, *19*(3), 339–383.

Lloyd, G. (2002). *The man of reason: "Male" and" female" in Western philosophy.* Routledge.

Lock, M. (1993). Cultivating the body: Anthropology and epistemologies of bodily practice and knowledge. *Annual Review of Anthropology*, *22*(1), 133–155.

Löfvander, M. B., & Furhoff, A. K. (1996). Backache in Greek immigrants to Sweden: A cultural interpretative approach. *Transcultural Psychiatric Research Review*, *33*(3), 319–332.

Loftus, E. F. (1993). The reality of repressed memories. *American Psychologist*, 48, 518–537.

Lopez-Pedraza, R. (2003). *Hermes and his children*. Daimon.

Lourdeaux, S. (1982). Toads in gardens for Marianne Moore and William Carlos Williams. *Modern Philology*, *80*(2), 166–167.

Low, S. M. (1994). Embodied metaphors: Nerves as lived experience. In T. Csordas (Ed.), *Embodiment and experience: The existential ground of culture and self* (pp. 139–162). Cambridge University Press.

Lu, Q., & Stanton, A. L. (2010). How benefits of expressive writing vary as a function of writing instructions, ethnicity and ambivalence over emotional expression. *Psychology and Health*, *25*(6), 669–684.

Luhrmann, T. M. (1991). *Persuasions of the witch's craft: Ritual magic in contemporary England*. Harvard University Press.

Luhrmann, T. M. (2001). The ugly goddess: Reflections on the role of violent images in religious experience. *History of Religions*, *41*(2), 114–141.

Luhrmann, T. M. (2011). *Of two minds: An anthropologist looks at American psychiatry*. Vintage.

Luhrmann, T. M. (2020). *How God becomes real: Kindling the presence of invisible others*. Princeton University Press.

Luhrmann, T. M., Dulin, J., & Dzokoto, V. (2024). The shaman and schizophrenia, revisited. *Culture, Medicine, and Psychiatry*, 1–28.

Luria, A. R. (1968). *The mind of a mnemonist*. Basic Books.

Lynn, S. J., & Rhue, J. W. (1988). Fantasy proneness: Hypnosis, developmental antecedents, and psychopathology. *American Psychologist, 43*(1), 35–44.

Lynn, S. J., McNally, R. J., & Loftus, E. F. (2023). The memory wars then and now: The contributions of Scott O. Lilienfeld. *Clinical Psychological Science, 11* (4), 725–743.

Lynn, S. J., Rhue, J. W., & Weekes, J. R. (1990). Hypnotic involuntariness: A social cognitive analysis. *Psychological Review, 97*(2), 169.

Lyon, J. K. (2006). *Paul Celan and Martin Heidegger: An unresolved conversation, 1951–1970*. Johns Hopkins University Press.

Lyotard J.-F. (1992). *The Inhuman: Reflections on time*. University of Chicago Press.

MacLean, P. D. (1949). Psychosomatic disease and the visceral brain: Recent developments bearing on the Papez theory of emotion. *Psychosomatic Medicine, 11*, 338–353.

MacLean, P. D. (1980). Sensory and perceptive factors in emotional functions of the triune brain. In A. O. Rorty (Ed.), *Explaining emotions* (pp. 9–36). University of California Press.

Macmillan, M. (1997). *Freud evaluated: The completed arc*. MIT Press.

Madison, A. A., Wilson, S. J., Shrout, M. R., Malarkey, W. B., & Kiecolt-Glaser, J. K. (2024). Intimate partner violence and inflammaging: Conflict tactics predict inflammation among middle-aged and older adults. *Psychosomatic Medicine, 86*(5), 379–386.

Maier, S. F., & Watkins, L. R. (1998). Cytokines for psychologists: Implications of bidirectional immune-to-brain communication for understanding behavior, mood, and cognition. *Psychological Review, 105*(1), 83–107.

Majno, G. (1975). *The healing hand: Man and wound in the ancient world*. Harvard University Press.

Malkomsen, A., Røssberg, J. I., Dammen, T., Wilberg, T., Løvgren, A., Ulberg, R., & Evensen, J. (2021). Digging down or scratching the surface: How patients use metaphors to describe their experiences of psychotherapy. *BMC Psychiatry, 21*, 1–12.

Malkomsen, A., Røssberg, J. I., Dammen, T., Wilberg, T., Løvgren, A., Ulberg, R., & Evensen, J. (2022). How therapists in cognitive behavioral and psychodynamic therapy reflect upon the use of metaphors in therapy: A qualitative study. *BMC Psychiatry, 22*, 433.

Mandell, B. (2002). *Is this heaven? The magic of the Field of dreams*. Roman & Littlefield.

Margalit, A. (2002). *The ethics of memory*. Harvard University Press.

Marks, L. E. (1996). On perceptual metaphors. *Metaphor and Symbolic Activity, 11* (1), 44–45.

Marriott, M. (1976). Interpreting Indian society: A monistic alternative to Dumont's dualism. *The Journal of Asian Studies, 36*(1), 189–195.

Marsella, A. J., Devos, G., & Hsu, F. L. K. (Eds.). (1985). *Culture and self: Asian and Western perspectives*. Tavistock Publications.

Martimianakis, M. A. T., Michalec, B., Lam, J., Cartmill, C., Taylor, J. S., & Hafferty, F. W. (2015). Humanism, the hidden curriculum, and educational reform: A scoping review and thematic analysis. *Academic Medicine*, *90*(11), S5–S13.

Martin, E. (2010). Self-making and the brain. *Subjectivity*, *3*(4), 366–381.

Matsuki, K. (1995). Metaphors of anger in Japanese. In J. R. Taylor & R. E. MacLaury (Eds.), *Language and the cognitive construal of the world* (pp. 137–151). de Gruyter.

Mattingly, C. (1994). The concept of therapeutic "emplotment." *Social Science and Medicine*, *38*(6), 811–822.

Maurer, D., Ghloum, J. K., Gibson, L. C., Watson, M. R., Chen, L. M., Akins, K., . . . & Werker, J. F. (2020). Reduced perceptual narrowing in synesthesia. *Proceedings of the National Academy of Sciences*, *117*(18), 10089–10096.

Mauss, M. (1902/1972). *A general theory of magic* (R. Brain, Trans.). W. W. Norton.

Mayer, G. (2008). The figure of the shaman as a modern myth: Some reflections on the attractiveness of shamanism in modern societies. *Pomegranate: The International Journal of Pagan Studies*, *10*(1), 70–103.

McAdams, D. P. (1989). The development of a narrative identity. In D. M. Buss & N. Kantor (Eds.), *Personality psychology* (pp. 160–174). Springer.

McAdams, D. P. (1991). Self and story. In J. Stewart, J. M. Healy, Jr., D. Ozer, & R. Hogan (Eds.), *Perspectives in personality* (Vol. 3, Part B, pp. 133–159). Jessica Kingsley Publishers.

McAdams, D. P. (2006). The problem of narrative coherence. *Journal of Constructivist Psychology*, *19*(2), 109–125.

McAdams, D. P. (2018). Narrative identity: What is it? What does it do? How do you measure it? *Imagination, Cognition and Personality*, *37*(3), 359–372.

McAllester Jones, M. (1991). *Gaston Bachelard: Subversive humanist*. University of Wisconsin Press.

McCreery, J. L. (1979). Potential and effective meaning in therapeutic ritual. *Culture, Medicine and Psychiatry*, *3*, 53–72.

McDougall, J. (2013). *Theaters of the mind: Illusion and truth on the psychoanalytic stage*. Routledge.

McLean, K. C., Lilgendahl, J. P., Fordham, C., Alpert, E., Maarsden, E., Szymanowski, K., & McAdams, D. P. (2018). Identity development in cultural context: The role of deviating from master narratives. *Journal of Personality*, *86* (4), 631–651.

McLean, K. C., & Syed, M. (2015). Personal, master, and alternative narratives: An integrative framework for understanding identity development in context. *Human Development*, *58*(6), 318–349.

McMullen, L. M. (1989). Uses of figurative language in successful and unsuccessful cases of psychotherapy: Three comparisons. *Metaphor and Symbolic Activity*, *4* (4), 203–226.

McMullen, L. M., & Tay, D. (2023). Research review of psychotherapists' use of metaphors. *Psychotherapy*, *60*(3), 255–265.

McNally, R. J. (2003). *Remembering trauma*. Harvard University Press.

McNally, R. J. (2024). The return of repression? Evidence from cognitive psychology. *Topics in Cognitive Science, 16*, 661–674.

McCrae, R. R. (2021). Music lessons for the study of affect. *Frontiers in Psychology, 12*, 760167.

Mehl-Madrona, L., & Mainguy, B. (2014). Introducing healing circles and talking circles into primary care. *The Permanente Journal, 18*(2), 4–9.

Meier, C. A. (1967). *Ancient incubation and modern psychotherapy*. Northwestern University Press.

Meier, C. A. (1989). *Healing, dream, and ritual: Ancient incubation and modern psychotherapy*. Daimon Verlag.

Meissner, K., & Wittmann, M. (2011). Body signals, cardiac awareness, and the perception of time. *Biological Psychology, 86*(3), 289–297.

Meltzoff, A. N., & Moore, M. K. (1977). Imitation of facial and manual gestures by human neonates. *Science*, 198, 75–78.

Melzack, R. (2005). The McGill pain questionnaire: From description to measurement. *Anesthesia, 103*(1), 199–202.

Melzack, R., & Casey, K. L. (1968). Sensory, motivational, and central control determinants of pain: A new conceptual model. *The Skin Senses, 1*, 423–443.

Mesman, J., van IJzendoorn, M. H., & Bakermans-Kranenburg, M. J. (2009). The many faces of the still-face paradigm: A review and meta-analysis. *Developmental Review, 29*(2), 120–162.

Mesquita, B. (2022). *Between us: How cultures create emotions*. W. W. Norton.

Mianji, F., & Kirmayer, L. J. (2020). The globalization of biological psychiatry and the rise of bipolar spectrum disorder in Iran. *Culture, Medicine, and Psychiatry, 44*, 404–432

Mianji, F., & Kirmayer, L. J. (2022). Women as troublemakers: The hard sociopolitical context of soft bipolar disorder in Iran. *Culture, Medicine, and Psychiatry, 45*, 864–888.

Mianji, F., & Kirmayer, L. J. (2023). Help-seeking strategies and treatment experiences among individuals diagnosed with bipolar spectrum disorder in Iran: A qualitative study. *Transcultural Psychiatry, 60*(2), 201–214.

Middlebrook, D. W. (1992). *Anne Sexton: A biography*. Vintage.

Midgley, M. (2011). *The myths we live by*. Routledge.

Miller, A. (2008). *The drama of the gifted child: The search for the true self*. Basic Books.

Miller, G. E., Cohen, S., & Herbert, T. B. (1999). Pathways linking major depression and immunity in ambulatory female patients. *Psychosomatic Medicine, 61*, 850–860.

Milloy, J. S. (1999). *A national crime: The Canadian government and the residential school system, 1879 to 1986*. University of Manitoba Press.

Miresco, M. J., & Kirmayer, L. J. (2006). The persistence of mind-brain dualism in psychiatric reasoning about clinical scenarios. *American Journal of Psychiatry, 163*(5), 913–918.

Mishler, E. (1984). *The discourse of medicine*. Ablex Publishing Co.

Mlodinow, L. (2011). *Feynman's rainbow: A search for beauty in physics and in life.* Vintage.
Moerman, D. E. (2002). *Meaning, medicine and the "placebo effect."* Cambridge University Press.
Morinis, A. (1985). The ritual experience: pain and the transformation of consciousness in ordeals of initiation. *Ethos, 13*(2), 150–174.
Mosès, S. (2009). *The angel of history: Rosenzweig, Benjamin, Scholem.* Stanford University Press.
Mould, T. J., Oades, L. G., & Crowe, T. P. (2010). The use of metaphor for understanding and managing psychotic experiences: A systematic review. *Journal of Mental Health, 19*(3), 282–293.
Mounin, G. (1985). *Semiotic praxis.* Plenum Press.
Mulder, R., Murray, G., & Rucklidge, J. (2017). Common versus specific factors in psychotherapy: opening the black box. *The Lancet Psychiatry, 4*(12), 953–962.
Munday, I., Kneebone, I., Rogers, K., & Newton-John, T. (2022). The language of pain: Is there a relationship between metaphor use and adjustment to chronic pain? *Pain Medicine, 23*(12), 2073–2084.
Mundt, C. (2014). Jaspers' concept of "limit situation": Extensions and therapeutic applications. In T. Fuchs, T. Breyer, & C. Mundt (Eds.), *Karl Jaspers' philosophy and psychopathology* (pp. 169–178). Springer.
Musolff, A. (2012). The study of metaphor as part of critical discourse analysis. *Critical discourse studies, 9*(3), 301–310.
Nabokov, V. (1966). *Speak memory: An autobiography eevisited.* G.P. Putnam's Sons.
Nabokov, V. (1969). *Ada.* McGraw-Hill.
Nachmanovitch, S. (1991). *Free play: Improvisation in life and art.* Penguin.
Nadeau, J. W. (2006). Metaphorically speaking: The use of metaphors in grief therapy. *Illness, Crisis & Loss, 14*(3), 201–221.
Naish, P. (2014). The perception of time in hypnosis. In V. Arstila & D. Lloyd. (Eds.), *Subjective time: The philosophy, psychology, and neuroscience of temporality* (pp. 621–636). MIT Press.
Nakamura, J., & Csikszentmihalyi, M. (2014). The concept of flow. In M. Csikszentmihalyi & R, Larson (Eds.), *Flow and the foundations of positive psychology* (pp. 239–263). Springer.
Nancy, J.-L. (2002). *L'intrus. CR: The New Centennial Review, 2*(3), 1–14.
Napier, A. D. (1986). *Masks, transformation, and paradox.* University of California Press.
Needleman, J. (1985). *The way of the physician.* W. W. Norton.
Neihardt, J. G. (1979). *Black Elk speaks.* University of Nebraska Press.
Neimeyer, R. & Mahoney, M. J. (Eds.). (1995). *Constructivism in psychotherapy.* American Psychological Association.
Neisser, U. (1994). Self-narratives: True and false. In U. Neisser & R. Fivush (Eds.), *The remembering self: Construction and accuracy in the self-narrative* (pp. 1–18). Cambridge University Press.

Nelson, K. (2003). Narrative and self, myth and memory: Emergence of the cultural self. In R. Fivush & C. A. Haden (Eds.), *Autobiographical memory and the construction of a narrative self: Developmental and cultural perspectives* (pp. 3–28). Lawrence Erlbaum Associates Publishers.

Neruda, P. (1969). *Twenty Love Poems and A Song of Despair* (W. S. Merwin, Trans.). Jonathan Cape.

Newen, A., Gallagher, S., & De Bruin, L. (2018). 4E cognition: Historical roots, key concepts, and central issues. In A. Newen, L. De Bruin, & S. Gallagher (Eds.), *The Oxford handbook of 4E cognition* (pp. 3–15). Oxford University Press.

Newitz, A. (2017). *Autonomous*. Tor Books.

Nicholls, A. (2014). *Myth and the human sciences: Hans Blumenberg's theory of myth*. Routledge.

Nicholls, D. (2004). What we talk about when we talk about anger. *MED Magazine, 18*. https://macmillandictionaries.com/MED-Magazine/April2004/18-metaphor-anger.htm#3

Nichter, M. (1981). Idioms of distress: Alternatives in the expression of psychosocial distress: A case study from South India. *Culture, Medicine and Psychiatry, 5*(4), 379–408.

Nichter, M. (2010). Idioms of distress revisited. *Culture, Medicine, and Psychiatry, 34*, 401–416.

Nichter, M. (2022). From idioms of distress, concern, and care to moral distress leading to moral injury in the time of Covid. *Transcultural Psychiatry, 59*(4), 551–567.

Niederland, W. G. (1968). The psychiatric evaluation of emotional disorders in survivors of Nazi persecution. In H. Krystal (Ed.), *Massive psychic trauma* (pp. 8–22). International Universities Press.

Niewöhner, J., & Lock, M. (2018). Situating local biologies: Anthropological perspectives on environment/human entanglements. *BioSocieties, 13*(4), 681–697.

Niezen, R. (2017). *Truth and indignation: Canada's Truth and Reconciliation Commission on Indian residential schools*. University of Toronto Press.

Nisbett, R. E., & Wilson, T. D. (1977). Telling more than we can know: Verbal reports on mental processes. *Psychological Review, 84*(3), 231–259.

Noel, M., Chambers, C. T., Parker, J. A., Aubrey, K., Tutelman, P. R., Morrongiello, B., . . . & Von Baeyer, C. L. (2018). Boo-boos as the building blocks of pain expression: An observational examination of parental responses to everyday pain in toddlers. *Canadian Journal of Pain, 2*(1), 74–86.

Noble, D. (2012). A theory of biological relativity: No privileged level of causation. *Interface Focus, 2*(1), 55–64.

Noble, D. (2016). *Dance to the tune of life: Biological relativity*. Cambridge University Press.

Norenzayan, A., & Heine, S. J. (2005). Psychological universals: What are they and how can we know? *Psychological Bulletin, 131*(5), 763–784.

Norman, D. (1990). *The hero: Myth, image, symbol*. Doubleday.

Nortje, G., Oladeji, B., Gureje, O., & Seedat, S. (2016). Effectiveness of traditional healers in treating mental disorders: A systematic review. *The Lancet Psychiatry*, *3*(2), 154–170.

Nussbaum, M. C. (2003). *Upheavals of thought: The intelligence of emotions.* Cambridge University Press.

Oakley, T. (2007). Image schemas. In D. Geeraerts & H. Cuyckens (Eds.), *The Oxford handbook of cognitive linguistics* (pp. 214–235). Oxford University Press.

Oakley, D. A., Walsh, E., Mehta, M. A., Halligan, P. W., & Deeley, Q. (2021). Direct verbal suggestibility: Measurement and significance. *Consciousness and Cognition*, *89*, 103036.

Oatley, K. (2019). The human unconscious in evolution. *Psychological Inquiry*, *30* (2), 76–78.

Obeyesekere, G. (1981). *Medusa's hair: An essay on personal symbols and religious experience*. University of Chicago Press.

Obeyesekere, G. (1991). *The work of culture: Symbolic transformation in psychoanalysis and anthropology*. University of Chicago Press.

O'Connor, M. F. (2019). Grief: A brief history of research on how body, mind, and brain adapt. *Psychosomatic Medicine*, *81*(8), 731–738.

Ogarkova, A., & Soriano, C. (2014). Emotion and the body: A corpus-based investigation of metaphorical containers of anger across languages. *International Journal of Cognitive Linguistics*, 5(2), 147–179.

O'Neill, J. (1985). *Five bodies: The human shape of modern society*. Cornell University Press.

Ongaro, G., & Kaptchuk, T. J. (2019). Symptom perception, placebo effects, and the Bayesian brain. *Pain*, *160*(1), 1–4.

Ongaro, G., & Ward, D. (2017). An enactive account of placebo effects. *Biology & Philosophy*, *32*(4), 507–533.

Onians, R. B. (1951). *The origins of European thought about the body, the mind, the soul, the world, time and fate*. Cambridge University Press.

Orange, D. M. (2011). *The suffering stranger: Hermeneutics for everyday clinical practice*. Routledge.

Orne, M. T., Whitehouse, W. G., Dinges, D. F., & Orne, E. C. (1988). Reconstructing memory through hypnosis: Forensic and clinical implications. In H. M. Pettinati (Ed.), *Hypnosis and memory* (pp. 21–63). Guilford Press.

Orr, G. (2002). *Poetry as survival*. University of Georgia Press.

Ortner, S. B. (1973). On key symbols. *American Anthropologist*, *75*(5), 1338–1346.

Ortony, A. (1979). Beyond literal similarity. *Psychological Review*, *86*(3), 161–180.

Ortony, A. (Ed.). (1993). *Metaphor and thought* (2nd ed.). Cambridge University Press.

Osgood, C. E. (1964). Semantic differential technique in the comparative study of cultures. *American Anthropologist*, *66*(3), 171–200.

Osgood, C. E. (1981). The cognitive dynamics of synesthesia and metaphor. *Review of Research in Visual Arts Education*, 56–80.

Osgood, C. E., May, W. H., & Miron, M. S. (1975). *Cross-cultural universal of affective meaning*. University of Illinois Press.

Osherson, S. & Amara Singham, L. (1981). The machine metaphor in medicine. In E. G. Mishler, L. R. Amara Singham, R. Liem, S. D. Osherson, S. T. Hauser, & N. E. Waxler (Eds.), *Social contexts of health, illness and patient care* (pp. 218–249). Cambridge University Press.

Oster, G. (1970). Phosphenes. *Scientific American*, *222*(2), 82–87.

Oster, S. B. (2020). Holocaust shoes: Metonymy, matter, memory. In V. Aarons & P. Lassner (Eds.), *The Palgrave handbook of Holocaust literature and culture* (pp. 761–784). Palgrave MacMillan.

Otgaar, H., Howe, M. L., & Patihis, L. (2022). What science tells us about false and repressed memories. *Memory*, *30*(1), 16–31. https://doi.org/10.1080/09658211.2020.1870699

Otis, L. (2019). *Banned emotions: How metaphors can shape what people feel.* Oxford University Press.

Ots, T. (1990). The angry liver, the anxious heart and the melancholy spleen: The phenomenology of perceptions in Chinese culture. *Culture, Medicine and Psychiatry*, *14*(1), 21–58.

Overing, J. (1990). The shaman as a maker of worlds: Nelson Goodman in the Amazon. *Man*, *25*(4):602-619.

Pagel, W. (1948). Jung's views on alchemy. *Isis*, *39*(1/2), 44–48.

Pajevic, M. (2001). The stance in the poetics of Paul Celan. *German Life and Letters*, *54*(4), 345–351.

Panksepp, J. (2004). *Affective neuroscience: The foundations of human and animal emotions.* Oxford University Press.

Panksepp, J., & Biven, L. (2012). *The archaeology of mind: Neuroevolutionary origins of human emotion.* W. W. Norton.

Paris, G. (1990). *Pagan grace: Dionysus, Hermes and goddess Memory.* Spring Publications.

Paris, J. (2019). *An evidence-based critique of contemporary psychoanalysis: Research, theory, and clinical practice.* Routledge.

Paris, J., & Frank, H. (1983). Psychological determinants of a medical career. *Canadian Journal of Psychiatry*, *28*, 354–357.

Paris, J., & Guzder, J. (1989). The poisoned nest: Dynamic aspects of exogamous marriage. *Journal of the American Academy of Psychoanalysis*, *17*(3), 493–500.

Parr, T., Pezzulo, G., & Friston, K. J. (2022). *Active inference: The free energy principle in mind, brain, and behavior.* MIT Press.

Patihis, L., Frenda, S. J., LePort, A. K., Petersen, N., Nichols, R. M., Stark, C. E., . . . & Loftus, E. F. (2013). False memories in highly superior autobiographical memory individuals. *Proceedings of the National Academy of Sciences*, *110*(52), 20947–20952.

Patten, S. B. (2015). Medical models and metaphors for depression. *Epidemiology and Psychiatric Sciences*, *24*(4), 303–308.

Peet, A. (2017). Epistemic injustice in utterance interpretation. *Synthese*, *194*(9), 3421–3443.

Peill, J., Marguilho, M., Erritzoe, D., Barba, T., Greenway, K. T., Rosas, F., . . . & Carhart-Harris, R. (2024). Psychedelics and the "inner healer": Myth or mechanism? *Journal of Psychopharmacology, 38*(5), 417–424.

Pennebaker, J. W. (2012). *Opening up: The healing power of expressing emotions.* Guilford Press.

Pennebaker, J. W. (2018). Expressive writing in psychological science. *Perspectives on Psychological Science, 13*(2), 226–229.

Pennebaker, J. W., & Smyth, J. M. (2016). *Opening up by writing it down: How expressive writing improves health and eases emotional pain.* Guilford Press.

Pepper, S. C. (1935). The root of metaphor theory of metaphysics. *The Journal of Philosophy, 32*(14), 365–374.

Pepper, S. C. (1982). Introduction: Metaphor in philosophy. *The Journal of Mind and Behavior, 3*(3/4), 197–205.

Perec, G. (1988). *W, or the memory of childhood.* David R. Godine.

Perec, G. (2005). *A void.* David R. Godine Publisher.

Perelman, C. (1982). *The realm of rhetoric* (W. Kluback, Trans.). University of Notre Dame Press.

Perricone, A., & Ahn, W. K. (2023). Reasons for the belief that psychotherapy is less effective for biologically attributed mental disorders. *Cognitive Therapy and Research*, 1–11.

Phelan, J. (2017). *Somebody telling somebody else: A rhetorical poetics of narrative.* The Ohio State University Press.

Pickering, A. (2017). The ontological turn: Taking different worlds seriously. *Social Analysis, 61*(2), 134–150.

Pietikainen, P. (1998). Archetypes as symbolic forms. *Journal of Analytical Psychology, 43*(3), 325–343.

Pillen, A. (2015). Atrocity and nonsense: The ethnographic study of dehumanization. In A. Hinton & D. Hinton (Eds.), *Genocide and mass violence: Memory, symptom, and recovery* (pp. 342–356). Cambridge University Press.

Pinsky, R. (1998). *The sounds of poetry: A brief guide.* Farrar, Strauss & Giroux.

Plato. (1961). *Plato: The collected dialogues.* Princeton University Press.

Pohlhaus Jr., G. (2012). Relational knowing and epistemic injustice: Toward a theory of willful hermeneutical ignorance. *Hypatia, 27*(4), 715–735.

Pollio, H. R., Barlow, J. M., Fine, H. J., & Pollio, M. R. (2023). *Psychology and the poetics of growth: Figurative language in psychology, psychotherapy, and education.* Taylor & Francis.

Ponge, F. (2008). *Mute objects of expression.* Archipelago.

Poole, G. D., & Craig, K. D. (1992). Judgments of genuine, suppressed, and faked facial expressions of pain. *Journal of Personality and Social Psychology, 63*(5), 797–805.

Pope, H. G., Jr., & Hudson, J. I. (1995). Can memories of childhood sexual abuse be repressed? *Psychological Medicine 25*, 121–126.

Porter, M. (2007). Global evidence for a biopsychosocial understanding of refugee adaptation. *Transcultural Psychiatry, 44*(3), 418–439.

Povinelli, E. A. (2001). Radical worlds: The anthropology of incommensurability and inconceivability. *Annual Review of Anthropology, 30*(1), 319–334.

Power, M. L., & Schulkin, J. (2008). Anticipatory physiological regulation in feeding biology: Cephalic phase responses. *Appetite, 50*(2-3), 194–206.

Powers, R. (2000). *Plowing the dark*. Farrar, Straus, and Giroux.

Powers, R. (2018). *The overstory*. Vintage.

Powers, W. K. (1990). When Black Elk speaks, everybody listens. In C. Vecsey (Ed.), *Religion in Native North America* (pp. 136–151). University of Idaho Press.

Prechtel, M. (1998). *Secrets of the talking jaguar: A Mayan shaman's journey to the heart of the Indigenous soul*. Jeremy Tarcher/Putnam.

Pribram, K. H. (1986). Mind, brain, body: Toward a convergence of psychoanalysis and neurobiology. *The Journal of Nervous and Mental Disease, 174*(6), 372–374.

Price, D. D., Milling, L. S., Kirsch, I., Duff, A., Montgomery, G. H., & Nicholls, S. S. (1999). An analysis of factors that contribute to the magnitude of placebo analgesia in an experimental paradigm. *Pain, 83*, 147–156.

Prince, R. (1980). Variations in psychotherapeutic procedures. In H. C. Triandis & J. G. Draguns (Eds.), *Handbook of cross-cultural psychology* (pp. 291–349). Allyn and Bacon.

Prince, R. (1982). Shamans and endorphins. *Ethos, 10*, 409–423.

Prince, R. H. (1976). Psychotherapy as the manipulation of endogenous healing mechanisms: A transcultural survey. *Transcultural Psychiatric Research Review, 13*(2), 115–133.

Pritzker, S. (2007). Thinking hearts, feeling brains: Metaphor, culture, and the self in Chinese narratives of depression. *Metaphor and Symbol, 22*(3), 251–274.

Prosser, C. L. (1970). Levels of biological organization and their physiological significance. In J. A. Moore (Ed.), *Ideas in evolution and behavior* (pp. 357–390). Natural History Press.

Puett, M., & Gross-Loh, C. (2016). *The path: What Chinese philosophers can teach us about the good life*. Simon and Schuster.

Qiu, A. H., Tay, D., & Watson, B. (2024). Metaphorical language and psychopathological symptoms: A case study of trauma victims' metaphor use. *BMC Psychology, 12*(1), 57.

Quinn, N. (1982). "Commitment" in American marriage: A cultural analysis. *American Ethnologist, 9*(4), 775–798.

Quinn, N. (1991). The cultural basis of metaphor. In J. M. Fernandez (Ed.), *Beyond metaphor: The theory of tropes in anthropology* (pp. 56–93). Stanford University Press.

Quinn, N., & Holland, D. (1987). Culture and cognition. In D. Holland & N. Quinn (Eds.), *Cultural models in language and thought* (pp. 3–40). Cambridge University Press.

Rabkin, R. (1977). *Strategic psychotherapy: Brief and symptomatic treatment*. Basic Books.

Radden, J. (2009). *Moody minds distempered: Essays on melancholy and depression*. Oxford University Press.

Rahimi, S. (2021). *A hauntology for everyday life*. Springer International Publishing.

Ramachandran, V. S., Marcus, Z., & Chunharas, C. (2020). Bouba-Kiki: Cross-domain resonance and the origins of synesthesia, metaphor, and words in the human mind. In K. Sathian & V. S. Ramachandran (Eds.), *Multisensory perception: From laboratory to clinic* (pp. 3–40). Academic Press.

Ramstead, M. J., Hesp, C., Tschantz, A., Smith, R., Constant, A., & Friston, K. (2021). Neural and phenotypic representation under the free-energy principle. *Neuroscience & Biobehavioral Reviews, 120*, 109–122.

Ramstead, M. J., Veissière, S. P., & Kirmayer, L. J. (2016). Cultural affordances: Scaffolding local worlds through shared intentionality and regimes of attention. *Frontiers in Psychology, 7*, 1090.

Ratcliffe, M. (2023). *Grief worlds: A study of emotional experience*. MIT Press.

Reaume, G. (2021). How is mad studies different from anti-psychiatry and critical psychiatry? In P. Beresford & J. Russo (Eds.), *The Routledge international handbook of mad studies* (pp. 98–107). Routledge.

Reddy, W. M. (2001). *The navigation of feeling: A framework for the history of emotions*. Cambridge University Press.

Reed, W. (1978). Shamanistic principles of initiation and power. In G. Hill (Ed.), *The shaman from Elko* (pp. 39–53). C. G. Jung Institute of San Francisco.

Reynolds, A. S. (2022). *Understanding metaphors in the life sciences*. Cambridge University Press.

Richards, B. A., & Lillicrap, T. P. (2022). The brain-computer metaphor debate is useless: A matter of semantics. *Frontiers in Computer Science, 4*, 810358.

Ricoeur, P. (1970). *Freud and philosophy: An essay on interpretation* (D. Savage, Trans.). Yale University Press.

Ricoeur, P. (1977). *The rule of metaphor: Multi-disciplinary studies of the creation of meaning in language*. University of Toronto Press.

Ricoeur, P. (1988). *Time and narrative* (Vol. 3). University of Chicago Press.

Ricoeur, P. (1991). Narrative identity. In D. Wood (Ed.), *On Paul Ricoeur: Narrative and interpretation* (pp. 188–199). Routledge.

Ricoeur, P. (1992). *Oneself as another*. University of Chicago Press.

Riley, D. (2019). *Time lived, without its flow*. Picador.

Rimke, H. (2020). Self-help, therapeutic industries, and neoliberalism. In D. Nehring (Ed.), *The Routledge international handbook of global therapeutic cultures* (pp. 37–50). Routledge.

Ripinsky-Naxon, M. (1993). *The nature of shamanism: Substance and function of a religious metaphor*. SUNY Press.

Riss, W. (1968). Overview of the design of the central nervous system and the problem of the natural units of behavior. *Brain, Behavior and Evolution, 1*, 124–131.

Robbins, P. E., & Aydede, M. E. (Eds.). (2009). *The Cambridge handbook of situated cognition*. Cambridge University Press.

Robcis, C. (2021). *Disalienation: Politics, philosophy, and radical psychiatry in postwar France*. University of Chicago Press.

Roch-Levecq, A. C. (2006). Production of basic emotions by children with congenital blindness: Evidence for the embodiment of theory of mind. *British Journal of Developmental Psychology, 24*(3), 507–528.

Rochberg-Halton, E. (1986). *Meaning and modernity: Social theory in the pragmatic attitude*. University of Chicago Press.

Rodríguez-López, R. (2023). Technologies of the self in culture: critical reflections on the self-managed subject. *Subjectivity, 30*(2), 152–166.

Roediger, H. L. (1980). Memory metaphors in cognitive psychology. *Memory & Cognition, 8*, 231–246.

Roesler, C. (2012). Are archetypes transmitted more by culture than biology? Questions arising from conceptualizations of the archetype. *Journal of Analytical Psychology, 57*(2), 223–246.

Rojtman, B. (1998). *Black fire on white fire: An essay on Jewish hermeneutics, from Midrash to Kabbalah*. University of California Press.

Roland, A. (1988). *In search of self in India and Japan: Toward a cross-cultural psychology*. Princeton University Press.

Rolls, E. T. (2015). Limbic systems for emotion and for memory, but no single limbic system. *Cortex, 62*, 119–157.

Rorty, R. (1979). *Philosophy and the mirror of nature*. Princeton University Press.

Rorty, R. (2016). *Philosophy as poetry*. University of Virginia Press.

Rosaldo, M. Z. (1980). *Knowledge and passion*. Cambridge University Press.

Rosaldo, M. Z. (1984). Toward an anthropology of self and feeling. In R. Shweder & R. A. LeVine (Eds.), *Culture theory: Essays on mind, self and emotion* (pp. 137–157). Cambridge University Press.

Rose, N. (1998). *Inventing our selves: Psychology, power, and personhood*. Cambridge University Press.

Rose, N., & Abi-Rached, J. M. (2013). *Neuro: The new brain sciences and the management of the mind*. Princeton University Press.

Ross, R. (1996). *Returning to the teachings: Exploring Aboriginal justice*. Penguin Canada.

Ross, R. (2014). *Indigenous healing: Exploring traditional paths*. Penguin Canada.

Rossi, E. L. (Ed.). (1980). *The collected papers of Milton H. Erickson, M.D.* (4 vols.). Irvington Press.

Rozin, P., Millman, L., & Nemeroff, C. (1986). Operation of the laws of sympathetic magic in disgust and other domains. *Journal of Personality and Social Psychology 50*(4), 703–712.

Rozin, P., & Nemeroff, C. (1990). The laws of sympathetic magic. In J. W. Stigler, R. A. Shweder, & G. Herdt (Eds.), *Cultural psychology: Essays on comparative human development* (pp. 205–232). Cambridge University Press.

Rubba, J. (1996). Alternate grounds in the interpretation of deictic expressions. In G. Fauconnier & E. Sweetser (Eds.), *Spaces, worlds, and grammars*. University of Chicago Press.

Saarinen, A., Harjunen, V., Jasinskaja-Lahti, I., Jääskeläinen, I. P., & Ravaja, N. (2021). Social touch experience in different contexts: A review. *Neuroscience & Biobehavioral Reviews, 131*, 360–372.

Sacks, J. (1997). *The politics of hope*. Jonathan Cape.
Sacks, O. (1982). *A leg to stand on*. Harper & Row.
Sahlins, M. (2022). *The new science of the enchanted universe: An anthropology of most of humanity*. Princeton University Press.
Salmon, P. (2020). *An event, perhaps: A biography of Jacques Derrida*. Verso Books.
Sampson, E. E. (1977). Psychology and the American ideal. *Journal of Personality and Social Psychology, 35*(11), 767–782.
Samuels, A. (1985). *Jung and the post-Jungians*. Routledge.
Sanchez-Ruiz, M. J., Santos, M. R., & Jiménez, J. J. (2013). The role of metaphorical thinking in the creativity of scientific discourse. *Creativity Research Journal, 25*(4), 361–368.
Sandner, D. F., & Wong, S. H. (2013). *The sacred heritage: The influence of shamanism on analytical psychology*. Routledge.
Sas, C., & Coman, A. (2016). Designing personal grief rituals: An analysis of symbolic objects and actions. *Death Studies*, 40(9), 558–569.
Sass L. A. (1992). *Madness and modernism: Insanity in the light of modern art, literature, and thought*. Basic Books.
Sass, L. A. (1998). Interpreting schizophrenia: construal or construction? A reply to Robert J. Barrett. *Culture, Medicine and Psychiatry, 22*(4), 495–503.
Sass, L. A. (2007). "Schizophrenic person" or "person with schizophrenia"?: An essay on illness and self. *Theory & Psychology, 17*(3), 395–420.
Sass, L., & Alvarez, E. (2023). Metaphor, magic, and mental disorder: Poetics and ontology in Mexican (Purépecha) curanderismo. *Transcultural Psychiatry, 60*(5), 781–798.
Saunders, B., Riesel, A., Klawohn, J., & Inzlicht, M. (2018). Interpersonal touch enhances cognitive control: A neurophysiological investigation. *Journal of Experimental Psychology: General, 147*(7), 1066.
Saunders, N. J. (2013). Architecture of symbolism: The feline image. In N. J. Saunders (Ed.), *Icons of power: Feline symbolism in the Americas* (pp. 12–52). Routledge.
Sax, B. (2009). The magic of animals: English witch trials in the perspective of folklore. *Anthrozoös, 22*(4), 317–332.
Sax, W. S. (2002). *Dancing the self: Personhood and performance in the Pāṇḍava Līla of Garhwal*. Oxford University Press.
Sax, W. S. (2010). Ritual and the problem of efficacy. In W. S. Sax, J. Quack, & J. Weinhold (Eds.), *The problem of ritual efficacy* (pp. 3–16). Oxford University Press.
Scarry, E. (1985). *The body in pain: The making and unmaking of the world*. Oxford University Press.
Schacter, D. L. (1999). The seven sins of memory: Insights from psychology and cognitive neuroscience. *American Psychologist, 54*(3), 182.
Schacter, D. L. (2022). The seven sins of memory: An update. *Memory, 30*(1), 37–42.
Schafer, R. (1992). *Retelling a life: Narration and dialogue in psychoanalysis*. Basic Books.

Schechtman, M. (2007). *The constitution of selves.* Cornell University Press.
Schechtman, M. (2024). Self-narrative, literary narrative, and self-understanding. *Philosophia, 52*(1), 11–20.
Scheff, T. J. (1979). *Catharsis in healing, ritual, and drama.* University of California Press.
Scheper-Hughes, N., & Lock, M. M. (1987). The mindful body: A prolegomenon to future work in medical anthropology. *Medical Anthropology Quarterly, 1* (1), 6–41.
Schieffelin, E. (1976). *The sorrow of the lonely and the burning of the dancers.* St. Martin's Press.
Schieffelin, E. (1979). Mediators as metaphors: Moving men to tears in Papua New Guinea. In A. L. Becker & A. A. Yengovan (Eds.), *The imagination of reality* (pp. 127–144). Ablex Publishing Co.
Schoeneman, T. J., Schoeneman, K. A., & Stallings, S. (2004). "The black struggle": Metaphors of depression in Styron's *Darkness visible. Journal of Social and Clinical Psychology, 23*(3), 325–346.
Scholem, G. (1961). *Major trends in Jewish mysticism.* Schocken Books
Scholem, G. (2006). *Alchemy and Kabbalah.* Spring Publications.
Schrempp, G. A., & Hansen, W. F. (Eds.). (2002). *Myth: A new symposium.* Indiana University Press.
Schulkin, J., & Sterling, P. (2019). Allostasis: A brain-centered, predictive mode of physiological regulation. *Trends in Neurosciences, 42*(10), 740–752.
Schwabe, L., Nader, K., & Pruessner, J. C. (2014). Reconsolidation of human memory: Brain mechanisms and clinical relevance. *Biological Psychiatry, 76*(4), 274–280.
Schwitzgebel, E. (2011). *Perplexities of consciousness.* MIT Press.
Searles, H. (1975). *Countertransference and related subjects.* International Universities Press.
Sebald, W. G. (1996). *The emigrants.* New Directions.
Sebald, W. G. (2001). *Austerlitz.* Random House.
Sebeok, T. A. (Ed.). (1965). *Myth: A symposium.* Indiana University Press.
Sedgwick, D. (2016). *The wounded healer: Countertransference from a Jungian perspective.* Routledge.
Segal, R. A. (2020). *Myth analyzed.* Routledge.
Seligman, R. (2014). *Possessing spirits and healing selves: Embodiment and transformation in an Afro-Brazilian religion.* Palgrave MacMillan.
Seligman, R. (2018). Mind, body, brain, and the conditions of meaning. *Ethos, 46* (3), 397–417.
Seligman, R. (2023). Metaphor and the politics and poetics of youth distress in an evidence-based psychotherapy. *Transcultural Psychiatry, 60*(5), 819–834.
Seligman, R., & Kirmayer, L. J. (2008). Dissociative experience and cultural neuroscience: Narrative, metaphor and mechanism. *Culture, Medicine and Psychiatry, 32*(1), 31–64.
Senju, A., Tucker, L., Pasco, G., Hudry, K., Elsabbagh, M., Charman, T., & Johnson, M. H. (2013). The importance of the eyes: communication skills in

infants of blind parents. *Proceedings of the Royal Society B: Biological Sciences, 280* (1760), 20130436.

Sennett, R. (1998). Disturbing memories. In P. Kara & K. Patterson (Eds.), *Memory* (pp. 10–26). Cambridge University Press.

Sexson, M. W. (1982). The wounder heals: A meditation on the serpent as mythic symbol of health. *Literature and Medicine*, *1*(1), 107–116.

Seyama, J., & Nagayama, R. S. (2007). The uncanny valley: Effect of realism on the impression of artificial human faces. *Presence*, *16*(4), 337–351.

Shah, N. J., Marshall, J. C., Zafiris, O., Schwab, A., Zilles, K., Markowitsch, H. J., & Fink, G. R. (2001). The neural correlates of person familiarity: A functional magnetic resonance imaging study with clinical implications. *Brain*, 124(4), 804–815.

Shallice, T. (1978). The dominant action system: An information-processing approach to consciousness. In K. S. Pope & J. L. Singer (Eds.), *The stream of consciousness*. Plenum Press.

Shamdasani, S. (1998). *Cult fictions: C.G. Jung and the founding of analytical psychology*. Routledge.

Shamdasani, S. (2017). Psychotherapy in society: Historical reflections. In G. Eghigian (Ed.), *The Routledge history of madness and mental health* (pp. 363–378). Routledge.

Shandler, J. (1999). *While America watches: Televising the Holocaust*. Oxford University Press.

Shapiro, L. (2010). *Embodied cognition*. Routledge.

Sheppard, G. (2006). *HA! A self murder mystery*. McGill-Queens University Press.

Sherman, G. D., & Clore, G. L. (2009). The color of sin: White and black are perceptual symbols of moral purity and pollution. *Psychological Science*, *20*(8), 1019–1025.

Sherzer, J. (1983). *Kuna ways of speaking: An ethnographic perspective*. University of Texas Press.

Shirokogoroff, S. M. (1935). *Psychomental complex of the Tungus*. Kegan Paul.

Shore, B. (2023). *The hidden powers of ritual*. MIT Press.

Shore, M. (2016). *Religion and conflict resolution: Christianity and South Africa's Truth and Reconciliation Commission*. Routledge.

Shoshana, A. (2020). "I am blacker than you": Mizrahiness and Ethiopianess in an educational boarding school in Israel. In U. Dochin & G. Djerrahian (Eds.), *Blackness in Israel* (pp. 147–164). Routledge.

Shulevitz, J. (2011). *The Sabbath world: Glimpses of a different order of time*. Random House.

Shusterman, R. (2000). *Pragmatist aesthetics: Living beauty, rethinking art*. Rowman & Littlefield.

Shusterman, R. (2006). The aesthetic. *Theory, Culture & Society*, *23*(2–3), 237–243.

Siegelman, E. Y. (1993). *Metaphor and meaning in psychotherapy*. Guilford Press.

Siegler, M., & Osmond, H. (1973). Aesculapian authority. *Hastings Center Studies*, *1*(2), 41–52.

Silove, D., Brooks, R., Bateman Steel, C. R., Steel, Z., Hewage, K., Rodger, J., & Soosay, I. (2009). Explosive anger as a response to human rights violations in post-conflict Timor-Leste. *Social Science and Medicine, 69*(5), 670–677.

Silove, D., Steel, Z., & Watters, C. (2000). Policies of deterrence and the mental health of asylum seekers. *Journal of the American Medical Association, 284*(5), 604–611.

Silverman, J. (1967). Shamans and acute schizophrenia. *American Anthropologist, 69*(1), 21–31.

Silverman, Y. (2020). *The story within: Myth and fairy tale in therapy*. Jessica Kingsley Publishers.

Silvonen, V., & Stepanova, E. (2019). Language, music, and emotion in lament poetry: The embodiment and performativity of emotions in Karelian laments. In S. E. Pritzker, J. Fenigsen, & J. M. Wilce (Eds.), *The Routledge handbook of language and emotion* (pp. 203–220). Routledge.

Simic, C. (2013). *New and Selected Poems: 1962-2012*. Houghton Mifflin Harcourt.

Simon, H. A. (1969). *The sciences of the artificial.* MIT press.

Singer, J. (2000). *Blake, Jung, and the collective unconscious: The conflict between reason and imagination*. Nicolas-Hays, Inc.

Sirois, S., Spratling, M., Thomas, M. S., Westermann, G., Mareschal, D., & Johnson, M. H. (2008). Précis of neuroconstructivism: How the brain constructs cognition. *Behavioral and Brain Sciences, 31*(3), 321–331.

Snell, B. (1982). *The discovery of the mind: in Greek philosophy and literature*. Dover.

Solms, M. (2019). A neuropsychoanalytic perspective. *Psychoanalytic Inquiry, 39* (8), 607–624.

Solms, M. (2020). New project for a scientific psychology: General scheme. *Neuropsychoanalysis, 22*(1–2), 5–35.

Sontag, S. (1978). *Illness as metaphor*. Farrar, Straus and Giroux.

Spence, D. P. (1982). *Narrative truth and historical truth: Meaning and interpretation in psychoanalysis*. W. W. Norton.

Spensley, J., & Blacker, K. H. (1976). Feelings of the psychotherapist. *American Journal of Orthopsychiatry, 46*(3), 542–545.

Sperber, D. (1974). *Rethinking symbolism*. Cambridge University Press.

Sperber, D. (1985). *On anthropological knowledge*. Cambridge University Press.

Spillane, R. (1987). Rhetoric as remedy: Some philosophical antecedents of psychotherapeutic ethics. *British Journal of Medical Psychology, 60*(3), 217–224.

Spiro, M. E. (1982). Collective representations and mental representations in religious symbol systems. In J. Maquet (Ed.), *On symbols in anthropology: Essays in honor of Harry Hoijer* (pp. 45–72). Undena Publications.

Stein, A. (1993). *Hidden children: Forgotten survivors of the Holocaust*. Penguin Books Canada.

Stein, D. (Ed.). (2023). *Archeology of metaphor: The art of Gilah Yelin Hirsch*. Skira.

Steiner, G. (1989). *Real presences*. University of Chicago Press.

Steiner, G. (2002). *Grammars of creation*. Yale University Press.

Sterling, P. (2012). Allostasis: A model of predictive regulation. *Physiology & Behavior, 106*(1), 5–15.

Stern, D. N. (2018). *The interpersonal world of the infant: A view from psychoanalysis and developmental psychology*. Routledge.

Sternberg, R. J. & Nigro, G. (1983). Interaction and analogy in the comprehension of metaphors. *Quarterly Journal of Experimental Psychology, 35A*, 17–38.

Stevens, W. (2011). *The necessary angel: Essays on reality and the imagination*. Vintage.

Stilwell, P., & Stilwell, C. (2024). Embracing metaphor in pain medicine. In A. Bleakley & S. Neilson (Eds.), *Routledge handbook of medicine and poetry* (pp. 133–141). Routledge.

Stoddard, J. A., & Afari, N. (2014). *The big book of ACT metaphors: A practitioner's guide to experiential exercises and metaphors in acceptance and commitment therapy*. New Harbinger Publications.

Stone, R. R. (2012). *The jaguar within: Shamanic trance in ancient Central and South American art*. University of Texas Press.

Stott, R., Mansell, W., Salkovskis, P., Lavender, A., & Cartwright-Hatton, S. (2010). *Oxford guide to metaphors in CBT: Building cognitive bridges*. Oxford University Press.

Strand, M. (2024). Opacity, difference and not knowing: what can psychiatry learn from the work of Édouard Glissant? *Medical Humanities*.

Straus, E. W. (1966). The upright posture. In M. Natanson (Ed.), *Essays in phenomenology* (pp. 164–192). Springer.

Strawson, G. (2004). Against narrativity. *Ratio, 17*(4), 428–452.

Stroebe, M., Schut, H., & Nauta, M. H. (2016). Is homesickness a mini-grief? Development of a dual process model. *Clinical Psychological Science, 4*(2), 344–358.

Stromberg, P. G. (1990). Ideological language in the transformation of identity. *American Anthropologist, 92*(1), 42–56.

Stromberg, P. G. (2018). Narrative and healing in dynamic psychotherapy: Implications for culture theory. In N. Quinn (Ed.), *Advances in culture theory from psychological anthropology* (pp. 247–284). Palgrave MacMillan.

Stromberg, P. G. (2023). Poetics and panic. *Ethos, 51*(2), 183–197.

Strupp, H. H., & Hadley, S. W. (1979). Specific versus nonspecific factors in psychotherapy: A controlled study of outcome. *Archives of General Psychiatry, 36*, 1125–1136.

Styron, W. (1992). *Darkness visible: A memoir of madness*. Open Road Media.

Sudnow, D. (1993). *Ways of the hand: The organization of improvised conduct*. MIT Press.

Sullivan, B. M. (2014). Fluid selfhood, human and otherwise: Hindu and Buddhist themes in science fiction. *Implicit Religion, 17*(4), 489–508.

Sulloway, F. (1979). *Freud: Biologist of the mind*. Basic Books.

Sweetser, E. (2000). Blended spaces and performativity. *Cognitive Linguistics 11* (3-4), 305–333.

Syed, A., & Jacob, M. S. (2024). Languaging psychopathology: neurobiology and metaphor. *Frontiers in Psychiatry, 15*, 1320771.

Szasz, T. (1961). *The myth of mental illness: Foundations of a theory of personal conduct*. Harper & Row.

Talbot, J., Convertino, G., De Marco, M., Venneri, A., & Mazzoni, G. (2024). Highly superior autobiographical memory (HSAM): A systematic review. *Neuropsychology Review*, 1–23.

Tambiah, S. J. (1968). The magical power of words. *Man*, *3*(2), 175–208.

Tauber, A. I. (1999). *Confessions of a medicine man: An essay in popular philosophy*. MIT Press.

Taussig, M. (2018). *Mimesis and alterity: A particular history of the senses*. Routledge.

Tay, D. (2022). *Navigating the realities of metaphor and psychotherapy research*. Cambridge University Press.

Tay, D., & Jordan, J. (2015). Metaphor and the notion of control in trauma talk. *Text & Talk*, *35*(4), 553–573.

Taylor, C. (1989). *Sources of the self: The making of modern identity*. Harvard University Press.

Taylor, C. (2016). *The language animal: The full shape of the human linguistic capacity*. Harvard University Press.

Taylor, C. C. (2014). Rwanda's Gacaca trials: Toward a new nationalism or business as usual? In A. Hinton & D. Hinton (Eds.), *Genocide and mass violence: Memory, symptom, and recovery* (pp. 301–320). Cambridge University Press.

Terr, L. (1994). *Unchained memories: True stories of traumatic memories, lost and found*. Basic Books.

Thagard, P. (2022). *Balance: How it works and what it means*. Columbia University Press.

Tham, D. S. Y., Sowden, P. T., Grandison, A., Franklin, A., Lee, A. K. W., Ng, M., . . . & Zhao, J. (2020). A systematic investigation of conceptual color associations. *Journal of Experimental Psychology: General*, *149*(7), 1311.

Thibodeau, P. H., & Boroditsky, L. (2011). Metaphors we think with: The role of metaphor in reasoning. *PloS One*, *6*(2), e16782.

Thompson, E. P. (1994). *Witness against the beast: William Blake and the moral law*. Cambridge University Press.

Thurman, R. A. F. (1995). *Inside Tibetan Buddhism: Rituals and symbols revealed*. Collins Publishers.

Tillman, J. G., Nash, M. R., & Lerner, P. M. (1994). Does trauma cause dissociative pathology? In S. J. Lynn & J. W. Rhue (Eds.), *Dissociation: Clinical and theoretical perspectives* (pp. 395–414). Guilford Press.

Timpanelli, G. (1993). The sacred does not shun the ordinary. In C. Simpkinson & A. Simpkinson (Eds.), *Sacred stories: A celebration of the power of story to transform and heal* (pp. 93–99). Harper Collins.

Tobias, R. (2006). *The discourse of nature in the poetry of Paul Celan: The unnatural world*. Johns Hopkins University Press.

Todorov, T. (1981). *Introduction to poetics*. University of Minnesota Press.

Tolbert, E. (2007). Voice, metaphysics, and community: Pain and transformation in the Finnish-Karelian ritual lament. In S. Coakley & K. Shelemay (Eds.), *Pain and its transformations: The interface of biology and culture* (pp. 147–165). Harvard University Press.

Tomlinson, R. A. (1983). *Epidauros*. Granada.

Törneke, N. (2017). *Metaphor in practice: A professional's guide to using the science of language in psychotherapy*. New Harbinger Publications.

Traugott, E. C. (1985). "Conventional" and "dead" metaphors revisited. In W. Paprotté & R. Dirven (Eds.), *The ubiquity of metaphor: Metaphor in language and thought*. John Benjamins Publishing Co.

Tronick, E., Als, H., Adamson, L., Wise, S., & Brazelton, T. B. (1978). Infants' response to entrapment between contradictory messages in face-to-face interaction. *Journal of the American Academy of Child and Adolescent Psychiatry*, *17*, 1–13

Trouillot, M. R. (2015). *Silencing the past: Power and the production of history*. Beacon Press.

Truth & Reconciliation Commission of Canada. (2015). *Canada's residential schools: The final report of the Truth and Reconciliation Commission of Canada*. McGill-Queen's University Press.

Tu, W.-M. (1985). Selfhood and otherness in Confucian thought. In A. J. Marsella, G. Devos, & F. L. K. Hsu (Eds.), *Culture and self: Asian and Western perspectives* (pp. 231–251). Tavistock.

Turner, B. S. (1984). *The body and society*. Basil Blackwell.

Turner, M. (1996). *The literary mind*. Oxford University Press.

Turner, V. (1969). *The ritual process: Structure and anti-structure*. Aldine De Gruyter.

Turner, V. (1974). *Dramas, fields, and metaphors: Symbolic action in human society*. Cornell University Press.

Turner, V. (1982). *From ritual to theater: The human seriousness of play*. PAJ Publications.

Uchino, B. N., Caioppo, J. T., & Kiecolt-Glaser, J. (1996). The relationship between social support and physiological processes: A review with emphasis on underlying mechanisms and implications for health. *Psychological Bulletin*, *119*(3), 488–531.

Ullman, M. T. (2004). Contributions of memory circuits to language: The declarative/procedural model. *Cognition*, *92*(1–2), 231–270.

Valente, D., Theurel, A., & Gentaz, E. (2018). The role of visual experience in the production of emotional facial expressions by blind people: A review. *Psychonomic Bulletin & Review*, *25*(2), 483–497.

van der Kolk, B. A. (2007). The developmental impact of childhood trauma. In L. J. Kirmayer, R. Lemelson, & M. Barad (Eds.), *Understanding trauma: Integrating biological, clinical, and cultural perspectives* (pp. 224–241). Cambridge University Press.

van der Watt, A. S. J., Van de Water, T., Nortje, G., Oladeji, B. D., Seedat, S., & Gureje, O. (2018). The perceived effectiveness of traditional and faith healing in the treatment of mental illness: A systematic review of qualitative studies. *Social Psychiatry and Psychiatric Epidemiology*, *53*(6), 555–566.

Varela, F., Thompson, E., & Rosch, E. (1991). *The embodied mind: Cognitive science and human experience.* MIT Press.

Vaughn Becker, D., & Neuberg, S. L. (2019). Archetypes reconsidered as emergent outcomes of cognitive complexity and evolved motivational systems. *Psychological Inquiry, 30*(2), 59–75.

Veissière, S. (2016). Varieties of Tulpa experiences: The hypnotic nature of human sociality, personhood, and interphenomenality. In A. Raz & M. Lifshitz (Eds.), *Hypnosis and meditation: Towards an integrative science of conscious planes* (pp. 5–78). New York: Oxford University Press.

Veissière, S. P., Constant, A., Ramstead, M. J., Friston, K. J., & Kirmayer, L. J. (2020). Thinking through other minds: A variational approach to cognition and culture. *Behavioral and Brain Sciences*, 43, e90.

Veissière, S., & Gibbs-Bravo, L. (2016). Language, ritual, and placebo sociality in a community of extreme eaters. In K. Cargill (Ed.), *Food cults: How fads, dogma, and doctrine influence diet* (pp. 63–86). Rowman & Littlefield.

Verene, D. P. (1981). *Vico's science of imagination.* Cornell University Press.

Vidal, F., & Ortega, F. (2020). *Being brains: Making the cerebral subject.* Fordham University Press.

Vidal-Naquet, P. (1992). *Assassins of memory: Essays on the denial of the Holocaust.* Columbia University Press.

Vitebsky, P. (2001). *Shamanism.* University of Oklahoma Press.

Viveiros de Castro, E. (2004). Exchanging perspectives: The transformation of objects into subjects in Amerindian ontologies. *Common Knowledge, 10*(3), 463–484.

von Franz, M.-L. (1972). *Problems of the feminine in fairytales.* Spring Publications.

von Franz, M.-L. (1975). *C.G. Jung: His myth in our time.* Little, Brown & Co.

von Franz, M.-L. (1979). *Alchemical active imagination.* Spring Publications.

von Franz, M. L. (1980). *Alchemy: An introduction to the symbolism and the psychology.* Inner City Books.

von Franz, M. L. (1981). *The problem of the Puer Aeternus.* Santa Monica.

von Franz, M. L. (2017). *Shadow and evil in fairy tales: Revised edition.* Shambhala Publications.

von Franz, M.-L., & Boa, F. (1988). *The way of the dream.* Windrose.

von Mohr, M., Kirsch, L. P., & Fotopoulou, A. (2017). The soothing function of touch: Affective touch reduces feelings of social exclusion. *Scientific Reports, 7* (1), 13516.

von Neumann, J. (1958). *The computer and the brain.* Yale University Press.

von Schnurbein, S. (2003). Shamanism in the Old Norse tradition: A theory between ideological camps. *History of Religions, 43*(2), 116–138.

von Stuckard, K. (2002). Reenchanting nature: Modern Western shamanism and nineteenth-century thought. *Journal of the American Academy of Religion, 70*(4), 771–800.

von Stuckard, K. (2023). Decentering humanism in philosophy and the sciences: Ecologies of agency, subversive animism, and diffractional knowledge. *Sophia,* 62(4), 709–722.

Vonnegut, K. (1969). *Slaughterhouse-five; or, The children's crusade, a duty-dance with death*. Delacorte Press.
Vosniadou, S., & Ortony, A. (1983). The emergence of the literal-metaphorical-anomalous distinction in young children. *Child Development, 54*, 154–161.
Vowles, David H. (1970). Neuroethology, evolution and grammar. In L. R. Aronson, E. Tobach, D. S. Lehrman, & J. S. Rosenblatt (Eds.), *Development and evolution of behavior: Essays in memory of T.C. Schneirla*. W. H. Freeman & Co.
Vygotsky, L. S. (1980). *Mind in society: The development of higher psychological processes*. Harvard University Press.
Wadhera, P. (2019). An omnipresent absence: Georges Perec's silent protest of the Holocaust in La Disparition. *Contemporary French and Francophone Studies, 23* (5), 576–583.
Wagner, R. (1986). *Symbols that stand for themselves*. University of Chicago Press.
Wagner, S., Winner, E., Cicchetti, D., & Gardner, H. (1981). "Metaphorical" mapping in human infants. *Child Development, 52*(2), 728–731.
Waitzkin, H., & Britt, T. (1993). Processing narratives of self-destructive behavior in routine medical encounters: Health promotion, disease prevention, and the discourse of health care. *Social Science and Medicine, 36*(9), 1123–1136.
Waldram, J. B. (2000). The efficacy of traditional medicine: Current theoretical and methodological issues. *Medical Anthropology Quarterly, 14*(4), 603–625.
Wallis, R. J. (2003). *Shamans/neo-shamans: Ecstasies, alternative archaeologies and contemporary pagans*. Routledge.
Wampold, B. E., & Imel, Z. E. (2015). *The great psychotherapy debate: The evidence for what makes psychotherapy work*. Routledge.
Wampole, C. (2016). *Rootedness: The ramifications of a metaphor*. University of Chicago Press.
Ward, J., & Simner, J. (2020). Synesthesia: The current state of the field. In K. Sathian & V. S. Ramachandran (Eds.), *Multisensory perception: From laboratory to clinic* (pp. 283–300). Academic Press.
Watkins, M. (1986). *Invisible guests: The development of imaginal dialogues*. Analytic Press.
Watzlawick, P., Beavin, J., & Jackson, D. D. (1967). *Pragmatics of human communication*. Random House.
Weaver, R. (2001). *Old wise woman: A study in active imagination*. Shambhala Publications.
Weinberg, S. (1992). *Dreams of a final theory: The search for the fundamental laws of nature*. Pantheon Books.
Weineck, S.-M. (1999). Logos and Pallaksch: The loss of madness and the survival of poetry in Paul Celan's "Tübingen, Jänner." *Orbis Litterarum, 54*, 262–275.
Weiskrantz, L., Elliott, J., & Darlington, C. (1971). Preliminary observations on tickling oneself. *Nature, 230*(5296), 598–599.
Welton, D. (Ed.). (1998). *Body and flesh: A philosophical reader*. Blackwell.
Whalley, G. (1997). *Aristotle's poetics*. McGill-Queen's University Press.

Whitbeck, L. B., Adams, G. W., Hoyt, D. R., & Chen, X. (2004). Conceptualizing and measuring historical trauma among American Indian people. *American Journal of Community Psychology*, *33*(3–4), 119–130.
White, L., Tursky, B., & Schwartz, G. E. (Eds.). (1985). *Placebo: Theory, research, and mechanisms*. Guilford Press.
White, M., & Epston, D. (1990). *Narrative means to therapeutic ends*. W. W. Norton.
White, S. H., & Pillemer, D. B. (1979). Childhood amnesia and the development of a socially accessible memory system. In J. F. Kihlstrom & F. J. Evans (Eds.), *Functional disorders of memory* (pp. 29–73). Lawrence Erlbaum.
Whitmont, E. C., & Perera, S. B. (1989). *Dreams: A portal to the source*. Routledge.
Whittington, J. C., McCaffary, D., Bakermans, J. J., & Behrens, T. E. (2022). How to build a cognitive map. *Nature Neuroscience*, *25*(10), 1257–1272.
Wickkiser, B. L. (2008). *Asklepios, medicine, and the politics of healing in fifth-century Greece: Between craft and cult*. Johns Hopkins University Press.
Wikan, U. (1990). *Managing turbulent hearts: A Balinese formula for living*. University of Chicago Press.
Wilce, J. M. (2017). Tradition, emotion, healing and the sacred: Revivalist lamenting in Finland in relation to three authenticities. In H. Basu, R. Littlewood, & A. S. Steinforth (Eds.), *Spirit & mind: Mental health at the intersection of religion and psychiatry* (pp. 227–252). LIT Verlag Münster.
Wilce, J. M., & Price, L. J. (2003). Metaphors our bodyminds live by. In J. M. Wilce (Ed.), *Social lives of immune systems* (pp. 50–81). Routledge.
Wilcox, R. A., & Whitham, E. M. (2003). The symbol of modern medicine: Why one snake is more than two. *Annals of Internal Medicine*, *138*(8), 673–677.
Wild, B., Erb, M., & Bartels, M. (2001). Are emotions contagious? Evoked emotions while viewing emotionally expressive faces: quality, quantity, time course and gender differences. *Psychiatry Research*, 102(2), 109–124.
Wilkinson, T., & Chemero, A. (2024). Affordances, phenomenology, pragmatism and the myth of the given. *Phenomenology and the Cognitive Sciences*, 1–17.
Wilkowski, B. M., Robinson, M. D., Meier, B. P., Carter, M. S., & Feltman, R. (2009). Hot-headed is more than an expression: The embodied representation of anger in terms of heat. *Emotion*, *9*(4), 464–477.
Williams, D. (2018). Predictive processing and the representation wars. *Minds and Machines*, 28(1), 141–172.
Williams, J. P., & Vannini, P. (2016). Saying what we mean; meaning what we say: Authentic dialogue in Aboriginal communities. In P. Vannini & J. P. Williams (Eds.), *Authenticity in culture, self, and society* (pp. 203–218). Routledge.
Williams, L. E., & Bargh, J. A. (2008). Experiencing physical warmth promotes interpersonal warmth. *Science*, *322*(5901), 606–607.
Williams, L. E., Huang, J. Y., & Bargh, J. A. (2009). The scaffolded mind: Higher mental processes are grounded in early experience of the physical world. *European Journal of Social Psychology*, *3*(7), 1257–1267.
Williams, R. (1976). *Keywords: A vocabulary of culture and society*. Fontana.
Wilson, E. A. (2004). *Psychosomatic: Feminism and the neurological body*. Duke University Press.

Wimmer, M. (2017). The afterlives of scholarship: Warburg and Cassirer. *History of Humanities*, *2*(1), 245–270.

Winet, E. D. (2010). *Indonesian postcolonial theatre: Spectral genealogies and absent faces*. Springer.

Winner, E. (1988). *The point of words: Children's understanding of metaphor and irony*. Harvard University Press.

Winner, E., McCarthy, M., Kleinman, S., & Gardner, H. (1979). First metaphors. *New Directions for Child and Adolescent Development*, *3*, 29–41.

Winnicott, D. W. (1971). *Playing and reality*. Penguin.

Winnicott, D. W. (2018). *Collected papers: Through paediatrics to psychoanalysis*. Routledge.

Wittgenstein, L. (1958). *Philosophical investigations* (3rd ed.). MacMillan.

Wittgenstein, L. (1979). *Remarks on Fraser's golden bough*. Humanities Press.

Wittgenstein, L. (1980). *Culture and value*. University of Chicago Press.

Wittmann, M. (2016). *Felt time: The psychology of how we perceive time*. MIT Press.

Wittmann, M., Jokic, T., & Pfeifer, E. (2019). Modulations in the experience of duration. In V. Arstilla, A. Bardon, S. E. Power, & A. Vatakis (Eds.), *The illusions of time: Philosophical and psychological essays on timing and time perception* (pp. 145–162). Palgrave Macmillan.

Witztum, E., & Goodman, Y. (1999a). Narrative construction of distress and therapy: A model based on work with ultra-orthodox Jews. *Transcultural Psychiatry*, *36*(4), 403–436.

Witztum, E., & Goodman, Y. (1999b). Further reflections on therapy, psychology, anthropology and the Haredim. *Transcultural Psychiatry*, *36*(4), 465–475.

Witztum, E., & Goodman, Y. (2004). Rewriting stories of distress: Culture-sensitive strategic therapy with ultra-orthodox Jews in Israel. In J. R. Ancis (Ed.), *Culturally responsive interventions: Innovative approaches to working with diverse populations* (pp. 134–164). Routledge.

Wohlman, A. (2022). *Metaphor in illness writing: Fight and battle reused*. Edinburgh University Press.

Wolin, R. (2022). *Heidegger in ruins: Between philosophy and ideology*. Yale University Press.

Wood, J. (2020). *Serious noticing: Selected essays, 1997-2019*. Farrar, Straus and Giroux.

Woods, A. (2011). The limits of narrative: Provocations for the medical humanities. *Medical Humanities*, *37*(2), 73–78.

Woods, A., Hart, A., & Spandler, H. (2022). The recovery narrative: Politics and possibilities of a genre. *Culture, Medicine, and Psychiatry*, *46*(2), 221–247.

Woodward, B. (2012). *Wired: The short life & fast times of John Belushi*. Simon and Schuster.

Woolf, C. J., & Salter, M. W. (2000). Neuronal plasticity: Increasing the gain in pain. *Science*, *288*(5472), 1765–1768.

Yancy, G. (2008). Colonial gazing: The production of the body as "other." *Western Journal of Black Studies*, *32*(1).

Yates, F. A. (2013). *Art of memory*. Routledge.

Yeats, W. B. (1910). *Poems of William Blake*. Routledge.

Yeats, W. B. (1961). *Essays and introductions*. Palgrave Macmillan.
Young, A. (1981). When rational men fall sick: An inquiry into some assumptions made by medical anthropologists. *Culture, Medicine and Psychiatry*, *5*, 317–335.
Young, A. (1982). Rational men and the explanatory model approach. *Culture, Medicine and Psychiatry*, *6*, 57–71.
Young, A. (1988). Unpacking the demoralization thesis. *Medical Anthropology Quarterly*, *2*(1), 3–16.
Young, A. (1995). *The harmony of illusions: Inventing posttraumatic stress disorder*. Princeton University Press.
Young, A. (2004). When traumatic memory was a problem: On the historical antecedents of PTSD. In G. M. Rosen (Ed.), *Posttraumatic stress disorder: Issues and controversies* (pp. 127–146). John Wiley & Sons.
Young, J. E. (1988). *Writing and rewriting the Holocaust: Narrative and the consequences of interpretation*. Indiana University Press.
Young, J. E. (1993). *The texture of memory: Holocaust memorials and meaning*. Yale University Press.
Young, K. (1989). Narrative embodiments: Enclaves of the self in the realm of medicine. In J. Shotter & K. J. Gergen (Eds.), *Texts of identity* (pp. 152–165). Sage Publications.
Yu, N. (1995). Metaphorical expressions of anger and happiness in English and Chinese. *Metaphor and Symbolic Activity*, *10*(1), 59–92.
Yu, N. (2008). Metaphor from body and culture. In R. Gibbs (Ed.), *The Cambridge handbook of metaphor and thought* (pp. 247–261). Cambridge University Press.
Zahavi, D. (2017). Thin, thinner, thinnest: Defining the minimal self. In C. Durt, C. Tewes, & T. Fuchs (Eds.), *Embodiment, enaction, and culture: Investigating the constitution of the shared world* (pp. 193–199). MIT Press.
Zajonc, R. B. (1980). Feeling and thinking: Preferences need no inferences. *American Psychologist* *35*(2), 151–175.
Zajonc, R. B. (1984). On the primacy of affect. *American Psychologist* *39*(2), 117–123.
Zerubavel, E. (2003). *Time maps: Collective memory and the social shape of the past*. University of Chicago Press.
Zerubavel, N., & Wright, M. O. D. (2012). The dilemma of the wounded healer. *Psychotherapy*, *49*(4), 482–491.
Zwicky, J. (2003). *Wisdom & metaphor*. Gaspereau Press.
Zwicky, J. (2014). *Lyric philosophy*. Brush Education.

# Index

For EU product safety concerns, contact us at Calle de José Abascal, 56–1°, 28003 Madrid, Spain or eugpsr@cambridge.org.

www.ingramcontent.com/pod-product-compliance
Lightning Source LLC
LaVergne TN
LVHW011659200926
848484LV00004B/994

* 9 7 8 1 0 0 9 6 1 7 7 8 9 *